WEBMASTER'S
Professional Reference

E. Loren Buhle, Jr.
Nancy Acosta
Rick Fairweather
Tim Ritchey
Mark Pesce
Larry J. Hughes, Jr.
Bill Weinman
Loren Malm
Mike Coulombe
Jim Vogel
James Ryans
Paul Singh
Mike Marolda
Fah-Chun Cheong
Lisa Morgan
Paul Buis
David Meeker

New Riders Publishing, Indianapolis, IN

Webmaster's Professional Reference

By Loren Buhle, Nancy Acosta, Rick Fairweather, Tim Ritchey, Mark Pesce, Larry J. Hughes, Jr., Bill Weinman, Loren Malm, Jim Vogel, James Ryans, Paul Singh, Mike Coulombe, Mike Marolda, Fah-Chun Cheong, Lisa Morgan, Paul Buis, David Meeker

Published by:
New Riders Publishing
201 West 103rd Street
Indianapolis, IN 46290 USA

Printed in the United States of America 1 2 3 4 5 6 7 8 9 0

Library of Congress Cataloging-in-Publication Data

```
Buhle, E. Loren.
   Webmaster's Professional Reference / E. Loren
Buhle, Jr.
      p.    cm.
   Includes index.
   ISBN 1-56205-473-2
   1. Internet (Computer network)    I. Title.
  TK5105.875.I57B84   1995
  004.6'7—dc20                              95-43372
                                                CIP
```


Warning and Disclaimer

Every effort has been made to make this book as complete and as accurate as possible, but no warranty or fitness is implied. The information is provided on an “as is” basis. The authors and New Riders Publishing shall have neither liability nor responsibility to any person or entity with respect to any loss or damages arising from the information contained in this book.

Publisher Don Fowley
Publishing Manager Jim LeValley
Marketing Manager Mary Foote
Managing Editor Carla Hall

Product Development Specialist
Julie Fairweather

Acquisitions Editor
Ian Sheeler

Development Editor
Suzanne Snyder

Project Editor
Cliff Shubs

Copy Editors
Lillian Duggan, Sarah Kearns, Peter Kuhns, Phil Worthington

Associate Marketing Manager
Tamara Apple

Acquisitions Coordinator
Tracy Turgeson

Publisher's Assistant
Karen Opal

Cover Designer
Karen Ruggles

Cover Illustrator
Jerry Blank

Cover Production
Aren Howell

Book Designer
Sandra Schroeder

Production Manager
Kelly Dobbs

Production Team Supervisor
Laurie Casey

Graphics Image Specialists
Stephen Adams, Brad Dixon, Sonja Hart, Clint Lahnen, Laura Robbins, Todd Wente

Production Analysts
Jason Hand, Bobbi Satterfield

Production Team
Angela Calvert, Dan Caparo, Kim Cofer, Tricia Flodder, Erika Millen, Beth Rago, Erich Richter, Karen Walsh

Indexer
Brad Herriman

Trademark Acknowledgments

All terms mentioned in this book that are known to be trademarks or service marks have been appropriately capitalized. New Riders Publishing cannot attest to the accuracy of this information. Use of a term in this book should not be regarded as affecting the validity of any trademark or service mark.

Dedications

My contribution to this book is dedicated to my loving husband, Hugo, and daughter, Alexandra, who have both been patient and understanding when I've had to work on the weekend to meet deadlines. Also, special thanks to Gary & Barbara Bouton, who have helped introduce me to this wonderful "author's world"; to Brete Root who helped with screen captures, and to Don Ristagno and my customers who all allowed me to publicize their great Web sites.

—Nancy Acosta

I would like to dedicate this book to my wife, Alycia Mallon-Buhle, and my daughter, Amanda Alycia Buhle, for their support and help in showing me the beauty and power of words.

—E. Loren Buhle, Jr.

In deep gratitude, I dedicate my contribution to this book to my wife, Lori, who selflessly supports my writing efforts in countless ways. My successes to date simply could not have taken the same shape without her. I pray my future successes will also be colored by her presence and love.

—Larry J. Hughes, Jr.

I would like to thank Chamath Palihalitiya for writing a key portion of my chapter. His knowledge is invaluable, and I'm sure Newbridge misses him. In particular, I would like to thank Susan, Adrian, and Katie.

—James Ryans

Thanks go to Larry Colwell for his invaluable help and collaboration in this adventure. A special thanks also to Carl H. Simpson for providing some amusing anecdotes, if not any helpful information.

—Jim Vogel

I would like to thank the excellent staff at New Riders, notably Ian Sheeler, Tracy Turgeson, and Sarah Kearns, for their hard work and dedication; my son, David, for preventing me from taking all of this too seriously (can you do anything but smile with a six-year-old laughing and playing in the house?); Lee, my partner-in-life, for her unending encouragement and support; and Spider Robinson for giving me something to read when I thought I'd run out of fresh Heinlein.

—Bill Weinman

More About Authors

Lisa Morgan has more than 15 years of business management and marketing experience. Her highly developed strategic abilities stem from her work with numerous companies, ranging from start-ups to multinational conglomerates. Ms. Morgan is president of Corporate Communication Strategies, a Silicon Valley-based business development and marketing firm serving high technology companies and professional organizations. In addition to representing client companies, Lisa was a Planning Committee member of Alliance 95 and founder of the Internet Society Bay Area Chapter.

Dr. Paul E. Buis started life in Kalamazoo, Michigan and moved around the Midwest. He attended Hope College in Holland, Michigan, where he majored in physics and mathematics. He graduated magna cum laude and was elected to Phi Beta Kappa, a liberal arts honorary; Sigma Pi Sigma, a physics honorary; and Pi Mu Epsilon,a mathematics honorary. He attended Purdue University where he received a Master's Degree in Mathematics and a Master's Degree in Computer Science. While attending Purdue, Paul was the software architect for a firm that sold veterinary cardiology systems to automatically diagnose heart problems in dogs and cats. Eventually, Paul completed his doctoral work in Computer Science at Purdue and was employed as a Professor in the Computer Science Department at Ball State University in Muncie, Indiana. He is an instructor for the Technology Exchange Company located in Reading, Massachusetts, which sends him around the country to give workshops on TCP/IP networking, the X Window system, C++ programming, and Unix System Administration.

David Meeker is a systems analyst for Computing Services at Ball State University in Muncie, Indiana. David's specialty is World Wide Web technology. He can be reached on the Internet at `dfm@marvin.bsu.edu`.

Contents at a Glance

Pt VI: Security

Pt VII: Beyond HTML Web Graphics

Pt VIII: Tomorrow's Technology

Appendix

Table of Contents

Part II: TCP/IP Connectivity

Part III: Server Setup: Administration and Maintenance

Part V: Web Application Design

Part VI: Security

Part VII: Beyond HTML Web Graphics

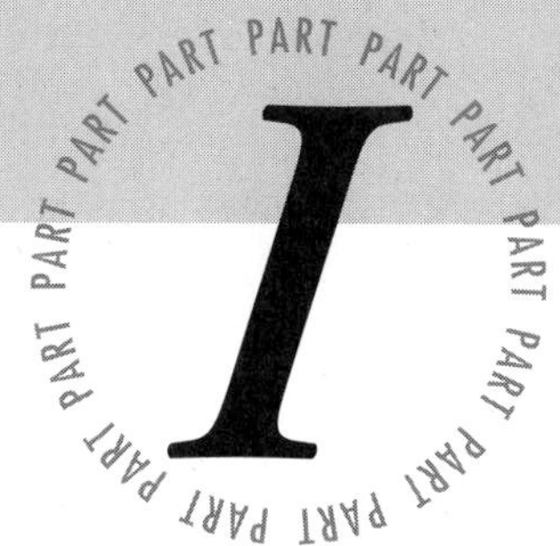

The Webmaster Profession

So Now You Are a Webmaster?

by Loren Buhle

One of the reasons why the World Wide Web (WWW or Web) has become so popular is the inherent capability to integrate networked information services under one umbrella. Through WWW integration, information is available to the user in many different formats and from many different sources. Web users can focus on solving problems and not concern themselves with the mechanisms of obtaining information. The simple and transportable graphical interface of the WWW browser provides one of the best means for access to huge amounts of information.

This chapter explores the following issues:

- The options available to a webmaster when planning a World Wide Web site. Issues concerning the Web maintainer and Web user are addressed.
- The various services that may be offered, and their ramifications in the design, setup, and maintenance of a Web site.
- One of the "torture tests" of a Web site: Does the design change over time and place increased demand on resources?

Many Web sites develop as quick and cheap assembled pilot projects. If these pilot projects fulfill the goals proposed by management, can they also support additional services and many users? Can the information stored on these Web sites be supported by a less informed provider base and still function with high standards? This chapter will briefly explore many of the services of a well integrated Web site.

What Is a Web Site?

A Web site is much larger than merely a Web server and a few text files. Many Web sites provide seamless integration of resources such as e-mail, news, an FTP archive, real-time activity, gopher access, Web access, search engines, and robots. The Web site becomes an integral information resource that must be maintained in terms of network and system support, often on a 24 hours per day, seven days per week basis.

World Wide Web sites are often configured as a firewall: They provide a secure interface that links a company's internal network to the external network serving the Internet. In this case, maintaining the integrity between the two networks is paramount. In other network topologies, the site is seen as "sacrificial," existing totally outside the company's firewall and overwritten periodically from an internal, secure site.

The Web site acts as the "front door" or first interface with the company for millions of Internet users. The Web site may be the only way some users get to know your company. Even if all the technical elements of a Web site, such as buttons and hot links, perform correctly, the information it presents to the user might not be helpful or organized properly. Issues such as company policies, liability, and auditing—areas that have nothing to do with how well the Web site functions—are also discussed in this chapter.

Determining the Purpose and Audience of Your Web Site

One of the most crucial questions to ask when designing a Web site is "What is the purpose of this site and who are its users?" Other questions that this chapter helps you answer will also help you narrow your target audience. If your site supports the marketing department by providing an online catalog, for example, who is the audience? Will the site be bidirectional, supporting user feedback on an individual level and also on the level of a public forum? Will the Web site support ongoing discussions by the millions of users of this product, requiring real-time messaging and search and thread functions? Or will the World Wide Web resource merely be a digital library acting as a backdrop for a larger "virtual community" of users existing in the interactive world of CuSeeMe and IRC-Chat? Perhaps the audience will be part of the 40 million Internet users of the near-interactive world of Listservs and newsgroups? Will this virtual community be segregated into selective customer groups, perhaps based on their skill set or ability to pay a larger subscriber fee and thus receive enhanced information? These policy issues greatly affect the technical design of a site in its infancy and over time.

If the Web site is designed for an "inside" audience and an "outside" audience, what will be the best way to provide useful information? The requirements of an inside audience—users completely within the firewall—may be substantially different from an outside audience. An outside audience includes the general public and employees that need access to confidential company information for their field work (such as price sheets and documents). These questions are answered in this chapter.

Network Requirements

The most difficult elements of setting up a Web site on a network include determining network bandwidth, designing for growth potential, ensuring network security, and addressing the requirements of the Internet provider.

Bandwidth

Bandwidth is the capacity of the information pipe connecting your network to the Internet. Efficient use of bandwidth depends on the nature and type of information interchanged with the Internet. Will the Web site be serving small packets of information, such as text-based classified advertisements less than 4 kilobytes in size, or will the Web site be serving ten- to hundred-megabyte videos? The former requires a bandwidth with fast turnaround that is capable of handling many small packets. Many existing networks are already set to accommodate this setup.

Large files, such as videos, place another type of demand on a network. Multiple requests for large quantities of data will saturate many existing networks, collide with intermittent users, and provide sluggish turnout times between the user and the Web server. Bandwidth requirements are even greater for real-time voice and video which require a given timeframe to preserve intelligible speech! Most Web sites are a mixture of each of these extremes: many small packets of information interspersed with a few large transfers from time to time.

Growth Potential

When the Web site becomes a central clearinghouse for information within the company and to users outside of the company, the bandwidth and processing power of the server will be stressed. Increased popularity can be easily translated into a budget justification for larger bandwidth; two ways to do this are to spend more on a T3 line (replacing a T1 or 56.6 Kbps Internet connection) or to purchase a more powerful computer. An alternative is to provide additional computers and additional Internet access. These additional resources provide a fall-back or fail-over solution if there are problems either with the computer hardware or the Internet connection. The information resource can be mirrored on other machines placed within the target audience. This redundancy is ideal for tackling acute and chronic problems. Acute problems are absolute failures, such as dead hardware, power failures, and Internet service disruptions. Chronic problems include noisy or congested Internet access, heavy computer activity due to servicing Web requests or any other processing load that consumes machine resources.

Additional resources provide a smooth and incremental growth path for the Web information to widen its capabilities and target audience.

Your Internet Service Provider

One critical element for creating a Web site is to partner with a suitable Internet Service Provider (ISP). In the early days of connecting to the Internet, simple questions of domain name registration, class of license, external Domain Name Service (DNS), and access to the Usenet news feed required hours of research. Concerns are just as numerous now, but not as difficult. For example, once your Web site becomes popular, questions should be directed to the method the ISP is using to access the Internet. Do they have a single T1 connection to the Internet? If the ISP has multiple connections to the Internet, usually to reduce congestion, are these connections all from the same vendor? Will the ISP be able to increase its bandwidth support as your Web enterprise expands? Is the ISP on firm financial ground to provide the promised level of support now and in the future?

Financial solvency of ISPs is particularly troublesome. The difference in price for a given method of Internet access (such as T1) varies enormously even within a single geographic region. Some vendors overcharge, while others undercharge to build a successful clientele. Some of these vendors operate on a shoe-string budget with a computer, router, and a rack of modems sitting in a backroom closet. Other vendors are so large that requests made to the ISP may take weeks before they are serviced. Cheaper prices might appear cost-effective in the short run, but you may be inviting trouble for the Web site. A low ball ISP may have insufficient resources to maintain demand, provide insufficient resources to service failing hardware, or outstrip financial projections and become fiscally insolvent. If the Web site is your company's interface to the public, a problematic ISP might reflect unfavorably on your Web site.

If you are starting with a new Internet Service Provider, try to create a unique Internet address domain (such as unicol.com, cardinal.com) to take with you if you leave the ISP. Any specific pointers to the ISP should be placed so they can be easily replaced. Setting up mirror sites at other locations, possibly using other ISPs will be useful in identifying dependencies on your first ISP.

Network Topology

A World Wide Web site can be placed in an existing network using several methods:

- Satellite model
- Pass-Through model
- Firewall gateway
- Sacrificial system

These four methods focus on network security.

Satellite Model

The Satellite model (see fig. 1.1) is the simplest Web site network configuration to design and implement. In the Satellite network, all the computers in the local network are connected directly to the Internet, operating completely independent of each other. This network model often is the result of having no planned network topology—the network grew in a haphazard fashion. Another reason to use this topology is if the network computers are widely dispersed with too few in any one place. Computers on a satellite network are connected directly to the Internet through the Internet Service Provider and must be configured for the Internet. Each computer is on its own for network support and network security.

Web sites placed in a satellite environment are best configured as full-featured facilities, capable of supporting all necessary functions on a single platform. This makes the Web site robust and independent of its environment. This lack of dependence on neighboring sites on the Internet also enables the Web site to be portable. Because each computer interacts directly with the Internet, there are no internal intermediates to slow the Web site. Thus, this model is highly efficient on a one-to-one basis.

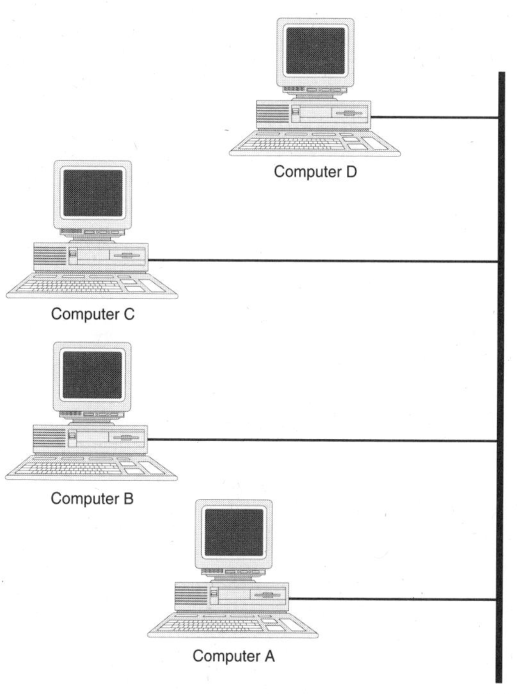

Figure 1.1
Satellite model.

Pass-Through Model

The Pass-Through model (see fig. 1.2) acts as a passive gateway between the Internet and the local environment. Information flows freely in both directions between the Internet and the local network. As in the Satellite model, all the computers that make up the local network are configured with valid Internet addresses and follow conventional Internet conventions. However, in this model, the Web site may provide local services, such as a Domain Name Service, a centralized e-mail hub, news, Listserv, and both private and public Web/gopher services.

Computers on the local network can pass their packets through the Pass-Through computer when network users want to surf the Internet or network computers can access the information on the Pass-Through computer. The Pass-Through model's additional benefits, centralized services such as e-mail and news, can be centrally supported without interfering with internal users who want to use Internet services directly.

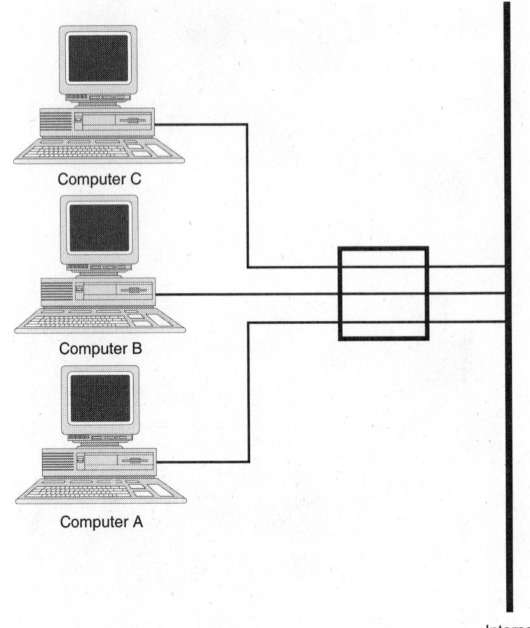

Figure 1.2
Pass-Through model.

Aside from maintaining the integrity of the Pass-Through computer, this model offers no security protection for local computers. On the other hand, this model is fairly efficient because the Pass-Through computer performs almost no processing and maintains an invisible presence unless it goes down. The Pass-Through model is frequently used in university environments with convenience services located on the centralized computers and most of the network security requirements handled by sysops responsible for internal computers.

Firewall Model

In the Firewall model (see fig. 1.3), packets traversing the boundaries between the Inside and the Internet are scrutinized and filtered. The filtration can be accomplished through network protocol, network address, application type, and other criteria. This model always works in a two-hop fashion, with no user on either the inside or outside ever directly interacting. Inside computers pass their packets to the Firewall computer, which then passes the packets to the Internet. Internet users interact with the Firewall computer, which then passes on the permitted packets to the internal computers. The outside and inside computers are completely separated from each other by the Firewall computer.

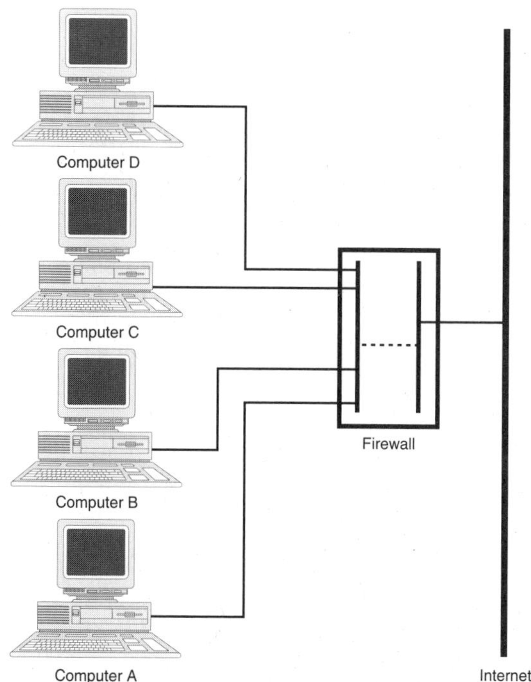

Figure 1.3
Firewall model.

A benefit of the Firewall model is that the internal computers may use their own network addressing scheme independently of the Internet rules. If the internal computers are configured using an addressing scheme that is illegal on the Internet (such as Class A license), any packet that may somehow propagate through any leaks in the Firewall will be rejected by most of the Internet routers as illegal. Likewise, an outside user attempting to break directly into the local network cannot use the local rules because they are illegal from the outside.

One of the problems with placing the Web site on the Firewall computer is the potentially high processing demands on the Firewall. While it processes all the traffic traversing the Firewall, the Firewall computer must process internal and external Web requests. If only one Firewall computer is used, a failure would be catastrophic for the network. Nonetheless, the Firewall model has tremendous benefit of providing security and monitoring network traffic. This model is often used in commercial installations. Multiple firewall computers may be used to help spread the network and processing load among several computers and to distribute the network traffic.

Sacrificial Model

The Sacrificial model builds on the Firewall model by placing the public Web outside the Firewall, allowing direct interaction with the Internet. The Sacrificial model is a compromise between the Firewall model and the Satellite model. The Web site sits on the Satellite computer, freely interacting with the Internet without any intervention of the Firewall.

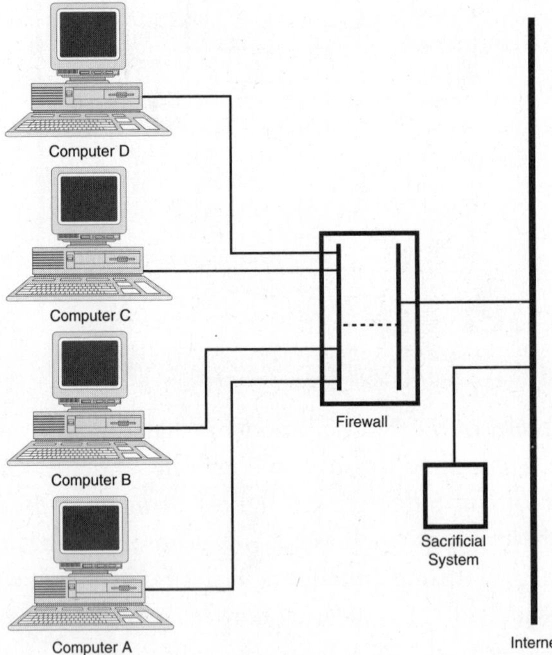

Figure 1.4
Sacrificial model.

The Sacrificial model differs from the Satellite model in that the Web site is updated by completely overwriting the Web contents from a Web site maintained inside the firewall. If the external Web is attacked or even completely destroyed, the external Web site can be easily restored by overwriting the external site with a copy from a "pristine" internal copy. This copying or *mirroring* of an internal, secured Web site to external sacrificial sites also allows for easy maintenance. Although many external sacrificial sites may exist, perhaps to support different parts of the world in different languages, there needs to be only a few (or one) internal master sites.

The concept of an internal site also allows for development and evolution of new Web features without involving the external "production" Web site. This model is becoming increasingly popular because it is fast, relatively easy to deploy and maintain, and secure.

An inexpensive variation of the sacrificial model is to rent space at an independent ISP's site. In doing so, you remove the connectivity of the Web site from your company's network except during the downloading of resource updates. For pilot sites, this option has an additional benefit of temporarily sidestepping the corporate computing resources (MIS). Many corporate network sites are not prepared for networking traffic, security details of a Web site, and the site's integration in their enterprise-wide network. Placing the Web site at the periphery or completely outside the sphere of the corporate network gives MIS the opportunity to study the pilot in isolation from the corporate network.

Internet Features

The following Internet options and services are available to a webmaster, and should be considered when planning a Web site:

- Electronic mail
- Newsgroups
- FTP archive
- Real-time activity
- Chats
- Resource reservation
- Multicast Backbone (MBone)
- Gopher support

The following sections describe the requirements of maintaining these Web capabilities and their usefulness to World Wide Web users.

Electronic Mail

Electronic mail (e-mail) is the most frequently used resource on the Internet. E-mail is the lowest common denominator, supported by almost all sites connected to the Internet—including primitive sites that use a modem to connect periodically.

E-mail is a time-delayed method of communication. A message is composed on the sender's system, sent across the Internet, and is received at some time in the future at the recipient's system. If the network topology includes a central collection point, such as the gateway of a firewall, the e-mail may either be stored or the e-mail may be further disseminated to specific computers in the local domain. Because of the time delay, e-mail is nearly the same as sending a conventional mail message, though hopefully the transmission speed is much faster! This differs from real-time communication, such as "chat sessions" which require real-time ("live") interaction of two or more parties.

For the Web administrator, e-mail provides a simple way of coordinating feedback between information providers and Web users. Well designed Web sites have numerous places for individual feedback using the mailto: directive. E-mail may be to the webmaster, who takes general responsibility for the Web site, or to individuals responsible for the content of the Web site. Often, the output of HTML forms on a Web site is submitted to sendmail for further processing. A Web administer may send e-mail to designated Web users notifying them of new material in their area of interest. Thus, e-mail provides bi-directional communication between the users and information providers.

Handling E-Mail

A commonly overlooked area of Web development is designating who will answer incoming e-mail. Although e-mail directed to the webmaster is usually handled by the team responsible for maintaining the Web software, e-mail directed to content providers of the Web is often not assigned.

Internet turnaround times usually are 24 hours. Many of the questions posed about information content tend to be repetitive, resulting in a frequently asked questions (FAQ) list. This FAQ may be posted directly on the Web site to reduce future questions or to help user queries be more specific. Repeated questions about a specific topic point to a deficiency in the site and suggest future information areas to be covered on the Web.

Searchable Archives

Many Web sites serve as a digital library of information and a backdrop for a "virtual community" comprising Listserv and newsgroup discussions that cover similar material. Listservs and newsgroups are e-mail–based and provide a lavish source of insight about Web information. If a Web resource bills itself as the ultimate information on baseball statistics, this is a natural electronic library to host and archive discussions regarding baseball. Questions arising from discussions can be researched in the Web site. Any deficiencies or inefficiencies of the Web site can be discussed and remedies proposed.

Many administrators are integrating automatic subscription forms and newsgroup pointers in their Web sites; more savvy Web administrators understand the value of older messages from a few days, months, or years ago. Questions tend to repeat over and over again. Why not organize the e-mail and news messages into a searchable archive, allowing a user to follow an earlier discussion? The capability to search a growing resource is a natural function of a Web site.

Warning If a Listserv or newsgroup is unmoderated, information slated for automatic archiving may be unacceptable to the needs and regulations of the Web site.

Audience-Specific Listservs

The types of questions posed and the content of the discussion groups are influenced by the Web site's audience. If a Web site supports three audiences: marketing, established vendors of the company, and customers of the company, the types of questions and range of the discussion may be quite different. The first audience can be viewed as "private" and "friendly." Company individuals, possibly only fellow marketing individuals in a department, may make up this group. Their message traffic can be reviewed by everyone participating in the group. The second audience is "private" and "unfriendly." The information present in this audience is competitive and may be extremely damaging if it is seen by a competing company or a competing vendor on a contract. The information in this second audience may be shared by a specific group within the company (such as legal affairs, purchasing), but is kept separate from each individual user. Nevertheless, both audiences might be supported by a company-sponsored Listserv hosted by the company running the Web site.

The third Listserv may be hosted elsewhere, requiring the Web administrator to obtain the message traffic either as an individual user or to obtain the message periodically from the Listserv owner. This open list is "public" and seen by everyone. Unless the list is moderated, all of the message traffic is seen by everyone.

E-mail is the basic commodity of the Internet; seamlessly integrating and archiving this simple medium is the sign of a well run Web site. E-mail provides the basic method of communication between the Web's users and information providers, making the Web site more useful to everyone. Like e-mail, newsgroups also measure the success of a Web site.

Newsgroups

Newsgroups have many of the same properties as the e-mail and Listservs. Newsgroups provide a slightly more efficient mechanism for the extensive traffic and flow of information. Web sites can archive and sort newsgroup messages, wait for suggestions and complaints about the site, and encourage Web usage by acting as a digital library. Many Web administrators may store a local copy of the newsgroup feed on a centralized machine in their company. This computer is often called the "News Machine." One machine of the company contacts the Internet Service Provider and downloads the designated newsgroups periodically. This local machine then provides rapid newsgroup access at the local company level. Company-specific newsgroups, which do not propagate to the Internet, can also be located on the News Machine.

A News Machine supporting approximately 5,000 active newsgroups must be capable of exchanging and updating 500–600 MB per day. The News Machine will store older news messages on the local server for a designated period of time ranging from a few days to indefinitely. The decision of how long to maintain news on the local News Machine depends on the amount of disk space, network bandwidth, and processing power of the computer serving as the News Machine. If the news is archived on a 1.2-GB disk drive and the news archive grows at a net rate of 500 MB per day, the retention rate of the existing news will be fairly short.

Note Not all newsgroups are of equal importance nor does each newsgroup have the same level of activity. Some newsgroups may have one or two 4 KB messages per day, while other newsgroups may have 300 messages of a given size per day.

The administrator presenting the newsgroups through a Web interface is then confronted with both a technical and political issue. Technically, does the News Machine have sufficient network bandwidth to quickly move the news between the local users and the Internet Service Provider at all times, including peak times of usage? If there is a delay, is it acceptable? Do bandwidth requirements of the news server compromise any existing network service? If the News Machine is inside a firewall, can the firewall machine handle the traffic? Does the News Machine have sufficient computing power to serve the users of a large news archive or should the News Machine be spread over several machines to present a virtual News Machine?

Note Over 20,000 newsgroups currently exist on the Internet.

FTP Archive

An FTP archive is a repository for static resources, such as software releases and other information commonly provided in binary form. One example would be to store the latest release of a World Wide Web browser, a special viewer, or some other binary data in a compressed format. The anonymous FTP site is often accessed by Web browsers because it allows administrators to post information pertaining to Web access, solicit user demographics, and direct specific releases to specific audiences. For example, a user might enter an anonymous FTP archive via a Web browser and be asked for the country of origin and desired language. If the software the user is looking for has import/export restrictions on certain versions or has software versions catering to specific international cultures, the user can easily obtain the correct software on his first pass.

One drawback to FTP access is that if a user accesses the site for a long period of time scarce system resources are consumed. This is particularly troublesome during long downloads (such as 10–15 minutes) because the resource cannot be used by another user. Popular Web sites releasing software updates on the Internet often exhaust the available FTP resources on a system. Many sites restrict the number of FTP connections within business hours to permit the system to function. Other sites use the Web server to determine a suitably idle FTP archive and attempt to perform simple load balancing by sending a user to this unsaturated site. In this load sharing setup, the Web server adds additional value to the conventional anonymous FTP facility.

The anonymous FTP site may also have an incoming site for users without an account who want to place information on the site. For example, the manuscript and illustrations for this chapter could be submitted to the editor in binary form at the publisher's anonymous FTP site. This information would be stored in a special directory (such as /incoming) until it is reviewed for security issues and content. Because this disk partition supporting incoming FTP access is not password controlled, a quota on the maximum amount of material should be enforced (or a separate disk used) to ensure system integrity cannot be compromised if all the disk space in the /incoming partition is filled.

Real-Time Activity

Listservs and newsgroups provide a method of peer-to-peer communication over time. This time-delayed nature of communication also allows some lag time to update the Listserv and newsgroups information on the Web server. Time-delayed communication also inherently lets participants operate at their own pace. The flip side is the lack of real-time conversation, or the ability to read body language and assess nontext-based cues through a video signal.

The network requirements for real-time communication are much greater than for time-delayed communication. If real-time communication involves transmitting speech, it must be transmitted at a sufficient rate to ensure it will be both intelligible and interactive. If the communication uses video in addition to audio, the network bandwidth of this large signal also becomes an issue.

The following sections discuss the use of text-based real-time communication methods and their integration into Web servers, following the model proposed for Listserv and newsgroup communication. Sections also explore the potential use of new technology, such as the Internet phone and MBone in the context of the Web site.

Chats

Chats involve real-time communication of one individual with many individuals in the chat audience. This function emulates the "talk show" environment, allowing the audience to listen to other conversations and chime in when they feel it is appropriate. Some Chat sessions also assign users to "virtual seats" to facilitate private communication to participants sitting in the "nearby virtual seats." The chat session is similar to newsgroup participation in that communication is usually immediate, impromptu, and may be heard by an openly defined audience. From the Web administrator's point of view, a chat session is a rapidly evolving Listserv or newsgroup archive; a transcript of the entire chat session is preserved and made available when the session ends.

Live Video and Audio

Direct communication tools, such as Chat, are text-based and consume little network bandwidth and processing power. If packets of information between parties are slightly delayed (usually the case), the text transcript may be awkward, but it does continue. Tools for communicating with audio (such as Internet phones) and video exist, but they reveal the design limitations of today's Internet. Internet packets are expected to arrive at some time in the future without any type of prioritization, which is perfect for Internet chat. Interactive video and audio transmission, on the other hand, require a guaranteed time and sequence for the delivery of packets. If the packets are delayed due to excessive collisions, the video and audio will break up, be bursty, and render the transmission unintelligible.

The Internet obtains its cost benefit by sharing communication lines. Whenever communication resources are shared, the probability of these resources being busy is always present. When the Internet gets busy, the network slows down. Following the standards employed on the Internet today, each packet of information is treated with equal priority. This is tolerable for delayed communication, but for direct communication requiring real-time performance, such as the delivery of a certain number of video frames per second, this is intolerable. Video goes into slow motion, jerks, and sometimes stops on or between frames. Audio transmission also breaks up. Nevertheless, real-time video and audio currently can be sent over the Internet because the paths taken during the transmission are not busy. As more people interact with voice and video, the demands on the Internet will increase rapidly. Two methods to handle this load have been proposed: resource reservation and multicasting.

Resource Reservation

A Web administrator may suggest using interactive video during "quiet times" on the network (or Internet) when there is less network traffic. As Internet use increases, quiet times on the Internet decrease. If the interactive video will be used inside the firewall, the network administrator might be able to rearrange the network to isolate resources for this purpose. Indeed, if all the interactive video users are within a specific network locale, a quiet period may be possible, such as at night. Users needing guaranteed access at their own convenience may agree to pay their Internet provider a higher price for faster access. This might work as long as all the parties involved exist within the Internet provider's portion of the Internet. If the parties are spread throughout the world, the messages are subject to traffic outside the Internet provider's computer.

Multicast Backbone (MBone)

The Multicast Backbone (MBone) protocol and transmission process offers live, worldwide audio and visual feeds across the Internet. MBone is a virtual network existing as a layer on top of the physical Internet to support routing of Internet Protocol (IP) packets. The network is composed of nodes that directly support IP multicast LANs like Ethernet, connected by virtual point-to-point links called *tunnels*. The connecting points of these tunnels are usually workstation-class computers running the "mcast" multicast routing daemon and capable of supporting IP multicast transmission. Multicast packets encapsulate data with the traditional datagrams they pass between the intervening routers and subnets composing the Internet. When the encapsulated packets reach another point on the tunnel, the packets are unencapsulated and the multicast packets are reassembled into the desired message. The MBone is fairly new and not widely used. Nevertheless, it is one approach to delivering time sensitive packets across the Internet.

The technology for multimedia—real-time delivery of interactive media across the Web—is still in its infancy. Text-based chat sessions can be archived on the Web site following the example of the time delayed Listservs and newsgroups. In principle, the feeds from interactive video could also be archived and indexed via hypermedia search engines to create a video-on-demand network. At present, this approach is still experimental and has not been implemented on a commercial scale.

Gopher Support

Gopher was one of the original tools for surfing the Internet. This system selects resources from menus and is often still supported in many institutions. The Internet gopher supports the basic client-server architecture seen in the client-server environment of the World Wide Web. Gopher predated the Web and will probably disappear as an interesting relic of the past. Fortunately, Web browsers can access existing gopher resources. In some situations, gopher browsers are still being used where Web browsers are unusable. If your user base requires gopher support, you can either run a combination Web/gopher server (GN is public domain software that provides these capabilities) or run two processes, one to support gopher and the other to support Web activity. Gophers are fairly easy to support because the documents require no hypertext markup, contain no hypertext, and are efficiently organized for the end user.

Gopher support involves maintaining the information base underlying the servers. The GN software allows the same information resource to be served to both gopher and Web browsers, but the Web version has no HTML formatting and appears as a <PRE>...</PRE> document. Without the capability to embed hypermedia links, make use of the Common Gateway Interface (CGI) and format text and multimedia, these documents are not attractive to the Web user accustomed to conventional HTML. In this case, the information base tends to diverge. Clearly, when an information resource makes heavy use of multimedia (such as images and sound), the gopher is unable to support this media. If there is a divergence in the contents of the gopher site and a corresponding Web site, maintaining the two resources will become more difficult. Some Web administrators support the gopher site as a subset of the Web, with a goal of retiring the gopher site in the near future.

World Wide Web

The first steps in designing a successful Web site are asking yourself:

- What is the purpose of this Web site?
- What are the measurable goals of this Web site?

The first question addresses the vision for the information resource. This vision often includes a central theme of the corporation. The second question addresses why the Web site should be started and maintained. This information must be translated into user demographics, frequency of access, and other market research.

Three general questions underlie the technical design of the Web site:

- What is the central information structure of the resource?
- What World Wide Web server software and ancillary software will be used?
- What is the source of the initial information and all subsequent information for the Web site?

Central Information Structure of a Web Site

How will the Web site be structured to allow maintenance and growth? This concern can be addressed by considering the following:

- The most traditional use of static links to specific files
- The integration of legacy software into the Web site
- The updating of meta-menus
- The use of dynamic links pointing to a variety of resources

Many older Web sites provided information directly from the file system of the computer running the Web server. Examination of the URL in the hypertext link shows explicit links to a specific file for each link. This is the simplest approach and, presuming the file system has few restrictions on the namespace of a file, is widely transportable to a large range of Web servers. Exceptions include the DOS filesystem, where the filename is restricted to the eight plus three rule and Macintosh filesystems, where filenames may include blanks characters. Unix filesystems are case sensitive, which presents a problem if the URL contains upper- and lowercase letters. Some Web browsers alter the case of the URL to all uppercase or all lowercase, making it impossible to access a URL that explicitly requires a case match (a filename such as TheTrueFile.html).

Use of the filesystem of the computer operating system to structure the information on the Web site also suffers from the inability to support version control of the Web documents. A successful Web site is revised over time. While most Web sites maintain only the "latest and greatest" pages, there may be a legal reason to maintain earlier pages so that the Web administrator can reconstruct the Web site at a particular point in time. Version control also allows the administrator to trace bugs, find the origin of changes, and document the overall evolution of the Web site. This tracking information is difficult to maintain when relying on the computer's operating system to order the information.

Static Links

The fundamental way to represent menu items and hypertext links in a Web site is by providing statically defined pointers to a predetermined resource. When the user activates a specific link, a known resource is provided. If this known resource is a specific file, it is known as a static link. What if several files could be used as a target for the hypertext link? Should the static link point to yet another menu (that is, a meta-menu) of existing links? A meta-menu is a solution when the Web site is fairly small and the choices for hypertext links are limited.

Meta-Menus

The model of meta-menus has problems when the Web site grows. How are these menus updated as more and more documents are added to the Web site? Will each static link have to be revisited to reflect the new additions to the Web site? This isn't practical if there are 3,000 links that must be manually updated. If there is hypertext link to "oil exploration sites," will the meta-menu contain all possible information on the Web site pertaining to oil exploration? Perhaps the user is interested in environmental impact of oil exploration? A common meta-menu serving all different types of user questions will serve them all poorly. The static link and the meta-menu therefore are neither scaleable enough nor flexible enough to help users at large sites.

Dynamic Links

One solution is to use a search engine, which can rapidly find information. Presenting menu after menu of information is useful for the casual browser, but for the user seeking specific information, it is an enormous waste of time. Suppose, for example, that you are interested in environmental impact statements for oil exploration in the Alaskan area between 1980 and 1990. You find a Web site with environmental information for the USA. You must then traverse many menus to find the specific topic. If this question could be posed to a search engine integrated into the Web site, the correct menu would appear immediately from the search request. This is extremely useful because it contains all the information available on the Web site regardless of when it was added.

Static links can be replaced with links composed of preset search queries. In the previous example, a static link could be replaced with a search query containing "oil exploration" + "environmental impact" + "Alaska" + "1980-1990." This type of dynamic link helps make the Web site a comprehensive information resource and also allows automatic updating of these links every time the search index is recomputed.

Dynamic links can also be constructed to provide information to the user based on demographics. If a user indicates that his or her primary interest is finance, the search engine can be biased to find and return documents oriented to a financial audience.

User-Customized Web Services

Dynamic links that are sensitive to the user's interests are another way to structure information; this type of design involves user-customized Web resources. One requirement of good Web design is to provide high quality information to users in a fast, reliable, and transparent process. Rigid information structure is easy to maintain for the Web administrator, but it might be counterproductive to the Web user whose model of approaching the information may be quite different. Borrowing an analogy from the newspaper world, the conventional newspaper is organized into sections such as: world news, local news, sports, business, classified, and comics. Newspaper customers are free to read the newspaper in any order, perhaps starting with the sports section, followed by the business section, and so forth. If readers are interested in sports business, the newspaper company might rearrange the preset sections, possibly throwing out the weather page and other irrelevant international news. If the newspaper reader must hurry, only a short amount of time can be spent on each article. Repackaging the rigid format of the newspaper is difficult.

On the Web, repackaging existing modules of information to allow users to specify their own personal view of your Web site is fairly simple. The use of the search engine to support a dynamic hypertext link is just one way. Tuning the dynamic links to questions the user answered when he or she filled out their demographic profile is another solution. The closest analogy in the conventional print world is the clipping service, which focuses on specific areas of interest.

Legacy Applications

Information provided on the Web may also be generated on the fly, based on the user's request. The Web administrator is often requested to provide an interface to an existing legacy software application. In this chapter, we shall consider two such classes of legacy applications. In both of these classes, the resulting document served to the Web user is transient and is generated for each user request. This method uses the Common Gateway Interface (CGI) discussed later in this book. The CGI links the Web server with ancillary programs coexisting in the Web environment. In both classes of application, the user fills out an HTML form supplying the input. The first class of application takes the input and processes it, producing HTML output for the user. This application may be a simple calculation of a tax form or a multimedia visualization of the user-specified model.

The second class of application takes user input and applies it to a database lookup. The database results are then processed through a report writer in HTML and presented to the user. The database might be a Search Engine for the Web site or a commercial database (such as Oracle, Sybase, or Foxpro). These applications are accessed outside the user's view and may be running on any machine connected on the network with the Web server. Indeed, the database query may search local databases and databases maintained in other areas of the world that may use different search methods and different protocols. All of this transparent to the user.

Use of the Web as a front-end for existing legacy applications is a powerful way to provide quality information and to encourage the use of legacy software. The Web browser is a convenient, portable, and inexpensive graphical user interface for existing applications.

World Wide Web Server Software

What should you look for when selecting a Web server software package? The best Web server software depends to some degree on the Web site's design (satellite, pass-through, or others) and on your budget. Many freeware and shareware Web server packages are available, but they presume the administrator is prepared to actively support the package with freeware upgrades, patches, and customizations. With freeware and shareware, you get what you pay for. If you have sufficient staff and can review the software package, public domain software is obviously cost-effective (it's free!). For facilities that must support gopher and Web resources using a single information resource, the public domain package GN is the only way to go. GN has been superseded with a Web-only WN server that is also freeware and supports the high level security of GN. (GN is currently in a maintenance phase.) The CERN and NCSA's httpd software provide other inexpensive Web servers for the Linux environment.

Note Some Web sites must support multiple Internet addresses on a single platform. Web software that supports different IP addresses simultaneously can handle this configuration. This is called a multihomed server (such as Apache server). A single computer may have several ethernet interfaces. A separate homepage is assigned to each ethernet interface, all running from one Web server process. Thus, several Web sites can be maintained on one platform, reducing the administrative load and hardware requirements substantially.

Commercial packages for Web servers and ancillary software are beginning to proliferate. These packages tend to bundle more features and ancillary tools around a common Web server core. Features may include the ability to restrict access to portions of the Web site, such as a pre-approved audience or pay-per-view monitoring. Many of the commercial packages also provide either Secure Socket Level (SSL) or SHTTP (Secure Hypertext Transmission Protocol) capabilities for future use in conducting commerce over the Internet. Support contracts from the commercial vendor also are available for the frustrated Web administrator. Freeware packages, on the other hand, quickly add new features and provide a huge audience of help online via newsgroups and Listservs. Because the code base is available in the public domain to "helpers" and "hackers," responsibility for software upgrades rests with the Web administrator.

Web Software Requirements

A Web site integrates ancillary databases that contain access control, billing information, and user demographics. If a portion of the Web site is restricted to a pre-qualified user population, it is critical that the username/password access control of this area of the Web site works flawlessly. If billing is associated with the Web site, the appropriate measurement of either time spent or resources consumed must be carefully tabulated. Is the Web software equipped to handle billing per resource or per time duration of use? Does the Web software allow for the collection and measurement of user demographics? Can the Web software support dynamic links so that the Web users can customize information to their liking?

Access and Security Log Files

A critical requirement of a Web site is to maintain a record of how the Web site is being used and who is using the Web site. All Web server software generates access and security logs. These logs are invaluable in the design and implementation of a Web project. Before the site becomes public, the logs help identify glitches. When the Web site goes online, the logs establish security problems and monitor patterns of usage. A substantial amount of data from the log files can help answer the question: How is the Web site performing?

Depending on the topology of the Web site, the log files will indicate who is reading what type of material and how they are reading it. These are merely measurements of services requested and result in a "hit" count. A *hit* is a request for an individual resource and is fairly meaningless. A document with six inline images will produce seven hits when it is requested by a Web browser supporting graphics (that is, 1 document + 6 images = 7 "hits"). Hits are also skewed by curiosity; this is similar to children in a museum. When they are confronted with buttons in front of a display, they generally press every button to see what will happen. A hit count does not measure the impact of the information on the user's decision making process; it merely indicates a resource was requested.

The Web server log file can be quite useful. The overall hit count can give some indication of which documents are "hot" and which documents have never been accessed. Perhaps the document has never been retrieved because there is no easy access link. Perhaps there is little interest in the subject matter. Unfortunately, the log file does not address the key question: What is the impact of the Web resource in the user's decision making process in their business and lives? This can be accomplished by physically watching users and discussing their use via the virtual communities mentioned earlier.

If the user comes from a unique Internet (IP) address, his or her progress through your Web site can be traced by examining the log file. The log file will tell you which resources were requested and in what order. A user might request an article discussing an "Introduction to Cancer," followed by an "Introduction to Breast Cancer," followed by "Clinical Trials for Breast Cancer." This pathway gives some information about the user. If the user activates many of the hypertext links defining medical terms used throughout these articles, this implies the user is not a healthcare professional conversant with oncology terms. If the information resources are arranged in discrete modules, the order of the request can be reviewed to establish the user's train of thought. Those who "press all the buttons" (like the child in the museum) will traverse discrete modules in a different path. Often this path depends on the proximity of the hypertext links on the user's screen. An user who activates each hypertext link in the exact order it appears in a document, with an identical time delay between activations, is usually a robot or knowbot, covered later in this book.

This analysis breaks down if the user is coming through a gateway shared by other users accessing the Web site simultaneously. If several users from America Online (AOL) are accessing your Web site at the same time, the IP address will not be unique. AOL uses 6–10 gateways to the Internet for all of its users. In this scenario, a discrete IP address during a given timeframe will reveal "the user" following several lines of thinking simultaneously. Several users are following different lines of thinking as they simultaneously browse your Web site. Distinguishing individual pathways of AOL users at this time is difficult.

In principle, the log file also gives some demographics. Users can be grouped by their Internet domain, separating commercial users from education users. Country codes can be discerned, if they are used. However, demographics of users from large carriers such as CompuServe, AOL, and Prodigy do not reveal the user's country of origin. Domain addresses ending in "net" and "org" also make identification of geographic origin difficult.

Search Engines

Search engines allow Web users to move rapidly to desired information without wasting time traversing menu after menu. Search engines can also index other Web sites so that users can search thousands of Web sites with a simple query. Searching other Web sites for information will be covered later in the book in the discussion of robots and knowbots. Search engines such as the Wide Area Information Service (WAIS) and Glimpse are available in the public domain to provide a full text indexing and search index.

Tip One of my design goals of the cancer information resource, OncoLink, was to ensure the user finds something useful within two minutes of entering this multimedia resource—even if the user doesn't know enough to ask the first question. I learned that most people can't spell the search terms very well, which necessitated the use of a phonics algorithm to guess probable search terms.

When exploring the realm of a World Wide Web site, the question of "where do I begin" may pop into mind. Browsing menu after menu may be appropriate for the casual Web surfer, but for users who need detailed information quickly, search capabilities are the answer. WAIS is one way to provide full-text indexes of Internet Web sites. WAIS was developed by Thinking Machines in collaboration with Apple Computer, Dow Jones, and KPMG Peat Marwick. This consortium developed a generalized retrieval system for accessing data around the world. Like the World Wide Web, WAIS uses the client-server model. On the server side, WAIS software indexes the documents and creates an inverted index to be accessed by WAIS and Web browsers. This index is run regularly to reference the documents composing the Web site. Active agents, covered later in this book, can be used to create indexes of external Web sites. These indexes are searched by the user's WAIS clients or Web browsers.

WAIS is a distributed information service that takes its input in a simple natural language format, offers indexed search for fast retrieval, and has a "relevance feedback" mechanism to bias future searches. For example, suppose your query to the WAIS client is relatively vague, producing a long list of resources for further examination. You might select a subset of this list and request "something similar to these selections." WAIS servers can be used to index resources such as telephone directories, reports, catalogs, spreadsheets, graphics, and video. WAIS search engine capabilities can even be used from the Web interface as the target of a hypertext link.

WAIS search engines also support Boolean queries, supporting syntax such as: "red and green not blue." This search will get all items containing both red and green, and excluding all records with blue. Partial requests, such as "hum*" might show "hum," "hummingbird," and "humid." For users who don't know how to spell their search term, WAIS can use the soundex and phonics search algorithms to "guess" correct matches.

The soundex and phonics algorithms are very handy when you aren't sure how to spell what you are looking for. In reviewing the search terms for the cancer information resource, OncoLink, it was obvious that many people can't spell the medical terms for which they are seeking information. If the search engine attempts a literal match, it will only report similar misspellings in the literature. If the soundex and phonics routines are employed on the incoming search term, the desired information is found very quickly. Hopefully, the frustration level also drops significantly.

Policy, Liability, and Auditing

This section explores the issues of information content of the Web site, the liability of the information, and the tracking of the Web site information. The first policy of the Web site is to address its goal. What is its purpose? What functions should the Web site not perform? What is the process for approving information destined for placement on the Web site? Who evaluates the "look and feel" as well as the information once it is placed on the Web site? What are the liabilities for placing traditional or new information on electronic media, especially when the Web site is now seen throughout the world?

A Web site should continually evolve over time, bringing new information and resources to users. There should be something new on the Web site at frequent and predictable intervals. The Web administrator needs to establish sufficient channels to facilitate a continual stream of new information. In keeping with established policies, this new information needs to be reviewed for accuracy and timeliness. This review process takes time and adds to the delay in producing information for the Web site. If several channels are simultaneously feeding information to the Web site, individual delays can be buffered from the Web site users.

A public Web site is currently the most popular type of interface for corporations on the Internet. The information posted on a public Web site should undergo the same review as any other information targeting the public.

Information generated under contract to an outside firm should be reviewed to see who owns the electronic rights.

In addition to review prior to placement on the Web, the information should be reviewed after it appears on the Web site. The Web site's unique design may alter the information's original intent. Large figures with much detail might be illegible or misinterpreted on today's small screens. Perhaps some mode of multimedia (such as sound or video) will enhance the message. Information parceled into discrete modules to facilitate rapid navigation will be read in a sequence chosen by the user. Thus, some modules might be skipped or seen in a different context. Does this modular presentation obscure the flow of information, perhaps by omitting frequent links? Ready access to the Web server's logs to track "what" and "how" information is accessed is crucial in reviewing the purpose of new information.

Refining the Web site is often neglected. If you place conventional printed documents on the Web the process may be quick, but it will ultimately fail in the long run. The ability to rapidly find information on a Web site requires an intuitive and flexible interface. A good interface starts with a good information architecture; a successful Web site with real usability requires recognizing what is wrong and making it right. Often it takes successive rounds of critical appraisal, revision, and refinement to remove defects. This usually takes time, requires open communication and cooperation between users, and is aided by input from information providers and technical parties. Refinement is usually an evolutionary process for the life of the Web site.

If the Web site hosts a moderated public forum, perhaps via Listserv or newsgroup, the cost and liability of the public forum must be planned for appropriately. An active Listserv or newsgroup might have 200–300 transmissions per day. Although the scope of allowed activities on the service should be clearly posted, a moderated forum presumes the Web administrator has someone actively reviewing each message. Moderation also implies checks for accuracy and intent. If a forum moderator allows slanderous and willfully inaccurate information on the forum, existing precedents allow the sponsor of the forum to be liable. A moderated forum purporting "safe and responsible" information may have to show suitable research into the information contained in each message to demonstrate "responsible moderation." Some forums find this degree of moderation unmanageable and take the position of the common carrier, much like a telephone company. Instead of censoring information on these forums, superior quality and information quantity usually become the norm.

Cost

What is the value for the company of providing information? All discussions of cost should be reviewed in the context of goals of the Web service. If the purpose of the Web site is to maintain internal documents for a peripheral component of the company's business, a bare bones approach to constructing and maintaining the site should be considered. If the Web resource is a pilot site for a corporate-wide information facility, a more robust and scaleable facility is required. Many Web site considerations, such as the location of the Web server in the information topology of the company, are beyond the control of the Web administrator.

When you are researching the cheapest and most common Web server software, always start with public domain software. Linux is a cost-effective (it's free!) software platform that can be used to create a Web site. Linux can run on a variety of Intel platforms and soon may run on Digital Equipment Corporation's AXP computers for high-speed work. The principle costs of a Web site are the Internet access costs and the management of information flow into and out of the Web site. Internet access costs depend on the required bandwidth, security considerations, and the widely varying access charges of local Internet Service Providers.

It is difficult to calculate the cost of maintaining information on the Web site. The Web administrator may employ a technical staff for scanning and incorporating printed documents, maintaining the linkages of the Web site to the databases and other legacy software, and maintaining the HTML of the Web site. The services of a graphics artist for the initial design and subsequent artwork should be retained. Many Web sites employ an outside consultant for the overall design and then maintain them on retainer to assist in the evolution of the Web site.

If the Web site operates as a separate entity, information must be purchased or licensed from existing information resources or constructed under contract to the company. Existing material already employed within the company may be useful, presuming distribution rights are granted.

If the Web site is an integral part of the information flow of the company, the cost of the site can be merged with existing corporate information costs. The Web site is merely another part of marketing, product support, and product evaluation.

The main consideration when designing a new Web site is to understand its goals. What are the intentions of the site today and in the future? Addressing this question will help determine the necessary network bandwidth, network security, and various ancillary services to be integrated in the Web site. Many Web site features, such as e-mail, Listservs, newsgroups, FTP archives for incoming and outgoing information, real-time activities, support for gopher, and search engines for both internal use and use throughout the Internet need to be considered in your goals for the site. These services need to be addressed at a technical level and a policy level; the Web administrator will soon realize the two levels are intertwined.

Core Competency for the Webmaster

by Loren Malm

This chapter discusses issues you will need to be aware of as a webmaster. Because you are likely to be just getting started with the development of your site, particular attention is given to issues you should address early in the process. The chapter gives more attention to the planning and design phases of development than to specific technical issues because the latter are covered in detail in later chapters of the book. The topics discussed in this chapter include these:

- *Important considerations preliminary to site design*
- *An introduction to Web servers and network issues*
- *The function of the webmaster*

- Web site management tools
- Elements of good page design

If you follow the advice in this chapter, you will spend considerably more time planning the layout and organization of your site than you will coding HTML or setting up your server. When you complete this chapter, you will have a thorough understanding of webmaster issues and how you should begin the process of designing and implementing your site.

Before You Build

A good way to find new ideas for your site is to become acquainted with Web sites that have already been created and consider what you observe in terms of what you intend to do with your own site. Peruse the Web with several different browsers if possible; examine the Web sites of others, and ask yourself some questions:

- Do any pages take an unusually long time to display?
- Does the initial screen look awkward in any particular browser?
- Are some of the links broken?
- How will you address these issues in your own site?

These questions concern basic technical problems that can generally be solved by making appropriate changes to the affected pages. If a particular page takes a long time to display, it is probably overloaded with high-resolution graphics. Removing unnecessary graphics and reducing an image's "color-depth" will both speed up a page transmission and cut-down on the workload of the server. Problems with a particular browser are generally due to unsupported functions that can be changed or removed. Broken links can easily be fixed. Also consider the following types of issues:

- Is the site's purpose readily apparent from its initial page?
- Is the order of the site well conceived?
- Is the use of graphics on the page appealing or does it feel cramped?

- Do the pages follow a consistent format?
- Do different browsers display the pages similarly?

These questions address broad areas of site design and go beyond simple technical considerations. Because problems such as lack of organization and inconsistent format involve deeper issues than technical problems such as broken links, they are more difficult to solve, and unfortunately are also the very areas in which sites are most likely to falter. These problems can be avoided by planning your site effectively and following some simple rules described later in this chapter.

Before you begin to plan your site, know what's possible using current Web technology. First, consider that all Web pages are written in a standard code referred to as the HyperText Markup Language (HTML), which is interpreted by Web client software (such as Netscape) to display text, graphics, and links to other pages. Although HTML is considered an official standard, many vendors of Web client software have chosen to support their own "extensions" to HTML in order to provide increased functionality. Therefore, what's possible using current Web technology depends on which vendor you ask. Many consider Netscape to lead the way in the area of HTML extensions, some of the most important of which are the ability to:

- Set the background of a document to a specific color
- Use a graphic image for the background of a document
- Change the size of text, allowing several different sizes
- Do simple animation with dynamic document update
- Arrange text into tables
- Send or "push" documents from the client to the server

Although they are not part of the official HTML specification, Netscape's HTML extensions have become widely supported, even by other vendors. Other Netscape extensions are also available on Netscape's HTML extension Web page:

`http://cgi.netscape.com/assist/net_sites/html_extensions.html`

Even more exciting than HTML extensions are the growing number of "plug-ins" and "helper" applications. *Plug-ins* are small programs that enable Web clients to display animation, live video, and an almost endless variety of other information. For example, the *Shockwave* plug-in from Macromedia can provide animation, video movies, and sound capability, all within a single Web page. Plug-ins that perform virtual reality and three-dimensional animation are also available. Helper applications are similar to plug-ins except that they work outside of Web pages as opposed to within them. When a helper application is used to display a digital movie, for example, the movie is shown in a separate window outside the Web page. Netscape maintains a directory of both plug-ins and helper applications, which can be found at the following locations:

Information about Netscape compatible plug-ins can be found here:

`http://home.netscape.com/comprod/products/navigator/version_2.0/plugins/index.html`

Information about Helper Applications is found at this URL:

`http://home.netscape.com/assist/helper_apps/index.html`

Considering the growing list of available plug-ins, helper applications, and HTML extensions, it is clear that the functionality that can be built into a site is almost limitless. There are even more capabilities on the horizon, detailed in Part VIII of this book, "Tomorrow's Technology." Before you plan your site, look into some of the tools described previously and determine which ones would be most appropriate in helping to get the message of your site across. Remember, however, that special extensions, plug-ins, and helper applications might fail to function or even crash particular Web clients. For example, the Shockwave animation capability will fail to function unless a user's Web client has installed and properly configured the Shockwave plug-in. Because many beginning Web users have probably not yet installed plug-ins such as Shockwave, relying on them to convey important pieces of a site's message can substantially narrow the scope of users who are able to receive it.

Before filling your site with large graphics files, HTML extensions, animation, or movies that make use of special plug-ins or helper applications, consider carefully whether or not your site really needs them to adequately convey its message. One way to help make these decisions is to define a site's intended audience at the outset of the design process.

Defining Your Audience

Although your potential audience is the entire Internet (assuming your site is public) you cannot possibly design your site to meet the needs of everyone everywhere. Given that, you can't be all things to all people; refining your definition will help you zero in on the people you most want to serve. This task is not that difficult. Suppose, for example, these types of Web purposes: you want to sell directly over the Internet as a primary business; you're a mass market advertiser who wants to attract as many people as possible; you need to provide a public information service for your local community; you are setting up an internal Web server for use by employees only. Each of these sites caters to a different group of people. To help define your intended audience and the purpose for your Web page, ask yourself these questions:

- Who will use your site?
- Why has your organization decided to build a Web site?
- How will your pages look, and what types of services will you offer?
- What do you want users to gain by visiting your site?

For example, a luxury hotel developing a Web site to promote its services might determine that in addition to textual and graphical images, a "tour" of the hotel using an online movie would be beneficial. Because the hotel wants its message to reach many potential customers, it takes care to provide as much information as possible in the text and still graphic images. Furthermore, information that does not need to be in a graphical format, such as phone numbers and pricing schedules, is provided in plain text.

In the case of the local community server, it might be known that the residents in the local population generally have only low-speed connection capabilities to the Internet that prohibit large graphic files and other special features such as digital movies.

A person setting up a Web server internal to a corporation is in an excellent position to evaluate what the local network and server will provide, how the user's Web clients are configured, and what services are necessary.

Your Purpose for Building a Site

Like most people, you are probably building a site because your organization recognizes a market for your goods or services on the Web. The goal of your site is therefore likely to be increasing sales, improving customer relations, and delivering product information. If the mission of your site has already been established by top-level management, the design process might be easier than trying to muster a grass-roots development. Building a site will undoubtedly require the collective talents of many employees from various groups within your organization, and top-level direction is necessary to make that kind of collaborative effort a reality.

Evaluating the purpose for your site will help answer important technical questions about how the site should be built. Taking orders for goods and services directly through a Web site, for example, might require advance planning to ensure that the Sales department can access order information collected through the Web, and that the Web server can interface with any existing order processing system currently in place. In this case, such advance planning would include selecting a platform and Web server software compatible with the corporate database server. Defining the purpose of your site will also help:

- Estimate how busy your site is likely to be
- Determine who should be involved in the design process
- Identify who will be responsible for keeping information updated
- Determine how other computing systems will be integrated
- Select a method of connecting your site to the Internet

Although these issues are covered in depth in later chapters, it is important that you consider your network, server software, and server hardware early in the design process. The equipment and software used will affect the site's future development and functionality. The following sections introduce these hardware/software considerations in the design of a Web site.

Server Software Considerations

This section introduces you to some of the options you should consider when deciding which server software to use. This topic is covered extensively in Chapter 16, "Planning for Web Productions," but is briefly discussed here to point out key issues surrounding the selection of Web server software.

Features to Look for in a Web Server

Web server software is currently available for nearly every computer platform—collectively, well over a hundred different varieties of server software are in existence, and more are on the way. Each server offers a different set of features, and evaluating which features are most important to your situation will help you decide which Web server software package is right for you. Some features that might be important to your site include the following.

Easy Interface to Administrator Functions

Some Web server software packages provide a graphical, or "forms" based interface to management functions. This can help speed the process of setting up a Web server as well as making ongoing server maintenance easier.

Highly Configurable

Web servers that are highly configurable lend themselves to increased functionality, such as custom reporting options, advanced error handling, and user defined functions.

Fault-Tolerant

Stability should be an important consideration for every site. Reliable server software seldom crashes and provides mechanisms for handling errors gracefully, such as automatically restarting after a crash. The most common servers (outlined in table 2.1) are generally considered "robust" because they are widely used and tested.

Secure Connections

Accepting credit-card numbers or transmitting other sensitive information over the Web requires some form of secure communications between the client and server. This is generally done through the Secure Socket Layer, or SSL, and is available in the major server packages. Some vendors charge extra for a version of their software that supports SSL communications.

Selecting a Server for Your Existing Platform

Using an existing computer platform saves the expense of purchasing an additional computer and may speed the development process because of familiarity with the platform. Choosing this route, however, means you will have to select one of the server software packages available for your system, instead of picking the features you want in a server and then basing your hardware selection on that decision. Because each server software package only runs on a few platforms, your choices will be somewhat limited. Table 2.1 lists several servers for each of the most common computing platforms.

Table 2.1
Web Server Software for Various Common Platforms

Operating System	Server Name	Server Contact Information
Unix	Apache	`http://www.apache.org/`
	Netscape	`http://home.netscape.com/`
	NSCA	`http://hoohoo.ncsa.uiuc.edu/`
	CERN	`http://www.w3.org/`
Windows NT	Microsoft	`http://www.microsoft.com/infoserv`
	Netscape	`http://home.netscape.com/`
	WebSite	`http://website.ora.com/`
	WebStar	`http://www.quarterdeck.com/`
Macintosh	WebStar	`http://www.starnine.com/`
VAX/VMS	DECThreads	`http://kcgl1.eng.ohio-state.edu/`

Each of the servers in the table is widely used and will likely continue to enjoy third-party software support and ongoing updates. If your platform is not listed, check the server comparison list at `http://www.webcompare.com/` —this site provides extensive information on many different server software packages as well as a comparison of the various features of each server.

When Price Is the Major Consideration

When price is a controlling factor, consider the Apache, NSCA, Microsoft, CERN, or DECThreads servers, which are available free of charge. The remaining server software packages are fee based, although generally the cost for each is under $1,000. The fee-based (or commercial) packages are also generally more fully featured than the freely available options and come complete with additional utilities and documentation.

Web Server Software Support

Free software may be attractive, but consider that "free" generally implies "as is" and is without support. In contrast, the commercial packages generally offer professional telephone support services as well as regular software fixes and enhancements. Commercial packages are also more likely to provide extended features such as secure communications.

If you decide to use one of the freely available server software packages, consider using one of the most widely used packages outlined subsequently. The popularity of these packages helps ensure that you will be in good company if you run into problems; you may be able to get all the help you need through online discussion groups with other users.

Site-Specific Factors in Selecting Web Server Software

Most sites want to offer services beyond "flat" pages that can only display text and graphics. User interaction, such as the ability to fill out a response card or an online order form are generally a necessity. This type of advanced functionality requires advanced techniques such as CGI scripting and database connection. Database connectivity and other programming "hooks" are complex issues that require considerable planning and coordination (see the New Riders book, *Building Internet Database Servers with CGI*, for more information on this). Some Web servers may provide native database connectivity to your existing systems, while others may not connect at all. For example, a site already running a Microsoft SQL Server as its corporate database engine should consider using the Microsoft Web server to provide Web services if interaction between the server and the database is desired.

Note The Common Gateway Interface, or CGI, used to allow the Web client to pass data, such as information from form pages to the server for processing. By enabling users to send information to the server, CGI is responsible for the Web's interactive capability. CGI scripting is covered in Part V, "Web Applicaion Design," and the security issues surrounding CGI are covered in Part VI of this book, "Security."

Netscape servers provide native support for Sybase and Oracle databases, offering a tremendous advantage for sites running either of those as a primary database server. Both the Microsoft server and the Netscape server provide support for the Open Database Connectivity standard (ODBC), which can be used for connecting to a variety of databases when native support is not available.

These examples are oversimplifications and are presented only to show that the best Web server for your site is dependent on several factors within your environment.

Note *Flat Pages* are Web pages that only display text, static graphic images, and links to other pages. This is in contrast to pages that provide interaction, such as the capability to transmit information back to the server by filling out a form.

Network Considerations

An on-site Web server requires a connection to the "outside world" so that people can get to it from outside your organization. Usually this means that you will have to negotiate with an Internet Service Provider (or ISP) to provide you with a connection. Unless you are located in a remote location, a number of ISPs are probably available. ISPs also offer different plans depending on the amount of traffic you need to support. Another requirement is a steady connection to the Internet; options are described in the following sections.

Dial-Up SLIP or PPP Access

This type of service requires the least initial overhead because it involves the use of a standard modem and existing telephone lines. Most ISPs charge for this type of account by the hour. Although this type of setup can be used to manage a server, it is difficult to keep a modem connection "up" all the time, and because pricing is often based on usage it may not be a cost effective solution.

If you can find SLIP/PPP access billed on a flat-rate for unlimited service, however, it can be a good deal. Flat rate connections are widely available for under $100 a month, and are decreasing. Of course, you need to figure in the cost of maintaining a dedicated phone line for this type of access, which is usually around $25 a month.

Note The *Serial Line Internet Protocol* (SLIP), which, together with the Point-to-Point Protcol (PPP), allows connection to the Internet without having to purchase special hardware or telephone lines. Instead, a standard modem and connection software is used to establish connection. ISPs that provide SLIP or PPP connection can recommend the appropriate software and provide help with its configuration.

Dedicated 56 Kbps line

A dedicated line ties directly into the phone company through a direct digital connection. This type of service requires special equipment, and is therefore more costly than modem access. The advantages, however, are substantial; your connection is virtually uninterruptable, and the speed is much faster than what a modem can offer. Charges for this type of connection have an initial setup cost of around $1,000 and incur an additional $450 a month.

Integrated Services Digital Network (ISDN)

An Integrated Services Digital Network combines the efficiency of using existing telephone wiring with the benefit of true digital communication. If ISDN service is available in your area, it often costs only a little more than a dedicated phone line. A dial-up/ISDN combination can provide connection more than twice as fast as dedicated 56 Kbps line; around 128 Kbps without data compression. An ISDN connection usually requires special equipment (some workstation and server class machines, such as Digital Alpha computers, come with ISDN jacks) that will add to your setup cost. Setup charges can be anywhere from $50 to several hundred dollars, and monthly rates are generally between $50 and $200.

Fractional T1

A fractional T1 is a high-speed connection for large installations that support several servers. It is called a "fractional T1" because you are allotted a fraction of a T1 connection. Setup charges for this type of connection are usually in the $2,000 range and require special on-site equipment. Monthly charges for fractional T1 service vary depending on the size of the "fraction" you purchase; expect to pay around $1,500 a month for a standard 256 Kbps connection. For a 128 Kbps connection, expect to pay at least $500 a month.

Dedicated T1

A dedicated T1 line is the fastest possible connection for most locations. It offers about 20 times the speed of a 56 Kpbs dedicated line, which equates to a throughput of about 1.544 million bits per second. A dedicated T1 connection costs at least $2,500 for initial setup charges, and around $650 to $1,800 a month for service, depending on your location. Because T1 connections are generally cost prohibitive, they are usually used only to connect major universities, large corporations, and other high-volume customers.

Faster than T1

A T1 type connection is generally as fast as you need to consider, although higher-end options are available in some locations. A dedicated 10 Mbit

Ethernet connection, for example, would provide about six times the bandwidth of a dedicated T1 connection. Even more advanced is a full T3 connection, which is offered by some ISPs and provides about 20 times the bandwidth of a full T1. T3 connections are generally reserved for use between high volume ISPs and other "backbone" interconnections, such as those that link major cities.

How Much Speed Do You Really Need?

How you connect to the Internet affects the number of clients you can reasonably support at one time, the services you can offer, and how many graphics you can put into your Web pages. The amount of speed you need depends on what you intend to do with your connection; however, unless you plan to be one of the busiest sites on the Web, a minimal investment is all you need for adequate service. Most sites, including those with multiple servers and extended services, work well with a 56 Kbps dedicated line or its equivalent.

Modem connections, however, should be avoided if possible; their reliance on standard telephony makes them somewhat unreliable, and they also tend to slow down while handling traffic.

Using an Internet connection for purposes other than a Web site such as telnet connections, "outbound" Web browsing, file transfers, or e-mail places extra demand on an Internet connection and if applicable to your situation should be considered when estimating expected traffic level for your site. For example, sites that provide a large file transfer area in addition to Web services will have to acquire a higher speed connection than those that simply provide Web services.

Regardless of the connection you choose, be it a useful 56 Kbps dedicated line or a full-blown T1, at some point you will probably outgrow it. Before you commit to a particular technology, check with your ISP or whatever company will lease you a line and ask about its recommended growth path.

Setting Up Web Services on an ISP Machine

The right platform, server software, and network connection are perhaps the most important and lasting decisions a webmaster has to make. These decisions often have to be made early in the development process, when you know very little about the type of service you need to provide. One tactic you can use to delay these important considerations is to develop your initial Web service on a machine maintained by the ISP. You don't connect any of your machines to the Internet; you simply pay a monthly fee for an account on a machine at the ISP's central office.

This type of account gives you access to a standard set of tools for developing your site, a dial-in type connection for site maintenance, and a quota of disk space on the ISP's server. You usually also are given a separate registered domain name that will make your Web server appear as if it's a separate host site, although it's really being served by the ISP's computer system. This sort of arrangement offers several advantages for start-up Web sites, including:

- Pricing for this kind of service is usually inexpensive. An unlimited access account can be as little as $50 a month; some ISPs advertise similar monthly services for as low as $30. Geographic location isn't as important a consideration as with physical connection ISPs, which means you can afford to shop around for the best service and price.

- You save the expense of setup and maintenance of a dedicated connection and do not have to pay for server software or the server. The only things you need on-site are a modem and occasional use of a phone line for site maintenance.

- You don't have to worry about network configuration or server setup because the machine, server software, and server are maintained by the ISP. You can devote your time almost exclusively to developing your site. In addition, start up time is short for this type of arrangement.

- No additional capital investments are required if you need more disk space or want to provide additional features. You are not locked into current technology as you would be with a system purchase, and you usually can pull out of this type of arrangement if things don't go well or if your needs change.

- You can use this type of arrangement to "test drive" the ISP before you make long-term commitments. If the ISP isn't as flexible or as helpful as you think it should be, you can easily move on to another provider.

Drawbacks of Using an ISP Server

One ISP arrangement you want to avoid is services that are billed based on the number of "hits" made to your Web page. This should not be a problem because most ISPs now offer unlimited service for a set monthly fee.

Although this type of arrangement offers a good path for building an initial site, its limitations become apparent as your site grows. Information updates and upkeep are a little harder to distribute among employees if your server is off site because you may be limited to one dial-up session at a time. If the information in your site is updated often, this may become a tedious process.

If you want to use advanced functions such as online ordering and forms processing, an ISP site probably won't fit your needs. Advanced functionality generally requires control of the server and the server software, which you would not have with an account on a remote machine.

Functions of the Webmaster

The "webmaster" is conceptually a new position, and the webmaster's primary responsibilities in your organization are likely just as open to definition. This section discusses some of the most common responsibilities of a webmaster.

Maintenance of a complex and successful Web server within your organization requires a number of people with particular skills. These skills will be required to fulfill the following webmaster responsibilities:

- Selecting the Web server and its software and hardware
- Managing the system and the Web server

- Determining network bandwidth requirements
- Assisting individuals who are responsible for maintaining content
- Selecting a standard set of authoring tools for editors
- Implementing the Web server
- Performing periodic backup of the system and Web server
- Initial testing of the Web server
- Registering your server and basic promotion
- Regular monitoring and reporting of server activity
- Responding to "webmaster" mail
- Regular system and server maintenance
- Integrating the Web server with other systems at your site
- Planning for growth

One thing you might notice about this list of responsibilities is that none of the webmaster duties has anything to do with organizing or maintaining Web pages. This is not an oversight; a good rule to follow is that the webmaster should not become responsible for authoring many of a site's Web pages. Although this might seem to be a contradiction, consider that webmaster responsibilities outside of a Web page's content are pretty substantial for one person.

Note Notice the difference between "server" and "system." Web *server* software runs on a computer *system*. Many times webmasters are responsible not only for managing the Web server software, but also for managing the computer system where the Web server resides.

A Team Approach to Initial Site Development

The development of a good Web site requires expertise and continual work in many diverse areas. A team approach to Web site development uses the collective strength of your organization to address these areas in the best possible way.

The capabilities and depth of how far and wide you can spread the collective tasks of a Web site are affected by the size of your organization and the number of people you are able to bring into the process. The larger and more diverse your organization, the more difficult it may be to pull in all the people you will need for the Web server and site. For a small site, you may be responsible for everything from creating the graphics to doing the backups. This is obviously not an optimal situation and it is one you should try to avoid if possible.

The ideal Web site involves employees from virtually every part of the organization. The best group or person to maintain information on the Web site is the group or individual who maintains the site for other functions unrelated to the Web.

If your site will have marketing information about products your company sells, someone from marketing who understands your company's products would be the best person to maintain the marketing section of the Web site. If you are going to have an online "customer relations" desk, customer support should maintain that particular part of the site.

Note Splitting up a site into several sections, each managed by different groups or individuals within an organization, requires that you also segregate the way Web pages are stored on your system. This segregation prevents one area from accidentally modifying information maintained by someone else. Segregating data on your server will not be apparent to clients visiting your site.

Conceptual Design and Initial Planning

The initial design of your Web site doesn't have to be fancy, but it should be the product of a collaborative effort among different groups and individuals in your organization. Everyone involved in the project should agree who will be responsible for the ongoing maintenance of each section of information. The webmaster does not generally control this process, but does play an important role in facilitating smooth operations. Some things the webmaster should do to keep things moving and to facilitate participation by others are as follows:

- Keep initial site development as simple as possible while maintaining a professional appearance. For example, do not attempt to incorporate fancy Web gadgets or overload graphics into your initial design; these generally add little to your message, increase the traffic level on your network, add processing overhead to your server, and are more prone to failure. In addition, the issues you have to contend with during initial site development provide enough headaches.
- Standardize the tools used to maintain information on the Web site. Even though you probably will not be one of the people maintaining information on the site, you may have to select the appropriate tools. You also will generally be responsible for training people who maintain information in the use of these tools. The "Web Development Tools" section later in this chapter offers more information on this topic.
- Develop a standard method for others to contribute and update information. Ideally, you will configure your site so the people responsible for maintaining each section of information in your site are the ones that perform the actual updates. The first generation of tools that can do this effectively are just starting to become available on the market.

Anticipate that the initial planning and layout of your site will take a lot of time. This is in no way a bad thing; developing a good plan with clear responsibilities smoothes the implementation process. After you finish the design you are ready to begin implementing your server.

Implementation of Your New Web Server

Server "implementation" basically involves getting the Web server up and running with test data to ensure the software works efficiently and effectively. Technical considerations of implementing a Web server are covered in Part III of this book, "Server Setup: Administration and Maintenance," and they vary, depending on the software and platform you decide to use. For example, some Web servers are configured using a graphical interface and others that have no graphical interface are configured by editing configuration files. One easy way to implement a server without broadcasting your site to the world is to start your server on a non-standard port. This allows you to test the features of your server without having to worry about casual users bumping into your site expecting to see the finished product.

If you chose to implement your initial server on an ISP system, setup will probably be as simple as creating the initial directory and file locations. Server implementation for all platforms is relatively simple and can be completed in a "cookbook" manner by following instructions provided by the software publisher. If you decided to use server software that provides technical support, now is the time to check with technical support to see if there have been any late-breaking developments with your software.

Initial implementation is also the only time you will have very little valuable information on your server. If your server is solely for Web use, you probably only have the operating system and server software installed at this point. Because you don't have anything on your server, this is also a great time to implement and test your backup strategy.

Backup and Recovery Procedures

One important part of webmaster responsibilities is regular backup of the Web server. Even if your data changes infrequently, it's essential that you have a sound backup strategy in place before you begin putting information into your site.

If your server runs on a dedicated machine, you can perform backups with a tape or optical disk device connected to the machine. For most servers, this means your Web server has to be down while you do your backup. A backup strategy usually involves nightly backups to tape or some other reliable medium such as an optical disk. A thorough backup solution should be available for less than $2,000 total; backup hardware continues to decrease in price.

An important part of proper backups, whether to tape or disk, is to test them periodically to ensure they are working properly. Backups should always be done with full-verify but even this does not guarantee your backups are working. The only way to verify that backups work is to perform a restore, which you should test before you put data you can't afford to lose on your server.

An uninterruptable power supply (UPS) is a cost effective and worthwhile investment for protecting data and equipment. Most Web servers are no larger than a workstation-class machine, which only requires a basic UPS costing no more then $500.

Quality UPS units (such as those from American Power Conversion—APC) come with software that enables you to shut down the server in the event of an extended power failure. This is an invaluable feature because most platforms, especially Unix machines, can't handle power failures very well.

Server Testing

Verifying that your server is running is usually as easy as connecting to it with a browser. This can be a tedious process, however. Fortunately, there are now automated verification systems that go through all the links and pages of your site to verify their addresses are valid.

No matter how you choose to test your server, it's important that you test it regularly, especially if you have links to services that are not under your direct control. This topic is addressed more fully in Chapter 18, "Monitoring Server Activity."

Initial Setup of Your Web Server and Site Promotion

The initial setup of the Web pages on your Web server involves working with everyone who contributes information and services to ensure that their information is in the proper format. If a number of people are involved, appointing an "editor" will help keep material organized and assure consistent formatting between sections.

After the initial setup of a site is complete, the next task is site promotion. The promotion of your site can take several forms, including posting messages in appropriate newsgroups (such as comp.infosystems.announce) and registering your site with the various Web-indexing servers available on the Web. The largest and most popular Web-indexing servers are shown in table 2.2.

Table 2.2
Popular Web-Indexing Servers

Index Server Name	Server Location
Alta Vista	`http://altavista.digital.com/`
Excite	`http://www.excite.com/`
Lycos	`http://www.lycos.com/`
Magellan	`http://www.mckinley.com/`
Yahoo	`http://www.yahoo.com/`

Each of these sites contains an "Add Site" or "Suggest Site" button that can be used to add your URL to the index server's database. Because these servers are used extensively (the Alta Vista server, for example, handles over two million requests per day), adding your site's location is one of the best ways you can promote your site.

Your Web server software may also provide the capability to create "referrer" logs, which are useful for determining how people are finding out about your site. A *referrer* log records the last site a client was connected to before they came to your site.

Monitoring and Reporting

Reports of server activity is one important task the webmaster should do regularly. Popular server packages include fairly sophisticated activity logging capabilities, and some have integrated reporting facilities that can provide you with statistics on just about any area of use you need. Reporting logs can help you:

- Justify expansion of your server and network bandwidth
- Identify popular areas of your system and build on them
- Obtain general information about who is using your server
- Discover how people located your site

Third party freeware is available on the Web to help you analyze server logs if your server software does not provide the capability.

User Questions, Problems, and Other Feedback

As the webmaster, one of the first things you will want to do is provide some way for users to send you e-mail in the event they have problems with your server or want to provide feedback.

This is an important feature that should appear prominently on your home page. Webmaster mail will be easier to manage if you set up a special account on your system specifically for handling mail coming from the Web server. Most users assume this is the setup you are using and will not indicate in messages that they are sending from a link off your Web server.

To make Web user feedback even easier, include your company's phone number and general contact information with your e-mail address. Of course, the addition of contact information on your home page creates a responsibility that your company must be prepared to accept.

At the very least, employees at the other end of the phone numbers you list should have some knowledge about information on your Web site. It is surprising how many companies overlook this important requirement; the bad impression these mistakes leave with the caller and the frustration phone representatives experience is harmful to public relations.

System and Server Maintenance

Perhaps the most important webmaster duty is the ongoing maintenance of the Web server. This usually involves installing server software updates and keeping the server properly configured. Most webmasters also serve as administrators of the system that is being used for the server, and are therefore responsible for system software maintenance.

System and server maintenance will be easier if you obtain a support agreement with the vendor from whom you purchased the system. Most vendors provide different levels of support (for different priority levels and hours of availability) so there is generally a plan available that will fit your needs and budget.

If you select a server for which no support is available (free servers) your only support option is whatever information you can obtain from Internet Usenet groups and mailing lists. Distributors of the free software usually point you to these sources. Servers available from vendors that offer fee-based support plans also have their own newsgroups and mailing lists, and often are worth checking out. These sources provide a wealth of hints and other information that you probably will not get through a paid support service.

If you paid for support, regularly contact technical support even when you don't have a particular problem. Periodically checking in to verify you are running the most recent software version and patch level is a good habit that can save you a considerable amount of time.

Tip

> When you encounter problems, check the documentation, but if you are paying for support, don't be afraid to pick up the phone. Keep in mind that sometimes a situation can be made worse by "tinkering" with a problem not covered in the documentation.

Integrating Your Web Server with Other Systems

Building interoperability among Web servers and other computing systems is probably the most complex function you can build into a Web server. The applications for this capability are essentially boundless, which means that many organizations will eventually want to plan for this type of service.

Nevertheless, this type of functionality is not something you want to attempt early in the development of your site. If you want to demonstrate that you plan to offer such services, you may want to create a "Coming Soon" link to a page explaining these functions and then see how often users connect to this location. This helps determine if the service is really even necessary.

Another reason to hold off integrating your Web server with other systems is that this setup creates substantial security risks. These security issues exist with any CGI application, but a breach becomes especially dangerous when a Web server is linked to other systems in your organization. A breach of security may mean exposure of information not only stored on your Web server but also on the production environment. This is precisely the reason many sites choose to run their Web server on a dedicated, stand-alone machine that is isolated from the other systems in the enterprise. An isolated Web server amounts to what is known as an "air gap" between systems.

Creating an air gap between your Web server and other systems in your organization is recommended early in the development of the Web site. The reason is that accidental security holes are most likely to occur when you are first learning about your system. Over the long term, however, this policy may be limiting because it precludes any interoperability with other systems in your organization. This level of restriction can sharply limit the legitimate services you are able to provide. For example, if your Web server is isolated from other systems, extended services, such as searching a corporate database located on another system, will be impossible. Generally, the only way to move information between systems in such a totally isolated environment is by disk or tape copy. Security issues related to Web servers and CGI are covered in detail in Part VI.

Planning for Growth

Part of what will determine the success of your site is how well your server is able to keep pace with demand. You might lavish your site with wonderful high resolution graphics, but if pages take too long to display, the user will simply hit the stop button and move on to something else. As a site grows, the webmaster must track performance and determine whether a larger server or more network bandwidth is necessary to keep up with demand. Chapter 20 discusses specific methods and tools you can use to track server and connection performance.

What Is HTML?

The HyperText Markup Language is used to create and access resources on the World Wide Web. HTML uses *tags* or commands embedded inside a document that determine how a document will appear. Tags are also used to indicate functionality instead of plain text and are used to define services.

Web Development Tools

Before you get started developing your site, you need to determine which Web development tools will be used to author Web pages. Several different types of tools are available, including HTML editors, graphics design and manipulation tools, document converters to transform existing documents into HTML, and page authoring tools to help you integrate text and graphics.

As the webmaster, you are probably not going to be doing the majority of page layout or editing for your site; whatever Web authoring software you use should reflect the needs of Web designers who will be creating the pages and performing updates. The following sections introduce you to tools you can use for Web page development. Page creation tools and techniques are discussed extensively in Chapters 27 and 28, "Web Page Graphics Techniques" and "Web Page Layout and Design."

HTML Editors

HTML editors are basically screen editors that also provide syntax checking of HTML code. Most HTML editors alert you when you enter incorrect HTML sequences. One advantage of using an HTML editor is that you can debug your code as you develop your document and see the results of your work almost immediately. Some of the more popular HTML editors are shown in table 2.3.

Table 2.3
Popular HTML Editors

Platform	Name	Contact Information
Windows	HoTMetaL	`http://www.sq.com/`
Windows	HotDog	`http://www.sausage.com/`
Windows	Gomer	`http://clever.net/gomer/`
Mac	Web Weaver	`http://www.northnet.org/best/`
Mac	BBEdit	`http://www.barebones.com/bbedit.html`

HTML editors still offer one advantage over page-oriented tools, however—greater control over the HTML code itself. This is because HTML editors allow direct manipulation of HTML code, and page-oriented tools insulate the user from HTML by providing a completely graphical interface. HTML editors are being replaced by page-oriented authoring tools, however, because of the ease of use the graphical interface provides.

Page Authoring Tools

Page-oriented authoring tools are more advanced than HTML editors in that pages are developed by laying out text and graphics on-screen as would be done with a standard page layout program such as Adobe PageMaker. Documents are saved as HTML code that can be inserted directly into a Web server. Graphically oriented page authoring tools isolate the user from HTML code; the code is not seen while the pages are being created.

Page-oriented editors are not intuitive for people already familiar with how HTML editing works, but are excellent for those with little HTML experience or those who need to concentrate exclusively on page layout.

The biggest advantage to using a graphically oriented page design program is the dramatic reduction in the learning curve associated with the HTML language. The ease of use associated with this program helps enable Web managers to distribute responsibilities for the development and maintenance of information. Two promising graphically oriented page layout tools on the market are PageMill from Adobe and Netscape Gold from Netscape Communications. Specific information about tools is shown in table 2.4.

Table 2.4
Further Information about Tools

Platform	Name	Contact Information
Win/Mac	Netscape	`http://home.netscape.com/`
Win/Mac	IA For Word	`http://www.microsoft.com/`
Win/Mac	PageMill	`http://w1000.mv.us.adobe.com/Apps/`

Graphics Tools

Web pages are graphical by nature, so you will want to include high quality graphic images in many of your pages. Creating and working with graphic images requires a special set of tools and the proper skills. Fortunately, whatever graphical development tools are currently in use at your company to create graphic files will probably also work with the Web.

To properly insert graphics into the Web the designer needs to know the proper graphic file formats and color depth for images. To be displayed by Web browsers, graphic files must be saved in either GIF or JPEG file formats. If your paint or draw software does not save in these formats, you have to use a paint/draw program that does or obtain some conversion software. Most graphics programs that are out now can save in these formats, so you should not have a problem. Graphic file formats are discussed in Chapter 26, "Graphics and Audio File Formats."

Document Converters

Document converters take existing documents from a word processor, for example, and convert the documents to HTML. These tools generally aren't as useful as they sound because documents created for other mediums (such as a word processor) differ from Web pages in layout and organization.

Documents that were created on a word processor and later converted to HTML almost always require heavy *post conversion* steps, which lessens the advantages of the conversion process. For the most part, it is easier to save documents as plaintext and insert HTML code into the documents by hand. Converters are available for the most common document formats however, including Microsoft Word, Microsoft PowerPoint, and WordPerfect. Each of these converters is available free of charge at the locations listed in table 2.5

Table 2.5
Freeware Converter Locations

Converter	Location
Microsoft Word	`http://www.microsoft.com/`
Microsoft PowerPoint	`http://www.microsoft.com/`
WordPerfect	`http://wp.novell.com/elecpub/inttoc.htm`

Systems Management Tasks

Webmasters usually have to manage the system on which the Web server resides. Fortunately, this is generally not difficult or time consuming. The easiest platform to manage with scaleable "server" class power is probably Windows NT; the most complicated and time-consuming is Unix.

If you believe in strength in numbers, you should know that the number of Unix Web servers on the Internet currently outranks every other platform by a wide margin. Windows NT is fairly new to the Web and is still only found in several places. No matter which platform you choose, you need to be concerned with only a few systems management tasks for basic operation:

User Maintenance

The webmaster will need to establish the basic accounts used to maintain system and server software. An *account* consists of a user name and a password and provides the mechanism for verifying identity with the computer system. Each person or group responsible for authoring functions will require an account, which will have to be created and maintained by the system administrator. The system administrator is generally also responsible for teaching each user how to connect to the system and to use the account properly. User maintenance can be simplified by the following:

- Keeping the system configuration as simple as possible
- Installing only the software absolutely necessary
- Giving each user only the access privileges needed

Backup

How you perform backups depends on the platform. Windows NT and most flavors of Unix provide built-in backup software; the only thing you need to add is a tape drive. Systems that don't have built in backup capabilities, such as the Macintosh, require backup software such as Dantz's excellent Retrospect product. Information about Retrospect can be obtained at `http://www.dantz.com/` on the Web.

Security

Maintaining the security of your server typically involves tasks such as accounting for system activity and periodically reviewing who has access to the machine. If you isolate your Web server from the rest of your company's networked systems, security concerns are less pressing than if your site provides interoperability with other systems. CGI scripting generally requires additional security measures and should be done with care. Part VI of this book discusses security issues in general, and Chapter 25, "CGI and SHTML Security," specifically discusses security issues inherent to CGI scripting.

System Maintenance

Basic system maintenance includes monitoring system performance, installing system software updates, and installing programming language tools. Make sure you keep in regular contact with your system software vendor to learn about patches and system updates.

Web Resources

If you need more information about your system, brand of server software, or network connection, the best place to look is the Web. All the major vendors maintain extensive Web sites and provide software updates and other changes. Another place to look for helpful information is the online indexes on Web design. Yahoo, for example, maintains an impressive index of Web design related documents. The address for this index is

```
http://www.yahoo.com/Computers/World_Wide_Web
```

Usenet newsgroups also can be a treasure-trove of information on just about every topic that has to do with the Web. A few groups you should examine include:

For General Information

- comp.infosystems.www.misc
- comp.infosystems.www.announce
- comp.infosystems.www.authoring.misc
- comp.infosystems.www.browsers.misc
- comp.infosystems.www.servers.misc

For Information on Page Authoring Topics

- comp.infosystems.www.authoring.cgi
- comp.infosystems.www.authoring.html
- comp.infosystems.www.authoring.images

For Information on Specific Browsers

- comp.infosystems.www.browsers.mac
- comp.infosystems.www.browsers.ms-windows

For Information on Specific Servers

- comp.infosystems.www.servers.mac
- comp.infosystems.www.servers.ms-windows
- comp.infosystems.www.servers.unix

Page Design Considerations

Some of the basic design issues involved in developing Web pages include the need for style conventions, which will help maintain a professional looking site, and differences in how the page displays using different types of browsers. Chapter 28 covers this topic in detail.

Page Appearance Depends on the Browser Used

Different browsers, and even different versions of the same browser, display pages differently. The biggest problem right now regarding different browsers is that companies and groups are moving ahead with their own specifications faster than the official standards. Netscape, for example, supports many different proprietary extensions to universal standards. Don't expect everyone to download the latest copy of Netscape simply because you include a link to their download site on your homepage, however; many people can't use Netscape on their machines, and others simply don't want to.

Fortunately, the simpler you keep your Web site, the less you have to worry about particular browser inconsistency. Most standard graphic formats, basic text formatting (such as bolding and underlining), and link formatting are consistent between all browsers. Because every browser is constantly being updated, however, the only way to tell for sure how your site will appear to each browser is to test your pages.

Text browsers are another consideration because they cannot display graphics of any kind. Some text browsers simply skip all graphics tags; others display a test message indicating that a graphic file was supposed to appear in that location. It's difficult to say what percentage of Internet use is text-based, but be aware that some clients probably will connect to your site with this type of browser. Some sites allow for text-based browsers by including an entirely separate text-based view of their Web services. This is certainly a helpful addition if your site is not too large, but keeping the text-based pages and graphics pages in sync can be a tough job even on a small site. The best solution is to create your site so that it does not over-stress graphics and displays acceptably on text browsers.

Page Layout Basics

It should be readily apparent from your homepage what your site is about, even if the person viewing it had no idea what he or she was about to see when they were linking to it. Many times your pages will be accessed through a search; controls such as links and other functions should be clearly marked and easily distinguishable, and should be presented in some type of order wherever they occur in your site. Remember that graphics display differently on various types of computers and from different browsers, so the use of graphic images as control buttons may be confusing to some users. Chapter 28 discusses page layout and design extensively.

Using Graphics in Your Web Page

Graphics are an important part of a Web page, but it is easy to overdo it. If graphics don't convey additional meaning, they probably are not necessary or appropriate. Keep in mind that if your Web pages take too long to download, users will just hit the "stop" button and miss your site altogether. The content of your pages is more important; this is why users come to your site.

To encourage users to stay at your site, keep graphics file sizes small. Most paint and draw programs are capable of saving in different file formats and "color depths." *Color depth* affects how accurately your graphic file displays on-screen. The best Web images are not high resolution and more closely resemble cartoon characters than photographs. The reason for this is files with a smaller color depth take considerably less space and time to download.

How "deep" should your images' color depth be? To find out, set your color depth smaller and smaller until the graphic degrades substantially. Keep in mind that graphic images display differently on different systems; you will have to test your browser extensively to ensure that the graphic looks correct across different browsers. Getting graphics to look right while keeping image size to a minimum can be challenging. Chapter 27 discusses Web graphics techniques in detail.

Maintaining a Consistent Interface

Using a standardized in-house template for page design can help provide rapid access times for your clients because templates usually have fewer graphics than custom pages. A standard format is easy to set up; all you have to do is build the outline of the page and let those responsible for maintaining the information in your site fill in the blanks. Many sites currently use this format.

If you have to have jazzy effects on your site, one approach is to customize your home page, then keep all subsequent pages in a standard format. The consistency of subsequent pages looks professional and helps users locate information quickly.

Elements of a Great Site

No site is perfect, although some sites distinguish themselves by putting function before form, and regarding content as more important than the Web medium. All the links are checked regularly and updated as necessary. The most popular section of the site is arranged so that it is easy to access, and the site provides useful information. In addition, each section of the site is regularly updated by people who understand the site's information.

CHAPTER 3

Internet Commerce

by Lisa Morgan

Internet commerce is the capability to buy and sell goods and services using the Internet. For network managers, Internet commerce presents another layer of complexity for enterprise systems and management. This chapter overviews the basics of Internet commerce: What it is; what companies are involved; and what concepts you might want to consider as the Internet becomes a more integral part of your enterprise system.

If your company is contemplating joining the ever-growing Internet community, there are many points to consider. The following list covers some of the benefits:

- **Start-up Costs.** *Setup costs typically range from $10,000–$200,000, a fraction of what is typically required to start a business or division.*

- **HR Costs.** Very little human intervention is required versus the need for a physical storefront.
- **Maintenance.** Maintenance is limited to system maintenance costs; virtually no traditional "overhead" costs exist.
- **Market size.** Anyone with Internet access is a potential customer. More than 30 million people are connected to the Internet, and this number is growing at approximately ten percent per month.
- **Reduced production, storage, and shipping costs.** A server replaces packaging and distribution; the Internet replaces warehousing and order fulfillment, shipping, and transportation; N copies can be "produced" (downloaded) and distributed on demand and at unprecedented, low costs.
- **The Digital Revolution.** Anything digital can be distributed.

Internet Commerce Isn't New

Although the commercialization of the Internet has been the basis for much controversy, people have been buying and selling goods and services for years. Shareware, for example, has been available for many years for free or for a small price. In line with Internet culture, the selling paradigm of shareware has been "Try it, and if you think it's worth it, buy it." Similarly, people have offered other products or services, often at a special price for Internet users. In many cases, the orders might have been placed over the Internet, but payment was sent by regular mail to a physical address (usually in the form of a check). For individuals or very small businesses, this system can work, but a lot can go wrong along the way, as noted in table 3.1.

Table 3.1
Ordered Through the Internet—The Check's on the Way

Ideal	More Likely	Worst Case
Buyer orders	Buyer orders	Buyer orders
Buyer sends check	Buyer gets distracted	Buyer sends bad check

Ideal	More Likely	Worst Case
Seller delivers product	Seller receives payment	Seller delivers product late or not at all
	Seller does or does not deliver product	Payment unlikely

Credit Cards

Businesses have been accepting credit card numbers over the Internet for years, but the ongoing viability of that strategy is the subject of great debate for the following reasons:

- Risk to the individual buyer
- Substantial risk to the credit card company
- Risk on the part of the seller

Businesses and individuals in favor of transmitting credit card numbers over the Internet claim that the act is no different from providing credit card data over telephone lines or handing a credit card to a waiter. Those against transmitting credit card numbers over the Internet claim that it is relatively easy to develop software that searches for credit card details—not on an individual basis, but on a mass basis.

Several companies, such as Godiva Chocolatier, Inc., accept unencrypted credit card numbers over the Internet. For some companies, this might represent a substantial amount of their potential revenue. As the Internet grows and becomes more commercial, there will be an increasing resistance to sending sensitive information (such as credit card numbers) over the Internet.

If sending credit card information over the Internet is so dangerous, why not encrypt the number before sending it?

Encryption has historically been a very expensive proposition for both buyers and sellers. As new techniques emerge and usage increases, the costs will fall. Therefore, it has been easier and more cost-effective to transmit numbers over the Internet. But as cyber-based crime increases and the cost of security falls, a smaller percentage of credit card numbers will travel over the Internet unprotected. Figure 3.1 illustrates remote monitoring of commericial traffic.

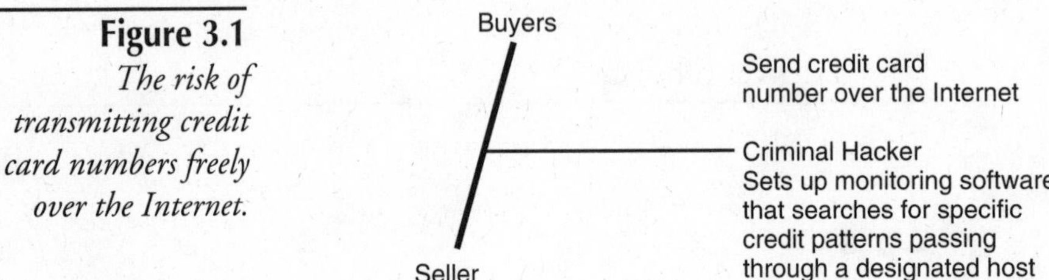
Buyers
Send credit card number over the Internet
Criminal Hacker
Sets up monitoring software that searches for specific credit patterns passing through a designated host
Seller

Figure 3.1
The risk of transmitting credit card numbers freely over the Internet.

Modern Internet Commerce

Today it is possible to not only order online, but also to complete the transaction using an Internet buyer account, a credit card number, a checking account number, or a debit card number. In the future, it will also be possible to settle financial transactions using digital cash, digital checks, and digital credit cards. If your company is serious about conducting business online, you will have to understand the different types of payment mechanisms and systems available, as well as how those technologies relate to your company's overall online strategy (see table 3.2).

Table 3.2
Digital Equivalents

Cyberspace	Physical World
Digital cash	Cash
Digital checks	Checks
Digital credit cards	Credit cards
Checking account number	Debit cards
Server	Product packaging Product duplication (production) Warehousing

Cyberspace	Physical World
Internet	Postal service Overnight delivery Parcel delivery services FAX Phone Channel distribution
Virtual storefronts	Retail stores
Data warehouses	Superstores

Internet Commerce—What's the Big Deal?

Thirty million people are connected to the Internet. That represents only a fraction of all computer users. Further, not everyone connected to the Internet is buying or selling something. So why should your company care?

The number of people connected to the Internet is growing at approximately ten percent per month, according to the Internet Society. This estimate indicates that the number of Internet connections worldwide will someday outnumber the total population.

That may sound farfetched to you and to the executives at your company. However, it is an indisputable fact that the Internet is growing at an unprecedented rate and that it is becoming a major focal point for many American businesses.

Because the Internet is open and unregulated, it is outpacing the development of Vice President Al Gore's National Information Infrastructure (which, by the way, has been appropriately repositioned as the Global Information Infrastructure). With the advent of inexpensive computers, cheap Internet access and security, and a potentially staggering market, the Internet is now open for business.

In *The Death of Money*, author Joel Kurtzman makes the following observations about what he calls megabyte money:

> Every day, through the "lobe" in the neural network that is New York, more than $1.9 trillion electronically changes hands at nearly the speed of light. These dollars—and the cards, hopes, and fears they represent—appear as momentary flashes on a screen.
>
> Every three days a sum of money passes through the fiber-optic network underneath the pitted streets of New York equal to the total output for one year of all of America's companies and all of its workforce. And every two weeks the annual product of the world passes through the network of New York—trillions and trillions of ones and zeros representing all the toil, sweat, and guile from all of humanity's good-faith efforts and all its terrible follies.

Electronic commerce is now headed for the Internet. Given its global structure and staggering growth, its effect on business cannot be overlooked by executives, entrepreneurs, users, or network managers.

Management Issues

Whether you are responsible for running a business or working with management to set up employee network usage policies, you will soon have to examine the possible effects Internet commerce might have on your business. Some Internet commerce models, for example, support transactions among individuals and require only e-mail access for both buyers and sellers. So not only can your network users buy goods and services, they can also sell them.

More likely, your company may soon consider Internet commerce part of its overall business strategy, which will require you to integrate hardware and software designed specifically for Internet commerce into your existing enterprise system.

Threats from Employees and Criminal Hackers

Your own employees pose the largest risk to your organization even though criminal hackers are getting most of the publicity. Now that information is considered a corporate asset, security has become an imperative part of any network. When financial transactions become part of the mix, the risks to your company—and the potential payoffs for employees or other saboteurs—increases dramatically.

It is much easier for employees to sabotage your system than someone outside your company. Employees have passwords; outside hackers do not. Employees can observe network design and deployment first hand; whereas most people outside the company cannot. Employees can get access to internal procedures; outside hackers usually have to make educated assumptions. Worse, people inside companies regularly share passwords and other information to save time or avoid perceived "hassles." For smart internal saboteurs, all this information can be invaluable.

That said, if enough weaknesses exist in your system or if the potential payoff is well worth the risk, your company is a prime target for external infiltration, especially when money is flowing down the wire. That is why financial systems have been closed systems off the Internet until now; why mathematicians are furiously working on security algorithms for open systems; and why you need to know what your options and their associated risks and benefits are.

Online commerce underscores the need for network security and the importance of the network manager. When selecting Internet commerce systems and transaction companies, make sure that the systems you choose can support your company's internal security procedures:

- Employee use policies
- Security methods
- Management systems and controls
- Process flow
- Auditing and reporting

VANs and Internet Commerce

If your company already uses value added networks (VANs) for financial transactions, chances are that you have already had to consider the added risks. VANs, however, are closed networks; the Internet is open and therefore more susceptible to attack from any point on the globe.

If you have a VAN in place for financial transactions, learn from it. VANs have been around for years; Internet Commerce is new. Companies in the VAN business may not necessarily be considering Internet support at this time because it is comparatively unstable. Similarly, Internet companies may choose not to get bogged down by a VAN paradigm because it is too complex, and the Internet is moving too fast.

Ultimately, in this author's opinion, there will be a shakeout where some companies use VANs (which are expensive, but reliable and proven); some companies will use the Internet solely for commerce (because it is cheap and represents a market that is growing exponentially); and others will use a combination of the two that makes sense for their unique corporate needs. Internet commerce, when it becomes big business several years from now, will force the prices of VANs down. Likewise, business paradigms for Internet commerce have not yet been defined, and the functions of Internet commerce may ultimately emulate VANs as we know them today.

How Real Is Internet Commerce?

In Autumn, 1994, the first Internet commerce companies were announced. Some of these companies had products or services immediately available; whereas others, like digital cash companies, have yet to deliver. To the surprise of some, Internet commerce hasn't yet delivered on the hype due to a lack of standards and increasing fears about Internet security. Later, this chapter examines Internet commerce companies, the underlying infrastructure, how Internet commerce fits into your company's business plan, and what you need to look for to conduct safe Internet commerce.

How Does Internet Commerce Relate to Existing Financial Systems?

The Internet already exists and so do electronic financial systems. Until Autumn, 1994, the two did not coexist in a formal business relationship that was apparent to the general public.

The Internet is far too unstable to be the backbone of any established financial system. The Internet is open to anyone and is not governed or regulated. The Internet was built by some of the world's brightest hackers, and it almost ran out of address space. Anyone can contribute to it, and virtually any computer can connect to it. Its biggest weakness has been and still is security.

How Financial Systems Are Affected by Online Capabilities

Setting the Internet aside for a moment, computers and computer networks have had huge effects on the financial community. Many formerly manually intensive practices are now automated, and money can be transferred instantaneously. In the case of investments, fortunes can be made or lost much faster than ever before possible. Banks regularly exchange funds electronically, and anyone with a computer and modem can electronically pay bills or buy airline tickets, goods, and services.

The parallel development of the Global Information Infrastructure (GII), electronic financial systems, and the Internet may not remain completely parallel forever. Many companies that are defining the GII are also offering (or plan to offer) Internet products and services. Similarly, members of the financial community are beginning to take notice of the Internet as a potential new market, which is illustrated later in this chapter.

Internet Commerce Companies and Organizations

This section describes the following Internet commerce companies and organizations:

- CommerceNet
- CyberCash, Inc.
- DigiCash
- First Virtual Holdings, Inc.
- Internet Shopping Network
- Netscape Communications Corporation
- Open Market

CommerceNet

CommerceNet is an industry association of information providers, Internet service providers, financial institutions, software companies, semiconductor manufacturers, consultants, and more. Originally funded by the government, CommerceNet is rapidly growing, attracting companies representing a broad range of sizes, industries, and interests.

CommerceNet has established several working groups and pilot programs that should greatly influence how Internet commerce evolves in terms of technology, standards, and regulation. Three pilot programs having to do with security are underway. One is a server certification authority; one deals with software licensing; and another focuses on key safeguarding.

Catalog projects are also underway having to do with search techniques and catalog architectures. Payment technology pilots, focused on credit cards and the design and manufacturing process, have also been launched, but digital cash has not yet been addressed.

Company Information:	800 El Camino Real Menlo Park, CA 94025 415-617-8790 415-617-1516 `http://www.commerce.net` E-mail: `info@commerce.net`
Description:	Industry association
Services:	Internet connectivity, directories, pubic key certification services
Sponsors:	Smart Valley, Inc.; Joint Venture: Silicon Valley Network; The California Trade and Commerce Agency
Participants:	Amdahl Corporation; Apple Computer, Inc.; (partial list)Bank of America; Bank One; Bellcore; Citibank N/A., Digital Equipment Corporation, Dun & Bradstreet Corporation, First Interstate Bank, Hewlett-Packard Company, Intel Corporation, International Business Machines (IBM), Pacific Bell, RSA Data Security, Inc., Wells Fargo & Co.
Annual Membership Dues:	Sponsor: $35,000 Subscriber: $1,250

Information current as of 3/27/95

CyberCash, Inc

CyberCash, Inc., located in Reston, VA, was founded by Dan Lynch and William Melton. In 1983, Lynch switched the non-standard ARPAnet (the seedlings of the Internet) to TCP/IP and remains active as an Internet advisor and visionary. William "Bill" Melton founded Verifone, which provides online credit-card verification to retailers. CyberCash, which is in the business of financial transactions, supports digital cash, credit cards, and debit cards.

CyberCash client software will be available free via servers on the Internet. The software will allow customers, merchants, and banks to establish links that support seamless financial transactions. Individuals will also be able to establish links among themselves to settle personal transactions.

Security and ease of use are two key features of the CyberCash system. All transactions are cryptographically protected, and the consumers' identities can be concealed from the merchants. According to CyberCash, the CyberCash PAY button will be added to online user services and graphical user interfaces. This will simplify the process of buying and selling over the Internet because customers are not required to have an established relationship with CyberCash to access the payment system.

The CyberCash system works as follows:

1. Customer selects a good or service and presses the CyberCash PAY button.
2. The CyberCash software is initiated.
3. The customer receives a detailed invoice from the merchant.
4. If the customer approves the purchase, a credit card number or debit account personal identificaton number is added to the invoice for processing.
5. This information is encrypted and transmitted to the merchant.
6. The merchant adds his identification information to the invoice and sends it to CyberCash for processing.
7. The CyberCash server forwards an authorization request to the bank or credit card company.
8. When the transaction is authorized, CyberCash notifies the merchant, and the transaction is completed.

Company Information:	2100 Reston Parkway, Suite 430 Reston, VA 22091 Phone: 703-620-4200 FAX: 703-620-4215 `http://home.cybercash.com` E-mail: `info@cybercash.com`
Description:	Transaction processing company
Product:	CyberCash client software
List Price:	none
Transaction Fees:	Not specified yet; however, estimated by CyberCash to be equivalent to a postage stamp
Software Support:	TBD
HTTP Support:	Yes
DNS and IP Support:	Yes
MIME Support:	Yes
Scalable:	Yes
Security:	Enterprise Integration Technologies, Trusted Information Systems and RSA Data Security, Inc.; Digital Encryption Standard (DES) that is already used in electronic commerce systems; public key encryption by RSA.
Unique Attributes:	High security and ease of use; embedded CyberCash PAY buttons in popular online service software and graphical-user interfaces.

DigiCash

DigiCash bv was founded by Dr. David Chaum, a digital cash and electronic security expert. DigiCash announced the first software-only product, called Ecash, that allows the transfer of digital cash over the Internet. Currently, DigiCash technology is being used in electronic wallets and smart cards; but in the long-term, the technology will be used for many more applications.

An Ecash experiment is now being conducted on the Internet, a precursor to the official service. According to DigiCash, approximately 4,000 people from some 50 countries volunteered to participate in the test as of January 1, 1995. 1,000,000 CyberBucks, with a virtual (as opposed to real) value of $1 each have been issued to accounts in quantities up to 100.

Company Information:	Kruislaan 419 1098 VA Amsterdam The Netherlands Phone: 31 20 665 2611 Fax: 31 20 668 5486 `http://www.digicash.com` E-mail: `info@digicash.nl`
Description:	Developer and provider of digital cash and related security technology
Product:	Ecash software enabling digital cash transactions; software distributed through third parties
List Price:	User (client) software is free
Transaction Fees:	None
Software Support:	Microsoft Windows, Macintosh, and most Unix operating systems
HTTP Support:	Yes
DNS and IP Support:	Yes
MIME Support:	Yes

Scalable:	Yes
Security:	RSA Data Security public key cryptography including encryption, authentication, and digital signatures, as well as proprietary blind signature technology.
Unique Attributes:	Blind signature technology ensures anonymous transactions.

First Virtual Holdings, Inc.

First Virtual Holdings, Inc. recently announced the first Internet commerce system that allows anyone with access to e-mail to buy and sell information over the Internet. The system's minimum requirement for buyers and sellers is access to e-mail.

The First Virtual system was designed by Internet leaders Marshall Rose, Ph.D, Einar Stefferud, and Nathaniel Borenstein, Ph.D. Dr. Rose is a network management expert and the author of several books on the Simple Network Management Protocol (SNMP). Einar Stefferud is a world-class e-mail expert. Dr. Borenstein is the primary author of the Multipurpose Internet Mail Extention (MIME) protocol that enables any binary object to be transported over the Internet.

First Virtual's system is based on selling information rather than hard goods. Information in this case pertains to anything digital, including text, graphics, video, audio, images, and so on. The First Virtual system has two unique features. First, you only need access to e-mail to become a buyer or seller. Second, First Virtual's system maintains Internet Culture by only requiring customers to pay for those things that have value to them (similar to the shareware concept).

Unlike most companies that are focusing on heavy security schemes to protect sensitive data, First Virtual keeps such information off the Internet completely. Customers who want to establish an account can call in a credit card or checking account number to get started and set their own account limit. Further, financial transactions are separated from business transactions so that encryption isn't necessary. For example, order processing is done over the Internet, but credit card verification is not.

Company Information:	No physical address Phone: 1-800-570-0003 `http://www.fv.com` E-mail: `info@fv.com`
Description:	Merchant Banker of the Internet
Product/Service:	InfoMerchant and InfoConsumer Accounts
Set-up Costs:	\$5–\$10
Monthly Fees:	None
Transaction Fees:	29 cents
Hardware requirements:	80286 computer or higher 2400 baud modem (or better) access
Software Support:	Any e-mail package that supports TCP/IP
DNS and IP Support:	Yes
MIME Support:	Yes
Scalable:	Yes
Security:	The First Virtual Payment System separates business transactions from financial transactions so that sensitive information never travels over the Internet. Credit card numbers, used to set up First Virtual accounts, are specified by the cardholder via phone or fax.
Unique Attributes:	Supports Internet Culture by allowing buyers to download and review information before committing to a purchase. The system only requires access to e-mail.

Internet Shopping Network

The Internet Shopping Network, which is owned by the Home Shopping Network, is the cyberspace version of a computer superstore. Available via the World Wide Web, the Internet Shopping Network contains more than 20,000 computer hardware and software products, InfoWorld magazine, and more. Its parent company, the Home Shopping Network, expects major retailers to set up virtual shops on the Internet Shopping Network, which would result in a major Internet shopping mall.

Company Information:	535 Middlefield Road Menlo Park, CA 94025 Phone: 1-800-677-SHOP Fax: 415-462-1248 `http://shop.internet.net` E-mail: `info@internet.net`
Description:	Online microcomputer software and hardware superstore
Set-up Costs:	\$2–\$10
Membership Fees:	None
Transaction Fees:	None; ISN acts as an online dealer of hardware and software products and receives a percentage of the sales, which is negotiable with the supplier.
Hardware requirements:	80286 computer or higher 2400 baud modem (or better) access
Software Support:	Any World Wide Web browser
DNS and IP Support:	Yes
MIME Support:	Yes
Scalable:	Yes
Security:	Buyers call or fax in their credit card numbers to set up an account.

Unique Attributes:	The Internet Shopping Network is the first true computer hardware and software superstore on the Internet.

Netscape Communications Corporation

Netscape Communications Corporation was founded by Jim Clark, former chairman of Silicon Graphics, and Marc Andreessen, designer of the National Center for Supercomputing Applications (NSCA) Mosaic browser. Netscape offers a commercial version of Mosaic that supports Internet purchases through First Data Corporation, a credit card processing company. The company also sells an HTTP-based server called the Netsite Communications Server and an enhanced, secure version called the Netsite Commerce Server, which is designed for Internet commerce and electronic data interchange (EDI).

Company Information:	650 Castro Street, Suite 500 Mountain View, CA 94041 Phone: 415-254-1900 `http://home.mcom.com` E-mail: `info@mcom.com`
Product:	Netsite Commerce Server
List Price:	$5,000
Monthly Fees:	None
Software Support:	Supports major Unix operating systems including DEC OSF/1 2.0, Hewlett-Packard HP-UX 9.03, IBM AIX 3.2.5, Silicon Graphics IRIX 5.2, Sun Solaris 2.4 and 2.4, SunOS 4.1.3, operating systems based on Intel 386, 486, or Pentium processors.
HTTP Support:	Yes
DNS and IP Support:	Yes

MIME Support:	Yes
Scalable:	Yes
Security:	RSA Data Security public key cryptography including encryption and server authentication
Unique Attributes:	SSL architecture that supports encryption, server authentication, and operates independently of higher level protocols such as HTTP, FTP, NNTP, Telnet, and so on.

Open Market

Open Market was founded by Shikar Ghosh who was previously CEO of Appex Corporation, which established payment systems for cellular phone "roaming." Open Market offers a complete system including hardware and software that enables users to easily set up shop online. Open Market's initial product offering enables merchants of all sizes to establish a virtual storefront on the Internet and to conduct secure financial transactions with their customers.

Open Market's StoreBuilder kit is a combination of hardware and software that enables users to catalog and index their products, adapt products for the online world, or to develop new products specifically designed for the Internet. The system supports secure payment, real-time credit card authorization, account statements, administrative interfaces for storefront management, and a customer feedback mechanism. Intelligent agents are embedded in the Open Market environment so that buyers can easily locate specific products and services.

Company Information:

215 First Street
Cambridge, MA 02142
Phone: 617-621-9500
Fax: 617-621-1703
`http://www.openmarket.com`
E-mail: `info@openmarket.com`

Description:	Developer and provider of end-to-end electronic commerce systems
Product:	StoreBuilder
Configuration Costs:	\$300–\$1,500
Monthly Fees:	\$50–\$300 + transaction fees + storage fees
Hardware requirements:	80386 or better recommended V.32 bis 14,400 or better modem
Software Requirements:	TCP/IP World Wide Web access software
HTTP Support:	Yes
DNS and IP Support:	Yes
MIME Support:	Yes
Scalable:	Yes
Security:	Encryption, firewall security, buyer authentication, Netscape Secure SocketLayer, and Secure Hypertext Transport Protocol
Unique Attributes:	Document fingerprinting stamps and numbers documents automatically to track fradulent distribution and \$50 to \$300 per month in monthly fees, in addition to transaction fees and additional storage fees.

Proprietary Systems

A formal infrastructure is required to support Internet commerce, which includes Internet service providers, banks, credit card companies, transaction processing companies, Internet commerce companies, and more. Some strategic relationships have been established to enable the first Internet commerce systems.

At the present time, no ubiquitous system exists for Internet commerce. Given that this industry is in the formative stage, vendors are establishing cooperative relationships with members of the financial community to provide customers with a system that can handle complete financial transactions. The problem with these systems is that they are proprietary and therefore may not (probably do not) interoperate for competitive reasons.

The advantage to these proprietary systems is the establishment of end-to-end financial systems designed for Internet commerce today. The disadvantage is that both the buyer and seller must be on the same system to complete a transaction. For example, you might have to set up an account on a specific system to purchase a product or service from a certain vendor. Ultimately, this may mean that a buyer will have several accounts with different passwords and keys.

Many industry observers agree that Internet commerce systems will have to eventually establish standards that allow money to flow among systems ubiquitously. Table 3.3 shows which companies are teaming up with whom.

Table 3.3
New Bedfellows

Internet Commerce	Partner Company
First Virtual	First USA, VISA, Electronic Data Systems
CyberCash	Wells Fargo
DigiCash	Not specified
Internet Shopping	The Home Shopping Network
Open Market	First Union Corporation
Netscape	BankAmerica Corporation, First Data Corporation, MasterCard

Digital Cash

Digital cash is the binary equivalent of currency. Like currency, it offers anonymity, but requires the stringent security of public key cryptography. Digital cash sounds sexy, but the concept is not really new; the application is.

Since the early 1980s companies in several countries have been experimenting with smart cards. Smart cards are plastic cards that contain a microchip. These cards are programmed with a certain value that decreases with purchases. In the mid-1980s Fujitsu conducted an experiment among banks and retail stores in Japan. The goal was to test a "cashless" society, which at the time to those unfamiliar with the concept sounded as ridiculous as the paperless office.

Smart cards have become much smarter over the years, and the concept of a cashless society doesn't seem so far-fetched. For example, prepaid phone cards are available from local drug stores, and similar card-based payments are being used to pay for bridge tolls or treats from vending machines. Due to advances in microchip design, more information can be stored in less space, which means that more transactions can be stored on a card; and the balance may be modified positively as well as negatively (depending on the design of the card).

A more popular example of a digital interface to financial systems is automatic teller machine (ATM) cards, which are very popular and ubiquitous, although they do not represent digital cash. ATM cards are debit cards that can be used for payment at grocery stores or gas stations, but the transaction is more complicated than a cash (or digital cash) transaction because the amount of the purchase must be verified before the amount is deducted from the customer's account.

Digital cash, even in the form of smart cards, yields instant payment like paper cash. In the physical world, you might offer a dollar to a retailer for a candy bar and receive $0.45 change. Using the smart card version, the amount would be instantaneously deducted from the smart card without the need for change or verification of monies in a bank account. Using digital cash generated by and residing on a computer, you can use digital notes or coins to pay for goods and services immediately and anonymously, and receive digital change back for overpayment. Because digital cash must be authorized by a bank prior to circulation, there is again no need to verify funds from a bank account or identify who the customer is in the first place.

The Importance of Digital Cash Anonymity

Like paper cash, using digital cash has several benefits. Payments for goods or services can be made instantly and without interest charges. Also, payments can be made anonymously, which becomes increasingly important in an ever more connected world.

Most people rarely consider the benefit of the anonymity of cash transactions unless there is something they want to hide from another party. The use of cash is virtually untraceable unless the serial numbers are monitored whenever the notes or coins are used. This is particularly advantageous if the buyer does not want to be associated with the purchase, or the buyer wants no traceable record of the purchase. Although these concepts may seem suspicious to the average person, they in fact take place more often than they are acknowledged.

Cash transactions are popular among criminals, but they are also a part of everyday life for most people. And although the concept of privacy is blatantly evident for a criminal, it may escape the average person until he or she wants to purchase something illegal, immoral, forbidden, or otherwise discouraged for reasons of status, religion, sex, and so on. Or perhaps the person might want to surprise a spouse or other person who might have access to check receipts, bank statements, credit card receipts, or credit card statements.

Another reason a person might want anonymity is to avoid being traced for reasons of direct marketing. As networks are interconnected, it is becoming easier to track the buying behavior of consumers. The more lists a name appears on, the more direct mail the subject receives and the more susceptible the person is to being added to even more lists. Some online criminals monitor spending habits to identify lucrative burglary sites!

In any case, there are real advantages to anonymous cash and digital cash transactions that should not be overlooked by those who want to buy or sell goods or services in cyberspace. As a network manager, it is important to understand not only how digital cash works, but why it exists (that is, understanding the technical and business issues of online payment systems).

How Digital Cash Is Generated

Digital cash must inherently be secure. Therefore, forms of digital cash necessarily employ encryption, authentication, and digital signature techniques to ensure that the digital cash generated is authentic, safe to use, and spent only once.

The following is an example of an Ecash transaction:

1. The user establishes a digital account at an appropriate bank.
2. The user deposits funds into the account.
3. The user requests a withdrawal via his computer.
4. The computer determines the necessary amount and type of digital currency required.
5. The computer generates random serial numbers using DigiCash's "blinding" technique and sends the data to the bank.
6. The bank verifies the funds and encodes the blinded numbers using its digital signature.
7. The amount is debited from the customer's account, and the authenticated coins are transferred to the user.
8. The customer removes the blinding factor (which he included in his original transmission).
9. Ecash is now available for use.
10. The customer uses the digital money to purchase a good or service.
11. The merchant deposits the digital cash to a bank that supports digital transactions.
12. The digital bank verifies the authenticity of the coins.
13. The seller's account is credited, and the amount may be converted into real money, transferred to a credit card account, or otherwise converted into a different payment mechanism.

The Internet: The First Nation in Cyberspace

Industry observers assert that Internet commerce systems will have to be ubiquitous to support widespread use. Given that most Internet commerce companies are headquartered in the United States, you might assume that the flow of money translates to dollars and cents.

In the beginning, most Internet commerce systems will support U.S. denominations; but given that the Internet is worldwide (representing 134 countries at present), other denominations will also have to be supported such as yen, francs, Deutch marks, pounds, lire, and more. As other forms of money are supported, these systems will have to automatically adjust the exchange rate depending on where and when the purchase was made. Tariffs and import and export charges may also come into play although the Internet is moving faster than the underlying economic, social, or judiciary systems.

In any case, with the emergence of Internet commerce, your role as a network manager will be increasingly tied to your executive management responsible for the business, financial, technical, and legal aspects of your company.

Digital Checks

Digital checks enable electronic payments in sums other than what is generally available using digital cash coins. Using digital cash, for example, you might purchase a software program for $10.00 plus tax; render $11.00 for the purchase; and receive $0.17 in digital change. Using a digital check, you could purchase the software for an electronic note valued at exactly $10.83.

Blind Signatures—An Added Measure of Privacy

Dr. David Chaum, founder of DigiCash, developed blind signature technology as an alternative form of identification that can be used for anonymous digital cash transactions. The technology protects the user from being identified by information collection systems (such as direct marketing firms, banks, the government, and so on) by allowing a new pseudonym to be created for each transaction.

Digital Signatures

Digital signatures are a means of authentication that enables the receiver to verify that the sender is who he says he is. This is accomplished using private keys to "sign" messages that can only be read by someone who has the corresponding public key.

Digital signatures are the basis for digital cash. For example, when a user wants to obtain digital cash, his computer generates a set of numbers that represent the number of coins requested, as well as the denominations of those coins. The bank verifies that the customer has enough funds in his account to cover the request. The bank then issues coins with its own signature, making the electronic currency valid. Then any insitution that has the bank's public key can verify that the coins are indeed valid.

Sales, Marketing, and IS

The Internet as a sales channel has yet to be proven effective on a grand scale, yet the future of cyberselling is eminent. With the advent of the World Wide Web and graphical browsers, the Internet has quickly become the hottest new marketing vehicle, but the same does not hold true for sales at this time.

In fact, most users are surfing the Web for information and entertainment, rather than purchases. This is because people are not used to purchasing goods and services online yet. Security remains an issue, and most companies haven't yet learned how to sell in cyberspace.

For IS and network managers, the Internet wave challenges their roles within an organization. Where e-mail and Internet connectivity have been within the IS domain, the demand for Web sites and online commerce systems is now coming from sales and marketing. This has the potential effect of relegating IS services to a support role, if IS itself does not keep up with its own competition.

The usefulness of Web sites as part of the marketing mix is becoming more apparent as more sites begin to attract up to several hundred thousand hits per day. But what sometimes looks great from a marketing perspective is disappointing in practical application if IS is unable to counterbalance creativity with sound implementation. For example, multimedia is expected to become an integral part of future Web sites, yet many Internet users lack the bandwidth necessary to benefit from it. Even graphics can be a problem for dial-up users. So sometimes Web pages get passed by if the graphics take too long to download.

IS can play an effective role in helping sales and marketing make the best use of the Internet based on the state-of-the-art and the state of Internet use. If potential customers choose not to visit your company's Web site and if they decide not to return once they get there, the marketing benefits are virtually nil.

Similarly, if your company is considering Internet commerce, your knowledge of alternatives and the potential implementations of those alternatives within your enterprise system can help make for a more sound application of these new products and services. Knowledge of competitive systems will also be useful and may help you avoid costly mistakes.

Keeping an Eye on Implementation

The Internet explosion has yielded many great ideas but fewer well-executed strategies. Internet commerce—the business of buying and selling over the Internet—must be an integral process co-developed by management, sales/marketing, and IS.

Like the many Internet commerce companies that are separating business transactions from financial transactions, users who are using the Internet as a sales vehicle are also separating front-end Internet processing from back-end operations. Although many improvements have been made in the area of Internet commerce, the general opinion remains: If you want completely secure operations, don't connect servers with sensitive information directly to the Internet.

Companies such as Netscape and DigiCash that are employing the best security technology available to Internet applications will break down the current barriers to widespread Internet commerce. In the meantime, some very real concerns exist regarding security that will influence which vendors you choose and how you integrate Internet commerce into your existing enterprise system.

The Role of the Network Manager

Electronic commerce underscores the important role of network managers. If your company has an Internet host connection, you are already aware of the need for security. As financial transactions become a part of this equation, it will be even more necessary for you to maintain control of technology planning, testing, and deployment, not only to preserve your company's information technology assets but also to preserve financial assets (to some degree) and the reliability of the network.

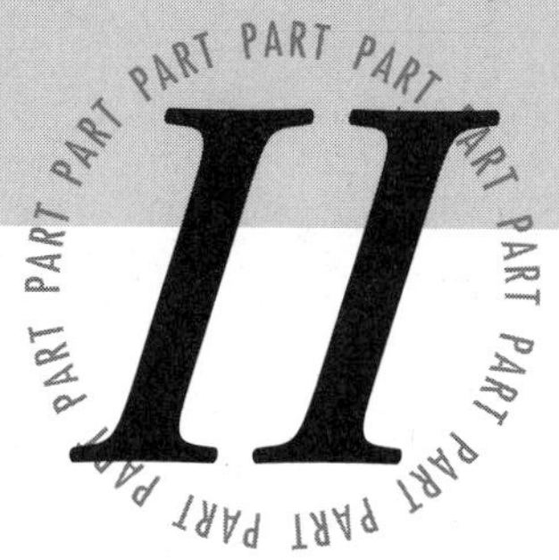

TCP/IP Connectivity

Overview of DNS for Website Administration

by Mike Coulombe

In the early days of the Internet, a simple text file translated host names to IP addresses. For this scheme to work, each host on the Internet had to have the same copy of this text file. As new machines were connected to the network, a new entry in the text file would need to be added before existing systems could reference the new machines by name. As the Internet grew exponentially, it did not take long before this method was completely inadequate. The Domain Name System (DNS) was created to replace this antiquated method and to perform the same host name to IP address translation, and allow for a distributed management model.

This chapter covers the following topics:

- Do you need a DNS Server?
- How DNS works
- Registering a domain name
- Setting up a DNS server
- DNS server example
- DNS in a firewalled network

Do You Need a DNS Server?

There are many different ways to connect to the Internet or to have an "Internet presence." The simplest solution is to have a Web server and use Internet email without installing a single piece of hardware at your office. On the other end, your organization can install a direct T-3 connection to the Internet backbone complete with high-end routers and Unix workstations to run Internet services. Many options between these two extremes are also possible. Many of these options require you to configure a DNS server.

If you decide to use a unique domain name, a DNS server is required. This server can be located literally anywhere on the Internet; the two most logical places are at your office or that of your Internet service provider. You might choose both of these locations for redundancy and performance reasons. In fact the InterNIC, the central registration service for Internet Domain Names, requires that each registered domain have a minimum of two DNS servers. With multiple servers for any given domain, DNS queries can still be resolved if one of the servers is down for any reason.

Your Internet service provider can provide one or both of the required DNS servers for your domain. If you are going to be renting space on a host system for your Web server, DNS services will usually be a part of the service. If your service provider manages both servers, updates to your domain become the responsibility of the provider. This can slow down the creation of new host names if a phone call or email is required for every new entry. This may be an acceptable limitation if you do not have to manage your systems directly.

Most installations place one DNS server at the company and the other at the service provider location. This configuration allows for redundancy. Domain changes made on one server will be updated on the second server automatically over the network. This feature will be discussed in more detail later.

How DNS Works

The Domain Name System is essentially one distributed database with thousands of servers. Each server is responsible for its own domain or section of the name space. The entire name space can be thought of as an inverted tree (see fig. 4.1).

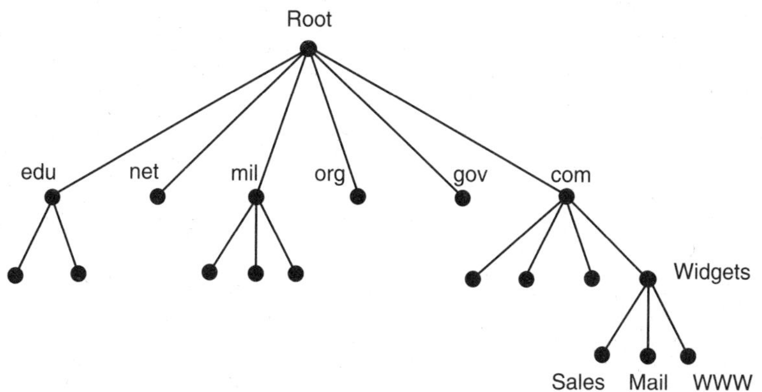

Figure 4.1
Domain name space pictured as an inverted tree.

This tree structure is similar to a directory structure of a computer's file system. Each node on the tree is a domain. At the top of the tree is the root domain labeled with a single period (.) called a *dot.* When creating Internet host names, the fully qualified domain name is interpreted from right to left. For example the host name `www.widgets.com` locates a machine three domains deep from the root domain. The name is broken down as follows: the root domain, followed by the com domain, the widgets.com domain, and finally the host name www within the widgets.com domain. When writing down Internet host names, often the root domain's final dot is assumed and left off.

Note The domain name used in these examples, widgets.com, did not exist when this chapter was written. The class C IP addresses used in this chapter, namely 192.168.148.0, are a part of a block of addresses reserved by the InterNIC that will never be assigned. These addresses are intended for internal TCP/IP networks that do not connect to the Internet.

These addresses are ideal for TCP/IP networks that sit behind a firewall and never have direct contact with the Internet. Their use in this chapter is only for illustration; these addresses should never appear in any DNS servers that are on the Internet.

Converting Names to IP Addresses

Computers on the Internet use the TCP/IP protocol to communicate to each other through the use of packets of information. These packets are sent back and forth using IP addresses that identify the sender and receiver of the data. Although these numeric addresses were created to help computers identify and communicate with each other, they can be quite cumbersome for people to use directly. People prefer to use names rather than numbers when referring to objects. DNS translates between names and numbers.

As with any database, the DNS database holds data. The majority of this data are IP addresses; the fully qualified domain name is the index to the stored data. Your phone number is an index that points the phone company to your account information—a fully qualified domain name points a DNS server to a computer's IP address.

Converting IP Addresses to Names

If a user starts a Web browser program and enters the host name www.widgets.com, the browser will use DNS to find out which IP address matches the server's name. The Web server receives the data and sends the response back to the IP address that made the request. If name to address translation was the only function the DNS database could perform, the server in the previous example would be at a disadvantage. The browsing computer has been told by the user the name of the system to communicate with, and the computers are communicating with each other using only their IP addresses. There needs to be a way for the second computer, in this case the server, to identify the name of the computer sending data to it. This information is essential for logging and security purposes. Administrators will want to know which computers are using their services and perhaps restrict access to certain services from computers within a specific domain. Without an IP-address-to-name translation, these types of administrative functions would be impossible.

The Domain Name System has a special domain called *in-addr.arpa.* This inverse address breaks the computer's IP address into a hierarchical name. With regular Internet host names, the most specific information is on the left and the most general is on the right. IP addresses are just the opposite. In the address 192.168.148.1, the most specific information is on the right, and the most general is on the left. If the IP addresses are reversed, the result is the same specific to general direction that exists with Internet host names. Figure 4.2 shows how this inverse domain would appear in a tree structure.

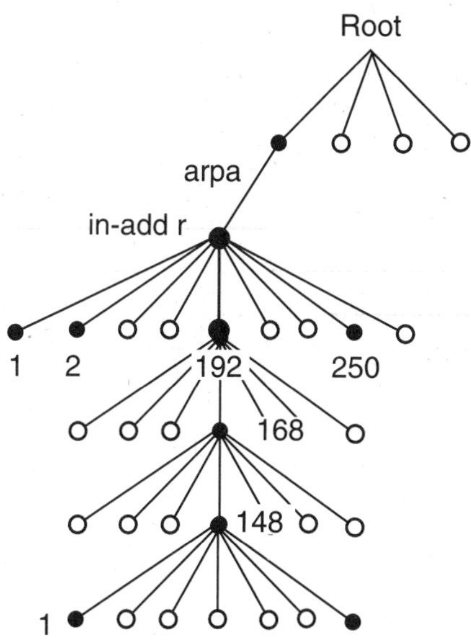

Figure 4.2
Logical view of the inverse domain name space.

Just as the fully qualified domain name www.widgets.com can be an index to the IP address 192.168.148.1, the inverse domain name 1.148.168.192.in-addr.arpa can be an index to the host name www.widgets.com. This allows the receiving computer to take the sender's IP address, reverse it, add on the `in-addr.arpa` domain, create an inverse name to send to a DNS server, and get a host name back.

The Role of Root Name Servers

The tremendous growth and size of the Internet and the Domain Name System requires a structured way to traverse the name space when searching for data. The DNS is a distributed database. Each domain name server only has data specific to the domain that it is serving. To prevent each name server from having to know about every other name server, *root name servers* hold the authoritative list of name servers for the top-level domains, such as com, edu, org, net, mil, us, and others.

The name servers in the top-level domains hold the list of name servers for the domains immediately below them. The com domain name server lists the location of the name server for the widgets.com domain, and any other domains immediately below com. Without root name servers, the functionality of the Domain Name System would fall apart. To ensure the DNS is always running, several root name servers are scattered throughout the Internet. If a name server has a list of these root name servers, the server will always be able to traverse the name space tree.

Each name server performs two functions. They answer requests made by other name servers for data the server maintains, and the server must answer requests made by local client computers. Requests made by local clients will include domains other than the ones maintained by the local server. To answer these requests, the server must be able to identify the name servers that will hold the requested information without having to know each one. Root name servers solve this problem. For example, to find the IP address for www.widgets.com, a request must be sent to the widgets.com name server. To help locate this name server, root name servers will return where this information can be found.

Name Resolution Example

This section takes a closer look at the name resolution process step-by-step. If you have ever configured a computer to use the TCP/IP protocol, you know many parameters have to be set before communication can take place. One of these parameters is the computer's domain name and the IP address of the computer's domain name server. This server will be where all name to IP address resolution requests are sent. For every destination a computer attempts to communicate with via e-mail, FTP, or HTTP, the name of the host system the user enters is converted to an IP address before any packets are sent. Figure 4.3 shows how the name resolution process might occur for a computer attempting to access a web page out on the Internet.

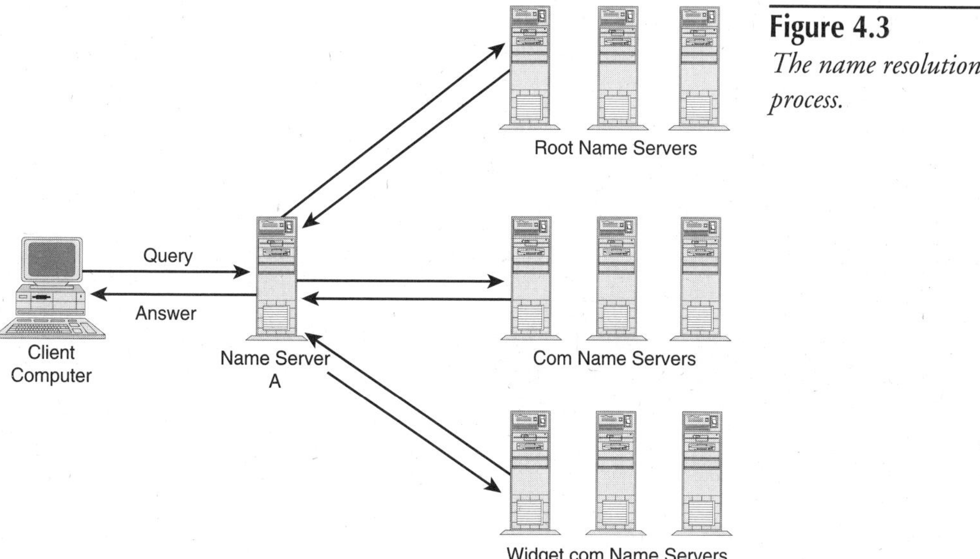

Figure 4.3
The name resolution process.

The following steps outline the process illustrated in figure 4.3:

1. Client computer needs to make a connection with an Internet host system www.widgets.com.

2. Client computer sends a DNS query to name server A to obtain the proper IP address for the desired Web server.

3. Name server A contacts one of the root DNS servers for an IP address of a name server for the com domain.

4. Name server A then contacts the com name server obtained from step 3 and requests the IP address for the widgets.com name server.

5. Name server A then contacts the widgets.com name server via the IP address obtained in step 4 and requests the IP address of the host system www.widgets.com.

6. Name server A returns the IP address obtained from step 5 to the client computer.

7. The client computer can now send its Web page request to the www.widgets.com server.

The client computer only sends on request to its name server. The name server must determine all the appropriate systems to contact to resolve the query. This process is known as a *recursive query*. Each step gets the name server a little closer to the answer. The preceding steps illustrate a worst case scenario. The DNS servers keep a cache of data over time. If another computer had requested the IP address of www.widgets.com, this information would be stored in the name server's cache, and subsequent queries would be answered using the cached data. At the very least, if the name server has been running for a while, the server should already know the IP address of the name server for the com domain. This would eliminate step three.

A name server's cache size is limited by the amount of memory allocated to the name server itself. All entries in the cache are labeled with a "time to live" parameter that controls how long the information can stay in the cache. After a record's time-to-live is exceeded, the record is purged from the cache. This keeps only the most recent DNS query results in the cache.

The Role of Primary and Secondary Servers

The Domain Name System has some redundancy built into it to make the service more reliable. For each domain, a minimum of two servers must exist: the primary and secondary server. The primary server holds the data, and the secondary holds a backup copy of the same data. Multiple redundant name servers are allowed, but they are still referred to as secondary servers.

To keep the secondary server synchronized with the primary server, the primary server keeps a serial number indicating the version of the data that it holds. When the data is updated, the serial number is increased to signal that a change has occurred in the data. When the secondary servers first start, a current data file is downloaded from the primary server.

Periodically, the secondary servers contact the primary server and compare serial numbers between the two systems. If the serial number of the primary is higher than that of the secondary server, the secondary downloads a new copy of the data with the new serial number. If the serial numbers match, no transfer occurs.

There are two important points to note about primary and secondary servers:

- The serial number is a field in the primary server's data file that must be updated by hand. The data files themselves are simple text files that can be updated with any text editor. If the administrator makes changes to the primary server's data and forgets to update the serial number, the secondary server will not download a new copy of the data.
- The secondary servers only check for an increase in serial numbers. Depending on the format chosen for the serial numbers, this check can be important. If a simple counter that is continually incremented with each change is used, this is not a problem.

Note A counter does not give much information about when the data was last updated. Often, a date stamp is used for serial numbers. A four digit year starts the serial number, and leading zeros are used for months and days. Without leading zeroes, November 31st (1131) is numerically larger than December 2nd (122). Similarly, with only a two digit year, 2000 (00) is smaller than 1999 (99).

Registering a Domain Name

All Internet Domain Name registrations are coordinated with the InterNIC. The registration form required to register domains and to make changes or deletions is included in this section. The URL at the top of the form indicates where the most recent copy of the form may be obtained. Only the completed form—items zero through nine—should be sent via e-mail to HOSTMASTER@INTERNIC.NET. If you cannot send Internet e-mail, have your service provider submit the form for you. To identify your request, indicate "NEW DOMAIN," "MODIFY DOMAIN," or "REMOVE DOMAIN" in the subject of your e-mail. Also include the name of the domain being registered.

An auto reply response will be sent back with a tracking number. This number may be used in further correspondence with InterNIC regarding the registration. When the registration is completed, a notification e-mail will be sent. InterNIC has automated software that parses the e-mail form, looking for the appropriate section numbers, periods, and colons (see the following code). If the form's format is altered, the e-mail message will most likely be rejected. Only send one form per e-mail message.

```
[ URL ftp://rs.internic.net/templates/domain-template.txt ]  [ 09/95 ]
********* Please DO NOT REMOVE Version Number *************
Domain Version Number: 2.0
******** Please see attached detailed instructions ********
** Only for registrations under ROOT, COM, ORG, NET, EDU, GOV **
0.   (N)ew (M)odify (D)elete....:
1.   Purpose/Description........:
2.   Complete Domain Name.......:
Organization Using Domain Name
3a.  Organization Name..........:
3b.  Street Address.............:
3c.  City.......................:
3d.  State......................:
3e.  Postal Code................:
3f.  Country....................:

Administrative Contact
4a.  NIC Handle (if known)......:
4b.  Name (Last, First).........:
4c.  Organization Name..........:
4d.  Street Address.............:
4e.  City.......................:
4f.  State......................:
4g.  Postal Code................:
4h.  Country....................:
4i.  Phone Number...............:
4j.  E-Mailbox..................:
```

```
Technical Contact
5a.  NIC Handle (if known)......:
5b.  Name (Last, First).........:
5c.  Organization Name..........:
5d.  Street Address.............:
5e.  City.......................:
5f.  State......................:
5g.  Postal Code................:
5h.  Country....................:
5i.  Phone Number...............:
5j.  E-Mailbox..................:

Billing Contact
6a.  NIC Handle (if known)......:
6b.  Name (Last, First).........:
6c.  Organization Name..........:
6d.  Street Address.............:
6e.  City.......................:
6f.  State......................:
6g.  Postal Code................:
6h.  Country....................:
6i.  Phone Number...............:
6j.  E-Mailbox..................:

Primary Name Server
7a.  Primary Server Hostname....:
7b.  Primary Server Netaddress..:

Secondary Name Server(s)
8a.  Secondary Server Hostname..:
8b.  Secondary Server Netaddress:

Invoice Delivery
9.   (E)mail (P)ostal...........:
```

InterNIC charges a domain name registration fee of $100 U.S., which covers the $50 maintenance fee for two years. After the two year period, an invoice will be sent on an annual basis. Further information on billing of domains and invoices can be found at `ftp://rs.internic.net/billing/README`.

The following instructions have been taken from the domain-template.txt registration form. They are included here to help you complete the registration form for new domain names.

Section 0—Registration Action Type

Following the colon, place the character **N** or the word **New** to indicate a new domain registration. Changing a name from DOMAINNAME1 to DOMAINNAME2 is treated as a new registration. The transfer of a name from one organization to another is also treated as a new registration. If you want to transfer a domain name from one organization to another, clearly indicate this in Section 1 and include a statement from the current holder of the name that it is being transferred.

Section 1—Purpose of Registration

Briefly describe the organization and the purpose for which this domain name is being registered. The description should support the choice of top-level domain in Section 2. If the domain name is for an organization that already has a domain name registered, describe the purpose of this domain and why the additional name is needed. Indicate why existing names cannot be used or why the proposed second-level name cannot be used as a third-level name under a domain name that is already registered.

Section 2—Complete Domain Name

Top-level country domains may be registered by inserting the two-letter country code in this section. See RFC1591 for the duties and responsibilities of top-level domain administrators.

Note RFCs, or Requests for Comments, are documents that define the standards used on the Internet. More information about RFCs can be found at `http://www.yahoo.com/Computers_and_Internet/Standards/RFCs/`.

For second-level domain names under COM, ORG, NET, EDU, and GOV insert the two-part name of the domain you want to register—for example, ABC.COM. The total length of the two-part name may be up to 24 characters. The only characters allowed in a domain name are letters, digits, and the dash (-). A domain name cannot begin or end with a dash (see RFC952).

Consult RFC1591 to determine the most appropriate top-level domain to join. In general, the domains have the following organization:

- **COM** is for commercial, for-profit organizations
- **ORG** is for miscellaneous; usually non-profit organizations
- **NET** is for network infrastructure machines and organizations
- **EDU** is for four-year, degreed institutions
- **GOV** is for United States federal government agencies

U.S. state and local government agencies, schools, libraries, museums, and individuals should register under the U.S. domain. See RFC1480 for a complete description of the U.S. domain and registration procedures. GOV registrations are limited to top-level U.S. Federal Government agencies (see RFC1816).

Section 3—Organization Using the Domain Name

The domain name is considered to be registered to an organization, even if the "organization" is an individual. It is important in Section 3 of the form to list the name and address of the end-user organization, not the provider organization.

If the organization has the same name as one that is already registered, explain this in Section 1. Item 3b may be copied as many times as necessary to reflect different lines of the Street Address. If item 3c, 3d, or 3e is not applicable for your country, leave that item blank.

Section 4—Administrative Contact

The administrative contact is the person who can speak on behalf of the organization listed in Section 3. This person should be able to answer non-technical questions about the organization's plans for the name. This contact should also know procedures for establishing sub-domains, and should be able to represent the organization regarding use of the name. See RFC1032 for more detail on administrative contacts.

Each contact in the InterNIC database is assigned a "handle:" a unique tag consisting of the person's initials and a serial number. This tag is used on records in the database to indicate a point of contact for a domain name, network, name server, or other entity. Each person should have only one handle.

If the person's handle is known, insert just the handle in item 4a and leave the rest of Section 4 blank. If a person's handle is unknown or the person has never been registered, leave item 4a blank. The registration software will check for an existing user record. If a matching user record is found, the record will be updated with any new information contained in the template.

Warning All contacts *must* include information in items 4i and 4j. Templates that do not have this information will be returned.

Section 5—Technical Contact

The technical contact tends to the technical maintenance of the domain's name server, resolver software, and database files. This person keeps the name server running and interacts with technical people in other domains to solve problems that affect the domain. The Internet Service Provider often performs this role.

The procedures for completing Section 5 are the same as those for Section 4. If Section 5 is left blank, the information from Section 4 will be assumed, and vice versa.

Section 6—Billing Contact

The billing contact will be sent invoices for new domain registrations and re-registrations. The procedures for completing Section 6 are the same as those for Section 4. If Section 6 is left blank, the information from Section 4 will be assumed.

Section 7—Primary Name Server

Domains *must* provide at least two independent servers for translating names to addresses for hosts in the domain. The servers should be in physically separate locations and on different networks if possible. The servers should be active and responsive to DNS queries *before* this application is submitted. Incomplete information in Sections 7 and 8 or inactive servers will result in delay of the registration.

The registration software makes a cross-check between the host name given and the IP addresses given to see if there are matches with either in the database. If a match with an IP number in the database is found, the name in the database will be assumed. Neither the name nor number of a registered name server will be changed as a result of a new domain registration. A Modify registration request *must* be sent to change either of these values.

Provide the fully qualified name of the machine that is to be the name server; for example: "machine.domainname.com," not just "machine."

Section 8—Secondary Name Server(s)

The procedures for completing Section 8 are the same as for Section 7; at least one secondary name server is required. If you plan on using several secondary servers, copy Section 8 as many times as necessary, but do not renumber or change the copied section.

Section 9—Invoice Delivery

If you want to receive your invoice electronically, place the character **E** or the word **Email** in item 9. If you want to receive your invoice by postal mail, place the character **P** or the word **Postal** in item 9.

Setting Up a DNS Server

This section discusses in detail the configuration of a DNS server on a Unix system. Other non-Unix implementations of DNS exist, but Unix is by far the most common platform for a DNS server and, from a software standpoint, can also be free. Most implementations of Unix come bundled with a DNS server. The server software itself is usually called "in.named" or just "named." All the examples in this chapter were developed on a Linux system, but they should run without modifications on any version of Unix that supports BIND—*Berkeley Internet Name Domain.* If your version of Unix does not come with BIND, or you would like a recent version, the source code can be obtained from `ftp://gatekeeper.dec.com/pub/misc/vixie/4.9.2-940221.tar.gz`.

This file is compressed with GNU zip. GNU zip is available for anonymous ftp from `ftp://prep.ai.mit.edu/pub/gnu/gzip-1.2.4.tar`.

BIND File Formats

The data files used by the BIND software themselves are just simple text files that can be created with any text editor, such as vi or emacs. Comments begin with a semi-colon and finish at the end of the line. Individual fields are separated with white space (tabs and space characters). There are no restrictions on the amount of white space used between fields; however care should be taken to make data files that are readable.

Unlike most Unix commands and configuration files, DNS data and queries are case-insensitive. To demonstrate this point, the data fields in the files are usually kept in all lowercase.

Name Server Boot File

When your name server starts, the first file read by default is the boot file located in /etc/named.boot. This default location can be overridden by using a command line parameter when starting the server. The following command, **/usr/sbin/named -b /var/named/named.boot**, would start the name server and use the boot file named.boot in the /var/named directory.

The boot file consists of a series of directives that instruct the server exactly what domains it will be serving, how it will serve those domains, and where the data can be found.

Using the Directory Directive

By default, the name server looks for any data files relative to the /etc directory. Most configurations store DNS data in a separate directory, such as /var/named, which keeps the data in one location and reduces clutter in the /etc directory. To tell the server to read its data files from the /var/named directory, put the following line in the boot file:

```
directory       /var/named
```

Using the Cache Directive

In the previous name resolution example, the name server had to contact one the of the root name servers to begin the resolution process. The DNS server must be "primed" with some initial data that contain the locations of the root domain servers. Without this information, the server would not know where to begin to resolve incoming queries. The *cache* directive tells the server to initialize its list of root domain servers from the given file. The following line tells the server to read the root server list from the file db.root.

```
cache       .       db.root
```

All DNS servers maintain a cache of recent query results. The *cache* directive no longer supports loading any type of DNS data directly into the server's cache. Even though the keyword "cache" remains the same, the purpose now is only to prime the server with a list of root name servers. This list of root name servers is available for FTP from `ftp.rs.internic.net`. This file is already formatted for DNS servers. A new copy of this file should be downloaded periodically to keep up with changes in the root name server addresses.

Using the Primary Directive

The *primary* directive tells the name server that it will be a primary name server for a specific domain. This means that an original copy of the domain's data will exist on the server. A server can be primary for some domains, and secondary for others at the same time. Although possible, it would not make any sense for a server to function as primary and secondary for the same domain.

The following line instructs the server to be a primary DNS server for the widgets.com domain and to read its data from the db.widgets file:

```
primary    widgets.com      db.widgets
```

Using the Secondary Directive

The *secondary* directive tells the name server that it will be a secondary name server for a specific domain. This means that the server will hold a copy of the domain data that exists on the primary server.

The following code line instructs the server to be a secondary DNS server for the widgets.com domain and to obtain its data from the name server at 192.168.148.1. After the data is retrieved, a copy will be saved in the file widgets.backup.

```
secondary    widgets.com    192.168.148.1     widgets.backup
```

Configuring Forwarding Servers

The *forwarders* directive instructs the name server to send all queries that cannot be answered from the cache to another name server, usually off-site. This can be used to reduce the amount of DNS traffic heading out of your organization. The purpose of a forwarding server is to build a large cache of DNS data that can answer most queries sent to the server and only send new queries off-site for resolution. The forwarding directive can also be used when setting up DNS servers in a firewalled network.

If the name server in the previous resolution example had the following line in its boot file, it would either answer the query from its cache or forward the query to one of the specified servers.

```
forwarders      192.168.150.10 192.168.150.12
```

The off-site name server is then responsible for doing all the leg work to resolve the query. The answer is sent back to the original name server and then to the client computer. If the forwarding name server does not receive a response back from the forwarded query, it will resolve the query just as it would without the forwarding feature enabled.

Configuring Slave Servers

The *slave* directive restricts the name server even more than the *forwarders* directive. A *slave name server* can only answer queries from its authoritative data or cache; all other queries are forwarded to another name server. If a name server is going to be configured as a slave, the forwarders directive must appear in the boot file. This feature is useful if a name server does not have direct access to the Internet, but has access to another machine with access to the Internet. This is often the case in a firewalled network. A more complete configuration of DNS servers in a firewalled network appears later in this chapter. To configure a slave DNS server, include the slave directive on a line by itself in the boot file.

DNS servers can have several combinations of directives presented here in the boot file. Servers can be configured as forwarders and slaves as well as primary and secondary servers. Primary, secondary, or forwarding-only name servers are also allowed.

Resolver Configuration File

The /etc/resolv.conf file lists the domain name and the name server to be used by the Unix system's resolver library routines. These routine are used by end programs such as Ping, FTP, and Telnet to resolve the host names they are given. A sample resolver file would look like the following.

```
domain widgets.com
nameserver 192.168.148.1
```

This file is not actually a part of the DNS server configuration; it applies to the DNS server's Unix clients. A server does not have to be its own client, but this is often the case.

Resource Records

The domain data files are usually referred to as *zone* files. This section will present the different record types and their syntax allowed in the zone files. The zone files consist of one or more resource records. Resource records contain the data on which the domain database is built. These records follow a specific syntax, shown here:

```
<domain name>   [<TTL>]   [<class>]   <type>   <data>
```

The domain name is the name of the record being described. This field will contain either host names or aliases. The optional TTL field stands for time-to-live. This controls how long the data is kept in the server's cache. The optional class field tells the server what type of class the data is in. The only class of data in common use is "IN" which stands for the Internet. Other classes are supported, but their use is specific to only a few networks. If a specific value for the TTL of class field is not specified, the last explicitly stated values are used.

Start of Authority Record (SOA)

The *start of authority record* is the first resource record in a zone file. It indicates that this name server will store the best or most authoritative data for the specified domain. Here is an example of an SOA record.

```
widgets.com. IN SOA foo.widgets.com. root.foo.widgets.com (
                    199602101         ;serial number YYYYMMDDR
                    10800             ;refresh (3 hours)
                    3600              ;retry (1 hour)
                    604800            ;expire (1 week)
                    86400 )           ;Min TTL (1 day)
```

The domain name widgets.com. indicates that the name server will be authoritative for this domain. The class IN stands for the Internet class of data. The type of record is SOA, or start of authority. This next field is the host on which this data resides—here the data on foo.widgets.com. The next field is the email address of the person responsible for the zone. The *at* character (@) is not supported here, so a period (dot) is used instead.

The parentheses enable the record to take up more than one line. The values within the parentheses control the behavior of the name server and any secondary servers. Consideration should be given when setting these values. The values listed are reasonable for a zone that does not change very often.

The serial number indicates the version of the zone data. This is the value used by the secondary server to check for any updates to the zone. Here a date format is used with a revision digit on the end. This only allows for ten changes per day, but that should be plenty.

The refresh time, specified in seconds, indicates how long the secondary server should wait before contacting the primary server to check for an update. This value should be set low, around one hour, when the domain is just being created. Initially, you will probably want to make many changes to your zone. You will want your secondary servers to update themselves with the new data as soon as possible.

After your domain has been created, you can extend this value to reduce the amount of time the secondary server contacts the primary. The retry time, again in seconds, indicates how long to wait after a failed refresh before attempting to contact the primary server again. If the primary server cannot be contacted within the expire time, all zone data is discarded by secondary servers. The minimum time-to-live value is used by records in the zone that have no explicit TTL value.

Name Server Record (NS)

The name server resource record indicates the name servers that will be serving the zone. The following records show that there are two name servers for the widgets.com domain: foo.widgets.com and secondary.provider.net. In this case, the first server is the primary server, and second NS record is the secondary DNS server run by the company's Internet provider.

```
widgets.com.        IN NS    foo.widgets.com.
widgets.com.        IN NS    secondary.provider.net.
```

Address Record (A)

Address records provide the name-to-address translation capability of the domain name system. An address record looks like this:

```
foo.widgets.com.      IN A  192.168.148.1
```

This creates an address record for the host foo.widgets.com, whose IP address is 192.168.148.1.

Canonical Name Record (CNAME)

Often you may want a host to be known by more than one name. It is customary to create host addresses that indicate which types of services are available on them. Addresses such as ftp.widgets.com, www.widgets.com, and news.widgets.com often point to the same machine. The canonical name resource record allows the creation of host aliases in the DNS.

The following records map the name foo.widgets.com to the address 192.168.148.1. The other host names are aliases for the first. When an address is requested for one of these aliases, the widgets.com server will return the actual host name instead. Then the address of the actual host can be requested. The use of CNAME records over A records allows for easy moving of services from one system to another without having to change any IP addresses. A site may start with one server for FTP and WWW, but may later decide to move each service to a separate server if the combined server is overloaded.

```
foo.widgets.com.     IN A   192.168.148.1
ftp.widgets.com.     IN CNAME  foo.widgets.com.
www.widgets.com.     IN CNAME  foo.widgets.com.
news.widgets.com.    IN CNAME  foo.widgets.com.
```

Mail Exchange Record (MX)

Mail exchange records provide a critical function in the delivery of Internet email. These records control where email is sent. For example, the following MX records direct all e-mail of the form `user@widgets.com` to the host foo.widgets.com:

```
widgets.com.         IN MX 0   foo.widgets.com.
widgets.com.         IN MX 5   mail.provider.net.
```

The MX record with the lowest preference is considered to be the final destination. If this host is unavailable, additional MX hosts are contacted in ascending order of preference. If no MX hosts can be contacted, the mail is considered undeliverable. In the preceding example, mail.provider.net receives email bound for widgets.com if the host foo.widgets.com were down.

When the system comes online, the e-mail that spooled onto the provider's system would be delivered to its final destination. If the final destination were to be down for an extended period of time, the e-mail collected on the provider's system would eventually be returned to the sender.

Pointer Record (PTR)

Just as the address records provide name-to-address translation, the pointer (PTR) resource records provide address-to-name translation. The following record creates an inverse address name for the IP address 192.168.148.1 that points to the host foo.widgets.com.

```
1.148.168.192.in-addr.arpa.     IN  PTR     foo.widgets.com.
```

Although the A, MX, and CNAME, records appear in the domain name zone files, the PTR records will appear in the inverse zone files. The use of different zone files will be demonstrated later in this chapter.

Other Records

The domain name system supports several resource record types, but only the most useful ones have been presented here. Additional record types existed when DNS was first created, and have been made obsolete over time. Other data types provide detailed information about hosts and services, but this data have not been exploited by applications, and therefore are only anecdotal information.

DNS Server Example

This section provides a detailed DNS implementation for the hypothetical domain widgets.com. This company has a dedicated connection to the Internet and provides its own primary DNS. Its service provider, provider.net, has been configured as the secondary name server for widgets.com. The company has also agreed to be a secondary name server for the gadgets.com domain. The IP addresses used here cannot be used to connect to the Internet, but are fine for this example.

Boot File

The boot file, `named.boot`, is located in the /etc/ directory. Most Unix systems on startup will look for this file; if it exists, the system will start the name server process. The directory statement listed in the following sample file indicates that all other zone files will be stored in the /var/named directory. The cache directive loads the file named.root into the server's cache. This file contains the list of DNS servers for the root domain.

```
;       File:   /etc/named.boot
;
;       Domain Name Service boot file for widgets.com
;
directory       /var/named
;
; TYPE        DOMAIN                            Source File or Host
; ----        ------                            -----------------
cache           .                                named.root
primary       widgets.com                       db.widgets
secondary     gadgets.com     192.200.10.2      db.gadgets.backup
primary       148.168.192.in-addr.arpa          db.192.168.148
primary       0.0.127.in-addr.arpa              db.127.0.0
```

The server is configured to serve as primary for the widgets.com domain; the zone file db.widgets contains the data for this domain. The server is configured as secondary for the gadgets.com domain, and will download the zone data from the name server at 192.200.10.2 and store this information in the file /var/named/db.gadgets.backup. The server also acts as primary for two inverse domains—the local class C subnet 192.168.148.0 and the TCP/IP loop back address (127.0.0.1).

Root Name Server List

The following file initializes the server with a list of root name servers. Without this file, the name server would not know where to start when resolving outside DNS queries. A current copy of this file can be obtained from `ftp://ftp.rs.internic.net/doamin/named.root`.

```
;       File:   /var/named/named.root
;
;       List of root DNS servers
;
;       This file is made available by InterNIC registration
;       services under anonymous FTP as
;           file                /domain/named.root
;           on server           FTP.RS.INTERNIC.NET
;       -OR- under Gopher at    RS.INTERNIC.NET
;           under menu          InterNIC Registration Services
;                               (NSI)
;              submenu          InterNIC Registration Archives
;           file                named.root
;
;       last update:    Nov 8, 1995
;       related version of root zone:   1995110800
;
.                       3600000  IN  NS    A.ROOT-SERVERS.NET.
A.ROOT-SERVERS.NET.     3600000      A     198.41.0.4
;
.                       3600000      NS    B.ROOT-SERVERS.NET.
B.ROOT-SERVERS.NET.     3600000      A     128.9.0.107
;
.                       3600000      NS    C.ROOT-SERVERS.NET.
C.ROOT-SERVERS.NET.     3600000      A     192.33.4.12
;
.                       3600000      NS    D.ROOT-SERVERS.NET.
```

```
D.ROOT-SERVERS.NET.      3600000     A     128.8.10.90
;
.                        3600000     NS    E.ROOT-SERVERS.NET.
E.ROOT-SERVERS.NET.      3600000     A     192.203.230.10
;
.                        3600000     NS    F.ROOT-SERVERS.NET.
F.ROOT-SERVERS.NET.      3600000     A     192.5.5.241
;
.                        3600000     NS    G.ROOT-SERVERS.NET.
G.ROOT-SERVERS.NET.      3600000     A     192.112.36.4
;
.                        3600000     NS    H.ROOT-SERVERS.NET.
H.ROOT-SERVERS.NET.      3600000     A     128.63.2.53
;
.                        3600000     NS    I.ROOT-SERVERS.NET.
I.ROOT-SERVERS.NET.      3600000     A     192.36.148.17
; End of File
```

Widgets Zone File

The following zone file loads the name server with authoritative data for the widgets.com domain. The SOA record indicates that the file is located on foo.widgets.com; any questions about the domain should be directed to root@foo.widgets.com.

```
;
;       File:   /var/named/db.widgets
;
;       DNS information for widgets.com
;
;    NOTE always change serial number when editing
;
widgets.com.    IN  SOA    foo.widgets.com. root.foo.widgets.com. (
                199602101     ; Serial # YYYYMMDD
                3600          ; Refresh count 1 hour
                1800          ; Retry count 30 minutes
                604800        ; Expire count 1 week
                86400 )       ; Minimum ttl count for data
;-----------------------------------------
                NS         foo.widgets.com.
                NS         secondary.provider.net.
                MX 0       foo.widgets.com.
                           MX 10    mail.provider.net.
;-----------------------------------------
```

```
foo             A          192.168.148.1
ftp             CNAME      foo.widgets.com.
gopher          CNAME      foo.widgets.com.
www             CNAME      foo.widgets.com.
sales           A          192.168.148.2
;
; Individual PC addresses
;
pc1             A          192.168.148.10
pc2             A          192.168.148.11
pc3             A          192.168.148.12
```

The serial number follows a date format to give a better idea when the zone file was last updated. The refresh count has been set to 3,600 seconds, or one hour. This means the secondary server will check once an hour to see if a new zone file needs to be downloaded. The secondary server will try every 1,800 seconds, or 30 minutes if the first refresh attempt fails. The secondary server expires all the zone data if the primary server cannot be contacted within 604,800 seconds—one week. Finally, a minimum time-to-live of 86,400 seconds—one day—will be used for all records without an explicit TTL value.

If there is no entry in the domain name field of a resource record, then the last name entered will be used. This is why the NS and MX records do not start with a domain name. The domain name used in the SOA record, widgets.com, will be used. The same applies to the class field. The class used in the SOA record "IN" will be used for all records that follow and do not contain a class field. The host foo.widgets.com is the preferred mail exchange for widgets.com. If this server is down, e-mail will be sent to the Widgets' service provider's mail system, mail.provider.net.

The rest of the entries in this zone indicate host addresses and aliases within the widgets.com domain. Whenever a trailing dot is missing from zone data, the current domain name will be appended. This can reduce the amount of typing and increase the readability of zone files. All the host names on the left side starting with foo will have the domain name widgets.com appended to them. The domain name could have been left off the CNAME records, but it is stated for clarity.

Note Always check to see if if you are leaving a trailing dot on or off your data. Even though an entry such as the following might look correct, there is no trailing dot and therefore the current domain will be appended.

```
foo.widgets.com       IN A      192.168.148.1
```

This small oversight results in the unusable foo.widgets.com.widgets.com

Inverse Zone Files

The following zone file configures the name server for the inverse domain 148.168.192.in-addr.arpa. An @ appears in the domain name instead of the actual domain value. The @ is a shortcut for the current domain. The current domain, 148.168.192.in-addr.arpa, was specified in the "primary" configuration line in the named.bot file. This shortcut could have been used in all the SOA records presented in this example.

```
;       File:    /var/named/db.192.168.148
;
;       DNS information for 148.168.192.in-addr.arpa
;
;    NOTE always change serial number when editing
;
@        IN  SOA       foo.widgets.com. root.foo.widgets.com. (
           199602101     ; Serial # YYYYMMDD
           3600          ; Refresh count 1 hour
           1800          ; Retry count 30 minutes
           604800        ; Expire count 1 week
           86400 )       ; Minimum ttl count for data
;----------------------------------------
    NS     foo.widgets.com.
    NS     secondary.provider.net.
;----------------------------------------
1          PTR        foo.widgets.com.
2          PTR        sales.widgets.com.
10         PTR        pc1.widgets.com.
11         PTR        pc2.widgets.com.
12         PTR        pc3.widgets.com.
```

The PTR records set up the address-to-name mappings for this zone. Notice that the trailing dot must appear for the host names because you do not want the current inverse domain name appended to the host names. The trailing dot has been left off the left hand side to help readability.

The following file is similar to the previous inverse zone file. The only real difference is that there is only one host, localhost, that exists in 0.0.127.in-addr.arpa domain. This zone, though not really needed, is included for a complete DNS configuration.

```
;       File:   /var/named/indnet/db.127.0.0
;
;       DNS information for 0.0.127.in-addr.arpa
;
;    NOTE always change serial number when editing
;
@        IN  SOA       foo.widgets.com. root.foo.widgets.com. (
           199602101    ; Serial # YYYYMMDD
           3600         ; Refresh count 1 hour
           1800         ; Retry count 30 minutes
           604800       ; Expire count 1 week
           86400 )      ; Minimum ttl count for data
;-----------------------------------------
     NS     foo.widgets.com.
1          PTR     localhost.
```

Checking a DNS Configuration with nslookup

After you have created all the necessary configuration and zone files, how do you know your DNS server is actually working the way you want? For secondary servers, you can quickly check to see if the zone data has been saved to the file you specified in the named.boot file. The nslookup program provides a more robust way of checking the status of your DNS server. The program is usually located in the /usr/sbin directory. To run it, type **/usr/sbin/nslookup**.

When the program starts, you should see something like the following:

```
Default Server:  localhost
Address:  127.0.0.1
>
```

Nslookup defaults to the domain name and server specified in the /etc/resolv.conf file. From the nslookup prompt, you can submit queries to the name server, as in the following example:

```
> set type=SOA
> widgets.com
Server:  localhost
Address:  127.0.0.1
widgets.com
        origin = foo.widgets.com
        mail addr = root.foo.widgets.com
        serial = 199602101
        refresh = 3600 (1 hour)
        retry   = 1800 (30 mins)
        expire  = 604800 (7 days)
        minimum ttl = 86400 (1 day)
widgets.com         nameserver = foo.widgets.com
widgets.com         nameserver = secondary.provider.net
foo.widgets.com     internet address = 192.168.148.1
```

First, the type of records to query is set to SOA. Then the server is asked for information about the widgets.com domain. If the server is functioning properly, the SOA record is returned. The nslookup program can be used to troubleshoot many DNS problems. Type **help** at the > prompt for a detailed list of commands that can be used. For further information about nslookup, consult your system's online manual pages with the command **man nslookup**.

DNS in a Firewalled Network

A few different setups are possible for DNS in a firewalled network. The type of firewall in use dictates the DNS configuration. If a simple packet filter is being used, then the firewall can be configured to allow DNS traffic through securely. If the firewall uses proxy services preventing direct Internet connectivity, then the firewall itself must be able to resolve DNS requests made by its clients.

If the proxy firewall is a Unix system, configuring DNS is no different from the example presented in an earlier section of this chapter. In this configuration, you may not want to include much, if any, DNS information about internal TCP/IP devices.

Dual DNS Server Configurations

Another approach to running DNS with a Unix proxy firewall is to run two DNS servers. This option is recommended if the domain has quite a bit of data you do not want the rest of the Internet to know about. This could be the case if you are using unregistered IP addresses, either from the reserved blocks from RFC-1597, or addresses you simply made up at one point and are now unable to change.

In this configuration, two name servers are used. One runs on the firewall and only contains a minimal set of data the rest of the Internet can access. The second server runs on the protected side of the firewall and contains the complete set of data for your domain. Figure 4.4 shows how a network might appear with this configuration.

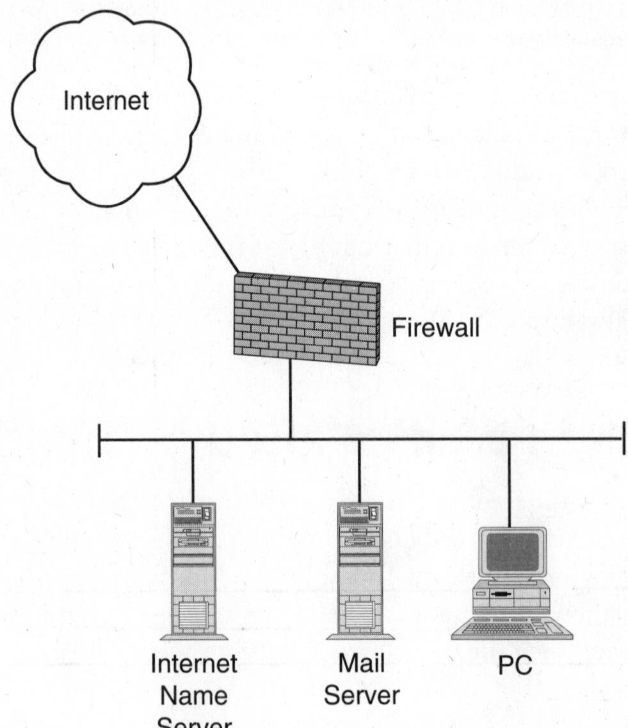

Figure 4.4
Dual DNS servers in a firewalled network.

The boot file for the firewall name server will look no different from the others presented in this chapter. The boot file on the internal name server will need some minor changes, however. The forwarders and slave directives are necessary. The internal name server cannot contact Internet name servers directly, so it must forward all queries to the firewall name server for resolution.

All internal TCP/IP devices will use the internal name server for resolving, *including the firewall.* Even though the firewall will be running its own name server, the internal name server contains the most complete data for the domain. The firewall will only contain a small portion of this data. This dual setup allows e-mail to be delivered properly. The firewall's DNS files should list themselves as the mail exchange for the Internet. The internal name server will have the proper mail exchange for the domain in its files. This way, incoming mail will be delivered to the firewall, and the firewall will then consult the internal name server for the e-mail's final destination.

IP Addressing and System Configuration

by Rick Fairweather

The purpose of an Internet Protocol (IP) address is very similar to an address used by the postal system on every letter we send and receive each day—it provides a means to reliably locate something and deliver relevant material. As you will see in this chapter, many of the characteristics of a mailing address are similar to the addressing structures and methods used by the IP protocol.

This chapter discusses the principles of IP addressing, including the structure and format of the IP address, subnetting IP addresses, and the implementation of IP addresses in typical networks.

IP Addressing—A Foundation

Every device that utilizes the IP protocol has an IP address. The device might be a computer, such as a personal computer, a file server, or a mainframe, or a network device, such as a router, a LAN switch, or an intelligent wiring hub. The use of IP addresses is, however, not limited to computer and network devices. Today, the IP protocol is being used for a wide range of devices, such as electrical monitoring systems, on-demand video services, or even traffic control systems. This wide array of uses for IP addresses, coupled with the rapid growth in computer and network deployment, is currently straining the number of IP addresses supported by the current implementation of the IP protocol, known as IP version 4. You will see in this chapter several solutions to this capacity issue. However, the real solution is a new IP protocol, known both as IP version 6 and IP Next Generation, which is discussed in detail in chapter 30, "IPng–The Next Generation."

IP Addressing Components

The IP protocol is a layer 3 or network layer protocol just as protocols such as IPX, AppleTalk, and DECnet are layer 3 protocols. Although these protocols are very different in their technologies and implementations, one aspect that they have in common is the two-part structure of their addressing implementations.

By definition, network layer protocol addresses are comprised of two components: a network number and a host number. The network number is used to denote a particular logical network, and the host number is used to identify a specific device on that network. Figure 5.1 illustrates the two parts of the addressing structure for several commonly used network layer protocols.

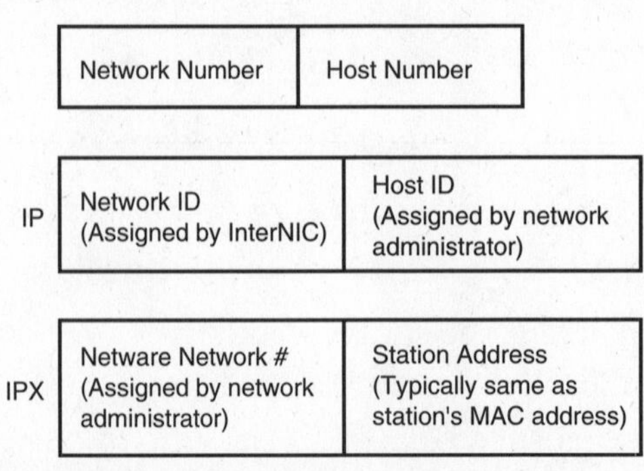

Figure 5.1
The two parts of network layer addresses.

One of the primary benefits of this two-part addressing structure is that the structure facilitates the delivery of packets to a destination based in part on the knowledge that all addresses having a specific network address are located on a particular network. This transport and delivery of packets based on the layer 3 network address is often referred to as routing. For this reason, network protocols that do have a two-part network layer address are often referred to as *routeable protocols*.

Note Not all network protocols utilize a two-part network layer address structure. Some protocols, such as LAT, commonly implemented in equipment from the Digital Equipment Corporation, or NetBios, commonly found in equipment from IBM, do not have a two-part network layer address and are therefore referred to as *non-routeable protocols*. Therefore, for these packets to be transported from one physical network to another, they must be bridged.

Now look at the postal sample letter again. Today, the use of ZIP codes is virtually universal within the United States. By quickly referring to a ZIP code, the postal system can direct or "route" the letter to the local post office depot, just as a router would do upon looking at the destination network address. Then, the name and street address, analogous to the host number, identifies the specific recipient of the letter.

Dissecting the IP Address

The actual numerical structure of the IP address presents some new challenges and concepts for many network implementers. With some proper instruction and practice, IP addressing can quickly become secondhand for nearly anyone.

IP addresses are 32 binary bits long and are broken into 4 bytes or octets. Each of these bytes or octets is 8 binary digits long. Typically, IP addresses are depicted in *dotted-decimal*, meaning that each of the octets is represented in decimal format separated by a period instead of in a traditional binary format. For example, a device might have the address 175.185.1.1, which is the dotted-decimal representation of an IP address. This same address would appear much differently in a binary format. Dotted decimal notation is frequently used for readability purposes.

IP network devices generally do not, however, view a number in decimal format as one might expect. Rather, network devices treat most numbers in binary format. Each of the octets in the IP address can range from 00000000 to 11111111, and each of the digits in the octet have a specific value as illustrated in table 5.1.

Table 5.1
Determining Decimal Values of Binary Numbers

Binary Numbers	Decimal Values
1st	128
2nd	64
3rd	32
4th	16
5th	8
6th	4
7th	2
8th	1

Therefore, a binary number with a value of 1 in the 8th position would have a value of 1. A binary number of 1 in the 1st position would have a value of 128. A binary number can be converted to a decimal value by adding the values of each of the binary digits that have a value of 1. Being that the octets in the binary representation of an IP address can range from 00000000 to 11111111, you can determine that these octets can range from a decimal value of 0 to 255.

Decimal to Binary Conversions

To illustrate this point, consider the binary number 10101111. First, determine which positions in the octet have a value of 1. This binary number has a value of 1 in the 1st, 3rd, 5th, 6th, 7th and 8th positions. By adding together the decimal values of each of these characters, you can determine the decimal value. The values of these characters are 128, 64, 32, 8, 4, 2 and 1. By adding these values together, the result is 175. Therefore, the binary number 10101111 also can be represented as the decimal number 175.

To further the concept, convert a decimal number to a binary number. It is often easiest to do this by determining the largest value of the characters in the binary numbers so it can be subtracted from the original value, subtracting to receive a result value and repeating this process on the resulting value. If you have the decimal number 185, you know immediately that the first position of the binary number is 1 because the decimal number, 185, is greater than the value of the 1st character in the binary number. If you then subtract 128 from 185, the result is 57. Because this result is less than the value of the 2nd digit in the binary octet, 64, then the value in that character is 0. If you continue this process, you will determine that the 1st, 3rd, 4th, 5th, and 8th characters of the binary octet will have a value of 1, whereas the remaining characters will have a value of 0. If you add the decimal values of each of these binaries, you receive the sum value of 185. Therefore, you have determined that the decimal number 185 can be represented as the binary number 10111001.

Although the process of converting values between binary and decimal representation is a skill worth learning, it is often considerably easier and quicker to have a reference guide to provide this function. For that reason, table 5.2 lists each of the binary and decimal values from 0 to 255.

Table 5.2
Binary and Decimal Listing up to 255

Decimal	Binary	Dec	Bin	Dec	Bin	Dec	Bin
0	00000000	64	01000000	128	10000000	192	11000000
1	00000001	65	01000001	129	10000001	193	11000001
2	00000010	66	01000010	130	10000010	194	11000010
3	00000011	67	01000011	131	10000011	195	11000011
4	00000100	68	01000100	132	10000100	196	11000100
5	00000101	69	01000101	133	10000101	197	11000101

continues

Table 5.2, Continued
Binary and Decimal Listing up to 255

Decimal	Binary	Dec	Bin	Dec	Bin	Dec	Bin
6	00000110	70	01000110	134	10000110	198	11000110
7	00000111	71	01000111	135	10000111	199	11000111
8	00001000	72	01001000	136	10001000	200	11001000
9	00001001	73	01001001	137	10001001	201	11001001
10	00001010	74	01001010	138	10001010	202	11001010
11	00001011	75	01001011	139	10001011	203	11001011
12	00001100	76	01001100	140	10001100	204	11001100
13	00001101	77	01001101	141	10001101	205	11001101
14	00001110	78	01001110	142	10001110	206	11001110
15	00001111	79	01001111	143	10001111	207	11001111
16	00010000	80	01010000	144	10010000	208	11010000
17	00010001	81	01010001	145	10010001	209	11010001
18	00010010	82	01010010	146	10010010	210	11010010
19	00010011	83	01010011	147	10010011	211	11010011
20	00010100	84	01010100	148	10010100	212	11010100
21	00010101	85	01010101	149	10010101	213	11010101
22	00010110	86	01010110	150	10010110	214	11010110
23	00010111	87	01010111	151	10010111	215	11010111
24	00011000	88	01011000	152	10011000	216	11011000
25	00011001	89	01011001	153	10011001	217	11011001
26	00011010	90	01011010	154	10011010	218	11011010
27	00011011	91	01011011	155	10011011	219	11011011
28	00011100	92	01011100	156	10011100	220	11011100
29	00011101	93	01011101	157	10011101	221	11011101
30	00011110	94	01011110	158	10011110	222	11011110
31	00011111	95	01011111	159	10011111	223	11011111

Decimal	Binary	Dec	Bin	Dec	Bin	Dec	Bin
32	00100000	96	01100000	160	10100000	224	11100000
33	00100001	97	01100001	161	10100001	225	11100001
34	00100010	98	01100010	162	10100010	226	11100010
35	00100011	99	01100011	163	10100011	227	11100011
36	00100100	100	01100100	164	10100100	228	11100100
37	00100101	101	01100101	165	10100101	229	11100101
38	00100110	102	01100110	166	10100110	230	11100110
39	00100111	103	01100111	167	10100111	231	11100111
40	00101000	104	01101000	168	10101000	232	11101000
41	00101001	105	01101001	169	10101001	233	11101001
42	00101010	106	01101010	170	10101010	234	11101010
43	00101011	107	01101011	171	10101011	235	11101011
44	00101100	108	01101100	172	10101100	236	11101100
45	00101101	109	01101101	173	10101101	237	11101101
46	00101110	110	01101110	174	10101110	238	11101110
47	00101111	111	01101111	175	10101111	239	11101111
48	00110000	112	01110000	176	10110000	240	11110000
49	00110001	113	01110001	177	10110001	241	11110001
50	00110010	114	01110010	178	10110010	242	11110010
51	00110011	115	01110011	179	10110011	243	11110011
52	00110100	116	01110100	180	10110100	244	11110100
53	00110101	117	01110101	181	10110101	245	11110101
54	00110110	118	01110110	182	10110110	246	11110110
55	00110111	119	01110111	183	10110111	247	11110111
56	00111000	120	01111000	184	10111000	248	11111000
57	00111001	121	01111001	185	10111001	249	11111001
58	00111010	122	01111010	186	10111010	250	11111010

continues

Table 5.2, Continued
Binary and Decimal Listing up to 255

Decimal	Binary	Dec	Bin	Dec	Bin	Dec	Bin
59	00111011	123	01111011	187	10111011	251	11111011
60	00111100	124	01111100	188	10111100	252	11111100
61	00111101	125	01111101	189	10111101	253	11111101
62	00111110	126	01111110	190	10111110	254	11111110
63	00111111	127	01111111	191	10111111	255	11111111

Registering for IP Addresses

Just like a mailing address, each IP address is unique. If two devices were to have the same IP address, there would be no way to determine which device should receive data destined for that specific IP address. The same is true with a mailing address. If two individuals had precisely the same address printed on the outside of an envelope, how would the postal deliverer know who should actually receive the letter without opening the letter and reading the contents? Just as in the case of a postal address, no two devices can share the same IP address at the same time.

So exactly how do we ensure that IP addresses are unique? Just as the postal service allocates ZIP codes, an organization, known as InterNIC, registers and allocates IP network numbers. Based on the number of networks and the number of addressable devices involved, the InterNIC assigns an IP network number to an individual or organization. You can receive an IP network number assignment either through an Internet Access Provider (IAP) or by contacting InterNIC directly using one of the methods shown in table 5.3.

Table 5.3
Methods for Getting an IP Address

Contact Medium	Address or Number
Via electronic mail	hostmaser@internic.net
Via telephone	(703) 742-4777

Contact Medium	Address or Number
Via facsimile	(702) 742-4811
Via postal mail	Network Solutions InterNIC Registration Services 505 Huntmar Park Drive Herndon, VA 22070

Note One might ask, "Why don't I just make up my own IP address rather than obtain an address from the InterNIC?" RFC 1597 does document a process for implementing non-registered IP addresses in a private, non-Internet connected network. The improper use of non-registered IP addresses can lead to significant problems for Internet-connected networks. If two different organizations happen to establish the use of the same IP network number, traffic cannot be accurately routed to the proper destination network. The same is true with a postal address. If two homeowners decided to use the address of 150 Main Street within the same ZIP code, how could the postal service actually know which home should actually receive a letter? The use of non-registered IP addresses is strongly discouraged.

IP Address Classes

One of the objectives of the addressing structures implemented in IP version 4 is to provide addressing capabilities for networks of all sizes. To help in accomplishing this objective, the IP address space has been divided into several classes.

As was discussed earlier, an IP address is made up of two components: a network address and a host address. To accommodate networks of all sizes and to make efficient use of network addresses, five different classes of IP addresses have been established (see fig. 5.2). All five classes utilize the same 32-bit address structure. However, as you will see, what varies is the number of bits allocated to the network portion of the address and the number of bits allocated to the host portion of the address.

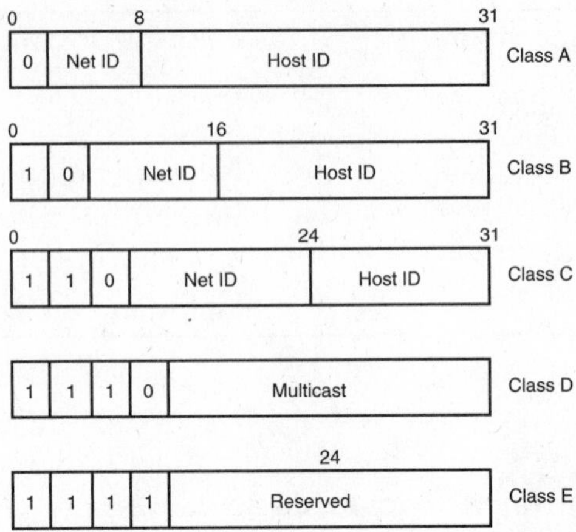

Figure 5.2
The five classes of Internet addresses.

Class A addresses have a network address, often referred to as a network ID, that is 7 bits long. The first binary digit of the first octet in a class A address will always be 0, as shown in figure 5.2. Thus, there can only be 127 (2^7–1) class A network numbers. These network numbers have been exhausted some time ago. The class A address allows for the remaining 24 bits to be assigned to host addresses. This allows for 16,777,216 (2^{24}) host addresses, often referred to a host ID. Two of these addresses, however, are actually reserved for specific functions, subnet addresses and broadcast addresses, which are discussed later in this chapter. Therefore, each class A network number can have a total of 16,277,214 addressable devices. Class A addresses are suited to extremely large networks, but, as mentioned earlier, the number of class A network addresses has long since been exhausted.

Class B addresses, often suitable for large companies, consist of a 14-bit network ID and a 16-bit host ID. There can be a maximum of 16,383 (2^{14}–1) class B addresses. Each class B network can have a total of 65,534 (2^{16}–2) addressable devices. Again, the majority of class B network numbers have already been allocated, leaving only class C addresses for those who are currently procuring approved IP addresses.

Class C addresses consist of a 21-bit network ID and an 8-bit host ID. There can be a maximum of 2,097,152 (2^{21}) class C networks each with a total of 255 (2^8–1) host IDs.

Class D and E addresses are not currently assigned. Class D addresses are reserved for protocols and devices that utilize multicast transmissions to communicate. Multicasts are generally a one-way transmission for a single source device to multiple destinations or receivers. One example of mulitcast implementation is the MBone, which is discussed in Chapter 32, "System Administrator's Guide to the MBone," and class E addresses are reserved for future use.

Table 5.4 illustrates the capabilities and address capacities of each of the classes of IP addresses.

Table 5.4
Class Capabilities and Address Capacities

Address Class	First Octet Range (Decimal)	Number of Network IDs	Number of Host IDs
A	1–127	127	16,277,214
B	128–191	16,383	65,534
C	192–223	2,097,152	255

Now that you have an IP network number assigned, one might be tempted to ask, "Are we done yet?" Well, in reality, you have only begun. The next step is to determine how to implement the IP addresses you have available.

Implementing IP Addresses

There are two guidelines you must consider before determining a strategy for deploying IP addresses:

1. Each device that will utilize or transport the IP protocol requires a unique IP address. If a device, such as a router, has multiple network interfaces, it will then have multiple IP addresses—one per network interface.

2. Each logical network that is bound by a router interface will need to have a unique IP network number. An Ethernet segment that is connected to a router will, for example, require a unique IP network number.

In summary, every device on a single logical network shares a common network ID, but has a unique host ID. It is worth noting that an IP network number can actually span multiple physical network segments. If one were to connect multiple physical segments with a device that provides level 2 forwarding of packets such as a bridge or Ethernet LAN switch, for example, all of those segments would share a common IP network number.

Reserved IP Addresses

As mentioned earlier in this chapter, two addresses from a network or subnet are "reserved" for special functions. These two functions are broadcast and subnet addresses. These addresses are identified by a host ID of all zeroes or all ones.

A host ID of all zeroes specifies a subnet address. This address, such as 198.100.100.0, would specify the subnetwork as a whole, not any specific device. An address of all zeroes is also used for machines that do not know all or part of their own host ID. For example, a diskless workstation might send out an address request to a bootP or address server using an address of all zeroes. The server would then respond and provide the IP address for the diskless workstation.

A host ID of all ones which would be a value of 255 in decimal notation in the case of a class B address, denotes a broadcast address. If data is sent to a broadcast address, all hosts on the specified network or subnetwork will receive that data. For example, if data is sent to the address 198.100.100.255, that data would in fact be sent to all hosts on the network 189.100.100.0.

Because of the need for these two reserved addresses, an adminstrator should never assign a device a host ID of either all zeroes or ones.

Subnetting IP Addresses

As was discussed previously, each of the IP address classes allows for a specific number of possible IP network numbers, each having a specific number of host IDs. For example, consider the IP network number 150.100.0.0. This network would allow for a total of 65,534 host IDs. If you review the IP address deployment guidelines discussed earlier, these 65,534 would all be on a common logical network.

This sample presents several potential issues.

- Many would consider the idea of implementing 65,534 network devices on a common logical network a poor network design, if not a ludicrous one. Given that some LAN technologies have limitations based on electrical parameters, the number of devices connected, and the total length of the network cable, such an implementation might not even be possible.
- Such an implementation would waste much potential address space by leaving many IP addresses unutilized.
- Such a network might actually be geographically dispersed, comprised of multiple smaller networks, perhaps based on different network technologies.

There are two primary solutions to these issues. First, the organization might seek to acquire a unique IP network number for each cable. Given the limited availability of IP network numbers, this is not a viable option. A more ideal solution to these issues is a concept known as subnetting.

Understanding the Subnetting Process

Subnetting is the process of further dividing the host ID portion of the IP address in order to create multiple logical subnetworks or subnets. The portion of the host ID that is allocated to the subnet is identified by a subnet mask. Like the IP address itself, the subnet mask is comprised of 32 bits broken into 4 octets. There essentially will be three components to the subnet mask: the network, the subnetwork, and the host. The network and subnetwork portions of the subnet mask will always be binary ones and the host portion will always be binary zeroes.

The process of subnetting IP networks requires the ability to derive three items: the subnet number, the range of valid host IDs, and the broadcast address. First, the subnet number is derived by performing a position-for-postion comparision of the binary representation of subnet mask with that of a specific address. If both of the relating bits are a 1, then a resulting 1 is placed in the corresponding bit location in the subnet number. If the bit in either the subnet mask or the IP number is a 0, then a resulting 1 is placed in the subnet number. This is often refered to as a logical and/or function. Consider the following example:

IP Number	10000011 . 01111100 . 00001110 . 11010111
Subnet Mask	11111111 . 11111111 . 11111111 . 00000000
Subnet Number	10000011 . 01111100 . 00001110 . 11010111

This example illustrates the use of an 8-bit mask, 255.255.255.0, on the IP address 131.122.14.215. The broadcast address is determined by converting all of the bits in the host portion of the subnet number to 1s. In the previous example, this involves converting the fourth octet to all 1s. In binary, this would be 10000011 . 01111100 . 00001110 . 11111111 or in decimal 131.122.14.255. If a host were to transmit data to all of the devices on the subnet 131.122.14.0, it would use a destination address of 131.122.14.255.

The valid range of host IDs falls between the subnet number and the broadcast address. In the example above, the range would be from 131.122.14.1 to 131.122.14.254.

If you apply the same process to the address 131.122.128.33, you can easily derive the same three items.

IP Number	10000011 . 01111100 . 10000000 . 00001111
Subnet Mask	11111111 . 11111111 . 11111111 . 00000000
Subnet Number	10000011 . 01111100 . 10000000 . 00001111

Converting this binary subnet number to dotted decimal notation, you will see that our subnet number is 131.122.128.0, and if you convert all of the bits in the host ID to 1s, you see that your broadcast address is 131.122.128.255. You can then see that your first valid host ID is 131.122.128.1, and the final host ID is 131.122.128.254. All IP devices that are assigned IP addresses on this logical segment must be given an IP address in this range.

Figure 5.3 illustrates the implementation of such a subnetting scheme in a network comprised of two Ethernet segments connected with a router.

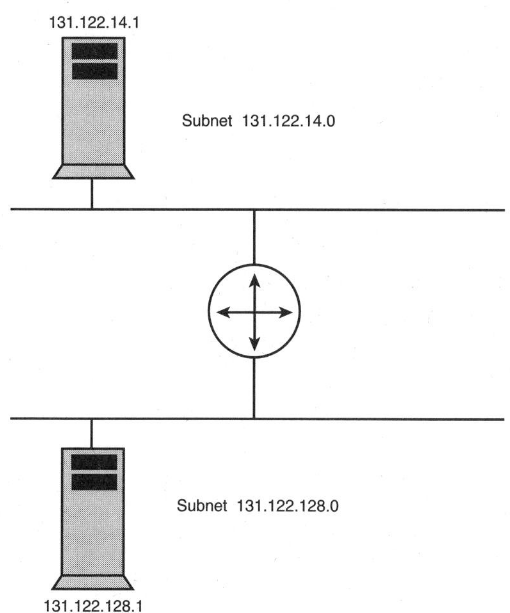

Figure 5.3
The implementation of the sample subnetting scheme.

Valid Subnet Mask References

Depending on the class of the address and the subnet mask used, a specific number of subnets and a specific number of host IDs can be derived from a network number. For reference purposes, tables 5.5 and 5.6 detail the resulting number of subnets and host IDs from the valid subnet masks for class B and class C network addresses respectively.

Table 5.5
Class B Subnetting

# Bits	Subnet Mask	# Subnets	# Hosts
2	255.255.192.0	2	16,832
3	255.255.224.0	6	8,190
4	255.255.240.0	14	4,094
5	255.255.248.0	30	2,046
6	255.255.252.0	62	1,022
7	255.255.254.0	126	510

continues

Table 5.5, Continued
Class B Subnetting

# Bits	Subnet Mask	# Subnets	# Hosts
8	255.255.255.0	254	254
9	255.255.255.128	510	126
10	255.255.255.192	1,022	62
11	255.255.255.224	2,046	30
12	255.255.255.240	4,094	14
13	255.255.255.248	8,190	6
14	255.255.255.252	16,832	2

Table 5.6
Class C Subnetting

# Bits	Subnet Mask	# Subnets	# Hosts
0	255.255.255.0	254	254
1	255.255.255.128	510	126
2	255.255.255.192	1,022	62
3	255.255.255.224	2,046	30
4	255.255.255.240	4,094	14
5	255.255.255.248	8,190	6
6	255.255.255.252	16,832	2

Subnetting Considerations

Subnetting only has local significance, which means that devices outside the subnetted network are not aware of the individual subnetworks, but rather see the entire network as a single network.

Another important concept is the nature of both inter- and intra-subnet communications. Devices that are on a common subnet will be able to communicate directly with each other without reliance on other hosts. Devices that are on separate subnets will, however, require the services of a gateway or router to exchange data. For this reason, it might be necessary to specify a default gateway or default router in the configuration of a host to facilitate "off-subnet" communication. The default gateway parameter is usually the IP address of a router interface that can provide routing services to other subnetworks.

Variable Length Subnet Masks

Generally, a single subnet mask is used throughout an entire network address. However, this often leads to wasted address space due to unused IP addresses.

This issue can be resolved through the use of variable-length subnet masks or VLSM. For example, an organization with a registerd class B network might implement an 8-bit mask for portions of the internetwork comprised principally of local area networks and perhaps a 14-bit mask for point-to-point wide area network circuits.

Although outside the scope of this text, the implementation of variable length subnet masks presents significant problems if not implemented correctly. It is recommended that the reader consult with an experienced professional prior to implementing VLSM.

Routing with TCP/IP Basics

by Rick Fairweather

Routers provide a critical function for both small and large internetworks—they provide connectivity between both similar and dissimilar networks. As figure 6.1 illustrates, routers function primarily at layer 3, the network layer of the OSI model, although they can also provide functionality at layers 4 and even 5.

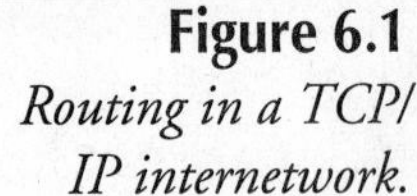
Figure 6.1
Routing in a TCP/IP internetwork.

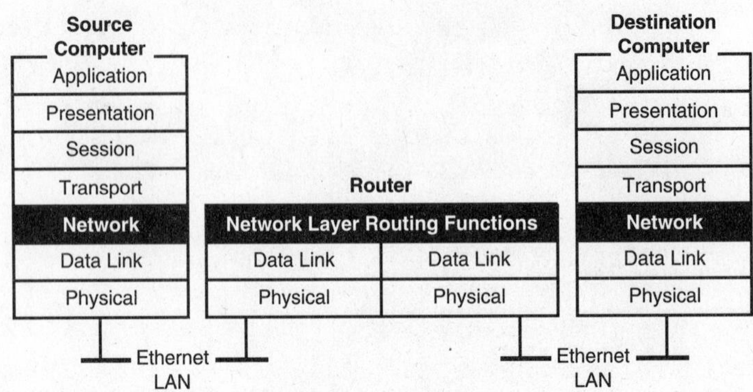

This chapter focuses on one particular aspect of this function—the protocols that actually make routing possible. In doing so, it examines two specific areas:

- The concepts and technologies fundamental to understanding routing protocols
- Several of the routing protocols in use today in many TCP/IP-based internetworks

Both positive and negative aspects of several routing protocols are discussed. This chapter's purpose, however, is not to determine the ideal routing protocol. There is no single ideal protocol—each protocol has both advantages and disadvantages. Rather, the goal is to objectively present the features, capabilities, and underlying technologies of these protocols.

What Is Routing?

So what exactly is routing? To properly understand routing, it is appropriate to dissect routing into two distinct functions:

- **Determining suitable and ideal paths through an internetwork.** This function, often termed route discovery or route determination, can be a fairly complex function of determining the optimal path from a source computer to a destination computer via an internetwork. Hence, routing protocols often are called route discovery protocols.

- **Transporting packets through an internetwork.** This function, often referred to as switching, is far less complex than path determination. *Switching* is typically a function performed in hardware and therefore implementations vary significantly between different vendor's products. This chapter doesn't address switching.

This chapter focuses on routing protocols that provide route discovery in an internetwork. Being able to distinguish routing protocols from routed protocols is critical. Routing protocols, such as RIP, OSPF, EGP, or BGP, provide route discovery services to hosts in an internetwork.

Routed protocols, such as the Internet Protocol (IP), the Internet Packet Exchange (IPX), and DECnet, are layer 3 or network layer protocols implemented in many host computers.

Fundamentals of Routing Protocols

Before you can properly understand routing protocols in general (and specifically, those examined later in this chapter), you need to grasp several of the fundamental underlying aspects of these protocols.

Classifications of Routing Protocols

Controversy swirls around the debate over link state versus distance vector routing algorithms. *Link state algorithms,* also known as *shortest path first* algorithms, flood routing information to all nodes in the internetwork. However, each router sends only that portion of the routing table that describes the state of its own links. *Distance vector algorithms* (also known as *Bellman-Ford* algorithms) call for each router to send its entire routing table, but only to its neighbors. In essence, link state algorithms send small updates everywhere, whereas distance vector algorithms send large updates only to neighboring routers. Later in this chapter, you will look closely at a common distance vector protocol, the routing information protocol, as well as a common link state protocol, the open shortest path first protocol.

Because they create a consistent view of the internetwork, link state algorithms are somewhat less prone to routing loops than are distance vector algorithms. However, because advertisements are flooded to all nodes within the network, link state algorithms can cause significant and widespread control traffic. They also are computationally difficult compared to distance vector algorithms, requiring more CPU power and memory than distance vector algorithms. Link state algorithms, therefore, can be more expensive to implement and support. Despite their differences, both algorithm types perform well in most circumstances.

Routing Algorithms

The heart of all routing protocols is one of a series of routing algorithms. These algorithms are used as the basis for calculating route metrics between a source host and a destination host, and fall into one of the following three catagories:

- **Destination/next hop based algorithms.** These algorithms essentially tell a router that a specific destination, such as an IP subnet, can be reached by switching the packet to the device identified as the next hop. Figure 6.2 illustrates a destination/next hop routing table.

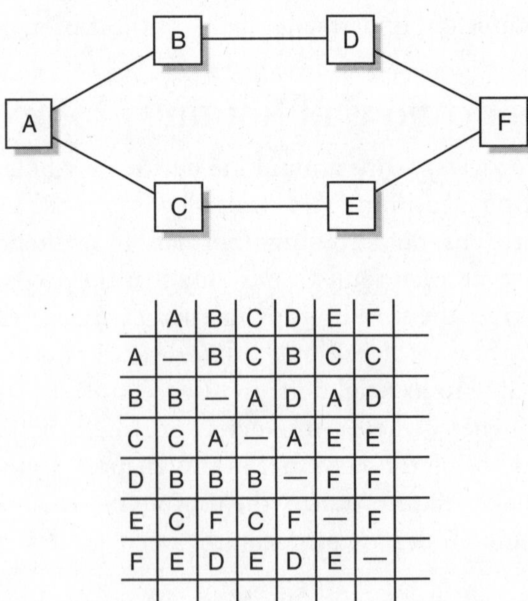

	A	B	C	D	E	F
A	—	B	C	B	C	C
B	B	—	A	D	A	D
C	C	A	—	A	E	E
D	B	B	B	—	F	F
E	C	F	C	F	—	F
F	E	D	E	D	E	—

Figure 6.2
A destination/next hop based routing table.

- **Destination/metric based algorithms.** These algorithms tell a router that a specific destination is some metric, or *distance*, away from the source (see fig. 6.3). This metric might be computed, for example, based on network bandwidth, network delay, or link utilization. Routers would then compare various metrics between the source and destination devices to select the optimal route for packet switching.

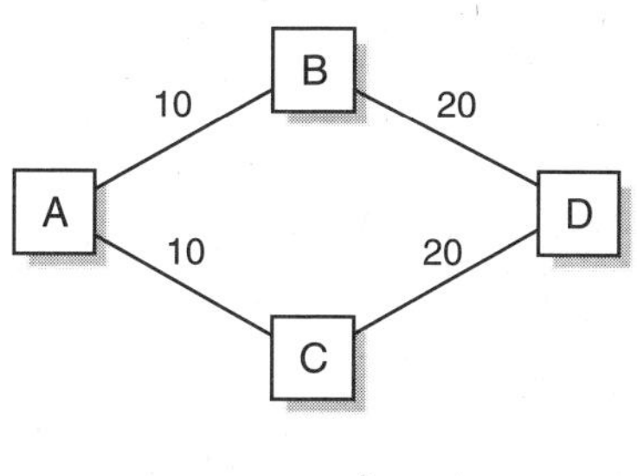

	A	B	C	D
A	—	10	10	30
B	10	—	20	20
C	10	20	—	20
D	30	20	20	—

Figure 6.3
A destination/metric based environment.

- **Destination/path algorithms.** These algorithms build routing tables that dictate the path for packets to take to reach a specific destination. This concept often is termed *source routing*, is widely deployed in IBM SNA and NetBios environments, and likely will see additional implementation in deployments of IP version 6 or IP Next Generation. Figure 6.4 illustrates this concept.

Routing protocols follow one of two general types of architecture: flat or hierarchical. The *Open Shortest Path First* (OSPF) protocol, for example, implements a hierarchy by deploying routing areas, each of which connect to a backbone area or area zero. Traffic switched from one area to another must pass through the backbone area. One of the most significant advantages of using a hierarchical protocol is that it facilitates scaling, and, therefore, can accommodate much larger networks. It does this by limiting the scope of transmission of routing exchanges. Routing updates are exchanged only between routers at the same level of hierarchy or within the same area. Figure 6.5 shows a hierarchical-based routed environment.

Figure 6.4
A destination/path based environment.

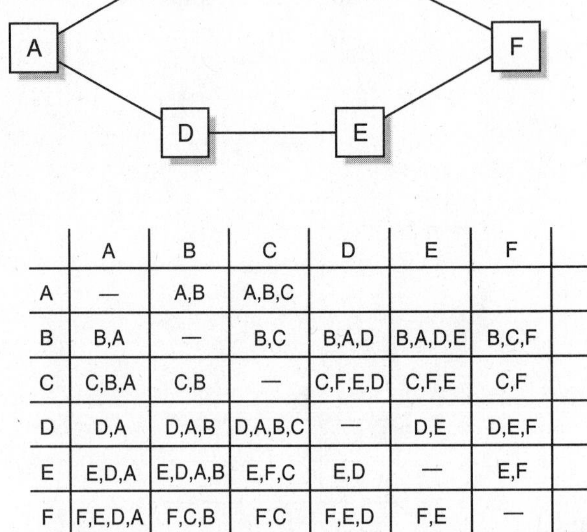

	A	B	C	D	E	F
A	—	A,B	A,B,C			
B	B,A	—	B,C	B,A,D	B,A,D,E	B,C,F
C	C,B,A	C,B	—	C,F,E,D	C,F,E	C,F
D	D,A	D,A,B	D,A,B,C	—	D,E	D,E,F
E	E,D,A	E,D,A,B	E,F,C	E,D	—	E,F
F	F,E,D,A	F,C,B	F,C	F,E,D	F,E	—

Figure 6.5
A hierarchical-based routed environment.

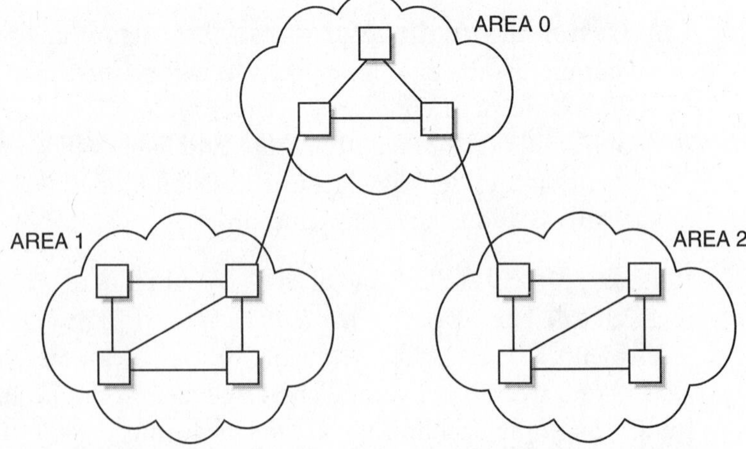

On the other hand, the *Routing Information Protocol* (RIP) doesn't employ any sort of hierarchy. All the routers in a RIP network essentially are peers, which is one of the primary shortcomings of RIP and has been the impetus for development of protocols such as the Open Shortest Path First protocol, which will be discussed later in this chapter in the discussion of interior gateway protocols.

Routing algorithms have several objectives, as follow:

- **Accuracy.** An algorithm's accuracy refers to its capability to detect the best route between a source and destination. The best route depends on the metric. If hop count is the metric, the best path would be the one containing the fewest hops. If the routing protocol uses delay as a metric, the best path would be the one that has the lowest delay.
- **Efficiency.** Efficiency can be a factor in terms of the networks in use as well as the hosts/routers that use these algorithms. If the algorithm involves frequent updates of routing information, for example, utilization of network segments and particularly wide area circuits can become an issue. If the algorithm involves frequent and complex calculations, memory and utilization of the routers and/or hosts that run these algorithms can become exhausted.
- **Rapid convergence.** Convergence is the process of all routers within an autonomous system agreeing on the best routes based on the metric in use. Rapid convergence is a requirement, not only to detect and use optimal routes, but also to eliminate routing loops. If convergence takes a significant amount of time after a topology change, routing loops can be formed, causing packets to be discarded. Ideally, not only should the process of convergence occur quickly but also the routing algorithm should be able to quickly detect the need for convergence. The capability to rapidly detect that a network segment is no longer available, that a change in network bandwidth or network delay has occurred, is critical for achieving optimal network stability.

Routing Metrics

Routing tables contain information used by the switching mechanisms in routers to select the best route. But how, specifically, are routing tables built? What is the specific nature of the information they contain? This section on algorithm metrics attempts to answer the question, "How do routing algorithms determine that one route is preferable to others?"

For example, one might ask what is the best route to take between New York and Los Angeles. The best route might have different paths depending on the perspective of what the best route is. Three people surveyed might have different opinions as to which the best route is: one person might say the best route is that with the fewest miles, another might say the path with the least amount of travel time, or perhaps the third might say the path with the most attractive scenery. Each of these opinions could be correct given their "metric" or what each person uses to quantify advantage of one path over another.

Many different metrics have been used in routing algorithms. Sophisticated routing algorithms can base route selection on multiple metrics, combining them in a manner resulting in a single (hybrid) metric. All of the following metrics have been used:

- **Hop Count.** Hop count indicates how many internetwork hops (routers) must be traversed before the destination can be reached. For example, a path that passes through one router would be considered to be a better route than a path that must transit four routers because it involves fewer hops.
- **Reliability.** Reliability, in the context of routing algorithms, refers to the reliability of each network link. Some network segments may display a high number of frame errors or retransmissions, perhaps due to faulty equipment or cabling problems. Some network links do go down more often than others. Obviously, failure of the circuit is a factor in determining the reliability of a connection. Once down, some network links are easier or faster to repair than other links. Any reliability factors can be taken into account in the assignment of reliability ratings. For example, if a particular network segment experiences a 20 percent frame error rate it might be assigned a reliability value of 5, whereas a segment with a frame error rate of 5 percent might be given a reliability value of 10. The segment with the higher reliability value would be selected as the path because it has a better reliability metric.
- **Delay.** Routing delay refers to the length of time required to move a packet from source to destination through the internetwork. Delay depends on many factors, including the bandwidth of intermediate network links, the port queues at each router along the way, network

congestion on all intermediate network links, and the physical distance to be traveled. Because it is a conglomeration of several important variables, delay is a *common metric.*

- **Bandwidth.** Bandwidth refers to a link's available traffic capacity. All other things being equal, a 10 Mbps Ethernet link would be preferable to a 64 Kbps leased line. Although bandwidth is a rating of the maximum attainable throughput on a link, routes through links with greater bandwidth do not necessarily provide better routes than routes through slower links. If, for example, a faster link is much busier, the actual time necessary to send a packet to the destination could be greater through the fast link. For this reason, utilization of a segment is also a common metric used in conjunction with bandwidth in routing.
- **Load.** Load refers to the degree to which a router is busy. Load can be calculated in a variety of ways, including CPU utilization, memory utilization, and packets processed per second. Monitoring these parameters on a continual basis can itself prove to be resource intensive.
- **Maximum Transfer Unit (MTU).** The Maximum Transfer Unit refers to the maximum size of a packet that can traverse a particular network link. An Ethernet network, for example, can handle frames as large as roughly 1,500 bytes. FDDI can handle frame sizes up to roughly 4,000 bytes.
- **Communication Cost.** Communication cost is another important metric. Some companies might not care about performance as much as they care about operating expenditures. Even though line delay might be longer, they want to send packets over their own lines rather than through public lines that cost money for usage time.

Autonomous System

An *autonomous system* is a group of networks under single authority; for example, an academic campus, a corporate complex, or a hospital complex. The autonomous system is identified by an autonomous system number, a number InterNIC typically assigns.

The other characteristic of an autonomous system is that a single interior gateway protocol (IGP), such as the Routing Information Protocol, typically addresses its system routing requirements within the autonomous system. Routing between autonomous systems generally is serviced by an exterior gateway protocol (EGP). Both protocols are discussed in detail later in this chapter.

Convergence

Convergence often is described as the process of rerouting around failed links. And that's true, but still more accurate would be to define it as the process of all routers within an autonomous system agreeing on optimal routes. When a network change occurs, such as a topology change or a change in network characteristics, routers exchange update messages causing the routers to recalculate optimal routes according to the metric in use. Consider the simple internetwork illustrated in figure 6.6.

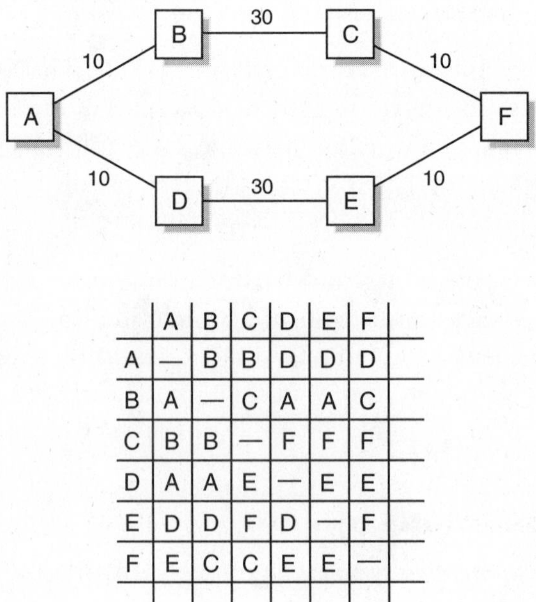

	A	B	C	D	E	F
A	—	B	B	D	D	D
B	A	—	C	A	A	C
C	B	B	—	F	F	F
D	A	A	E	—	E	E
E	D	D	F	D	—	F
F	E	C	C	E	E	—

Figure 6.6
A simple routed network and its routing table.

Using hop count as the metric in this example, each router builds a routing table as illustrated by the sample routing table shown figure 6.6.

However, in figure 6.7, if the segment between routers B and C were to fail, the routers would then have to converge or agree on the optimal paths between any given source and destination device. Each router would then revise its routing table to reflect accurate routes between the various devices. Figure 6.7 depicts the routing table after convergence has occurred.

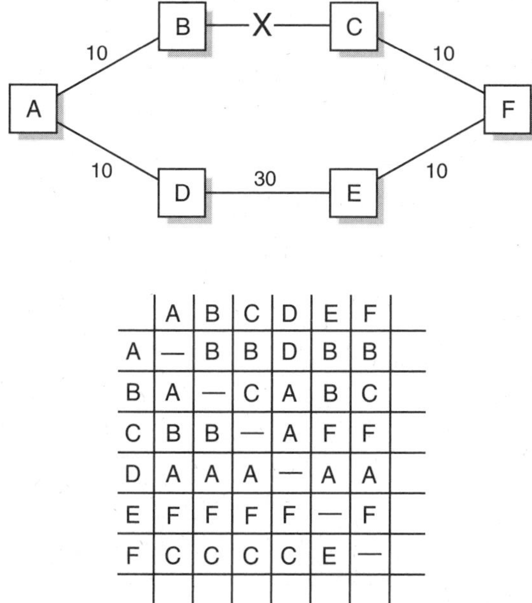

	A	B	C	D	E	F
A	—	B	B	D	B	B
B	A	—	C	A	B	C
C	B	B	—	A	F	F
D	A	A	A	—	A	A
E	F	F	F	F	—	F
F	C	C	C	C	E	—

Figure 6.7
Convergence in a simple internetwork.

Static Routing

Static routing algorithms are some of the earliest deployed routing technologies and still are used in many networks today. They're hardly what one would normally consider to be an algorithm since a network administrator creates and manually maintains them. Static routing algorithms do not react to network segment failures, topological changes, and changes in network characteristics.

Networks based on static routing algorithms offer several advantages. They are simple to design and implement and work well in networks that have highly predictable network traffic and a relatively simple overall network design. For example, most IBM SNA based networks use a form of static routing. A combination of static and dynamic routing algorithms frequently are implemented. Many IP networks, for example, statically designate a *router of last resort*, a specific router to which all unroutable packets are sent. This is a form of static routing.

Because static routing algorithms cannot react to network changes or topological changes, they are not appropriate for many of today's more complex and dynamic internetworks, such as those based on the TCP/IP protocol suite. These networks are best served by using dynamic protocols that can react to changing network characteristics in real time. In the following sections, several of the more common dynamic routing protocols used in IP networks are discussed in detail.

- **Interior gateway protocols.** Interior gateway protocols, or IGPs, are routing protocols that provide route discovery and route determination within an autonomous system. For this reason, interior gateway protocols are most commonly deployed in private internetworks. Two of these protocols, the routing information protocol and the open shortest path first protocol will be the focus of the following section.

- **Routing Information Protocol (RIP).** RIP is a distance vector, interior gateway protocol designed to address routing needs in autonomous systems. Originally designed for PUP, the Xerox PARC Universal Protocol in 1980, it gained much wider acceptance when it was integrated with the Berkeley Standard Distribution (BSD) implementation of Unix in 1982. The implementation in Unix, typically referred to as routed (pronounced *route dee*) has made it readily available to thousands of Unix-based hosts and gateways. Since then, RIP often has been considered an integral part of TCP/IP and Unix and is extensively deployed in workstation and host-based gateways today. The majority of routers manufactured by today's leading internetworking vendors, such as Cisco Systems, also support RIP. RIP is formally defined in the XNS Internet Transport Protocols publication and in RFC 1058.

  Not only has RIP experienced extensive deployment in TCP/IP environments, it also has served as the basis for routing protocols developed by other common networking protocols. AppleTalk's routing protocol (RTMP), for example, is a modified version of RIP. RIP also served as the basis for the routing protocols of Novell, 3COM, Ungermann-Bass, and Banyan. Some of these implementations, such as Novel and 3COM RIP, use RIP with minimal modifications, whereas other implemtations, such as Banyan and Ungermann-Bass, have been modified considerably to suit protocol requirements.

RIP was designed for reasonably small- or moderate-sized networks, and it's quite useful in this capacity. The maximum network diameter or number of hops between two routers in a RIP network is 16. The following section examines RIP in closer detail and concludes by presenting some issues concerning RIP in today's networks.

Routing Table Format

Each entry in a RIP routing table provides a variety of information, including the ultimate destination, the next hop on the way to that destination, and a metric. The metric indicates the distance in number of hops to the destination. The routing table also can include other information, such as various timers associated with the route. Figure 6.8 shows a typical RIP routing table.

Destination	Next Hop	Distance	Timers	Plays
140.100.1.0	140.100.2.1	4	t1,t2,t3	x,y
198.92.54.0	198.92.53.8	3	t1,t2,t3	x,y
201.1.2.0	198.92.53.8	2	t1,t2,t3	x,y

Figure 6.8
A typical RIP routing table.

RIP maintains only the best route to a destination. When new information provides a better route by having a better metric, this information replaces old route information. Network topology changes can provoke changes to routes, causing, for example, a new route to become the best route to a particular destination. When network topology changes occur, routing update messages reflect them. When a router detects a link failure or a router failure, for example, it recalculates its routes and sends routing update messages. Any router that receives a routing update message that includes route metrics that are different from what it currently has stored automatically updates its tables and propagates the change.

The Inner Workings of RIP

As Douglas Comer discusses in his book, *Internetworking with TCP/IP,* Volume II, a RIP network has two basic types of participants: active and passive. The basic model is active propagation and passive acquisition. Let's take a closer look at these two particpants.

Gateways or routers function as active participants in a RIP network, meaning they actively propagate or broadcast routing information through a network. Like all distance vector routing protocols, these updates contain a specific router's routing table. In the figure 6.9, for example, router Alpha would propagate its routing table to all of its neighbors; in this case, routers A, B, C, and D.

Figure 6.9
Routing information propogation in a RIP network.

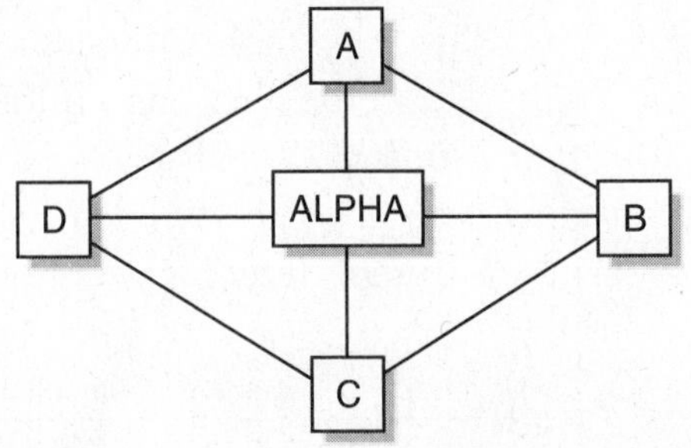

This function demonstrates the first aspect of active participation in RIP routing: the *transmission* of routing information or route tables. These transmissions utilize UDP port 520. In standard implementations, these updates are transmitted every 30 seconds. In environments in which many routers or gateways are on a single network, they tend to synchronize their updates, which can lead to network performance problems during these updates. To prevent this problem, many implementations use a random offset to the 30 second timer so the updates don't synchronize.

Compared to the second aspect of active participation, *reception,* transmission is relatively simple. When a router receives a RIP update, it compares the entries in the update with entries in its own routing table. If the router receives new destinations in an update, it adds those destinations to its routing table. If the router already has an entry for a specific destination, it ascertains whether the new routing information has a better or worse metric for that destination. It discards entries that have a worse metric for a specific destination that already exists. If the metric in the update for a specific destination is better than the metric reflected in the current table, the next hop location is updated with the relevant metric and next hop information. Consider the example shown in figure 6.10.

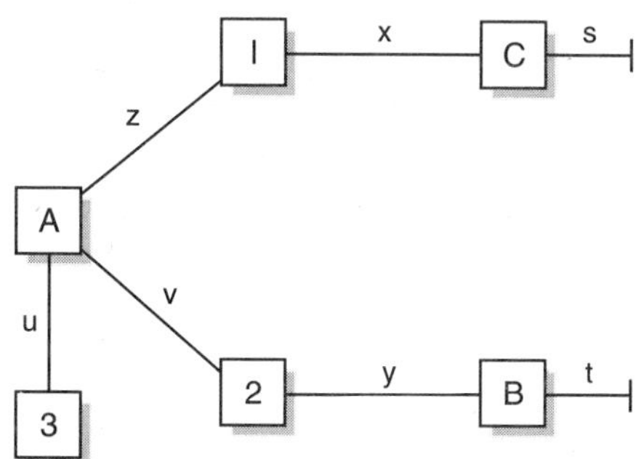

Figure 6.10
Receiving routing information in a RIP network.

Routing Table 1

Destination	Next Heep
u	A
v	A
x	1
y	2
z	A

Routing Table 2

Destination	Next Heep
s	1
t	2
u	A
v	A
x	1
y	2
z	A

As illustrated in Routing Table 1, router A only knows of entries of routers 1, 2, and 3. When it receives routing updates from its neighbor routers, it adds routes to new destinations to its table and adjusts the next hop location for entries that have a better metric in the update received, as shown in Routing Table 2.

RIP Timers

Every 30 seconds, the output process is instructed to generate a complete response to every neighboring gateway. When a single network has many gateways, those gateways tend to synchronize with each other and issue updates at the same time. This can happen whenever the processing load on the system affects the 30 second timer. Update messages becoming synchronized can lead to unnecessary collisions on broadcast networks—and nobody wants that. Thus, implementations must take one of two precautions.

- The 30-second updates are triggered by a clock whose rate is not affected by system load or the time required to service the previous update timer.
- The 30-second timer is offset by adding a small random time each time it is set.

Two timers are associated with each route, a *timeout* and a *garbage-collection time.* The timeout is initialized when a route is established and is reinitialized any time an update message is received for the route. If 180 seconds elapse from the last time the timeout was initialized, the route is considered to have expired, and the deletion process that is about to be described is started for it.

Deletions can occur for one of two reasons: the timeout expires or the metric is set to 16 because of an update received from the current gateway. In either case, the following events happen:

- The garbage-collection timer is set for 120 seconds.
- The metric for the route is set to 16 (infinity), causing removal of the route from service.
- A flag is set noting that the entry has been changed, and the output process is signalled to trigger a response.

Until the garbage-collection timer expires, the route is included in all updates that this host sends, with a metric of 16 (infinity). When the garbage-collection timer expires, the route is deleted from the tables.

Should a new route to this network be established during the garbage-collection timer's run, the new route replaces the one about to be deleted. In this case, the garbage-collection timer is reset.

Packet Format: IP Implementations

Figure 6.11 shows the RIP packet format for IP implementations, as specified by RFC 1058. Some other RIP variations make slight modifications to the format and/or to the field names listed here, but the basic routing algorithm is functionally identical.

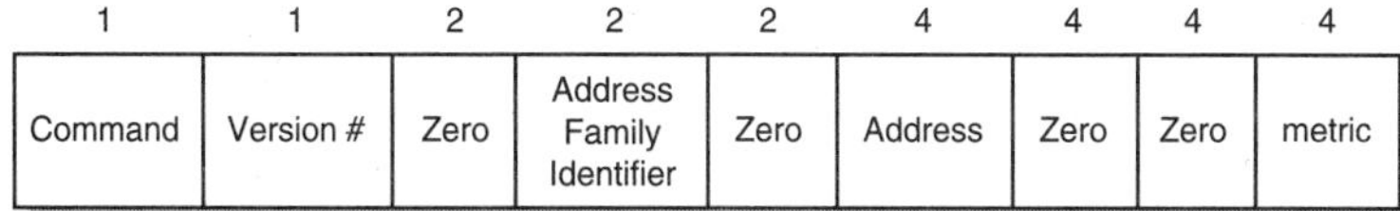

Figure 6.11
The format of a RIP packet.

The fields of the RIP packet are as follows:

- **Command.** Indicates that the packet is a request or a response. The request command requests the responding system to send all or part of its routing table. Destinations for which a response is requested are listed later in the packet. The response command represents a reply to a request or, frequently, an unsolicited regular routing update. In the response packet, a responding system includes all or part of its routing table. Regular routing update messages include the entire routing table.
- **Version number.** Specifies the RIP version being implemented. With the potential for many RIP implementations, this field can serve in an internetwork to signal different, potentially incompatible, implementations.
- **Address family identifier.** Follows a 16-bit field of all zeros and specifies the particular address family being used. On the Internet, this address family typically is IP (value = 2), but other network types also can be represented.
- **Address.** Follows another 16-bit field of zeros. In Internet RIP implementations, this field typically contains an IP address.
- **Metric.** Follows two more 32-bit fields of zeros and specifies the hop count.

As many as 25 occurrences of the address family identifier field through metric field are permitted in any single IP RIP packet. Therefore, up to 25 destinations may be listed in any single RIP packet. Multiple RIP packets are used to convey information from larger routing tables.

Stability Features

RIP specifies a number of features designed to make its operation more stable in the face of rapid network topology changes, including a hop-count limit, hold-downs, split horizons, and poison reverse updates.

Hop-Count Limit

RIP permits a maximum hop count of 15. Any destination greater than 15 hops away is tagged as unreachable. RIP's maximum hop count greatly restricts its use in large internetworks, but prevents a problem called *count to infinity* from causing endless network routing loops. Figure 6.12 illustrates the count-to-infinity problem.

Figure 6.12
The count-to-infinity problem.

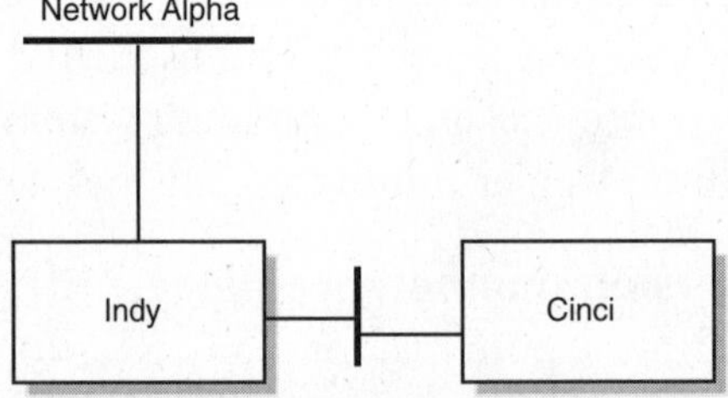

Consider what happens when Router Indy's link (link 1) to Network Alpha fails (refer to fig. 6.12). Indy examines its information and sees that Cinci has a one-hop link to Network Alpha. Since Indy knows it is directly connected to Cinci, it advertises a two-hop path to Network Alpha and begins routing all traffic to Network Alpha through Cinci, which creates a routing loop. When Cinci sees that Indy now can get to Network Alpha in two hops, it changes its own routing table entry to show that it has a three-hop path to Network Alpha. This problem and the routing loop will continue indefinitely, or until some external boundary condition is imposed. That boundary condition is RIP's hop-count maximum. When the hop count exceeds 15, the route is marked unreachable. Over time, the route is removed from the table.

Hold-Downs

Hold-downs are used to prevent regular update messages from inappropriately reinstating a route gone bad. Neighboring routers detect it when a route goes down, and then they calculate new routes and send out routing update messages to inform their neighbors of the route change. This activity begins a wave of routing updates that filter through the network.

Triggered updates do not instantly arrive at every network device, so a device that has yet to be informed of a network failure could send a regular update message (indicating that a route that has just gone down is still good) to a device that has just been notified of the network failure. In this case, the latter device now contains (and potentially advertises) incorrect routing information.

Hold-downs tell routers to hold down any changes that might affect recently removed routes for some period of time. The hold-down period usually is calculated to be just greater than the period of time necessary to update the entire network with a routing change. Hold-downs prevent the count-to-infinity problem.

Split Horizons

Split horizons derive from the fact that sending information about a route back in the direction from which it came never benefits anyone (see fig. 6.13).

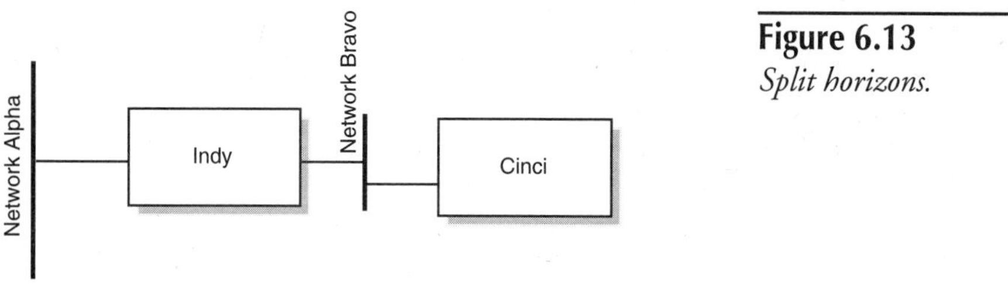

Figure 6.13
Split horizons.

Router 1 initially advertises that it has a route to Network Alpha (refer to fig. 6.13). Router 2 has no reason to include this route in its update back to Indy because Indy is closer to Network Alpha. The split-horizon rule says that Cinci should strike this route from any updates it sends to Indy.

The split-horizon rule helps prevent two-node routing loops. Consider what would happen if Indy's interface to Network Alpha were to go down. Without split horizons, Cinci would continue to inform Indy that it can get to Network Alpha through Indy. If Indy didn't have sufficient intelligence, it might actually pick up Cinci's route as an alternative to its failed direct connection, causing a routing loop. Although hold-downs should prevent this, split horizons provide extra algorithm stability.

Poison Reverse Updates

Whereas split horizons should prevent routing loops between adjacent routers, poison reverse updates are intended to defeat larger routing loops. The idea is that increases in routing metrics generally indicate routing loops. Poison reverse updates then are sent to remove the route and place it in hold-down.

Limitations of RIP

Unfortunately, in larger, more complicated internetworks, RIP has several drawbacks. First, RIP's hop count limit is 16, so destinations may not be more than 16 hops distant. Second, the protocol cannot choose routes based on real-time parameters, such as delay or load. Because of these inadequacies, RIP has been replaced in many installations with more modern routing protocols. Finally, because RIP is based on fixed update and timeout timers, it often isn't suitable for networks that experience frequent topology changes that would cause changes in routing tables. These issues are some of the primary issues that have driven the development of more suitable routing protocols such as OSPF.

Open Shortest Path First Protocol

Open Shortest Path First (OSPF) is a relatively recent intra-domain, link state, hierarchical routing protocol developed for IP networks by the Internet Engineering Task Force (IETF). OSPF was derived from several research efforts, including the following:

- Bolt, Beranek, and Newman's (BBN's) SPF algorithm developed in 1978 for the ARPANET

- Dr. Perlman's research on fault-tolerant broadcasting of routing information (1988)
- BBN's work on area routing (1986)
- An early version of OSI's Intermediate System-to-Intermediate System (IS-IS) routing protocol

As its acronym indicates, OSPF has two primary characteristics. The first is that it is open, in that its specification is in the public domain. The OSPF specification is published as RFC 1247. The second principal characteristic is that it is based on the SPF algorithm, sometimes referred to as the *Dijkstra algorithm* in honor of the person credited with its creation.

Technology Basics

OSPF is a link-state routing protocol. As such, it calls for the sending of link-state advertisements or LSAs to all other routers in the same hierarchical area. OSPF LSAs include information on attached interfaces, metrics used, and other variables. As OSPF routers accumulate link state information, they use the SPF algorithm to calculate the shortest path to each node.

As a link-state routing protocol, OSPF contrasts with RIP, which is a distance vector routing protocol. Routers running the distance vector algorithm send all or a portion of their routing tables in routing update messages, but only to their neighbors.

Information on attached interfaces, metrics used, and other variables are included in OSPF routing updates. This information is flooded throughout the routing area. As OSPF routers accumulate link-state information, they can calculate the shortest path to each node. Updates are required only when a link state changes. OSPF routers exchange periodic Hello messages that act as *keepalives* to let routers know that other routers are still functional.

Routing Hierarchy

Unlike RIP, OSPF can operate within a hierarchy. The largest entity in the hierarchy is the autonomous system. An autonomous system can be divided into a number of areas. An *area* is a group of contiguous networks and attached hosts. Routers with multiple interfaces can participate in multiple areas. These routers, called *area border routers,* maintain separate topological databases for each area.

A topological database essentially acts as an overall picture of networks in relationship to routers. The topological database contains the collection of LSAs received from all routers in the same area. Because routers within the same area share the same information, they have identical topological databases.

The term *domain* sometimes describes a portion of the network in which all routers have identical topological databases, and frequently is used interchangeably with autonomous system.

An area's topology is invisible to entities outside the area. By keeping area topologies separate, OSPF passes less routing traffic than it would if the autonomous system were not partitioned.

Area partitioning creates two different types of OSPF routing, depending on whether the source and destination are in the same or different areas. Intra-area routing occurs when the source and destination are in the same area; inter-area routing occurs when they are in different areas.

An OSPF backbone is responsible for distributing routing information between areas. It consists of all area border routers, networks not wholly contained in any area, and their attached routers. Figure 6.14 shows an example of an internetwork with several areas.

In figure 6.14, routers 4, 5, 6, 10, 11, and 12 form the backbone. If host H1 in area 3 wants to send a packet to host H2 in area 2, the packet is sent to Router 13, which forwards the packet to Router 12, which sends the packet to Router 11. Router 11 forwards the packet along the backbone to an area border router, Router 10, which sends the packet through two intra-area routers (Router 9 and Router 7) to be forwarded to host H2.

The backbone itself is an OSPF area, so all backbone routers use the same procedures and algorithms to maintain routing information in the backbone as any area router. The backbone topology is invisible to all intra-area routers, as are individual area topologies to the backbone.

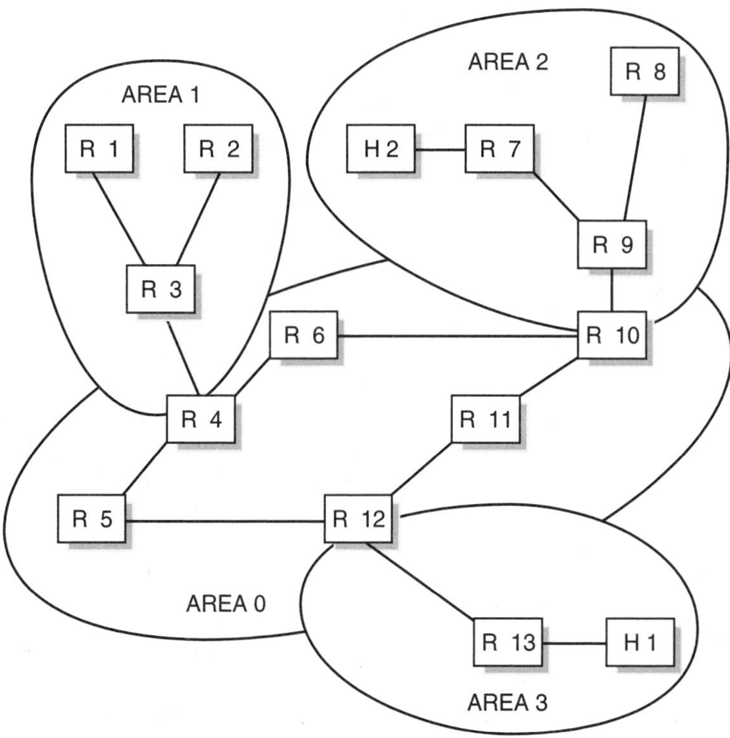

Figure 6.14
A hierarchical OSPF internetwork.

Areas can be defined in such a way that the backbone is not contiguous. In this case, backbone connectivity must be restored through virtual links. Virtual links are configured between any backbone routers that share a link to a nonbackbone area, and function as if they were direct links.

Autonomous system border routers running OSPF learn about exterior routes through exterior gateway protocols (EGPs), such as the Exterior Gateway Protocol (EGP) or the Border Gateway Protocol (BGP), or through configuration information. Later in this chapter, you will examine several viable exterior gateway protocols including both EGP and BGP.

SPF Algorithm

The SPF routing algorithm is the basis for OSPF operations. When an SPF router is powered up, it initializes its routing protocol data structures and then waits for indications that its interfaces are functional from lower-layer protocols.

After a router is assured that its interfaces are functioning, it uses the OSPF Hello protocol to acquire neighbors. The router sends hello packets to its neighbors and receives their hello packets. In addition to helping acquire neighbors, hello packets also act as keepalives to let routers know that other routers are still functional.

On multiaccess networks (networks supporting more than two routers), the Hello protocol elects a designated router and a backup designated router. The designated router is responsible, among other things, for generating LSAs for the entire multiaccess network. Designated routers allow a reduction in network traffic and in the size of the topological database.

When the link-state databases of two neighboring routers are synchronized, the routers are said to be *adjacent.* On multiaccess networks, the designated router determines which routers should become adjacent. Topological databases are synchronized between pairs of adjacent routers. Adjacencies control the distribution of routing protocol packets, which are sent and received only on adjacencies.

Each router periodically sends an LSA. LSAs also are sent when a router's state changes. LSAs include information on a router's adjacencies. By comparing established adjacencies to link states, failed routers can be detected quickly and the network's topology altered appropriately. From the topological database generated from LSAs, each router calculates a shortest-path tree, using itself as root. The shortest-path tree, in turn, yields a routing table.

Packet Format

All OSPF packets begin with a 24-byte header, as figure 6.15 shows.

Figure 6.15
The OSPF header format.

1	1	2	4	4	2	2	8	Variable
Version #	Type	Packet Length	Router ID	Area ID	Checksum	Authentication Type	Authentication	Data

The fields of the OSPF header are as follows:

- **Version number.** Identifies the particular OSPF implementation being used.

- **Type.** Specifies one of five OSPF packet types:

  Hello. Sent at regular intervals to establish and maintain neighbor relationships.

  Database description. Describes the contents of the topological database, and are exchanged when an adjacency is being initialized.

  Link-state request. Requests pieces of a neighbor's topological database, which are exchanged after a router discovers (by examining database description packets) that parts of its topological database are out of date.

  Link-state update. Indicates a response to link-state request packets. They also are used for the regular dispersal of LSAs. Several LSAs may be included within a single packet.

  Link state acknowledgment. Acknowledges link-state update packets. Link-state update packets must be explicitly acknowledged to ensure that link-state flooding throughout an area is a reliable process. Each LSA in a link-state update packet contains a type field. The four LSA types are as follows:

  - **Router links advertisements.** These describe the collected states of the router's links to a specific area. A router sends an RLA for each area to which it belongs. RLAs are flooded throughout the entire area, and no further.

  - **Network links advertisements.** Sent by the designated routers, these describe all the routers attached to a multiaccess network and are flooded throughout the area containing the multiaccess network. An example would be all of the routers that share connections to a common ethernet.

  - **Summary links advertisements.** These summarize routes to destinations outside an area but within the autonomous system. They are generated by area border routers and are flooded throughout the area. Only intra-area routes are advertised into the backbone. Both intra-area and inter-area routes are advertised into the other areas.

- **Autonomous system external links advertisements.** These describe a route to a destination that is external to the autonomous system. Autonomous system external links advertisements are originated by boundary routers. This type of advertisement is the only type forwarded everywhere in the autonomous system; all others are forwarded only within specific areas.

- **Packet length.** Specifies the packet's length (in bytes), including the OSPF header.
- **Router ID.** Identifies the packet's source.
- **Area ID.** Identifies the area to which the packet belongs. All OSPF packets are associated with a single area.
- **Checksum.** Checks the entire packet contents for potential damage suffered in transit.
- **Authentication type.** Contains an authentication type. "Simple password" is an example of an authentication type. All OSPF protocol exchanges are authenticated. The authentication type is configurable on a per-area basis.
- **Authentication.** Contains authentication information and is 64 bits in length.

Additional OSPF Features

OSPF supports one or more metrics. If only one metric is used, it is considered to be arbitrary, and type of service (TOS) is not supported. If more than one metric is used, TOS is optionally supported through the use of a separate metric and, therefore, a separate routing table. OSPF supports multiple TOS classes, identified by the eight unique combinations of the three IP TOS bits (the delay, throughput, and reliability bits). If the IP TOS bits specify low delay, low throughput, and high reliability, for example, OSPF calculates routes to all destinations based on this TOS designation. TOS-based routing supports those upper-layer protocols that can specify particular types of service. For example, an application might specify that certain data is urgent. If OSPF has high-priority links at its disposal, these can be used to transport the urgent datagram.

IP subnet masks are included with each advertised destination, enabling variable-length subnet masks. This capability is not possible with a routing protocol such as RIP. With variable-length subnet masks, an IP network can be broken into many subnets of various sizes, which provides network administrators with extra network configuration flexibility.

Additional OSPF features include equal-cost, multipath routing. This capability makes load sharing across parallel network paths possible in a redundant network.

Exterior Gateway Protocols

Exterior gateway protocols provide routing services between autonomous systems. Because of this, exterior gateway protocols are typically implemented by Internet access providers and those responsible for routing in the Internet. In many situations, a webmaster might not have any direct interaction with these protocols because they are not typically used for intra-autonomous system routing. Therefore, the objective of this section on exterior gateway protocols is to provide more of an overview of these protocols.

EGP

The Exterior Gateway Protocol (EGP) is an interdomain reachability protocol used in the Internet. Originally documented in RFC 904, EGP is used for communication between the "core" Internet routers that form the Internet's routing backbone.

Although EGP is a dynamic routing protocol, it uses a very simple design. It does not use metrics and, therefore, cannot make true intelligent routing decisions. EGP routing updates contain network reachability information. In other words, they specify that certain networks are reachable through certain routers. Because of this, EGP has often been referred to as being a reachability protocol rather than a routing protocol.

EGP updates are sent to neighboring routers at regular intervals. In the updates, each router indicates those networks to which it is directly attached. This network reachability information eventually permeates the EGP environment. The information is used to construct and maintain routing tables.

Technology Basics

EGP was designed to communicate reachability to and from the Advanced Research Projects Agency Network (ARPANET) core routers. Information was passed from individual source nodes in distinct Internet administrative domains, called *autonomous systems*, up to the core routers, which passed the information through the backbone until it could be passed down to the destination network in another autonomous system. Figure 6.16 shows this relationship between EGP and other ARPANET components.

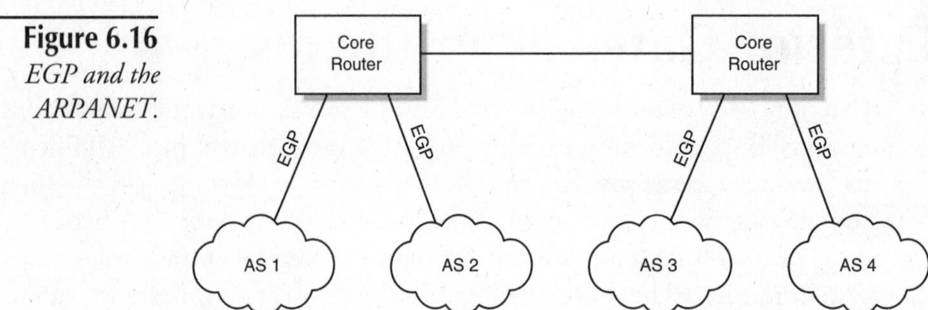

Figure 6.16
EGP and the ARPANET.

EGP has three primary functions. First, routers running EGP establish a set of neighbors. These neighbors simply are routers with which an EGP router wants to share reachability information, without implying geographic proximity. Second, EGP routers poll their neighbors to see if they are alive. Third, EGP routers send update messages containing information about the reachability of networks within their autonomous systems.

Packet Format

EGP can perhaps be best understood by examining the packet structure of an EGP update. As we will see, the packet format is relatively simple and provides basic functionality to address communications between neighboring routers and provide a means to exchange the networks a router is aware to its neighbors.

Figure 6.17 shows an EGP packet.

1	1	1	1	2	2	2	Variable
EGP Version Number	Type	Code	Status	Checksum	Antonomous System Number	Sequence Number	Data

Figure 6.17
The EGP packet format.

The fields of the EGP packet are as follows:

- **EGP version number.** Identifies the current EGP version and is checked by recipients for any matches between sender and recipient version numbers.
- **Type.** Identifies the message type. EGP defines the following five separate message types, which are listed briefly here and will be discussed in more detail later in this section:

  Neighbor Acquisition. Establishes/de-establishes neighbors.

  Neighbor Reachability. Determines whether neighbors are alive.

  Poll. Determines reachability of a particular network.

  Routing Update. Provides routing updates.

  Error. Indicates error conditions.
- **Code.** Distinguishes among message subtypes.
- **Status.** Contains message-dependent status information. Status codes include insufficient resources, parameter problem, protocol violation, and others.
- **Checksum.** Detects possible problems that might have developed concerning the packet in transit.
- **Autonomous system number.** Identifies the autonomous system to which the sending router belongs.
- **Sequence number.** Allows two EGP routers exchanging messages to match requests with replies. The sequence number is initialized to zero when a neighbor is established and incremented by one with each request-response transaction.

Message Types

Additional fields follow the EGP header. The contents of these fields vary depending on the message type and are identified by the value in the type field.

Neighbor Acquisition

The neighbor acquisition message includes a hello interval field and a poll interval field. The hello interval field specifies the interval period for testing whether neighbors are alive. The poll interval field specifies the routing update frequency.

Neighbor Reachability

The neighbor reachability message adds no extra fields to the EGP header. These messages use the code field to indicate whether the message is a hello message or a response to a hello message. Assessing reachability and exchanging routing information are distinct functions in EGP. They are handled separately primarily to reduce the amount of network traffic between EGP routers. Routers will frequently exchange hello messages to verify reachability but will exchange routing only when a change in reachability has been detected. If a specified number of reachability messages have not been received, then the router will access the route to be down and will therefore remove it from its routing tables.

Poll

To provide correct routing between autonomous systems, EGP must know the relative location of remote hosts. The poll message allows EGP routers to acquire reachability information about the networks on which these hosts reside. These messages only have one field beyond the common header: the IP source network field, which specifies which network to use as a reference point for the request.

Routing Update

Routing update messages provide a way for EGP routers to indicate the locations of various networks within their autonomous systems. In addition to the common header, these messages include many additional fields.

The number of interior gateways field indicates the number of interior gateways appearing in the message. The number of exterior gateways field indicates the number of exterior gateways appearing in the message. The IP source network field provides the IP address of the network from which reachability is measured. A series of gateway blocks follows this field. Each gateway block provides the IP address of a gateway and a list of networks and distances associated with reaching those networks.

In the gateway block, EGP lists networks by distances. In other words, at distance three, there might be four networks. These networks then are listed by address. The next group of networks might consist of those that are distance four away, and so on.

Error

Error messages identify various EGP error conditions. In addition to the common EGP header, EGP error messages provide a reason field, followed by an error message header. Typical EGP errors (reasons) include bad EGP header format, bad EGP data field format, excessive polling rate, and the unavailability of reachability information. The error message header consists of the first three 32-bit words of the EGP header.

Note Although it has served the Internet well for a number of years, EGP's weaknesses now are becoming more apparent. EGP offers no way to deal with the routing loops that can occur in multi-path networks. Also, EGP routing updates often are large and cumbersome. Finally, EGP cannot make intelligent routing decisions because it does not support link metrics. Consequently, EGP is slowly being phased out of the Internet and in many cases is being replaced with BGP, the Border Gateway Protocol.

Border Gateway Protocol (BGP)

The Border Gateway Protocol represents an attempt to address EGP's most serious problems. Like EGP, BGP is an interdomain routing protocol created for use in the Internet core routers. Unlike EGP, BGP was designed to detect routing loops and to use a metric so that intelligent routing decisions could be made. BGP can be thought of as "next-generation EGP." Indeed, BGP is (slowly) replacing EGP in the Internet. BGP is specified in RFC 1163.

Although designed as an interdomain protocol, BGP can be used both within and between domains. Two BGP neighbors communicating between domains must reside on the same physical network. BGP routers within the same domain communicate for two reasons:

- To ensure that they have a consistent view of the domain
- To determine the BGP router within that domain to serve as the connection point to/from certain external domains

Some domains merely act as pass-through channels for network traffic. In other words, some domains carry network traffic that did not originate in and is not destined for them. BGP must interact with whatever intra-domain routing protocols exist in these pass-through domains. These interactions, although beyond the scope of this document, are detailed in the BGP protocol specification.

BGP update messages consist of network number/domain path pairs. The domain path contains the string of domains through which the specified network may be reached. These update messages are sent over the TCP reliable transport mechanism.

The initial data exchange between two routers is the entire BGP routing table. Incremental updates are sent out as the routing tables change. Unlike some other routing protocols, BGP doesn't require periodic refresh of the entire routing table. Instead, routers running BGP retain the latest version of each peer routing table. Although BGP maintains a routing table with all feasible paths to a particular network, it advertises only the primary (optimal) path in its update messages.

The BGP metric is an arbitrary unit number that specifies the "degree of preference" of a particular path. These metrics typically are assigned by the network administrator via configuration files.

Degree of preference might be based on any number of criteria, including domain count (paths with a smaller domain count are generally better), type of link (is the link stable? fast? reliable?), and other factors.

Technology Basics

Although BGP was designed as an inter-autonomous system protocol, it can be used in and between autonomous systems. Two BGP neighbors communicating between autonomous systems must reside on the same physical network. BGP routers within the same autonomous system communicate to ensure that they have a consistent view of the autonomous system and to determine the BGP router within that autonomous system to serve as the connection point to or from certain external autonomous systems.

Some autonomous systems merely are pass-through channels for network traffic. That is, some autonomous systems carry network traffic that did not originate within the autonomous system and is not destined for the autonomous system. BGP must interact with whatever intra-autonomous system routing protocols exist within these pass-through autonomous systems.

BGP update messages consist of network number/autonomous system path pairs. The autonomous system path contains the string of the autonomous system through which the specified network can be reached. These update messages are sent over the Transmission Control Protocol transport mechanism to ensure reliable delivery.

Packet Format

Figure 6.18 shows the BGP packet format.

16	2	1	Variable
Marker	Length	Type	Data

Figure 6.18
The BGP packet format.

BGP packets have a common 19-byte header consisting of the following three fields:

- **Marker.** Contains a value that the receiver of the message can predict. Used for authentication.
- **Length.** Contains the total length of the message, in bytes.
- **Type.** Specifies the message type. There are four types of messages that can be identified in the BGP header: open, update, notification, and

keepalive. Each of these message types is discussed in more detail in the section below.

Open

After a transport protocol connection is established, the first message sent by each side is an *open* message. If the recipient finds the open message acceptable, a keepalive message confirming the open message is sent back. After a successful confirmation of the open message, updates, keepalives, and notifications can be exchanged.

In addition to the common BGP packet header, open messages define several fields. The version field provides a BGP version number and allows the recipient to check that it is running the same version as the sender. The autonomous system field provides the sender's autonomous system number. The hold-time field indicates the maximum number of seconds allowed to elapse before receipt of a message that the transmitter is assumed to be dead. The authentication code field indicates the authentication type being used (if any). The authentication data field contains actual authentication data (if any).

Update

BGP *update* messages provide routing updates to other BGP systems. Information in these messages is used to construct a graph that describes the relationships of the various autonomous systems. In addition to the common BGP header, update messages have several additional fields. These fields provide routing information by listing path attributes that correspond to each network.

BGP currently defines the following five attributes:

- **Origin.** Can take on one of three values: IGP, EGP, or incomplete. The IGP attribute means that the network is part of the autonomous system. The EGP attribute means that the information was originally learned from the EGP. BGP implementations would be inclined to prefer IGP routes over EGP routes, because EGP fails when faced with routing loops. The incomplete attribute is used to indicate that the network is known via some other means.

- **Autonomous system path.** Provides the actual list of the autonomous system on the path to the destination.
- **Next hop.** Provides the IP address of the router that should be used as the next hop to the networks listed in the update message.
- **Unreachable.** If present, indicates that a route is no longer reachable.
- **Inter-autonomous system metric.** Provides a way for a BGP router to advertise its cost to destinations within its own autonomous system. This information can be used by routers outside the advertiser's autonomous system to select an optimal route into the autonomous system to a particular destination.

Notification

Notification messages are sent when an error condition has been detected and a router wants to tell another router why it is closing the connection between them.

Aside from the common BGP header, notification messages have an error code field, an error subcode field, and error data. The error code field indicates the type of error and can be one of the following:

- **Message header error.** Indicates a problem with the message header, such as an unacceptable message length, an unacceptable marker field value, or an unacceptable message type.
- **Open message error.** Indicates a problem with an open message, such as an unsupported version number, an unacceptable autonomous system number or IP address, or an unsupported authentication code.
- **Update message error.** Indicates a problem with the update message. Examples include a malformed attribute list, an attribute list error, and an invalid next-hop attribute.
- **Hold time expired.** Indicates a hold-time expiration, after which a BGP node is declared dead.

Keepalive

Keepalive messages do not contain any additional fields beyond those in the common BGP header. These messages are sent often enough to keep the hold-time timer from expiring.

Multi-Routing Protocol Environments

The majority of IP networks utilize a single routing protocol for route determination and discovery. Many networks have multiple routing protocols deployed, however, perhaps owing to policy, perhaps owing to a multivendor router environment, or perhaps to achieve specific network protocol results. Two specific features, administrative distance and route redistribution, can be of vital importance in these environments.

In large networks, some routers and routing protocols are more reliable sources of routing information than others. This is often referred to as the *relative believability* of one protocol over another. The network administrator can use the administrative distance metric to quantify the reliability of information sources. Given a specific administrative distance, the router can select between sources of routing information based on the source's reliability. If a router uses both OSPF and RIP, for example, one might set the administrative distances to reflect greater confidence in the OSPF information. The router then would use OSPF information as available. If the source of OSPF information fails, the router automatically uses RIP information as backup until the OSPF source becomes available again.

Translation between two environments using different routing protocols requires that routes generated by one protocol be redistributed into the second routing protocol environment. Route redistribution enables a company to run different routing protocols in workgroups or areas in which certain protocols are particularly effective. Routing protocol redistribution provides a unidirectional or bidirectional transfer of routing metrics between both dynamic protocols, such as OSPF and RIP, and static route information.

As discussed earlier, there is no single routing protocol that is ideal for all situations. Each protocol has its advantages and disadvantages. There are obviously situations where depending on the nature of the network, its topology, its characteristics, and the hardware that is being utilized that would make one protocol more applicable than another. Using the information in this chapter, the webmaster should be equipped with the information necessary to select which routing protocol meets the present requirements.

Bibliography

Comer, Douglas E. and David L. Stevens, *Internetworking with TCP/IP, Volume II*, Prentice Hall, 1991

Hedrick, C. , "Routing Information Protocol," RFC 1058, June 1988

Lougheed, Y. Rekhter, "A Border Gateway Protocol 3 (BGP-3)," RFC 1267, October 1991

Rekhter, T. Li, , "A Border Gateway Protocol 4 (BGP-4)," RFC 1771, March 1995

CHAPTER 7

WAN Access Services

by Paul Singh

Most network managers say that they can never have enough bandwidth, especially when it comes to wide area networking (WAN). Unlike LAN bandwidth, however, WAN bandwidth is not free. Generally, bandwidth price is directly proportional to its size—a 384-Kbps link costs more than a 56-Kbps link, for example. The monthly cost of WAN services is a significant portion of the total monthly cost of Internet access. Selecting the right amount of bandwidth and the right type of WAN access service is critical.

Realistically assess your bandwidth needs, evaluate different services in relation to your needs, and then select an Internet Access Provider (IAP) that offers the best type and WAN bandwidth service.

This chapter provides guidelines for determining the optimum WAN service for your needs, including bandwidth calculations and types of service. The following WAN services are discussed:

- Analog dial-up services
- Switched digital services, including ISDN and Switched 56
- Dedicated WAN services, including Frame Relay and Point-to-Point Leased (or Dedicated) lines

In addition to discussing different services, information is also provided on the types of devices needed at the customer premises to take advantage of different WAN services.

Note This chapter focuses on layer 4 of the Internet connectivity matrix.

Understanding WAN Services

Before delving into a discussion of the different WAN services, it is essential to understand how WAN services function. Traditional data and voice networks connecting any two offices within the U.S. use a local and a long distance provider. The local access provider connects your premises to its nearest central office, where the call is then handed off to the long distance access provider. The same process is mirrored at the receiver's end, where the long distance provider hands off the call to the local access provider. The geographic location of the hand-off points on the long distance network is referred to as *Point of Presence* (POP). Sometimes the same telephone company is both the local and long distance provider. Figure 7.1 illustrates a typical scenario for traditional WAN services.

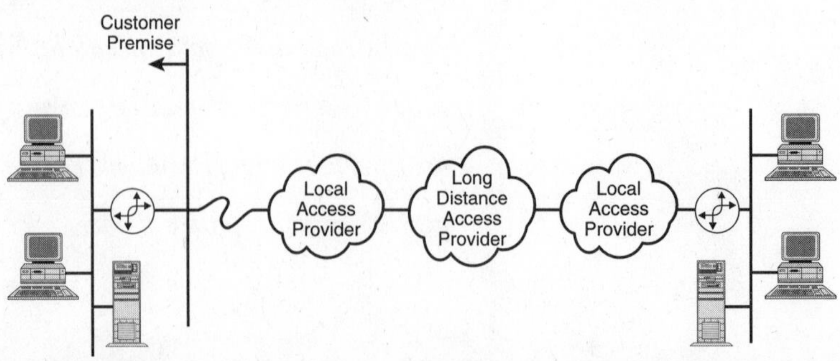

Figure 7.1
An example of typical call routing for traditional WAN services.

Local access in the U.S. is generally provided by the seven regional bell operating companies (RBOCs)—Ameritech, Bell Atlantic, Bell South, NYNEX, Pacific Bell, Southwestern Bell, and US West. In addition, many smaller local access providers exist. Telephone companies such as AT&T, MCI, and Sprint provide long distance access for WAN services. In most of the European and Asian countries, local and long distance access is provided by one centralized telephone company. There is a recent trend in many European countries (such as the U.K.), however, toward decentralized and multiple telephone carrier systems.

As in a traditional WAN service, you need two types of WAN service providers for Internet access—local and long distance. Internet Access Providers are in a sense the long distance carriers for Internet access, while local access is still provided by the RBOCs. Most IAPs lease their lines from long distance carriers, thus acting as distributors for the long distance services. Figure 7.2 shows a typical arrangement of Internet access, with local access being provided by an RBOC going into the POP of the IAP. The IAP then in turn connects to the Internet, using telephone lines leased from the telephone companies.

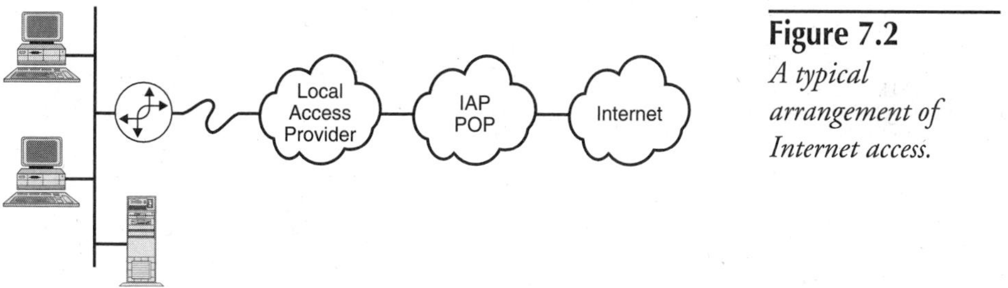

Figure 7.2
A typical arrangement of Internet access.

Telephone companies such as MCI and Sprint have recently entered the Internet access business, while many of the other telephone companies, such as AT&T and the RBOCs, have also announced their intentions to enter the business. Some online services like CompuServe have their own private networks, giving you the choice of using just their network or using their network as an access point to the Internet. Only a few IAPs have their own private network.

Types of WAN Services

There is no universal way to categorize services offered by telephone companies. For the purpose of this book, WAN services are categorized into the following two areas:

- Dial-up or switched WAN services
- Dedicated WAN services

Dial-Up Services versus Dedicated Services

As the name indicates, dial-up services are not always "on," whereas dedicated services are up 24 hours a day whether someone is using them or not. In dial-up, you pay for what you use (the amount of time the connection is up)—the connection times are metered. With dedicated connections, however, you essentially "lease" the line and pay a fee that is independent of the usage level. Your dial-up service can be used in a dedicated line mode, however, if the connection is kept open all the time to a pre-set location. This is very common for Internet access in cases where only a local "unmetered" call is needed from your house or office to the nearest IAP.

From an IAP's standpoint, if the IAP does not have to assign a static IP address and dedicate a port and a modem specifically for the customer, it is a dial-up service. The IAP will not wake up your host for a dial-up connection—in other words, it won't call your computer if someone on the Internet wants to access your host when you are not connected to the Internet. In figure 7.3, for example, if User X wants to FTP or Telnet into Host A on a LAN that is connected to the Internet using a dial-up service, the user won't be able to complete the connection unless someone from the LAN first dials a connection to the Internet.

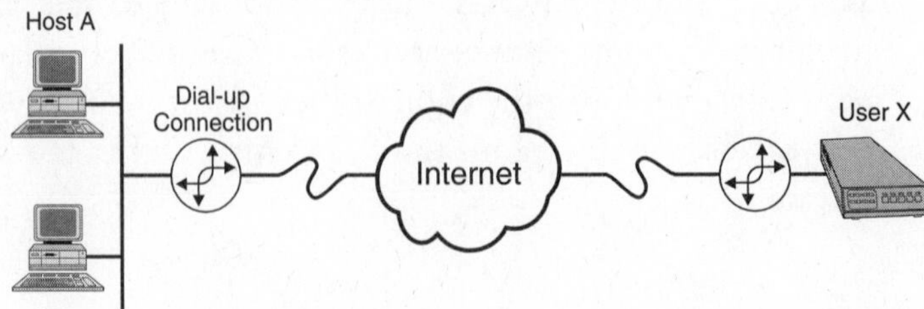

Figure 7.3
The outside user can't initiate a call into the dial-up account.

When an IAP assigns a static IP address, and dedicates a port and a modem specifically to a customer, it becomes a virtual dedicated link. The type of WAN service can be either a permanent connection or a dial-up connection that is kept on all the time. Most IAPs that provide dedicated analog service (as discussed in the following sections) recommend leaving the dial-up link connected all the time to make it a virtually dedicated link.

Figure 7.4 shows an example of a dial-up service, which appears as a dedicated link to users dialing in from the Internet because the connection is kept on all the time. When User X requests a connection to Host A, the IAP dials into Host A's LAN. The delay caused by setting up the dialed connection is small. From User X's perspective, Host A has a permanent connection to the Internet.

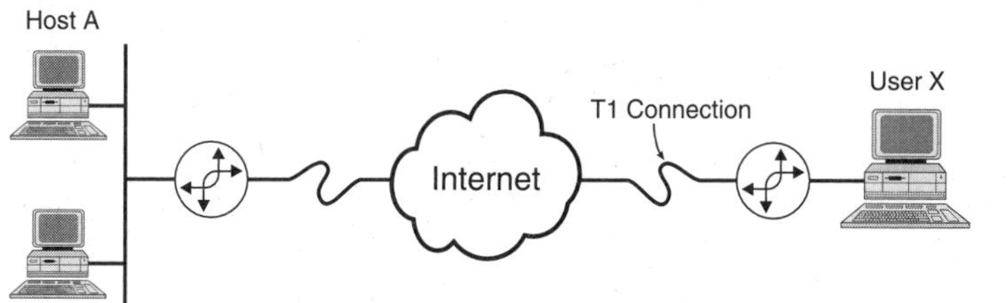

Figure 7.4
A dial-up connection can appear as a permanent connection to outside users.

A dial-up service from an IAP's standpoint thus may not always be the same as it is from a WAN access provider's point of view. In the past, all dial-up services were predominately analog, while most of the dedicated link services were digital. That distinction is no longer valid due to new advances in dial-up technology. The next section provides details on different dial-up WAN services from the standpoint of the WAN access provider.

Dial-Up WAN Services

Dial-up WAN services, which enable you to connect any two points in the world, do not provide a permanent connection. The connection is made on an as-needed basis, and you pay only for the time duration of the connection. A device such as a telephone or a modem is required to initiate the connection. Dial-up WAN services can be further categorized into universally available analog dial-up services and dial-up digital or switched digital services, which include ISDN (most popular), Switched 56 Kbps, and others. The discussion that follows first focuses on analog dial-up services, and then progresses into switched digital services.

Analog transmissions follow voice patterns and have voltage levels that vary continuously. Digital transmissions translate all data into 1s and 0s. All of the computer-generated data that is digital in form is thus converted into analog signal (using modems) before being sent on the telephone wire. The physical telephone wiring for both analog and digital dial-up is the same—it is a copper wire pair that runs into the majority of houses within the U.S. The difference in the analog and digital dial-up, however, comes from the central office switch to which the lines are connected.

Analog dial-up service—also called Plain Old Telephone Service (POTS)—is the only service that is available worldwide. Most homes in the U.S. and the rest of the world receive this type of service from their telephone companies. Analog dial-up delivers the most economical service, but it offers the least amount of bandwidth. In most places, selecting an IAP that has a POP in the local calling area is economical—analog dial-up services are not metered within a local calling distance.

Accessing Analog Dial-up Services

Analog dial-up service can be obtained either directly from your local telephone company or by putting an analog line card in a private branch exchange (PBX). All data applications, as opposed to voice applications, require a modem. The modem converts the digital data generated by computers into analog signals for sending it over the telephone wire. The maximum theoretical bandwidth from an analog line is 32 Kbps. With the recent advance in modem technology, today's modems can provide 28 Kbps of raw throughput.

Modem Standards

You know that your old modem was rated for 57.6 Kbps, but the maximum theoretically possible bandwidth is only 32 Kbps. How is that possible? Both are correct statements, but the statements refer to different data rates. The following list explains the modem terms that are important to understand before you can make an intelligent modem selection:

- **Raw throughput.** This is the maximum throughput in bits per second (bps) that you can expect from your modem with no compression. Depending on the line conditions and the modem at the other end, you may make a connection at this speed or drop down to the next fallback speed. A modem with raw throughput of 14.4 Kbps may not be able to connect with another modem at 14.4 Kbps, for example, and therefore may only make an actual connection at 9,600 bps, due to either line conditions or the receiving modem. Some of the standards, such as V.32, V.32bis, and V.34, set by CCITT, specify the maximum throughput.

- **Error correction.** V.42 and MNP4 are the most common standards; most modems come with the V.42 error correction protocol. The error correction protocols were developed to counter some of the errors introduced by line quality and distortion. MNP10 is another standard used in cellular systems for error correction.

- **Compression.** Most modems today use the V.42bis as the default compression standard. Under the ideal condition for compression (generally a blank file), V.42bis will yield a 4:1 compression, which is how a 14.4-Kbps modem was marketed as a 57.6-Kbps modem; the reality, however, is a compression rate of 2:1. V.42bis only provides compression for text files, and not for binary files. Most binary files available for download on the Internet are compressed with PKZIP or some other compression scheme.

- **Fallback.** Before the V.34 standard came into existence, most modems dropped to the next lower speed standard if they could not make a connection at their rated speed. With the V.34 standard, modems fall back in decrements of less than 100 bps. Because V.34 is still a new standard, the same vendor's modem should be used at both ends of the connection to get the full performance benefit.

Table 7.1 provides a list of the most commonly available modems and their specifications.

Note Contrary to popular opinion, you can have your own domain name even if you have a dial-up account. You can have domain name of mycompany.com, for example, even if you have an analog dial-up service.

Table 7.1
Modem Specifications

Modem Modulation Standard	Maximum or Advertised Throughput*	Raw Throughput	Average Throughput**	Fallback
V.32	38.4 Kbps	9,600 bps	19.2 Kbps	4,800 bps, 2,400 bps
V.32bis	57.6 Kbps	14.4 Kbps	28.8 Kbps	12, 9.6, 7.2 Kbps
V.34	115.2 Kbps	28.8 Kbps	57.6 Kbps	<100 bps increments

* Advertised throughput is 4 times the raw throughput and assumes that the modem has V.42bis compression.

** Average throughput is generally twice that of the raw throughput.

Internet Connection

For a single user Internet connection, many people choose the analog dial-up service because it provides an easy platform for connecting to the Internet. For a LAN connection to the Internet, the decision to select analog dial-up services depends on your current and estimated future usage of the Internet.

The following criteria can be used to help determine if analog dial-up is the appropriate choice for your LAN-based Internet connection:

- Do you need both inbound and outbound Internet access? If you only need outbound Internet access, analog dial-up is sufficient. Outbound access enables users on your LAN to access the Internet, but customers could not access your servers unless you initiate the connection to the Internet. Inbound access permits outside users to access your Internet servers that are made available for their use, thus making your Web server available for your customers to access product information. For inbound access to servers like FTP, Gopher, and Web, analog dial-up is insufficient.

- How many users on your network have access to the Internet? The general rule of thumb is that analog dial-up access may suffice for a network of up to five users.

- What are the most common applications used? Each application has a different Internet bandwidth requirement. If the application does not require a large bandwidth, an analog dial-up service is usually an acceptable option.

  On most networks, e-mail is the number one Internet application. If e-mail is your only Internet application, analog dial-up service is sufficient for large numbers of users; however, if you need to receive your e-mail instantly, analog dial-up service is inadequate because you have to dial your IAP's host to check mail. Also, dial-up service is inadequate if your users send files frequently with their e-mail.

  FTP access is generally not very bandwidth-intensive except when a file is being transferred. In average settings, not many people are transferring files with FTP simultaneously, so an analog service should be adequate.

  Web access requires more bandwidth than any other Internet applications. Even for a single user, analog access at V.34 speeds is inadequate. If your users want Web access, analog dial-up access is not recommended for LANs.

- What about my budget? There are two types of monthly charges—one for the local telephone access into the nearest location of the IAP, and one for the services provided by the IAP, such as access into the Internet. Analog access is the cheapest of all WAN access services, costing between $25 and $100 for unlimited usage depending on your local phone company's tariff structure. Most IAPs charge anywhere from $20 to $150 for unlimited analog access.

  In some states, like California, ISDN access is very competitive with analog access. Therefore, you must compare access prices before making a decision.

Switched Digital Services

Switched digital (or dial-up digital) services have become popular in the last few years. The most commonly available switched digital service in the U.S. is Switched 56 Kbps. ISDN, however, is quickly becoming the universal standard for switched digital access in today's environment. ISDN is now readily available in most metropolitan areas within the U.S. and in most industrial countries such as Japan, Germany, U.K., and France.

Integrated Services Digital Network (ISDN)

Integrated Services Digital Network is a set of digital transmission protocols defined by CCITT, the international standards organization for telephony and telegraphy. The protocols are accepted as standard by virtually all the world's telecommunications carriers. ISDN provides end-to-end digital connectivity. Unlike dial-up analog service, data travels in digital form all the way from the sender's computer or telephone, to the central office of the telephone company, to the long distance provider, to the central office, and then to the computer or telephone of the receiver. Unlike dial-up analog services, ISDN also offers the ability to carry both data and voice simultaneously over the same connection. In addition to providing an integrated voice and data service on a digital network (hence its name), ISDN also offers higher bandwidth than dial-up analog services.

There are different types of ISDN services, with Basic Rate Interface (BRI) being the most common. The other type of ISDN is called Primary Rate Interface (PRI), which is equivalent to T1 services. PRI is discussed later in this chapter. BRI consists of two 64 Kbps B channels and one 16 Kbps D channel (see fig. 7.5). The two B channels carry the actual customer data, whereas the D channel carries the signaling information that is needed by the telephone company. The D channel is therefore a separate out-of-band signaling channel for ISDN services.

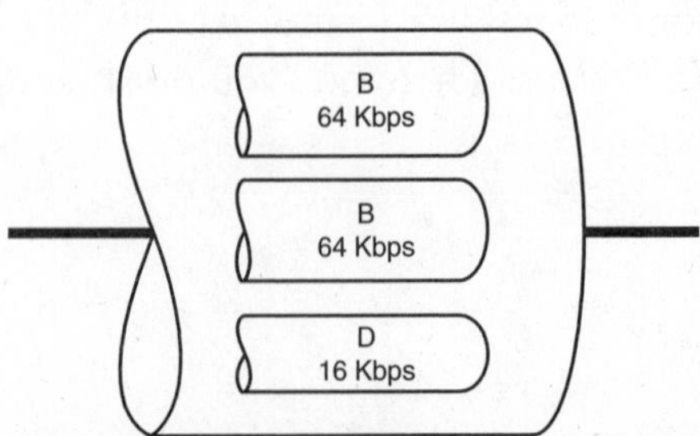

Figure 7.5
BRI is comprised of two B channels and one D channel.

Note ISDN can be thought of as a collection of independent channels—you can reserve specific channels for certain applications, or you can combine channels together for higher throughput.

In the first case, one of the B channels is used for voice, and the other B channel is used for data application, such as Internet access. In the second case, both B channels are used for data, but are going to different locations within the network. Two B channels can also be connected to the same location, with each B channel's bandwidth combined for data applications to generate a higher throughput.

The process of combining two B channels to give a higher resultant throughput is called inverse multiplexing. In an ideal situation, inverse multiplexing of two B channels will result in a bandwidth of 128 Kbps (64×2). The telephone system within North America has not been completely upgraded to accommodate ISDN signaling. Therefore, you may not get more than 56 Kbps from each B channel or 112 Kbps from the two B channels.

One of the other benefits of ISDN, besides the higher throughput, is having a very fast call set-up. Analog call set-up takes as long as 30 seconds, whereas the call set-up on ISDN is less than five seconds. Users with their LANs connected to the Internet with ISDN will thus be able to make the connection much more quickly than users connected with analog dial-up lines.

Also, the pricing of ISDN ranges from $25–$100 depending on the region. In some areas, the price directly correlates with the amount of usage, whereas other areas simply charge a flat rate. Table 7.2 lists the typical pricing structures available through the telephone companies.

Table 7.2
ISDN Pricing Structure

Carrier	Monthly Rate	Usage Charges
Ameritech	$34.15	Voice and data: 1–16 cents per minute (depending on time of day)

continues

Table 7.2, Continued

Carrier	Monthly Rate	Usage Charges
Bell Atlantic	$23.00	Voice: 2.9 cents per minute Data: 5 cents per minute
BellSouth	$99.50	Circuit-switched voice and data: Telecommunications no charge Packet-switched data: 0.000214 to 0.000257 cents per minute
GTE Telephone	$69.37	Voice: no charge Operations Data: 3–5 cents first minute; 2–3 cents each additional
NYNEX	$28.23	Voice: 8 cents first minute; 1.3 cents each additional Data: 9 cents first minute; 2.3 cents each additional
Pacific Bell	$26.85	Voice and data: 4 cents first minute; 1 cent each additional
Southwestern Bell Telecommunications	$46.00	No usage charges
U.S. West	$35.00	Voice and data: 4–4.5 cents Communications first minute; 1.5–2 cents each additional

Depending on the tariff structure and your usage, ISDN may turn out to be cheaper than Point-to-Point Dedicated lines for the same bandwidth. For areas where there are no usage charges, an ISDN line can be left connected all the time, thus getting a virtual leased line connection for the price of ISDN. Generally, the installation charges for ISDN are also less than the Point-to-Point Dedicated lines.

Accessing ISDN Services

ISDN service, like analog dial-up service, can be ordered either directly from your local telephone company or by putting an ISDN line card in a private branch exchange (PBX). ISDN utilizes the same pair of copper wiring that is used by analog dial-up lines. Therefore, if you wanted to get an ISDN service at home, no additional wiring would be needed in most cases. ISDN is now available in all major metropolitan areas—Bell Atlantic, Pacific Bell, and Ameritech are leaders in providing ISDN access within their respective service areas.

Connecting ISDN to Your Network

Just as connecting to the Internet using analog services requires a modem, ISDN requires a terminal adapter. The terminal adapter connects the computer with the telephone company network. Figure 7.6 shows how to connect your network to the ISDN network. The terminal adapter doesn't connect directly into the telephone jack. A network termination unit (NT1) is needed, in addition to the terminal adapter. The NT1 device provides the power for the network, as well as the proper signaling protocol. More and more terminal adapter vendors are incorporating the NT1 into the terminal adapter. With an integrated NT1/terminal adapter, you can connect directly to your telephone jack. Most of the time, it is preferable to have an integrated NT1 because it is one less external device to manage.

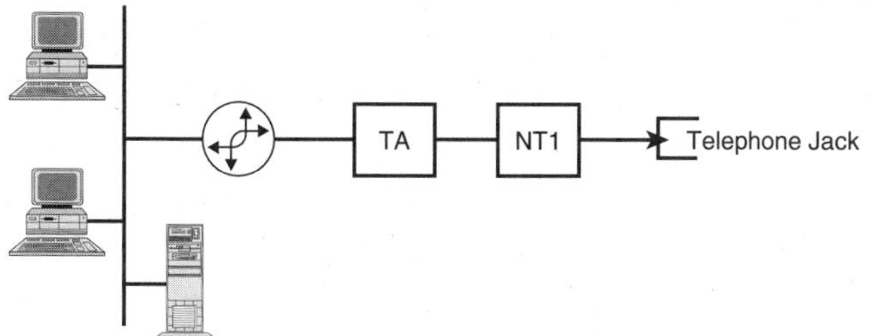

Figure 7.6
BRI ISDN connections require a terminal adapter and NT1 device.

Because terminal adapters are all different, it is important to understand your requirements. If you are getting ISDN specifically for an Internet connection, you will need a terminal adapter that supports two data channels and the capability to inverse multiplex the two channels for a higher throughput.

The standard on the Internet for inverse multiplexing is called *multilink point-to-point control* (an extension of the PPP protocol). Currently, no products conform to that standard. This situation is likely to change very quickly; at this time, however, most of the terminal adapters have their own proprietary method of inverse multiplexing, which means you must use the same terminal adapter on both ends of the ISDN connection. This is why many IAPs insist you use a particular brand of terminal adapter for ISDN service.

The raw throughput you can expect from a BRI connection is 64 Kbps or 128 Kbps. You would expect that you could increase the throughput with some compression scheme, as is the case with modems. Unfortunately, there is no standard compression scheme for ISDN terminal adapters yet; however, an effort is under way to come up with a compression standard. You will start to see standard-based compression in all the ISDN terminal adapters in the near future. As is the case with inverse multiplexing, standards for compression don't exist, leading to incompatibilities between different terminal adapters. For now, keep in mind that the equipment at your end must be compatible with the equipment at the service provider's end.

Switched 56 Kbps

Switched 56 Kbps is another switched data service that is similar to ISDN. In the same manner as ISDN, you can call up bandwidth when needed. Unlike ISDN, however, Switched 56 Kbps is a single channel service that can only carry data. Switched 56 Kbps is only available in the North American circuits—no equivalent exists in Europe and Asia. Switched 56 Kbps, unlike ISDN, has no separate signaling channel, has only in-band signaling, but is available in most places. When you compare it to either ISDN or to analog services, it is relatively expensive. Switched 56 Kbps probably won't be a very desirable service beyond the next few years because of the advent of ISDN and Frame Relay, a packet switched service discussed later in this chapter.

In order to connect to a Switched 56 Kbps service, you need a *data service unit/channel service unit* (DSU/CSU). A DSU/CSU connects any external Switched 56 Kbps connection to your network. The DSU part of the system converts data into the correct format, and the CSU part of the system terminates the line condition, conditions the signal, and participates in the testing of the connection.

Choosing a Switched Digital Service for Your Internet Connection

For a LAN connection to the Internet, the decision to select a switched digital service depends on your current and estimated future usage of the Internet. The same criteria discussed previously under "Choosing Analog Dial-Up for Your Internet Connection" can also be used to help determine if a switched digital service is the appropriate choice for your LAN-based Internet connection.

Outbound Internet Access?

For outbound access, switched digital services offer two benefits over analog connections—faster call setup time and more bandwidth. For inbound access, ISDN can be used in place of Point-to-Point Dedicated lines if it is economical to leave the line connected all the time.

Internet Usage

The following rule of thumb may help you estimate your company's Internet usage amount. ISDN access with two B channels inverse multiplexed is sufficient for between 25–50 users; whereas for 25 users or less, ISDN single B or Switched 56 Kbps is appropriate.

Internet Application Usage

What are the most common applications used? Each of the applications, along with its usage pattern, requires a different bandwidth. Some applications, such as e-mail and Telnet, take up less bandwidth, while applications such as Web access require large bandwidth.

E-Mail and FTP Bandwidth Requirements

E-mail does not require much bandwidth because it is a store-and-forward system. Users do not expect mail they send to arrive instantly, and their computer is not tied up while the mail is making its way through the Internet to its recipient. ISDN or analog access are both appropriate for traditional e-mail users, but as users begin using more MIME-based e-mail (which tends to have many file attachments, such as Microsoft Word documents or Lotus spreadsheets), the e-mail application will require a high bandwidth connection such as ISDN.

File transfer with FTP will benefit by higher bandwidth provided by ISDN. If your users download many files from the Internet, they will save significant time with an ISDN connection.

Web Access

The application that benefits the most from an ISDN connection is the World Wide Web. Most Web browsers are not optimized for slower speed modems, so any amount of high bandwidth provided to a Web application will make a noticeable difference. The increase in ISDN bandwidth by four times over the analog connection delivers dramatic improvements when it comes to Web access.

Note The following is a guideline for calculating bandwidth requirements for a LAN:

- E-mail (ASCII-based)—2 Kbps/user
- E-mail (MIME-based)—5 Kbps/user
- Web access—10 Kbps/user

For a five-user LAN with two active e-mail users and three active Web users, you thus need a bandwidth of 50 Kbps for optimum access.

Budget

In some parts of the country, such as the area served by Pacific Bell, a small monthly price difference exists between analog access and ISDN access. ISDN gives you substantially more bandwidth than analog—therefore, choosing between the two is an easy decision. Most of the IAPs charge more for ISDN access than for analog access, however. Some IAPs offer a fixed price ISDN service, where the IAP actually pays for the cost of the ISDN access and usage. These access and usage charges are budgeted, however, into the fixed price that is actually offered, so it may or may not be a less expensive option.

If you are accessing the Internet 4–6 hours per day or more, a Point-to-Point Dedicated line or Frame Relay (both discussed later in this chapter) may be more economical than using switched digital services. Carefully consider your usage pattern before choosing ISDN or Switched 56 Kbps.

Dedicated WAN Services

Dedicated services are the second most used services after analog access because they are available everywhere and can be configured for different speeds. The most common speed for dedicated lines is 56 Kbps in the U.S., and 64 Kbps in Europe and Asia. Dedicated services can be further categorized into Packet Switched services and Point-to-Point Dedicated services.

Packet Switched Services—Frame Relay

One of the newest technologies to emerge in the last few years in the area of wide area networking is called Frame Relay. Frame Relay is a packet switching protocol with speed ranges from 56 Kbps to 45 Mbps. Frame Relay delivers a low delay, high throughput connection. Frame Relay is similar to the X.25 protocol, but it does not correct errors or request retransmission. Instead, Frame Relay relies on availability of superior quality lines, such as fiber optics, that are common in today's telephone networks. Frame Relay expects clear, high-quality lines to guarantee virtually error-free transmissions. If errors do occur, it is the responsibility of intelligent end devices to request retransmission.

Frame Relay is yet another wide area service that provides high-speed connections. Frame Relay is more of a substitute for dedicated connections than for an analog dial-up or switched digital connection. One of the big benefits Frame Relay offers is that the price is distance-insensitive—the distance the call travels does not affect the hourly rate for the call. That is why Frame Relay is being used extensively in the wide area networking environments of different companies. If Frame Relay is already a standard for your wide area communications, use it to connect to the Internet. Frame Relay standards already guarantee interpretability with the Internet protocol, and are set by the Frame Relay Forum.

Frame Relay is a lower layer service—there are implementations available for both IPX and IP over Frame Relay. In the OSI model hierarchy shown in figure 7.7, Frame Relay is at the data link layer. If you are using Frame Relay to connect to the Internet, you need to run IP over your Frame Relay connection. Standard RFC 1274 exists to ensure the interoperability of different vendors' implementation of IP over Frame Relay, which is suitable for all the bursty applications. Because the traffic on the Internet is not constant but goes up and down, Internet access can be classified as a bursty application.

Figure 7.7
Frame Relay protocols versus the OSI model.

Frame Relay	OSI Model
	Application
	Presentation
	Session
TCP or SPX	Transport
IP or IPX	Network
Frame Relay	Data Link
Physical	Physical

Permanent Virtual Circuits

A Frame Relay connection is made up of one or more *permanent virtual circuits* (PVCs). A PVC is a dedicated, end-to-end, logical connection that is used for data transfer. Unlike Point-to-Point Dedicated lines, PVCs are not connection-oriented. They get set up like a dedicated line and remain active until the service is terminated, creating virtual dedicated connections as opposed to real permanent connections.

Committed Information Rate (CIR)

The *committed information rate* is defined as a minimum average data rate that the network guarantees to carry over a given PVC for a specified period. The data rate is chosen at the time of subscription, but it can be modified if users find that their transmission needs have changed. CIR is important because a Frame Relay network may specify a throughput of 64 Kbps or 56 Kbps and a CIR of zero. A CIR is a guarantee that whenever you connect, your throughput will not fall below the threshold specified. In order to provide a CIR above zero, the phone company or access provider must reserve a physical line for your connection. If you purchase a PVC with 56 Kbps of throughput and a CIR of zero, you are not guaranteed any bandwidth. Today, the current state of the Frame Relay infrastructure is such that most users are able to get the full extent of the bandwidth. Frame Relay offers some interesting possibilities when it comes to looking at Internet connections.

Some IAPs, such as PSI, have their own private networks, enabling them to offer multiple PVCs into your network—one PVC is dedicated to one application while the other PVC is designated for a different application. One of the PVCs might be dedicated to newsgroups, for example, guaranteeing newsgroups bandwidth regardless of the level of user activity in other Internet applications. A PVC dedicated to outside users dialing in to a network prevents the network from getting bogged down for inside users. This is one benefit Frame Relay offers over T1 leased lines or other dedicated lines. This advantage may also apply when comparing Frame Relay and switched digital services (that is, ISDN, Switched 56 Kbps, and so forth), depending on the customer usage of the Internet.

Figure 7.8 provides a visual example of the PVCs going to different locations.

Tip Reserving PVCs for particular applications is one way to effectively manage your Internet bandwidth.

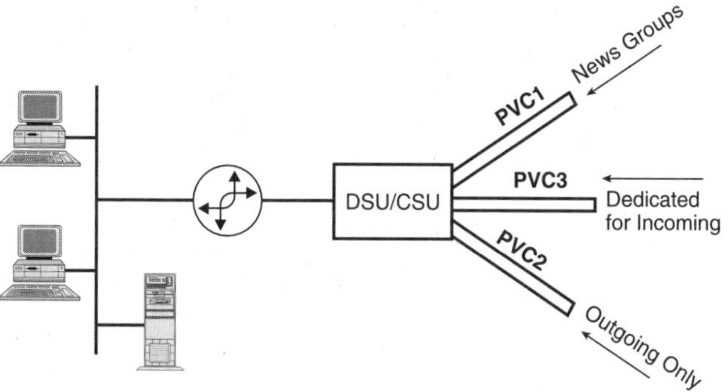

Figure 7.8
Frame Relay PVCs can be set to guarantee bandwidth for different applications.

Procuring Access Lines for the Frame Relay

Your local access provider can deliver Frame Relay, but if you already have a data multiplexer within your company and you subscribe to the Frame Relay service, use one of the PVCs to access the Internet. Most IAPs that offer a Frame Relay service assist with all the procurement of the local access services. To connect your network to the Internet using Frame Relay, a DSU/CSU is needed. In addition, you will need a router that supports routing of IP over Frame Relay protocol.

Frame Relay Pricing

Frame Relay pricing, like all other services, involves installation charges and monthly usage charges. The monthly usage charge for 56 Kbps Frame Relay is around $200 to $300. The Frame Relay pricing appears more attractive than a 56 Kbps dedicated line until you read the fine print and see that these prices are for 0 CIR. The installation charges for Frame Relay can sometimes be quite costly—as high as $1,000. Most of the IAPs offer Frame Relay access either at the same or lower pricing than an equivalent Point-to-Point Dedicated line.

Point-to-Point Dedicated Services

Previously, the T1 trunk was the high-end option for Point-to-Point Dedicated lines, and is the one that is still most frequently used. A T1 trunk supports transfer speeds up to 1.544 megabits per second. In Europe, E1 is the equivalent service, offering bandwidth of up to 2.048 Mbps. For companies that don't require this much throughput, telephone companies have begun offering *Fractional T1* (FT1) services. FT1 services are configured as a number of 56 Kbps channels. In spite of the popularity of the T1 service, the emerging high end option for a Point-to-Point Dedicated connection is the T3 line, which supports a 45-Mbps connection. Today, very few sites in the country require a T3 line as their Internet connection, and this will most likely continue to be the case for the immediate future. Only when you start using much higher bandwidth applications, or start to use the Internet as a wide area backbone, is this likely to change.

An important difference between Point-to-Point Dedicated lines and Frame Relay is that with the latter, you are not guaranteed any bandwidth above your CIR. At first glance, Point-to-Point Dedicated line prices may look expensive for long distances (they are priced based on bandwidth and the distance between two points). Because you only need the dedicated line from your LAN to the nearest point of presence of your IAP, however, the actual cost for a dedicated line can be very reasonable. Of course, this depends on finding a suitable Internet Access Provider close to your network. Actual costs of Point-to-Point Dedicated lines range from $200–$300 within a 20-mile radius. These numbers vary between different telephone companies. Many sites connect to the Internet using Point-to-Point Dedicated lines because of the numerous benefits this type of service offers.

Accessing Point-to-Point Dedicated Services

First, check with your telecommunications manager. You may already have leased a full T1 line for voice and other services. In this case, your company may have spare channels that can be used for your Internet connection. This happens frequently when the cost of a full T1 is less than the cost of buying exactly the needed amount of FT1 services. If your company does not already have a dedicated line, contact your telephone company or Internet Access Provider.

Choosing a Dedicated Service for Your Internet Connection

Frame Relay and Point-to-Point Dedicated lines are both recommended services if you need to support both inbound and outbound Internet connections, or if you intend to host your own Web server. If you are using Frame Relay for 56 Kbps connections, your actual bandwidth will be identical to a Switched 56 Kbps or ISDN connection.

The actual throughput your applications see does not vary significantly between Frame Relay and Point-to-Point Dedicated lines. The primary economic benefit of Frame Relay—distance-insensitive pricing—is inconsequential when connecting to the Internet since most companies can find an Internet Access Provider located relatively nearby. For this reason, Point-to-Point Dedicated lines are a popular alternative for companies requiring a high-speed permanent Internet connection.

Table 7.3 summarizes the types of connections you should consider for your Internet connection.

Table 7.3
Comparison of WAN Access Services

	Analog	ISDN	Switched 56 Kbps	Frame Relay	Point-to-Point Dedicated
Bandwidth	14.4 or 28.8 Kbps	56/64 or 112/128 Kbps	56 Kbps	56 Kbps to 1.5 Mbps	56 Kbps to 1.5 Mbps
Call Setup Time	30 seconds and up	Less than 5 seconds	Less than 20 seconds	Negligible	None
Tariff Structure	Fixed or Per Minute	Fixed or Per Minute	Fixed or Per Minute	Fixed	Fixed
Availability	High	Medium	High	Medium	High
Suitable for Inbound Access	Only if line is kept on all the time	Only if line is kept on all the time	Only if line is kept on all the time	Yes	Yes

Dial-up analog access is appropriate for single users or small LANs with up to five users. If ISDN is available in your area, its pricing may be very competitive with the dial-up analog, especially when you consider the extra bandwidth provided. For a LAN of up to 50 users, ISDN is a good alternative. For more than 50 users, or to set up your own Web servers, use either Frame Relay or a Point-to-Point Dedicated line, depending on which is cheaper in your area. Choosing the right connection up front is important because of the specialized hardware and installation charges involved.

Once you've made the critical decision concerning which WAN service type to use for your Internet connection, the next step is to select the appropriate equipment you will need to complete the connection. Chapter 8, "WAN Access Devices," provides information on the various alternatives to help you make the correct decisions for your environment.

WAN Access Devices

by Paul Singh

Having determined your wide area bandwidth and service needs, you are now ready to examine the hardware alternatives for connecting to the Internet. The equipment required for enabling this connection is termed wide area network (WAN) access devices. The choice of WAN access devices is dependent on the wide area networking service, LAN environment, existing equipment, and support from your Internet Access Provider (IAP).

For the purpose of this chapter, WAN access devices include routers, modems, and other devices that make the actual wide area connection. In many cases, your Internet Access Provider may recommend or even resell WAN access devices. This chapter provides details on the various choices for WAN access devices so that you can evaluate and decide on the best option for your environment.

This chapter is divided into four sections based on the types of WAN services available, as follows:

- Dial-up analog service
- ISDN service
- Leased-line and Switched 56 services
- Combined access

Note This chapter focuses on layer 5 of the Internet connectivity matrix.

7 SECURITY AND MANAGEMENT
6 Internet Access Providers
5 WAN Access Devices
4 WAN Access Services
3 Internet Application Servers
2 Internet Navigation Software
1 Network Communication Protocols

Connecting LANs to the Internet

Before delving into the details of each of the services, it is important to understand the different software and hardware components needed to connect a LAN to the Internet. The equipment needed is very similar to that needed to connect to another LAN over a private or public wide area network. The WAN access devices for Internet access can, however, be much simpler because there is only one protocol (IP) required. Also, the routing information, in most cases, is very simple—there is only one network to connect to. The WAN access device (or router, in this case) at your premise is connected to the router at the Point of Presence (POP) of the Internet Access

Provider. The router at the POP, on the other hand, needs very complex routing information tables. This situation is analogous to the private corporate networks where the central site routers, like the routers in the POP, need very complex routing tables and configuration; the branch office router, like the router at your premise for Internet access, can have a much simpler configuration.

Each of the workstations on a LAN—whether it is Ethernet, Token Ring, or FDDI—can either run its own TCP/IP stack or each can use the server's TCP/IP stack. Whenever a workstation uses any Internet application such as e-mail, FTP, or Mosaic, it effectively generates a TCP/IP packet destined for router B, located in the Internet Access Provider's POP (see fig. 8.1).

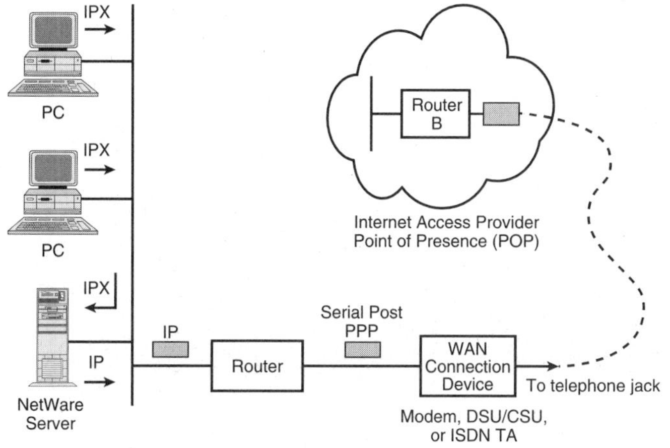

Figure 8.1
Taking IP packets from a network to the Internet.

For the packet to reach router B, however, it has to go through a telephone network. For the telephone network connectivity, a wide area access device such as a modem, a DSU/CSU, or an ISDN terminal adapter (TA) is needed. These devices are connected physically to a serial port on the router, which is in turn connected to the network. In addition, an IP router is needed to route the packets appropriately. Therefore, a router with a LAN connection and a serial port for the WAN access device connection is needed.

In order for the packet transmission to occur on a serial link connection, the IP protocol has to be encapsulated in a layer 2 WAN protocol, such as SLIP, PPP, or Frame Relay. Most routers encapsulate the IP received over their LAN into an appropriate WAN protocol, such as PPP, over their WAN ports.

The WAN protocol in the router at the customer's premises must be understood by the router at the IAP's POP—this is why most IAPs insist on customers using a router that they have tested for compatibility with their POP equipment. As IP over PPP and Frame Relay are becoming universal standards, however, the issues of incompatibility are becoming less important.

Note Point-to-Point Protocol (PPP) is the serial line protocol that is a predecessor to SLIP and is universally used for data encapsulation over the wide area network. Unlike SLIP, however, PPP has implementations of IP, IPX, and other protocols running over it. RFCs 1548, 1332, and 1334 define IP over PPP implementation—the only PPP implementation needed to connect to the Internet.

For connecting to the Internet, a router that supports IP is sufficient—this is the protocol of choice for the Internet. The router has to be attached to a wide area networking device, which connects a corporate network to the wide area network. The following software and hardware is thus needed to provide Internet access for a LAN:

- An IP router with serial ports for connecting WAN devices
- WAN encapsulation software such as SLIP, PPP, or Frame Relay, one of which is generally provided with the router software
- A WAN connection device such as a modem, DSU/CSU, or ISDN TA
- A WAN connection from the telephone company

The different equipment possibilities are discussed in subsequent sections, and are based on the chosen WAN service.

Dial-Up Analog Service

If you have determined that dial-up analog service is the best alternative for your needs today, it might be appropriate to review the WAN access device choices. With dial-up analog, you are restricted to a maximum raw throughput of 28.8 Kilobits per second (Kbps)—most areas average 14.4 Kbps. The types of devices that can be used to provide dial-up analog connectivity are as follows:

- Direct attached modem
- Remote access servers
- Internal routers
- External router

Direct Attached Modem

The most common start-up connection is a modem directly attached to a user's PC with SLIP or PPP, and dialer software to dial the IAP POP (see fig. 8.2). In this particular case, the user's PC needs a TCP/IP protocol stack. In order to take full advantage of modem speed, the user's PC must also have a high-speed serial card.These types of connections don't work well for LAN-connected environments, however—only one user can connect to the Internet at any time with the company's domain name. Furthermore, it requires a modem at each user's workstation to dial the Internet.

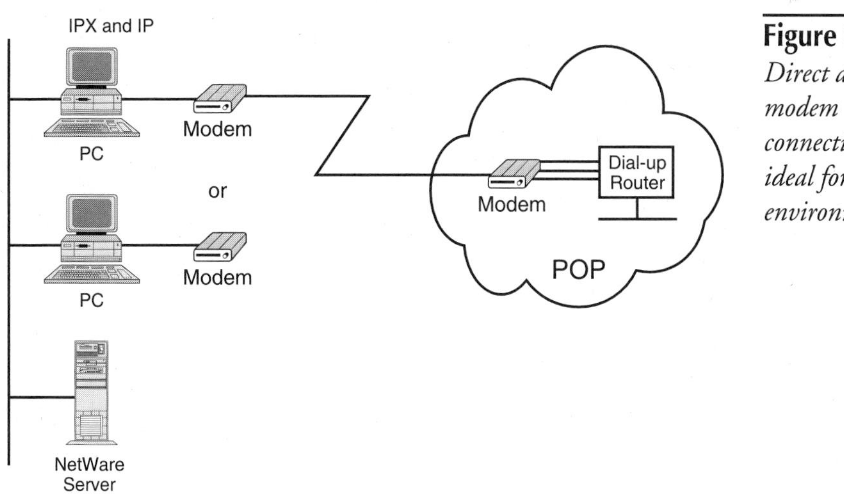

Figure 8.2
Direct attached modem connection—not ideal for LAN environments.

Most IAPs don't permit LAN connections with direct attached modems. This alternative, therefore, is not recommended unless only one or two users in the organization need slow and occasional Internet access.

Remote Access Servers

Many organizations are using remote access servers to provide network access to their telecommuters and mobile workers. The majority of remote access servers provide remote node access, whereby the remote user appears as another LAN node that is directly attached to the network. In addition, most of the remote access servers also provide routing capabilities and support IP and IPX protocols. For companies that have been exploring Internet access options and have determined that dial-up access is adequate for their current needs, the existing remote access servers could be used to connect to the Internet in the manner shown in figure 8.3. In this case, you need a spare WAN port, which can be connected via a modem to the IAP POP from where the connection to the Internet is made.

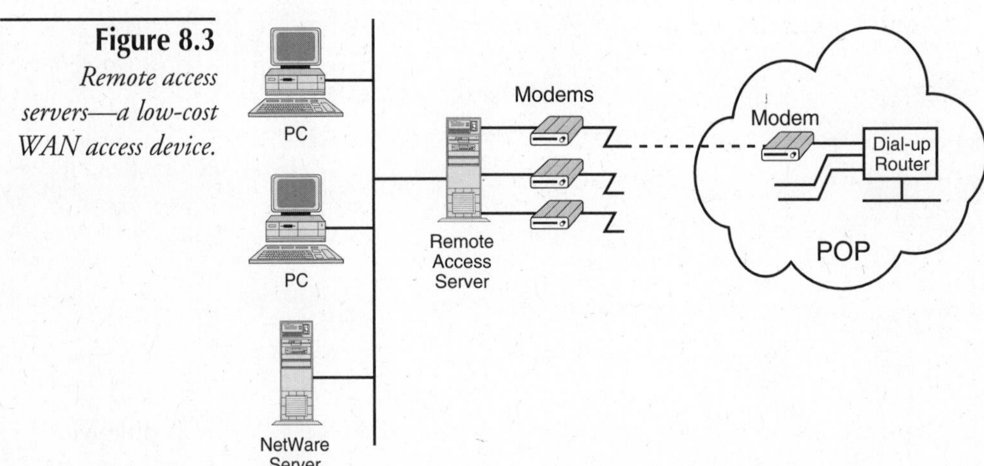

Figure 8.3
Remote access servers—a low-cost WAN access device.

Before using a remote access server, you must ensure that it meets the following criteria:

- Availability of an extra WAN port—this alternative is only recommended when a remote access server is already available and is being used for another purpose.

- Dial-on-demand routing capability—any packet sent to the remote access server automatically initiates the modem dialing.
- Routing of IP protocol—must be able to route IP protocol.
- SLIP or PPP support—make sure that PPP implementation is compliant with the latest standard and supported by your IAP.

Most remote access servers are available in 4-port, 8-port, or 16-port configurations—4-port units are in the $1,500 to $2,500 price range, 8-port units in the $2,500 to $4,000 price range, and 16-port units in the $4,500 to $7,000 price range. None of these prices include modems, which are also required. Therefore, it does not make sense to buy a remote access server just for Internet access.

Some of the well-known remote access servers include LAN Rover from Shiva Corporation, RLA from DCA Corporation, NetBlazer from Telebit, Portmaster from Livingston, LANA from LAN Access Corporation, Access Builder from 3Com Corporation, and NetHopper from Rockwell Information Systems. Novell sells a software version of its remote access server called NetConnect. It does not support PPP and dial-on-demand routing at this time, however. Funk Software and Stampede Technology also offer a software version of their remote access servers, which supports PPP access.

Internal Routers

The term internal router refers to the routers that are installed on the network server itself, and includes a software/hardware combination that enables a server to connect directly to the Internet. The most common router in this category is Novell's multiprotocol software—MPR. It is a software-only router that supports PPP and can be installed as a NetWare Loadable Module (NLM) on a NetWare server, or on a dedicated PC running NetWare Runtime software that comes with MPR. You can attach a modem directly to the computer running MPR, provided the computer supports a high-speed serial card. It is recommended, however, that a third-party WAN card compatible with MPR be used for performance reasons. It should be noted that you must use MPR version 3.0 or higher for dial-on-demand support. As shown in figure 8.4, this alternative eliminates external routers or remote access servers, but puts additional load on the server.

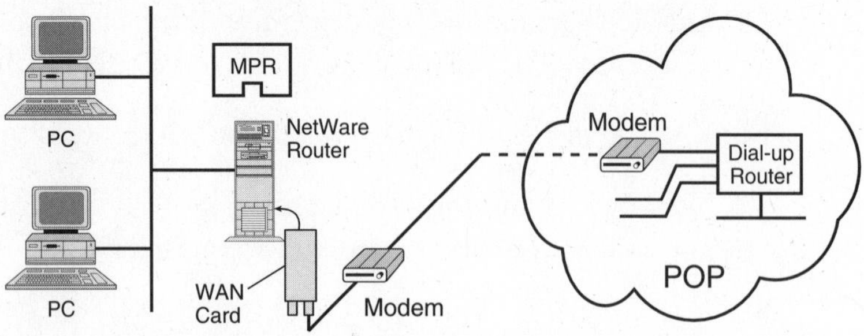

Figure 8.4
An internal router uses the network server as the router.

Note NetWare Runtime is a limited version of NetWare. It enables you to run NetWare NLM Applications—such as MPR and NetWare LANalyzer—on a dedicated machine that can't be used as a file or print server.

This alternative is quite expensive, with MPR priced at about $1,000, plus the add-on cost of $1,000 to $1,500 for the WAN card and an additional modem. Most WAN cards come with two ports, however. This alternative is thus recommended only if one of the WAN ports on the existing MPR is not being utilized. In this case, it would not be cost-effective to make a new purchase just for Internet connectivity.

Microdyne and Eagle Technology (now owned by Microdyne) sell WAN cards for Novell's MPR. Most of these cards are designed for high-speed networks, but could easily support low-speed analog dial-up service at 14.4/28.8 Kbps. There are also other card vendors, such as Newport/Cisco and Eicon Technology, that include routing software integrated with their cards and WAN ports.

External Dial-Up Routers

The term external router refers to a router that is a stand-alone device connected to the LAN on one side and to a WAN/WAN port on the other side. Even though it is not directly connected or mounted inside the network server, it takes all the traffic destined for a WAN away from the LAN and redirects it to the WAN. For Internet access over dial-up lines, an external dial-up router is recommended. Dial-up routers are designed to support LAN interfaces, such as Ethernet or Token Ring, and they provide asynchronous and synchronous serial ports. These routers provide dial-on-demand capability and support PPP. Many of these routers now come with integrated modems, as shown in figure 8.5.

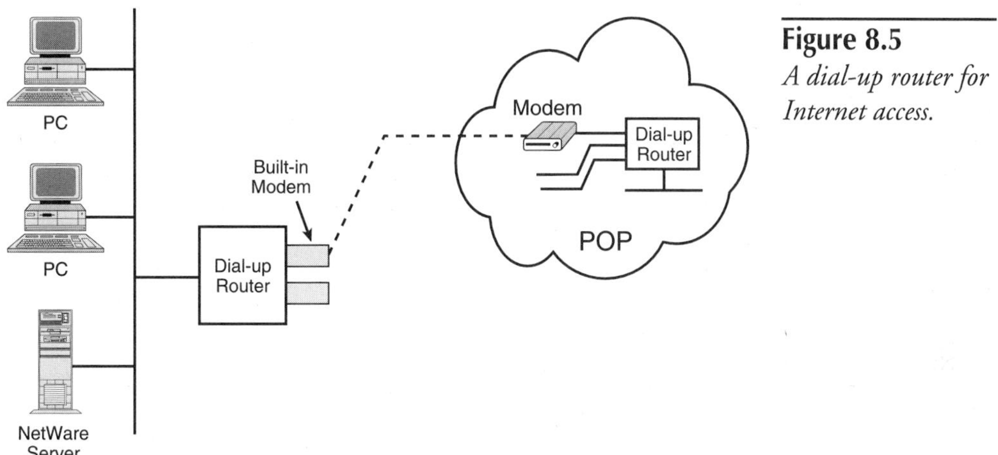

Figure 8.5
A dial-up router for Internet access.

Dial-up routers range in price from $1,000 to $2,000, including the modem. The following criteria may be used in choosing a dial-up router:

- Support of WAN protocols—SLIP, PPP.
- Upgradability of modem—if not compliant with the V.34 standard.
- Availability of additional sync (serial) port—if a sync port is available, the same dial-up router could later be used to support higher speed digital services, such as leased-lines or ISDN.
- Ease of set-up—for most smaller sites where a dial-up router is adequate, a dedicated network administrator is not provided.

Some of the dial-up routers include NetBlazer PN from Telebit, NetHopper from Rockwell, and Dr. BonD from NEC America.

Table 8.1 summarizes the four devices discussed in this section that can be used to provide dial-up analog connectivity. The price range, connectivity to LANs, protocols, expandability, and pros and cons of each device are included in the table.

Table 8.1
Comparison of Dial-up Analog WAN Devices

	Direct Attached Modem	Remote Access Server	Internal Router	External Router
Price Range	$300 to $500 per user	$2000 to $3000	$2500 to $3000	$1000 to $2000
LAN Connectivity	No	Yes	Yes	Yes
Protocols	Needs TCP/IP at every workstation	Can work with both workstation or server TCP/IP solutions	Can work with both workstation or server TCP/IP solutions	Can work with both workstation or server TCP/IP solutions
Expandability	None	None	Can be used to support higher speed services	Can be used to support higher speed services
Pros	Low initial investment	Can use existing remote access server	Expandable; can be integrated with the NetWare server	Expandable; lowest price per unit
Cons	Need separate modem for every user	Expensive if used only for Internet access	Expensive for slow speed access; increases risk for failure	More expensive than direct modem

Note The "Expandability" line in table 8.1 refers to the flexibility of upgrading the WAN device to support other services besides dial-up analog.

ISDN Service

Where readily available, ISDN may be the best WAN service for Internet access because it offers the cheapest price per Kbps. ISDN offers a maximum throughput of 128 Kbps, however, with normal throughput restricted to 112 Kbps in the United States. Most sites may only be using one B channel in the ISDN service, limiting throughput to 64/56 Kbps.

To provide ISDN access to networks, the available WAN devices can be categorized into the following areas:

- Internal routers
- External routers
- Integrated ISDN routers

A terminal adapter that is directly attached to a PC serial port is not considered a viable alternative in this case—it only offers single user access and still does not offer many cost advantages over the other alternatives. Also excluded from consideration are remote access servers—most do not support ISDN to its full potential because the serial port speed is limited and most support TAs in the asynchronous mode. When remote access servers start supporting ISDN to its full potential, however, they will also be a viable alternative, involving the same type of issues as found for analog dial-up access.

Internal Routers

As discussed in the "Dial-Up Analog Service" section of this chapter, the term internal router refers to the routers that are installed on the network server itself. Internal routers include a combination of hardware and software that allows for connecting a network server directly to the Internet. The most common router in this category is Novell's multiprotocol software—MPR. Until recently, MPR didn't support ISDN services. ISDN support is now available with MPR version 3.0 and higher. There are three alternatives available for achieving ISDN connectivity (see fig. 8.6):

- Novell's MPR software, in combination with a WAN card and an external ISDN TA
- Novell's MPR software, in combination with an ISDN TA card
- Integrated ISDN TA and router on a card

The first alternative of using MPR in conjunction with a WAN card and a TA is expensive, with prices ranging from $2,500 to $3,500. This alternative is only desirable when a WAN card and an MPR are already in place, and a second WAN port is available for connecting ISDN TA. Most ISDN TAs now come with an optional NT1 interface, which is needed to provide power and connect to the public telephone network. If your TA does not have integrated NT1, you must also purchase a separate NT1 in all cases.

The second alternative, using MPR and MPR-compatible ISDN TA, is more attractive than the previous alternative. Any ISDN TA, such as from ADC Kentrox and Motorola UDS, that supports V.25bis dialing protocol can be connected to the WAN card for supporting ISDN. Alternatively, a PC card

TA that does not require a separate WAN card is preferable. At the time of writing this book, however, no U.S.-certified, MPR-compatible ISDN cards are available. That will likely change soon, though, because there are many vendors that make ISDN TAs, such as Digiboard and IBM. Some of the vendors who have TAs available include the following:

- Australia (ITEC Manufacturing)
- France and Belgium (OST and SCii Telecom)
- Germany (AVM GmbH, Diehl Electronics, ITK GmbH, and Loewe ISCOM)
- United Kingdom (Dataflex Design Ltd, First Source Limited, and KNX Limited)

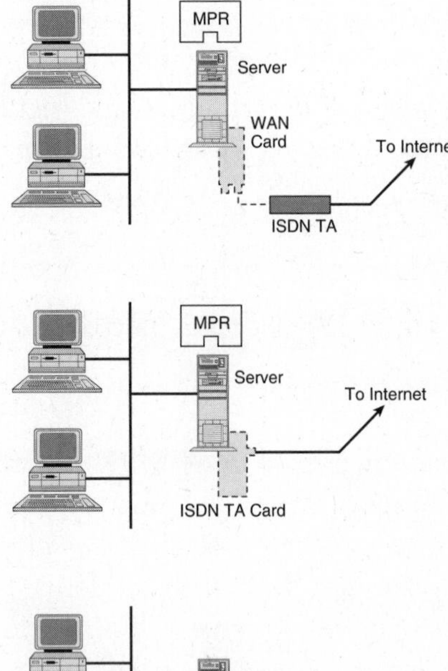

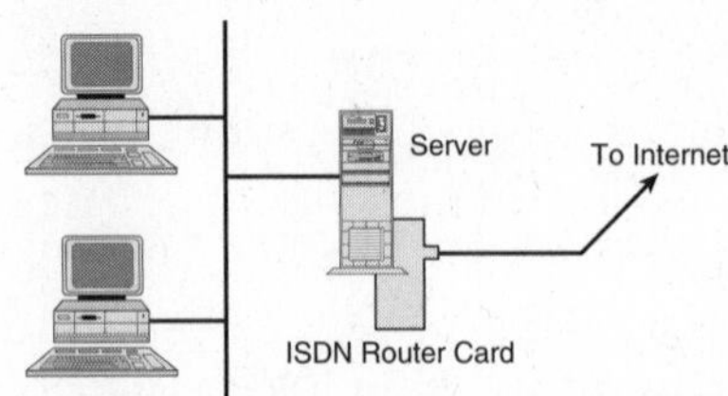

Figure 8.6
The three alternatives for achieving ISDN connectivity with MPR.

The most economical alternative in this category is the Integrated ISDN TA and router on a card. Unfortunately, at the time of writing this book, no vendor is shipping such a product. Digiboard and Combinet provide an integrated ISDN TA and a bridge on a PC card, but those products are focused on single user access, rather than for a LAN, and don't route IP protocols. Eicon Technology and Newport/Cisco also supply router cards, but their products don't have an integrated TA at this time.

External Routers

Any router that has a LAN and a WAN port can be used for this purpose with an external ISDN TA if it supports the following features:

- Support of PPP protocols and routing of IP
- Dial-on-demand software with support of dialing commands such as AT, V.25bis, or X.21
- Sync port with port speeds of a minimum of 128 Kbps

Some of the dial-up routers discussed in a previous section for analog dial-up access also offer a sync port for ISDN connectivity. In addition, all major router manufacturers, such as ACC, Bay Networks, Cisco, and 3Com, provide routers with one LAN and one WAN port that can be used with an external TA.

These routers range in price from $1,500 to $3,000. For sites intending to migrate to leased-line connections, these routers may be a good choice. The stand-alone ISDN TA are made by many manufacturers, with Motorola UDS and ADC Kentrox leading the pack. As pointed out earlier, most of these TAs come with a built-in NT1 or will work with external NT1, as shown in figure 8.7. The ISDN TAs range in price from $500 to $1,000.

Integrated ISDN Routers

Unlike the previous alternative, integrated ISDN routers provide a LAN an ISDN interface, thereby combining a router, ISDN TA, and NT1 (generally an optional device) in one device. On one end, these devices connect to the Ethernet or Token-Ring LAN interface; on the other end, they provide a direct connection to the telephone jack for ISDN service, as displayed in figure 8.8.

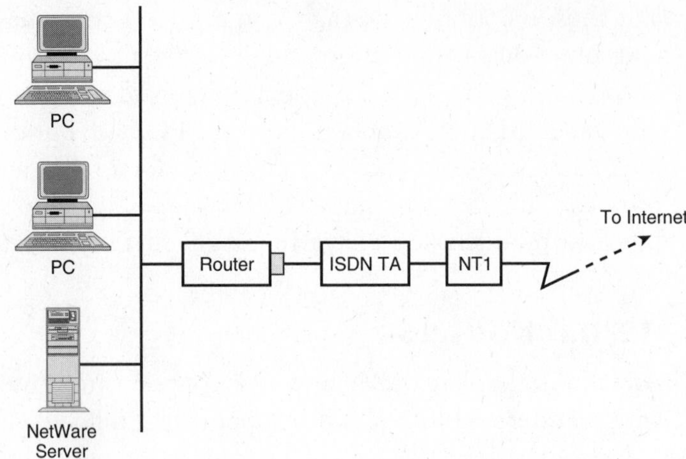

Figure 8.7
External routers with ISDN connectivity.

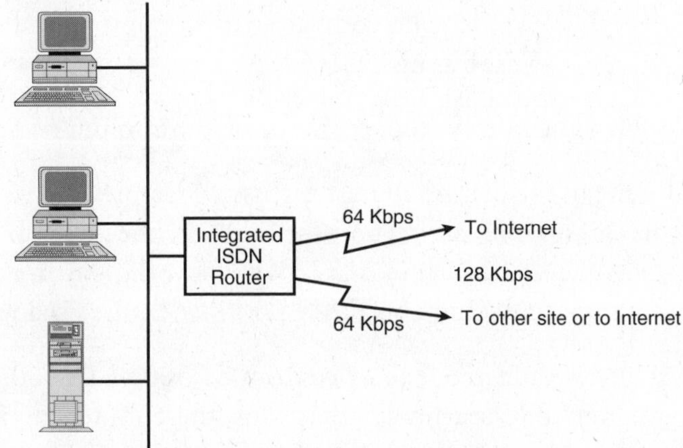

Figure 8.8
An integrated ISDN router combines many components.

Most integrated ISDN routers provide two B interfaces. One of the B interfaces can be used for connection to the Internet, while the other B channel can be used to dial another destination, such as another branch office. It is also possible to combine two B channels to get up to 128 Kbps of raw throughput. Most of the routers use proprietary inverse multiplexing schemes (combining of different B channels)—however, the standard for inverse multiplexing of two B channels, called multilink PPP, is just emerging. You thus need the same vendor's routers at both ends for getting 128 Kbps connections. If you intend to use ISDN for 128 Kbps connection, you must check with your Internet Access Provider to find out if it supports the same equipment as you intend to use at your end.

ACC, Ascend, Cisco, Telebit, and many other vendors provide integrated ISDN routers ranging in price from $1,500 to $3,000. Some of the other router vendors like Cisco also provide additional WAN ports for upgrading to higher speed, leased-line services in addition to built-in ISDN ports, but this comes at a price premium over other vendors. In addition, there are many vendors that sell integrated ISDN bridges, such as Combinet, Digiboard, Intel, and Gandalf. In theory, all of these products can also be used for Internet connectivity. Because these products do not route IP or provide IP over PPP, however, most IAPs do not support these devices.

Table 8.2 summarizes the three WAN devices discussed in this section. The price range, LAN connectivity, protocols, expandability, and pros and cons of each device are included in the table.

Table 8.2
Comparison of ISDN WAN Devices

	Internal Router	**External Router**	**Integrated ISDN Router**
Price Range	$2500 to $3000	$2000 to $4000	$1500 to $3000
LAN Connectivity	Yes	Yes	Yes
Protocols	Can work with both workstation or server TCP/IP solutions	Can work with both workstation or server TCP/IP solutions	Can work with both workstation or server TCP/IP solutions
Expandability	Can be used to support higher speed services	Can be used to support higher speed services	Can be used to support higher speed services
Pros	Can use familiar NetWare environment	Offers more flexibility and expandability	Most integrated solution; reduces installation and maintenance costs
Cons	Expensive; needs extensive integration	Expensive; needs extensive integration	Least flexible; can't be used for other services

Leased-Line and Switched 56 Services

The most common leased-line connections used for Internet access start out in the 64/56 Kbps bandwidth. These could be obtained either from DDS56 type of service or from Frame Relay type of service. Like ISDN, Switched 56 is a switched service, but it requires a DSU/CSU like other leased-line services. The other most common type of leased-line connection is T1, having a bandwidth of 1.544 Mbps. In addition, there are many fractional T1 services, called FT1, which could vary from 56/64 Kbps to N* 64 Kbps where N=24.

In Europe, E1 is the predominant standard instead of T1. Though T1 offers a maximum speed of 1.54 Mbps, E1 offers a speed of 2.04 Mbps. A T1 service can be thought of as a combination of 24 pipes, each delivering 64 Kbps, while E1 is a combination of 30 pipes, each delivering 64 Kbps.

For the leased-line connections, a DSU/CSU is needed to connect to the telephone network. The DSU/CSU is connected in turn to the WAN serial port on the IP router. Most of the routers support Frame Relay encapsulation, in addition to the PPP encapsulation. There are two possible categories of solutions for leased-line connectivity, as follows:

- Internal routers
- External routers

In addition, there are some routers, such as those from Imatec and Ascend, that integrate DSU/CSU within the router itself for Switched 56, Leased 56, and Frame Relay services. These routers are limited to 56 Kbps connections, however, and are therefore not suitable for customers with FT1 and T1 needs.

Internal Routers

This alternative assumes Novell's MPR in conjunction with the integrated DSU/CSU WAN card, as shown in figure 8.9. There are many vendors that provide integrated DSU/CSU WAN cards for Novell's MPR router, including ADC Kentrox, Arnet Corporation, Eicon Technology, Microdyne Corporation, and Newbridge Microsystems. The total cost of this solution is in the range of $2,500 to $3,500, unless you have to dedicate a PC for this operation. If this is the case, the cost would increase by the value of the dedicated PC.

Alternatively, there are many other vendors, such as Newport/Cisco and Eicon Technology, that provide a router and a WAN device on a card for use in the network server.

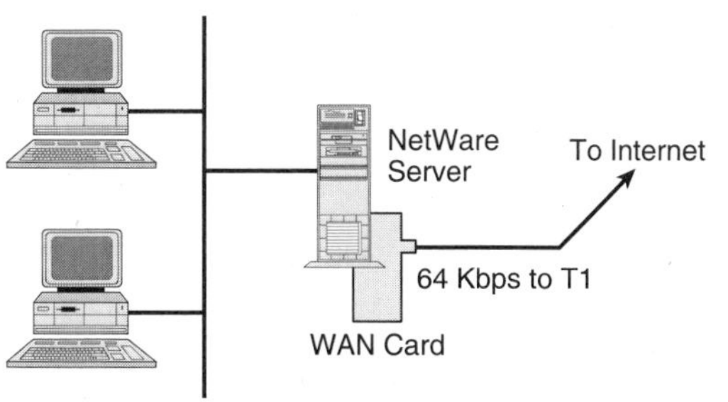

Figure 8.9
MPR integrated with WAN cards for Internet access.

External Routers

This alternative assumes an external router that, when connected to a DSU/CSU, provides Internet access (see fig. 8.10). These types of routers are provided by all major router vendors, including ACC, Bay Networks, Cisco, and 3Com. The DSU/CSU for leased lines can be obtained from ADC Kentrox, Digital Link, Larsecom, Motorola UDS, and others. The total cost of this solution ranges between $2,500 to $3,500.

This alternative of using external routers is similar to the previous alternative of using internal routers. The selection of one alternative over the other is controlled by your comfort with a particular vendor and your company's philosophy on external versus internal routers.

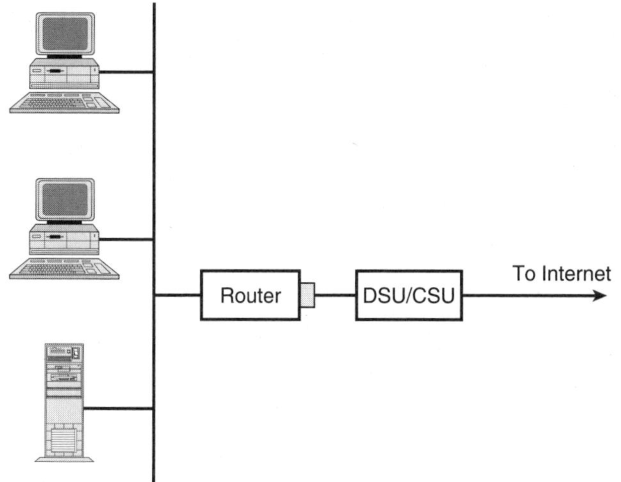

Figure 8.10
External routers and DSU/CSU for Internet access.

Combined Access

The Internet offers many other possibilities, some of which are useful today, while others will become more practical over time. This section provides discussion on some unconventional scenarios of Internet access, including the following:

- Providing Internet access to remote offices
- Providing Internet access to telecommuters
- Using the Internet as a private virtual WAN

Providing Internet Access to Remote Offices

Depending on the size of the remote office and the company structure, it may be more desirable to provide Internet connectivity to the remote office using the corporate office's Internet connection. Consider the example of a company with a remote office in San Jose linked to the corporate office in Boston with a dedicated 56-Kbps link, as shown in figure 8.11.

The corporate office is linked to the Internet over a T1 line. The router in the remote office and the corporate office could be configured in such a way that all of the remote office users can also transparently access the Internet, just as users in the corporate office do. Therefore, both the remote office and the corporate office users benefit from the Internet connectivity.

Providing Internet Access to Telecommuters

With growth in telecommuting, many organizations use remote access servers to enable their telecommuting users to access the corporate LAN resources. With the Internet becoming another corporate LAN resource, it is possible to provide Internet access to telecommuters using the company's Internet connection. The remote users could be dialing in directly with a TCP/IP package, or they may be dialing with a remote node software and using server-based TCP/IP access on the LAN to get to the Internet. Figure 8.12 displays a graphical representation of this scenario.

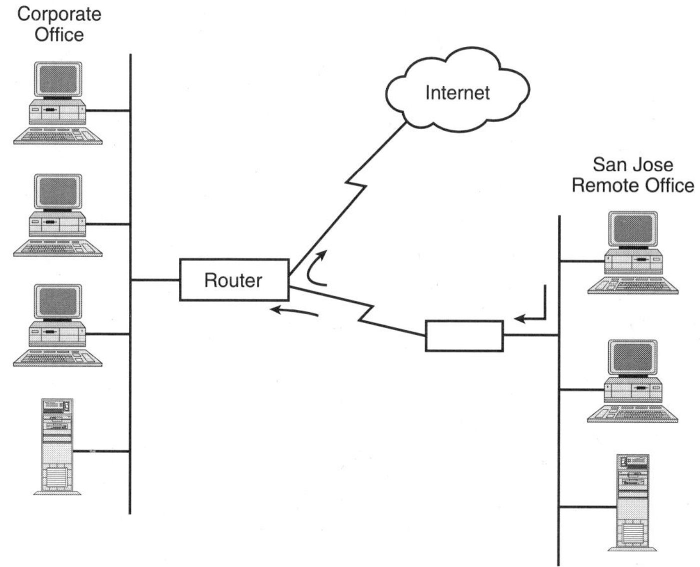

Figure 8.11
Connecting remote offices to the Internet using the corporate Internet link.

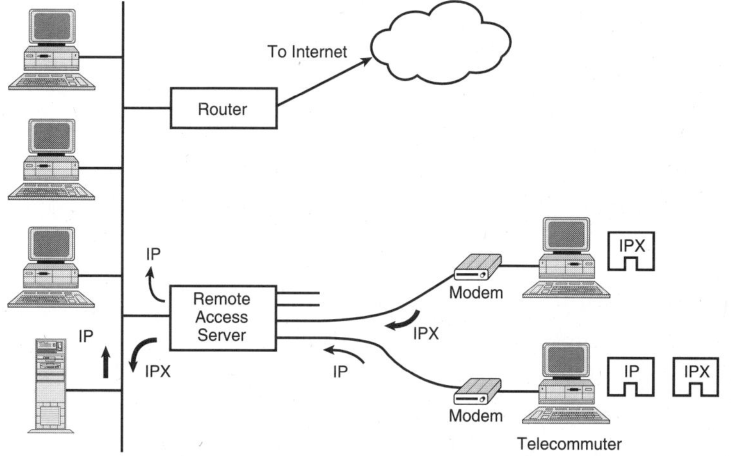

Figure 8.12
Providing Internet access to telecommuters.

Using the Internet as a Private Virtual WAN

It is possible to use the Internet as a wide area network, connecting a company's multiple offices over the Internet. For this to be an effective and viable alternative, however, an utmost level of security must be established.

The security devices at both ends should not only authenticate the users, but should also encrypt all conversations traveling through the Internet (see fig. 8.13).

At this time, these security devices are very expensive. It is expected that within a couple of years, however, these devices will become more affordable and will help to make the Internet more suitable for use as a private virtual WAN.

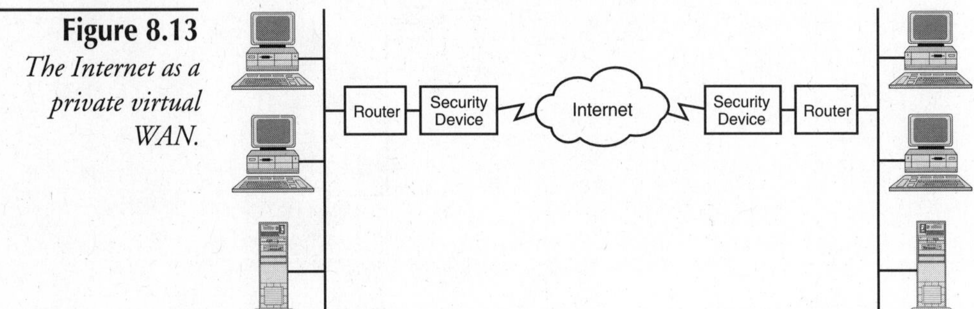

Figure 8.13
The Internet as a private virtual WAN.

To connect to the Internet from your LAN, you need a router that provides a LAN interface, a WAN port, and support for WAN protocols such as SLIP, PPP, and Frame Relay. In addition, you need a WAN connection device to complete the LAN-to-Internet connection. This device might be a modem for analog access, an ISDN TA for ISDN services, or a DSU/CSU for Switched 56, Leased 56/64 Kbps, Frame Relay, FT1/E1, or T1/E1 services.

For analog access, dial-up routers are the preferred alternative because they incorporate integrated modems with the option to upgrade to higher-speed line services. Overall, dial-up routers offer an economical solution for a network's analog access to the Internet. For ISDN access, integrated ISDN routers are the best alternative because they incorporate integrated ISDN TA and are priced aggressively. For leased-line access, both Novell's MPR with WAN cards from third parties or external routers with external WAN devices are equally attractive, depending on a site's needs and policies.

There are many choices available for WAN access devices, but the objective of all WAN devices is to provide a connection to the POP of the Internet Access Provider.

Client SLIP and PPP Connectivity

by Rick Fairweather

There are numerous methods and technologies used to connect networks and individual users to today's Internet. Options include dial-up modem access, Integrated Services Data Network (ISDN), point-to-point leased-line services such as T1 or 56 K circuits, switched technologies such as Frame Relay, X.25, Switched Multimegabit Data Service (SMDS), Asynchronous Transfer Mode (ATM), or traditional local area network (LAN) technologies such as Ethernet or the fiber distributed data interface (FDDI). Because each of these technologies has features, benefits, and perhaps even shortcomings, not any single technology is appropriate for everyone, let alone all of the users within a single organization.

One of the fastest growing areas in Internet usage is the individual user using access technologies such as asynchronous dial-up modems or circuit-switched technologies such as ISDN. Specifically, the growth in asynchronous, dial-up access to networks and the Internet is enormous. This is in part due to the fact that nearly every computer sold today has a modem or serial ports that can be easily used to access networks via asynchronous dial-up connections. Although these technologies provide the physical transport for data, they do not provide the complete solution in terms of the protocols required to transport higher layer protocols. The objective of this chapter is to discuss two key technologies that complete the solution for remote access communications.

This chapter discusses two protocols: the Serial Line Internet Protocol (SLIP) and the Point-to-Point Protocol (PPP), both of which provide the means to transport higher layer TCP/IP protocols over point-to-point communications media such as modem dial-up or ISDN.

SLIP—Serial Line Internet Protocol

The SLIP protocol has received fairly wide acceptance, in part due to the fact that SLIP is included in Berkeley Unix, Digital Equipment's Ultrix, Sun Microsystems' Unix, and many PC-based TCP/IP implementations. SLIP was developed in the mid-1980s specifically to address the transmission of IP datagrams over serial point-to-point communications links such as dial up modem connections. However, it can function over synchronous leased lines as well.

It was intended to address host-to-host, host-to-router, router-to-router, and workstation-to-host communications. SLIP was specifically defined to operate over 1,200 bps to 19.2 Kbps but can operate over higher speed circuits. Later, we will discuss some issues present with SLIP in relation to connection speed.

Physical Layer Requirements of SLIP

By definition, SLIP was designed to operate over a single kind of connection: dedicated, character-oriented, asynchronous lines such as RS-232. These communications lines generally range in speed from 1,200 bps to 19.2 Kbps.

This is an issue because many of the transmission technologies found today are bit-synchronous in nature and are frequently higher speed, such as 56 kilobits or 1.544 megabits. One of the reasons for this is that asynchronous technologies such as SLIP rely on start and stop bits to designate the beginning and end of characters, whereas synchronous technologies utilize sophisticated clocking mechanisms. Furthermore, as we will discuss later, the SLIP packet does not provide for the transmission of the ASCII characters used by most modems to provide flow control.

SLIP Internals

Perhaps the greatest attraction of SLIP is its simplicity. The SLIP protocol defines two special characters: ESC and END. ESC is actually octal character 333 (decimal 219) and END is octal character 300 (decimal 192).

Note It should be noted that the ESC character described here is not the same as the ASCII ESCape character.

The function of the ESC character is to mark the beginning of the SLIP packet. Figure 9.1 illustrates the structure of the SLIP packet.

INFO*	Flag

Figure 9.1
The structure of the SLIP packet.

After the ESC character, designated by the INFO field in figure 9.1, the higher layer protocol, such as IP, simply streams data, byte by byte, until all of the packets have been transmitted or until the maximum SLIP packet size has been reached. Then the SLIP packet is marked as being complete by terminating with the END character.

One potential problem with this structure is demonstrated when a data byte from the data to be transmitted has the same coding as either the ESC or the END characters. This could incorrectly mark the beginning or termination of the SLIP packet. If a data byte in the queued data has the same coding as the ESC character, then that character is replaced by a two-byte sequence of ESC and octal 335. If the data byte has the same coding as the END character, that byte is replaced by a two-byte sequence of the ESC and octal 334. Then the SLIP protocol stack on the receiving station will return these values to their original values prior to passing the datagrams to the higher layer protocols.

There is no defined maximum packet size for SLIP. Most implementations follow the Berkeley Unix SLIP driver maximum of 1,006 bytes (not including the framing characters). Therefore it is best that new implementations support at least 1,006 byte datagrams and should not send datagrams larger than 1,006 bytes in order to ensure interoperability.

Problems Associated with SLIP

Perhaps one of the more attractive aspects of SLIP is also its greatest problem—its simplicity. As explained above, SLIP is a fairly simple protocol, and, therefore, does not address several issues that are critical in today's networking arena. It is somewhat ironic that RFC 1055 devotes nearly a third of its text to the discussion of the shortcomings of SLIP. The limitations of SLIP can be broken down into several critical areas:

- Addressing
- Type identification
- Error detection and correction
- Compression

Addressing

SLIP does not provide a mechanism for the connected hosts to transmit addressing to each other. Because of this, two devices in a SLIP connection must know each other's IP address before TCP/IP packets can be transmitted.

Type Identification

As discussed earlier, a SLIP transmission is little more than a series of bytes preceded by an ESCape character and terminated by an END character. There is no field to identify the protocol being transmitted. This means that SLIP cannot provide protocol multiplexing—each SLIP session can support a single network-layer protocol only. Therefore, if two computers supporting TCP/IP and OSI are communicating via a SLIP connection, the two protocols cannot be transmitted over the SLIP connection simultaneously. While SLIP can in fact support any higher-layer protocol information, it can only support one protocol over a single SLIP line.

Error Detection and Correction

SLIP provides no error detection or error correction capabilities. This is increasingly consequential with protocols that do not include higher layer error detection and correction. However, it should be noted that SLIP was originally designed for transmission speeds ranging from 1,200 bps to 19.2 Kbps, which are less likely to be prone to transmission errors than today's higher speed transmission technologies.

This is ever more important with protocols such as IPX that rely on the link layer protocols to discard bad packets. SLIP actually relies on the higher level protocols, such as the IP header, to detect and handle malformed packets. If neither the link layer protocol, in this case SLIP, nor the higher level protocols provide error detection and correction, the integrity of the communications session can be significantly impeded.

Compression

Being that SLIP is primarily used for slower dial-up connections such as 2,400 bps, packet compression could bring large improvements in packet throughput. Unfortunately, this capability is not present with SLIP. Compression could also address the protocol overhead by either compressing the headers themselves or actually eliminating potentially unnecessary headers. For example, in RFC 1055, J. Romkey suggests the following possibility:

> Usually, streams of packets in a single TCP connection have few changed fields in the IP and TCP headers, so a simple compression algorithm might just send the changed parts of the headers instead of the complete headers.

Unfortunately, SLIP does not define either of these possibilities. While some implementations of SLIP do provide various forms of compression, it is possible that these solutions are not universally supported and may cause problems between different vendor's implementations.

To be fair, it should be noted that many of the problems and issues that face us today were not relevant when SLIP was developed. Numerous vendors have tried to address these limitations and issues by providing extensions to the SLIP protocol. Unfortunately, these extensions reduce the guarantee of interoperability between various vendor's products.

In the early 1980s when SLIP was developed, it met the majority of the requirements that faced network professionals at that time. Networks were predominately single protocol, transmission speeds were considerably lower and the use of these technologies was not ubiquitous. That has changed. Today's networks are frequently multi-protocol, transmission speeds are exponentially higher than in earlier times and these networks are being used extensively. These factors necessitate a protocol that addresses these issues—that protocol is PPP.

PPP—The Point-to-Point Protocol

PPP, like SLIP, was primarily designed as a standards-based encapsulation protocol for network layer protocols such as IP across serial, point-to-point links. However, unlike SLIP, it was designed to have the capability to support other network layer protocols such as IPX, AppleTalk, DECnet, and OSI. Also, while it was primarily designed for serial point-to-point links, it can also function over other types of communications technologies such as ISDN.

PPP also includes features to support network-protocol multiplexing, link configuration, link quality testing, authentication, Van Jacobson TCP/IP header compression, error detection, and link-option negotiation. These features will be discussed in detail later in this chapter.

Physical Layer Requirements of PPP

The Point-to-Point protocol does not have specific requirements as to the type of signaling or even the transmission speed of the communications circuit. PPP is frequently employed on connections ranging from relatively slow 1,200 bps dial-up connections to 45 Mbps DS3 point-to-point circuits.

PPP was designed to function with virtually any asynchronous or synchronous, dedicated or dial-up, or circuit switched full-duplex circuit. It can utilize the majority of common serial-communications protocols, including EIA-232-E (also known as RS-232-C), EIA-422, EIA-423, EIA-530, and CCItt V.24 and V.35.

Like TCP/IP, PPP is in fact a suite of protocols and not a single protocol. The suite contains a series of protocols—which provides the functionality found in PPP—as well as individual protocols to support the various network layer protocols such as IP, AppleTalk, DECnet, or OSI. Figure 9.2 illustrates the PPP protocol suite. Later in this chapter we will look at several of these protocols in depth.

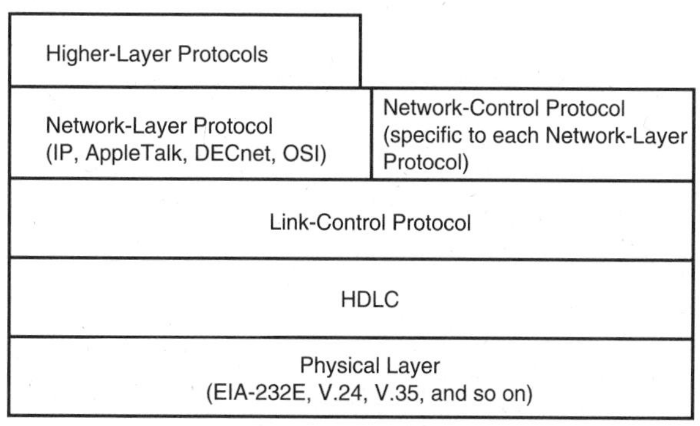

Figure 9.2
The components of the PPP protocol suite.

Unlike SLIP, PPP was from the beginning intended to be an Internet standard, with support from numerous vendors and technologies. Therefore, a great deal of work has gone into the development of this protocol to ensure that it addresses the majority of the known issues present in other similar data-link protocols. Further information on these technologies can be found in the Internet Request for Comment (RFC) documents noted in table 9.1.

Table 9.1
Useful Internet Request for Comment (RFC) Documents

RFC Number	Title
1220	PPP Extensions for Bridging
1331	Point-to-Point Protocol
1332	PPP Internet Protocol Control Protocol (IPCP)
1333	PPP Link-Quality Monitoring
1334	PPP Authentication Protocols
1376	PPP DECnet Phase IV Control Protocol (DNCP)
1377	PPP OSI Network-Layer Control Protocol (OSINLCP)
1378	PPP AppleTalk Control Protocol (ATCP)

The PPP Frame Format

As you will see in this section, the PPP frame is more complex than the frame structure of a SLIP packet. This additional complexity is actually the result of additional functionality and features, many of which are discussed in this chapter. First, it might be helpful to visualize the structure of the PPP frame to properly understand some of these features. A graphical depiction of the SLIP packet is provided in figure 9.3.

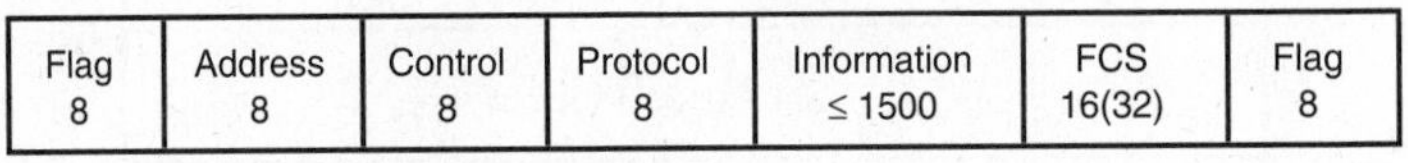

Figure 9.3
The structure of the PPP packet.

Flag	Address	Control	Protocol	Information	FCS	Flag
8	8	8	8	≤ 1500	16(32)	8

- **Flag.** The function of the flag field is to specify both the beginning and end of the PPP frame. This one octet field will always have the binary value of 02220 (hexadecimal value 7E). When a receiving station sees this value in a transmission, it will know that this is either the beginning or termination of the PPP frame.

- **Address.** This one octet field will always have the binary value of 2222 (hexadecimal value FF) specifying the HDLC All-Station address. PPP does not assign individual station addresses.

- **Control.** This one octet field will always have the binary value of 0000002 (hexadecimal value 03) denoting HDLC unnumbered information. HDLC uses this field to indicate frame type and sequence numbers. However, PPP only uses a value of 03.

- **Protocol Field.** This two octet field identifies the protocol encapsulated in the information field. Per HDLC guidelines, the first octet must end in a 0 and the second octet must end in a 1. Table 9.2 lists some of the protocols and protocol values currently supported by PPP.

Table 9.2
Some Protocols and Protocol Values Currently Supported by PPP

Value (in hex)	Protocol Name
0001 to 001f	Reserved (transparency inefficient)
0021	Internet Protocol

Value (in hex)	Protocol Name
0023	OSI Network Layer
0025	Xerox NS IDP
0027	DECnet Phase IV
0029	AppleTalk
002b	Novell IPX
002d	Van Jacobson Compressed TCP/IP
002f	Van Jacobson Uncompressed TCP/IP
0031	Bridging PDU
0033	Stream Protocol (ST-II)
0035	Banyan Vines
0037	Reserved (until 1993)
00ff	Reserved (compression inefficient)
0201	802.1d Hello Packets
0231	Luxcom
0233	Sigma Network Systems
8021	Internet Protocol Control Protocol
8023	OSI Network Layer Control Protocol
8025	Xerox NS IDP Control Protocol
8027	DECnet Phase IV Control Protocol
8029	AppleTalk Control Protocol
802b	Novell IPX Control Protocol
802d	Reserved
802f	Reserved
8031	Bridging NCP
8033	Stream Protocol Control Protocol

continues

Table 9.2, Continued
Some Protocols and Protocol Values Currently Supported by PPP

Value (in hex)	Protocol Name
8035	Banyan Vines Control Protocol
c021	Link Control Protocol
c023	Password Authentication Protocol
c025	Link Quality Report
c223	Challenge Handshake Authentication Protocol

- **Information.** This field, which may be as large as 1,500 bytes, contains the datagram from the network layer protocol identified in the Protocol field.
- **Frame Check Sequence.** This field is used to detect bit errors. This field is usually 16 bits in length but can be extended to 32 bits if both devices in the PPP connection support this option.

Now, having dissected the PPP frame and described its components, several of the key functionalities and features of PPP that are made possible by the relevant components of the frame are discussed.

The Principal Functions of PPP

PPP can be best understood by breaking down the breadth in functionality in this protocol to three primary components:

- Encapsulation
- Link Management
- Network-Control Protocols

Encapsulation

PPP provides a technique for encapsulating data over communications links, based on the ISO High-Level Data-Link Control (HDLC) protocol. The

PPP Data-Link layer is not an entirely new protocol. PPP provides an encapsulation protocol for both bit-oriented synchronous and asynchronous links with eight bits of data and no parity. The links must be full-duplex but may be either dedicated links such as 56 KB and T1 circuits or circuit-switched links such as dial-up, ISDN, or switched 56K services. In fact, it borrows heavily from the concepts and frame structure of HDLC.

Link Management

A *Link-Control Protocol* (LCP) provides the functions of establishing, configuring, authenticating, and verifying the integrity of the connections. The LCP is also used to terminate the connection when transmission is complete.

All LCP packets have the same general format but may vary in length. This format is illustrated in figure 9.4.

Code	Identifier	Length

Figure 9.4
The structure of the LCP packet.

The fields of the LCP packet identified in figure 9.4 provide PPP with some key capabilities not found in more simple protocols such as PPP. These functions enable PPP to provide a high level of transmission reliability for higher layer network protocols. The following list analyzes each of the fields of the LCP packet and discusses many of the benefits they bring to this protocol suite.

- The one octet Code field identifies the type of LCP packet. The various types of LCP packets are listed in table 9.3.

Table 9.3
LCP Packet Types

LCP Packet Code	LCP Packet Type
1	Configure-Request
2	Configure-Ack

continues

Table 9.3, Continued
LCP Packet Types

LCP Packet Code	LCP Packet Type
3	Configure-Nak
4	Configure-Reject
5	Terminate-Request
6	Terminate-Ack
7	Code-Reject
8	Protocol-Reject
9	Echo-Request
10	Echo-Reply
11	Discard-Request
12	RESERVED

- The one octet Identifier field is a number chosen at random and is used to correlate requests and replies. Any packet that is sent in response to a request must contain the same value in the Identifier field.
- The two octet Length field indicates the length of the entire LCP packet in octets. Any information following this field in the PPP packet is data or configuration options.

LCP packets can be broken down into three types based on the functionality they deliver:

- Link-Configuration
- Link-Termination
- Link-Maintenance

Link-Configuration Packets

Link-Configuration packets are used to establish and configure the PPP connection. There are four types of Link-Configuration packets with specific functions:

- **Configure-Request packets** are sent by a PPP device that is attempting to open an LCP connection. The establishment of the LCP connection must be complete before any Network-Layer transmission can occur. In the data/options field of the LCP packet, the device can communicate configuration options such as maximum packet size, asynchronous control characters, type of authentication protocol, link-quality monitoring reporting period, and compression type. The device that receives the configure-request packet will respond with one of the following packets.

- **Configure-Ack packets** are sent back to the originating station when all of the options requested in the configure-request packet are acceptable. A configure-ack response indicates that the LCP connection has been successfully established.

- **Configure-Nak packets** are sent back to the originating device when all of the options requested in the configure-request packet are recognizable but some of the requested options are not acceptable to the receiver. The configure-nak response lists which of the configuration options specified in the configure-request packet were unacceptable, as well as those that were accepted. In some situations the originating station may send a new configure-request packet with new option values, or the two sides may negotiate the values for specific options. It should be noted that the LCP session will not be established until the two devices agree on all options.

- **Configure-Reject packets** are sent to the originating device when one or more of the options in the configure-request packet are not recognizable or are unacceptable and cannot be negotiated. The configure-reject packet will contain those options that are rejected. In order for the LCP connection to be established, the originating device will need to send a new configure-request packet that does not contain any of the values that were rejected.

Link-Termination Packets

Link-Termination packets are obviously used to terminate the PPP link. In order to terminate the PPP link, one station will send a terminate-request packet and the receiving station will reply with a terminate-ack packet.

Link-Maintenance Packets

Link-Maintenance packets are used to manage and troubleshoot a PPP link. PPP supports the following four types of link maintenance packets that ensure a high level of integrity and reliability to PPP-based communications.

- **Code-Reject packets** are sent if a PPP host receives a packet that contains an invalid Code-field value.
- **Protocol-Reject packets** are sent if a PPP host receives a PPP frame with an invalid Protocol-field value. This would occur if a device is attempting to establish a PPP connection to another device to transport a network-layer protocol that is not supported by the receiving device.
- **Echo-Request and Echo Reply packets** provide a loopback function that can be useful in troubleshooting, performance testing, verifying link quality, and other functions.
- **Discard-Request packets** are also used in debugging or performance testing situations. Unlike the echo-request and echo reply packets, these packets are discarded by the receiving station.

So far, the aspects of PPP that have been discussed focus primarily on the capabilities of PPP to ensure reliable and trouble-free wide area communications. Many of these features are noticeably absent from more fundamental protocols such as SLIP. However, these features encompass only part of the appeal of PPP. Perhaps the strongest aspect of PPP, as is discussed in the following section, is its capability to support multiple protocols, even simultaneously over a single PPP connection.

Network-Control Protocols

A collection of *Network-Control Protocols* (NCPs) provides lower layer support for the various supported Network Layer Protocols. These protocols, as illustrated earlier in figure 9.3, function at the network layer in parallel with the network layer protocols such as IP, AppleTalk, or IPX.

PPP Operational Phases

The establishment of a PPP connection is not an instantaneous event—it actually occurs in phases and occurs one layer at a time. For example, a physical layer and the HDLC data-link layer connection must be established before LCP packets can be exchanged. As explained earlier, an LCP session must be established before any network-layer data can be transmitted.

The Link-Dead Phase

This phase is where the PPP session begins and ends. In this phase, the physical layer is in a "dead" state and is not capable of communications. When a communications device, such as a modem or ISDN terminal adapter, begins a dialing sequence, the PPP session moves to the link-establishment phase.

The Link-Establishment Phase

The first step in the link-establishment phase is the establishment of a connection at the physical layer, such as the response from the remote device's modem. At this point, the two devices will exchange LCP Configure packets and possibly negotiate on LCP options in order to establish an LCP session.

Note In the link-establishment phase, only LCP options are negotiated. Any network-layer options will be negotiated during a later phase.

This phase is complete when the originating device sends a configure-request packet and the receiving device replies with a configure-ack. If this negotiation is unsuccessful, PPP will return to the link-dead phase.

The Authentication Phase

In some situations, PPP devices may be required to authenticate themselves before network layer communications can take place. This phase is optional and therefore may not always occur. If this authentication is successful, then PPP progresses to the network-layer protocol phase; if it is not, then PPP advances to the link-termination phase. Detailed information on the authentication techniques used in PPP can be found in RFC 1334.

The Network Layer Protocol Phase

This phase clearly illustrates one of the most significant aspects of PPP. Each network layer protocol, such as IP, has a unique NCP that will provide transmission support. If the device has IP packets to transport, the appropriate NCP connection will be established to transport those packets. Likewise, if the device has AppleTalk packets to transport, the appropriate NCP connection will be established to transport those packets. If packets are received for which there is not a supporting NCP, those packets will be discarded.

The first NCP to be defined was to support the IP protocol and is referred to as the Internet Protocol Control Protocol (IPCP). PPP frames that transport IPCP packets can be identified by the Protocol-field value of 8021. The format of an IPCP packet is shown back in figure 9.4.

To transport IP frames across a PPP connection, the originating station would first send an IPCP Configure-Request packet. This packet might include options such as the originator's IP address, maximum frame size information, and compression techniques. The receiving host will then either agree to all options, begin a negotiation of options or perhaps refuse the connection altogether. After the IPCP connection has been made, then the two hosts are able to transmit IP datagrams to each other. These packets can be identified by a Protocol-field value of 0021 in the PPP header information. After all of the IP datagrams have been exchanged, then the IPCP connection can be ended through the exchange of IPCP Terminate LCP packets. This process is very similar for other NCPs that support protocols such as AppleTalk, IPX, DECnet, or OSI.

The Termination Phase

A PPP termination may be a deliberate event, such as a user wishing to terminate a connection to a host; it can also be an automatic event due to a loss of carrier, authentication failure, poor link quality, or the expiration of an idle-period timer. One station will transmit a terminate-request packet and the other will respond with a terminate-ack packet. At this point, PPP will return to the Link-Dead phase. This termination will allow the graceful termination of all NCP connections that have been operating over the PPP link.

Security with PPP

One of the positive aspects of PPP is the ability for two hosts to negotiate an authentication protocol in order to validate the two devices that intend to communicate prior to the transmission of any network layer protocol data. The process of authentication takes place during the establishment of the LCP connection. As discussed earlier, if the authentication is not successful, then PPP immediately proceeds to terminate the link, thereby preventing the transport of any network layer protocol information.

Currently, two authentication protocols are in wide acceptance in PPP implementations; *Password Authentication Protocol* (PAP) and Challenge *Handshake Authentication Protocol* (CHAP). Both of these protocols are implemented after a successful LCP connection establishment and must be successful prior to proceeding to the Network-Layer Protocol phase.

Password Authentication Protocol (PAP)

PAP is a relatively simple method of authentication in which the two PPP peers establish their identities using a two-way exchange or an ID/Password pair or handshake. This handshake, which takes place after the link is successfully established, involves the repeated transmission of the ID/Password combination until it is either accepted by the other peer or until the link is terminated. After that point, PAP is not active; once PAP authenticates the remote peer, there is no further verification of the PPP traffic.

The actual PAP verification process is very similar to the establishment of the LCP connection. PAP frames can be identified in a PPP transmission by a protocol-field value of c023. First, a PAP packet is transmitted with a Code field set to 1 denoting it as an authenticate-request packet. This authenticate-request packet contains the peer-ID and peer password. As mentioned earlier, this packet will be sent repeatedly until accepted. This authenticate-request packet is sent repeatedly in case the response packet from the authenticator is lost.

There are several possible responses to the authenticate-request packet. If a valid peer-ID and password pair is transmitted, the authenticator will respond with an authenticate-ack packet. This packet is identified by a code value of 2. If the authentication is not successful or a predefined retry counter expires before a valid peer-ID/password pair is exchanged, an authenticate-NAK, which can be identified by a code value of 3, is sent by the authenticator.

Warning PAP presents a potential security exposure in that ID/password pairs are transmitted across the link in plain text and not encrypted. This allows the possibility of "sniffing" or recording of the ID/password pairs as they are exchanged. Also, since by design these pairs are exchanged repeatedly until accepted, there is virtually no protection from repeated trial and error attempts at finding a valid ID/password pair.

PPP is most commonly used in situations where a clear text username and password combination is required, such as when logging into a host computer.

One solution to these exposures is the encryption of the PAP password. In this situation, the server host must be capable of decrypting the password using the same algorithm as the client. The server can then decrypt the password and forward the password to the login process on the server. The encryption of the PAP password does address the issue of transmission of clear text passwords across a network but does not verify the authenticity of the peer during the session.

Some of these exposures are addressed in the second PPP authentication protocol, CHAP.

Challenge-Handshake Authentication Protocol (CHAP)

CHAP utilizes a three-way handshake process to authenticate peers. Unlike PAP, CHAP not only conducts this authentication upon link establishment but can repeat this authentication during the PPP session.

After the link is established, the authenticator sends a "challenge" to the peer. The peer sends back a value calculated using a "one-way hash" algorithm. The authenticator compares this value to its own calculation of what it expects the value to be. If the two values match, the authentication is successful and the connection is established. If not, the session establishment should be refused and the connection is immediately terminated.

The authentication is based on a "secret," a value used to calculate the one time hash value. This value is known only by the authenticator and the peer and is never transmitted across the communications link.

This process illustrates one of the most significant advantages of CHAP versus PAP. First, passwords are never transmitted in clear text form. This prevents the potential exposure due to possible scanning for passwords. Furthermore, each time an attempt is made to authenticate the peer, the peer-ID is incrementally changed. These measures greatly reduce possible penetration through the use of repeated attempts or random password generations.

As the number of sites accessing the Internet and other TCP/IP hosts and networks via serial point-to-point communications links increases, the use of PPP continues to grow exponentially. Although SLIP has been used widely and continues to be used today, PPP is being deployed at a much greater rate because it addresses the multiprotocol, performance-orientated, and security-conscious needs of today's environment. PPP is, therefore, rapidly becoming today's and tomorrow's choice of a standards-based protocol for network connectivity.

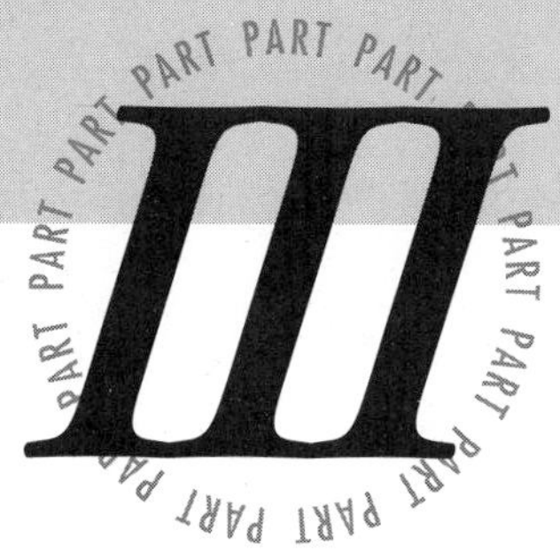

Server Setup: Administration and Maintenance

Building and Managing an HTTP Server

by James Ryans with Chamath Pali

The Internet is a magic body of information just waiting for you to ask it a question. At least that is what most users think until it becomes their turn to make something available on the Web. The World Wide Web is that fast growing area of the Internet that dishes out multimedia information about millions of companies, institutions, and computer nerds who insist on having a homepage. It is also one of the hottest areas for advertising and public relations investment.

As technology improves, the Web is becoming much more sophisticated and useful. Currently, you can get your news, order a pizza, and watch live fish swimming in their tank at Netscape; for the future, the possibilities are vast. Now that many corporations are being forced to develop a Web presence, be it from customers or competition, there is a growing need for a solid reference on how to install an HTTP or Web server.

HTTP, or HyperText Transfer Protocol, is the language of the Web. It allows a computer to demand and receive a variety of file types using the Internet as the transmission medium. To get your company on the Web, you start with the installation of an HTTP server. If you're ambitious or bored, you can even create your own server software. For the rest of us, there are a number of options, some of them free, which will more than meet your needs.

This chapter is designed to give you all the information needed to get an HTTP server up and running. If that is your goal, the only part of this chapter you need is the section "Installing an HTTP Server." For those of you who like to learn a little more about the workings of the software you will be using, there is a good introduction to the protocol HTTP, secure communication, and more advanced server issues. For those who have a need to incorporate encryption, or who want to learn about the options for Web commerce, there is a section explaining the current options, as well as some proposed technologies.

You will find that this chapter provides step-by-step instructions for installing an HTTP server on a Unix machine, as well as information for someone looking for general information about Web servers. This chapter is focused, however, upon those readers who need to get a server up and running, with maximum reliability, in a minimal amount of time.

For administrators who have growing Web sites to manage, the maintenance and administration of your server will be an important task that cannot be overlooked. Methods for managing users and groups of users, ways of securing your data, and other management techniques will be discussed.

To achieve these goals, there are a number of steps you must undertake. First, you have to analyze the goals of the server and make sure you have the required hardware. Once the hardware and the Internet connection are available, you need to choose the software that meets the needs defined by you or your company. Next, you have to get the software and install it on your system. Finally, you need configure the server to provide all the features needed, in addition to securing the rest of the system from unwanted access.

Hardware

An HTTP server can be run on virtually any modern desktop computer. To be certain, there are some choices that are much better than others, but you will not have to spend a great deal of money to get a serviceable server. Consider the main factors:

- Processor speed
- Memory
- Storage capacity
- Operating system
- Internet connection

By examining each of these factors as they relate to your current and future needs, you will be able to devise a solid foundation for your HTTP server.

Processor Speed

Processor speed is the least of your worries when it comes to designing your server. If your expected traffic flow is not going to be massive (that is, hundreds of thousands of requests per day), then you should not need anything faster than a desktop PC with a 486 or a Pentium processor.

Memory

You do, however, need to consider memory a little more carefully. As a rule of thumb, have 0.5–1 MB of RAM for each simultaneous request. For large files, this should be upped to at least 1 MB per simultaneous request. It is important to note that you cannot average your daily number of hits to get the number of simultaneous requests, but you must take the maximum at any one time during the day. For example, if you have a peak usage of 1,000 hits per hour with an average download time of 10 seconds per request, you would have about three simultaneous users. This would require 2–3 MB of RAM above what the operating system and other software requires. Performance is severely hampered by a shortage of RAM, so don't skimp in this area. For a lightly used server, you will want at least 16 MB, and a heavily used system should have 32 MB or more.

Storage Capacity

With hard drives being as inexpensive as they are today, you should make sure you have an excess of storage capacity to avoid time-consuming upgrades in the future. One consideration is the speed of the drive. If you have the money and the need for performance, be sure to use fast SCSI hard drives instead of the cheaper IDE versions. Your users will notice a difference if there is heavy traffic on your site.

Operating System

This is probably the most important area to consider when planning your server. The operating system is the foundation of the server and will determine the stability and even the performance of the system. First, the system should be multitasking. A true multitasking system will enable you to serve several documents simultaneously without worry. Secondly, you need a system that is supported and has other users whom you can ask for help should the need arise.

Most of the development and support will be for Unix environments, and this should be the first operating system you examine. Keep in mind that Unix does not preclude you from using that spare 486 PC you have lying around. In fact there are excellent Unix operating systems for the PC, including Linux, which is free, and BSD, a commercial PC Unix operating system. Both perform very well, and you can find lots of helpful users on the Internet who would be glad to help solve your problems.

Internet Connection

Connecting the HTTP server to the Internet could be the subject of a whole other book, so if you do not have the expertise to do it yourself, you will need professional help. What you need to plan for is the speed of your connection. Of course, with lots of users, you want the fastest connection you can afford.

If you are connected to an Ethernet LAN, your connection should be at 10 Mbps, more than fast enough for most needs. Of course, many people do not have access to a LAN, so they must consider other options, such as ISDN service. The best place to find information about these service is with a reputable local service provider.

Possible Uses of HTTP Servers

If you already know what services you want to offer, a good question you should be asking is "Can I do that?" The following are techniques currently in use on the Web:

- **Sell things.** This can be done, but some ways are far better that others.
- **Provide information.** This is what the Web was designed for, and it does this best.
- **Restrict access to your information.** This can be done, although the browser software of the user plays a role.

Most anything that is currently being done on the Web falls into one or a combination of these categories. By restricting access to files, services such as online magazine subscriptions are being provided. Some companies, such as Cisco Systems, are giving customer support information, but this information is restricted to registered customers only.

The selection of the complete server is a combination of hardware and software choices. Assuming you have a particular hardware platform in mind, you must choose the best software solution. The best solution will have the desired performance and features demanded by your users, but also future upgradeability and support from other server administrators.

Selecting HTTP Server Software

One of the first things to consider in selecting the software for building an HTTP server is why you are setting up a Web server. More often than not, the mission is somewhat undefined; something along the lines of "We want to provide information for our customers." Although this is not much to go on, it is usually enough. You only start getting into trouble when your goal is to sell products using the Web as the medium for the financial transaction.

When selecting HTTP server software, there are a number of factors to evaluate:

- Is it fast?
- Is it easy to set up?
- Is it easy to maintain?
- Is it secure?

These criteria are met by a few popular servers, notably the Netscape family of servers and NCSA httpd. Netscape is a commercial server that is known for high performance and a wide variety of features. For the purpose of this chapter, you will be using the NCSA httpd server software. The reasons for choosing this particular software will be discussed in more detail later in this chapter.

Note If NCSA httpd is just as good as Netscape, then you must be wondering why people buy Netscape at all. The reason is in the browsers. Netscape has developed a security standard that is currently only supported by its own browser, the Netscape Navigator. Because the vast majority of Web users use the Netscape browser, if you want to offer secure transactions, the easiest way to do this is by using a secure Netscape server.

Performance Considerations

One of the initial considerations when planning your server and Web site is performance. Performance differences among different server software packages can be negligable until heavy demand is placed on a system. To control the demand placed on your hardware and software, you have to be careful when designing the system so that it takes into account the size and types of files you will be serving. By looking at both the content and the platform, you can understand if your server will be viable.

When a client accesses your server to request some data, it has to follow a defined set of rules. Simplified, this procedure forces a client requesting a hypertext page to request and retrieve the page, followed by a series of requests to retrieve any images that were included in that page. After the whole page has been downloaded, the user can select another hyperlink, and the process repeats itself.

This might seem trivial since you are immediately concerned with performance; however, it demonstrates the biggest problem with the existing HTTP standard. If you were to study how the document request process is divided into time slices, you would see that most of the time is spent waiting, not transmitting or receiving data.

The reasons why a lot of time is spent waiting for confirmations are problems inherent in TCP/IP, the underlying transmission protocol, which is poorly suited to carrying HTTP data. The reasons are somewhat complicated—suffice it to say that there are no cheap solutions to improving document retrieval speeds. To increase the retrieval speed, the protocol, TCP/IP, would itself have to be changed. This is clearly an impossible task, so if you are to work with TCP/IP, the only reasonable solution is to improve the network speed.

When setting up a WWW site, one of the most crucial decisions is bandwidth, or the throughput of your connection. Small companies have to consider if they can afford to pay steep monthly fees for a high-speed fiber connection. Another option is to house your site on the server of a local service provider. This may be the best solution currently, but with the growth of ISDN, a high-speed digital phone service offered by the phone companies, it will soon be almost as cheap to manage your own server. Needless to say, if you are reading this, you are interested in setting up your own server, and it is assumed that you have examined the options.

There are two ways to address this performance situation. One, if you already have Internet access at a given speed, then you will have to work around this to define the proper size of the documents you will be serving given your expected number of hits. The other way to address performance is to examine the services you want to offer and buy a connection based on that estimate.

More often than not, you will fall into the first category, and you will have to create guidelines so that your users get a good level of service.

Note A major misconception companies needlessly worry about is simultaneous access. Unless your site is extremely busy, simultaneous access is not a problem. In the worst case scenario where your company uses all of its bandwidth for HTML pages, it would be serving tens of thousands pages per day. Although the speed of your Internet connection will become inadequate before you get to that point due to swells in demand at certain times of the day, most dedicated connections will be adequate—*most* meaning anything faster than a 28.8-Kbps modem.

Some guidelines you should follow to help ensure a high level of HTTP server performance include:

- Pages that users are meant to view should be readable within five seconds
- Avoid posting very large documents on the same server if you want other users to get good access
- Test the connection speed regularly from outside your LAN and upgrade when slowdown is apparent
- Check the statistics regularly and move very large but infrequently used files to a secondary server

Introducing HyperText Transfer Protocol (HTTP)

A *protocol* is really just a set of rules governing the communication between two systems. People have an informal protocol that usually consists of a greeting, a handshake, the two-way exchange of information, and the dismissal. Computer protocols work in much the same way. The *HyperText Transfer Protocol* (HTTP) was designed as a small, quick protocol to access distributed, collaborative hypermedia systems. In other words, the designers were looking to design a protocol that could handle lots of different types of data on different computers to achieve a virtual community.

Features of HTTP

Initially, it was supposed to be fairly simple, although it has outgrown the early days and has become a complex protocol with numerous features. The protocol has been used by the World Wide Web since 1990. It was designed to be generic and stateless. This allows it to be used for numerous tasks through its command set. The current evolution of HTTP has met these design goals, and we are finding that HTTP is being used as the medium for a wide variety of new interactions. Almost all of these interactions are being developed for the World Wide Web, and they will provide a wealth of unimaginable features in the future. The command set itself provides for some powerful transmission, interaction, and control over distributed systems.

Resource Locators

HTTP is built on the direction or address given to it by a Uniform Resource Identifier (URI)—a Uniform Resource Locator (URL) or Uniform Resource Name (URN). These directives indicate where a given request should be applied. The present version of HTTP supports FTP, TELNET, WAIS, Gopher, SMTP, Mailto, Prospero, and NNTP, as well as others. HTTP also allows these resources to be applied through a proxy server, gateway, or firewall without the loss of data conveyed in earlier versions of those resources.

Request and Response

The protocol works through a request and response dynamic. A client (usually the end-user with a browser) establishes a connection with an HTTP server. It then submits a request that includes the resource type to apply, the URI to apply it to, protocol version, and a Multipurpose Internet Mail Extension (MIME) message. When the server receives a request, it sends out a response, which includes a success or error code, server information, and entity meta-information. Both the request and response could initially contain body content.

In addition, the HTTP protocol requires that the connection be made by the client before it submits a request where it is closed by the HTTP daemon after a response is sent. Both the client and the server must be aware of premature termination or loss of connections no matter the status of transmission. This is so that errors do not occur due to impatient clients or poor connections.

Tip Although HTTP is usually run on a TCP/IP network, the protocol only assumes it is a reliable transport method. Therefore, any protocol that can provide this stability can be used to transport and house HTTP-related data. Usually, the HTTP daemon is run on TCP port 80 and assumes as much unless it is given other instructions in a URI.

HTTP and Security

In general, HTTP works fairly well, except that security is not adequately addressed in the protocol, but is left to the server. HTTP provides a means to gain access and to directly manipulate a remote file system, and this results in an inherent danger of the protocol.

Caution must therefore be taken when setting up an HTTP server. With established products, such as Netscape and NCSA servers, you can be reasonably assured that your server will be safe from attack, but there are no guarantees that your data or even your network will be bulletproof.

Due to the powerful command set given to the HTTP protocol, there are built in ways to create and delete directories and files. Given that the server software controls whether or not the requests are carried out, you need that much faith in your software if sensitive files and systems are accessible via this HTTP server.

Installing an HTTP Server

Now that you know about HTTP and how an HTTP server works, it is time to get one up and running. There are a few steps to follow for the best chance of getting a satisfactory server up and running:

1. Choose the server software that meets your needs and growth expectations.

2. Buy or download the software and install after carefully reading all the instructions.

3. Configure the software using either a Netscape Navigator based interface (Netscape servers only) or by manually editing the configuration files.

Each of these steps is explained in detail, and the last two are covered for the NCSA httpd software, which is available for free.

Choosing the Best Server Software

When deciding which HTTP server to use, consider the framework of the services that you want to offer. Among other concerns, consider the following:

- Who will the users of this service be?
- Who will be providing the information?
- What are the current proposed services?
- Are there indications of which services will be offered in the future?

Each of these will have a bearing on which software you will use, and how to configure it once you get it.

In the vast majority of cases, the company that wants to install an HTTP server already has access to the Internet. Usually, the motives for having a Web server are that everyone else has one and so should you. This argument has some merit to it, but a more important concern is the services that can be provided on the Web. Some companies want to sell their products, others want to advertise, and more still want to provide corporate and product information to customers. In many cases, a combination of these three approaches is used, and it must be decided whether the server will need security features such as encryption and access control.

If a company wants to sell products over the Web and make it convenient for the user to buy, then the capability to handle financial transactions over the Internet is required. In this case, the most pressing concern is security. If credit card numbers and other personal information are going to be transmitted, then some form of encryption or data security must be used to protect all parties involved. Secure transmission is a volatile and fast developing area on the Internet, and the various options currently available are discussed later in this chapter.

If you have no need for secure transmission, your decision making has been simplified. The aspects that will be of concern to you are price, options, speed, robustness, security, and ease-of-installation. There are a number of competing products that have different strengths. On the commercial side, there is the popular Netscape family of servers that will meet a variety of needs, but will make you pay for it. Freeware servers are very popular, and, although they can be a little harder to install than Netscape, they can be just as capable or better. Leading the pack is the NCSA httpd server, which is continually being improved by the National Center for Supercomputing Applications. Currently at release 1.4, the NCSA server is widely used and has been tested to be at least as fast as Netscape servers in some conditions at the time of writing.

Because most people start with the free NCSA software, it has been chosen as the demonstrated installation software in this book. NCSA is a very robust server that will serve all your needs, except secure communications.

Benefits of Using NCSA

First of all, you should use NCSA because it is free. If this is not a good enough reason, there are other more technical reasons. These include the following:

- NCSA httpd serves documents to browsers using either HTTP/1.0 and HTTP/0.9
- NCSA supports virtual directories
- Efficient use of system resources

- Users can have their own Web pages
- Support for executable server scripts and programs and server side includes
- Some user management and security features

Virtual Directories

With NCSA httpd, you can serve your documents from a virtual directory, which means that the browsers will never see the physical location of the documents. This enables you to move documents to different directories without rewriting the HTML documents or republicizing them. When documents may move from one server to another, NCSA allows you to point to the new location without the user being aware. You can, for example, make a directory appear like it is in the tree on your main server, but in actuality all the files exist on another server at another location.

An effective benefit of this feature is that you can move large or popular documents to a new server so that the traffic can be spread around. The rest of your files need not be re-referenced, and your directory structure will appear seamless and familiar to your users.

Resource Efficient

A great benefit of NCSA httpd is that it has little impact on system resources, as well as its capability to serve a large number of documents simultaneously. With the release of version 1.4, the performance is top-of-the-line. NCSA makes very efficient use of memory, and little tricks, like having a pool of waiting server processes ready, ensures that new requests are quickly handled.

Another benefit to stressed out system administrators is the ability, under NCSA httpd, to allow users to serve files to the Web from their own directories with no aliasing required. This allows users to have their own directory whose contents can be made available for HTTP access without you having to create links to them.

In the past, webmasters had to create directories for each user who wanted a homepage. For schools and large companies, this is a major task. Now you can specify a name, usually *public_html*, for a directory located in your users home directories. All the files they keep in this directory are accessible from the Web simply by including *~user_name* in the URL.

Scripts and Includes

NCSA enables you to use server scripts and server side includes. This feature lets you include scripts or programs that can be implemented in addition to simple HTML pages. These scripts are run on the server machine and can provide different output based on input from the browser. They are useful for a number of purposes; some examples currently in widespread use are imagemaps, forms, and searches. This is one of the most powerful features that differentiates excellent sites from just good ones. Scripts and programs can provide the most useful information if they are well implemented. One example that everyone frequently uses is search engines. These services take a search string that you supply, and a server side script will pass it to a database and return a list of relevant pages. *Server side includes* allow you to include the output of commands or programs, which will change over time. An example could be the inclusion of access counts or the current date and time on the header of your page.

Security and Access Control

NCSA also supports a number of security features. Directories can be protected so that only requests from certain domains will be served. If a user's browser supports user authentication, then that user will be asked for a userid and password before he is granted access to certain files or directories. These features allow you to limit outside access, as well as to charge for access to particular information. One area where NCSA httpd is lacking is in encryption support. The vast majority of browsers in use either support Netscape's SSL encryption technology or none at all. The fault is not of the server software, but that most browsers cannot make use of the encryption features.

Downloading NCSA httpd

To install NCSA httpd, you must first get a copy of the source code or a precompiled binary. NCSA has made available binaries for the following platforms:

Silicon Graphics, Inc.
SGI Indy, IRIX 5.2.

Sun Microsystems
SPARCserver 690MP, SunOS 4.1.3.

Sun Microsystems
Sparc 20, Solaris 2.4

International Business Machines
IBM RS/6000 Model 550, AIX 3.2.5

Hewlett-Packard
HP 9000 model 715, HP-UX 9.05

DEC
Dec Alpha, OSF/1 3.0

Intel-Based PC
Pentium 90, Linux 1.2.7

The binaries are available by FTP at ftp.ncsa.uiuc.edu in the directory /Web/ncsa_httpd/current/ and the file is httpd_*your-system*.tar.Z

If your system type is available as a binary, then your installation process is somewhat simplified. If you have to compile, then you can step to the next step.

To install the binaries, you need to decide in which directory the files will reside in (usually /usr/local/etc/httpd). Copy the tarred file to that directory and uncompress and untar it using this command:

```
uncompress file_name
```

```
tar -xvf file_name
```

The files and directories should expand into their appropriate directories. Once this has occurred, you are ready to configure the system.

Compiling NCSA httpd

If you need the server for a platform that was not listed previously, you will have to get the source and compile it yourself. The source is located at the same place as the previous binaries, but it is called http_source.tar.Z.

The first step in compiling the server is to create the directory where httpd will reside. This is up to you, but the usual location is /usr/local/etc/httpd. Download the source to /usr/local/etc and uncompress it. Untar the source using **tar -xvf source_name** and the files and directories should be created for you.

Before compiling, edit the Makefile in src/Makefile. Set the correct AUX_CFLAG by uncommenting the line that corresponds to your system if it is available. To compile the server, you must compile three separate items: the server, the scripts, and the support programs; the Makefiles are located in /src, /cgi-src, and /support respectively. Use the **cat Makefile | more** commands on the Makefile to find the name used for your particular system as it appears in the file, then build the binaries by typing **make linux** (if you were running a Linux system).

Follow this procedure in each of the three directories. After you have created the binaries, edit the configuration files as described in the following sections to ensure that the server runs correctly.

Configuring NCSA httpd

There are three configuration files you need to edit before NCSA httpd will run correctly: httpd.conf, access.conf, and srm.conf. You will first see the minimum changes you need to make to get httpd running. In the next section, you will see how to configure the more advanced features and set up services such as user authentication.

The httpd.conf Configuration File

The first file you will need to edit is httpd.conf. Open it using your favorite text editor and make the following changes. You do not have to edit every directive in the configuration files, but you should read through them all to familiarize yourself and to make sure you do not miss an important command.

ServerType

The first server directive is *ServerType.* There are two choices, inetd or standalone. The difference between them is that inetd causes the system to handle the socket and child management, and standalone allows the server to handle them. When httpd is run under inetd, the system loads httpd as a new process and parses all the configuration files before it can begin to serve the request. This is contrasted with standalone where httpd makes a copy of itself, which requires no loading of binaries, and can start serving files much sooner.

Syntax: `ServerType standalone`

Port

The next directive is *Port,* which is the port that standalone listens to. If you insist on running inetd, you can skip to the next directive, ServerAdmin. Generally, you will run httpd on port 80, but you have to start httpd as [root] to use ports lower than 1023. If you are not root, therefore, you will have to pick a larger port.

Syntax: `Port 8080`

User

The directive *User* tells the server which user ID the server's children will answer as. To use this directive, the standalone server has to be run as [root]. Normally, you can leave this as the default setting of User #-1

Syntax: `User userid`

Group

Following User is the *Group* directive. Only one Group directive can be used and this group name must be found in /etc/group. This can also be left as the default of Group #-1

Syntax: `Group groupid`

ServerAdmin

ServerAdmin is a directive where you can store an e-mail address so users can notify you if an error message is given. If you leave this address out, httpd will not assume any address and will simply give no response address during an error.

Syntax: `ServerAdmin cyote@acme.dynamite.com`

ServerRoot

The *ServerRoot* directive is the root directory for httpd. The server expects to see the directory tree including conf and cgi-bin under the root directory. This is so the server knows where to find the configuration files. Try not to stray from the standard configurations because other directives and configuration files will use this root directory for other relative paths. The default directory is /usr/local/etc/httpd/.

Syntax: `ServerRoot /absolute/path/`

ServerName

The *ServerName* directive is used to define a hostname should the server be using a DNS alias.

Syntax: `ServerName www.acme.com`

If you do not specify a ServerName, httpd attempts to find it through a system call. If you want your HTTP server to run using a different DNS alias than the host machine, use this directive. Make sure that this is a valid name; you cannot just make one up.

StartServers

StartServers defines how many children NCSA httpd will launch at startup. This is a pool of servers that wait until requests come in. By having these children launch at startup, the server saves time on each request by not having to load a new copy of itself. This directive works in combination with the next directive, MaxServers. As more processes are required, children of the process stay around as long as there are less than the MaxServers value. If more copies than MaxServers are required, then these extra processes will die when they are finished. Linux's compiler currently does not support file descriptor passing, and you will have to comment out these two directives before NCSA httpd will start under Linux. Hopefully, this fault in Linux will be fixed soon because these extra servers are the reason most of the efficiencies that make NCSA httpd run so fast.

Syntax: `StartServers 5`

`MaxServers 20`

TimeOut

TimeOut sets the elapsed time, in seconds, that the server will spend waiting for a client to accept information. If you plan to serve large files over slow networks, such as dial-up lines, you should have a large time out. Eight hundred to 1,200 seconds should be fine for files less than 1 MB if your minimum speed is a 14.4 modem.

Syntax: `TimeOut 600`

ErrorLog

The log files are useful to a webmaster for diagnosing problems and tracking usage. If you are sure you have no use for any log files, they can be disabled by substituting /dev/null for the filename by entering the directive as: `ErrorLog /dev/null`. The ErrorLog directive tells NCSA httpd in which file to record error occurrences. As of version 1.4, it logs the following errors:

- Client time outs
- Bad scripts (no output)
- .htaccess files that attempt to override things they do not have permission to
- Server bugs that produce segmentation violations or bus errors
- User Authentication configuration problems

The standard location for the log files is the directory /ServerRoot/logs. If the directory does not already exist, you will have to create it.

Syntax: `ErrorLog logs/error_log`

TransferLog

TransferLog is a log file which records client accesses. It is also a useful logfile because it provides a way to analyze your server traffic. There are many shareware logfile analyzers available on the Internet that will produce reports based on your logfiles, or you can write a simple one yourself.

The logfile format is similar to the following:

```
host rfc931 authuser [DD/Mon/YYYY:hh:mm:ss] "request" ddd bbbb
```

All of the above fields are fairly obvious except:

- rfc931: information returned by identd for this person
- *ddd*: the status code returned by the server
- *bbbb*: the total number of bytes sent

Syntax: `TransferLog logs/access_log`

AgentLog

AgentLog records the user browser or agent. This may be useful for statistical purposes, if, for example, you want to know how many of your users are using Netscape. Other than that, it seems to be somewhat useless.

Syntax: `AgentLog log/agent_log`

RefererLog

This is a log file that stores referrers. A *referrer* is the document that contained the link to the requested document. This can be useful for tracking usage patterns around your site or the links from which people discover your site.

Syntax: `RefererLog logs/referer_log`

RefererIgnore

This tells httpd to avoid writing to the referrer log any lines coming from a given place. You place a string after the directive, and if the string matches part of the Referrer header, then the line is not logged.

Syntax: `RefererIgnore string`

PidFile

The *PidFile* directive sets the file to which httpd will record the process ID of each httpd process. To disable it, set PidFile /dev/null. You normally should not have this file disabled because it is used to simplify the task of restarting the server.

Syntax: `PidFile logs/pidfile`

AccessConfig

AccessConfig sets the file where NCSA httpd can find the access configuration file. This file is very important for managing authenticated users, as well as restricting access to certain parts of the Web site. The file is usually found in conf/access.conf. You will be editing this file in the section "The access.conf Configuration File."

Syntax: `AccessConfig conf/access.conf`

ResourceConfig

The resource configuration file, which will be edited in a later section, describes various methods of controlling the appearance of your Web site. Among other things, it decides if users may have their own homepages, and how indexes will look.

Syntax: `ResourceConfig conf/srm.conf`

TypesConfig

The *TypesConfig* directive gives httpd the location of the typing configuration file. The TypesConfig file maps filename extensions to MIME types. If you want to support additional MIME types, you should not edit the TypesConfig file, but place the information with the AddTypes directive in the srm.conf file instead.

Syntax: `TypesConfig conf/mime.types`

IdentityCheck

This directive enables RFC931-compliant logging of the remote username for sites that run identd. This information is logged in access_log. Do not trust this information to be accurate, and indeed many sites will not be running a supported process. If you have no direct use for this information, it is better to keep the directive off to save on bandwith.

Syntax: `IdentityCheck off`

The srm.conf Configuration File

The resource configuration file is essential to the operation of a Web site. Beyond defining directory aliases and document location, it enables you to access some features which will save you a great deal of time.

One example is a directive that allows your system's users to set up a homepage. On other servers, you might have to alias each individual who wants a Web page. Using the UserDir directive, you can allow every user to have a homepage, provided they put the files in a standard directory directly off of their home directory. An outsider who wants to view one of the user's homepages would simply reference `http://www.acme.com/~user/`.

Other important aspects of this configuration are the aliasing capabilities, which allow long directory paths to be called using a shorter or easier-to-remember alias. More about the individual alias directives will be included in the directive description.

The following are the directives for the resource configuration file, which is usually located in conf/srm.conf or the filename you defined in httpd.conf.

DocumentRoot

The *DocumentRoot* directive defines the root directory from which httpd will serve files. Only files located below this root directory can be accessed by the server. If you have to give access to other files on the system, they can be accessed using the alias directive or by creating a link to the desired file.

Syntax: `DocumentRoot /usr/local/etc/httpd/htdocs`

UserDir

UserDir defines the directory in a user's home directory that can be used to serve files. If UserDir is set to public_html, then the client request for

/~user/file would be aliased to /home/user/public_html/file or whatever the user's home directory is given as in /etc/passwd.

Syntax: `UserDir public_html`

If the keyword DISABLED is substituted for the directory name, the user directory feature will be turned off.

DirectoryIndex

NCSA httpd can generate an index for a directory if the client does not request a specific file. Use *DirectoryIndex* to set the name of the file that will be served if no specific filename is given. The de facto standard is index.html. This means that if you do not want clients to see an index of your directories, then you would create a page called index.html, and that would be the default file.

Syntax: `DirectoryIndex index.html`

AccessFileName

This is the name of the file that contains access restrictions. It can restrict access to certain directories or branches based on user groups or authentication. Refer to the section on configuring the access.conf file for more details.

Syntax: `AccessFileName .htaccess`

AddType

This directive enables you to add entries to the server's default MIME type information. It causes a certain file extension to be mapped to a specific MIME type. AddType directives override entries in the file defined by the TypesConfig directive.

Syntax: `AddType type/subtype extension`

Example: `AddType text/plain txt`

Type/subtype is the MIME type for the document, and *extension* can be either of a filename extension, a filename, or a complete pathname. You can use as many AddType directives as you want, and you must use them when serving new types of files, such as PDF or MPEG.

AddEncoding

This directive enables you to serve encoded documents to a client. For clients who support the encoding scheme, the document is decoded upon receipt. Otherwise, the document is saved to disk.

Syntax: `AddEncoding type extension`

Example: `AddEncoding x-gzip gz`

Where *type* is the encoding type for the document, and *extension* is the filename extension for this encoding. You can use as many AddEncoding directives as you want.

DefaultType

If httpd cannot discern a file's type through the AddType or TypesConfig directives, it will send it using DefaultType.

Syntax: `DefaultType type/subtype`

The default assignment is DefaultType text/html.

Redirect

This directive causes requests for redirected files to be translated to a request from a different server. This is useful if you move documents from one server to another but cannot change all links to the old location.

Syntax: `Redirect virtual URL`

Example: `/location http://new.acme.com/location`

Alias

The *Alias* directive creates a virtual directory or document on this server. This directive provides a means to make long or complicated URLs easier to remember, or gives them a more prominent position without arranging your physical directory structure. You can include as many alias directives as you want.

Syntax: `Alias virtual path`

Example: `Alias /dynamite /products/descriptions/dynamite`

ScriptAlias

The *ScriptAlias* directive creates a virtual directory which serves CGI server scripts. You will usually want to assign the /usr to /cgi-bin so that script calls are easier to implement. You can include several of these aliases.

Syntax: `ScriptAlias virtual path`

Example: `ScriptAlias /cgi-bin/ /usr/local/etc/httpd/cgi-bin/`

OldScriptAlias

The *OldScriptAlias* directive sets the virtual directory from which the server returns the output of an NCSA server script.

Syntax: `OldScriptAlias virtual path`

Example: `OldScriptAlias /htbin /usr/local/etc/httpd/htbin`

FancyIndexing

This directive specifies whether fancy directory indexing (with icons and file sizes) or standard directory indexing is generated. It does not really matter which one you use, but fancy looks better.

Syntax: `FancyIndexing on`

ReadmeName

This directive enables you to create a file that gives a description for the contents of a directory. NCSA httpd automatically adds the contents of the readme file to the end of the index it generates.

Syntax: `ReadmeName README`

HeaderName

HeaderName adds a custom header to a directory index. It displays the header file as plaintext at the top of the directory index.

Syntax: `HeaderName HEADER`

AddDescription

You can add a single line description to go beside a filename in your directory index. It is somewhat important to keep the description small and concise. You can have as many AddDescriptions declarations as there are files.

Syntax: `AddDescription "description of this file" filename`

The output will look something like:

```
no_description.txt (800 KB)
filename : description of this file
```

AddIcon

AddIcon tells httpd what kind of icon to show for a given MIME filetype in a directory index.

Syntax: `AddIcon icon name1 name2...`

Example: `AddIcon /icons/image.xbm .gif .jpg .xbm`

AddIconByType

This directive lets httpd know which icon to show for a given filetype in a directory index. You can use multiple AddIconByType declarations.

Syntax: `AddIconByType icon type1 type2...`

Example: `AddIconByType /icons/image.xbm image`

IndexIgnore

IndexIgnore tells the server to ignore all files with a certain extension, in addition to individual files during the indexing of a directory. The syntax example will omit the file INDEX_README and any file with the gif extension from the directory index.

Syntax: `IndexIgnore INDEX_README gif`

IndexOptions

IndexOptions specifies a number of indexing options in one directive. You can select fancy indexing and a number of other, less important options.

Syntax: `IndexOptions opt1 opt2...`

The options are as follows:

- IconsAreLinks makes the icons part of the anchor for the filename.
- ScanHTMLTitles causes httpd to fill in the description field of an HTML file with its title.
- FancyIndexing turns FancyIndexing on.
- SuppressLastModified will cause httpd not to print the last date of modification in index listings.
- SuppressSize will cause httpd not to print the size of the files in index listings.
- SuppressDescription will cause httpd not to print descriptions for any files.

ErrorDocument

This specifies an error message to send instead of the standard bulletin.

Syntax: `ErrorDocument type filename`

Type is one of the following:

302—REDIRECT

400—BAD_REQUEST

401—AUTH_REQUIRED

403—FORBIDDEN

404—NOT_FOUND

500—SERVER_ERROR

501—NOT_IMPLEMENTED

Example: `ErrorDocument 500 /oops.html`

The access.conf Configuration File

To get your server up and running initially, there are only two lines in the /conf/access.conf file that you have to change. In the first uncommented line, you have to change the default directory to your server root directory, but chances are this will remain the default of /usr/local/etc/httpd. In the fourth uncommented line, you should change the directory to the document root directory, usually usr/local/bin/httpd/docs. These are the only lines you have to change initially, but this file is very useful for setting up some other server functions.

The access.conf file defines directories that are only accessible to certain users or groups of users. To learn more about how to set up access restrictions, refer to the access section.

Starting Your Server

If you were working on the configuration files and building the source in a working directory, then you will have to move all the files into the directories you specified in the configuration files. Once the directories and files are in place, do a final check to ensure that all the requirements are met.

1. The configuration files are edited correctly.
2. The configuration files are located in their specified directory.
   - Configuration files in ServerRoot/conf
   - Log files in ServerRoot/logs

- Support files in ServerRoot/support
- cgi-bin scripts in ServerRoot/cgi-bin
- httpd the server binary itself

3. You have created the specified directory for the log and made sure that the directory is writeable for User.
4. Use the mkdir command to create the directory httpd/htdocs.

To start the server as standalone, you can simply type the following from the server's root directory.

```
/usr/local/bin/httpd# httpd &
```

If all went according to plan, you should be ready to serve files. To test the server, start Netscape or another browser by your usual method and enter **http://*your.server.name*** in the location field and press Enter.

Maintaining Your Web Server

Now that you have an HTTP server up and running, you will have to maintain it as the needs of your Web site change and grow. From an initial offering of documents and other information, you may want to expand into subscription information; in other words, make certain documents available to certain users. You might have an interest in online sales. Selling over the Web vastly complicates the issues and really requires professional developers to ensure security and an easy-to-use system. There are other issues that a webmaster should be able to address, such as users wanting home pages and management demanding more advanced services. These issues can be addressed in the scope of this chapter, although not in depth, and a system administrator usually will not have time to learn all that is required to make some of these changes without the help of additional instruction or consultation.

The best way to keep an easy-to-manage HTTP server is to plan the structure from the beginning. This is easier said than done since you rarely will know what the purpose of the site will be in a few months, nevermind a year from now. Despite this uncertainty, there are few common-sense rules that will help you.

- Do not simply dump all your HTML files in one directory.
- Keep the directory tree as short as possible.
- Let users have their own directories, but disable some features for added security.

To get the most out of your server, there are some small issues you should be familiar with.

Uniform Resource Locators (URLs)

A Uniform Resource Locator (URL) is the address of a particular document. Every file on your server will have a URL of the form `http://server.name:port/path/to/file.html`. If the port is omitted, then port 80 is assumed. All URLs are made with reference to your DocumentRoot path or to the alias paths you created during the configuration.

It is important to keep in mind the length of the URLs that users might have to type. Try to keep them short and self explanatory so users have an idea which type of information the current page displays. For example, the following line…

```
http://158.95.22.80:8080/~bsd3156/000a/334-123/doc_1.html
```

…is not as clear as this:

```
http://www.acme.com/products/sales/dynamite/TNT.html
```

For this reason, try to pick a clear and concise way for organizing and naming your files and directories.

Changing the Configuration Files

As you get more confident and experienced as a webmaster, you will want to have more features available on your site. As your site grows, you may want to add user groups and access restrictions. These changes will require modifying the access.conf file and are examined with a detailed example in the section on access control.

When you make changes to the configuration files, you will have to restart the server for the changes to take effect. To restart the server, type the following:

```
kill -HUP 'cat logs\pidfile'
```

Using the Log Files

The log files play an important role in analyzing the statistics for your website. They record information about access times and volumes, and should be used as tools to improve the quality of your site. You can write programs to sift through this data—perl being especially useful for this task—or get one that is already in existence. One that is very popular is called WebStat, and is distributed on the Internet.

If you want to play with the data in your log files, you have to be careful when running the server in standalone mode. You should move or copy the log files to the new position and restart the HTTP daemon right away. You can then perform whatever atrocities you want on the moved log files. Errors will result if the log files go missing while httpd is running. If httpd is re-started and the logs have been moved, it simply creates new log files.

Installing the Imagemap Script

Imagemaps are special pictures whereby clicking on different parts of the image will send you to different files as if different parts of the picture pointed to different URLs. To have the ability to use imagemaps in your pages, you have to compile the imagemap.c source and place the executable in the cgi-bin directory. Almost every page with graphical content will use imagemaps, and you will cause a lot of headaches for your users and HTML page designers if you inadvertently forget to install the imagemap script.

To compile the imagemap.c program, change directories so you are in the httpd/cgi-src directory. If you want to build all the supporting programs at this time, you can type the following:

```
cat Makefile ¦ more
```

Scroll through this file until you find the name of your system, then type:

```
make your_system
```

Your_system should be exactly the same as it appears in the Makefile.

If you do not want to build all the accessory files or your system is not available in the Makefile, you can follow the following procedure:

```
gcc -c -g imagemap.c
```

You may have to replace gcc with the C compiler that is available on your system. When this is done, type the following line:

```
gcc imagemap.o -o ../cgi-bin/imagemap
```

Now the imagemap program is compiled and located in the cgi-bin directory. Your users can now implement imagemaps without requiring imagemap configuration files as was the case with older versions of this program. To make use of imagemaps in your HTML pages, you can refer to virtually any book about HTML or at hundreds of online HTML and imagemap resources.

Forms Support

One of the first value-added features that is implemented on a system is forms. A *form* is a page with locations for a client to type in information and send it to your server. As a system administrator, it is your job to provide the foundation so that programmers and HTML page designers can provide dynamic and pertinent information to the users. Forms are an excellent way to get information from your users, or to provide them with an interface to various features of your system. Everything that is required to handle forms is built into NCSA httpd, so there is nothing extra that you will have to do as an administrator to support these features. You might want to be careful with the security implications of letting your users install scripts because, when run, these programs effectively have [root] privileges. You will therefore want to check the source code for any file installed in the cgi-bin directory, or, if this is not possible, only give access for trusted users.

For information on how to design and implement forms, refer to the chapter about forms. You will find an excellent introduction to using the Web as a database interface in Chapter 20, "Introduction to Perl and Oracle CGI Scripting."

If these rules are followed, and you can get the support files for basic Web features set up, then your Web site will run smoothly, and your administration jobs will be few and far between. Inevitably, there will be a growth of services, if only for the simple reason that you may be missing a large source of revenue by giving away information for free. An important issue with commercial servers is keeping certain information out of prying (and non-paying) eyes. This brings up the issues of securing access to all or portions of your server. To control access, you have to edit various portions of the access.conf file.

Access Control

Access control comes in several forms. The first is user authentication. *User authentication* is the process whereby a client is prompted for a userid and password when he selects a secure document. If you have a browser that supports user authentication—Netscape and Mosaic are two—then you will be admitted to the document and any other document that your userid satisfies. You will not have to be authenticated again unless you try to access files to which your current userid does not have access.

To create users, NCSA httpd ships a program in the support directory called *htpasswd.* Here is an example of how to secure a directory for single user access. Say you are the Acme Dynamite company, and you want to protect the directory called /ordering. The only users you want to have access are Coyote. The first thing to do is create a file called .htaccess in the /ordering directory. It should look something like this:

```
# Begin
AuthUserFile /somedirectory/.passwdfile
AuthGroupFile /dev/null
AuthName ByPassword
AuthType Basic

<Limit GET>
require user coyote
</Limit>
#End
```

Your next step is to create a password file. To do this, use the htpasswd program supplied in the support directory. Create a password by typing the following line:

```
htpasswd -c /somedirectory/.passwdfile coyote
```

The program asks you to supply the password twice. Once this is done, your directory is secure from anyone who does not know the name and password of Coyote.

Your next problem is to restrict access of a directory to a group of users. Now assume that the user Roadrunner has earned his blasting license and wants access to the ordering directory. You will want to set up a group for all registered buyers; it will be called "toons." The first step in creating group access is to start a group file. This file will list all the valid members of that group and will be called .groupfile. It would resemble the following:

```
# Begin .groupfile

toons: coyote roadrunner yosemite

# end .groupfile
```

To give toons access to the /ordering directory, create a password entry for each of them using htpasswd, like in the example, except leave out the -c option, which creates a new password file. Next, you have to edit the .htaccess file in /ordering so it appears like this:

```
# Begin
AuthUserFile /somedirectory/.passwdfile
AuthGroupFile /somedirectory/.groupfile
AuthName ByPassword
AuthType Basic

<Limit GET>
require group toons
</Limit>
#End
```

Now this directory is protected against any access except by anyone in the group toons. Through the use of scripts and programs, you can automatically add users to groups. This is not very secure, but it provides a good way to keep track of users or provide special services. If your protected files are somewhat sensitive, using the automated method to add users to a group is not recommended; instead, you should add these individuals separately. If your files are very important, protecting them with httpd is not recommended, nor is having them located on a server with outside access.

Security Issues

With all the benefits that came about with distributed computing and open networks, there also come a great deal of security concerns. These problems are inherent with non-secure computing in general and are not specific to HTTP servers. There are several areas of concern that should be noted, such as the following, especially if you will be conducting commercial operations using your HTTP server.

- Unauthorized access to sensitive files
- Eavesdropping on confidential transmissions
- Theft or destruction of important information

Tip

> Probably the best rule of thumb is that if information is too important to be seen or destroyed, do not protect it with an HTTP server.

Virus Threats

The HTTP protocol defines that a client read and interpret data that is downloaded from a server on the Internet. If the proper precautions are not taken, there is nothing to stop the passage of viruses, malicious code, and so forth.

Due to this concern, many companies have decided to set up *firewalls.* These barriers, which come in different forms, can help to isolate and protect a LAN from the Internet, while still providing access. Most firewalls come as either turnkey solutions from LAN security experts, or as software toolkits that programmers can use to create and interface with their own firewall. A firewall can define the blockage of certain services or access to certain sites, as well as providing one-way access to a network. A firewall may, for example, allow members of your LAN access to the Web, but will not allow HTTP requests to come in to you. However, URLs support Gopher, WAIS, NNTP, Mailto, Prospero, FTP, HTTP, Telnet, and RLOGIN, which do not operate under the same channels that would be blocked out by the firewall—that is, it does not use the same process of opening a TELNET session as a node would. Therefore, it is possible to subvert the intentions of the firewall. In general, there are a wide variety of security solutions that use the name "firewall," and they all have different methods of operation. If you are on a firewalled LAN, you will have to contact the vendor to determine if you can set up an HTTP server, and if you are installing a firewall, check to see if your server will still work.

Exploitation of Network Servers

Another security issue brought about by a Web presence is the threat to a corporation's network servers. These threats include the unauthorized modification of server data, access to userids, passwords, access to sensitive server data, and the complete downing of the server through the exploitation of any bugs in the Web server software employed.

Because HTTP allows several methods for writing data to a server, it is possible that these methods could be used for an ulterior purpose. While work is still in development to secure HTTP servers, nothing concrete is currently available at the time of this publishing, and you are putting your faith in the programmers who developed the HTTP daemon.

Note Although the previous issues are important for securing the site, most of today's security developments have occurred in the field of transactions between the client and server. These developments have occurred in authentication, confidentiality, and integrity. Such developments are so pervasive because it directly affects the most lucrative aspect of the World Wide Web—electronic commerce.

Authentication

Authentication is very important for electronic commerce. *Authentication* allows a server to recognize valid users. This authentication must also occur, however, by the client which must recognize a valid server. This authentication must be robust so that it is not easily cracked.

Confidentiality

Confidentiality is important because if a client submits credit card information, the client must be assured that it will not be compromised. This is also very applicable when various types of sensitive information, such as medical records, government files, and sensitive corporate information, start traveling the Web.

Integrity

Integrity implies that the data arrives at the client or server in the exact manner in which it left. If it arrives modified, it could be an indication of a potential breach. As you can see, these three items are inter-related and co-dependent. You cannot achieve one aspect without the other.

To address these problems, several standards have evolved. No cryptographic standard can offer a guaranteed secure solution, since there must always be a way to decode the information.

Standards for Server Security

Although a secure server is still a problem with many solutions, there have been two standards in use on the server level. These two competing standards are Secure-HTTP (S-HTTP) and Secure Socket Layer (SSL). The former was developed by NCSA, while the latter is the choice of Netscape Communications Corp. At the time of this writing, SSL would probably be the method of choice because it is supported by more than 60 percent of the browser market. Netscape has indicated the intention to include S-HTTP compatibility in the near future which would allow secure transactions to occur using an S-HTTP or SSL-compliant server.

Secure Hypertext Transfer Protocol (S-HTTP)

S-HTTP is an enhancement to the object transport protocol HTTP. Therefore, it does not give any independent certification of documents or other objects outside the transfer of such objects. As well, S-HTTP is a layer independent of services offered at underlying network layers. This means that

S-HTTP coexists with other mechanisms in single transactions, each providing security at their appropriate level, even at the sake of redundancy.

The main idea behind S-HTTP is that it can provide a secure mechanism to support spontaneous commercial transactions for a wide range of applications. The design supports key management mechanisms, trust models, cryptographic algorithms, and encapsulation formats from an interaction between the client and server. S-HTTP is robust enough to handle various types of security mechanisms depending on the type of interaction between the client and server. It also provides equal treatment of both client and server requests and responses, all while preserving the underlying HTTP preferences of each.

Many cryptographic message format standards have been incorporated into the S-HTTP clients and servers. Among them are PACs-7, POEM, and PPG. S-HTTP, however, does not need a client public key certificate which supports symmetric session key operation modes. This allows spontaneous secure transactions without the need for the client having an established public key.

A major enhancement on HTTP that S-HTTP provides is the capability to encrypt documents fully so that sensitive data never has to be sent out in the clear—that is, only part of the form is encrypted. Therefore, it is not possible to isolate a certain aspect of a form as the field that contains credit card information for example. You would have to de-encrypt the whole document to discern what it contained. This flexibility gives users an added feeling of safety that HTTP fails to provide.

S-HTTP's mode of operation is to provide three independent forms of message protection. These are signature authentication and protection. Any message can be protected, authenticated, and signed or any combination thereof. S-HTTP also recognizes parties who lack a key and prearranges one before transmission, thereby ensuring security even with the most primal browsers. Additionally, transactions are coded with a 'nonce' or seal of freshness which is used to ensure that a genuine legitimate transaction is occurring.

Note *Signature authentication and protection* is one term. However, it provides three forms of protection. You can sign a message, protect a message, and authenticate a message. Neither of them necessarily involves the others, but they can involve any combination. For example, a message can be protected without being signed, or it can be authenticated without being protected. It acts as sort of a three-in-one thing.

Secure Socket Layer (SSL)

The other competing standard for secure HTTP is Netscape's SSL. This has been incorporated into Netscape's Commerce Server. SSL also provides privacy between the client and server while its protocol was designed to authenticate the server and the client for each and every transaction.

The layer works by providing a channel security to ensure a secure transaction. This channel security includes three basic properties. The channel is *private* so that messages use the same form of secret key encryption once a simple handshake defines that key. The channel is *authenticated* by authenticating the server to the client and optionally authenticating the client to the server. Finally, the channel has *integrity* where messages are transported with a message integrity check.

Using SSL, all data is encapsulated in a record—that is, the header and any following data. The most important aspect of SSL occurs when the server establishes a secure channel with the client. This SSL handshake has two phases. Initially, the client and server exchange "hello" messages. These hello messages give the client and server enough information to determine whether a new master key is needed. If one is needed, the client uses the information in the server's "hello" message to generate one. This key contains the server's authenticity certificate. After a key has been generated, the client requests a SERVER-VERIFY of that master key. Finally, once the key has been established, the client authenticates the server with that newly generated key.

After the client has authenticated the server, the second phase occurs where the server must authenticate the client. This is done through the same channel by requesting given information from the client. If the client responds with the requested information, authentication occurs and the transaction continues. If the client does not have the information, however, the error message generated will result in the closure of the channel.

Breaking Encryption

It is obvious to see that S-HTTP and SSL both perform the same things in slightly different ways. Although S-HTTP builds directly on the shoulders of HTTP, SSL is a transparent layer that was customized to conform to the HTTP standard. Though both work, it is still to be seen which one will be cracked first. Public key encryption is generally very hard to break unless there is a trap door or the key is of limited size. Even with limited keys, such as are required by U.S. export laws, the amount of traffic would make it prohibitive to try and crack every secure transmission to look for financial or sensitive data. While there is no clear winner in the race for the better secure HTTP daemon, they both provide major blockades to malicious users lurking on the Internet.

Both standards were built around four publicly known ways that could potentially break an encrypted message. These four methods, while complicated and requiring lots of resources, can still work in certain cases. These types of piracy, each of which are discussed in greater detail in the next section, are commonly known as

- Brute force
- Clear text attacks
- Replays
- Man in the middle

The worst case scenario is that public key encryption is easily crackable. This is possible because it has not been definitively proven that it is hard to factor large prime numbers (in the range of 150 digits); this is the mathematical puzzle on which public key encryption is based. If some brilliant mathematician could find a way to factor extremely large prime numbers easily, then this encryption method would be useless.

Although S-HTTP and SSL use several cryptographic technologies, usually only one constant type of algorithm is used for client/server authentication. Therefore, if someone successfully broke those algorithms then S-HTTP and SSL would no longer be secure.

Brute Force Method

Brute force attacks are done by recording a specific communication session that is known to be using a certain cryptographic technology. An algorithm would then try all possible public and session keys until it breaks the encrypted message. However, because S-HTTP and SSL use keys that are as long as 1,024 bits, it is unlikely that any person or group would engage in such a time- and money-consuming attack.

Clear Text Method

Another form of attack is the *clear text* attack. This attack is brought about when the hacker has an idea of the type of data being encrypted. The hacker simply creates a database that is indexed by the encrypted value of the known text and whose values are the session cipher key. Thereby, the hacker has created a "dictionary" that allows her to make a quick reference to see which cipher key created which type of message. However, assembling such a dictionary is a time-consuming process. As well, S-HTTP and SSL use session keys that are large enough to make the amount of hardware needed to crack such a code extremely large.

Replay Method

The *replay* attack works by recording a communications session between a client and server. Then the attacker reconnects to the server and replays the message. This might sound like a useless attack, but you could rack up charges to someone's credit card by repeating a known purchase session over and over. S-HTTP and SSL defeat this with their use of a *nonce*, which serves to authenticate the message and make it somewhat unique. Therefore, in theory, it would be impossible to predict the nonce in advance because it is based on a random set of events outside the attacker's control.

One obvious way to crack the nonce problem is to record enough sessions so that if you could determine the nonce used by the server in its hello message, you could replay the recorded session which contained that nonce. However, to record enough sessions to break a 128-bit nonce is 2^{64} sessions. And this only gives you a 50 percent chance of success; also, it is not economically feasible to construct a device that could record 2^{64} sessions and store them. Therefore, the replay method is not likely to become a cost-effective method of causing damage to SSL and S-HTTP protected systems.

Man in the Middle Method

Finally, there is the *man in the middle* method, which involves the hacker sitting between the client and server, thereby intercepting the traffic before it reaches its destination. The hacker pretends to be the server to the client and the client to the server. However, with S-HTTP and SSL's authentication certificates, this kind of emulation is not possible. Within this certificate is the server's public key and the name of the certificate issuer. The client verifies this by checking the name of the issuer, as well as the signature of the certificate.

Included with the certificate is data that has been encrypted with that server's private key. Therefore, only a legitimate server could respond properly with the certificate and private key. If a phony certificate is issued then the signature check would fail. If the certificate is legitimate, then the name check would fail unless the attacker knew a certificate authority's private key. Finally, if the attacker knew the server's certificate that caused the signature and the name check to pass, the attacker could still not properly encrypt any requests or responses because he still does not know the server's private key. If the attacker is lucky and guesses the public key, he still does not have the private key to de-encrypt any responses and view the data.

Where to Go From Here

Beyond basic site planning and installation, there are time constraints on a system administrator that limit the services she can provide. Over an extended period of time, the administrator can learn the scripting skills needed to provide more advanced features, such as forms and scripts, so users can add themselves to user groups. If you have some time on your hands and are eager to learn how to tie different aspects of your computer system together, there are opportunities to learn tricks like providing access to a database, real-time generation of HTML documents, and other custom services that are only limited by your imagination.

To find out about such services, and other new developments, you should be able to see some examples on the Web if you can recognize them. Literature on the cutting edge features will be hard to come by, so you should try to do a little surfing and newsgroup reading in your spare time to keep abreast of important developments. Few programmers can afford to give up the time and personal advantage by letting everyone know the tricks of their trade, so try to be as innovative as you can.

You will find the use and maintenance of your Web server a challenging and profitable investment for your company. With the quick and dramatic changes occurring on the Internet, you will always have room to grow and expand your services.

Building and Managing an FTP Server

by Loren Buhle

File Transfer Protocol *(FTP) is a method of copying binary and ASCII files between computers on the Internet. FTP allows files to be copied regardless of the types of computers connected or operating systems being used. If both computers understand the FTP protocol, they can exchange files. Although FTP commands vary slightly from one implementation to the next, the basic FTP structure remains the same.*

Files can be in many different formats on different types of computers; the FTP protocol can handle these variations. This chapter discusses the FTP process for users and system administrators, who often use the FTP client to obtain software from the Internet. The first part of this chapter discusses the differences inherent in FTP, explores conventional uses of FTP, and explains how users can take advantage of anonymous FTP sites. The second part of this chapter demonstrates FTP advantages for the system administrator.

Note The File Transfer Protocol is defined in the RFC 959 of October 1985.

Getting Started with FTP

To help you learn the basics of FTP, suppose you have accounts on both computers between which you want to copy files. Presuming you are already logged on to your local machine, execute the following command:

```
ftp remote-computer-name
```

This command starts the FTP application on the local or client machine. The client level FTP application sends out a request to the remote machine and attempts to connect to the remote machine. The remote machine must be running as an FTP server waiting for incoming FTP requests for a connection to be successful between the two computers.

The following output is what a user would see on the client machine after the FTP application has been executed.

```
ftp buhle.medicine.org

Connected to buhle.medicine.org
220 buhle ftp server (OSF 3.0) ready.
Name (loren.upenn.edu:buhle): buhle
331 Password required for buhle.
Password:
230 User buhle logging in.
```

Note Not all remote machines ask for a password after logging in. Some machines, such as MSDOS and the Macintosh system, do not use passwords. If your remote machines do not use passwords or if you merely want to inhibit FTP access, you can prevent the FTP server process from running, thus making it impossible to service incoming FTP requests.

When you are prompted for the Name of the user on the remote machine, the default username will be chosen as the username currently in use on the remote machine. If the author is logged in locally as "buhle," the default username on the remote machine will also be "buhle." If a valid account for "buhle" exists on the remote machine and the correct password of this remote account is entered, access will be given to the directory controlled by buhle on this remote machine. Keep in mind the username and password requested by the FTP process is of the remote computer's account. The privileges available for manipulating files in this remote account are defined for buhle on this remote machine.

Transferring Files between Machines

After the remote system has accepted the login with a valid username and password, you may begin transferring files in either direction. The `ftp>` prompt appears waiting for more FTP commands. To move a file from the local machine to the remote machine, use the *put* command. To move files from the remote machine to the local machine, use the *get* command. These commands have the following syntax:

```
ftp> get source_file destination_file

ftp> get destination_file source_file
```

The *source_file* is the existing file to be copied; the *destination_file* is the name of the newly created copy. If the *destination_file* name is omitted, the *source_file* is used.

The following output provides an example of what you might see on the client machine after successfully logging in to the remote machine and then entering the get command. Note that the *quit* command appears on the last line to denote that the file transfer is complete and that you are ready to exit the FTP application.

```
ftp buhle.medicine.org
     Connected to buhle.medicine.org
     220 buhle FTP server (OSF 3.0) ready.
     Name (loren.upenn.edu:buhle): buhle
     331 Password required for buhle.
     Password:
230 User buhle logging in.
```

```
ftp> get README
200 PORT command successful
150 ASCII data connection for README (1.2)(32bytes)
32 bytes received in 0.002 seconds
ftp> quit
```

Browsing a Remote Machine

When you access a remote machine, you first may want to review the directory of the remote system. You may not know exactly where the desired file is stored or you might just be curious and want to poke around the directory structure. The basic commands for listing directories are dir and ls. These two commands have the same format:

```
ftp> dir directory_name local_filename
```

```
ftp> ls directory_name local_filename
```

Both commands list the files contained in the remote *directory_name* and place the directory list in *local_filename*. If you neglect the *local_filename*, the directory will be printed to the screen. If you neglect the *directory_name*, the current directory of the remote machine will be listed.

Using Wildcards

If you want to be more specific when searching for files in the FTP environment, the asterisk (*) is frequently used as a *wildcard* to match an unspecified number of characters. For example, the following command might generate filenames such as lunatic or lunar-lander:

```
ftp> dir luna*
```

Exactly which files are listed depends on whether the asterisk wildcard includes the period character. If the remote system uses the Unix operating systems, the period is merely another character, and filenames such as lunatic and lunatic.txt will appear. On VMS and MSDOS system, filenames are composed of a filename and an extension, separated by a period. Because no extension was specified, the example would only return the filename lunatic. To obtain the same results on a VMS or MSDOS system as a Unix system, the following command would have to be used:

```
ftp> dir luna*.*
```

The *ls* command provides a simple list of the directory. This command is often used for producing a list of files that will be input for another program. Generation of a simple list of files for internal use with the *mget* command will be shown later. The result of the ls command appears as follows:

```
ftp> ls
150 Opening ASCII mode data connection for file list
README
file_1
file_2
subdirectory_1
wildthing
```

If the command ls filename were used, the list of files on the remote system would be stored in the file "filename" on the client system.

On most systems, the asterisk is a wildcard for any number of characters. On Unix systems, the question mark can be used as a wildcard for one character in a specific position, as in the following example:

```
ftp> ls l?re
lore
     lure
lyre
ftp>
```

In an earlier example with the ls command, a file called README.FIRST appeared in the directory. You could "get" this file, exit FTP, and read the file locally. Or, you could get this file directly to the screen as follows:

```
ftp> get README ~
150 Opening ASCII mode connection for README 1230bytes)
This is the first line of the file README
This file explains the contents and layout of this
directory and
subsequent subdirectories . . .

. . . lines deleted . . .

226 Transfer complete
1230 bytes received in 0.20 seconds (6.8 Kbytes/s)
```

Unfortunately, used in this manner, get sends the entire file to the screen, without any flow control. If the file has more lines than the screen can hold at one time, the lines will scroll by on-screen. To see the file a screen at a time, you would use the following command:

```
ftp> get README  "¦more"
```

This particular command uses the pipe mechanism in Unix to pause the screen. You must press Enter to request the next screen. The pipe feature is not universal to all versions of client FTP.

Changing Directories

To determine your current location on the remote system, use the *pwd* command:

```
ftp> pwd
/pub/directory/loren
```

When you know where you are in the directory structure, you can move around between subdirectories using the following commands:

```
ftp> lcd directory
```

```
ftp> cd directory
```

cd moves around the remote directory; lcd moves around in the local directory. The lcd command has several rules:

- If no directory is given, lcd moves you to the default directory of the client's account. This is the directory where client finds itself after logging in.
- If the command lcd .. is used, the client moves up one directory in relative motion.
- If the directory starts with a slash, lcd moves to this directory regardless of the current location, in an absolute fashion.
- If the directory starts with an alphanumeric character, the client attempts to move to a subdirectory in the current directory with the same name. This is a relative motion.

The cd command has similar rules:

- If the command cd .. is used, the remote directory immediately above the current directory is selected.
- If the directory starts with a slash, cd moves to this directory regardless of the current location, in an absolute fashion.
- If the directory starts with an alphanumeric character, the remote directory will attempt to move to a subdirectory in the current directory with the same name, in a relative motion.

ASCII and Binary Transfers

The default method for FTP transfers is ASCII. The dir and ls FTP commands illustrate this distinct transfer mode when you use either command to see filenames; two common modes—binary and ASCII—appear. A binary transfer preserves the exact bit sequence of the file on the remote system when it is copied to the client system. Keep in mind that if the bit-sequence between the client and the remote system is not identical, executable files, such as applications, might not run on the client machine.

If you have a program on a PC and use the binary FTP mode to move this file to a Macintosh, it will not be able to run on the Macintosh because the bit-sequence is different for the two systems. If the file is copied from a PC to a Macintosh and then to another PC, all in binary mode, the file should be able to be run on the second PC because the bit-sequence is the same as the first PC. Some files, such a GIF files, have a defined bit-sequence and can be processed on machines with different bit-sequences.

ASCII mode is really a text mode. The client side of FTP attempts to transfer the contents of the file in a readable fashion from the remote system. In the previous example, the bits composing the file on the PC are meaningless on the Macintosh. In ASCII mode, the client translates the file to readable text. A directory list or a README file is translated to text on the client machine so that it can be read. If the remote machine, for example, contains a document in French, and the client machine only understands English, a binary transfer would give the client an exact copy of the document in French. In ASCII mode, the client would attempt to make the translation from French to English to make it understandable on the client.

FTP does not know what the contents are of the files being transferred. If the default (ASCII) mode is set, FTP will attempt to translate to ASCII the requested file. If the file was meant to be copied in binary mode (a GIF image file, for example), the client will translate it to ASCII and irreparably damage the file after its transfer. If the file is transferred in binary mode, an exact copy is made.

The binary or image mode (I) can be set by typing **binary**. The ASCII mode can be set by typing **ascii**:

```
ftp> binary
Type set to I.
ftp> get loren.gif
ftp> ascii
Type set to A.
ftp> get README
```

Most database and spreadsheet programs store their data in binary mode, even if the data is text-oriented. To be safe, it is a good idea to transfer all files in binary mode.

Transferring Multiple Files

The get and put commands transfer individual files. To transfer several files at a time, *mget* and *mput* are used. When you transfer files, FTP by default prompts you before the transfer of each file. This is particularly useful if you want to transfer some but not all files, and when you want to prevent overwriting different files with identical names.

```
ftp> ls b*
200 PORT command successful
150 ASCII data connection for /bin/ls (127.0.0.1.1234)
red_file.doc
blue_bills.gif
howard_cook.doc
wilder.wp
wipple.doc
```

```
226 ASCII Transfer complete
ftp> binary
Type set to I.
Type set to Image
ftp> mget *.doc
red_file.doc? y

howard_cook.doc? y
wipple.doc? n
```

FTP generated comments have been omitted from this example for clarity. If you dislike being prompted before the transfer of each file, type **prompt** to turn it off. Note that the following command does not take the local copy of wipple.doc and place it on the remote machine as howard_cook.doc, as you would expect with the put command.

```
ftp> mput wipple.doc howard_cook.doc
```

Instead, this is how you move both files from the local file to the remote filesystem with the mput command. mput copies multiple files, but it cannot be used to transfer a directory. To copy all the files in the subdirectory, from a remote filesystem to your local filesystem, you need to change directories (cd) until you are in the appropriate directory on the remote system and then execute mget.

Not all mget commands are the same. This command's behavior depends on the implementation of FTP running on the local machine. mget works by internally issuing the **ls** command to generate an internal list of files to transfer and then performing multiple get operations based on this list.

Common Problems

One of the most common problems when working with FTP is to mistype the username or the password. If you make this mistake, you will receive a `Login incorrect` message. You can handle this in one of two ways: either execute a quit command and start again, or issue the user command to restart the login process. You will be prompted for the password, as in the following example:

```
ftp buhle.medicine.org
     Connected to buhle.medicine.org
     220 buhle FTP server (OSF 3.0) ready.
```

```
     Name (loren.upenn.edu:buhle): buhle
     331 Password required for buhle.
     Password:
530 Login failed.
ftp> user buhle
331 Password required for buhle.
Password:
230 User buhle logging in.
```

Although it is confusing to see the ftp> prompt even if you haven't successfully logged in, the ftp> command prompt does not have anything to do with the status of the link between the local and remote machine.

Other mistakes include misspelling the name of the remote machine, misspelling the username, or misspelling the name of the file requested. If you misspell the remote machine or request a non-existent machine, the error `host unreachable`, `connection timed out`, or `host not responding` will appear. If you misspell the username, the correct password will never let you log on. If you misspell the name of the requested file, you will receive the error `no such file or directory` or something similar. Please keep in mind that filenames on the remote system are governed by the remote system's operating system naming scheme. Thus, if the remote system is case sensitive, the file Junk.txt differs from junk.txt. Case sensitivity isn't a concern in MSDOS, VMS, or NT systems, but is very important in the proper names of files in Unix systems.

Understanding Anonymous FTP

The FTP examples cited so far presume the user has an account on the remote machine. Anonymous FTP enables a user to access a remote machine without the need for a password. This type of access is perfect for access to public domain files, such as freeware or shareware. Anonymous FTP sites have restrictions, however: Users can only get files and are restricted to specific subdirectories (using the cd command). In addition, the anonymous FTP site may only work at certain times to minimize the load on the machine.

When anonymous FTP is enabled on a remote machine, you log in with the username *anonymous* and, if asked, use your email address as the password.

You can then examine the area on the remote machine set up for anonymous users. Expect to use the *image* mode for transferring files that are not obviously text.

Creating an Anonymous FTP Server

Anonymous FTP sites on a remote server are simple to use. Setting up an anonymous FTP service on your system is slightly more complicated. To set up an anonymous FTP service, follow these steps:

1. Add the user *ftp* to the /etc/passwd file.

2. Create an *ftp* home directory owned by ftp that can be written to by anyone.

3. Create a *bin* directory under the *ftp* home directory that is owned by *root* and that cannot be written to by anyone. The ls program should be placed in this directory and changed to execute-only mode (mode 111).

4. Create an *etc* directory in the *ftp* home directory owned by *root* that cannot be written to by anyone. Create special *passwd* and *group* files in this directory, and change the mode of both files to read-only (mode 444).

5. Create a *pub* directory in the *ftp* home directory that is owned by ftp and allows read, write, and execute modes (mode 777). This is the only directory where anonymous FTP users can store files. If you want this directory to be used for retrieval only (no uploading of files by the user), change the mode of this directory to read-only (mode 444).

Demonstrating FTP Server

The following example shows the commands for each of these steps, with the entries of the system administrator in boldface. This example creates the *ftp* home directory and then the required subdirectories. The ftp directory will be under the /usrc directory.

```
# mkdir /usrc/ftp
# cd /usr/ftp
```

```
# mkdir bin
# mkdir etc
# mkdir pub
```

Copy ls to /usrc/FTP/bin and set the appropriate file permissions.

```
# cp /bin/ls /usrc/ftp/bin
# chmod 111 /usrc/ftp/bin/ls
```

Create a group only used by anonymous FTP. This group should have no other members. In this example, the group will be called "anonymous" and assigned to group 15. The new group must be entered into the /etc/group file:

```
anonymous:*:15
```

A separate file containing only the preceding line is placed into /usrc/ftp/etc/group of the anonymous FTP directory.

A user named *FTP* is placed into the /etc/passwd file. In this case, a file named /usrc/ftp/etc/passwd containing only this line will also be created. This is the entry appearing in both files:

```
ftp:*:15:15:Anonymous ftp:/usrc/ftp:
```

The uid and gid can be anything you want as long as they are not used for anything else on the system. After the /usrc/ftp/etc/group and/usrc/ftp/etc/passwd file are created, their modes should be set to 444.

```
# chmod 444 /usrc/ftp/etc/passwd
# chmod 444 /usrc/ftp/etc/group
```

The ownership of the other files is changed for the other directories. The ownership of /usrc/ftp/bin and /usrc/ftp/etc need not be changed because these directories were created by the root directory.

```
# cd /usrc/ftp
# chown ftp pub
# chmod 777 pub
# chmod 555 bin
# chmod 555 etc
# cd ..
# chown ftp ftp
# chmod 555 ftp
```

Organizing FTP Files

Files placed in an FTP archive should be organized. It is frustrating to find directories full of disorganized files because of the time it takes to list directories and discern the logical pattern for locating current and older editions of software. Whenever possible, material in an archive should be broken into logical groups. These logical groups should reside in separate directories. If your company supports sixteen products, have at least sixteen directories to support each product line. Each product line may require subdirectories to separate further such information as bug patches, archives, incoming submissions, and FAQs, as in the following code:

```
/pub
/pub/product_1/
/pub/product_1/patches
          /pub/product_1/archives
          /pub/product_1/FAQ
          /pub/product_1/incoming
          /pub/product_1/meetings
          /pub/product_2/
          /pub/product_2/distribution
                etc.
```

Individuals responsible for maintaining the contents of a specific area of the FTP archive will need appropriate write permission to place new contents on the FTP site. In addition to keeping each section current, the site administrator will be responsible for creating links to other parts of the archive, creating subdirectories, and maintaining the README and ls-lr files that describe each directory's contents. The FTP site administrator must also check security on the system; she must ensure the write-protected portions (all but the incoming directories, if any) remain protected.

Note The ls-lr file is a long-format (ls -l) recursive list of everything in the FTP archive. This ls-lr file should be shared with neighboring Archie sites so that the contents of the archive will be publicized to the world.

Standardized Naming Conventions

FTP enables users to download files (get) either in the ASCII or BINARY format. A binary file downloaded as an ASCII file is useless. Some FTP clients try to autosense the type of file before downloading it. Guessing the appropriate type of download is much easier if the archive filenames follow some sort of convention. For example, if Postscript files have a ps extension, or image files use gif, tiff, and jpg for CompuServe GIF, TIFF, and JPEG, you will quickly know what type is listed. This type of naming convention helps Web browsers, such as Netscape and Mosaic, guess the type of file and preferred method of transfer. Another reason to stick to some type of common naming convention is Web browsers automatically display GIF files if the filename ends in .gif.

Many files on an FTP archive are compressed to save disk space and decrease the number of bytes that must be transferred by the FTP client. Several types of compression are available, though some compression methods are only accessible on certain clients. Table 11.1 shows common compressed file formats:

Table 11.1
Compressed File Formats Found at FTP Sites

Compression Program	Decompression Program	File Suffix	Typical Filename
compress	uncompress	.Z	patch.txt.Z
gzip	gunzip	.z or .gz	wn.tar.gz
pack	unpack	.z	textfile.z
Stuffit	unsit	.Sit	program.Sit
PackIt	unpit	.pit	census.pit
PKZIP	unzip41	.zip	pceudora.zip
zoo210	zoo210	.zoo	monkey.zoo

Making It Easy to Find Files

Logical presentation helps users find a file among thousands. Symbolic links enable FTP administrators to use obvious names to point to archive files, making it easy for the users to find what they are seeking. Suppose, for example, you are maintaining a freeware Web server package on an FTP site. In the distribution subdirectory, you maintain the current distribution and several of the older versions. The filenames of the distribution software contain the version number of the release. The following file is version 12 of the first release:

```
wn-1.12.tar.gz
```

It is a gzipped compressed tar set. Is this the most recent release or is there some other release (such as wn-1.12a.tar.gz)? Why not set a symbolic link, using the name wn.tar.gz to point to the most current release. Thus, users seeking the latest and greatest need only download wn.tar.gz and not worry about the release number. If the user wants an earlier version, he or she can select the appropriate filename.

Symbolic pointers do not consume disk space and are fantastic aids for users. In addition to the pointer to the latest version of the software, you can include a pointer to the uncompression executable in the same directory as the compressed distribution. You could place a copy of the uncompression software in every subdirectory, but this would be wasteful, and when you upgraded the decompression software, you would have to upgrade every copy. If you kept the decompression software in a separate subdirectory, would the user know where to find it? The best setup for finding the decompression software is to place it in a separate subdirectory, then place symbolic pointers to this subdirectory in every distribution area.

Limiting User Access

The FTP administrator may want to restrict access to an anonymous FTP site because of abusive users or if the site is being overrun with users. The WU Archive FTP software enables the FTP administrator to limit access to the archive based on Internet address, time of day, or by placing information in hidden directories that only "informed users" can access. The last category of hidden directories can be done by any FTP administrator.

The WU archive software prevents access to the FTP archive by placing an entry into the FTPaccess file using the deny command:

```
deny   abc.com   /etc/ftpmsgs/denied
```

This means any user trying to access this FTP archive from the domain abc.com will receive the file /etc/ftpmsgs/denied and then the connection will be dropped. If you want to deny specific users on a site from accessing the file, specify the username in the line:

```
deny  bob abc.com /etc/ftpmsgs/denied
```

In this case, bob cannot access the FTP archive from the domain abc.com.

If the FTP archive's popularity is so great that the computer's CPU cycles cannot support the increasing load, the FTP access "limit" directive limits the number of active FTP connections from a specific class of users. If you want to limit the number of anonymous users from outside your domain (named anonym_out) to a maximum of ten users, the command sequence would be as follows (the ➥ indicates the code normally fits on one line):

```
   limit anonym_out 10 Any /etc/ftpmsgs/too_many_users.msg
Perhaps this limit can be relaxed on the weekends to a higher
➥limit:
 limit anonym_out 20 SuSa /etc/ftpmsgs/too_many_users.msg
 limit anonym_out 10 Any /etc/ftpmsgs/too_many_users.msg
Perhaps this limit during the weekday can be raised after 6pm
➥until 8 am:
 limit anonym_out 10 Any1800-800 /etc/ftpmsgs/too_many_users.msg
 limit anonym_out 20 SuSa /etc/ftpmsgs/too_many_users.msg
 limit anonym_out 10 Any /etc/ftpmsgs/too_many_users.msg
```

A simple way of restricting access to a given set of files, perhaps a new beta release of software, is to place these files in a hidden directory. Only users who know the location of the files can access them. This method uses Unix filesystem permission tricks and can be done on any Unix platform. The trick is to make a directory with execute permission and no read permission. If the user issues the commands ls or dir to review the directory, the file will appear as unreadable. Actually, the directory is unreadable. If the user knows the exact filename, he or she will be able to download the file.

The FTP Protocol

FTP uses a client-server model. The server side is implemented by a daemon called either ftpd or in.ftpd. The client side is implemented by the FTP program. Figure 11.1 shows a simplified model of FTP interaction.

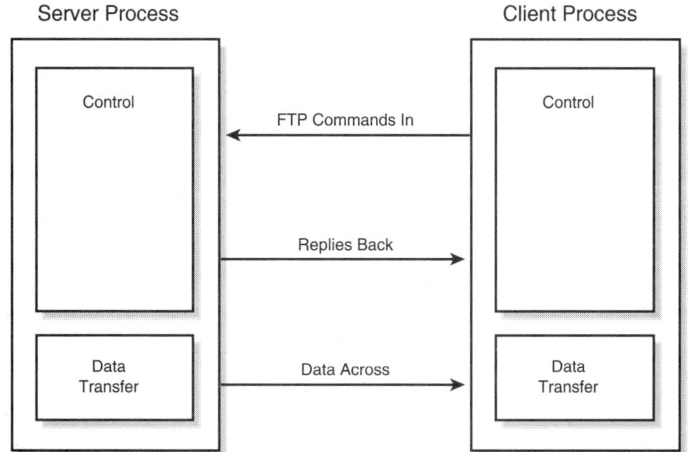

Figure 11.1
The basic FTP interaction model.

The FTP client begins each session by opening a control connection with the server. The client sends its port number and network address to port 21 using the TCP protocol. The client sends its port number and network address in the connection request. If FTP is not available on the network address, the transport provider returns a message `connection refused message`. If the request for a control connection is accepted, the FTP server sends back a reply code 220, saying the server is ready and the authentication process should begin. This reply code is a three-character digit code followed by a text string. The text string is for human use and is not fixed by the protocol. The digit code is used by the client process and is fixed by the FTP protocol. The digits can be summarized as follows:

- The first digit tells whether the reply is positive or negative
- The second digital relays the reply's category
- The third digit, presuming it is not zero, is a gradation of the reply

Table 11.2 lists several definitions of the first two digits.

Table 11.2
Explanation for the First Two Reply Code Digits

Number	First Digit Description	Second Digit Description
0	Not specified	Syntax: syntax error; command not implemented; message not fitting in other categories
1	Positive Preliminary: more to come, do not send command	Information: status or help data
2	Positive Completion: done, send next command	Connections: control and data connection
3	Positive Intermediate: request for more data, send command completing request	Authentication: login
4	Transient Negative Completion: command not accepted, try again at beginning of command sequence	Not specified
5	Permanent Negative Completion: command not accepted, do not try exact same command again	File system: status of server file system for a given request

When authentication has occurred and a confirming reply is returned, the client issues commands and the server responds with replies on the control connection. If there is data to transfer (the user has issued a command such as get, put, or ls), the server opens and manages a new connection to transfer the data. The server uses port 20 and the TCP protocol to connect to corresponding ports on the client side. The FTP command may have between 70–100 commands and command options. Table 11.3 presents the most commonly used FTP commands.

Table 11.3
FTP Command Summary

Command	Description
ascii	Enters ASCII mode, for transferring files.
binary	Enters binary mode, for transferring files.
cd *remote_directory*	Changes the working directory on the remote filesystem.
close	Terminates the local FTP session with the remote machine without terminating FTP. After using close, you can use the open command.
delete *filename*	Deletes a file on the remote system.
dir *file destination*	Generates a full directory list of the remote directory. *File* and *destination* are optional. *File* can be an individual file or a wildcard construct. If the *destination* is present, the output from the file command is stored in this file on the local machine.
hash	Tells FTP to generate a hash symbol (#) for every block of data moving from a get or put command. This command is useful if you question whether the network is functioning. *Hash* is a toggle. Typing **hash** a second time will stop its action.
help *command*	Produces documentation on the *command* on-screen.
lcd *directory*	Changes the location of the local directory to *directory*.
ls *file destination*	Generates a short directory list of the files in the directory of the remote machine. The arguments for ls are the same as for dir.

continues

Table 11.3, Continued
FTP Command Summary

Command	Description
mget *file_list*	Obtains multiple files matching the *file_list* from the remote machine. The *file_list* can be a wildcard construct or a list of multiple files.
mput *file_list*	Moves multiple files matching the *file_list* from the local machine to the remote machine. The *file_list* can be a wildcard construct or a list of multiple files.
open *machine_name*	Connects to a computer designated by the *machine_name*. This command is used when FTP accesses multiple remote machines without restarting the FTP application. The converse operation to open is close.
prompt	Used prior to the mget and mput commands to select whether the user is queried for transfer of the files.
pwd	Prints the current directory on the remote machine.
quit	Closes any existing FTP session and terminates FTP.
user *username*	Sends the username (if omitted, the user will be prompted) to the remote machine for logging in to the remote system.

Note One of the best (and free) FTP daemons to run is the Washington University (in St. Louis) version of *ftpd*. The WU FTP has many features perfect for heavy traffic sites and is being used on many major Internet FTP sites. You can download this daemon by anonymous FTP from wuarchive.wustl.edu in /packages/wuarchive-ftpd/wu-ftpd-2.x.tar.Z, where the "x" in 2.x.tar.Z is some number larger than 4.

Building and Managing an E-Mail Server

by Loren Buhle

Since the advent of the first network, electronic mail, or e-mail, has been one of the most prominent uses of networking. E-mail began as a simple service that copied a file from one machine to another, appending it to the recipient's so-called mailbox file. This model is still the mode of most e-mail implementations, although the ever-increasing complexity of the routing, e-mail enclosures, and volume of messages has made more elaborate schemes necessary. Various standards of e-mail exist, with Internet e-mail adhering to the structure of RFC 822 and augmented by various RFCs to describe machine-independent ways of transferring special characters, multimedia mail (sounds and pictures) and other extensions from the ASCII text-based foundation of e-mail. Another e-mail standard, X.400, has been defined by the CCITT.

The Linux system supports several different types of mail programs. The most common mail transport program on Linux is smail-3.1.28, written and copyrighted by Curt Noll and Ronald Karr. This shall be called *smail* and is included in most Linux distributions. This mail facility is fairly new and handles small sites with simple routing requirements. For larger sites with potentially more extensive e-mail routing requirements, *sendmail* from the University of Berkeley, has a much more flexible (and complicated) configuration scheme. Both smail and sendmail have configuration files that must be customized to the site. In addition to placing the hostname in the files, both of the configuration files are fairly complicated to configure and there are books (Bryan Costales, Eric Allman, and Neil Rickert's *sendmail*, by O'Reilly & Associates, 1993) devoted to this process.

This chapter defines e-mail, provides concepts regarding e-mail routing, discusses automated e-mail servers, e-mail ethics, and other concepts necessary to administer a robust e-mail presence on the Internet.

Components of a Mail Message

A mail message consists of a message or *mail body* containing the body of the information sent. This body of information generally is the text the sender composed. The mail message may also contain special data specifying the e-mail's recipients, transport medium and other things you would associate with the envelope of a piece of conventional mail. This latter administrative data falls into two categories. The first category is called *the envelope* and contains data specific to the transport of the information, such as the address of the sender and the recipient. It may be transformed by the transport software as the message goes from the sender to the recipient. The second category is any data necessary for handling the mail message, such as the message subject line, the list of all recipients, and the date and time the message is sent. In many networks, it has become a standard to prepend this data to the mail message in a *mail header*. This header is offset from the *mail body*. Optionally, a signature or ".sig" is appended to a mail message. This *signature* usually contains information on the author's name, address, and phone number, or a joke or motto. This information is offset from the *mail body* by a line containing '-.'

Mail Headers

The mail transport software from the Unix world uses a mail header defined in RFC 822. This RFC was designed to supply a standard for use in the entire ARPAnet, the predecessor of the Internet. As a result, the mail header became independent of its environment and has been adapted to other networks. RFC 822 has been extended by more recent standards in an effort to cope with newer needs of data encryption, the international character set, and Multipurpose Internet Mail Extensions (MIME). In all of these standards, the header consists of several lines separated by newline characters. A line is composed of a field name, beginning in the first column, followed by a colon and some white space, and then the field itself. The format and semantics of each field vary depending on the field name. A header field may be continued across a newline, if the next line begins with a TAB character. Fields can appear in any order. A typical mail header may appear as:

```
From: buhlel01@mcrcr6.med.nyu.edu <Loren Buhle>
Return-Path: <mcrcr0.med.nyu.edu>
Received: from mcrcr0.med.nyu.edu by
howard.med.nyu.edu with smtp
Date: Wed, 25 Oct 1995 18:43:29 -0500
Message-Id: <139643234.PARQ07738@amanda>
From: Mandy@AOL.COM (Mandy Whitehouse)
To: buhlel01@mcrcr6.med.nyu.edu
Subject: Your blasted e-mail...
```

All of these fields are generated by the mail client. The sender is usually asked for the recipient's e-mail address and a suitable subject line. The rest of the information is added by mail transport software. A list of some of the common header information is shown in table 12.1.

Table 12.1
Common Header Information

Field	Meaning
From:	This contains the sender's e-mail address and possibly their real name. This format varies enormously.
To:	The recipient's e-mail address.
Subject:	A general description of the mail contents as described by the sender.
Date:	The date the mail left the recipient.
Reply-To:	Optional field, specifying the address to which you want the recipient to direct their reply.
Organization:	Optional field, specifying the organization that owns the machine where the sender originated.
Message-ID:	A string generated by the mailing program on the sender's computer.
Received:	Information from every machine processing your e-mail, from the sender all the way to the recipient's machine. This shows the path the e-mail took to get to you. Each machine inserts its site name, message ID, time and date it received the message, and so on. This is how you can follow a message and complain to the appropriate postmaster if there is a problem.

Note The one exception to this structure is the first line. The first line starts with the keyword From, followed by a blank instead of a colon. To distinguish this from the From: field (generally shown in this book as "From"), it is frequently referred to as *From_*. This is a holdover from the UUCP bang-path styles to be discussed later in this chapter. This field contains the message route, time, and date from the machines handling the mail and an optional part from the recipient host. Because this field is regenerated by every system that processes the message, it is sometimes subsumed under the data envelope. The From_ is mostly around for backward compatibility with older mailers and is not used much anymore.

How Is Mail Delivered?

Mail is composed with Linux programs ranging from the very simple mail or mailx to the more sophisticated mail handling programs such as elm, mush, or pine. The user may compose their mail message on their PC or Macintosh and then use Linux's mail system. These programs are called mail user agents (MUAs). The mail message is then handed to another program, a mail transport agent (MTA), for delivery. On some systems, there are different mail agents for local (lmail) and remote delivery (rmail). Other systems support one mail delivery system.

Local mail is much more complicated than appending the message to the recipient's mailbox file. The local MTA must be capable of understanding aliasing, forwarding, and bounced mail. Aliasing involves setting up local recipient addresses pointing to other address. The most common alias used is the "postmaster" alias. Mail sent to the postmaster usually has an alias (contained in /etc/aliases) to the e-mail address of the individual designated to handle the postmaster responsibilities. Forwarded e-mail redirects a user's mail to some other destination. This is often used if a recipient has several e-mail addresses, but only uses one of them to read their e-mail. Messages that cannot be delivered for whatever reason are *bounced*, meaning they are returned to the sender with a relevant error message. If the mail involves the Unix to Unix Copy Protocol (UUCP), mail will usually not be delivered directly, but will be forwarded to the destination host by a number of intermediate systems. In this case, the MTA will execute rmail on the forwarding system using *uux*. This is a considerable amount of work for a major mail hub and thus the workload is often batched to deliver several e-mail messages simultaneously.

E-Mail Addresses

The e-mail address is composed of the recipient's user identification and the name of the machine handling the recipient's mail. The recipient's user identification is usually the recipient's login name, though it can be something else. Mail addressing schemes, such as X.400, use a more general set of attributes to look up the recipient's host in an X.500 directory server. The way the machine name is handled and how the recipient's name is managed depends on the network and their individual mailers. If the site follows the RFC 822 standard, the e-mail address will be *user@host.domain*, where *user* is the recipient's name and *host.domain* is the host computer's fully qualified domain name. These two names are separated by the "@" symbol, known as the "at" sign. This is called the *absolute address* and does not invoke a route to the destination host.

The UUCP environment used the form "*path!host!user*", where *path* described the sequence of machines the message had to traverse to reach the *host* machine where the *user* resided. This construct is called the *bang* notation, because the exclamation mark is called a bang. Mixing this type of addressing with the RFC 822 address produces a mess. Consider the address `hostG!user@hostQ`. Which host takes precedence, hostG or hostQ? Should the mail be sent to hostG, which then sends it to `user@hostQ`, or should the mail be sent to hostQ, which will attempt to use UUCP to send it to `hostG!user`? These mixed addresses are called *hybrid addresses*, and the convention is to give precedence to the @ sign and deliver the message to hostQ first. The RFC 822 document allows for a *route-addr address*, taking the form of `@hostF,@hostG:user@hostH`. This denotes a user on hostH, which can be reached through hostF and then hostG, in that order.

Finally, there are addresses that use the "%" sign, such as `user%hostM@hostN`. Mail will first be sent to hostN, which expands the rightmost % sign into an @, causing hostN to send mail to `user@hostM`. There are other conventions, but the predominate address scheme is the `user@host.domain`.

Mail Routing

Mail routing involves directing a mail message from the sender to the recipient. It also involves error checking and speed and cost optimization. There is a substantial difference in the way the UUCP site handles mail from an Internet site. On the Internet, the routing of e-mail is done via the IP networking layer. For UUCP, the route the mail takes is supplied either by the sender or is generated by the mail transfer agent. In this chapter, we will discuss only the mail routing on the Internet.

Mail routing on the Internet depends on the destination host. The default mode is to deliver a mail message directly to the IP address of the recipient's machine. Any actual routing of the data composing the mail message occurs at the IP transport layer. If a destination site has a firewall computer or a designated handler of e-mail for a company, this computer handles the distribution of all external mail to the internal addresses. This functionality of a central mail hub is announced to the outside world via the MX record of the Domain Name Service (DNS) database.

The MX record, or *Mail Exchanger*, states the server host is willing to act as a mail forwarder for all machines in this main, including traffic for hosts that are disconnected from the Internet, such as UUCP networks or internal company networks segregated by a firewall. Most MX records have a preference to them, so if the primary mailhub is unavailable, there are secondary mailhubs to handle the load. This preference is a positive integer in the MX record. If several mail exchangers exist for a given host, the mail transport agent will transfer the mail to the exchanger with the lowest preference value, and failing this transfer (that is, the host is unavailable, the host is so busy the attempt to connect times out, and so on), will try to connect to a host with a higher value. If the mail still cannot be delivered, most sites will hold the mail and attempt to deliver it again at set intervals for up to three days. After three days of being unable to deliver the mail, the mail is then returned to the sender as "undeliverable."

Note The capability to redeliver the mail is a lifesaver for administrators that must take an e-mail destination machine out of service. The administrator generally has three days to bring the machine back online before all the incoming mail is flushed back to the senders.

If all users of the domain cardinal.com want their e-mail handled by a mailhub named mailhub.cardinal.com, the MX notation in the DNS table might be as follows:

```
cardinal.com     IN    MX   5   mailhub.cardinal.com
                 IN    MX   7   backup.mailhub.cardinal.com
```

A host wanting to deliver e-mail destined for `buhle@outland.cardinal.com` would look into the DNS and realize all mail destined for the domain cardinal.com would be delivered to mailhub.cardinal.com. If this site were unavailable, backup.mailhub.cardinal.com would be used next.

National Character Sets

The RFC 822 standard is being reexamined to extend mail support beyond plain text and support various non-text messages, such as binary data, PostScript files, images, and sound. This set of new standards and RFCs covering these aspects is referred to as MIME, or Multipurpose Internet Mail Extensions. These standards would also extend the standard ASCII to support the French accents, German umlauts and other international characters. The character set used internally by Linux is the ISO-8859-1 or Latin-1 set. Any e-mail message using characters from this character set should have the following line in its header:

```
Content-Type:   text/plain; charset=iso-8859-1
```

The receiving system should recognize this field and attempt to display the message appropriately. The default type (when not specified) of e-mail messages is:

```
Content-Type:  text/plain; charset=us-ascii
```

E-Mail Services

This section discusses two types of e-mail services:

- E-mail information servers
- Mailing lists

E-mail information servers or archive servers are a type of program that receives specific requests for information and satisfies this request by sending back the requested index, file, or error message. One example is an e-mail file server, where a user sends an e-mail message requesting certain files and the e-mail file server reads the message and sends the files back. Another approach is ftpmail and wwwmail, which allow the user to access an FTP site or World Wide Web site via e-mail. These latter two categories have fallen by the wayside as direct Internet connections are becoming more popular.

A mailing list is a group of e-mail addresses that can be reached by sending a message to one address, the list address. Mail sent to this address is redistributed to all of the addresses or subscribers of the list. Subscribers have a discussion with all the participants by sending messages to the list address (that is, "posting to the list") and each mail message is broadcast to all of the list's subscribers. These lists can be maintained by list server software such as: Listserv, Majordomo, or Listprocessor. Mailing lists range in size, depending on their usage. They are used for disseminating information from a centralized source, such as to all Linux Internet Administrators. They can also be small and target a list of developers on a project. Questions and answers are posted for all to see and contribute.

Archive E-Mail Servers

Archive servers are programs that send files by e-mail in response to incoming e-mail addresses. To obtain a file, help, or a directory of the archive, the user sends an e-mail message to the archive e-mail server's mailbox requesting attention. This e-mail message usually contains one instruction per line, ranging from something as simple as **help**, to **index**, to **get filename.txt**. In the first case, the program sends the standard help file containing all of the commands recognized by the program. The "index" is usually a directory of the resources to be served by the archive server. The command "get filename.txt" varies in the syntax, but implies a request to send the file named filename.txt, as it is listed in the index.

CancerNet Archive Server

A heavily used archive server is CancerNet or PDQ, a cancer information resource maintained by the (United States) National Cancer Institute for use by patients, physicians, and the "worried well" throughout the world. Users of this service send e-mail to `CancerNet@icicc.nci.nih.gov` with no subject, and the word **help** as the message. The archive server will reply with a help file and the directory of the resources, combining the function of "help" and "index." To obtain information about a specific form of cancer, such as breast cancer, you send e-mail to the same address, and place the respective code for either the patient version or the physician version of the information. For each line, a separate e-mail reply is sent. Thus, if you wanted information about breast cancer and prostate cancer, your message would look like this:

```
To: CancerNet@icicc.nci.nih.gov
Subject:  <leave this blank or put a period ".")
cn-100013  <this will send you the physician's version for breast
cancer>
cn-200013  <this will send you the patient's version for breast
cancer>
cn-101229  <this will send you the physician's vers. for prostate
cancer>
cn-201229  <this will send you the patient's version for prostate
cancer>
```

This is a one-time interaction with this archive server. Each message line will result in only one reply, unless the reply message is so large it must be broken into several pieces and reassembled by the user. If the physician's file on prostate cancer is updated after you have retrieved it, you will not be notified. The National Cancer Institute realizes this is a flaw in the archive server and thus encourages users who are interested in the monthly updates of this service to subscribe to their list server. This is the second functionality to be discussed in the section on e-mail services. Subscribers will be sent a directory of the monthly updates. The subscribers must still use the archive server to retrieve the specific file that has been updated.

Sending Non-Text Information

Archive servers can send non-text information without resorting to MIME extensions on the recipient's machine. Pictures, sounds, executable programs, and so on, can be *UUENCODED* at the server side into 80 columns of text and sent to the recipient. The recipient must UUDECODE these files to turn them back into the non-text file. If the non-text file is fairly large (less than 32 KB), it is often broken down into parts. Some of the steps your mail takes as it is routed from the sender's machine to the recipient's machine have limitations on the size of the individual mail message. Messages that are too large are either rejected or truncated. This is less of a concern than it was ten years ago, but the concept of breaking down large e-mail messages into several packages is well established. The recipient reassembles the packages into the order specified, usually stated as part of the subject header of the e-mail. If the total package was UUENCODED, the reassembled package is UUDECODED.

List Server Services

The list server is a program to automatically manage a list of subscribers and handle message traffic. There are two general ways to manage mailing lists:

- Using a Mail Transport Agent (MTA), such as sendmail or MMDF
- Using a dedicated program, such as Listserv, Majordomo, or ListProcessor

An in depth discussion of each of these methods is beyond the scope of this book. We shall discuss the advantages and disadvantages of each of these categories of managing mailing lists.

Mail Transport Agents

Small mailing lists can be handled by the sendmail program already used by Linux. Other MTAs, such as MMDF, can be set up to handle the same problem. The list of subscribers is stored as a mail alias in the /etc/aliases file. When the MTA goes to send mail to the user named "book_authors", the program realizes there is no username identified as such and looks to the /etc/

aliases file to resolve this name. In this file, book_authors are aliased to the real e-mail addresses. A line in the /etc/aliases file might appear as follows:

```
book_authors: larry@aol.com curley@ix.netcom.com  moe@prodigy.com
```

Any mail sent to book_authors would be sent to three authors, either locally or remotely. Thus if this /etc/aliases existed on the machine with a domain name of stooges.com, e-mail sent to `book_authors@stooges.com` would be received by `larry@aol.com`, `curley@ix.netcom.com`, and `moe@prodigy.com`.

Someone with access to this aliases file is in charge of maintaining the subscription list by hand. Additions, deletions, and corrections are sent to this individual to make the changes. The changes are implemented as soon as the aliases file is processed. There are no restrictions on who, how, or what can be posted to this list. There are software packages to allow this functionality to be executed by someone with conventional privileges.

There are three advantages to using an MTA:

- No new programs are needed
- The maintenance is simple
- Allows a "personal touch" for subscribers

The disadvantages follow:

- All subscription additions, deletions, and corrections must be done manually
- Subscribers have to wait for the list maintainer if they are not available
- There is little or no control over the messages, their size, frequency, or content, without adding more software

List Server Software Packages

The list server software is used for more extensive subscriber lists where more control and automation is necessary. The three general software packages with this functionality include Listserv, Majordomo, and ListProcessor. Some of the features of these list server packages include:

- Most of the subscriber additions, deletions, temporary deletions (nomail), etc. are handled automatically, allowing the subscriber to participate within minutes of subscribing.
- Allows a moderator (human intervention) to control which messages appear.
- Allows the implementation of filters to control spamming or contributions from users who are not subscribers to the list server.
- Can distribute the messages in a *digest* form to allow bundling of an entire day's batch of e-mail messages into one message. A digest contains all of the messages normally sent during the time interval (usually one day) and may contain a summary of the subjects covered.
- Archives previous postings to a list and makes them available to subscribers. This archive may contain frequently asked questions and other information of value to the subscribers that may not have been posted to the general list.
- Provides some help in resolving bounced messages. A bounced message is one that is sent to a subscriber and is returned as undeliverable.

List Server Addressing

List servers use two special addresses:

1. An address to handle administrative details
2. Another to handle the normal message flow

The administrative e-mail address handles the process of subscribing and unsubscribing to the list server, converting to digest or undigest, setting the nomail flag to temporarily halt mail when you are on vacation, and so forth.

An example is the breast-cancer list server (using the Listserv software):

To subscribe, send a message to this address:

```
listserv@morgan.ucs.mun.ca
```

Leave the subject line blank and set the first message line to

```
subscribe breast-cancer <yourfirstname> <yourlastname>
```

E-mail received at the address `listserv@morgan.ucs.mun.ca` is interpreted by the Listserv program and the verb "subscribe breast-cancer" is executed and the user is added to this list server. If the verb in the message were "unsubscribe breast-cancer," the user would be deleted from this list server. The message generally must come from the individual's e-mail account to prevent other users from deleting specific subscriptions. The actual commands vary between the Listserv, Majordomo, and ListProcessor commands. This administrative e-mail address is often forgotten after the user subscribes. This presents a problem when the user wishes to unsubscribe and posts numerous requests to unsubscribe to the general mail address.

The second address is the general mail address where all users exchange messages. In the example above, the general address is `breast-cancer@morgan.ucs.mun.ca`. Messages posted to this list by subscribers are rebroadcast to the subscription list.

The list server is generally moderated by one or more list owners, who control the additions or deletions and potentially, approve every message before it is sent to the subscribers of the list. The list owner can also change the configuration of the list itself. Many list servers are not moderated, mostly because of the demands of time on the moderator and the implied presumption of endorsement by the moderator of any messages "approved" for list serve dissemination. This is a gray area in the legal community when a list server moderator promises to maintain a "safe, accurate, and appropriate" list. How can this be done? Is the list moderator responsible for evaluating and exploring all of the ramifications of each message to ensure no one on the list might find it inappropriate, unsafe, or inaccurate? This is impossible and some moderators are relaxing the criteria for posting messages on their list servers. Moderators have other demands on their time and a list that generates 100+ messages per day can quickly generate a backlog. Many moderators are implementing filters to flag suspicious messages. Some of the filters include restricting posting of messages to only the subscribers, removing messages from any address containing the word "Postmaster" to weed out rejected e-mail before it cascades back to every subscriber on the list, and so on.

Note There is a mailing list for people who manage mailing lists, called list-managers. This list covers discussions of issues related to managing Internet mailing lists, such as software, methods, mechanisms, security, etc. To subscribe to the list-managers list, send your subscription request to `majordomo@GreatCircle.com`, following the information received from a help request.

The previous messages sent to list-managers are stored in compressed archive files and are accessible by anonymous FTP from ftp.greatcircle.com in the directory /pub/archive. You can also access these files from e-mail by using (to the e-mail address above) the index and get commands. This list server is managed by Majordomo.

List Server and E-Mail Ethics

The culture of the Internet plays a large role in how the Internet is used. E-mail has its own set of rules and new users should be reminded of these rules. A good rule of thumb is to be very explicit about the purpose of a list server. What is the list server for and what is not permitted on the list server? When you announce the presence of a new list server, you should be explicit about its purpose, the degree of moderation, the identity of the list owner, and so forth.

You should invite people to join at their own volition and not draft subscribers from another list. E-mail flowing through your list server should reflect content that is desired by the subscribers. Unsolicited e-mail or junk mail is widely despised. E-mail originating from outside the subscriber population, especially if the material is foreign to the purpose of the list server, is also disliked.

Subscribers should use intelligent subject lines in their e-mail. When confronted with a day's e-mail of several hundred entries, the user screens the subject lines for information to be read first. The subject line should contain something relevant to the contents of the message. If the message is a reply to previous posting, the subject line should contain "RE: *old message subject*" in the subject line. It is considered a good policy when replying to a previous message to give a brief quote from the previous message of the material being addressed. This allows the casual reader to understand the context of the reply. It is not necessary to quote entire pages of the original message, but a few relevant sentences to bring everyone back to focus on the specifics of this communication. This quotation is usually done by placing a special character (such as > or ; in the first column of each line) to denote a quotation. When a message is quoted back and forth several times, the level of these characters gives a clue as to the extent of the conversation.

One of the problems with several replies to an earlier posting, using the convention of the "RE: *old message*" is thread drift. The original posting may have asked several questions or several different discussions may have emanated from a single posting. Because there are now several *threads* of conversation originating from a single posting, the original subject line becomes irrelevant. This is called *thread drift.* Changing the subject line to reflect the message content is a good idea.

E-Mail and Mailing List Security

With e-mail, it is trivial to forge the return address. A user's address, especially in the From field can be forged. Any plain-text e-mail message can easily be injected into the Internet with a bogus or forged address, giving the recipient the impression of a genuine e-mail message from `Bill_Clinton@whitehouse.gov`. Though possible, the probability is remote. Unless there is some token ensuring the identity of the sender, examine the sender's address with some skepticism. As stated earlier, the contents of an unencrypted e-mail message can be seen by a wide variety of people. You should expect the contents of your e-mail, especially if it is sent over the Internet, to be read by anyone. The volume of e-mail is very large, so it is unlikely for your e-mail to be read on a regular basis, but it is easy to do.

It is sometimes possible to detect forged messages by looking at the From: (with colon) header field and comparing its contents with the Received and From_ (no colon) field. If the pathway of the e-mail is present in the message header, does it make sense? If the header shows an IP address, does the IP address match the sender's domain name (that is, using nslookup)?

A slight security problem for list owners is the fact that they use e-mail to maintain the list. Many list owners manage the list remotely, sending their privileged commands with a list owner password in clear text across the Internet. In principle, this password could be seen and the list owner's password compromised.

Administrative Policies for E-Mail Use

All administrators of e-mail should have policies on e-mail in place for review by both their users and corporate management. Is the e-mail received on a given machine private to recipient(s)? When does the system administrator have authority to read someone else's mail? Just like the employee's use of the phone, what is the appropriate use of e-mail in the workplace? What is inappropriate use of these resources and ramifications if they are violated? These subjects should be addressed and be made known to all parties involved, before they begin using the system.

Privacy of e-mail is a large concern for everyone involved. The system administrator may maintain an archive of all e-mail traffic traversing the system, reviewing it for message bounces, and so on. How much leeway does a system administrator have to review messages? Is the system administrator required to review the contents of their users' e-mail to see if company secrets are being shared? If this falls in the domain of the system administrator, does this individual have the authority to do anything when something is found amiss? Should this authority to review and enforce company policy rest in the hands of one individual? If e-mail is being reviewed by neither the sender nor recipient, is this made public to both parties?

How long should transmitted e-mail be stored? If company business is transacted by e-mail, these records should be stored in some manner so they can be audited and reviewed by an independent counsel. Are these archives secure from tampering?

How are forged e-mail messages handled? How are message bounces or strange addresses handled? Is there a company policy against spamming other individuals? What defines spamming in your organization? Is posting the time and place of a company-wide meeting spamming? How about hourly updates to the entire company on the status of the yet-to-be-adopted kittens?

In the first chapter of this book, some of the policies behind the technical considerations of running a Web site on the Internet were discussed. These same considerations should be identified and made company policy with corporate support.

This chapter discussed the concept of a mail message, showed how these messages are delivered, and dissected the e-mail address. It touched upon the extension of the standard RFC 822 to a larger character set and suggested the role of extensions beyond the traditional text-only e-mail. At this point, the discussion focused on two categories of e-mail servers: the archive information servers and mailing servers. The advantages and disadvantages of these two methods were discussed.

Building and Managing a News Server

by Loren Buhle

This chapter discusses Usenet news from the perspective of the user and administrator. To provide an efficient implementation, it is important to understand how the user population perceives Usenet news. This chapter begins with a general description of network news, followed by a brief history, a discussion of the Usenet, and the general design of managing news.

Defining Network News and Newsgroups

Network news, also called Usenet news, is the name for the collection of ever-growing news archives and all its related programs. The data within Network news is organized into discrete discussion sets called *newsgroups.* Each of these newsgroups can be accessed by a variety of news programs to present these discussions in an orderly way. Of the 20,000 or so existing newsgroups, the user might want to subscribe to a menu composed of a few hundred selections. These selections constitute a menu of the newsgroups, such as current news in Florida, developer tips on Microsoft NT, discussions on visual computing, and so on. Within each menu is a submenu of specific message threads of ongoing discussions. The individual elements within a message thread are called *news.*

There are two parts of the news software: the client and the server.

- The news *server* is the software than handles the delivery of these articles to other machines on the network.
- The news *client,* sometimes called the newsreader, is a program that connects to a local server to allow the user to read and post news.

History of Network News

Network news was born in 1979 when two graduate students used UUCP to facilitate information exchange between three Unix machines in North Carolina. The traffic was originally handled by shell scripts. This was recoded in C and then evolved to "A" news for public release. Network news became very popular and exceeded the capability of A news, giving rise to "B" news in 1982. B news continued to grow and eventually gave rise to "C" news. Up until C news, these programs were designed around the use of UUCP networks.

Note UUCP stands for Unix-to-Unix Copy Program. This is one of the early methods of communicating between computers, usually by one Unix computer calling another Unix computer and passing files via the modem connection. This method is still used on rare occasions, when only intermittent connection to the Internet is deemed necessary.

Despite numerous enhancements to C news, the load of C news on sites that carry a substantial amount of newsgroups was substantial. The Performance Release of C news appears on most Linux distributions and is the most efficient implementation of C news to date. Unfortunately, it is not clear if C news can scale as traffic continues. To handle this ever increasing number of newsgroups and news traffic, the Network News Transfer Protocol (NNTP) was introduced in 1986. This protocol was based on TCP/IP connectivity and specifies a number of commands to interactively transfer and retrieve news articles. Several news packages, such as nntpd and Internet News (INN) were built around NNTP. *Internet News* can provide both front end and news server capability. INN is capable of maintaining a sophisticated news relay daemon to maintain concurrent NNTP links with efficiency. INN is the news server of many Internet sites.

The Usenet

The *Usenet* is a loose collaboration of sites that exchange Usenet news. To become part of the Usenet, an administrator needs only find a collaborative site, hammer out an agreement with this other site's owners and maintainers, and exchange news, or *feed*, with this site.

The basic unit of Usenet news is the article. An *article* is a message, much like an e-mail message, that the user writes and "posts" to the network. In this stage, the user is performing the same type of task as a subscriber of a list server posting a message to their fellow subscribers. In this case, however, the message comes from a newsreader and not an e-mail package.

The news package prepends an article header onto this message to allow the news software to maintain the message. This header is much like the Internet mail standard RFC 822 in that it consists of several lines of text, each beginning with a field name terminated by a colon, followed by the field's values. The format of the news header is specified in RFC 1036, "Standard for Interchange of USENET messages."

Articles are submitted to specific *newsgroups.* The newsgroups follow the example of the list servers in providing a forum for articles relating to a common topic. The newsgroups are better organized in that they are arranged in a hierarchy. This can be seen in the following sample of some of the Linux-oriented groups and is discussed at greater length in the following section:

comp.os.linux.admin

comp.os.linux.answers

comp.os.linux.development

comp.os.linux.development.apps

comp.os.linux.development.system

comp.os.linux.networking

comp.os.linux.system

The Newsgroup Hierarchy

Newsgroups are organized in a hierarchy, with the broadest reaching groups first, followed by an arbitrary number of subgroupings. The name of each group is separated from its parent in the hierarchy by a period. Thus the "rec" group stands for recreational, which is followed by music, followed by rock, and so forth, to arise in a newsgroup called "rec.music.rock."

Newsgroup Categories

There are more than 15,000 newsgroups, with many additional ones being added daily. Traditionally, these newsgroups fall into specific categories that once made sense. For example, the computer oriented newsgroups were placed in the computer hierarchy. The science oriented newsgroups were placed in the sci.* hierarchy. Some of the groups covered "the rest," such as alt.* and misc.* and now contain a fairly wide variety of newsgroups under this umbrella. An explanation of the major categories of newsgroups follows:

- **alt.** This is the "alternate way of looking at things." The newsgroups in this section have topics ranging from the truly incoherent fringe to very serious material. The alt group includes groups like alt.sex, alt.support.cancer, alt.gopher, and a huge variety of others. Because of the wide-ranging content of this subgroup, the alt newsgroups are sometimes omitted from the offering. Unfortunately, for people with cancer searching for "virtual community" support from people involved with cancer, this broad censorship eliminates such topics as alt.support.cancer and alt.support.cancer.prostate.
- **bit.** The most popular BITNET LISTSERV discussions groups are often archived in this area.
- **comp.** This is one of the original newsgroups and targets computer science and related topics, such as computer hardware and software issues, operating systems, new events, and topics of general interest to people involved in the computer field.
- **news.** This group is concerned with news of the network and newsreader software. This includes groups such as news.newsusers.questions (questions from new users) and news.announce.newusers (important information for new users).
- **rec.** This newsgroup focuses on hobbies, recreational activities, and arts and entertainment.
- **sci.** This group discusses scientific research and applications unrelated to computer science. For example, sci.med.diseases.cancer appears in this section. Other areas include many of the established scientific and engineering disciplines, including some social sciences.
- **soc.** This group discusses social issues, ranging from political to socializing and everything in between.

- **talk.** These groups are famous for long, unresolved discussions that range over many message threads, involve lots of people, and are often unresolveable. Issues like religion, how history should be rewritten, and so on, often end up in this section.
- **misc.** This is the original miscellaneous group of newsgroups that did not have a home anywhere else. Groups such as misc.jobs (jobs offered and wanted) and misc.forsale ensure this group will be here for a long time.

The following list provides a sense of the diversity of topics covered in various newsgroup categories.

- In the alt group:

  alt.sport.bowling

  alt.sport.pool

  alt.sport.baseball.phila-philles

  alt.sport.football.pro.phila-eagles

  alt.startrek.creative

  alt.startrek.klingon

  alt.suburbs

  alt.support

  alt.support.divorce

  alt.support.diet

  alt.support.grief

  alt.support.phobias

  alt.support.spina-bifida

- In the bit group:

  bit.med.resp-care.world

  bit.listserv.confocal

  bit.listserv.movie.memorabilia

- In the comp group:

  comp.databases

  comp.databases.informix

  comp.databases.ingres

  comp.databases.ms-access

  comp.databases.object

  comp.databases.oracle

  comp.databases.paradox

  comp.databases.pick

  comp.databases.rdb

  comp.databases.sybase

  comp.databases.theory

  comp.databases.xbase.fox

  comp.databases.xbase.misc

  comp.editors

  comp.graphics

  comp.graphics.algorithms

  comp.graphics.animation

- In the misc group:

  misc.consumers

  misc.consumers.house

  misc.education

  misc.education.adult

  misc.education.language.english

  misc.education.multimedia

  misc.fitness

misc.forsale

misc.jobs.contract

misc.jobs.offered

misc.jobs.offered.entry

misc.jobs.resumes

misc.kids

misc.kids.computer

misc.kids.vacation

misc.legal

misc.wanted

- In the news group:

  news.announce.important

  news.announce.newsgroups

  news.announce.newusers

  news.answers

  news.groups

  news.groups.questions

  news.groups.reviews

  news.lists

  news.newsites

- In the rec group:

  rec.answers

  rec.aquaria

  rec.arts.cinema

  rec.arts.startrek.current

  rec.arts.theater

rec.autos.tech

rec.aviation.owning

- In the sci group:

sci.chem

sci.gonitivie

sci.cryonics

sci.econ

sci.econ.research

sci.edu

sci.electronics

sci.med

sci.med.aids

sci.med.dentistry

sci.med.nursing

sci.med.nutrition

- In the soc group:

soc.answers

soc.college

soc.couples

soc.couples.intercultural

soc.culture.afgahanistan

soc.culture.african

soc.culture.african.american

soc.culture.japan

soc.culture.jewish

soc.culture.feminism

soc.religion.quaker

soc.singles

soc.veterans

soc.women

- In the talk group:

talk.abortion

talk.environment

talk.politics.china

talk.politics.medicine

Local Newsgroups

Some newsgroups are created for local use only, such as a company-wide or university-wide newsgroup. These newsgroups are generally interesting to the local community only, such as a newsgroup for a specific college class or a discussion of the local social events. Local newsgroups are named and run by the local newsgroup administrator who only needs to ensure there is no name conflict with another Internet newsgroup with international distribution.

The administrators of these newsgroups also decide what subset of newsgroups will be received from their Internet provider's centralized network news archive. The subset of news feed might provide 3,000 newsgroups with a machine load of 60–100 MB of new material per day. The news administrator may decide not to carry certain newsgroups because of the content of the newsgroup, or a particular newsgroup may be too active for the computer and its limited disk space. Indeed, a newsgroup archive containing very active groups may saturate a computer and its neighboring network, allowing for little else than newsgroup processing!

How Usenet News Is Delivered

Usenet news is enormously popular and has grown to tremendous proportions. Major university sites may clear 500 MB of new Usenet news messages per day. This news processing is more than shoveling of bytes through the network. Network news comes from a variety of sources simultaneously; for instance, some neighboring archives might maintain the comp and sci groups, but not the alt and biz newsgroups. If your site requires all of these groups, you will need to establish links to each of these neighboring archives.

Message Flooding

The coordination and flow of information follows the principle of flooding. Each site maintains a number of links or newsfeeds to other sites. Any article that is generated or received by the local news system is forwarded to them, unless it has already been received at that site. If the message is a duplicate, it is discarded. A site can examine the Path argument in the news message header field to list all of the systems that this message has visited.

Articles and their duplicates are distinguished by the message ID number specified in the Message-Id header field. The message ID combines the posting site's name and serial number into a resource at `"<serial@site>" (that is usually a file)`. For each article processed, the news system logs this ID into a history file. Each new article ID is compared against the history file to see if it is a duplicate. This list holds all unique message ID numbers to maintain an efficient way of insuring complete coverage without duplication.

Message Batching and the ihave/sendme Protocol Scheme

This scheme of message flooding is very inefficient. A simple solution is to batch process groups of articles in periodic intervals. On slower systems, news servers collect articles over a period of time and combine them into a single file, compress it, then send it to the remote nodes. This is called *batching*.

Another scheme, used by the C-news server, is to use a *ihave/sendme* protocol designed to compare message ID numbers before they are transmitted. Instead of transmitting the news messages, the message ID numbers of a batch are placed into a file, and sent to the remote node in a giant "ihave" file. The remote node compares the list in this ihave file to its history file and selects the unique message ID numbers missing. This new list is called the "sendme" list and is sent back to be satisfied. The final batch of articles is then sent. This ihave/sendme interaction works best when both sites are large, receive newsfeed from several independent sites, and poll each other enough to maintain consistency between their news archives.

Transferring NNTP News

TCP/IP network-based news uses the Network News Transmission Protocol (NNTP). TCP/IP-based sites using an NNTP news archive have two different ways to transfer news. One method is a real-time version of ihave/sendme, called *pushing* the news. Information generated at the local news server site is *pushed* to the surrounding news server sites for general dissemination. The concept of flooding, discussed earlier in this chapter, is one way for a news server to push news to the outside world. Pushing is used by the NNTP news server software and is essentially the same as the C news ihave/sendme protocol. The client offers an article to the server through tthe "IHAVE <varmsgid>" command, and the server returns a response code indicating whether it has the article or needs it. If the server needs the article, the client sends it, terminated by a single dot (or period) on a separate line. Pushing news has the disadvantage of seriously loading a server system, because it has to search its history database for every article.

The second method is called pulling the news. The opposite of pushing, *pulling* news is where the client requests a list of all available articles from a group that have arrived after a specified date. This request is performed by a NEWNEWS command. From the returned list of message IDs, the client selects those articles it doesn't have and uses the ARTICLE command to download individual articles. One of the problems with pulling news is the need to retain tight control by the server over which newsgroups are made available to which clients. The server, for example, has to ensure that no confidential material from local newsgroups is sent to unauthorized clients.

Some implementations of news clients use "convenience commands" to permit them to retrieve the article header and body separately, allowing the news to stay on a central host. A problem with this method used by NNTP-based news services it the ability for a sophisticated user to insert articles into the news stream with a false sender specification. This is called *news faking* or *spoofing* a news message. An extension to NNTP has been implemented to provide user authentication on some of the news commands between news servers and news clients.

At the news server site, the news hierarchy is kept below the filesystem hierarchy of /var/spool/news with each article in a separate file and each newsgroup in a separate directory. The directory name is the newsgroup name. Thus, comp.os.linux.answers is kept in /var/spool/news/comp/os/linux/answers.

As the articles enter the newsgroup, they are assigned a number, which serves as the file's name in the filesystem. The range of articles currently online in the news archive is kept in a file called *active*, which also serves as a list of the newsgroups active on the news archive. The archive is periodically purged, or *expired*, of articles within certain groups after a fixed number of days after they arrive. This may be overridden by changing the date of expiration in the Expires file of the news article header.

The User Perspective of News

Newsgroup users activate their newsreader software on their computer and interact with a local newsgroup server. This newsgroup server maintains local copies of a selection of the Usenet newsgroups. The user of a newsgroup may elect to subscribe to a subset of the newsgroups on this local server for his or her daily perusal of interesting newsgroups.

When users run their newsreader software (nn or tin, for example) and select a specific newsgroup, such as sci.med.disease.cancer, most newsreaders see a collection of message threads. These message threads are similar to the e-mail subject header in that the message threads segregate the contents by topic. Threading enables the user to follow certain conversations and sidestep uninteresting conversations. A user may elect to send a public message and thus continue the thread, or send private e-mail in response to the previous public message.

Not all newsreaders thread the messages within a specific conversation. Some of the less advanced newsreaders merely list all of the news in chronological order of receipt. Even without threading of the message traffic, newsgroups still present an advantage over list servers. A list server delivers e-mail to all the subscribers for every submission. For the newsreader, only the top header information of the news message is downloaded into the client's newsreader program. If the user selects a specific news message, the message is then transferred into the user's machine. This allows the user to be more selective on what is downloaded to his machine.

Eventually, the contents of a news server archive are removed from the archive. The length of time that individual news messages are stored in a local archive is determined by the local network news administrator. The length of time a message stays around is often dependent on the amount of disk space available and similar constraints. When the quota of space for the individual newsgroup is consumed, the news software will purge the oldest messages from the archive.

Note A very active newsgroup tends to limit the lifetime of a message within a newsgroup before it scrolls off. The scrolling of messages from a newsgroup appears to the user to happen in two ways.

After a user reads a specific message within a news thread, it will not appear in any subsequent news session. This focuses the user on incoming news. The user can, however, override the default conditions of his or her newsreader software and reread previous messages. Ultimately, the messages, read or unread, will scroll out of the news server completely.

The amount of time any article remains on the computer system depends entirely on how long the administrator allows these items to be stored. This can vary from days to months and also depends on the volume of traffic within a specific newsgroup.

Most newsreader clients maintain a pointer to where the user has been in the archive, returning him to the point where he left off in each newsgroup. After a user concludes a news session, the news reader client updates the local pointer indicating the last news message within each newsgroup. The next time the user starts the newsreader software, only the message headers from the unread news messages are presented. To reread previously read messages, the user must reset this pointer to an earlier time. If the message thread has not been purged from the local network news archive, the old message can be reread.

Designing a News Service

Linux provides a number of different facilities to handle electronic news. You can choose to set up a local news server on your system and operate locally or within your company. You might also choose to connect via the Internet and participate in Usenet and enjoy their worldwide news service.

There are several news servers available on the Linux platform. They all follow the same basic protocols and design. The two main servers are C News and INN. Client software can include newsreaders such as rn and tin. Your choice of a newsreader depends on your user population and their specific tastes. The news server operates independently of the news client; you can, therefore, have a completely open mixing and matching of news clients and servers. Often, users will access the news server with clients on their personal computers (Forté's "Free Agent," for example), workstations, or mainframes using different news client software. All of these clients can interoperate with the different news servers to achieve the same function. The expected differences in news servers will be the inclusion of local news groups, the choice of which Usenet groups are represented, the message storage time of these individual groups (how long before their material is deleted), and the frequency of the archive updates.

If news will only run locally on your computer, you need to set up a local server and maintain a newsreader. The news server stores the articles in the directory /usr/spool/news, and the newsreaders should be configured to review this directory for news articles.

If you want to run news over the network, there are several options available. As mentioned previously in this chapter, TCP/IP network-based news uses the *Network News Transmission Protocol*. NNTP enables a user to read and post news over a network. Most businesses and universities have one or more NNTP servers configured to handle Usenet news for the entire site. Thus, the archive of the news articles only needs to be stored in one or two computers within a given site. All the other machines on this site access this server via an NNTP-based newsreader. There are several possible configurations:

- Run news locally, with no network connection. In this case, you will need to run both the client and server on the local machine.
- Connect to the Internet via TCP/IP and speak NNTP via a newsreader to a local NNTP news server. In this scenario, neither the news server nor the articles need to be stored on the machine.
- If you have a connection to the Internet, but have no NNTP server. In this case, you can run the NNTP news server on your Linux system. You can either install a local or NNTP-based newsreader and the server will store news articles on your system. In addition, you can configure the server to communicate with other NNTP news servers to transfer news articles.

Implementation of the News Server NNTP

Both news servers and news clients were traditionally compiled by hand. Some of the news software did not use static configuration files, allowing instead the configuration options to be determined at compile time. Most of the "standard" news software will compile "as is" on Linux. This software can be obtained via anonymous FTP from ftp.uu.net in the directory /news. Necessary patches can be found on the sunsite.unc.edu site in the /pub/Linux/system/Mail.

There are a number of NNTP packages available. One of the most commonly used, called the reference implementation, is the NNTP daemon. Originally written by Stan Barber and Phil Lapsley to explain RFC 977, the most recent version is nntp-1.5.11. This package must be compiled from the source because various site-specific values must be compiled into the executable.

There is also Rioch Salz's package called "InterNet News," or INN. INN provides both NNTP and UUCP-based news transport and is more suitable for large news hubs. The kit for building INN on a Linux environment is available by anonymous FTP from sunsite.unc.edu in the /pub/system/mail directory. INN's FAQs are posted regularly on the newsgroup news.software.b.

Installing NNTP

The NNTP server can be compiled in two ways, depending on the load of the news server. All of the options for configuring this news server are defined in the macro of common/conf.h. NNTP runs as the daemon *nntpd.* This daemon can be configured as either a standalone server started at boot time from rc.inet2 or as a daemon managed by inetd. If *nntpd* is handled by inetd, the entry in /etc/inetd.conf would appear as:

```
nntp   stream    tcp  nowait   news    /usr/etc/in.nntpd  nntpd
```

If *nntpd* is running as a stand-alone server, make sure any lines in inetd.conf are commented out and the following line appears in /etc/services:

```
nntp   119/tcp   readnews  untp   # Network News Transfer Protocol
```

To temporarily store incomnig articles, *nntpd* also needs a .tmp directory in the news spool. This can be created by the following commands:

```
# mkdir /var/spool/news/.tmp
# chown news.news /var/spool/news/.tmp
```

Security Restrictions for NNTP Access

Access to NNTP resources is governed by the file nntp_access in /usr/lib/news. Each line in the file grants access rights to foreign hosts, using the following format:

```
site read¦xfer¦both¦no  post¦no  [!exceptgroups]
```

If the client connects to the NNTP port, the *nntpd* process takes the host's incoming Internet address and obtains the Internet Protocol address (192.131.131.3, for example) by reverse lookup. The client's hostname and IP address are checked against the site field of each entry in the order in which they appear. Matches may be partial or exact. If the match is exact, it applies. If the match is partial, it applies only if there is no other match following that is more exact. The "site" field can be specified using the following terms:

- **[hostname].** This is the fully qualified domain name of the host. If this matches the client's canonical hostname literally, the entry applies and all following entries in the nntp_access file are ignored.
- **[IP address].** This is the IP address in the dotted decimal notation. If there is an exact match, all subsequent lines are ignored.
- **[domain name].** This is the name of the domain, as specified by *.domain. If the client's hostname matches the domain name, the entry matches.
- **[network name].** This is the site name of the network specified in /etc/networks. If the network number of the client's IP address matches the network number associated with the network name, the entry matches.
- **[default].** Any client is allowed through.

Entries of the more general nature should be placed near the beginning of the file, as they can be overwritten by more exact matches appearing later in the file.

The second and third field describe the access rights of specific client. The second field describes the permissions to retrieve news by pulling and transmit news by pushing. A value of *both* enables both, while *no* denies access altogether. The third field grants the client the right to post an article. This third field is ignored as irrelevant if the second field says *no.* The fourth field is optional and contains a comma-delimited list of groups the client is denied access to.

In this example, three entries are shown:

```
#
# by default, anyone may transfer news but not read or post
#
default              xfer     no
#
# howard.nbc.com offers public access to the rest of the domain
# to read and post to any group EXCEPT for the local.* groups
#
howard.nbc.com       read     post     !local
#
# allother hosts at nbc may read and post
#
*.nbc.com            read     post
```

There are some experimental implementations of NNTP where the client is asked for a username and password prior to exchanging news. This uses a new NNTP command, AUTHINFO. When this command is used, the client transmits a username and password to the NNTP servier. *nntpd* will validate the username and password by comparison with the /etc/passwd file and verify the user belongs to the nntp group. Unfortunately, this works only against plain-style password databases and does not work on shadow password databases. In addition, there is the exposure of the username and password in clear (unencrypted) text. The client must maintain an account on the news server, which may be a problem.

C-News

C-news (or Cnews) has been around for many years and is mentioned for completeness. Cnews originated with the UUCP style of transmission, so many of the commands reflect its heritage. Cnews has been upgraded to use the nntp protocol. Cnews contains its own documentation for installation, which should be examined closely because the installation differs depending on the site of origin. The newspak distribution of Cnews from the sunsite.unc.edu contains working configuration files for the "Cnews Cleanup Release under Linux." In this area, you will see references to using a "doexplode" to get around some problems with Linux's bash1.12. The installation continues with a "quiz" script. Answer the questions and generally stick to the default answers. The installer may have to examine the /usr/include tree of her filesystem to find specific items in the installation, but otherwise the installation is quite straightforward. The following files to be examined prior to configuration are found in /usr/local/lib/news:

- **active.** The active file.
- **batchparms.** Batch parameters.
- **explist.** Article expiration list.
- **mailname.** Name in headers for mailed replies.
- **mailpaths.** Path to mail moderated posts.
- **organization.** Your "organization."

- **sys.** Control what you take (pull) and feed (push).
- **whoami.** Your hostname for the Path: line.

Cnews is managed by utilities. In general, a news administrator should always check to see if there is a utility to perform the task and not try to perform tasks manually. To set up newsfeeds, the script "addfeed" should be run. The active file is maintained using the "addgroup" file. Articles are expired by running updatemin. Essentially, all the functions have utilities to handle the operations and nothing should be run by hand. A sample crontab file to perform periodic manipulation appears below:

```
# take the compressed batches of news grom other systems
# and post (local) articles
20 *    * * * * /usenet/sw/news/bin/input/newsread
#
# batch the outgoing news and send it out
#
0 *     * * * *  /usenet/sw/news/bin/batch/sendbatches myfeedsite
#
# expire C-news
59 0    * * *    /usenet/sw/news/bin/expire/doexpire
#
# monitor and report as needed
#
10 5      * * *  /usenet/sw/news/bin/newsdaily
00 5      * * *  /usenet/sw/news/bin/newswatch
#
# turn processing of incoming news batches off 0630 to 1600 hrs
# to guard against saturating the computer during prime time
30 6      * * * /usenet/sw/news/bin/input/newsrunning off
00 16     * * * /usenet/sw/news/bin/input/newsrunning on
```

InterNet News (INN)

INN is one of the hottest and most recent news servers in the Unix environment. Its main benefit is speed and the complete integration of the nntp protocol. INN has been built for Linux and functions "out of the box" very well. A distribution of INN appears on the InfoMagic Linux CD, as well as several anonymous FTP sites. It can be found at the ftp.win.tue.nl site in the directory /pub/linux/ports/inn-1.4.linux.tar.gz and builds flawlessly with bash version 1.13 or later. Documentation on installation is provided and the frequently asked questions for INN comes out monthly. Archives of the FAQ can be obtained at rtfm.mit.edu in directory /pub/usenet-by-hierarchy/news.

INN works with essentially no maintenance. My crontab file has the following entries:

```
# daily maintenance, expire the .overview database and articles
➥1 0 * * *  /usenet/sw/inn/bin/news.daily expireover delayrm <
➥/dev/null
```

Other newsreaders known to work under Linux include dynafeed and slurp1.05.

Newsreader Configurations

This section discusses the configuration and maintenance of the newsreaders discussed previously. The focus is on three of the newsreaders based in the Linux environment: tin, trn, and nn. Newsreaders based in the personal computer area often need only be configured by entering the Internet name of the news server.

The most versatile newsreader in the Linux environment is tin. Written by Iain Lea, it is loosely designed around an older newsreader named "tass." tin does its threading when the user enters the newsgroup. If tin is using NNTP in a distributed fashion, it is somewhat slower. For example, on a 486DX50 machine, it takes about 30–45 seconds to thread 1,000 articles when reading directly from a local disk. Using NNTP to a loaded news server, this can take about 5 minutes. If the local news server does its own threading, such as INN-1.4, tin can retrieve the threads database produced by INN and work very fast. By default, tin dumps its client's threading databases in the user's home directory below .tin/index. This can consume lots of disk space if every user maintains his or her own threads database. The news administrator might consider keeping a centralized threads database for all the users of a particular machine. This can be achieved by making tin setuid to the news group or some other entirely unpriviledged group (though *not* "nobody," because no files or commands should ever be associated with the group nobody). tin will then keep all thread databases below /var/spool/news/

.index. Should a user attempt any file access or shell escape, they will be reset to their original uid.

A far better solution is to use the tind indexing daemon that runs periodically to update the index files. At this time, this daemon is not a standard part of Linux distributions and needs to be obtained and compiled. If tin is invoked as "tin -r" or "rtin," tin tries to connect to the NNTP server specified in the file /etc/nntpserver or in the NNTPSERVER environmental variable. The nntpserver file contains the name of the new server on a single line.

The trn server is the sucessor of rn and was written by Wayne Davidson. "rn" stood for *read news.* The "t" of trn stands for *threaded*, though trn has no provision for generating its own threading database at run-time (as is done in tin). trn's threaded database is prepared by the mthreads program that is run regularly from crontab to update the index files. trn can be run without a threaded database, though all the messages come unthreaded.

mthreads is invoked with a list of newsgroups on the command line. An example of the list appears as follows:

```
mthreads com,rec,alt,!alt.sex
```

This command enables threading for all of the comp, rec, and alt groups, with the exception of the alt.sex newsgroups. If the news administrator only wants to handle news updates at night, mthreads needs only to be run once in the morning. Very active sites run mthreads in daemon mode. This is done by starting the mthreads daemon at system boot time with the -d option, which places the process in the background, awakening it every 10 minutes to check for newly arrived articles and threading them. To run mthreads in daemon mode, the following line needs to be in the rc.news script:

```
/usr/local/bin/rn/mthreads -deav
```

The -a option allow mthreads to be turned on automatically for new newsgroups as they are created; -v enables verbose output; -e expires articles once a day, usually just after midnight. Articles whose number is below a low water mark in the active file are expired.

The nn newsreader was written by Kim Storm and is reputed to stand for "No News." No News stands for the motto "No news is good news. nn is better." To achieve this goal, nn has a vast collection of utilities to perform thread generation, consistency checks of the databases, accounting, gathering usage statistics, access restrictions, and so on. There is also an administrative program called nnadmin to allow these tasks to be performed interactively. Most of these tasks are intuitive, so we shall turn our attention to the generation of index files.

nn threads messages into a database using nnmaster. nnmaster is usually run as a daemon, started in either rc.news or rc.inet2 and invoked as the following, which enables threading all newsgroups in the "active" file:

```
/usr/local/lib/nn/nnmaster -l -r -C
```

Another way to handle threading is to invoke nnmaster periodically from cron, giving nnmaster a list of target groups. This list is very similar to the subscription file used in the trn example, except it uses blanks instead of commas. Instead of a fake group called "all," an empty argument of " " should be used to denote all groups. An example:

```
#/usr/local/lib/nn/nnmaster !alt.sex alt comp rec
```

The group order from left to right is significant. The leftmost group specification that matches always wins. Thus, if !alt.sex had appeared to the right of alt, all groups from alt would have been indexed, regardless of the following exclusions.

nn expires entries from its database using a variety of methods. The first method is to update the database by scanning the newsgroup directories and discarding the entries whose corresponding article is no longer available. This is the default operation when invoking nnmaster with the -E option. It is reasonably fast, unless NNTP is used.

The second method of expiration operates just like the mthreads example of trn, in that it only removes those entries that refer to articles whose article numbers are below the low water mark in the active file. It can be enabled using the -e option. The third strategy is to discard the entire database and recollect all the articles. This is accomplished using the -E3 option of nnmaster.

The list of groups to expire is given by the -F option in the same manner given above. If nnmaster is running as a daemon, the news administrator must kill it (using -k) before the expiration process can take place and restart it with the original options after the expiration is complete. The command to expire all groups using the first method is:

```
# nnmaster -kF ""
# nnmaster -lrC
```

There are quite a few flags to fine tune nn in your environment. These flags and their effects are detailed in the appropriate manual pages.

nnmaster uses a file called GROUPS, located in the /user/local/lib/nn directory. If it does not exist, nnmaster will create it. For each newsgroup, this file contains a line that begins with the group's name, optionally followed by a time stamp and flags. The news administrator may edit these flags to enable certain behaviors for specific groups in question. Be especially careful not to alter the order in which the groups appear as this order in the GROUPS file is synchronized with the binary MASTER file.

Building and Managing a Finger Server

by Loren Buhle

Finger is an old Unix utility based on RFC 1288 to examine the user login file and learn something about the user. For one thing, you can learn if the user is logged into the system at that very moment and perhaps learn the last time the user logged on. If the user has configured his account for interrogation by outside users, it can also reveal the user's e-mail address and other information.

The original finger program was written by Les Earnest. Earl Killian and Brian Harvey were jointly responsible for implementing the original protocol. The first documentation was provided by Ken Harrenstien in the RFC 742 where he called it the "Name/Finger," reflecting its capability to return information about a system's users to a remote client. This document evolved into RFC 1288, written by David Paul Zimmerman in later years.

Flow of Events in Finger

Finger is based on the Transmission Control Protocol (TCP), using TCP port 79 (decimal or 117 octal). The local host opens a TCP connection to a remote host on the Finger port. A remote process becomes available on the remote end of the connection to process the finger request. The local host sends the remote process a one-line query based upon the Finger query specification, and waits for the remote process to respond. The remote process receives and processes the query, returns an answer, then initiates the close of the connection. The local host receives the answer and the close signal, then proceeds to close its end of the connection.

Finger Data Format

Any data transferred *must* be in ASCII format, with no parity, and with lines ending in CRLF (ASCII 13 followed by ASCII 10). This excludes other character formats such as EBCDIC, and so on. It also means that any characters between ASCII 128 and 255 should truly be international data, not 7-bit ASCII with the parity bit set.

Finger Query Specifications

The remote process must accept the entire finger query specification. The query specification is defined as follows:

{Q1} ::= [{W}|{W}{S}{U}]{C}

{Q2} ::= [{W}{S}][{U}]{H}{C}

{U} ::= username

{H} ::= @hostname | @hostname{H}

{W} ::= /W

{S} ::= <SP> | <SP>{S}

{C} ::= <CRLF>

{H}, being recursive, means there is no arbitrary limit on the number of @hostname tokens in the query. In examples of the {Q2} request specification, the number of @hostname tokens is limited to two, simply for brevity.

Be aware that {Q1} and {Q2} do not refer to a user typing **finger user@host** from an operating system prompt. It refers to the line that a remote process actually receives. So, if a user types **finger user@host<CRLF>**, the remote process on the remote host receives "user<CRLF>," which corresponds to {Q1}.

Remote Process Behavior

A query of {Q2} is a request to forward a query to another RUIP. A remote process *must* either provide or actively refuse this forwarding process. If a remote process provides this service, it *must* conform to the following behavior:

Given that:

> Host <H1> opens a Finger connection <F1-2> to an RUIP on host <H2>.
>
> <H1> gives the <H2> RUIP a query <Q1-2> of type {Q2} (for example, FOO@HOST1@HOST2).

Then:

> Host <H3> is the right-most host in <Q1-2> (that is, HOST2)
>
> Query <Q2-3> is the remainder of <Q1-2> after removing the right-most "@hostname" token in the query (that is, FOO@HOST1)

And so:

> The <H2> remote process then must itself open a Finger connection <F2-3> to <H3>, using <Q2-3>.
>
> The <H2> remote process must return any information received from <F2-3> to <H1> via <F1-2>.
>
> The <H2> remote process must close <F1-2> in normal circumstances only when the <H3> remote process closes <F2-3>.

The actual output of the remote process depends on the administrator's implementation and the individual's implementation. The information returned is designed to be read by people and not a program. This output should be informative, but might also be a major security risk.

{C} Query

A query of {C} is a request for a list of all online users. A remote process must either answer or actively refuse. If the remote process answers, it provides the user's full name and possibly more information such as the following:

- Terminal location
- Office location
- Office phone number
- Job name
- Idle time (number of minutes since last typed input, or since last job activity).

{U}{C} Behavior

A query of {U}{C} is a request for in-depth status of a specified user {U}. If the system administrator doesn't want to provide this service, they should seriously consider removing the finger daemon from their system. An answer must include at least the full name of the user. If the user is logged in, at least the same amount of information returned by {C} for that user must also be returned by {U}{C}.

Because this is a query for information on a specific user, the system administrator should be allowed to choose to return additional useful information such as the following:

- Office location
- Office phone number
- Home phone number

- Status of login (not logged in, logout time, and so on)
- User information file

A *user information file* is a feature wherein a user may leave a short message that will be included in the response to finger requests. This is sometimes called a *.plan* file and is easily implemented by having the finger program look for a specially named text file in the user's home directory or some common area. Often, this is the .plan file. Instead of reading a predetermined file, the system administrator can also allow the finger query to run a program.

{U} Ambiguity

Allowable "names" in the command line must include *usernames* or *login names* as defined by the system. If a name is ambiguous, some finger implementations will ignore the username and presume it is blank, while other implementations will attempt possible derivations to return something of possible use.

/W Query Token

The token /W in the {Q1} or {Q2} query types is an option to request a verbose response from the remote process handling the finger request. This token may be ignored.

Information Provided

Some finger implementations allow the system administrator to tailor what *atoms* of information are returned in a finger query. For example, an administrator might want to send the following information:

- Administrator A chooses to return office location, office phone number, home phone number, and logged in/log out time.
- Administrator B chooses to return only office location and office phone number.
- Administrator C chooses the minimum amount of required information, which is the person's full name.

User Information Files

The remote process servicing a finger request can also read a user-modified file and send this along. This user file may be an executable file, as seen with the weather example discussed later in this chapter. Although this is usually seen as a security nightmare and thus rarely implemented on systems, there are some precautions that can be taken if this behavior is allowed. The remote process handling the finger request usually filters out any unprintable data, leaving only printable 7-bit characters (ASCII 32 through ASCII 126), tabs (ASCII 9), and CRLFs. This filter is an attempt to protect against sending terminal escape codes, changing the recipient's X-Window names, or committing some other unexpected behavior on the finger recipient's system. Unfortunately, this filter is too restrictive for users expecting the ability to view international or control characters. Thus, this filtering process, if present, may be an option. Though often too late to be useful, finger inquiries can be logged for system administrator review, which is useful if there are repeated inquiries from one site in an effort to learn the names and habit of users on your site.

Using Finger

The finger program included with Linux was written by GNU, based on the Berkeley 4.3 finger routine. Linux installs both the client and server portions of this utility as part of its basic installation. The server part of the program, /etc/fingerd, listens to socket 79 for the TCP protocol spoken by a finger client request. When a response is obtained on this TCP socket, the finger protocol between the client (finger) and server (fingerd) ensues. The finger service is generally available to anyone on the network, both locally and remotely. Finger has three main uses:

- If you run finger with no arguments, the program prints the username, full name, location, login time, and other information stored on the user in the /etc/passwd file.
- If you run finger with a name argument, the program searches through the /etc/passwd file and prints detailed information for every use with a first, last, or username that matches the name specified in the finger request.

- Finger can be used to provide short bits of information from a system by changing the normally static information field to provide dynamic information.

These three usage patterns are detailed in the following section.

Finger's Command Structure

The command structure for finger follows:

```
finger username@hostname
```

The *username* is optional and requests specific information about a user whose first or last name matches the *username* on the *hostname* system. If you are using the user's login name, the name match is case sensitive, meaning "Joe" is different from "joe." If you are using the user's actual name (such as the GECOS filed of /etc/passwd of Unix systems), the search is case insensitive. To be safe, you can use all lowercase and will find a match most of the time.

The *hostname* is the name of the computer where you are making the inquiry. If you execute only the finger command without arguments, you will make an inquiry on the system on which you are currently logged on. In this example, the finger command is executed without any arguments; the local fingerd process listening on socket 79 will provide a brief list of the users currently logged in to the local machine:

```
finger
[www.lifecare.org]

                        CPU load: 0.50 0.73 1.00
Login Name      Tty         Idle        Login         Office Home
buhle   Loren Buhle p0     0:10     Oct 23 12:23    Rm 323 Beachfront
buhle   Loren Buhle t1     0:02     Oct 23 12:24    Rm 323 Beachfront
buhle   Loren Buhle t2     2:10     Oct 23 12:24    Rm 323 Beachfront
manny     Manny Moe p4     0:15     Oct 23 18:23    30 Rockefeller Ctr
```

This command can also be directed to a system out on the Internet, often yielding the same result:

```
finger @www.lifecare.org
[www.lifecare.org]
```

```
                   CPU load: 0.50 0.73 1.00
Login Name        Tty     Idle       Login           Office Home
buhle  Loren Buhle p0     0:10    Oct 23 12:23    Rm 323 Beachfront
buhle  Loren Buhle t1     0:02    Oct 23 12:24    Rm 323 Beachfront
buhle  Loren Buhle t2     2:10    Oct 23 12:24    Rm 323 Beachfront
manny  Manny Moe   p4     0:15    Oct 23 18:23    30 Rockefeller Ctr
```

In both the local and remote examples, three user processes assigned to the username buhle are currently running. The actual user is Loren Buhle who, according to the information contained in the /etc/passwd file, maintains an office in Rm 323 Beachfront. The list of current users and login times is derived from the /etc/utemp file. The three processes with rapid initial login times infer the use of an X-window terminal. The user manny has only one process running and has been logged on since 6:23 p.m. on October 23. This user process has not performed any CPU or input/output operations for the 15 minutes.

Finger Features

The CPU load is a feature implemented on only some finger servers. The three numbers give a rough estimate of the average load on the computer in the last 5, 10, and 15 minutes. A userload of 1.00 means the machine was 100 percent busy. A userload of more than 1.00 (such as 2.30) means the system was saturated at least two times a single CPU processor load. If there is more than one CPU in a symmetric multiprocessor system (SMP) where each CPU can work independently, a two-processor system fully loaded could tolerate a load of 2.0 without becoming saturated. A load of 0.85 means a single-processor system isn't loaded to capacity.

The finger daemon also enables you to learn more information about an individual user of this system. If you are a local user on the system, you can neglect the information after the username (that is, omit @www.lifecare.org because this is your local system):

```
finger buhle@www.lifecare.org
[www.lifecare.org]

Login name: buhle                    In real life: Loren Buhle
Directory: /usr/usrc/buhle          Shell: /bin/csh
```

```
Last Login: Mon, Oct 23, 1995 on ttya1 from ix.netcom.phila.com
No Plan.
```

In this case, the information regarding the default directory, default shell, login name, and username came directly from the respective fields in the /etc/passwd file. If the implementation of fingerd shows the last time the user logged on, this is derived from the /usr/adm/wtmp file. If username buhle had a file called .plan with world read permission in an administrator's home directory and the corresponding home directory has world read and execute permissions, you would see buhle's plan. If there is a file called .project present in the home directory, it would also be displayed. If these files were located in this directory, you would see the following:

```
finger buhle@www.lifecare.org
[www.lifecare.org]

Login name: buhle                    In real life: Loren Buhle
Directory: /usr/usrc/buhle          Shell: /bin/csh
Last Login: Mon, Oct 23, 1995 on ttya1 from ix.netcom.phila.com
Project: Finish the chapters of this book
Plan: Work day and night to complete this deadline...
```

Finger as a General Information Processor

Because finger displays the .plan and .project files to outside requests, this becomes a simple way of providing small bits of information. By selectively placing this information in these files, information such as the weather might easily be obtainable to the general public. On a purely fictitious server machine called hostname.org, a process might periodically overwrite the .plan file with the latest weather information. Thus, a user could type **finger weather@hostname.org** and get this:

```
finger weather@hostname.org
[hostname.org]

Login name: weather                       In real life: Who knows
Directory: /usr1/weather                  Shell: /bin/ksh
Plan:

Recent weather in the San Francisco Area on October 23, 1995
4 p.m. PST - This evening, there is a chance of darkness with a
small chance of scattered light, depending on the phase of the
```

```
moon and the cloud cover. At about 6:30am PST, the darkness will
give way to increasing amounts of light.
```

The GNU fingerd included with Linux enables a user to set up a .fingerrc file in her home directory. The source of this version of fingerd can be obtained by anonymous FTP from ftp.gnu.ai.mit.edu in the file /pub/gnu/finger-1.37.tar.gz. This is a script that is executed when a remote user fingers the local user's account. The standard output is sent to the remote user. To help customize the output, three arguments from the normal finger output are sent to the fingerrc script:

- The domain name or IP address of the domain host
- The keyword *local* if the requester is local or *remote* if the requester is not local
- The name of the user doing the fingering (the user running the finger client) or a null string if the fingerd cannot tell.

The designers of the fingerrc script set the following security considerations on their script:

- The script must be owned by the user who owns the home directory.
- The script must be writeable only by the user who owns the home directory.
- The script must not be setuid or setgid.
- The script must by run by the user "nobody."

Further security matters are discussed in the following section.

Problems with Finger

The finger client sends a TCP request to socket 79 of the target machine, anticipating a response from the fingerd program. If the target machine is unresponsive to this socket, perhaps because the machine is down, socket 79 has been commented out of the /etc/services file, or some similar reason, the user will obtain the following message:

```
finger buhle@www.lifecare.org
[www.lifecare.org]

connect: Connection refused
```

There is insufficient information from this message to discern the status of the remote server. The fingerd is often disabled, either by killing the fingerd process or commenting out socket 79 from /etc/services because the information provided by fingerd may be used to compromise the system (see the following discussion). Finger makes it easy for intruders to get a list of users on your system, which dramatically increases the odds of the intruder's successful penetration into your system. Many sites disable finger for this very reason. This can often be a nuisance to outsiders trying to determine mail addresses or phone numbers. fingerd programs older than November 5, 1988 were exploited by the Internet Morris worm (also discussed presently) and should be replaced with a newer version.

Security Issues

The remote process handling the finger request is expected to sample the entire input string and process it according to the criteria discussed earlier; thus it provides an avenue for direct security penetration into a system. The Morris worm, a program that shut down many Unix computers on the Internet in 1988 (discussed in greater detail presently), pointed out these sources of penetration quite vividly.

Like telnet, FTP, and Simple Mail Transfer Protocol (SMTP), finger is one of the protocols at the security perimeter of a host. Finger's activity, even when used correctly, can be seen as a security breach because it discloses information about the system's users. This information might be considered sensitive by some users. Indeed, some implementations of finger provide the time a user last logged in, the time they last read their mail, whether unread mail awaits the user, and who sent the unread mail. This information makes it possible to track conversations in progress and see where the party's attention is focused. Some sites find this information disclosure unreasonable and turn off finger completely.

Turning off Finger

The responsible way to turn off finger is to have the remote process handling the incoming finger socket reply to all inquiries with a simple refusal of service message, such as `Finger forwarding service denied`. The incoming finger input string should *not* be interrogated because this might provide a source of penetration. Some system administrators prefer to close the socket by removing the finger entry from the /etc/services file and terminating the fingerd process. Mere termination of the fingerd process is not sufficient because the fingerd process could be restarted, or it's possibly that a larger security breach could be launched occupying the fingerd socket. If a fingerd process is running and denying service, this covers the socket in an active way.

Security Hole of Finger

Finger was one of the ways the infamous Internet Morris worm spread in the late 1980s. As you saw earlier, the fingerd receives a variable length argument. The Morris worm exploited this variable length by sending the fingerd process new code. The fingerd was not expecting to receive code and thus there were no provisions in the finger protocol for receiving code. The fingerd process executed a *gets* call, which does not specify a maximum buffer length. The worm filled fingerd's read buffer and more with its own code and continued to fill the buffer until it had overwritten the return address in gets' stack buffer. When the subroutine within fingerd finally returned, the program jumped into the new code downloaded by the worm and the system was compromised. This bug was corrected in versions of fingerd after November 5, 1988 and should not be in your Linux distribution. This discussion is intended to allay fears of compromising your system via fingerd gets hole.

This chapter discussed the use of finger to gain information about users on a remote system. Finger works in a client-server fashion, using a TCP connection to the default socket of 79 on a remote host. At the remote end, a remote process handles the process and returns the specified information according to the constraints set by the remote system administrator. These constraints may be to ignore the input stream and announce a denial of service, thus returning no useful information about the remote system's users. If the input stream is blank, the remote process will provide a list of users currently logged in to the remote system.

Options on the input stream of the finger process may request specific information, resulting in the reading of specific files or the execution of specific processes. Several examples are given of this, such as reading the .plan file or executing a program to interrogate the corresponding weather prognosis. In a security-conscious world, finger is seen as an unnecessary breach of information. A properly working finger interaction provides information that can be used to compromise a system or its users. Finger also presents an opportunity to break into a system, so appropriate ways to deny finger service were discussed.

Building and Managing a Telnet Server

by Loren Buhle

Telnet, the Network Terminal Protocol, *provides a bidirectional, eight-bit, byte-oriented communication facility to provide a way of interfacing terminal devices and terminal-oriented processes to each other. Most people use Telnet to provide a remote login over the Internet and emulate a VT100 or IBM 3270 character interface. Telnet is defined by RFC 854 and uses the Transmission Control Protocol (TCP) to transmit telnet control information and data.*

General Considerations

The Telnet protocol is built upon three ideas:

- The concept of a Network Virtual Terminal
- The principle of negotiated options
- A symmetric view of terminals and processes

Understanding Network Virtual Terminal

When a telnet connection is first established, each end is assumed to originate and terminate a Network Virtual Terminal (NVT). The NVT is an imaginary device—described in greater detail later in this chapter—that provides a standardized way of representing a terminal. This standard eliminates the need to create a unique list of terminal servers and hosts containing information about the characteristics of everyone's terminals and their handling conventions. (The user *host* is where the physical terminal is connected and usually initiates the connection. The *server* is the destination of the connection.) All hosts, both the user and server, map their local device characteristics and connections over the network.

Negotiated Options

Many hosts have additional properties that need to be communicated prior to engaging a communication. These properties may include sophisticated terminal options, flow control between the user and server, and other customizable properties. The Telnet protocol allows a degree of negotiation between the user and server, breaking down into a "DO, DON'T, WILL, WON'T" structure to allow a user and server to agree on a common set of conventions to govern the particular telnet connection. These options might include changing the character set, the echo mode, and so on.

Note When a Telnet connection is initiated, the user and server processes pass a flurry of option requests back and forth in an attempt to get the best possible service from the other party.

The negotiation begins by one of the parties initiating a request for some option to take place. The other party then accepts or rejects the request. If the request is accepted, the option takes effect immediately; if it is rejected, the associated aspect of the connection remains as specified as the default condition for an NVT. The Telnet negotiation always permits a party to refuse a request to enable an option, but it must never refuse a request to disable an option. If both parties request an option simultaneously, each sees the other's request as the positive acknowledgment of its own.

Symmetric Rules

One problem in the options negotiation process is that both parties might see acknowledgements as new requests, giving rise to an ever-increasing spiral of negotiation. To bring control over these potential nonterminating acknowledgement loops, both parties in the process may only request a change in the option process; they cannot merely announce their current status. If a request is received to change to a mode the recipient already occupies, this request is ignored. This nonresponse prevents endless loops of negotiation. On the other hand, if a request for change is made, a response is generated—even if no change in mode is made.

Mechanics of a Telnet Session

The Network Virtual Terminal (NVT), described in general terms earlier, can be defined more specifically as a bi-directional character device consisting of a printer (output) and keyboard (input). The printer responds to incoming data (placing it on the console screen), and the keyboard produces outgoing data to be sent over the Telnet connection.

If the mode between the user and server has "echoes" enabled, the Telnet process may put the character on the printer (user's screen) as well. In most cases, the Telnet mode operates in full duplex, meaning a character typed on the user's Telnet session is sent to the host and echoed back to the user's screen. The fact that a keystroke on a full-duplex telnet session must journey to the host and back before it is seen on the screen is often most noticeable when there are delays or interruptions in the Internet session. Users might be typing far ahead of what they see on their screen. Eventually, the screen catches up with what is typed. If the mode is set to half-duplex, the characters are sent to the host and are not echoed back to the user.

A typical Telnet session is traditionally full-duplex mode, passing each character as it is entered. In some older Telnet sessions, however, the NVT operates by locally storing a full line of text in a half-duplex device operating in line-buffered mode. This was done because of the high cost of transmission. In line mode, characters are stored in a local buffer and locally echoed to the user's screen (printer). When a signal is generated either by a host process or the human user, the contents of the local buffer are downloaded to the server. The typical signal for transmission from the local buffer is the Enter or Return key on the keyboard. Indeed, many Unix editors permit "in-line" editing until the user sends the line by hitting the Enter key. This older mode of transmission deserves mention because there are still some computers today that send only lines or screens of data.

When large amounts of data pass between the host and server, there is a dialog of control sequences controlling the flow of information. Consider the process of listing the contents of a long file on the host terminal. The host can only display information from the server at a given rate. The host terminal may have a local buffer to store the information coming from the server prior to display to the user. When this local buffer is full, the host needs to tell the server to stop transmitting information, or the host will be overrun with information. The host sends the server a control sequence (Ctrl+S) to stop transmitting until the host is ready for more information. When the host is ready for more information, it sends another control sequence (Ctrl+Q) to the server to continue transmitting information.

Note Neither the host nor the server machine can take over the other end of the NVT connection. This fact is particularly important when considering the transmission of large amounts of data.

Standard Representation of Control Functions

The purpose of the Telnet protocol is to provide a standard interface between terminal devices and terminal-oriented processes via a network. Lessons learned in the early days of connecting terminals to computers through networks resulted in the standardization of certain functions, but the implementation of the functions differed widely. For humans interacting with several different server systems, the different implementations were frustrating. Telnet was designed to automatically handle these different implementations, using a standard representation for five of these functions, which follow:

- Interrupt Process (IP)
- Abort Output (AO)
- Are You There (AYT)
- Erase Character (EC)
- Erase Line (EL)

Interrupt Process (IP)

Many systems provide a function that suspends, interrupts, aborts, or terminates the operation of a user process. This function is frequently used when a user believes his process is in an unending loop, or when an unwanted process has been inadvertently activated. IP is the standard representation for invoking this function.

Abort Output (AO)

Aborting output allows a process to run to completion (or reach the same stopping point it would reach if it ran to completion) without sending the output to the user's terminal. Thus, the process is not interrupted and any functions the process may perform (updating and closing files, for example) are allowed. This function usually clears any output produced and queued prior to display on the user's terminal. AO is the standard representation for invoking this function. Some processes, for example, might normally accept a user's command, send a long text string to the user's terminal in response, and finally signal readiness to accept the next command by sending a "prompt" character (preceded by <CR><LF>) to the user's terminal. If the AO were received during the transmission of the text string, a reasonable implementation would be to suppress the remainder of the text string, but transmit the prompt character and the preceding <CR><LF>. (This is possibly in distinction to the action that might be taken if an IP were received; the IP might cause suppression of the text string and an exit from the process.)

Are You There (AYT)

Many systems provide a function that provides the user with some visible (that is, printable) evidence that the system is still up and running. This function can be invoked by the user when the system is unexpectedly "silent" for a long time because of the unanticipated (by the user) length of a computation, an unusually heavy system load, and so forth. AYT is the standard representation for invoking this function.

Erase Character (EC)

Many systems provide a function that deletes the last preceding undeleted character or *print position* from the stream of data being supplied by the user. This function is typically used to edit keyboard input when typing mistakes are made. EC is the standard representation for invoking this function.

Erase Line (EL)

Many systems provide a function that deletes all the data in the current *line* of input. This function is typically used to edit keyboard input. EL is the standard representation for invoking this function.

The NVT Printer/Screen and Keyboard

The NVT printer or screen has an unspecified width and page length and can produce the USA ASCII codes between 32–126, inclusive. ASCII control codes between 0–31 are generally control characters. Characters between 128–255 are defined as uncovered codes and represent the extended ASCII set. Some of the control codes are shown in table 15.1.

Table 15.1
A Sampling of Control Codes Meanings

Name	Code	Meaning
NULL (NUL)	0	No Operation.
Line Feed (LF)	10	Moves the printer to the next print line, keeping the same horizontal position.
Carriage Return (CR)	13	Moves the printer to the left margin of the current line.
BELL (BEL)	7	Produces an audible or visible signal (which does *not* move the print head).
Back Space (BS)	8	Moves the print head one character position toward the left margin.
Horizontal Tab (HT)	9	Moves the printer to the next horizontal tab stop. It remains unspecified how either party determines or establishes where such tab stops are located.
Vertical Tab (VT)	11	Moves the printer to the next vertical tab stop. It remains unspecified how either party determines or establishes where such tab stops are located.
Form Feed (FF)	12	Moves the printer to the top of the next page, keeping the same horizontal position.

The sequence CR LF, as defined, causes the NVT to be positioned at the left margin of the next print line (as would, for example, the sequence LF CR). However, many systems and terminals do not treat CR and LF independently, and have to exert some effort to simulate their effect. Some terminals do not, for example, have a CR independent of the LF, but on such terminals it might be possible to simulate a CR by backspacing.

Therefore, the sequence CR LF must be treated as a single "new line" character and used whenever their combined action is intended; the sequence CR NUL must be used where a carriage return alone is desired; and the CR character must be avoided in other contexts. This rule gives assurance to systems that must decide whether to perform a new line function or a multiple-backspace that the telnet character stream contains a character following a CR that will allow a rational decision.

The Telnet Command Structure

All telnet commands consist of at least a two-byte sequence: the Interpret as Command (IAC) escape character, followed by the code for the command. The commands dealing with option negotiation are three-byte sequences, the third byte being the code for the option referenced. This format was chosen so that more comprehensive use of the "data space" is made. Table 15.2 shows some of the telnet commands, their code sequences, and subsequent meanings.

Table 15.2
A Sampling of telnet Commands

Name	Code	Meaning
SE	240	End of subnegotiation parameters.
NOP	241	No operation.
Data Mark	242	The data stream portion of a Synch. This should always be accompanied by a TCP Urgent notification.

Name	Code	Meaning
Break	243	NVT character BRK.
Interrupt Process	244	The function IP.
Abort output	245	The function AO.
Are You There	246	The function AYT.
Erase character	247	The function EC.
Erase Line	248	The function EL.
Go ahead	249	The GA signal.
SB	250	Indicates that what follows is subnegotiation of the indicated option.
WILL (option code)	251	Indicates the desire to begin performing, or confirmation that you are now performing, the indicated option.
WON'T (option code)	252	Indicates the refusal to perform, or continue performing, the indicated option.
DO (option code)	253	Indicates the request that the other party perform, or confirmation that you are expecting the other party to perform, the indicated option.
DON'T (option code)	254	Indicates the demand that the other party stops performing, or confirmation that you are no longer expecting the other party to perform, the indicated option.
IAC	255	Data Byte 255.

Telnet is the client program and telnetd is the server program. The Telnet TCP connection is established between the user's port U and the server's port L. The server listens on its well known port L (23) for such connections. Because a TCP connection is full-duplex and is identified by the pair of ports, the server can engage in many simultaneous connections involving its port L and different user ports U. Telnetd can be configured to provide a normal login, a customized login procedure, or no login at all.

Telnet provides remote users most of the services available to a local character terminal, including the curses screen handling package or escape sequences to get customized graphical effects. Telnet services provide a good alternative to direct dial-in service without the hassle of phone lines and sufficient modems per simultaneous users. If the standard Linux telnetd server is used, users see a normal login prompt when they connect using the Telnet client. After the user has logged in via the Telnet client using port 23 and the TCP protocol, the telnetd daemon looks to the /etc/passwd file for the appropriate login shell and runs it. This login shell is the program that implements the actual service.

The program specified within the /etc/passwd shell can be any program that reads from standard input and writes to standard output. Usually, this program or script works by supplying questions to the user in a form of a menu and requests the user to select a number or letter to indicate her choice. The rest of this chapter explores the elements of security in conventional login via Telnet, captive accounts, and specialized versions of the telnetd.

Installation and Maintenance of Telnet

Both the client and server portions of telnet are installed in the default options of the Linux installation. With few exceptions, maintenance of either the Telnet client or the telnetd server process is non-existent because they are quite robust and work quite well. There are two things a Linux administrator might want to consider:

1. The number of Telnet sessions allowed on the Linux platform
2. The role of Telnet in the network topology of the specific Linux computer

Telnet sessions consume a finite amount of memory in any Unix host. In these days of limited memory, this memory consumption might be viewed as a problem and a limitation on the number of active sessions that could be implemented in the Unix kernal configuration file. This need to control the number of active sessions was abrogated by efficient memory management. Inactive Telnet sessions were merely paged to disk. Telnet is almost never a major consumer of computer resources. On the rare occasion when Telnet consumes more than an occasional burst of computer resources, it is often because a process is running out of control.

If the Linux platform is operating as a firewall computer segregating the inner network from the Internet, the system administrator might want to remove the telnetd and Telnet process. Normally, a user from the Internet who wants to access an internal computer would first have to log in to the firewall computer using telnetd and use the firewall computer's telnet process to log in to the internal network. If the administrator removes Telnet and telnetd from the computer, this cannot occur.

The Security of Using Telnet

Logging in to a computer via telnet may pose a greater security risk than dialing directly into your computer because your username and password traverse the Internet unprotected. On ethernet networks, such as the Internet, the packets of information are connected by some physical connection, such as coaxial wire or fiber optics. The packets of TCP/IP data are transmitted to every computer connected to this wire.

Note Not every computer on the Internet will be able to see your username and password. Your network might have implemented routing of packets to ensure only a limited set of computers, such as those within your subnet; see your ethernet packet. One of the purposes of a firewall and subnetting within this firewall is to provide some security and keep internal packets out of the reach of the world at large.

Normally, the computers on this network will examine each packet and only listen to those packets destined for their specific Internet address. It is possible to write a *sniffer* program to list and record every packet transmitted. Some sniffer programs examine the first 100 bytes of each packet, going in each direction, to capture the user's username and password. It is best to use a sniffer if unauthorized personnel have direct, physical access to your network.

There are some heightened disadvantages to using Telnet over a dial-in access. Although very few dial-up modem numbers are publicly available, the Internet address is widely published or can often be guessed by following established conventions. If a user telnets across the country, say from the East Coast of the U.S. to the West Coast, the exposure of their packets along the specific route to sniffing is heightened. By the nature of the Internet, the route the packets takes varies from one session to the next. Access to the Telnet ports of a computer can be done very efficiently and cheaply over the Internet, although use of a direct modem connection is slower (especially when guessing a few thousand passwords), more costly (long distance phone charges), and easier to trace. Establishing an Internet connection to your hardware brings thousands of potential hackers to your telnetd port every minute.

Clients as Login Shells

When a user logs in over Telnet, he is handed to the shell program identified in the /etc/passwd file for that particular user. For a traditional programmer, this shell program may be the csh, ksh, bsh, or some other standard Unix shell. For a more specialized user, such as a system operator, a Gopher client in line-mode might be used. One advantage to using the line-mode Gopher client is that the user needs only the Telnet client and not the Gopher client, to access the service. The other advantage is the ability to use a username and password to access the Gopher client, instead of opening the system operator's account to any Gopher client on the Internet. If a Gopher server is not running on the server machine, a line-mode Web client, such as Lynx, could deliver the same functionality.

> **Warning** The menu items available on a gopher menu should be careful to restrict the user only to the desired items and functionality on the menu. The user should *never* be able to escape to a full-featured shell (that is, csh, ksh, or bsh) or command interpreter. If you do, a user might be able to exploit security holes on the system to gain root privilege and wreak havoc on the system. Even without root privilege, the user may be able to cause damage or learn sensitive information, all from being able to jump out of the captive menu.

The use of a Gopher or Web menu introduces the concept of a captive account for incoming Telnet sessions. The *captive account* provides only a limited set of options to the user, steering them through the customary usage patterns of a typical user. If the captive account is presented as a series of menu items, the user need not remember lists of commands and command options. In the following example, listing 15.1, a typical login session to an account at St. Johns University in New York is shown. The session begins with a telnet to the Internet address and successful completion of a username and password. The user sees the information shown in listings 15.1 through 15.3. Listing 15.1 welcomes the user.

Listing 15.1

```
Welcome to
                              The UNIBASE Global Network
                                University of St. Johns
                                   Jamaica, New York

                        Providing access to UNIBASE sites on the:

                                Gabriel Dumont Network
                             Yorkton Tribal Council Network
                            UNIBASE Global Education Network
                          Saskatchewan Schools Education Network
                         The Active Living and Environment Project
        St Johns University Rehabilitation and Educational Network

                      Education Databases, Discussions and Conferences
                                 Information Resources

                          Press Enter to continue:
```

This first screen greets the user and provides a common location for announcements. The second screen, demonstrated in listing 15.2, enables the user to change some of the terminal and account parameters, which is particularly important because this system makes use of escape characters of the curses program to position text on the screen.

Listing 15.2

```
This system makes extensive use of the screen
characteristics on your computer. It is important that you
have your local terminal settings and the settings on this
system agree.  The current profile settings are:

Home menu:                  Mainmenu
Terminal emulation:           vt100
Editor:                                 Unix Vi
Mailer:
Computer/Op.sys            msdos
File transfer mode:           kermit
Chat permission:              Y

If you are UNSURE about your configuration, or
if you NEED to change the settings at your end,
please do so now.

Enter  C to change or review your settings
   or  <RETURN/ENTER> to continue.
```

The third screen, as shown in listing 15.3, is the main screen presented to the user. This is where most of the user's activities are based and shows the possibilities available. After completion of an activity, such as item #7—reading the user's personal e-mail—the user is returned to this screen. Though there are many options, this program has the capability to make some options unavailable to specific individuals. Since I am not a student at St. Johns University, options pertaining to the "Classroom Activity Modules" are unavailable to me. It is critical to provide a way out of the menu. In this menu, it is the last item, "Q."

Listing 15.3

```
Current time: 00:07              at: St.Johns University
                          1 - System Bulletins
                          2 - System Manuals
                          3 - Usenet News
                          4 - Classroom Activity Modules
                          5 - Professional Development Activities
                          6 - Special Interest Centres
                          7 - Unibase Personal Mail
                         12 - Gateway to local Services
                         13 - Gateway to Internet Services
                         91 - Library Research System
                         92 - Conference/Chat
                         93 - Personal File/Directory Maint.
                         94 - System Utilities/configuration
                         98 - Explain This Menu
                          Q - Exit from Unibase

                         Enter your choice:
```

A simple version of this captive account can be implemented using the following Perl script, defined as the user's login shell in their /etc/passwd entry (the small arrow indicates the text would normally fit on one line).

```
#!/usr/bin/perl

$weatherpt = '/usr/bin/telnet um-weather.sprl.umich.edu 3000';

sub prompt{
    print
    "\n[P]rint weather\nGet [d]ate and time\n[H]elp\nE[x]it or
    ➥[q]uit\n\n";
    print "Please enter your choice:  ";
    chop($response = <STDIN>);
    return($response);
}

print "Welcome to the Generic Information Server!\n";

while ($retval = &prompt) {
    if ($retval =~ /[Pp]/) {
        open(QUOTE, "$weatherpt ¦") ¦¦ die "Couldn't access the
```

```
Weather Report!\n";
        print STDOUT <QUOTE>;
        next;
               }
     if($reval =~ /[Dd]/) {
        print STDOUT 'date';
        next;
     }
     if($reval =~ /[Hh]/) {
        open(HELP, "helpfile") || warn "No help available: $!\n";
        print STDOUT <HELP>;
        next;
     }
     if($reval =~ /[XxQq]/) {
        print STDOUT "Goodbye!\n;
        exit 0;
     }
     print STDOUT "Sorry, please choose one of [pdhxq]\n");
}
```

This code uses a specific telnet command to a nonstandard port on the computer called downwind.sprl.umich.edu to obtain the weather. This example also demonstrates how to use local commands, such as the date to perform local functions.

Another captive account, often used within organizations, is to start remote X-Window displays. A user would like a given machine to place an X-Window on their X-Window platform. The manual way to perform this task is to log in to a suitable machine using Telnet, set the DISPLAY environmental variable to the address of where you would like the X-Window display, and then start the X-Window program (for example, xterm, xclock, and so on). The user then logs out. This is very tedious and can be automated. A simple Perl script, based on Larry Wall's sample server in *Programming Perl* (O'Reilly & Associates, Inc.), can be written to simplify the process. This Perl script listens at a specific port (specified either on the command line or set to a default). When there is incoming activity, the server determines the hostname or IP address, perhaps compares this hostname against a list maintained by the system administrator, and prompts the user for the desired service. After the user has selected the desired X-Window service, the server runs the appropriate X-client with the display redirected to the user's display. Be careful that the X-Window client doesn't compromise your captive account by providing a way to escape to the operating system (giving them xterm, for example).

Customized Logins

The system administrator can replace telnetd with a program to perform additional functionality beyond the usual possibilities. You might want to replace telnetd's login procedure to implement billing or entry directly into a program without having a login procedure. This latter example avoids all logins via this TCP port and should be examined closely for security implications. This is often used within company firewalls to share a general function with a large group of people incapable of remembering a password.

Customizing the login can be done in two ways. One way is to leave telnetd alone and place your specialized login at another port, say at port 3000. Users logging in without a specific port would use the default port and receive the customary handling of the telnetd program. Users logging in to the special port, for example port 3000, would enjoy the special behavior permitted by the server program monitoring this port. This method allows almost infinite flexibility because different ports could have different functionality. Of course, these nonstandard ports would have to be advertised to your audience. This is indeed the function provided when you telnet to port 3000 of um-weather.sprl.umich.edu. Next time you are on the Internet, try the following:

```
telnet um-weather.sprl.umich.edu  3000

------------------------------------------------------------------
*                     University of Michigan
*                       WEATHER UNDERGROUND
------------------------------------------------------------------
*
*          College of Engineering, University of Michigan
*       Department of Atmospheric, Oceanic, and Space Sciences
*               Ann Arbor, Michigan  48109-2143
*               comments: ldm@cirrus.sprl.umich.edu
*
*       With Help from: The National Science Foundation
*       supported Unidata Project
*            University Corporation for Atmospheric Research
*                Boulder, Colorado  80307-3000
*
*      This program is running on a DEC Alpha 3000 donated by
*      Digital Equipment Co.
*
------------------------------------------------------------------
```

```
*       NOTE:----------> New users, please select option "H" on the
*       main menu:
*                     H) Help and information for new users
-----------------------------------------------------------------
```

And so on...

Another approach is to replace the telnetd with your own version, which saves your users from remembering which port gives what functionality. There are several starting points, such as Larry Wall's sample server from *Programming Perl*, available by anonymous FTP from ftp.uu.net at part of the archive /published/oreilly/nutshell/perl.tar.Z; David Noble's sock.pl Perl library posted to the newsgroup comp.lang.perl; and the FreeBSD telnetd source code available via anonymous FTP from freebsd.cdrom.com in /FreeBSD/FreeBSD-current/src/libexec/telnetd.

Commercial Telnet Clients

The typical Telnet client emulates the traditional terminal interface. The terminal interface of choice is usually some subset of Digital Equipment Corporation's VT100 terminal, though occasionally the IBM 3270 terminal is an option. The VT100 terminal had a large presence in the Unix world and is the de facto industry standard terminal to emulate. Most Telnet clients emulated the VT100 in a bare-bones fashion, though some will handle some of the extensions, such as double-wide character support, support for both 80 and 132 column width, and the support for the keypad of the VT100 terminals. Some Telnet clients support other formats, such as the more recent VT-family terminals, as well as the terminals of other manufacturers (such as HP).

Telnet sessions that run through a windowing environment, such as X-Window or Microsoft Windows, may also provide the capability to scroll back several screens and use the windowing environment's cut and paste functions to retrieve and replicate information from previous screens. The ability to cut and paste from a long history of screens is extremely useful for both software development and general usage in mundane areas ranging from e-mail to system management to program development. Often, the "power" user will start several telnet sessions simultaneously on her windowing environment and cut and paste between the Telnet screens. Because many of the older programs were written based on the capability to handle their I/O through a simple terminal interface, Telnet brought to the windowing environment remains a powerful client to the power user! The enhancements brought by some of the commercial telnet providers breathes new life into the VT100 format.

In this chapter, you have explored the Telnet functionality provided by the telnetd daemon. This daemon normally listens to socket 23 for TCP activity, handles the login of the user, and executes the login script found in the user's /etc/password entry. You have read about the actual protocol of the Telnet process, both the mode negotiation and the process of passing data along the Network Virtual Terminal. The ramifications of logging in across the Internet with unencrypted usernames and passwords was covered. The telnetd then executes the login script and then detaches from this user. This login script may be a Gopher or Web client with a controlled selection, a normal shell script, or a captive account. Examples of each type were given.

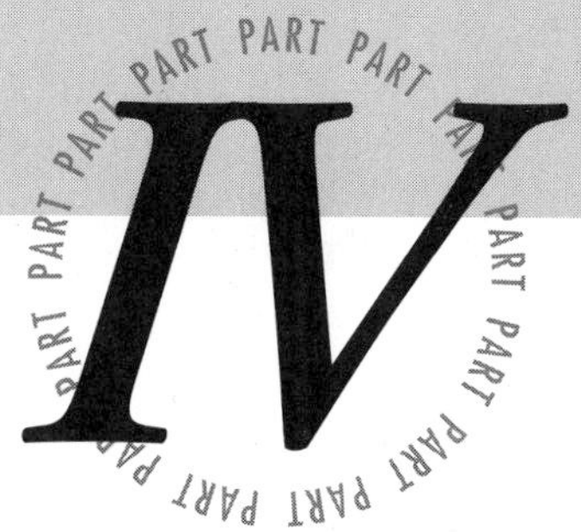

Web Site Administration and Primer

Planning for Web Productions

by David Meeker

The most important phase of Web productions—and the most often neglected—is the planning stage. Time spent carefully planning your Web presence has a huge impact on the appearance, ease of maintenance, and capabilities of your Web presence. Keeping these thoughts in mind, this chapter explores three of the key issues for which you must plan:

- *Server platform*
- *Server software*
- *Connection bandwidth*

As you read this chapter, you might want to make a few notes concerning the primary considerations you expect your organization to face. The end of this chapter presents two examples that illustrate the decision-making process of planning for Web productions. Having some notes about your organization's primary planning concerns can help you consider your own server's needs as you follow along with the examples.

Selecting a Server Platform

When you choose a platform to execute your Web server, a number of issues merit consideration, including interoperability, present environment, operating system, and hardware platform. Failing to consider these issues can result in a woefully inadequate server. The following sections discuss each of these issues in turn.

Interoperability

Interoperability is one of the most important issues to consider for a potential server platform and operating system. Does your organization have existing information services that you need to mesh with the Web server? If so, is the proper software available for the platform you're considering? For example, if your organization uses a centralized database server, you should be sure that the software to connect to that server is available for the platform you choose.

Present Environment

Your organization probably has a choice of hardware and software platforms. If your network is largely homogenous, you should consider keeping your current hardware and operating system combination, to assure that you have the proper software and employees with the necessary expertise to operate the platform. If your organization were completely standardized on the Macintosh platform, for example, you wouldn't need to think long and hard (if at all) before you determined that the most suitable server for your Web productions would be another Macintosh.

Operating Systems

The operating system has no perceptible effect on the appearance of a Web site, so you should choose a platform based on the ease with which it can be configured and maintained, as well as on how well it can be expected to respond to the demands of network serving.

MS-DOS

MS-DOS is a rapidly obsolescing operating system, by all accounts, superseded now by Windows 95. Microsoft has expressed no plans to continue DOS, although it remains available to Windows 95 users for the time being. Although there are Web servers available for DOS, most potential DOS machines can support a more flexible operating system, such as Windows NT, OS/2, or a flavor of Unix. Any more modern operating system would be a better choice than DOS.

Mac OS

The Mac OS is an operating system that most users either love or despise; the middle ground seems rather empty. In choosing your server, however, don't let its pastoral nature deceive you into discounting this very capable OS.

Apple has produced an integrated solution to Web publishing with their Apple Internet Server Solution, based on the Power Macintosh architecture. In addition, their Redundant Array of Independent Computers (RAIC) technology enables a site to begin with a single server and add servers as page demand grows. Together, they can provide an effective, scaleable server solution.

OS/2

IBM's wavering support of OS/2 has scared many potential customers away from this product. Although OS/2 remains a powerful, if under-appreciated, consumer OS, deployment has been slow in the dedicated server arena. Scalability also is an issue, because OS/2 is restricted to Intel's 80x86 family for the foreseeable future, which rules out the mammoth servers large sites might need.

Unix

Unix is one of the most flexible, if complicated, operating systems available. Its minimalist, utilitarian nature is suited perfectly to server applications, although it generally turns off neophyte users, and all but its most devoted advocates wouldn't want it on their desktop.

Unix is, given its obfuscated command set, one of the most difficult operating systems to administer. A manual is simply not sufficient to introduce someone to the system, so consider the choice carefully if no Unix systems are already present in your organization.

> **Warning** Owing to the tempting ease with which Web servers for Unix can fork, it's done quite frequently. It's a bad idea, however, and can lead to unacceptable performance on a server that carries a heavy load. Keep this in mind when you choose a server for your Unix system.

Virtual Memory System (VMS)

VMS, like Unix, is a strong server operating system. As an offering from Digital Equipment Corporation, VMS has what so many complain Unix lacks: a consistent command-line interface. Although the proprietary nature of the operating system means that not nearly as many free utilities are available for it, that same nature invalidates the need: Unix's "utilities" are VMS's built-in commands.

VMS is mildly difficult to administer. It's likely to bewilder the neophyte user, so if you use VMS to replace your current OS, plan on needing training.

VMS also shares one of Unix's traps: Creating new processes is easy, so many Web servers take advantage of this and fork a new process for each request. VMS incurs much greater overhead for each process, however, so the problem is more severe under VMS. To avoid this potential problem, try to find a server that uses the DECthreads package for multitasking, rather than multiple processes.

Three Web servers are available for VMS: CERN's HTTP Server, Process Software's Purveyor, and the Region 6 HTTP Server.

Windows NT

Windows NT, as Microsoft's flagship operating system, has taken off in the server market. With its partial device-independence, the new Microsoft Internet Information Server (which is tightly integrated with the Microsoft Back Office suite), as well as clustering technology on the way, Windows NT is poised to seize the Internet server market.

NT is much easier to administrate than VMS or Unix. Without further training or documentation, most competent users with a manual could set up and run a Web server, although interfacing with other information sources requires more expertise.

Hardware Platform

For the most part, your choice of operating system dictates the hardware platform, with a few notable exceptions. Unix in its various flavors, for instance, can run on a myriad of machines, from the humble Intel 386, to the impressive (and imposing) DEC AlphaServer 8400.

Unix

If you choose Unix for your host operating system, you face another major decision concerning the hardware platform on which to run it. Sun Microsystems, Hewlett-Packard, and Digital Equipment Corporation have staked out the high end of the market. All three offer extremely high-performance servers capable of serving in the most demanding environments. One notable example of DEC's premiere Alpha line is the AltaVista Web search engine, an annotated index of much of the Web. This monstrous database (30 GB at this writing) is served from an AlphaServer 8400, DEC's most powerful machine.

Choosing a hardware platform on which to run Unix isn't easy, given the diversity of available configurations. Generally, you probably want to buy as much power as you can afford. Small sites might be able to get by with an

Intel Pentium-based system, but others will want to contact DEC, Hewlett-Packard, or Sun and investigate more powerful systems.

VMS

VMS users face a rather trivial choice after selecting this operating system: the choice between the Alpha AXP and VAX architectures. For the most part, you can't go wrong if you opt for the newer, cheaper Alpha. Unless you have existing VAX machines, or for some reason the software you intend to run is only available for the VAX, choose the Alpha.

Windows NT

Windows NT, by design, is a portable operating system, available for a variety of systems, including MIPS, Alpha, and Intel's 80x86 family. As with other platforms, buy what you can afford, unless you can afford a great deal more than you anticipate ever requiring for your Web needs. Just remember that an idle CPU is better than an over-extended one, and that NT can serve most enterprise applications; filling out the extra load shouldn't prove too difficult.

Selecting Server Software

When you choose a server software, you want to ensure that your Web server can meet your current needs, as well as accommodate potential future needs as your site grows. A number of issues merit consideration, including the following:

- Multi-homed serving
- Logging facilities
- Browser compatibility features
- Headers and footers
- Access control

- Commerce security
- Administration method
- User-defined Web spaces

Multi-Homed Serving

Organizations that want to register multiple domain names but use a single server for all the domains need this feature. Multi-homed serving enables a single machine running a single server to differentiate between requests for www.somedomain.com and www.otherdomain.com and serve different Web pages for each. Internet presence providers utilize this feature extensively; it enables them to serve all their clients, each with their own domain name, from a few powerful machines.

Organizations that don't register multiple domains but have their own Domain Name Server (DNS) might also want to use this feature to serve different pages for different addresses within the domain.

Servers that have this feature include EnterpriseWeb, Internet Connection Server, NCSA httpd, Netscape Commerce, Netscape Communications, Open Market WebServer, Open Market Secure WebServer, Purveyor, Region 6 HTTP Server, Spinner, WebCommander, WebQuest, and WebSite.

Logging Facilities

Flexible logging facilities are essential for an enterprise server. Most servers write log files in the standard format established by the NCSA and CERN servers. This standard format enables third-party products to read and dissect your logs for analysis.

Also important are custom logging facilities, which enable CGI scripts to write log entries and enable administrators to customize log formats.

Servers that have either standard or custom logging facilities (or both) include the following:

CERN httpd (Standard Only)

EnterpriseWeb

Internet Connection Server (Standard Only)

NCSA httpd (Standard Only)

Netscape Commerce

Netscape Communications

Open Market Secure WebServer

Open Market WebServer

Purveyor (Standard Only)

Quarterdeck WebServer

Region 6 HTTP Server (Standard Only)

Spinner

WebCommander

WebQuest

Webshare (Standard Only)

WebSite (Standard Only)

WebSTAR

Browser Compatibility Features

In the current environment of splintering HTML specifications and features, server features that differentiate between browsers are essential for all but the most basic Web sites. Retaining compatibility with all forms of browsers used to require little more than careful HTML authoring, but it's becoming more and more difficult as features proliferate. A server that can deliver different documents based on the Accept: and User-Agent: fields in the HTML/1.0 specification enables a site administrator to have the most advanced, aesthetically pleasing pages, and still serve efficient, small pages to text-only browsers, unbloated by JavaScripts, client-side image maps, and other features useless to text-only browsers.

Servers that have this feature include the following: CERN httpd, EnterpriseWeb, Netscape Commerce, Netscape Communications, Open Market WebServer, Open Market Secure WebServer, Spinner, WebQuest, and WebSTAR.

Headers and Footers

To achieve a consistent look and feel, many site administrators rely on automatically created HTML headers and footers. Headers and footers is an important feature, because it eliminates the temptation to write a CGI script to do the same thing; CGIs take many more resources to run than do server-native functions and you should avoid them unless they're absolutely necessary.

Servers that have this feature include these: Netscape Commerce, Netscape Communications, Spinner, and WebCommander.

Access Control

Access control is an essential feature for any organization considering a pay-per-service site or considering using the same server for both Internet and Intranet publishing. Access control usually comes in two flavors: address-based and user-based. Address-based access control lets you permit or deny access based on the subnet from which a request comes. Address-based access restrictions provide a quick and easy way to limit access to Intranet materials to only the hosts that belong to your organization, minus the administrative hassles of user accounts.

User-based access control requires users to supply their username and password before they can access a particular document. Unfortunately, the increased control that this method permits brings with it the added administrative burden of creating and maintaining access lists. On the other hand, user-based control sometimes matches the necessary solution perfectly.

Servers that implement access control include these: CERN httpd, EnterpriseWeb, gn, Internet Connection Server, NCSA httpd, Netscape Commerce, Netscape Communications, Open Market Secure WebServer, Open Market WebServer, Purveyor, Quarterdeck WebServer, Region 6 HTTP Server, Spinner, WebCommander, WebQuest, WebSite, and WebSTAR.

Commerce Security

Any site considering electronic commerce that requires a customer to provide a credit card number over the network must choose a server that implements the Secure Sockets Layer (SSL). Not only are customers scared away when their browser warns them that the information they're submitting (their credit card number) could be monitored by a third party (no such warning will appear with an SSL-enabled server), but asking customers to submit their number by such an insecure means also is bad form.

Servers that implement SSL include Internet Connection Server, Netscape Commerce, Open Market Secure WebServer, WebCommander, and WebSTAR.

Administration Method

Web servers aren't simple applications. They require almost constant administration to keep them functioning optimally and delivering the content. To ease this task, most servers employ the graphical user interface (GUI) of their native operating system, or that of a graphical Web browser. Most people prefer a GUI-based method to editing text-only configuration files, which generally provide little more than slightly descriptive field names. Under a GUI-based administration system, the server generally provides a full description of what purpose the value serves and what effects modifying that value might have.

Servers that implement GUI administration include EnterpriseWeb, Internet Connection Server, Netscape Commerce, Netscape Communications, Open Market Secure WebServer, Open Market WebServer, Purveyor, Quarterdeck WebServer, Spinner, WebCommander, WebQuest, WebSite, and WebSTAR.

User-Defined Web Spaces

For those placing Web servers on existing multiuser machines, the capability to enable users to create their own Web spaces is important. Assume you administrate a Unix system, for example. Furthermore, assume your document hierarchy resides in /www/documents and your users reside in /home.

If you didn't have user-defined Web spaces, you would have to create a directory for each user in /www/documents just so users could create their own Web spaces. User-defined Web spaces would resolve http://myserver/~username to /home/username/www, or whatever specific subdirectory you define, without the administrative hassle of creating a directory for every user who wants to build a homepage.

Servers that enable user-defined Web spaces include CERN httpd, EnterpriseWeb, Internet Connection Server, NCSA httpd, Netscape Commerce, Netscape Communications, Open Market Secure WebServer, Open Market WebServer, Purveyor, Region 6 HTTP Server, Spinner, WebCommander, and Webshare.

Individual Server Products

This section serves as a starting point for considering which server to acquire, and offers sections on each of the following in turn:

- CERN httpd
- EnterpriseWeb
- gn
- Internet Connection Server
- NCSA httpd
- Netscape Commerce Server
- Netscape Communications Server
- Open Market WebServer
- Open Market Secure WebServer
- Purveyor
- Quarterdeck WebServer

- Region 6 HTTP Server
- Spinner
- WebCommander
- WebQuest
- Webshare
- WebSite
- WebSTAR

The preceding list and table 16.1 are far from complete; many other Web servers are available and new ones are released quite often. The list should serve as reference to the more dominant servers on the Internet, as well as to those that possess unique merits. If you have already selected your server platform, refer to table 16.1 to determine which servers are available.

Table 16.1
Servers Reviewed by Operating System

Operating System	Server Packages Available
Unix	CERN httpd, gn, Internet Connection Server, NCSA httpd, Netscape Commerce, Netscape Communications, Open Market Web Server, Open Market Secure Web Server, and Spinner
Windows 3.1	Quarterdeck WebServer
Windows 95	Purveyor, Quarterdeck WebServer, WebQuest, and WebSite
Windows NT	Netscape Commerce, Netscape Communications, Purveyor, Quarterdeck WebServer, WebQuest, and WebSite
OS/2	Internet Connection Server
Macintosh OS	MacHTTP and WebSTAR

Operating System	Server Packages Available
VMS	CERN, Purveyor, and Region 6 HTTPd
VM/CMS	Enterprise Web and Webshare

CERN httpd

The CERN httpd server is another of the reigning standards of the Internet. It is provided by CERN, the high-energy physics organization that created the Web and much of the software that makes it possible. One useful feature of the server is the capability to remap files and directories; a subdirectory can actually be another Web server halfway across the country. The redirection feature enables many ingenious solutions.

The W3 Consortium (W3C) maintains a page for the CERN server at `http://www.w3.org/hypertext/WWW/Daemon/Status.html`.

Server Features: Standard Logs, Browser Compatibility Features, Access Control, User-defined Web Spaces

Supported Operating Systems: Unix, VMS

EnterpriseWeb

EnterpriseWeb, from Beyond Software, is a fully featured Web server for the VM/CMS platform. Unlike WebShare, the other notable VM/CMS Web server, EnterpriseWeb's feature set is comparable to that of other servers running on more common platforms. The server has the potential to enable organizations to run entire Web sites from their existing VM/CMS machines, including new and advanced features, without extensive custom coding.

You can find product and purchase information about EnterpriseWeb at `http://www.beyond-software.com/`.

Server Features: Multi-homed Serving, Standard and Custom Logs, Browser Compatibility Features, Access Control, GUI Administration, User-defined Web Spaces

Supported Operating Systems: VM/CMS

gn

John Franks at Northwestern University created gn, a lightweight server designed to be small and simple. Although gn probably isn't well-suited to more demanding enterprise applications, it could prove useful to those with existing gopher trees. The gn server can ease the transition from gopher services by serving both gopher and HTTP requests from the same document tree. If a gopher hierarchy already is in place in an organization, running gn on the existing tree can get an HTTP server running quickly, enabling new HTML documents to be created without being rushed to publication.

You can find further information on gn at `http://hopf.math.nwu.edu:70/`.

Server Features: Access Control

Supported Operating Systems: Unix

Internet Connection Server

The Internet Connection Server, available from IBM, is the natural choice for enterprises already running on IBM mainframes. The server itself isn't unique, except that it's an IBM product, with all the implications that carries. This server merits serious consideration from any organization that already employs IBM applications and consultants; it's extensible by interconnection with other IBM products, and IBM's consultants can help you get it up and running the way you want it.

For more information on the Internet Connection Server, visit `http://www.ibm.com/internet/`.

Server Features: Multi-homed Serving, Standard Logs, Access Control, Commerce Security, GUI Administration, User-defined Web Spaces

Supported Operating Systems: OS/2 Warp, Unix (AIX)

NCSA httpd

NCSA, the organization that brought the world Mosaic, the original graphical Web browser, also created NCSA httpd, the standard in servers. The server only runs under Unix, and now is among the few servers that don't have a GUI-based administration function. However, NCSA httpd correctly serves from a gopher hierarchy, easing transitions from legacy gopher servers, and it also has an internal search engine.

Further information on NCSA httpd is available at `http://hoohoo.ncsa.uiuc.edu/docs/`.

Server Features: Multi-homed Serving, Standard Logs, Access Control, User-defined Web Spaces

Supported Operating Systems: Unix

Netscape Commerce Server

Netscape's Commerce Server is quickly becoming the platform of choice for cutting-edge Web developers. The server attracts users not because of any extraordinary features, but because of its association with Netscape, the leading company in Web browser development. Add Netscape's LiveWire Pro, however, and you transform the Commerce Server into the most advanced Web development platform on the market today. LiveWire includes Visual Site Management, Wizards and Templates, Java and JavaScript development tools, and SQL connectivity.

Netscape's site is at `http://www.netscape.com/`.

Server Features: Multi-homed Serving, Standard and Custom Logs, Browser Compatibility Features, Headers and Footers, Access Control, Commerce Security, GUI Administration, User-defined Web Spaces

Supported Operating Systems: Windows NT, Unix

Netscape Communications Server

Netscape's Communications Server is the non-secure version of Netscape's Web Server. The same industry-leading features of LiveWire Pro are compatible with this server, without the Secure Sockets Layer. Before choosing this server over its secure cousin, remember that any transactions that take place with this server are insecure, and subject to "snooping" by a third party. For further information on secure commerce, see Chapter 3, "Internet Commerce."

Further information on Netscape's server products is located at `http://www.netscape.com/`.

Server Features: Multi-homed Serving, Standard and Custom Logs, Browser Compatibility Features, Headers and Footers, Access Control, Commerce Security, GUI Administration, User-defined Web Spaces

Supported Operating Systems: Windows NT, Unix

Open Market's WebServer

Open Market's WebServer is among the more popular Web servers currently deployed on the Internet. It supports both Secure HTTP and the SSL. Open Market's distinction is its server's speed; it employs a multithreaded, multiprocess model. Unlike other servers' simpler multiprocess models, which are singlethreaded, Open Market made each process multithreaded as well, enabling each of the processes in the server pool to accomplish multiple actions at once. This design decreases server latency and increases both throughput and capacity.

Another extremely useful feature of the server is the way it employs the Tool Command Language (Tcl) in its configuration files; you can use Tcl to implement extremely complicated access controls. (For example, one could partially implement a system that maps hostnames to particular geographic areas and blocks access based on local times.)

Open Market's Web site is at `http://www.openmarket.com`.

Server Features: Multi-homed Serving, Standard and Custom Logs, Browser Compatibility Features, Access Control, GUI Administration, User-defined Web Spaces

Supported Operating Systems: Unix

Open Market's Secure WebServer

Open Market's Secure WebServer simply is a secure variant of its successful WebServer product. It supports both Secure HTTP and SSL, and includes WebServer's advanced capabilities for access management, as previously described.

Open Market's Web site is at `http://www.openmarket.com`.

Server Features: Multi-homed Serving, Standard and Custom Logs, Browser Compatibility Features, Access Control, Commerce Security, GUI Administration, User-defined Web Spaces

Supported Operating Systems: Unix

Purveyor

Process Software's Purveyor WebServer targets Intranet developers, but their server package is a capable member of the legions of Web products available. Process has created a server that offers simple, integrated ODBC query and update support (without programming), a custom log management application, and a broken-link detector. Purveyor also is an extremely capable proxy server, performing and caching requests for HTTP, FTP, and gopher protocols.

Process Software's Web site can be reached at `http://www.process.com/`.

Server Features: Multi-homed Serving, Standard and Custom Logs, Access Control, GUI Administration, User-defined Web Spaces

Supported Operating Systems: Windows 95, Windows NT, OpenVMS

Quarterdeck's WebServer

Quarterdeck's WebServer is a rather standard offering. It features a Windows-native setup GUI and enables you to create user groups (rather than the standard single access list). Quarterdeck has tested the server to support 25,000 document accesses per hour, with 16 simultaneous connections.

Quarterdeck also mentions that its server can run in the background, enabling you to use your PC for other tasks. Unless you use a Pentium with 32 MB (or stronger), you probably don't want to try doing so, however, especially if you have CGI scripts running.

> **Warning** Running a server in the background probably isn't a good idea; Windows is stable enough when running a server, but if you start running other things, Windows' tendency to crash becomes a factor. For an enterprise server, one missed connection is too many.

Server Features: Standard Logs, Access Control, GUI Administration

Supported Operating Systems: Windows 3.1, Windows 95, Windows NT

Region 6 HTTP Server

The Region 6 HTTP Server is a freeware, DECthreads-based Web server; a simple, efficient, and customizable alternative to the $CREPRC-happy CERN server for VMS. It provides all the basic necessities for serving under VMS.

Region 6 distributes the Threaded HTTP Server at `http://kcg11.eng.ohio-state.edu/www/doc/serverinfo.html`.

Server Features: Multi-homed Serving, Standard Logs, Access Control, User-defined Web Spaces

Supported Operating Systems: OpenVMS

Spinner

Spinner, a freeware offering from Informationsvavarna, is a somewhat unique Unix Web server. Although its lack of support for secure transactions makes it ill-suited for some enterprise applications, the fact that it's modular and customizable means that some organizations will find it perfect for their needs. By taking Spinner's freely available source code and replacing various modules, you could design a server to serve HTTP documents from virtually any source.

Informationsvavarna's Spinner information site is at `http://www.infovav.se/`.

Server Features: Multi-homed Serving, Standard and Custom Logs, Browser Compatibility Features, Access Control, GUI Administration, User-defined Web Spaces

Supported Operating Systems: Unix

WebCommander

WebCommander, from Luckman Interactive, is among the more advanced offerings in Web servers. It includes full S-HTTP support, in addition to the more common SSL standard, allowing for more secure transactions. It includes PERL support for CGI scripting, but also includes several features that usually require scripting to accomplish, such as real-time monitoring facilities, ODBC support for connecting to enterprise databases, Excite and WAIS search engines, and automated credit card clearing and verification. WebCommander also can serve as a POP3 and SMTP mail server.

For more information, visit Luckman Interactive's Web site at `http://www .luckman.com`.

Server Features: Multi-homed Serving, Standard and Custom Logs, Headers and Footers, Access Control, Commerce Security, GUI Administration, User-defined Web Spaces

Supported Operating Systems: Windows 95, Windows NT

WebQuest

Questar Microsystems' WebQuest server is among the more innovative servers when it comes to live content; Questar's implementation of Server Side Includes Plus (SSI+) enables many new dynamic tags for use within server-parsed HTML documents. WebQuest also is fully ODBC enabled, including updates, queries, and logging. A bundled product, Webmeister, performs concurrent diagnostics and hyperlink validation.

WebQuest's information page is located at `http://www.questar.com/`.

Server Features: Multi-homed Serving, Standard and Custom Logs, Browser Compatibility Features, Access Control (User-based Only), GUI Administration

Supported Operating Systems: Windows 95, Windows NT

Webshare

Webshare, from Beyond Software, is a freeware Web server implemented in the REXX language under VM/CMS. Although the server itself is rather limited in its features, it is designed to encourage users to write custom applications. Via CGI scripting, (in REXX,) the server can act as a powerful gateway to the masses of information currently stored on VM/CMS mainframes all over the world. The server enables user-defined Web spaces 2 (and control over the CGI scripting from those user-defined Web spaces), has forms support (GET and POST), automatic file conversions, filetype to MIME content-type mappings, multilingual support, and limited built-in image map support. For those interested in VM/CMS applications on the Web, check out the VM/World Wide Web discussion list, `www-vm@sjuvm.stjohns.edu`. To subscribe, send a message containing the body "Subscribe WWW-VM (firstname) (lastname)" to `listserv@sjuvm.stjohns.edu`.

For further information on Webshare, visit Beyond Software's Web site at `http://www.beyond-software.com/`.

Server Features: Standard Logs, User-defined Web Spaces

Supported Operating Systems: VM/CMS

WebSite

WebSite, from computer book publisher O'Reilly and Associates, has earned raves among its users for its ease-of-use, integration, and support. WebSite comes bundled with Webview, an application that generates a tree-like display of server documents and links, detects broken links, generates statistics from log files, and includes indexing and search tools. The package also includes HotDog, an HTML editor that supports both tables and forms. The server's most beloved feature, however, isn't in the software; it's the documentation. WebSite comes with a 480-page book that describes all the important considerations in maintaining the server, with O'Reilly's usual flair for making a computer book readable.

O'Reilly and Associates' Web site is located at `http://website.ora.com/`.

Server Features: Multi-homed Serving, Standard Logs, Access Control, GUI Administration

Supported Operating Systems: Windows 95, Windows NT

WebSTAR

Nine Technologies' WebSTAR is a direct descendant of the shareware MacHTTP server. This PowerPC native application rivals the speed of Unix-based servers, at three to four times faster than its ancestor, MacHTTP 2.0. The server provides full, built-in support for forms and image maps, provides access controls based on IP addresses and domain names, and enables remote administration via Web browsers on the Internet.

The WebSTAR server utilizes AppleScript as its CGI language; through AppleScript CGIs, the WebSTAR server can publish information from virtually any Macintosh application, which should come as welcome news to any organization looking to go online with its Macintosh databases.

Unlike MacHTTP, WebSTAR is a commercial product. For pricing and purchasing information, visit StarNine Technologies' Web site at `http://www .starnine.com/`.

Server Features: Standard and Custom Logs, Browser Compatibility Features, Access Control, Commerce Security, GUI Administration

Supported Operating Systems: Macintosh OS

Choosing Your Connection Bandwidth

Unless you decide on a really useless Web server, chances are that the bottleneck in your Web content delivery is your network's connection to the Internet. In the eyes of the impatient user, your potential customer, nothing is more important than the speed of delivery. A site might have the coolest interface or the most advanced graphics on the Web, but if it takes too long to load, nobody is going to stick around to see it. So, before you can balance network speed and content size, you need to determine exactly how long is too long.

For the initial HTML page, the accepted standard wait is five seconds, which means that after users click on a link to your page, it should be on the screen within five seconds, or they start to lose interest. Inlined images and small audio clips need to arrive within fifteen seconds, or users finish reading the page and move on before they arrive. If you plan to deliver files larger than 200 KB as an integral part of your Web presence, you need at least an ISDN link; if you plan to deliver files larger than 500 KB as an essential part of your Web site, buy all the bandwidth you can afford.

The following sections use these times as guidelines for illustrating file sizes that you can transmit over links of a given bandwidth.

Single-node Connectivity

For a single-node Web server on a dedicated line, a small bandwidth connection can suffice. Keep in mind, however, that running a Web server can consume most of a machine's memory, so that dedicated line to that single computer probably won't allow anyone at your organization to go surf the Web.

Single-node connectivity generally is provided by a local Internet Service Provider (ISP), which generally has a T1 or better connection to the Internet backbone and parcel out bandwidth to dialup and ISDN users.

Dedicated Dialup

A dedicated dialup line (operating at 28.8 kilobits per second) is the entry-level connection to the Internet. At this speed, initial HTML pages should be no larger than 14.4 KB in size. (HTTP protocol startup overhead accounts for approximately one second over modem links, plus four seconds of transmit time at 3.6 KB per second.) HTML plus external files should account for no more than 40 KB at this line speed.

A talented and driven Web designer takes limited bandwidth as a challenge to create the smallest, most efficient, but still aesthetically pleasing page possible. A 28.8 Kbps bandwidth certainly provides a challenging obstacle against which to work.

ISDN

ISDN, which has recently become widely available, allows connection throughput of 64 kilobits per second, which more than doubles the available bandwidth over dedicated modem lines. At this speed, permissible initial HTML page size increases to 36 KB, and total combined file size increases to around 110 KB. These file sizes allow for reasonable graphics capabilities for moderately busy sites. Be aware, however, that at these file sizes the bottleneck becomes the user's network connection, not the server's.

Whole-Network Connectivity

WAN routers (as described in Chapter 8, "WAN Access Devices") are essential for connecting multinode networks to the Internet. These access devices route TCP/IP packets into and out of your LAN over the dedicated line between it and your service provider. Various bandwidths are available, but most organizations want all the bandwidth they can afford if they intend to use their Internet connectivity.

WAN solutions generally are serviced by high-bandwidth providers, namely the major telecommunications companies, such as AT&T, MCI, and Sprint. They run a high-bandwidth connection from your location to their Point of Presence (POP), then backhaul the signal to their nearest Internet gateway. Bandwidth above ISDN could be prohibitively expensive for many organizations; T1 rates run upwards of $8,000 annually, while T3 rates can run in excess of $360,000 annually.

ISDN

For all but the smallest LANs, ISDN can't provide sufficient bandwidth for demands made by clients on both the inside and the outside of the network. One large application download taking place over the ISDN link slows the connection for several minutes.

T1

T1 is becoming the connection of choice for mid-sized enterprises connecting to the Internet. T1 provides bandwidth of 1.5 Mbps, enough for all but the most demanding WAN applications. If your Web site is overloading a T1, chances are that you're making enough money to afford the jump to a T3, or at least an NxT1.

A Web server running on a T1 can, in all likelihood, deliver whatever content you can come up with. Graphics, PDF, Audio, MPEG, and QuickTime are all fair game with this kind of bandwidth.

NxT1

NxT1 is the intermediate step between T1 and T3; Partial T3 bandwidth is delivered through inverse multiplexing over multiple T1 lines. Multiple routers on both ends break up multi-megabit signals, transmit them over the T1s, then reassemble them at the other end. The benefits of NxT1 are cost, availability, and scalability. Running multiple T1s in parallel scales the cost and bandwidth to fit the organization's budget and needs.

T3

T3 connections provide bandwidth of 45 Mbps from end to end. They are, for now, the paramount WAN solution for Internet access. Beyond this speed, the network backbone isn't fast enough to enable a significant speed increase.

T3s are unavailable in many markets. Most sites require special installation of a line from the DS3 POP to the nearest Internet Gateway, constituting an additional cost on top of the already expensive T3 link. Contact your telecommunications service provider for availability and pricing information.

Alternative Solutions

Although for the most part a Web server is the most flexible solution for your organization, it isn't the only possible solution to establishing a presence on the Web. Presence providers and dedicated Web devices are two possible alternatives worth considering. The following sections discuss these alternatives.

Presence Providers

Presence providers are businesses that have high-speed connections to the Internet backbone and parcel out space on their Web servers to organizations. Generally, these providers fall into two somewhat indistinct categories: hosting services and mall services. Both solutions, however, leave you with much less control over your publishing environment than does maintaining your own server. Presence providers generally impose throughput and size restrictions on your content, for example, among other things.

Hosting Services

A *hosting service* generally provides a directory on a machine, a certain quota of space, and a certain monthly throughput to each subscriber. Your pages are placed on their server, and perhaps in a "What's Here" list on the server. Advertising in the hundreds of pages on the Internet is up to you, and people generally visit the site because they're interested in your services or products.

Hosting services generally don't allow CGI scripting or other server-customizations over which you would have control on your own machine. Database connectivity and search capabilities probably aren't available, or are available but cost extra. Many service providers limit your available solutions but advertise for their consulting services, which can create any custom application or content you may want. For all but the most basic needs, service providers aren't worth sacrificing your flexibility.

Mall Services

Mall services generally are more restrictive than hosting services. *Mall services* organize a collection of vendors into a virtual mall configuration, each service with its own storefront. Users are attracted to the mall by the possibility of browsing, not necessarily for your service. Mall services take care of the advertising, for the most part; their responsibility is to provide their clients exposure, not simple hosting.

A mall might be just the solution you want, depending on the content of your planned Web site. Chances are, though, that it isn't. Some things are better done in-house, where everything's under your control.

Dedicated Web Devices

Another intriguing development in the Web market came in the form of a small, black device about the size of a cigar box. The WebBox, from Webtronics K.K., a Japanese venture development firm, is a dedicated, firmware-based Web server. It stores pages in its zippy Flash RAM (2 MB initially, expandable to 8 MB), serving them on demand. The server runs only on an Ethernet network, so it requires full-network connectivity to serve documents to the Web; you cannot connect it directly to a dedicated line.

The WebBox's httpd implementation is written in Tcl and executed by the built-in Tcl interpreter in ROM. The source to the server is included for customization, as are example scripts.

The WebBox also has a tamper-proof hardware lock, so you can place it outside a corporate firewall to serve content to the Internet. The WebBox's tamper-proof setting makes the Flash RAM read-only.

For technical information regarding WebBox, send e-mail to Webtronics at `info@wtnx.com`, and for sales information in North America, contact Corporate Source at `cs@ix.netcom.com`.

Example Cases

The following cases are presented to illustrate the decision process in selecting a Web server. They represent two extremely different environments, but the decision process is the same: Weighted considerations are made based on existing circumstances. The two cases represent the two distinct approaches to establishing a presence: starting small and expanding as necessary, and starting with a powerful server and a fast connection. For most purposes, your situation will probably parallel one approach or the other.

The Non-Profit Organization

This is a regional organization that provides social services. They have extremely limited preexisting hardware—just a few PCs and modems scattered at various sites used to exchange nightly data.

The goals of the Web site simply are to publicize exactly what the organization does and hopefully raise some money. To accomplish this effectively, they have decided that they need a somewhat graphics-intensive site.

The database that is exchanged nightly is completely separate from the information they want to publish on the Internet, so interoperability isn't a concern. The staff is used to using Windows, however, so it looks like Windows or a Macintosh machine will be used; Unix definitely is out.

The important features this organization requires are logging facilities, to know where people are being reached; browser compatibility features, to make sure the page is presented optimally for each browser; access control, for future possibilities of information exchange via the Web server; and GUI-based administration, because none of the staff has had to use a command line.

After considering their needs regarding features, the organization settles on WebSTAR for the Macintosh, from StarNine Technologies.

For connectivity, the organization chooses a dedicated ISDN line to their local service provider; anything less couldn't deliver the content required, anything more couldn't fit into the budget.

This organization's decision process mirrors what many small businesses and entrepreneurs do as they create a Web presence; they start with a baseline server and connection, and upgrade as finances and circumstances warrant. It is an approach that you may wish to consider as you establish your presence.

The Mid-Sized Corporation

This mid-sized corporation is simultaneously creating a dedicated Web server and connecting its 200-node LAN to the Internet. The network is extremely heterogeneous; Macintosh, Windows 95, a VM/CMS server, and several Unix boxes make up the more mainstream elements.

The purpose of the Web site is to publish general information about the company, serve the product catalog, and also enable electronic transactions to take place. The Board of Directors was recently introduced to the Web in an impressive (but canned) multimedia presentation by the Chief Information

Officer. After this presentation, they decided to have the server include the most advanced features available, including stills, image maps, frames, live applications, movies, and audio. Fortunately, they adjusted the budget to compensate for these high expectations.

The important considerations for this organization are interoperability, because it must be able to interface with the existing database system; multi-homed serving, because the company has agreed to provide Web presences for several local non-profits; logging facilities, because marketing wants to know what audience they're reaching; browser compatibility features, to serve pages optimized for the viewing platform; and commerce security, because purchases are to be made via the server.

The implementation team finally settles on the Netscape Commerce Server with LiveWire Pro as the server software, communicating with the VM/CMS server with ODBC, and a DEC AlphaServer running DEC Unix as the server platform.

For connectivity, the team decides on dual T1 lines in a NxT1 configuration to allow for future expansion, and to make sure they have plenty of bandwidth for now.

The case of the corporation illustrates just how important a consideration interoperability is. Upgrading your software, hardware, and your people can end up costing more than the server itself; don't do it unless you have to. Most importantly, plan ahead. Put everything down on paper, and let everyone involved mull over the details; if planning is done properly, most potential problems can be found and solved before they leave the planning stage.

System Optimization

by Mike Coulombe

When optimizing a Web server, especially on a Unix platform, you must consider many factors. The various hardware issues, for example, are adequate memory, swap space, disk space, and CPU utilization to name a few. Information on optimizing these resources typically is specific to a vendor's platform. In addition to these issues, Web server software comes with many configurable options that can hinder or improve performance. You can optimize your Web server by understanding these configuration options and using them to get the most out of your server.

This chapter focuses on the configuration files for NCSA HTTPd v1.5a. This free Web server is very robust and has many, and sometimes more of the advanced features that you find in commercial Web server products. Features, such as pre-forking, keepalive timers, and parsed HTML, enhance the performance and flexibility of the server. NCSA's HTTPd is available precompiled for a variety of platforms, and the source is also available should you need to compile the software yourself. You may download this software from `ftp://ftp.ncsa.uiuc.edu/Web/httpd/Unix/ncsa_httpd`.

HTTPd Configuration Files

HTTPd's behavior is controlled by a set of configuration files. These files, located in /usr/local/etc/httpd/conf for the examples used here, are plain text files that can be modified with your favorite Unix editor. The content of the configuration files is case sensitive. Comment lines begin with a number symbol (#). Comments must be on a line by themselves; they cannot be included after configuration directives. Only one directive is allowed per line. The format for server directives is:

```
Directive     data     [data2 … datan]
```

where *data2* through *datan* are optional parameters specific to the exact directive being used. White space must separate the data elements from themselves and from the directives.

For changes to the Web server's configuration files to take effect, restart the server by sending a kill signal to the server's process id. The server saves its process id to the location specified by the *PidFile* directive in the httpd.conf configuration file. To restart the server, use the command

```
kill -1 'cat pidfile'
```

or

```
kill -HUP 'cat pidfile'
```

where *pidfile* is the filename specified in httpd.conf. If you need to stop the Web server, use this command:

```
kill 'cat pidfile'
```

This command stops the Web server and any child processes. Avoid using `kill -9` to stop the Web server because it might not stop the child processes on some systems.

HTTPd Server Configuration File

The main server configuration file for the Web server is httpd.conf. This file controls how the server loads, what TCP port to use, what user and group IDs to run under, the name of the server, the location of your HTML documents and log files, and many other options. The server distribution comes with a sample file named conf/httpd.conf-dist. To start, copy this file to conf/httpd.conf. You must edit several of the settings in this file before you can start the server. A copy of this template is included here for reference as you read this section. Comments within the template have been made by NCSA to help you configure the server.

```
#==================================================================
# NCSA HTTPd (comments, questions to httpd@ncsa.uiuc.edu)
#==================================================================
# This is the main server configuration file. It is best to
# leave the directives in this file in the order they are in, or
# things may not go the way you'd like. See URL http:/
# hoohoo.ncsa.uiuc.edu/for instructions.
# Do NOT simply read the instructions in here without
# understanding what they do; if you are unsure, consult the
# online docs. You have been warned.
# Thanks to A. P. Harris for some of the organization and
# explanations contained here-in.
#==================================================================

#==================================================================
# Server Operation
# -----------------------------------------------------------------
# ServerType is either inetd, or standalone.
# Set to 'inetd' to run from inetd, or 'standalone', to run as a
# daemon.
# Default: standalone

ServerType standalone
```

```
# If you are running from inetd, go to "ServerAdmin".

# Port: The port the standalone listens to. For ports < 1023, you
# will need HTTPd to be run as root initially.
# Default: 80 (or DEFAULT_PORT)

Port 80

# StartServers: The number of servers to launch at startup.  Must
# be compiled without the NO_PASS compile option
# Default: 5 (or DEFAULT_START_DAEMON)

StartServers 5

# MaxServers: The number of servers to launch until mimicing the
# 1.3 scheme (new server for each connection).  These servers will
# stay around until the server is restarted.  They will be reused
# as needed, however.
# See the documentation on hoohoo.ncsa.uiuc.edu for more
# information.
# If compile option RESOURCE_LIMIT is used, HTTPd will not mimic
# the 1.3 behavior, and MaxServers will be the maximum number of
# servers possible.
# Default: 10 (or DEFAULT_MAX_DAEMON)

MaxServers 20

## TimeOut <seconds>
# The number of seconds the server will wait for a client to
# send its query once connected, or the maximum amount of time the
# server will spend waiting for a client to accept information.
# Default: 1200 (or DEFAULT_TIMEOUT)
TimeOut 1200

# If you wish HTTPd to run as a different user or group, you must
# run HTTPd as root initially and it will switch.
# User/Group: The name (or #number) of the user/group to run HTTPd
# as.
# Default: #-1 (or DEFAULT_USER / DEFAULT_GROUP)

User nobody
Group #-1
```

```
# IdentityCheck: Enables or disables RFC931 compliant logging of
# the remote user name for sites which run identd or something
# similar.
# This information is logged in the access_log.  Note that it
# *will* hurt responsiveness considerably, especially for non-unix
# clients.
# Default: off (or DEFAULT_RFC931)

#IdentityCheck On

# AssumeDigestSupport: Whether it's safe to assume that clients
# support md5 digesting.
# Default: off

#AssumeDigestSupport On

#==================================================================
# Server Customization
#------------------------------------------------------------------
# ServerName allows you to set a host name which is sent back to
# clients for your server if it's different than the one the
# program would get (i.e. use "www" instead of the host's real
# name).
#
# Note: You cannot just invent host names and hope they work. The
# name you define here must be a valid DNS name for your host. If
# you don't, understand this, ask your network administrator.
# Valid with <VirtualHost>
# Default: If you do not specify a ServerName, HTTPd attempts to
# retrieve it through system calls.

#ServerName new.host.name

# ServerAdmin: Your address, where problems with the server should
# be e-mailed.
# Valid within <VirtualHost>
# Default: <none> (or DEFAULT_ADMIN)

ServerAdmin you@your.address
```

```
#==============================================================================
# File Locations
#------------------------------------------------------------------------------
# ServerRoot: The directory the server's config, error, and log
# files are kept.
# Note: All other paths will use this as a prefix if they don't
# start with /
# Default: /usr/local/etc/httpd (or HTTPD_ROOT)

ServerRoot /usr/local/etc/httpd

# ErrorLog: The location of the error log file. If this does not
# start with /, ServerRoot is prepended to it.

ErrorLog logs/error_log

# TransferLog: The location of the transfer log file. If this does
# not start with /, ServerRoot is prepended to it.

TransferLog logs/access_log

# AgentLog: The location of the agent log file.  If this does not
# start with /, ServerRoot is prepended to it.

AgentLog logs/agent_log

# RefererLog: The location of the referer log file.  If this does
# not start with /, ServerRoot is prepended to it.

RefererLog logs/referer_log

# PidFile: The file the server should log its pid to
PidFile logs/httpd.pid

# TypesConfig: The location of the typing configuration file,
# which maps filename extensions to MIME types.
# Default: conf/mime.types (or TYPES_CONFIG_FILE)

#TypesConfig /usr/local/lib/mime.types
```

```
# CoreDirectory:  where to dump core.
# Default: SERVER_ROOT

#CoreDirectory /tmp


#=====================================================================
# Logging Directives
#---------------------------------------------------------------------
# LogOptions: This determines the type of log file you are using,
# Valid options currently are:
#   Combined for CLF with Referer and UserAgent tagged on
#   Separate for CLF in one file and Referer and UserAgent in
#   separate files
#   Servername for CLF + ServerName
#   Date for Referer and UserAgent logs with same date stamp as
#   access_log

LogOptions Separate

# LogDirGroupWriteOk, LogDirPublicWriteOk: Define either of these
# if you  want the server to start even if you have write
# permissions on the log directory.  Having write permissions set
# is a potential security hole. Only makes a difference if the
# server process is started by root.

#LogDirGroupWriteOk
#LogDirPublicWriteOk

# RefererIgnore: If you don't want to keep track of links from
# certain servers (like your own), place it here.  If you want to
# log them all, keep this line commented.

#RefererIgnore servername

# DNSMode allows you to control the amount of DNS activity the
# server will perform.  The default is Standard, which means it
# does a single lookup on every request. Minimum means the server
# will only do a lookup if
```

```
# necessary to fulfill a domain restriction.  Maximum means the
# server will do two lookups per request.  This will be slow, and
# not necessarily that much better security.  None will keep the
# server from doing any DNS resolution. Maximum is the same as the
# old MAXIMUM_DNS compile option, and none is the same as the old
# MINIMUM_DNS option.
# Default: Standard

DNSMode Standard

#=====================================================================
# KeepAlive Directives
#---------------------------------------------------------------------
# The directives below configure keepalive, the ability of the
# server to maintain a persistent connection with a client at the
# client's request

# The following line turns keepalive on. The default is off, so
# you can omit this line, or change 'on' to 'off'

# KeepAlive on

# The following line specifies the timeout in seconds of the
# persistent connection. If the client fails to issue another
# request on the socket within this window, the connection is
# closed

# KeepAliveTimeout 10

# The following line specifies the maximum number of requests
# that will be accepted on the persistent connection. If it
# is set to 0, then there will be no maximum.
# Default:

# MaxKeepAliveRequests 0

#=====================================================================
# Misc Options
#---------------------------------------------------------------------
```

```
# ProcessName: This is the prefix for the process name if compiled
# with SETPROCTITLE.
# Default: HTTPd

#ProcessName WebServer

#Annotation-Server: Name of our annotation server.  This will send
# back an Annotation: header with requests to denote where the
# annotation server is located.
#Default: None


#=====================================================================
# VirtualHost
#---------------------------------------------------------------------
# VirtualHosting is the ability to respond differently to
# different IP addresses.  It can be implemented either by having
# a single server respond to all, or by having a different server
# respond to each (the Unix(tm) OS setup precludes responding to
# some).  Every effort has been made to allow a single server to
# respond to all as effectively as possible, as this is more
# resource efficient.  There are some things which still aren't
# possible in that configuration, however.

# BindAddress: A '*', IP number, or host name.  Binds the server
# to a specific IP address.  * is all IP addresses.  Should not be
# used in conjunction with <VirtualHost>.
# Default: *

#BindAddress 127.0.0.1

# VirtualHost allows you to look differently depending on the
# hostname you are called by.  The parameter must be either an IP
# address or a hostname that maps to a single IP address.  Most of
# the normal httpd.conf commands are available, as well as the
# ability to denote a special ResourceConfig file for this host.
# You can also specify an error level with this setting, by
# denoting the VirtualHost as Optional or Required.
```

```
<VirtualHost 127.0.0.1 Optional>
DocumentRoot /local
ServerName localhost.ncsa.uiuc.edu
ResourceConfig conf/localhost_srm.conf
</VirtualHost>
```

Now that you have reviewed these settings, the following sections discuss each directive's meaning and possible use. You might want to start with a minimal amount of changes and make more as you become more familiar with the configuration files and the server.

Server Type (inetd versus Standalone)

The *ServerType* directive controls how the Web server loads. The two possible values are *inetd* and *standalone.*

Inetd is the "super-server" for Unix systems. The configuration files /etc/services and /etc/inetd.conf contain the list of services and server programs to load for incoming client requests. The /etc/services file identifies to which ports each service is assigned: 23 for Telnet, 25 for SMTP e-mail, 70 for gopher, 110 for pop-mail, and so on. The /etc/inetd.conf file identifies which server process to run for each service. As requests come in to TCP ports, the inetd process checks which port corresponds to which service and therefore which process to start. This method of execution prevents the system from needing to run every server simultaneously. The inetd process only starts the servers as needed. For occasional use services such as Telnet, FTP, pop-mail, and others, this mode of operation works well.

For higher use or more resource-intensive services such as databases, printing, and SMTP e-mail, however, this mode of operation is inefficient. For these services, a constantly running server eliminates the overhead associated with loading the program and reading configuration files, saving a considerable amount of time.

Your server performs faster in stand-alone mode than in inetd mode. When the system starts, the Web server loads, reads the configuration files, and listens for incoming requests. Requests are then serviced immediately, in contrast to the wait involved when the inetd process starts the Web server.

Starting with version 1.4, NCSA's HTTPd now supports Pre-Forking. This mode of operation is discussed in the section that addresses the topic of StartServers and MaxServers. Unless you have a specific reason not to, run your Web server in stand-alone mode.

Port Number

The *Port* directive tells the server which TCP port to listen to for incoming requests. The default port for the HyperText Transfer Protocol (HTTP) is 80. Unix platforms restrict access to ports below 1023 to the root or superuser account. To run your Web server on port 80, the process must be started by the root user. For servers running in inetd mode, the inetd configuration files determine which port Web requests are serviced.

Tip If your Web server is still in development, consider running the server at one of the port numbers above 1023, such as 8000. Using a higher port number makes it harder for outside users to inadvertently see your unfinished work.

To access a Web server on a port other than 80, include the port in the URL. The URL `http://www.widgets.com:8021/test.html` directs the Web browser to port 8021 on the server www.widgets.com and requests the page test.html. You also can run a production Web server on port 80 and a development server on a higher unused port.

StartServers and MaxServers

The *StartServers* and *MaxServers* directives control how many server instances to run in a server pool. One Web server listens to port 80. As requests come in, they are handed to one of the idle servers in the pool. As the load increases, additional idle servers up to a limit set by MaxServers may be started. This server pool creation is called *pre-forking*. Without the server pool, only a single server process runs. As requests come in, the server must "fork" a second process to handle the request while the original process continues to listen for incoming requests. Under heavy loads, the pre-forking server pool can save a considerable amount of time in servicing Web requests.

To use the pre-forked server pool, your operating system must support file descriptor passing. This support has been tested under SunOS4, Solaris2, Irix, HP-UX, AIX, Ultrix, OSF/1, NeXT, NetBSD, and SCO SVR3.2. The Linux kernel currently does not support file descriptor passing, but a work around exists using the /proc file system. If your Linux system is having trouble running the server in a pre-forked mode, comment out the StartServers and MaxServers lines in the configuration file.

TimeOut

The *TimeOut* directive controls how long the server waits for a client to send or receive a request after the client has connected. This time out value can have an adverse effect on modem users. If your Web pages contain many graphics, or you are using your Web server to download large binary files, this value can terminate a Web connection before all the data has been sent. Most modems run at transfer speeds of 1 to 2 KB per second. With a time-out setting of 1,200, any file download over 1,200 KB can be terminated before it is completed. Take care not to include too many large graphics in your Web pages. If your site offers large files to download, consider using an anonymous FTP server rather than the Web server.

User and Group

The *User* and *Group* directives control which user and group IDs the Web server uses when services are requested. These directives are only applicable if your server is running as stand-alone. The Web server itself must run as root to access port 80, but the forked processes created to service the request have their ID numbers changed to the ones specified in the configuration file.

If names are used, the user and group names used must be present in the /etc/passwd and /etc/group files. Most Unix systems have a user ID of "nobody" defined. Using this ID limits the security access the server is allowed while it services requests. Setting the server's user and group ID to an unprivileged account helps prevent unwanted access to your server.

IdentityCheck

The *IdentityCheck* directive either enables or disables RFC931 logging of the remote user name for sites running identd. This information appears in the second field of the access_log entry. The only two options allowed are On and Off. The default setting is Off. Enabling this feature can severely impact your server's performance. Unless you know you will be using this information, maintain the Off default setting.

AssumeDigestSupport

The *AssumeDigestSupport* directive sets a flag in the server that is never checked. At one time it was thought that some sort of prompt would appear to clients that did not support md5, but this feature was never implemented. The two possible values are On and Off. The default setting is Off.

ServerName and ServerAdmin

The *ServerName* directive sets the host name the Web server reports back to its clients. If this directive is not set, the system attempts to discover its own host name. Use this directive if you want to set the server's name to something other than the true system name, such as www.domain.name rather than host.domain.name. Any name you use must be a valid DNS host name.

The *ServerAdmin* directive sets the e-mail address sent back to a client browser when an error occurs. The person browsing then can send you an e-mail message notifying you of the error they received so you can fix it.

File Location Directives

The ServerRoot and ErrorLog directives are only slightly related to the previous ones. NCSA globbed them under one commented section, but they really don't fall into a server catagory.

The *ServerRoot* directive tells the Web server in which directory the server's configuration, log, and error files are kept. This directory path is prepended to the rest of the file location directives if a leading forward slash (/) is not given. The default location for *ServerRoot* is /usr/local/etc/httpd.

The *ErrorLog* directive tells the Web server in which file to log server errors. The file contains errors such as unauthorized access given to protected documents, or simply someone mistyping the URL of a page on your server. This file also logs the times at which your Web server has been restarted. The examples in this chapter have all log files located in the /usr/local/etc/httpd/ logs directory. The error log appears like the following:

```
[Sun Feb 18 12:08:49 1996] HTTPd: caught SIGHUP, restarting
[Sun Feb 18 12:08:49 1996] HTTPd: successful restart
[Sun Feb 18 12:17:44 1996] HTTPd: access to /usr/local/etc/httpd/
htdocs/nopage.html failed for hue, reason: No file matching URL:
/nopage.html from -
```

In the preceding example, the Web server process receives a kill signal and successfully restarts. Then an attempt is made to load the page nopage.html. Because this page does not exist on the server, an error is logged. The Web browser also receives a `404 not found` error message.

The *TransferLog* directive tells the Web server in which file to log all requests received by the server. This file records all attempts to access your Web server, successful or not. Unsuccessful access attempts also are logged in the *ErrorLog* file. The *TransferLog* file is the key file used to determine the amount of traffic on your Web site. Chapter 18, "Monitoring Server Activity," discusses in depth the format of this file and the ways to analyze it. The following are some sample entries from an access_log file:

```
hue - - [18/Feb/1996:12:09:05 -0500] "GET / HTTP/1.0" 200 111
hue - - [18/Feb/1996:12:09:08 -0500] "GET /two.html HTTP/1.0" 200 50
hue - - [18/Feb/1996:12:17:44 -0500] "GET /nopage.html HTTP/1.0"
➥404-
```

The computer "hue" made three requests to the server. The first two were successful, the last was not. The last field is supposed to be the amount of bytes transferred for the page. The first two pages had byte counts of 111 and 50, respectively. The last page request produced an error, therefore the error number, 404, and an empty byte count, represented by a hyphen (-), were recorded.

The *AgentLog* directive tells the Web server in which file to log Web agent information. Starting with version 1.4, the NCSA Web server can log the browser used to access your Web pages. This information is extracted from the request packets sent by all Web browsers. The output of the AgentLog file looks like the following:

```
Mozilla/2.0 (Win95; I)
Mozilla/2.0 (Win95; I)
Mozilla/2.0 (Win95; I)
```

Each line of the file represents one request. The browser used for each request is logged. Mozilla is the name that the Netscape browser reports to the server. The version number and operating system also are included in this log. Later in this section, you learn how to include date and time information when logging when browsers' requests are made.

The *RefererLog* directive tells the Web in which file to log Web referrals to your pages. Starting with version 1.4, the NCSA Web server can log which page the Web browser used to reach a page on your server. This information is useful to determine the external sites that have links to pages on your server. The majority of external references in this file most likely are from Web indexes such as Yahoo, WebCrawler, and others. This will have entries like the following:

```
http://borg/ -> /two.html
```

The server borg referred the browser to the page two.html. By default, references made by the server to itself are recorded in the *RefererLog* file. The previous example is such a reference. The home page index.html contained a link to the page two.html. When the link was selected, the reference was recorded.

The *PidFile* directive tells the Web server where to save the process id number of the first server process. Use this file when you send kill signals to the server. The PidFile directive is used only if the *ServerType* is stand-alone. This file is usually located in /usr/local/etc/httpd/logs/httpd.pid.

The *TypesConfig* directive tells the Web server where to read the MIME types information. The Web server uses this file to map filename extensions to MIME types to return to clients.

The *AccessConfig* directive, not shown in the distribution file, tells the Web server where to read the global access configuration file. This file controls all access to your server. If this directive is not included, and it is not in the template file, the server defaults to the following:

```
AccessConfig conf/access.conf
```

More information related to this file can be found in the "Global Access Configuration File" section later in this chapter.

The *CoreDirectory* directive tells the Web server where to save core dumps should they occur. A process typically dumps core due to unforeseen error conditions that force the process to terminate. The default location for core files is the *ServerRoot* directory. If your Web server is dumping core files on a regular basis, something is wrong either in the code or in your configuration. Check the error logs for any messages that might point to a problem. Check to make sure you have the most current version and patch level of software for both the server and the operating system.

Logging Directives

The *LogOptions* directive controls how the Web server formats the log files, and how many files to use. The four options available are:

- Separate
- Combined
- Servername
- Date

The *Separate* option produces output that matches the file formats presented previously in the log file locations section.

The *Combined* option combines the access, agent, and referrer information all on one line in the *TransferLog* file. This file looks like the following:

```
hue - - [18/Feb/1996:17:18:41 -0500] "GET / HTTP/1.0" 304 0 ""
➥"Mozilla/2.0 (Win95; I)"
hue - - [18/Feb/1996:17:19:15 -0500] "GET / HTTP/1.0" 200 111 ""
➥"Mozilla/2.0 (Win95; I)"
hue - - [18/Feb/1996:17:19:18 -0500] "GET /two.html HTTP/1.0" 200
➥50 "http://borg/" "Mozilla/2.0 (Win95; I)"
```

Client browser and referring information, if any exists, is included with each Web request. The Web server logs the additional information using the *Combined* format even if the AgentLog and RefererLog directives are commented out of the configuration file. If these directives are not commented out, and the combined format is used, they are ignored. The combined format is helpful in associating the Web browser with each request.

Note The Combined format is a relatively new option, and not many log analysis tools have been written to support it. Over time, this will not be as much of a problem as new tools are developed to support this format.

The *ServerName* option appends the server's name to each Web request logged into the *TransferLog.* This format is often useful in conjunction with the *VirtualHost* directives discussed later in the "Multihome/Virtual Host Support" section. With the *VirtualHost* directive, your server can be configured to run under different server names based on which IP address was used to access the site. If you use the *VirtualHost* feature, the *ServerName* log format helps sort out which requests were made to each server.

The *Date* option prepends a date stamp to the entries in the *AgentLog* and *RefererLog* files. The format of the *TransferLog* file remains unchanged. The *Date* option provides additional information that you can use to determine which clients were used to access your server and when.

The *DNSMode* directive controls how many DNS queries your server generates. The default setting of Standard generates one DNS lookup for each request. A setting of Minimum only generates a DNS lookup if an access restriction must be met. A setting of None prevents all DNS resolution, prohibiting you from limiting access based on host names.

KeepAlive Directives

By design, the HTTP protocol is *stateless*, meaning that each request made to the server is independent and generally unrelated to any others. The key benefit of this statelessness is simplicity. A Web server can communicate with one or many clients downloading the same or different pages—a connection is established, a request is made, the request is serviced, the connection is terminated, and then the process begins again.

A drawback to this model is the overhead involved in opening and closing the server/client connection. Most Web pages contain graphics of some kind, usually more than one. For a page with four graphics, five requests are generated: one for the page and four for each graphic. To help improve performance, NCSA's HTTPd now enables multiple requests to be handled over a single connection through the keepalive feature. The only catch to this feature is that your browser must support it as well. NCSA's Mosaic supports the keepalive feature, and NCSA claims a 30-percent increase in performance using it.

To enable the keepalive feature, set the *KeepAlive* directive to On. The *KeepAliveTimeout* directive controls how long the server holds the connection open awaiting new requests. The *MaxKeepAliveRequests* directive sets the limit of how many requests a Web server handles per connection.

Warning Consider some issues before turning on the keepalive feature. Because NCSA's HTTPd is a pre-forking server, the keepalive feature ties up a server process longer per connection, reducing the amount of available servers for other client requests. This reduction can lead to an increase in server processes and an increase in memory used by the server. Some care, therefore, should be taken in setting the keepalive parameters.

NCSA is currently studying the effect the keepalive feature has on overall server performance. Shortly after NCSA implemented its keepalive feature, a similar method was proposed by the Internet Engineering Task Force (IETF) for version 1.1 of HTTP. Future versions of HTTPd most likely will support the proposed standard.

Multihome/Virtual Host Support

Starting with version 1.5, HTTPd now supports multihome or virtual host capabilities. Most Unix systems allow support for multiple IP addresses per network interface. The implementation of these multiple addresses are specific to your version of Unix. Every Unix system can have at least two IP addresses, one for the network interface, and the second being the loopback address 127.0.0.1.

With virtual host support, you can configure the Web server to report back different server names based on the IP addresses used to access the server. A system that has two IP addresses on an Ethernet interface, for example, 192.168.1.1 and 192.168.1.2, can be configured to run separate servers on each interface, www.*first*.com and www.*second*.com. This configuration still requires that the IP addresses and DNS names are valid for the network in question. The following is an example of a virtual host configuration:

```
BindAddress 127.0.0.1

<VirtualHost 127.0.0.1 >
DocumentRoot /local
ServerName localhost.domain.name.com
ResourceConfig conf/localhost_srm.conf
</VirtualHost>
```

These directives configure a new server name of *localhost.domain.name*.com for any request that reaches the IP address 127.0.0.1. The server also uses a different resource configuration file for requests made using the loopback address. Requests using the loopback address must be made on the system running a Web browser locally.

Server Resource Configuration File

The *server resource configuration file*, srm.conf, controls how users see your system. This file translates the Unix directory structure into the Web directory structure on your server. The server distribution comes with a sample file named conf/srm.conf-dist. If you install your server in /usr/local/etc/httpd, copying the distribution file to srm.conf will suffice to get the Web server up and running. You may choose, however, to change this directory or enable features not enabled by default. A copy of the distribution file srm.conf-dist is included here for reference as you read this section:

```
#==========================================================================
# NCSA HTTPd (comments, questions to httpd@ncsa.uiuc.edu)
#==========================================================================
# This is the server resource configuration file.  With this
# document, you define the name space that users of your server
# see.
# See URL http://hoohoo.ncsa.uiuc.edu/ for HTTPd Documentation.
# Information specific to this file can be found at
# http://hoohoo.ncsa.uiuc.edu/docs/setup/srm/Overview.html
# Do NOT simply read the instructions in here without
# understanding what they do.  If you are unsure, consult the
# online docs.  You have been warned.
#==========================================================================


#==========================================================================
# Name Space Options
#--------------------------------------------------------------------------
# DocumentRoot: The directory out of which you will serve your
# documents. By default, all requests are taken from this
# directory, but symbolic links and aliases may be used to point
# to other locations.

DocumentRoot /usr/local/etc/httpd/htdocs

# UserDir: The name of the directory which is appended onto a
# user's home directory if a ~user request is recieved.

UserDir public_html
```

```
# Redirect allows you to tell clients about documents which used
# to exist in your server's namespace, but do not anymore. This
# allows you to tell the clients where to look for the relocated
# document.
# Format: Redirect fakename url

Redirect /HTTPd/ http://hoohoo.ncsa.uiuc.edu/

# Aliases: Add here as many aliases as you need. The format is
# Alias fakename realname

Alias /icons/ /usr/local/etc/httpd/icons/

# ScriptAlias: This controls which directories contain server
# scripts.
# Format: ScriptAlias fakename realname

ScriptAlias /cgi-bin/ /usr/local/etc/httpd/cgi-bin/

#=========================================================================
# Directory Indexing
#-------------------------------------------------------------------------
# If a user requests a document (URL) from your server ending in
# /, the server will attempt to "index" the directory.  It will
# first look for a file matching the DirectoryIndex directive in
# order.  If no files exist, and Indexing is allowed for that
# directory, the server will provide an index that it generates
# itself.  These options allow you to modify the look of that
# index.

# DirectoryIndex: Name of the file to use as a pre-written HTML
# directory index.  These files are used if a directory is refer-
# enced.

DirectoryIndex index.html index.shtml index.cgi

# IndexOptions

IndexOptions FancyIndexing
```

```
# AddIcon tells the server which icon to show for different files
# or filename extensions

AddIconByType (TXT,/icons/text.gif) text/*
AddIconByType (IMG,/icons/image.gif) image/*
AddIconByType (SND,/icons/sound.gif) audio/*
AddIcon /icons/movie.gif .mpg .qt
AddIcon /icons/binary.gif .bin

AddIcon /icons/back.xbm ..
AddIcon /icons/menu.gif ^^DIRECTORY^^
AddIcon /icons/blank.xbm ^^BLANKICON^^

# DefaultIcon is which icon to show for files which do not have an
# icon explicitly set.

DefaultIcon /icons/unknown.xbm

# AddDescription allows you to place a short description after a
# file in server-generated indexes.
# Format: AddDescription "description" filename

# ReadmeName is the name of the README file the server will look
# for by default. Format: ReadmeName name
#
# The server will first look for name.html, include it if found,
# and it will then look for name and include it as plaintext if
# found.
#
# HeaderName is the name of a file which should be prepended to
# directory indexes.

ReadmeName README
HeaderName HEADER

# IndexIgnore is a set of filenames which directory indexing
# should ignore This doesn't use full regexp syntax, perhaps it
# should . . .
# Format: IndexIgnore name1 name2...

IndexIgnore */.??* *~ *# */HEADER* */README*

#=============================================================================
```

```
# Content Type and Mime Configuration
#-------------------------------------------------------------------
# Although NCSA HTTPd doesn't fully support the content-negotia
# tion that exists in HTTP/1.1, it does attempt to correctly
# identify different encodings and types of files it serves.  The
# following options specify how it does this

# DefaultType is the default MIME type for documents which the
# server cannot find the type of from filename extensions.

DefaultType text/plain

# AddType allows you to tweak mime.types without actually editing
# it, or to make certain files to be certain types.
# Format: AddType type/subtype ext1

# AddEncoding allows you to have certain browsers (Mosaic/X 2.1+)
# uncompress information on the fly. Note: Not all browsers sup
# port this.
#AddEncoding x-compress Z
#AddEncoding x-gzip gz

# The following are known to the server as "Magic Mime Types."
# They allow you to change how the server perceives a document by
# the extension.
# The server currently recognizes the following mime types for
# server side includes, internal imagemap, and CGI anywhere.
# Uncomment them to use them.
# Note: If you disallow (in access.conf) Options Includes ExecCGI,
# and you uncomment the following, the files will be passed with
# the magic mime type as the content type, which causes most
# browsers to attempt to save the file to disk.

#AddType text/x-server-parsed-html .shtml
#AddType text/x-imagemap .map
#AddType application/x-httpd-cgi .cgi
```

```
#==========================================================================
# Misc Server Resources
#--------------------------------------------------------------------------
# AccessFileName: The name of the file to look for in each direc
# tory for access control information and directory specific
# configuration

AccessFileName .htaccess

# If you want to have files/scripts sent instead of the built-in
# version in case of errors, uncomment the following lines and set
# them as you will.  Note: scripts must be able to be run as if
# they were called directly (in ScriptAlias directory, for
# instance).

# 302 - REDIRECT
# 400 - BAD_REQUEST
# 401 - AUTH_REQUIRED
# 403 - FORBIDDEN
# 404 - NOT_FOUND
# 500 - SERVER_ERROR
# 501 - NOT_IMPLEMENTED

#ErrorDocument 302 /cgi-bin/redirect.cgi
#ErrorDocument 500 /errors/server.html
#ErrorDocument 403 /errors/forbidden.html
```

The sections that follow discuss each directive's meaning and possible use. You might want to start with a minimal amount of changes and make more as you become more familiar with the configuration files and the server.

DocumentRoot

The *DocumentRoot* directive sets the root directory that your Web users see. The sample setting /usr/local/etc/httpd/htdocs tells the Web server where to begin the Web directory tree. Web clients have access to this directory and all directories below it. Directories outside the document root are unavailable to Web clients. The few exceptions to this rule are presented later.

If a file called homepage.html exists in document root directory, the URL to the file is `http://servername/homepage.html`. When creating your Web pages, make all directory path names relative to the document root directory. Use subdir/file.html, for example, rather than /usr/local/etc/httpd/htdocs/subdir/file.html. Relative paths are required because at the time the Web page is read, the server has access only to the document root directory; all other directories are excluded for security purposes.

User Directories

One way to make directories outside of the document root available to Web clients is to use user directories. You often need to let individual user accounts on the Web server create their own Web pages. User directories enable any Unix account to create Web pages without access to the document root directory structure. The *UserDir* directive tells the Web browser from which directory under each user's home directory to access Web documents. The sample name public_html gives the Web browser access to this subdirectory, if it exists, of each user's home directory. The file /home/username/public_html/my_page.html, for example, has the URL `http://servername/~username/my_page.html`. The *~username* portion of the URL tells the Web server under which user's public_html to look. The public_html directory, and all documents below it, must allow read access to the user account used by the Web server set in httpd.conf. The keyword DISABLED turns off support for user directories.

Redirection and Aliases

The *Redirect* directive enables your server to redirect browsers from an URL on your server to another location. This feature is useful for documents that once were on your server and have been relocated. The syntax is straightforward:

```
Redirect    /old-location    http://new.server/new-location
```

The first field is the path to the old location, and the second field is the path to the new server and new directory.

The *Alias* directive works in a manner similar to *Redirect*, but can be used only for locations on your server. The *Alias* directive is another way you can include access to files outside of the server root directory. For example, consider the following alias:

```
Alias /icons/ /usr/local/etc/httpd/icons/
```

This alias enables any requests for files in the /icons/ directory to be serviced from the /usr/local/etc/httpd/icons/ directory. The server uses the icon files here for indexing directories that do not have an index.html page.

ScriptAliases

The ScriptAlias directive is a special form of the Alias directive. *ScriptAlias* enables executable scripts to be run by your server. Their output is then sent to the client browser. The following is an example of the ScriptAlias directive.

```
ScriptAlias /cgi-bin/ /usr/local/etc/httpd/cgi-bin/
```

In this directive, a request to /cgi-bin/test.cgi tells the server to run the script test.cgi and send the output of the script to the client browser that made the request. Any scripts in the /cgi-bin directory must have execute permissions before they can be run. CGI scripts keep your server from only using static documents. You can use these scripts to parse HTML forms and create dynamic HTML pages.

Always keep security in mind when writing scripts that any user with access to your Web server can execute. Never trust CGI input 100 percent. Always try to verify the validity of the input to prevent your scripts from being used in unintended ways. For more information about CGI scripts, see Parts V and VI of this book, "Web Application Design" and "Security."

Indexing Options

Requests made to directories without a specific filename force the server to index the directory requested. The server first looks for any file matching a name included in the *DirectoryIndex* directive. The following is an example of the *DirectoryIndex* directive.

```
DirectoryIndex index.html index.shtml index.cgi
```

This directive tells the server to look for files named index.html, index.shtml, or index.cgi. If the file index.html exists in your server root directory, then the URL `http://servername/` returns the index.html file because no specific file was requested in the URL. If no DirectoryIndex is specified, the server uses index.html by default.

In the absence of any files matching the DirectoryIndex, the server attempts to generate a directory index for the client browser. Without the FancyIndexing option specified, the server returns a bulleted list of files in the requested directory. If FancyIndexing is specified in the *IndexOptions* directive, the server attempts to match an icon to describe the contents of each file in the requested directory. The ScanHTMLtitles option tells the server to look in each HTML file in the directory and include the text within the TITLE tags as the file's description. The ScanHTMLtitles option can be CPU intensive; use it with caution. Figures 17.1 and 17.2 show the difference between standard and fancy indexing.

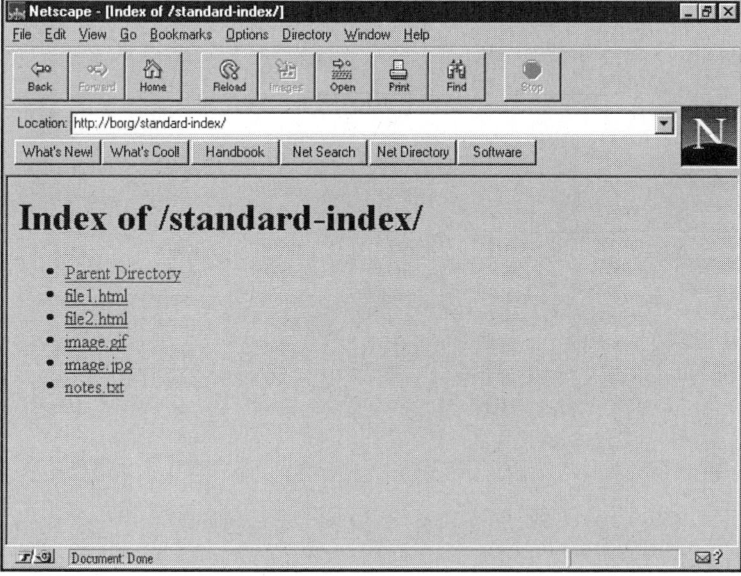

Figure 17.1
A standard directory index.

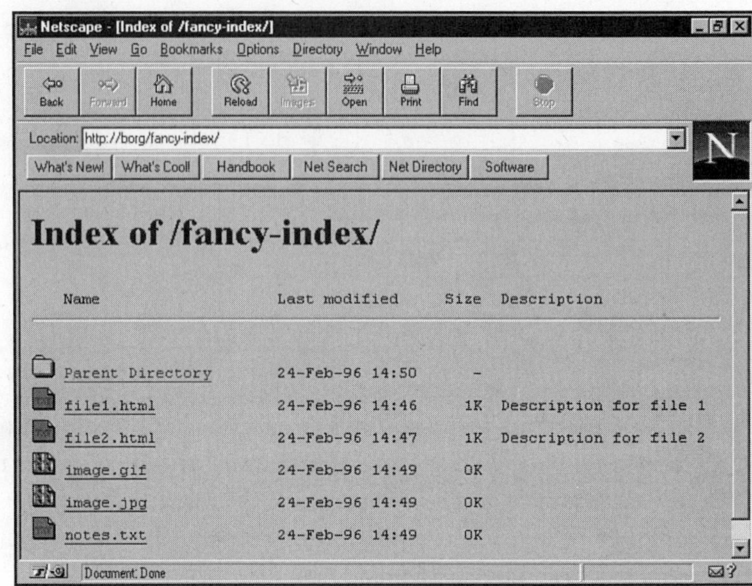

Figure 17.2
A directory index using the FancyIndexing option.

Using the *AddIconByType* directive, you can control which icons the server uses for each file based on the file type indicated in the mime.types file. The *AddIcon* directive controls which icon to use for a file based on the filename extension. The *DefaultIcon* directive is used for files the server cannot identify by extension or MIME type.

The *HeaderName* directive tells the server which filenames to prepend to the generated directory index. The *ReadmeName* directive tells the server which file to append at the end of a generated index. These files will contain information about the files that exist in that directory. The HEADER and README files also can contain HTML tags. Figure 17.3 shows a generated index that includes a HEADER and a README file.

The *IndexIgnore* directive specifies which filenames to ignore when generating a directory index. You can use this directive to leave out HEADER and README files. You also can use this directive to hide temporary files or other documents you do not want to appear in a directory index.

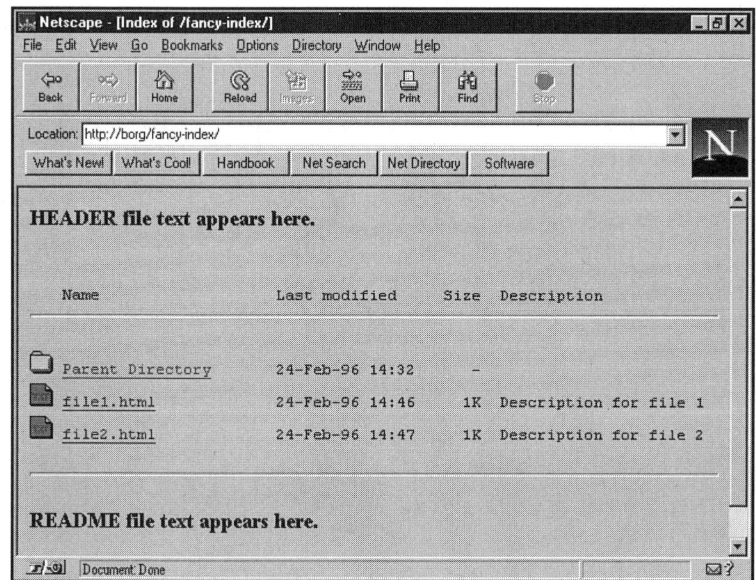

Figure 17.3
A directory index with HEADER and README files included.

You can add individual file descriptions to generated indexes by using the *AddDescription* directive rather than the ScanHTMLtitles option. The syntax follows:

```
AddDescription "description" filename
```

This directive can be useful, but it also can add considerable content to your srm.conf file if you use it frequently. If you need many AddDescription directives, consider creating your own index.html files instead.

Content Type and MIME Configuration

The HTTP/1.1 protocol has built-in content-negotiation capabilities. NCSA's HTTPd does not fully support this feature, but a set of directives exists that help identify basic file types.

The *DefaultType* directive tells the server how to treat files whose type cannot be identified. Use the default setting of text/plain. Do not change this default unless you have a specific reason to do so.

The *AddType* directive lets you add or override settings in the *TypesConfig* file. Three special MIME types are commented out of the srm.conf-dist file: text/x-server-parsed-html, text/x-imagemap, and application/x-httpd-cgi.

These MIME types control support for parsed HTML, image maps, and CGI scripts outside of the ScriptAlias directory.

Parsed HTML enables you to include other HTML or CGI scripts into a Web page. This feature is perfect for creating a standard look and feel for your site. You can use include tags to insert standard background images, HTML toolbars, contact information, and copyright notices. Using *include* tags, you only have to change the tagged information once to change all your documents that include the information. Parsed HTML is a feature specific to NCSA HTTPd. Other servers might support a similar feature, but the syntax could be quite different. An include tag looks like the following:

```
<!--#include file="footer.html"-->
```

This tag inserts the file footer.html into the requested HTML document as the document is sent to the browser. To use parsed HTML in your documents, pages that contain the parsed HTML tags must end with the extension specified in the AddType text/x-server-parsed-html directive. You have two choices here: you can create a second type such as .shtml for parsed HTML documents; or you can set all .html documents as parsed HTML. The latter choice simplifies maintenance of your site, but it adds the extra overhead of the server examining each HTML file before it is sent out. You also must enable includes in the access.conf file (see the "Global Access Configuration File" section). You can find additional information about parsed HTML at:

`http://hoohoo.ncsa.uiuc.edu/docs/tutorials/includes.html.`

The text/x-imagemap MIME type enables support for image maps. Image maps create clickable regions inside images. These regions can be linked to any URL. To support image maps using NCSA's HTTPd server, you must define the text/x-imagemap type and compile the imagemap.c file on your server. If you downloaded a pre-compiled server, you probably already have a compiled version of imagemap. Every major Web server supports image maps, but not all servers support them in the same way. You can find a comprehensive tutorial on HTTPd image maps at:

`http://hoohoo.ncsa.uiuc.edu/docs/tutorials/imagemapping.html.`

The *AddType* application/x-httpd-cgi directive enables the server to support CGI scripts anywhere in your Web directory. The only requirement is that the script file's extension match the extension used in the AddType directive. Using CGI scripts outside of the ScriptAlias directory adds to the flexibility of your site; however, you should limit the directories wherein CGI scripts can run. You set these limits in the access.conf file.

AccessFileName

By default, all Web documents on your server are available to any client that requests them. Sometimes, however, you might want to limit access to specific documents on your server to a specific set of users. The *AccessFileName* directive sets the name of the file to check for to establish access control lists. If no AccessFileName is specified, the default filename of .htaccess is used. Access control files enable you to limit access to your Web documents based on passwords, IP addresses, host names, or domain names.

For more information about securing your Web documents, consult Part VI, "Security." The following URL points to a detailed tutorial on how to set up access control files for NCSA's HTTPd.

`http://hoohoo.ncsa.uiuc.edu/docs/tutorials/user.html`

Global Access Configuration File

You can control access to your server by two means: the global access configuration file and per-directory access files. The filename for per-directory access files is established by the AccessFileName directive in the resource configuration file. Support for per-directory access files can be enabled or disabled, for the entire server or individual directories, from the global access configuration file.

Tip

> One advantage to using per-directory access files is that you do not have to restart the server when making changes to them. You must, however, restart the server before any changes made to the global access configuration file take effect.

The global access configuration file, access.conf by default, controls the overall security of your server. Certain options can be applied to the server as a whole, or to individual directories. You can use the distribution file access.conf-dist without modification if you install your server in /usr/local/etc/httpd. To use this file, copy it to conf/access.conf or the filename used in the *AccessConfig* directive in the httpd.conf file. It is strongly encouraged, however, to examine this file and only enable the options you intend to use. A copy of the distribution file access.conf-dist is included here for your reference as you read this section:

```
#========================================================================
# NCSA HTTPd (comments, questions to httpd@ncsa.uiuc.edu)
#========================================================================
# This is the global access configuration file.
# Documentation for NCSA HTTPd is available from
# http://hoohoo.ncsa.uiuc.edu/
# Documentation specific to this file is at
# http://hoohoo.ncsa.uiuc.edu/docs/setup/access/Overview.html
# http://hoohoo.ncsa.uiuc.edu/docs/tutorials/user.html
#
# NCSA takes no responsibility for any problems that result from
# the use of this server.  See the COPYRIGHT statement that came
# with this distribution.
#========================================================================


# /usr/local/etc/httpd/ should be changed to whatever you set
ServerRoot to.
<Directory /usr/local/etc/httpd/cgi-bin>
Options Indexes FollowSymLinks
</Directory>
# This should be changed to whatever you set DocumentRoot to.

<Directory /usr/local/etc/httpd/htdocs>

# This may also be "None", "All", or any combination of "Indexes",
# "Includes", or "FollowSymLinks"

Options Indexes FollowSymLinks

# This controls which options the .htaccess files in directories
# can override. Can also be "None", or any combination of
# "Options", "FileInfo", "AuthConfig", and "Limit"
```

```
AllowOverride All

# Controls who can get stuff from this server.

<Limit GET>
order allow,deny
allow from all
</Limit>

</Directory>

# You may place any other directories you wish to have access
# information for after this one.
```

Sectioning Directives

Sectioning directives control the scope of additional access restrictions. The format of these directives is similar to HTML tags. These directives begin with the word "Directory" and may be followed by additional directives that apply to the named directory structure, as shown in the following example:

```
<Directory /usr/local/etc/httpd/htdocs>
. . .
. . .
</Directory>
```

The previous directives establish a section for the directory /usr/local/etc/httpd/htdocs, the default document root directory.

The other type of sectioning directive is *Limit*. The Limit sectioning directive must appear inside a Directory section or inside an access file, such as .htaccess, within a document directory. For more information about securing your Web documents, consult Part VI of this book. The URL `http://hoohoo.ncsa.uiuc.edu/docs/tutorials/user.html` points to a detailed tutorial on how to set up access control files for NCSA's HTTPd.

Options

The *Options* directive controls which features the server supports for a specific Directory section. The format is as follows:

```
Options option1 option2
```

The options supported include the following:

- **None.** All options are disabled for the directory.
- **All.** All options are enabled for the directory.
- **FollowsymLinks.** Sybolic links within the directory are followed.
- **SynLinksIfOwnerMatch.** Symbolic links are only followed if the owner of the link and the destination file or directory match.
- **Indexes.** Allows server-generated indexes if a pre-compiled index file does not exist.
- **ExecCGI.** Allows the execution of CGI scripts in the directory.
- **Includes.** Allows parsed HTML and server-side includes in the directory.
- **IncludesNoExec.** Allows parsed HTML but disables the exec feature in the directory.

Consider the following example:

```
<Directory /usr/local/etc/httpd/htdocs>
Options None
</Directory /usr/local/etc/httpd/htdocs>

<Directory /usr/local/etc/httpd/htdocs/working>
Options Indexes
</Directory /usr/local/etc/httpd/htdocs/working>
```

These directives disable all options for the entire server, and then enable server-generated indexes for the subdirectory working under the document root directory. Disabling server-generated indexes is a popular feature of many Web sites. Without the generated indexes, your server lets your users see only what you want them to. Documents not referenced by HREF tags cannot be accessed if the user does not know their location. This helps keep unfinished documents unseen until you are ready to link them to your site. If a directory does not have an index.html file, and server-generated indexes are disabled, the browser receives an error message when it tries to access the directory by its name and not specifying a file within the directory.

AllowOverride

The *AllowOverride* directive controls which global access control directives can be overridden by per-directory access control files (.htaccess). The following are the possible values:

- **None.** .htaccess files are ignored in the directory.
- **All.** All features can be overridden by .htaccess files.
- **Options.** The *Options* directive is allowed in .htaccess files.
- **FileInfo.** *AddType* and *AddEncoding* directives are allowed in .htaccess files.
- **AuthConfig.** *AuthName*, *AuthType*, *AuthUserFile*, and *AuthGroupFile* authentication directives are allowed in .htaccess files.
- **Limit.** The *Limit* directive is allowed in .htaccess files.
- **Redirect.** The *Redirect* directive is allowed in .htaccess files.

Resource Configuration Directives per Directory

Many of the directives presented in the Resource Configuration section are supported within the global access configuration file or per-directory access control files. The syntax for these directives is the same as mentioned in the "Global Access Configuration File" section.

The following resource configuration directives are supported in both the global access configuration file and per-directory access control files: AddType, AddEncoding, AddIcon, IndexIgnore, DefaultIcon, and ReadmeName. The directives *DefaultType* and *AddDescription* are supported in only per-directory access control files. These directives enable you to change the behavior of your server on an individual directory basis.

HTTPd Server Configuration Checklists

The following checklists can help you configure your server quickly. Each checklist has a specific purpose, which might conflict with the others. The Quick Start checklist gives no consideration to security or performance, for example.

Quick Start Configuration Checklist

This checklist is designed to get your server up and running with minimal effort. The installation directory is assumed to be /usr/local/etc/httpd. The location of the server's installation is unimportant, but you have to change fewer settings if you use this directory.

1. Download the pre-compiled distribution for your Web server from `ftp://ftp.ncsa.uiuc.edu/Web/httpd/Unix/ncsa_httpd`. Save this file in /usr/local/etc.

2. Extract the archive with the command

   ```
   zcat <archive file name> ¦ tar xf -
   ```

3. Move the directory httpd_*version* to httpd.

4. Copy the distribution configuration files /usr/local/etc/httpd/conf/*.conf-dist to the actual configuration file names *.conf.

5. Set the ServerName directive if needed.

6. Set the ServerAdmin directive to your e-mail address.

7. Remove or comment out the VirtualHost configuration directives at the end of the httpd.conf file.

8. Create the directories /usr/local/etc/httpd/htdocs and /usr/local/etc/httpd/logs.

9. Create a test HTML document in the newly created htdocs directory.

10. Start your Web server with the following command, which must be run as user root.

    ```
    /usr/local/etc/httpd/httpd -d /usr/local/etc/httpd.
    ```

11. Try to access your test document from a Web browser.

If your document does not load, make sure the DNS names your are using are valid. Test to see if the client can access the server using ping or telnet. Finally, check the /usr/local/etc/httpd/logs/error_log file for any possible problems.

For a production Web server, spend more time optimizing your configuration files. This checklist is intended as a starting point for those new to NCSA's HTTPd server. After your server is up and running, experiment with the various configuration settings to find out which features you want to enable, and which ones you can leave disabled.

Security Configuration Checklist

This checklist can help you identify the configuration options that affect your server's security. Some of these options involve a tradeoff between functionality and security; for each option you must decide which is more important.

1. Make sure the server is running as an unprivileged user and group.
2. Make sure your server's log files are owned by root and are not writable by any other user (mode 644).
3. Verify the permissions of the document root directory, cgi-bin directory, and all files below them are not world writable.
4. If at all possible, disable user directory support and comment out the UserDir directive. If you must support user directories, disable CGI scripts and local .htaccess files.
5. Make sure none of your CGI scripts have the Set UID bit enabled.
6. If CGI scripts are allowed outside of the ScriptAlias directory, be aware which accounts have access to these directories.
7. If your server will support parsed-HTML, disable the exec feature.
8. Disable server-generated indexes by removing the Indexes option from the access.conf file.

9. Change the AllowOverride directive's default setting of All to None.

10. If you need to use symbolic links on your server, use the SymLinksIfOwnerMatch option rather than the less secure FollowSymLinks option.

11. If you are limiting access to your documents by DNS name or passwords, keep in mind a few points. DNS restrictions are only as secure as DNS itself. It is possible to spoof or corrupt DNS data. User passwords are sent across the network unencrypted. Do not use NCSA's HTTPd Web server if secure document transmissions are required.

Performance Configuration Checklist

This performance checklist should help you identify the performance-critical configuration options of NCSA's HTTPd server. No amount of configuration tweaking, however, makes up for a lack of memory, swap space, or CPU horsepower. If your server is dramatically slow, hardware upgrades or additional servers might be your only solution. With that in mind, consider these performance options:

1. Use the pre-forked server model if supported by your platform. Watch how many servers typically run with the ps command and adjust the StartServers and MaxServers directives as needed. Keep in mind that each server process consumes additional memory resources.

2. Always run your server in StandAlone mode.

3. Make sure the IdentityCheck directive is commented out in httpd.conf.

4. Keep the DNSMode set to Standard and use Minimum if at all possible.

5. Use caution when setting the KeepAlive time out values. A time out value that is too long can detract from the benefits of the pre-forked server pool.

6. Do not enable the ScanHTMLTitles indexing option.

7. If parsed-HTML is used, avoid setting all .html files as parsed HTML. Use a separate file extension such as .shtml for these documents.

Monitoring Server Activity

by Jim Vogel and Larry Colwell

The most straightforward method of tracking the usage of a Web server and the pages in its domain is to examine the log files it maintains. The large volume and raw format of log file data make log analysis tools an indispensable part of tracking the interests of a Web site's users and allocating resources to best advantage.

Fortunately, an abundance of log analysis tools are freely available on the Web; almost any conceivable format for reporting Web usage data from currently used log files is either in progress or already implemented. Most log analysis tools tend to be written in the scripting language Perl, so portability and user modification are not usually great concerns. Commercial Web tracking tools also are available for those webmasters who are critically interested in their audience, but the freeware tools serve the majority of log analysis demands.

This chapter provides a good introduction into the monitoring of WWW server activity, including both the actual HTTP server, and the computer and other hardware running that server. While looking at the HTTP server, the chapter also covers log files. Using the Common log as a basis, ideas covered include the format, maintenance, and analysis of logs. The single most important aspect contributing to the performance of the Web server is its network connection. Therefore we will look into different network topologies, and network monitoring tools. Likewise, a plethora of other tools ranging from HTML checkers to link checkers will be discussed. Finally, a discussion of Web server errors will round out the chapter.

Access Logs and Their Interpretation

The largest log file generated by the Web server is the *access log*. Most servers use the appropriately named Common Log File format to store information about hits to the pages in their domain. The Common format stores information in ten distinct fields separated by whitespace. The following excerpt from an actual log file in the Common format represents an access to a single Web page, including all its resources:

```
130.36.160.20 - - [28/Jan/1996:06:06:02 -0600] "GET / HTTP/1.0"
➥200 8265
130.36.160.20 - - [28/Jan/1996:06:06:13 -0600] "GET /~icons/
➥image.gif
HTTP/1.0" 200 935
130.36.160.20 - - [28/Jan/1996:06:06:13 -0600] "GET /~icons/
➥back.gif HTTP/1.0"
200 883
130.36.160.20 - - [28/Jan/1996:06:06:13 -0600] "GET /~icons/
➥text.gif HTTP/1.0"
200 926
130.36.160.20 - - [28/Jan/1996:06:06:13 -0600] "GET /~icons/
➥dblank.gif
HTTP/1.0" 200 836
130.36.160.20 - - [28/Jan/1996:06:06:15 -0600] "GET /~icons/
➥menu.gif HTTP/1.0"
200 929
130.36.160.20  - - [28/Jan/1996:06:06:16 -0600] "GET /~icons/
➥unknown.gif
HTTP/1.0" 200 921
```

The fields appearing in the log file are described as follows, using the home page access on the first line as an example:

1. **Remote IP Address/Name.** Contains the IP address (or name, if it can be resolved) of the site obtaining access. In this example, the IP address of the site is 130.36.160.20.

Note It is possible for the server to disable the next two fields in the log file. In fact, disabling these fields is recommended because the information could help an intruder in gaining unauthorized access to the client machine. The appearance of a hyphen, as in the example, shows that the server disabled the field.

2. **Remote Logname.** When enabled, this field contains the account name of the user obtaining access, if the name can be retrieved.

3. **User.** When enabled, this field contains the full name of the user who owns the account obtaining access, if name can be retrieved.

4. **Date and Time.** Contains the time and date of access. In the preceding example, access occurred at 6:06 a.m. on January 28, 1996. The military (24-hour) time format is used to record the time in the access log.

5. **GMT Adjustment.** Contains the offset from Greenwich Mean Time (GMT), the internationally recognized time standard, as seen by the server. In the example, the date and time of access is six hours earlier than GMT.

6. **Operation.** Contains the type of operation requested. For WWW page and resource accesses, this field always reads GET.

7. **File.** This field contains the path and filename of the WWW page being accessed. The following are the three types of path/filename combinations:

   - **Implied Path and Filename.** Accesses a file in the user's home directory and assumes the name of the file to be the host default.

   - **Relative Path and Filename.** Accesses a file in a directory relative to the user's home directory.

- **Full Path and Filename.** Accesses the specified file through the specified path. This is the most reliable access method.

8. **Server Protocol.** Contains the type of protocol used to access the page; HTTP version 1.0 in the example.

9. **Status.** Contains the HTTP error code generated during access. In the example, the value 200 was generated, denoting normal completion of the GET operation.

10. **File Size.** Contains the size in bytes of the file accessed. In the example, 8,265 bytes were retrieved.

Recognizing Path Name Ambiguities

In many cases, the server is configured to access a user's home page using implied path and filenames. These implied names can be difficult to analyze because the user must know the way the server is configured. The following are some examples of home page references using implied path and filenames:

- **/.** This implied pathname expands into a path that references the index.html page found in the (appropriately configured) WWW server default directory.

- **/~username/ or /%7Eusername/.** These implied pathnames expand into /dir/dir/ ... /dir/username/public_html/index.html. The %7E escape sequence represents a hex value, in this case the value for the tilde (~) character.

Using Log Analysis Tools

Many log analysis programs exist which distill the vast contents of the access log into a compact, readable form. Several of the more popular log analyzers appear in table 18.1. These attributes might help you determine which one is most appropriate for use with your server.

Three of the analyzers are shown in figures 18.1 through 18.3.

Table 18.1
The More Popular Log Analyzers

Name/Version	Language	Log Format	Output Format	Frequency	Market/Price	Author	Platform	URL
Access Watch 1.23	perl	Common	Tabular	Daily	Shareware/$40	Dave Maher	Unix/nt	http://www.eg.bucknell
Analog 1.2.5	C	Common/ Agent/Referrer	Tabular/Bar Graph	Hourly-Monthly	Freeware	Stephen Turner	Unix	http://www.statslab.ca
BrowserCounter 1.1.1	perl	Agent Log	Tabular	n/a	Freeware	Benjamin Franz	Unix	http://www.netimages.c
CreateStats 1.01 (1)	perl	Various	Tabular	Weekly/Daily	Freeware	Doug Stevenson	Unix	http://www-bprc.mps.oh
Gerstats 1.2 (2)	SunOS gcc	Various	Tabular/ ASCII Bar Graphs	Hourly-Monthly	Free2	Kevin Hughes	Various Unix	http://www.eit.com/sof
Statbot 3.0.2 (3)	(Executable)	Common	Tabular/Gif Charts	Daily	Shareware, $103	n/a	Various	http://www.xmisssion.co
wusage 3.2	C	Common/PLEXUS	Tabular/Gif Charts	Weekly	Freeware	Thomas Boutell	Unix	http://www.boutell.com

1. CreateStats requires Getstats

2. Requires License Agreement

3. $10 for personal registration; $20 for business

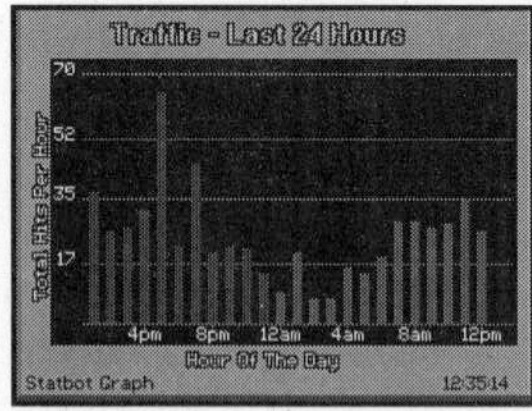

Figure 18.1
The results of the statbot analyzer.

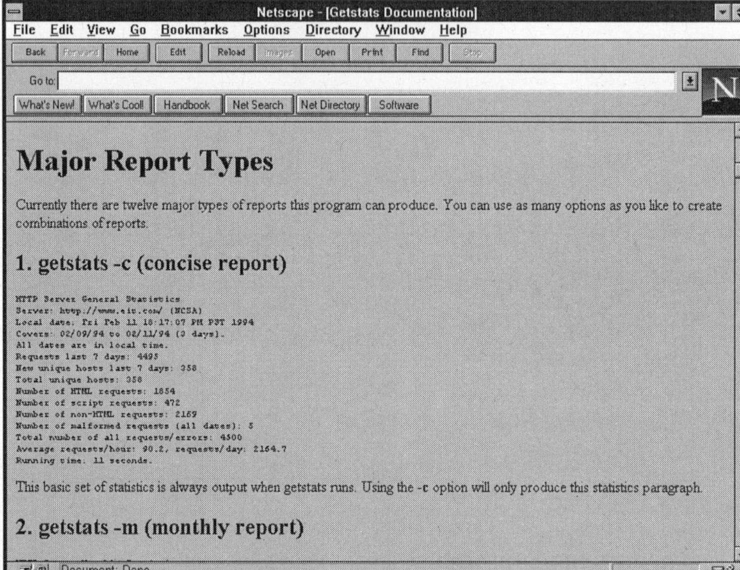

Netscape - [Getstats Documentation]
File Edit View Go Bookmarks Options Directory Window Help
Back Forward Home Edit Reload Images Open Print Find Stop
Go to:
What's New! What's Cool! Handbook Net Search Net Directory Software
Major Report Types
Currently there are twelve major types of reports this program can produce. You can use as many options as you like to create combinations of reports.
1. getstats -c (concise report)
HTTP Server General Statistics
Server: http://www.eit.com/ (NCSA)
Local date: Fri Feb 11 18:17:07 PM PST 1994
Covers: 02/09/94 to 02/11/94 (2 days).
All dates are in local time.
Requests last 7 days: 4495
New unique hosts last 7 days: 358
Total unique hosts: 358
Number of HTML requests: 1854
Number of script requests: 472
Number of non-HTML requests: 2169
Number of malformed requests (all dates): 5
Total number of all requests/errors: 4500
Average requests/hour: 90.2, requests/day: 2164.7
Running time: 11 seconds.
This basic set of statistics is always output when getstats runs. Using the -c option will only produce this statistics paragraph.
2. getstats -m (monthly report)
Document: Done

Figure 18.2
The getstats analyzer.

Netscape - [Web Server Statistics for Stephen Turner's pages]
File Edit View Go Bookmarks Options Directory Window Help
Back Forward Home Edit Reload Images Open Print Find Stop
Go to:
What's New! What's Cool! Handbook Net Search Net Directory Software

Daily Summary

(Go To: Top: Monthly report: Hourly summary: Domain report: Directory report: Request report)

Each unit (▬) represents 3 000 requests, or part thereof.

```
day:  #reqs:
---   ------
Sun:   93907:
Mon:  139581:
Tue:  139604:
Wed:  142507:
Thu:  147627:
Fri:  141653:
Sat:   97038:
```

Hourly Summary

(Go To: Top: Monthly report: Daily summary: Domain report: Directory report: Request report)

Document: Done

Figure 18.3
The analogex log analyzer.

Access Logs and What They Don't Mean

The analysis of Web access logs can provide useful information about the popularity and general use of a site. It is extremely easy, however, to misinterpret the results provided by most simple log analysis tools. Distortions arise in the log data from many different sources; although some are within the webmaster's purview to remedy, others are caused by the access methods of remote Internet service providers and browsers.

Reducing Distortions in Tracking Data

Every access to a Web page is actually a collection of several individual hits to the various resources comprising the page. Each hit is stored separately in the access log. Therefore, the log file is jammed with many times more hits to the site than actual interested viewers. The access log does not offer any information about the associations between the page and its resources, so maintaining a relationship between access to a page and its resources is difficult.

A simple solution is to instruct the log analyzer, if it is able, to count only the hits to the base page HTML file, ignoring incidental hits to the page's resources.

This scheme is not completely effective, however. If a Web page designer decides to establish a link to the resources on a local page, but not to the page itself, and the log analyzer is set to ignore the resource hits, then the resource hits might go unnoticed, and interest in the site will be underreported by the log analyzer.

In addition, requests intended for a local page and its resources might never reach the server. Many large Internet providers, such as America OnLine and Compuserve, perform a cache operation on Web pages. The cache operation is requested by users to reduce data transfer costs and to speed access.

Newer versions of several Web browsers also use this technique, which is unfortunate for the server administrator for two reasons. First, the inaccuracy of access statistics is completely out of the local administrator's control. There is no way to determine how many times the "virtual page," created behind the provider's firewall, is being encountered. Secondly, if a page has dynamic resources, perhaps providing real-time data in some form, the viewer of the virtual page sees the static cached resource rather than the dynamic resource painstakingly provided by the page's designer. To a large prospective audience, and to an incalculable degree, the effectiveness of the Web page is thereby diminished.

Archiving Log Files

Large log files develop quickly. One function of log analysis is to determine peak usage times and schedule log file archiving that does not interfere with Web access and yet keeps files to a manageable size. The actual process of log file archiving can range from a simple file deletion to a more complex periodic backup of log files, and perhaps log analysis results, to secondary storage. Ultimately, the perceived importance of saving historical data and the availability of system resources determine the method and scheduling of log archives.

Using Unix HTTPD Archiving Methods

The NCSA Web server daemon (httpd) serves as a good example for analyzing and archiving log files. The main concern when dealing with archives is how to carry out the file move and delete operations with minimal impact to the Web server. When httpd runs under inetd, the archive data can be moved or deleted without interfering with the server at all; the next request to the httpd simply creates a new log file. If httpd is running standalone, however, it holds the files open continuously, locking them. In this case, carry out the following steps:

1. Using the cp -f command, possibly under the control of cron, copy the log file to the archive directory.

   The destination filename may be the same for every archive, obliterating the previous contents, or it may vary to reflect the current archive date/time in the new filename.

2. Read the httpd process id from the file specified in the PidFile directive of the http.conf file.

3. Send the command `kill -hup` *`pid`*, where *pid* is the process number for the httpd.

   The daemon restarts, re-creating the log file by rereading the TransferLog path directive from http.conf.

Automating the Archive Process

A Perl or shell script can facilitate the automation of the archive process. The script functions as follows:

1. Generate a destination log archive path name, if needed. The date command provides several command-line switches for manipulating the date output into a filename-suitable form.

2. Copy the log file into the archive path. The archive path can be stored in an environment variable or in a file similar to that for storing the httpd process id.

3. Find the process id for the httpd. The PidFile directive indicates the location of the pid.

4. Send the `kill -hup` command to the httpd process. Use the pid found in step 3.

Using NT HTTP Service Archiving Methods

Generally, archiving the log files on an NT server is similar to archiving them on a Unix Web server. The NT Event Scheduler found in the Resource Kit, however, is used instead of the cron utility for scheduling the archive event.

Monitoring Connection and Server Performance

Monitoring network connection utilization and server performance are obviously intertwined with one another. The network connection is the primary factor in performance, and therefore it gets a lot of attention in the monitoring of server performance. Before delving into this relationship and server performance along with all the other topics left in the chapter, some realistic expectations for how the server should perform should be set. They serve as an overview of what should be expected; after everything is said and done.

Performance Guidelines

Considering the great variation in the speed of servers on the Web, it makes sense to throw out some general guidelines worth adhering to. Looking only at end results, it should require no more than 45 seconds from the moment the user makes a request for a page on your server, until they have the entire page before them. Realistically, ten seconds should be sufficient to send a page of text, and it should never take more than a minute to receive an external file. If you need more than one minute to load your entire home page, you are doing something incorrectly. Users will have already lost interest in your site before they even arrive.

Bitmapped graphics, inline images, real-time audio, video, and other frills are becoming almost mandatory on the Web; but they all carry an incurred price: speed. Obviously only a finite amount of data can be passed through your Internet connection per second, so there are definite limitations on what you can use in your HTML pages. If it takes more than a minute to load your home page you need to decide whether you are getting inadequate performance from your server, or if you are simply transferring too much data. The first case calls for a technical response, covered to a large degree in the remaining part of this chapter. The second case calls for a creative decision to be made in redesigning the page.

One of the goals of this chapter is to aid you, the aspiring webmaster, in implementing the most efficient Web site possible. To this end you need to understand what factors enable a Web server to perform to its full billing. These factors are a combination of hardware and software inseparably intertwined with each other.

On the hardware side, the important factors contributing to the performance of your server are processor, memory, and I/O subsystem. For most Web servers, the single most important part of hardware is the network I/O. Obviously this is not true for those servers connected to an ultra-high bandwidth connection (T3). On smaller systems, however, the network I/O is so slow relative to the rest of the system that in essence it becomes the bottleneck of the system that garners the most attention.

For the giant sites that receive up to 4.5 million hits a day, other important concerns exist in addition to network I/O. For the small to relatively large sites it is unlikely that the network waits on the rest of the computer. A quad Pentium processor-based machine with 64 or 128 MB of RAM is a good example of how unimportant the rest of the computer is, relative to the network connection. This machine is relatively inexpensive in terms of dollars, yet this system has sufficient resources to power almost any site on the Web.

Tip Try to set aside a disk just for logging. One other important thing to keep in mind is disk cache. Memory is fairly cheap, so keep your Web pages cached.

Sitting atop the hardware is the software. Web server performance is dependent upon the following: the HTTP server, TCP/IP stack, underlying operating system, and other related software such as Perl and CGI scripts. The following is a collection of concerns to keep in mind when looking for an increase in performance from software.

The most important single piece of software is the HTTP server. This server services all the requests from Web clients. The HTTP service, or daemon, needs to be tuned on an individual basis, corresponding to its environment.

When shopping for HTTP services be certain that the server you choose relies on threads rather than entire processes. The efficiency gain from using a multithreaded server as opposed to one that allocates entire processes for each request is considerable. One other alternative is to use a server that relies on pre-allocated processes. The improvement between an incorrectly installed or default installation of the service, and a finely tuned service can differ by an order of one fifth the original speed. For the same reason, they essentially are the part of the backbone of your server, the shell scripts and CGI interfaces need to be honed. Extra time spent optimizing scripts can make a huge difference in the long run.

Note On Unix machines there is a choice to make. The httpd can be run either as part of a larger service, inetd, or by itself. Be certain you are running the daemon in standalone mode as opposed to inetd. This saves you an exec system call on each request, in addition to any gain you merit from not having to reload the service continuously.

Lying directly beneath the HTTP server in terms of both importance and abstraction is the TCP/IP stack. The HTTP protocol by design is inefficient when implemented over TCP/IP. Try to offset this by making sure you are running the best version available. The same logic applies to the operating system (OS). The OS you use is a matter of personal preference, but use the newest version of whichever OS you choose. If your original choice proves unstable then use the previous version, with any and all necessary patches.

Note HTTP is an extremely simple protocol. Consisting of very high-level primitives, such as GET, an HTTP server could be fabricated in a weekend by a novice using Perl. Essentially, in an average session a client connects to a server and asks for the HTML page. The server sends the HTML page. Then the client interprets the page and asks for inline images and other sorts of files, referenced by the HTML page (see fig. 18.4). The unfortunate part of this scenario is the size of the files. An HTML page simply consists of ASCII characters, and relatively few of them.

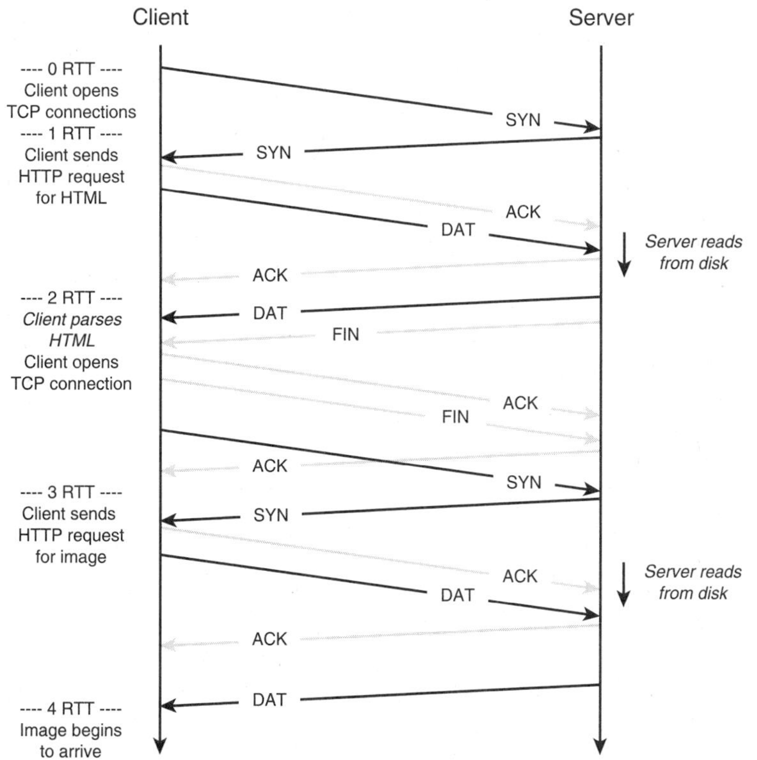

Figure 18.4
The basic client-server connection requesting an HTML page.

Now look at the establishment of a TCP connection. A three-way handshake establishes the connection. The client sends a connection request to port 80 of the HTTP server. Now the server sends back a response. Finally, upon acknowledgment from the server, the client can start sending the request. The process goes back and forth and back, and for what? The request is probably for no more than a few datagrams of data. To further compound the inefficiency, TCP regulates the size of packets sent using an algorithm known as *slow start*. Not knowing what kind of bandwidth is on either side of the connection, TCP starts sending small packets, and as they reach their destination, it starts increasing the size of the "window" or datagram. Eventually it sends too much, and when packets are lost, it starts shortening the size. This is an exemplary method; in general, it finds a nice equilibrium. Unfortunately, this method was obviously designed to be used with transactions of all sizes, but favoring the larger ones. The larger the transaction size, the better the equilibrium will be. The one instance where this protocol is not good is when dealing with small transactions, such as those associated with HTTP. This is because the transactions don't last long enough for TCP to get the "window" opened up.

Network Topology, Monitoring, and Tuning

Starting from scratch, one of the most important decisions you encounter is your choice of Internet connection. Choosing the correct network topology and service provider is extremely important; it plays a large role in determining the effectiveness of your company's presence on the Internet.

In a general sense, the connectivity options are divided into two groups: dialup and permanent based. When using a dial-up connection you connect remotely to your Internet provider using Point-to-Point (PPP) connections. PPP connections consist of a link established using a client program such as PPP or SLIP. Physical connection is established using an analog or ISDN modem. The client program (PPP or SLIP) establishes a gateway between client and server. The server assigns an IP number to the client, allocated either statically or dynamically, and you essentially are integrated onto the Internet for the duration of the connection. Packets to and from the client (your Web server) are then routed through your modem onto the Internet. When dealing with a network device of higher speed, such as a leased line, a full-time router is used. A *router* is an intelligent network device capable of forwarding IP packets from your LAN to the Internet.

The need for a fast connection is evident, although it can be costly. You must compromise, balancing speed for economy. Dial-up access via SLIP or PPP using an ordinary phone line is the least costly method of gaining Internet access. A 28.8-Kbps connection can provide a feasible solution if you are running a very small Web site and expect to only rarely have more than one person connected at a time.

Keep in mind two considerations when using a 28.8-Kbps connection. First, because you are using such a limited device, you want to maximize the efficiency of your modem by using the best one possible. Make sure that the modem does not use any proprietary features and is completely V.34 compliant. Additionally, check with your service provider to find out what brand of modem it uses, as most modems perform best when connected to identical models. Second, keep in mind the small amount of bandwidth you are using. If your company is running any other Internet services, or if more than a couple employees regularly access the Internet, you need a faster connection.

The next step up the ladder of performance is ISDN. With throughput of 168 Kbps over a double line, ISDN provides a comfortable level of performance for most small- to medium-sized companies. With the recently declining price of ISDN across much of the country, it is quickly becoming the most cost-effective choice. ISDN is quick enough to provide a complete Internet presence; meaning that in addition to running a Web server, it also can run a Telnet server, FTP server, and other services. ISDN should be adequate for serving one or two users on the Web server and covering the additional overhead of company employees who send e-mail, read news, or Web surf.

Leased lines lie at the top of the performance ladder. A T1 line provides ample bandwidth for all medium to large corporations. Passing data at speeds up to 1.54 Mbps, a T1 comes with a high price. Average installation fees can run upwards of $1,800, and monthly rates often are as high as $1,000. If you can afford it and you run a very popular Web site, a T1 is definitely the way to go. If you don't quite need the speed of the T1, a fractional T1 is available for less money.

On the other hand, at the extreme top of the ladder of performance lies one alternative if a T1 is insufficient. A T3 line provides 45 Mbps throughput, but its costs put it beyond the reach of all but the largest companies. Currently a T3 costs about $50,000 a month. T3 lines are used primarily to connect backbone links of the Internet.

Note Depending on what part of the Internet backbone you are connected to, a T3 might prove to be no improvement over a T1. This is because many segments of the Internet are connected by T1 lines. If the T3 happened to be connected only to T1 lines, then you would never see the speed increase. Packets move only at the speed of the slowest link.

Network Monitoring

Getting the most performance from your network can incur substantial effort on the part of the administrator. Logs should be reviewed and the Performance Monitoring data analyzed to gain enough insight into your specific networking situation. Every network topology, much less specific products, is different, and each has its own quirks.

Monitoring Network Connection Utilization

Gaining the most from your network is an immensely complex subject encompassing a huge domain of topics. The surest and easiest method for ensuring a smooth running network is prior planning: network needs should be assessed prior to purchasing. Checking hardware compatibility, consulting experts if needed, and using equipment known to perform in accordance to your expectations are key. Quick answers are often helpful and can sometimes be found from simple solutions such as using the newest device drivers and placing telephone calls to the technical support line; however, simplicity is not the norm.

Determining network loads is a prerequisite to analyzing the efficiency, quality, and productivity of your Web site. Two major OS alternatives exist for running a Web server: Microsoft Windows NT and Unix. This section discusses network tools for both. An important feature of NT is the Performance Monitor, which Microsoft includes with Windows NT Advanced Server. Because of the almost infinite varieties of Unix, however, an excess number of Unix utilities will not be explored.

Case Study: Tools available for Microsoft Windows NT

When you install NT on your server, Performance Monitor and the Simple Network Management Protocol (SNMP) should both be installed, along with TCP/IP (see fig. 18.5). At this point your monitoring options depend on your Internet connection. If you are using a modem, be it analog or ISDN, you need a PPP connection and the Remote Access Service (RAS) PORT and RAS TOTAL objects for monitoring purposes (see fig. 18.6). With RAS you also can use the Remote Access Monitor for a graphical display of modem use (see fig. 18.7).

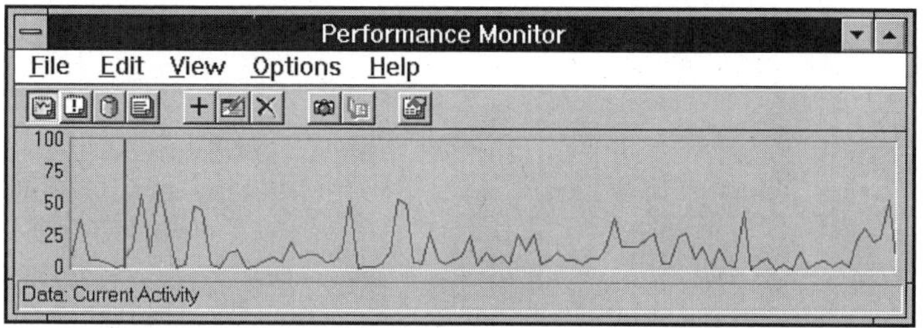

18.5
The Performance Monitor showing current activity.

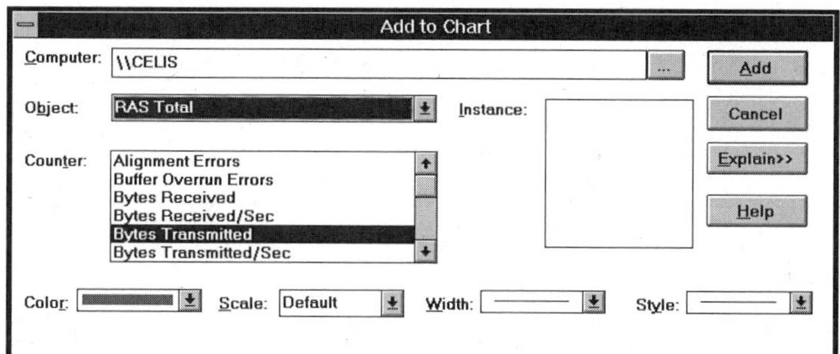

18.6
Adding counters to the RAS Total object monitor.

18.7
The graphical display of modem use.

If you use something faster than a PPP connection, you are obviously connected, via a router, from your LAN to the Internet and can make fuller use of the Performance Monitor tools, monitoring the Network Interface and Network Segment objects. In addition, the objects FTP Server, ICMP, IP, TCP, and UDP are of great use in looking at specific protocol-level network utilization.

Note Complete lists of objects and counters can be found at the end of the chapter.

There are other useful tools to keep in mind as well. In addition to the Performance Monitor, another important tool to use with NT is the Event Viewer, which records all sorts of system events (see fig. 18.8). Logged activities include server errors, application starts and stops, and security.

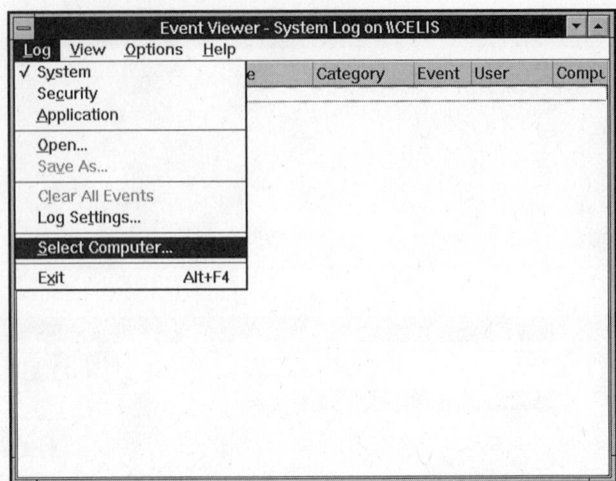

Figure 18.8 *Some of the many items you can track with the Event Viewer.*

An Alternative Tool for Virtually any Operating System

Netperf is a freely distributed network performance utility developed by Hewlett Packard. The source is available so it can be compiled on any Unix system, and an NT version has recently been released as well. Netperf is capable of measuring request/response performance, TCP stream performance, and UDP performance along with CPU utilization. A URL provided at the end of the chapter leads you to the manual and other information needed to install and run Netperf.

Webstone

Performance of your Web server can be monitored using a well known HTTP 1.0-compliant tool from Silicone Graphics called *Webstone.* In the near future, SPEC should release a benchmark; however, few exist now. SGI's white paper and corresponding FAQ are the authoritative sources of information about Webstone. The white paper describes what Webstone does and doesn't test and indicates that Webstone measures performance in the following fields:

- Average and maximum connect time
- Average and maximum response time
- Data throughput rate
- Number of pages retrieved
- Number of files retrieved

Webstone can provide a fairly clear picture of WWW performance. Of course the data gained from this tool is not perfect. Although it provides a ballpark figure of performance, a more thorough benchmarking tool is needed. Critics claim that Webstone is designed to weight favor toward SGI machines. Webstone's generated "tests contains unrealistic samples in terms of file set size and file size distribution." (SUN paper)

Understanding the Webstone Architecture

The centerpiece of the distributed Webstone architecture is the *WebMASTER*, an object that remotely spawns the client processes. WebMASTER comes configured to run not only on a separate machine, but on a machine not even on the same network as the client's machine. Therefore the WebMASTER, the clients, and the HTTP server can all be isolated. Upon execution, the WebMASTER parses the command line and the configuration files. Then a command line is constructed for each client, and the clients are remotely started. Upon the clients completion of its queries, the client updates the WebMASTER and a report is generated.

You can download Webstone from SGI. You need simply to compile it and edit a couple of configuration files. Compilation is a trivial matter using the makefile that comes with the distribution. Before attempting to set up the benchmark, read the entire README file that comes with the distribution. The FAQ is also a good source of information, probably the best for initial setup.

Webstone lends itself to individual configuration. In addition to changing the logging, length, and debugging parameters, you can customize the workload of the individual clients. Striving to match real-world situations, different data sets are available: general mix, general modem mix, media rich mix, and general and media rich mix.

The following is a typical run of the benchmark. First you see the output from the run. Then you see what hardware it was run on, and finally you see the configuration file that specified the test HTML pages to be loaded. As you can see from the file, it is a simple task to specify exactly what you want the server to be loading, so you can develop your own test cases using your own files.

The results of a test run for 10 minutes with the preceding page sets follows.

```
/usr/local/bin/webstone -w xpi0-alfalfa -c sulu:8636 -u filelist
-t 10 -n %d
Client: gateweb-indy8 Number of Clients: 6
Client: gateweb-indy9 Number of Clients: 6
Client: gateweb-indy10 Number of Clients: 6
Client: gateweb-indy11 Number of Clients: 6

Waiting for READY from 24 clients
All READYs received
Sending GO to all clients
All clients started at Tue Mar 7 01:33:16 1995
Waiting for clients completion
All clients ended at Tue Mar 7 01:43:41 1995
Page # 0
===============================================================
Total number of times page was hit 1888
Total time 1262.655230 seconds
Maximum Response time 1.758487
Total connect time for page 21.293520
Maximum time to connect 0.038234
Total amount of data moved 23199744
Page size 12288
Total number of connects 5664
```

Note The following parameters were modified to run the test:

```
nm_clusters
somaxconn = 50
nm_clusters = 4000
tcp_keepidle = (1200)
tcp_keep_timer_in_close = 1
```

Description of Server running the benchmark.

Hardware platform: 1 150 MHz IP22 Processor

FPU: MIPS R4010 Floating Point Chip Revision: 0.0

CPU: MIPS R4400 Processor Chip Revision: 5.0

On-board serial ports: 2

On-board bi-directional parallel port

Data cache size: 16 KB

Instruction cache size: 16 KB

Secondary unified instruction/data cache size: 1 MB

Main memory size: 256 MB

Integral ISDN: Basic Rate Interface unit 0, revision 1.0

XPI FDDI controller: xpi0, firmware version 9411032038, SAS

Integral Ethernet: ec3, version 1

Integral Ethernet: ec0, version 1

Integral SCSI controller 5: Version WD33C95A, differential, revision 0

Disk drive: unit 4 on SCSI controller 5

Disk drive: unit 3 on SCSI controller 5

Disk drive: unit 2 on SCSI controller 5

Disk drive: unit 1 on SCSI controller 5

Integral SCSI controller 4: Version WD33C95A, differential, revision 0

Integral SCSI controller 0: Version WD33C93B, revision D

Disk drive: unit 5 on SCSI controller 0

CDROM: unit 4 on SCSI controller 0

Disk drive: unit 2 on SCSI controller 0

The file set used for this test follows. In this case a general and media rich mix was used:

```
# This file is used to configure the pages and files to be tested
#for.
6
40 3
/file3k.html
/file4k.html
/file5k.html
5 3
/file10k.html
/file17k.html
/file20k.html
5 2
/file5m.html
/file1m.html
20 3
/file6k.html
/file7k.html
/file200k.html
20 2
/file3m.html
/file21k.html
10 2
/file500k.html
/file13k.html
```

Tools

As with any field of computing there is a wide selection of tools designed to make life easier. The problem lies in the fact that often more time is wasted learning to use and configuring the tool than is ever saved actually using it. This is especially true with the tools in this infant domain of computing. The majority of tools are either share- or freeware, which is good and bad. It is good in that they don't cost much, if anything. It is bad in that there is an inherent cost in terms of time in setting them up and getting them configured. Much of the configuration work is left to the user. Therefore, picking just a couple tools and investing the time to use them might be a good strategy.

HTMLFlow

One of the more helpful shareware utilities is *HTMLFlow*. Ported to Linux, SunOS, and DOS, if it runs on your platform it is worth checking out. HTMLFlow is a thorough utility; it checks every single link from all your Web pages, generating large log files.

HTMLFlow comes ready to run, right out of the box, so to speak. In the case of the DOS version, you merely need to unzip it and read the README file. The README file gives you all the parameters for setting up the utility, including a helpful section on setting up your parameter file. The parameter file includes all the parameters you want to pass to the program on the command line upon execution. The Unix version was even handier: it came with a Perl script to run the program.

HTMLFlow can be found at the following Web site:

```
HTTP://www.on-the-net.com/flow
```

Anchor Checker

Very similar to HTMLFlow, Anchor Checker is slightly more robust. It has been ported to quite a few varieties of Unix including HPUX, IRIX, SunOS, Linux, AIX, FreeBSD, SCO, and OSF1. Anchor Checker's biggest quirk is its dependence upon Lynx or WWW to track down links. Your WWW client needs to be in the same directory, unless you specify otherwise in the configuration file.

This utility comes with fair documentation. The following is a list of options, taken directly from the manual page:

SYNOPSIS

```
checker [options] html-documents
What do they do:
 -help          print a help screen(not much right now)
 -version       print out program name and version number
 -trace         turn on trace mode
 -base-address  http-address
relative address root(see below for
description)
 -current-address http-address
address up to directory of the documents(see
below)
 -config-file file  specify where can the program find config
file
 -only-errors       output only errors
 -remoteurl URL     check remote document
 -tmpdir directory  temporary directory
 -detail            Show last modified time and server type
 -verbal            Report total links after checking of each
document
 -update-notice     Tell you if the document has been changed
since your last visit
 -no-smtp           Do NOT check telnet and mailto tags
 html-documents     documents you want to check

Sample result file.
Scanning file "my-cat.html"...

line-number: SUCCESS http://XXXXXXXXX/YYYYY
line-number: OK      http://XXXXXX/YYYYY : connection SUCCESS!
line-number: FOUND   #foo : Section "foo" found
line-number: NOT FOUND  #bar : Section  "bar" not found
line-number: ERROR   gopher://XXXX/YYYY/ZZZZ
line-number: DENIED  ftp://ftp.wustl.edu/
line-number: ERROR   /home/john/home.html not found!
line-number: SUCCESS mailto:q7f192@ugrad.cs.ubc.ca : address
verified
line-number: SUCCESS telnet://gambier.ugrad.cs.ubc.ca : address
verified
```

```
  19: ERROR   telnet://foo.bar.com : host foo.bar.com not found
 111: SUCCESS
http://info.cern.ch/hypertext/WWW/Library/Status.html
        Last-Modified:  Wednesday, 05-Apr-95 01:47:38 GMT
Server: CERN/3.0pre6
  11: SUCCESS
http://www.ncsa.uiuc.edu/SDG/Software/WinMosaic/HomePage.html
        Last-Modified:  Fri, 19 May 1995 00:44:34 GMT  Server:
NCSA/1.4
        Notice: document's changed since last visit on Thu Apr  6
15:02:52 1995
```

Anchor Checker can be found at the following Web site:

```
HTTP://www.ugrad.cs.ubc.ca/spider/q7f192/branch/checker-man.html
```

HTMLChek

HTMLChek is one of the most extensive HTML checkers available. Unfortunately you need awk or Perl to run this program. The setup is fairly tedious. Those who take the time to set up HTMLChek, however, reap the rewards of a very powerful tool.

Using Perl as a foundation, this tool is a regular expression enthusiast's dream. As you can see from the excerpt from the manual pages, HTMLChek offers every kind of textual manipulation you can imagine. HTML 2.0 is supported, and HTML 3.0 and Netscape extensions can be added in the configuration file. Almost all HTML errors are detected and warnings are issued for poor style.

Although HTMLChek is obviously a useful tool, it is almost exclusively for use on a Unix machine. You can find a version of awk for MS-DOS and a version of Perl for Windows NT, but they are not nearly as powerful as their Unix counterparts.

The following list is a summary of HTMLChek command-line options:

```
append=1
     Cross-reference Checking Output option
arena=1 or arena=off
     Language Customization option
configfile=filename or cf=filename
     Language Customization option
```

```
deprecated=tag1,tag2...
     Language Customization option
dirprefix=urlprefix
     Cross-reference Checking URL Prefix option
dlstrict=1 or dlstrict=2 or dlstrict=3
     Language Customization option
html3=1 or html3=off
     Language Customization option
htmlplus=1 or htmlplus=off
     Language Customization option
inline=1
     Output option
listfile=filename or lf=filename
     Listfile option
loosepair=tag1,tag2...
     Language Customization option
lowlevelnonpair=tag1,tag2...
     Language Customization option
lowlevelpair=tag1,tag2...
     Language Customization option
map=1
     Cross-reference Checking Output option
metachar=1 or metachar=2 or metachar=3
     Language Customization option
netscape=1 or netscape=off
     Language Customization option
nogtwarn=1
     Language Customization option
nonblock=tag1,tag2...
     Language Customization option
nonpair=tag1,tag2...
     Language Customization option
nonrecurpair=tag1,tag2...
     Language Customization option
novalopts=tag1,opt1:tag2,opt2...
     Language Customization option
nowswarn=1
     Output option
refsfile=filenameprefix
     Cross-reference Checking Output option
reqopts=tag1,opt1:tag2,opt2...
     Language Customization option
strictpair=tag1,tag2...
     Language Customization option
subtract=pathprefix
     Cross-reference Checking URL Prefix option
sugar=1
     Output option
```

```
tagopts=tag1,opt1:tag2,opt2...
     Language Customization option
usebase=1
     Cross-reference Checking URL Prefix option
xref=1
     Cross-reference Checking Output option
```

HTMLChek can be found at the following Web site.

HTTP://uts.cc.utexas.edu/~churchh/htmlchekprog.html

ERRORS

Most of the errors your server is likely to produce, short of catastrophic failure, are not necessarily very harmful. Included at the end of this chapter is a list of simplified error codes for HTML 1.0. A couple of them are common—they pop up here and there and can be taken with a grain of salt.

The most common errors you see are time-out errors. If these occur often and for no obvious reason, they should be investigated. If you experience a few timeouts during peak usage, you cannot do much to help; you simply don't have the resources to contend with the clients. File-loading problems arise fairly often as well and need to be addressed immediately. Such an error might mean you have a corrupted file, or new files might need to have their permissions changed. One final error that arises regularly are log errors. Check and archive the log files regularly.

During the course of writing this book a test server was run. The following is part of the error file:

```
Error Log: Running a personal HTTP server over a 19.2
[01/Feb/1996:00:40:22 -0600] Access to
C:/WEB_SERVER/DATA/aol/images/other/loadartw.gif failed for
128.10.12.114, reason: file does not exist
[01/Feb/1996:00:40:22 -0600] Access to
C:/WEB_SERVER/DATA/aol/images/other/inetconn.gif failed for
128.10.12.114, reason: file does not exist
[01/Feb/1996:00:40:29 -0600] Access to
C:/WEB_SERVER/DATA/aol/images/other/inetconn.gif failed for
128.10.12.114, reason: file does not exist
[01/Feb/1996:00:40:29 -0600] Access to
```

```
C:/WEB_SERVER/DATA/aol/images/other/loadartw.gif failed for
128.10.12.114, reason: file does not exist
[01/Feb/1996:00:40:29 -0600] Access to
C:/WEB_SERVER/DATA/~jegelhof/maps/jumpbar.gif failed for
128.10.12.114, reason: file does not exist
[01/Feb/1996:01:08:59 -0600] Access to
C:/WEB_SERVER/DATA/default.html failed for 128.10.12.114, reason:
file does not exist
[01/Feb/1996:01:19:16 -0600] Access to
C:/WEB_SERVER/DATA/rwoman.htm failed for 128.10.12.114, reason:
file does not exist
[01/Feb/1996:01:23:53 -0600] Access to
C:/WEB_SERVER/DATA/default.html failed for 128.10.12.114, reason:
file does not exist
[01/Feb/1996:01:32:47 -0600] Access to
C:/WEB_SERVER/DATA/new_net.html failed for 128.10.12.114, reason:
file does not exist
[01/Feb/1996:01:36:19 -0600] Access to
C:/WEB_SERVER/DATA/new_net.html failed for 128.10.12.114, reason:
file does not exist
[01/Feb/1996:01:42:44 -0600] Access to
C:/WEB_SERVER/DATA/new_net.htm failed for 128.10.12.114, reason:
file does not exist
[01/Feb/1996:01:43:00 -0600] Access to
C:/WEB_SERVER/DATA/new_net.htm failed for 128.10.12.114, reason:
file does not exist
[01/Feb/1996:01:44:46 -0600] Access to
C:/WEB_SERVER/DATA/new_net.htm failed for 128.10.12.114, reason:
file does not exist
[01/Feb/1996:19:25:25 -0600] Access to
C:/WEB_SERVER/DATAgopher://olt.et.tudelft.nl:70/11/fun/sounds
failed for 130.36.160.40, reason: file does not exist
[01/Feb/1996:23:29:41 -0600] Access to C:/WEB_SERVER/DATA/t1.gif
failed for 128.10.12.114, reason: file does not exist
[01/Feb/1996:23:35:11 -0600] Access to C:/WEB_SERVER/DATA/t1.gif
failed for 128.10.12.114, reason: file does not exist
[01/Feb/1996:23:36:29 -0600] Access to C:/WEB_SERVER/DATA/t1.gif
failed for 128.10.12.114, reason: file does not exist
[01/Feb/1996:23:38:22 -0600] Access to C:/WEB_SERVER/DATA/t1.gif
failed for 128.10.12.114, reason: file does not exist
[01/Feb/1996:23:38:47 -0600] Access to C:/WEB_SERVER/DATA/t1.gif
failed for 130.36.160.20, reason: file does not exist
[03/Feb/1996:14:04:14 -0600] Access to
C:/WEB_SERVER/DATA/timeline.gif failed for 128.10.12.114, reason:
file does not exist
[03/Feb/1996:14:04:16 -0600] Access to
C:/WEB_SERVER/DATA/tvslrem.gif failed for 128.10.12.114, reason:
file does not exist
```

Evidently at one point some house cleaning was taken care of and a few loose ends weren't sewn up. There is nothing more disappointing than becoming excited over following a link to a particular point of interest, only to find the file is missing. As you can see, the errors span a three day period, meaning the referenced objects were unavailable for that period. Check the log as often as possible!

Simplified HTTP Error Codes

The following is a "simplified" error list found on the Web. It can be very useful in day to day server administration.

2xx **Success!** (These are rare and can be ignored.)

200 OK—normal completion of request

201

202

203

204

3xx **Redirection**

301 Moved. This file has permanently moved, and clients' records should be updated to reflect the new URL.

302 Found. The remote server is issuing a "redirect" to point the client toward another URL, but this original URL should be kept in the files. This is often used for Imagemap and "jump to random link" features.

303 Method. You shouldn't see this because this status code has not been formally approved.

304 Not modified. A client can request that a remote URL be sent only if it has been modified since a certain date. This response means that the URL exists but does not meet the date criterion.

4xx Error in Request

400 Bad syntax in request, perhaps due to an error in client software, but more likely to a broken server on the remote system.

401 Unauthorized.

402 Payment required.

403 Forbidden. Probably due to improper file permissions on remote files.

404 Not found. A true "broken link" that needs to be fixed in client HTML files.

5xx Server Error

500 Internal server error on the remote system.

501 Not implemented. This error could point to a problem on either system, or even in the URL we're trying to access.

502 Server temporarily overloaded. Some newer servers issue this "busy signal," which instructs clients to try their request again at a later time.

503 Gateway timeout. You should never see this if you're not using a proxy server.

6xx Client Error

600 The client could not decipher the requested URL.

601 Not implemented in client.

602 Connection failed. The initial connection to the remote system failed. This probably means that the other site is either down, busy, or unreachable from the local network.

603 Timed out. The initial connection was successful, but the remote server took too long servicing the client's request.

Commonly Used Internet Server Counters

FTP Server Counters

Bytes Received/sec

Bytes Sent/sec

Bytes Total/sec

Connection Attempts

Current Anonymous Users

Current Connections

Current NonAnonymous Users

Files Received

Files Sent

Files Total

Logon Attempts

Maximum Anonymous Users

Maximum Connections

Maximum NonAnonymous Users

Total Anonymous Users

Total NonAnonymous Users

ICMP

Messages Outbound Errors

Messages Received Errors

Messages Received/sec

Messages Sent/sec

Messages/sec

Received Address Mask

Received Address Mask Reply

Received Address Mask Reply

Received Dest. Unreachable

Received Echo Reply/sec

Received Parameter Problem

Received Redirect/sec

Received Source Quench

Received Time Exceeded

Received Timestamp Reply/sec

Received Timestamp Reply/sec

Received Timestamp/sec

Sent Address Mask Reply

Sent Destination Unreachable

Sent Echo Reply/sec

Sent Echo/sec

Sent Parameter Problem

Sent Redirect/sec

Sent Source Quench

Sent Time Exceeded

Sent Time Exceeded

Sent Timestamp Reply/sec

Sent Timestamp/sec

IP Server Counters

Datagrams Forwarded/sec

Datagrams Outbound Discarded

Datagrams Outbound No Route

Datagrams Received Address Errors

Datagrams Received Delivered/sec

Datagrams Received Discarded

Datagrams Received Header Errors

Datagrams Received Unknown Protocol

Datagrams Received/sec

Datagrams Sent/sec

Datagrams/sec

Fragment Re-assembly Failures

Fragmentation Failures

Fragmented Datagrams/sec

Fragments Created/sec

Fragments Re-assembled/sec

Fragments Received/sec

TCP Counters

Connection Failures

Connections Active

Connections Established

Connections Passive

Connections Reset

Segments Received/sec

Segments Sent/sec

Segments/sec

UDP

Datagrams No Port/sec

Datagrams Received Errors

Datagrams Sent/sec

Datagrams/sec

Hardware Objects

RAS Port

Alignment Errors

Buffer Overrun Errors

Bytes Received

Bytes Received/Sec

Bytes Transmitted

Bytes Transmitted/Sec

CRC Errors

Frames Received

Frames Received/Sec

Frames Transmitted

Frames Transmitted/Sec

Percent Compression In

Percent Compression Out

Serial Overrun Errors

Timeout Errors

Total Errors

Total Errors/Sec

RAS Total

Alignment Errors

Buffer Overrun Errors

Bytes Received

Bytes Received/Sec

Bytes Transmitted

Bytes Transmitted/Sec

CRC Errors

Frames Received

Frames Received/Sec

Frames Transmitted

Frames Transmitted/Sec

Percent Compression IN

Percent Compression OUT

Serial Overrun Errors

Timeout Errors

Total Connections

Total Errors

Total Errors/Sec

Network Interface

Bytes Received/sec

Bytes Sent/sec

Current Bandwidth

Output Queue Length

Packets Outbound Discarded

Packets Outbound Errors

Packets Received Discarded

Packets Received Errors

Packets Received Non-Unicast/sec

Packets Received Unicast/sec

Packets Received Unknown

Packets Received/sec

Packets Sent Non-Unicast/sec

Packets Sent/sec

Packets/sec

Network Segment

%Multicast Frames

%Network Utilization

Broadcast frames received/second

Multicast frames received/second

Total bytes received/second

Total frames received/second

Online Resources

The following are sites mentioned in this chapter.

Access Watch

`HTTP://www.eg.bucknell.edu/~dmaher/accesswatch/`

Analog

`HTTP://www.statslab.cam.ac.uk/~sret1/analog/`

BrowserCounter

`HTTP://www.netimages.com/~snowhare/utilities/browsercounter.html`

CreateStats

`HTTP://www-bprc.mps.ohio-state.edu/usage/CreateStats.html`

getstats

`HTTP://www.eit.com/software/getstats/getstats.html`

Statbot

`HTTP://www.xmission.com/~dtubbs/club/cs.html`

wusage

`HTTP://www.boutell.com/wusage/`

HTMLFlow

`HTTP://www.on-the-net.com/flow`

HTMLChek

`HTTP://uts.cc.utexas.edu/~churchh/htmlchekprog.html`

Anchor Checker

`HTTP://www.ugrad.cs.ubc.ca/spider/q7f192/branch/checker-man.html`

SGI's Webstone

`HTTP://www.sgi.com.au/Products/WebFORCE/WebStone/`

SGI's FAQ for Webstone

`HTTP://www.sgi.com.au/Products/WebFORCE/WebStone/FAQ-Webstone.html`

Netperf

`http://www.cup.hp.com/netperf/training/Netperf.html`

Handy Search Engines

Yahoo.com

`HTTP://yahoo.com/`

DEC's Alta Vista

`HTTP://www.altavista.digital.com/`

WWW FAQs

`HTTP://www.boutell.com/faq/`

`HTTP://clever.net/self/faq/faq.html`

Handy Sites for CGI Scripting Support

ABC Tutorial on CGI

`HTTP://www.lpage.com/cgi/`

HTML-Based Interfaces:

`HTTP://blackcat.brynmawr.edu/~nswoboda/prog-html.html`

CGI for the Non-Programmer

`HTTP://www.catt.ncsu.edu/~bex/tutor/index.html`

CGI Programmer's Reference

`HTTP://www.best.com/~hedlund/cgi-faq/`

Win-httpd CGI-DOS

`HTTP://www.achilles.net/~john/cgi-dos/`

Windows CGI 1.1 Description

`HTTP://www.city.net/win-httpd/httpddoc/wincgi.htm`

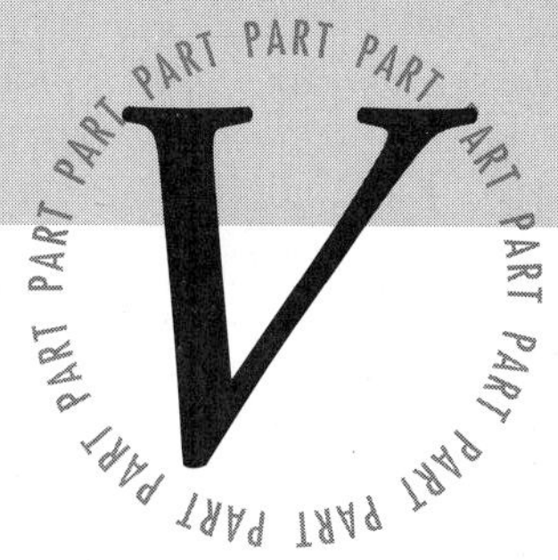

Web Application Design

The Basics of CGI

by Bill Weinman

The Common Gateway Interface *(CGI) is the interface between a HyperText Transfer Protoco*l *(HTTP) server (the program that serves pages for a Web site) and the other resources of the server's host computer.*

CGI is not really a language or a protocol in the strictest sense of those terms. It's really just a set of commonly named variables and agreed-upon conventions for passing information from the server to the client and back again. When viewed in this admittedly simplistic light, CGI becomes much less intimidating.

This chapter covers the following topics:

- *The environment of CGI*
- *Selecting a programming language*
- *Structure of a CGI program*
- *Using basic authorization*
- *A form-processing example that sends e-mail*
- *Non-parsed header CGI*

The Environment of CGI

CGI is closely tied to both HTTP, the protocol that links Web servers to clients (see the following Note), and the *HyperText Markup Language* (HTML), which is used to write Web pages. It is therefore important that you already have a working knowledge of HTML, and at least a basic understanding of how HTTP works, in order to fully understand CGI.

Note In this model, the browser is one of a class called clients. Not all HTTP clients are browsers. Spiders, robots, and even proxy servers are HTTP clients at least some of the time.

CGI programs run on the server's host machine. A CGI program gets its input from the server via environment variables and data streams. *Environment variables* are special memory areas set aside by an operating system for passing small amounts of static data between programs. *Data streams* are sequentially organized data that are commonly used for console and file I/O. The *standard input* stream (commonly abbreviated as *stdin*) is used by the server to pass streamed data to CGI programs.

Note Because CGI programs run in the server's environment, you cannot test your CGI programs on a machine that is not running an HTTP server. In other words, if you use the "Open File" command on your browser to read a file that uses CGI, the CGI program will not run.

You can write CGI programs in any language, although some languages are more suitable than others for any given application. CGI programs are commonly written in C, Perl, and shell scripts, as well as proprietary languages, such as Visual Basic, which are only available on certain machines.

Selecting a Programming Language

There are three major criteria you must consider when deciding what language you will use to write your CGI programs, as follows:

1. The language must be supported by the operating system on which the server is running.
2. The language must have sufficient facilities to perform the task that you need from it.
3. You (the programmer) must be comfortable enough with the language to code in it proficiently.

The first criterion is usually a major factor. According to Georgia Tech's latest GVU Survey, 64.6 percent of Web servers are running some flavor of Unix, where C is universally available, and Perl is also commonplace. The second and third criteria are more subjective. There are few languages today that don't have the power to perform the necessary tasks—although some are more capable than others. Attempts to quantify the suitability of any given language for any given application, however, usually leads to a discussion that more closely resembles a religious debate than a reasoned, objective analysis of facts and figures.

The examples in this chapter are written in Perl. Perl is available on most Unix systems, and on many other platforms as well. It is powerful enough to handle most CGI-related tasks efficiently, and most system administrators have some level of familiarity with the language—or they could benefit from learning it if they haven't already.

Note The version of Perl used for the examples in this chapter is version 4.0.1.8 patch level 36. Version 4 was chosen because it's a common denominator. Many systems still don't have version 5, and most systems with version 5 also have version 4 available.

Structure of a CGI Program

A CGI program can be broken down into three basic tasks that it may or may not perform, depending on the specific application. These tasks are as follows:

- Retrieving and decoding input from the server.
- Formatting the necessary MIME-style headers for HTTP.
- Creating, formatting, and delivering the correct output to the server.

What follows is a discussion of the specific requirements and protocols associated with each of these different segments of a CGI program. Small code fragments are included with the descriptions to illustrate the techniques involved.

Input from the Server

Most of the data for a CGI program will come from data typed into forms on the user's browser. This data is encoded in a *query string*, in a format that looks like this:

```
name=value&name=value&name=value . . .
```

These *name/value* pairs can be delivered by one of two methods: GET and POST. Both methods encode the query string in the same manner; they differ only in their delivery method.

GET uses part of the URL to send variable data from the client to the server. The data is then forwarded to the CGI program in an environment variable called QUERY_STRING. Listing 19.1 is a code fragment in Perl that retrieves the QUERY_STRING environment variable.

Note The Uniform Resource Locator (URL) is the common format of addressing objects on the World Wide Web. It is described in RFC 1630.

Listing 19.1
Retrieving the QUERY_STRING Variable

```
# put the QUERY_STRING into a variable
$qs = $ENV{'QUERY_STRING'};

# split it up into an array by the '&' character
@qs = split(/&/,$qs);
```

Because the query string is delivered as part of a URL, the use of certain characters are restricted. Therefore, the query string must be encoded to avoid using these characters. Space characters are replaced with plus (+) characters, and other restricted characters are replaced with their hexadecimal value, preceded by the percent (%) character. A typical QUERY_STRING might look like this:

```
Name=William+E.+Weinman&Email=wew@bearnet.com
```

Any code that retrieves the QUERY_STRING variable will have to decode these characters before it can use them. Listing 19.2 is a Perl code fragment that decodes a query string.

Listing 19.2
Decoding the QUERY_STRING Variable

```
foreach $i (0 .. $#qs)
  {
  # convert the plus chars to spaces
  $qs[$i] =~ s/\+/ /g;

  # convert the hex characters
  $qs  =~ s/%(..)/pack("c",hex($1))/ge;

  # split each one into name and value
  ($name, $value) = split(/=/,$qs[$i],2);

  # create an associative array
  $qs{$name} = $value;
  }

print "\nVariables:\n\n";

foreach $name (sort keys(%qs))
  { print "$name=", $qs{$name}, "\n" }
```

The POST method delivers data in the same format, but by a different method. Instead of using an environment variable, the POST method delivers the query string via the *standard input* stream.

The major advantage of the POST method over the GET method is that it's not limited by the size of the environment space on the host machine. With the GET method, you can only send as much data as there is space available for environment variables. Because the POST method uses a data stream, there is no such limitation on the amount of data you can send.

Listing 19.3 is a code fragment that retrieves and decodes a POST method query string.

Listing 19.3
Retrieving and Decoding *POST* Data

```
$ct = $ENV{"CONTENT_TYPE"};
$cl = $ENV{"CONTENT_LENGTH"};

# check the content-type for validity
if($ct ne "application/x-www-form-urlencoded")
  {
  printf "I don't understand content-type: %s\n", $ct;
  exit 1;
  }

# put the data into a variable
read(STDIN, $qs, $cl);

# split it up into an array by the '&' character
@qs = split(/&/,$qs);

foreach $i (0 .. $#qs)
  {
  # convert the plus chars to spaces
  $qs[$i] =~ s/\+/ /g;

  # convert the hex tokens to characters
  $qs[$i] =~ s/%(..)/pack("c",hex($1))/ge;

  # split into name and value
  ($name, $value) = split(/=/,$qs[$i],2);

  # create the associative element
  $qs{$name} = $value;
  }
```

```
print "Variables:\n\n";

foreach $name (sort keys(%qs))
  { printf "$name=%s\n", $qs{$name} }
```

The POST method identifies its data with the special MIME content type, `application/x-www-form-urlencoded`. According to MIME protocol, the length of the data is also specified with a MIME content-length. This MIME encoding is delivered via the environment variables, `CONTENT_TYPE` and `CONTENT_LENGTH`, respectively.

Warning You cannot rely on receiving any end-of-file indication from the standard input stream. It will not always be terminated. Therefore, you must read only the number of bytes specified by the value of the `CONTENT_LENGTH` variable.

After your program has retrieved the input from the server, it may begin formatting the output to send back to the client through the server.

Formatting MIME Headers

Before a CGI program can send data to a client, it must send a *response header* (sometimes called a MIME header because it follows many of the same rules) that identifies the type of data it is sending with a Multipurpose Internet Multimedia Extensions (MIME) content type. The simplest form of response header contains only the content type, like this:

```
Content-type: text/html
```

Note MIME is the specification commonly used for Internet mail. It is defined in RFC 1521. Sometimes the MIME content type is simply called the "MIME-type."

The response header must be followed by two newline characters. The following is a code fragment that sends a simple response header:

```
print "Content-type: text/html\n\n";
```

> **Note** Technically, newlines in the response header are supposed to be carriage-return/linefeed pairs, (0D Hex, 0A Hex), but common practice is to use a linefeed (0A Hex) by itself, which is in fact universally supported.

The content type is used by the browser to decide how to render the output that it receives from your program. There are several different content types in common use—table 19.1 contains a brief list.

Table 19.1
Some Common MIME Content Types

Content Type	Usage
text/html	HTML documents
text/plain	Plain text documents
image/gif	GIF-formatted images
image/jpeg	JPEG-formatted images
image/png	PNG[1]-formatted images
video/mpeg	MPEG-formatted video
video/quicktime	QuickTime-formatted video

1. PNG is a new graphics format designed to displace GIF. It has many of the same properties as GIF, with a larger possible palette and, more importantly, a non-proprietary compression algorithm. PNG stands for either "Portable Network Graphics" or "PNG's Not GIF."

MIME content types are coordinated by the Internet Assigned Numbers Authority (`http://www.isi.edu/iana/`). Many MIME content types, besides those listed previously, are in common use. For a more complete list, see `ftp://ftp.isi.edu/in-notes/iana/assignments/media-types`.

In most cases, the server will add more components to the response before sending it to the client. The exception to this rule is discussed later, under "Non-Parsed Header CGI."

Delivering the Output

Output from a CGI program is sent to the standard output stream. In most languages, this is the default behavior for the print command. Listing 19.4 is a Perl code fragment that sends a small HTML fragment to the client.

Listing 19.4
Sending Output to the Client

```
print "<html><head><title>Form Response</title></head>\n";
print "<body><h1>Form Response</h1>\n";
print "<p>The name you entered in your form was $name.\n";
print "<p>The address you entered was $address.\n";
print "<hr>\n</body></html>\n";
```

The format of your output must be the format specified in the content type of the response header. In this case, that content type was "`text/html`", so the output must be in proper HTML format. On the other hand, if the content type were `image/gif`, the output would have to be a valid GIF formatted image.

A Brief Discussion of the Standard CGI Variables

Input from the server includes a number of standard CGI environment variables. These variables represent all the information commonly available about the server and client with which your program will be interacting. This section is a brief description of each of those variables.

Tip

You will find that there are other variables available to your CGI program, besides those listed here. What variables your program gets depends on many factors, including the server you're using, the operating system you're using, and often the whims of your system administrator.

Here is a useful CGI program used to list all the environment variables available on a server:

```
#!/usr/bin/perl

print "content-type: text/plain\n\n";

foreach $v (sort keys(%ENV))
  { print "$v: $ENV{$v}\n"; }
```

The standard CGI environment variables fall into three general categories: information about the user, the server, and the specific request that initiated the CGI program.

About the User

Some of the standard CGI variables contain information about the user and their environment. The most useful of these are `HTTP_USER_AGENT`, `HTTP_ACCEPT`, `REMOTE_HOST`, and `REMOTE_ADDR`, discussed in the next sections.

HTTP_USER_AGENT

The `HTTP_USER_AGENT` variable contains the name and version of the user's browser in the format "*name/version library/version*". It also contains information about any proxy gateway (see Note) that the user may be going through. Typically, you won't need information about the proxy gateway, except to know that whenever there is one, the proxy is likely caching data and the connection may or may not represent an individual user.

> **Note** A *proxy gateway* is a computer that gets between the requests from a group of users and the responses from systems outside their realm. In the case of the World Wide Web, proxies are becoming more popular and are adding quite a bit of complexity to the standards process. In particular, there is a great deal of discussion about how to properly negotiate with proxies to keep their caches up-to-date and make sure their users have access to timely information, while preserving the attendant reduction in traffic they provide for the Net.

Generally, it's not a good idea to count on the format of the `HTTP_USER_AGENT` string without having a lot of information in advance about what each of the different browsers sends there. As you can see from the next examples, the format varies greatly. Listing 19.5 is a log of some `HTTP_USER_AGENT` strings from my Web site (`http://www.bearnet.com/cgibook/`).

Listing 19.5
HTTP_USER_AGENT Strings

```
PRODIGY-WB/1.4b
Mozilla/1.1N (Macintosh; I; 68K)
Microsoft Internet Explorer/4.40.308 (Windows 95)
TCPConnectII/2.3 InterCon-Web-Library/1.2 (Macintosh; 68K)
Mozilla/2.0b3 (X11; I; IRIX 5.3 IP22)
Lynx/2.3.7 BETA  libwww/2.14
NCSA_Mosaic/2.7b1 (X11;SunOS 5.4 i86pc)  libwww/2.12 modified
NCSA Mosaic/2.0 (Windows x86)
Mozilla/1.22 (compatible; MSIE 2.0B; Windows 95)
Microsoft Internet Explorer/0.1 (Win32)
Enhanced_Mosaic/2.10.17S Win16 FTP Software/Spyglass/17S
EINet WinWeb 1.1
IWENG/1.2.000  via proxy gateway  CERN-HTTPD/3.0 libwww/2.17
IBM WebExplorer DLL /v1.03
Mozilla/2.0 (Win95; I)
NetCruiser/V2.1
```

It's worth noting, in this context, that the preceding list is not representative of the ratios of different browsers that have visited my site. This log's source had 484 entries, of which 413 were Netscape (Mozilla) browsers.

Note The Netscape browser calls itself Mozilla. The official word is that the word "Netscape" is pronounced "Mozilla." (Consider that fact that the company is run by a 22-year-old whiz-kid on leave from college.)

The reason for "Mozilla" probably stems from the fact that Netscape was built on the Mosaic browser, then the college that owns Mosaic forced Netscape to change their name. The name Mozilla seems to be a play on words with the name Mosaic. Word-play is popular on the Net.

Listing 19.6 is a listing of some `HTTP_USER_AGENT` strings with proxies.

Listing 19.6
HTTP_USER_AGENT Strings with Proxies

```
Mozilla/2.0b2a (Windows; I; 16bit) via proxy gateway CERN-HTTPD/
➥3.0 libwww/2.1
NCSA Mosaic for the X Window System/2.4-2 libwww/2.12 modified via
➥proxy gatew
IBM WebExplorer DLL /v1.03 via proxy gateway CERN-HTTPD/3.0pre5
➥libwww/2.16pre
Mozilla/1.1N (X11; I; HP-UX A.09.05 9000/712) via proxy gateway
➥CERN-HTTPD/3.0
```

Warning Although the `HTTP_USER_AGENT` string is designed to let you know what brand and version of browser are connecting to your site, it is becoming more difficult to use it for that. The latest version of the *Microsoft Internet Explorer* (MSIE) identifies itself with Netscape's *User-Agent* string. Unlike previous versions of MSIE, there is no indication that it is not the Netscape Navigator. Unfortunately, since MSIE does not support all of the Netscape extensions, it is creating real problems by masquerading as Mozilla. Please see `http://www.bearnet.com/msie-ii.html` for more information.

HTTP_ACCEPT

The `HTTP_ACCEPT` string provides the MIME content types that the browser can accept. The format of the `HTTP_ACCEPT` string is *type/subtype, type/subtype, [. . .].* As you can see from the examples here, some browsers also add other information that may be used in future versions of HTTP.

In the following examples from my log file, I've put the name of the browser on one line and the HTTP_ACCEPT string on the next, so you can tell which browser is generating what string.

```
from Mozilla/2.0b1J --
image/gif, image/x-xbitmap, image/jpeg, image/pjpeg, */*

from Mozilla/1.22 (Windows; I; 16bit) --
*/*, image/gif, image/x-xbitmap, image/jpeg
```

```
from NCSA Mosaic/2.0.0 Final Beta (Windows x86) --
video/mpeg, image/jpeg, image/gif, audio/basic, text/plain, text/
➥html, audio/x-aiff, audio/basic, */*

from Lynx/2.3.7 BETA libwww/2.14 --
*/*, application/x-wais-source, application/html, text/plain,
➥text/html, www/mime, application/x-ksh, application/x-sh,
➥application/x-csh, application/x-sh

from NCSA Mosaic/2.0.0b4 (Windows x86) --
application/pdf, application/winhelp, application/freelance,
➥application/msword, audio/x-midi, application/x-rtf, video/
➥msvideo, video/quicktime, video/mpeg, image/jpeg, image/gif,
➥application/postscript, audio/wav, text/plain, text/html, audio/
➥x-aiff, audio/basic, */*

from NetCruiser/V2.00 --
text/plain, text/html, image/gif, image/jpeg

from NCSA Mosaic(tm) Version 2.0.0a8 for Windows --
audio/x-midi, application/x-rtf, video/msvideo, video/quicktime,
➥video/mpeg, image/jpeg, image/gif, application/postscript,
➥audio/wav, text/plain, text/html, audio/x-aiff, audio/basic, */*

from SPRY_Mosaic/v8.17 (Windows 16-bit) --
application/x-gocserve, audio/basic, audio/x-midi, application/x-
➥rtf, video/msvideo, video/quicktime, video/mpeg, image/targa,
➥image/x-win-bmp, image/jpeg, image/gif, application/postscript,
➥audio/wav, text/plain, text/html; level=3, audio/x-aiff, audio/
➥basic, image/jpeg, image/x-gif24, image/png, image/x-png, image/
➥x-xbitmap, image/gif, application/x-ms-executable, application/
➥x-sprymosaic-hotlist, application/x-airmosaic-patch,
➥application/binary, application/http, www/mime

from Lynx/2.3 BETA libwww/2.14 --
application/pdf, application/x-dvi, application/postscript, video/
*, video/mpeg, image/*, audio/*, */*, application/x-wais-source,
text/plain, text/html, www/mime

from NCSA Mosaic/2.0.0 Final Beta (Windows x86) --
video/x-msvideo, video format-quick movie format, video/mpeg,
text/x-sgml, image/tiff, image/jpeg, image/gif, image/bmp,
➥application/zip, application/x-zip, application/x-tar,
➥application/x-rtf, application/x-hdf, application/x-gzip,
➥application/x-compress, application/postscript, application/pdf,
```

```
➥application/octet-stream, application/msword, audio/x-wav,
➥audio/x-midi, audio/x-aiff, audio/wav, audio/basic, text/plain,
➥text/html, audio/x-aiff, audio/basic, */*

from IBM WebExplorer /v1.01 --
*/*; q=0.300, application/octet-stream; q=0.100, text/plain, text/
html, image/bmp, image/jpeg, image/tiff, image/x-xbitmap, image/
gif, application/zip, application/inf, audio/x-wav, audio/x-aiff,
audio/basic, video/avs-video, video/x-msvideo, video/quicktime,
video/mpeg, image/x-bitmap, image/bmp, image/tiff, image/jpeg,
image/gif, application/editor
```

The IBM WebExplorer appears to break the rules more than the other browsers by using semicolons, equal signs, and so on. This is what the MIME folks call *multilevel encoding*. It's not supported by the current HTTP specification, but it may be in the future and doesn't seem to provide any real problems. If you plan to decode the `HTTP_ACCEPT` variable, you just need to be aware that some browsers will do this.

REMOTE_HOST and REMOTE_ADDR

The `REMOTE_HOST`, and `REMOTE_ADDR` variables provide information about the IP address of the user. `REMOTE_ADDR` will contain the IP address in dotted-decimal notation. The `REMOTE_HOST` variable will contain the text-equivalent host name of the address.

Note *Dotted-decimal* notation is a common format for expressing the 32-bit IP address used by the Internet Protocol to locate a specific machine on an internet. See *The CGI Book* (New Riders), Chapter 5, "IP Addressing and System Configuration," for a complete discussion of URLs and IP addresses.

You will find that the `REMOTE_ADDR` field is always filled in, but the `REMOTE_HOST` field may not be. Because translating the dotted-decimal address to a host name (sometimes called *reverse hostname resolution*) takes both time and network bandwidth (it must send requests to a DNS server), many servers turn off this feature for performance and security reasons. If your server has reverse hostname resolution disabled, the `REMOTE_HOST` variable will be either blank (as it should be) or filled in with the value of `REMOTE_ADDR` (as it most often is).

About the Server

The following group of variables provide information about the server and the software that runs it:

- The SERVER_SOFTWARE variable contains the name and version of the server software in the format *name/version.*
- The SERVER_NAME variable contains the server's host name, DNS alias, or IP address for use in building self-referencing URLs. Note that this is not always the primary name of the server. The server I use, for example, is a *virtual server* set up by a provider service to look like a private server to the outside world. It should rightfully return the *virtual* name, `www.bearnet.com`, and it does.
- Finally, the `GATEWAY_INTERFACE` variable contains the revision of the CGI specification that this server uses in the format, *CGI/revision.*

Here's an example of how these variables are set on the server I use:

```
SERVER_SOFTWARE = Apache/0.6.4b
SERVER_NAME = www.bearnet.com
GATEWAY_INTERFACE = CGI/1.1
```

Request-Specific Variables

The following variables are request-specific in that they change based on the specific request being submitted. In addition to these, the user-specific variables discussed previously are request-specific as well:

- `QUERY_STRING` is probably the most important of these variables. This is the most common method of passing information to a CGI program.

  Commonly, a request is made to a CGI program by including a "?" followed by extra information on the URL. For example, if the URL `http://www.bearnet.com/cgi/test.cgi?quick.brown.fox` is submitted, all the characters after the `?` will be put in the `QUERY_STRING` variable. The value of the variable will be `quick.brown.fox`.
- `SCRIPT_NAME` is set to the file name of the CGI program. This may be useful if you are generating your scripts on-the-fly.

- `SERVER_PROTOCOL` contains the name and revision number of the protocol that this request came in from. It is in the format, *protocol/revision.* This will almost certainly be "`HTTP/1.0`" for now.
- The `SERVER_PORT` variable is the number of the port on which the request came in. It may be significant if your program is servicing requests coming in on different ports, perhaps for different domains or services.

  This field will usually be 80, the standard port for HTTP requests.
- `PATH_INFO` and `PATH_TRANSLATED` represent another way of passing information to a CGI program. You can pass another file path to the program by simply appending it to the URL, like this: "`http://www.bearnet.com/cgi/cgi-program.cgi/a/b/c`".

  Then, `PATH_INFO` will contain the extra path (`/a/b/c`) and `PATH_TRANSLATED` will contain the `PATH_INFO` appended to the document root path of the server (`/var/web/luna` on my server), like this:

  ```
  PATH_INFO = /a/b/c
  PATH_TRANSLATED = /var/web/luna/a/b/c
  ```
- `CONTENT_TYPE` is filled in for queries that have attached information; such as `POST` requests. It is the MIME content type of the data in the form `type/subtype`. `CONTENT_LENGTH` is the number of bytes of data.

  A typical set of values would be the following:

  ```
  CONTENT_TYPE = application/x-www-form-urlencoded
  CONTENT_LENGTH = 17
  ```
- `AUTH_TYPE` is used for user authentication. It contains the authentication method used to validate the user. User authentication is discussed further later in this chapter.
- `REQUEST_METHOD` is the method used for the request. It tells you where and how to look for whatever data is passed. Usually it will be either `POST` or `GET`.

That covers all the standard CGI variables. In addition to these variables, and whatever other environment variables your server provides to CGI programs, there may also be strings that a browser sends to your server, available with

"`HTTP_`" prepended to the name (the `HTTP_ACCEPT` string is one of these). Browser-specific variables vary greatly and tend to change from version to version.

Using Basic Authorization

For some applications, it's important to know authoritatively who is on the other end of the connection. If the service or information you are offering on your Web site is intended for a select group of people, or if you are charging for access to your service, or for any number of other reasons, you may need to implement some method of user authentication.

This section teaches how to use the Basic Authentication Scheme provided in the HTTP/1.0 specification. There are other methods of authentication available. SHTTP (Secure HyperText Transfer Protocol) and SSL (Secure Sockets Layer) are in limited use today. The GSS-API, which uses a secret key negotiated on-the-fly between the server and client; HTTP-NG, which provides performance improvements as well as authentication; and a digest authentication scheme from the HTTP working group of the IETF are also under development.

There are still many hurdles ahead, however, before any standard, secure method of user authentication can be widely implemented on the Internet. Not the least of these is that many countries, including the United States, classify encryption technology as munitions, thereby creating legal challenges—on top of the technical challenges—that must be overcome before a new standard may be deployed.

At the time of this writing, the HTTP Basic Authentication Scheme is the only means of user authentication that is widely supported.

Is Basic Authorization Secure?

The Basic Authorization Scheme, as described in the HTTP/1.0 specification, uses a BASE64 transfer-encoding scheme borrowed from the MIME specification. BASE64 is not an encryption scheme—it is simply an encoding method designed to ensure the integrity of the authorization data as it travels through the Net from the client to the server. Even if it were designed to be difficult to decode, you wouldn't have to decode it to use it for nefarious purposes—all a miscreant would actually need to break in would be the *encrypted* password, as transferred by the browser.

The HTTP/1.0 specification does not specify how the server should save the user names and passwords on the host. Most systems (including the NCSA, CERN, and Apache servers, which together represent about half of the servers on the Internet) use the `crypt()` function found on most Unix hosts to store the password in a concealed form on the host. This is the same method that many Unix systems use to store passwords in their user database.

Note Technically speaking, crypt() does not do encryption, in spite of what the Unix manual says. It uses a one-way hash algorithm to generate a value that is more of a cryptographic checksum than an encrypted string.

The current draft of the HTTP/1.0 specification has this to say about the security value of Basic Authentication:

> The basic authentication scheme is a non-secure method of filtering unauthorized access to resources on an HTTP server. It is based on the assumption that the connection between the client and the server can be regarded as a trusted carrier. As this is not generally true on an open network, the basic authentication scheme should be used accordingly.
>
> —From *http Working Group Internet-Draft*, October 14, 1995, Berners-Lee, Fielding, and Neilsen, Sec. 11.1

Thus, Basic Authorization is not designed to be secure—all the information a potential intruder needs is available in the response from the browser. A complete solution to the problems of security and user authentication may be forthcoming in time, but for now, all you have to work with is Basic Authorization.

Note If you are interested in such things, you can find a complete description of BASE64 transfer-encoding in RFC 1521, the document that defines MIME.

How Basic Authentication Works

The Basic Authentication scheme is a realm-specific method that can assign differing levels of access to different users in different realms of its data structure. Usually these realms are based upon directory trees.

The system works on a simple challenge-response scheme. When the browser requests a file from a restricted realm, the server initiates the authorization transaction with a challenge consisting of the authorization scheme ("basic" in this case), and an identifier representing the realm of the restriction. At this point, the browser will usually prompt the user for a user-ID and password, then respond to the challenge with a response string back to the server. The *response string* contains the credentials of the user for access within that particular realm on that server.

The server then checks the credentials of the user against those in its database to determine their authenticity and authority. Based on the results of the search, the server will respond by either providing the requested data (if it is satisfied that the user is allowed to have it), or an indication that the user is forbidden access.

The Challenge and the Response

When the server gets a request for a document in a secure area, it begins the authorization transaction by sending a "challenge" back to the client. This challenge includes the 401 (Unauthorized) response code and the `WWW-Authenticate` token as part of the header. The `WWW-Authenticate` token has the following format:

```
WWW-Authenticate: Basic realm="Elvis Presley"
```

where `Elvis Presley` is the name the server has assigned to identify the protected realm. This string is actually sent as part of the HTTP header that the server sends with each of its responses, so the whole response may look like this:

```
HTTP/1.0 401 Unauthorized
Date: Tue, 12 Dec 1995 04:05:58 GMT
Server: Apache/1.0.0
WWW-Authenticate: Basic realm="Elvis Presley"
Content-type: text/html
```

```
<HEAD><TITLE>Authorization Required</TITLE></HEAD>
<BODY><H1>Authorization Required</H1>
This server could not verify that you
are authorized to access the document you
requested.  Either you supplied the wrong
credentials (e.g., bad password),
or your browser doesn't understand how to supply
the credentials required.<P></BODY>
```

The HTML included after the header is the text that will be displayed if the user is not authorized. In most installations, it is customizable.

When the browser sees this response, it will prompt the user for credentials. Figure 19.1 displays the user authentication dialog box from the Netscape browser.

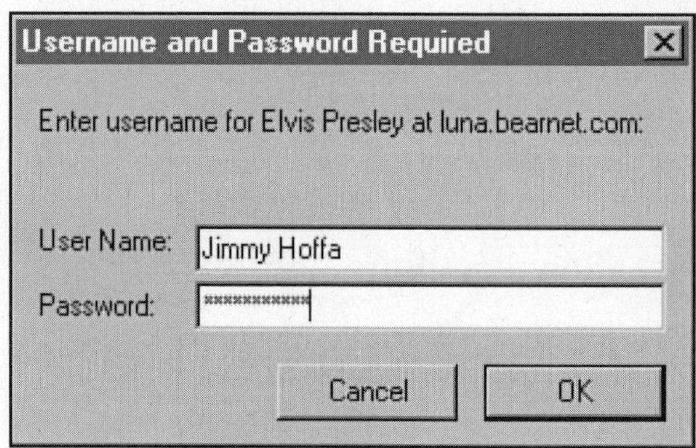

Figure 19.1 *The user authentication dialog box in Netscape.*

After the user enters the credentials, the browser sends them as part of its Authorization response in the form, *Userid:Password*, separated by a colon, and encoded with BASE64. Here's the authorization response from the Netscape browser for the preceding user-ID and password:

```
GET /cgibook/chap06/excl HTTP/1.0
Connection: Keep-Alive
User-Agent: Mozilla/2.0b3 (Win95; I)
Host: luna.bearnet.com:8080
Accept: image/gif, image/x-xbitmap, image/jpeg, image/pjpeg, */*
Authorization: Basic SmltbXkgSG9mZmE6YWJjZGVmZ2hpams=
```

If the credentials supplied are acceptable to the server, it will respond with the requested data; if not, it will respond with 401 (Unauthorized) again, just as in the initial challenge. This enables users to keep trying in case they have inaccurately typed their user-ID or password. Of course, this indefinitely repeatable exchange also enables a user to keep trying password after password in a surreptitious attempt to determine someone else's credentials—it's definitely a double-edged sword.

The Access Control File

Most servers—including NCSA, CERN, and Apache—use an *Access Control File* (ACF) to configure many aspects of the server's operation, including Basic Authorization. There are two possible types of ACFs—a *Global* ACF, usually named `access.conf` in the server's configuration directory; and *Per-Directory* ACFs, usually called `.htaccess`, which may exist in any directory. (Some servers disable Per-Directory ACFs, so ask your system administrator before you try to use one.)

Different servers use different formats for their ACF files, so check with your server documentation or your system administrator for help in setting it up. So that you know what sort of information is kept in an ACF, here is the format used by NCSA-based servers (this is an NCSA-style access control file):

```
<Directory {path}>
AuthType Basic
AuthName {name of area}
AuthUserFile {user-password path}
AuthGroupFile {group-file path}
<Limit {method} {method} ...>
order {order}
deny from {host} {host} ...
allow from {host} {host} ...
require {entity-type} {entity} {entity} ...
</Limit>
</Directory >
```

The preceding example has all the different directives and parameters listed. As a reference, table 19.2 contains a brief definition of each of them.

Table 19.2
NCSA Access Control File Directives

Directive	Description
	<Directory>
`</Directory>`	Sectioning directive. Valid only in the Global ACF. Specifies the directory tree that the included access controls apply to. Must be terminated with `</Directory>`.
`AuthType`	Authorization method. Currently the only valid parameter is `Basic`.
`AuthName`	The name of this restricted area.
`AuthUserFile`	The path to the password file.
`AuthGroupFile`	The path to the group file.
	<Limit>
`</Limit>`	Sectioning directive. Lists the access methods controlled by this section. `GET` and `POST` are the only currently implemented methods. `GET` is used for retrieving any files; `POST` currently applies to `POST`-method CGI calls. Must be terminated with `</Limit>`. `Order`, `deny`, `allow`, and `require` are the only directives allowed within a `<Limit>` section.
`order`	Defines the order in which the `deny` and `allow` directives are evaluated. Its parameter must be one of the following: `deny,allow`—deny before allow `allow,deny`—allow before deny

<Limit>	
	`mutual-failure` is synonymous with "`deny from all`" followed by specific `allow` and `deny` directives.
`deny`	For listing hosts from which users are denied access. Valid parameters include the following: Host names Domain names IP addresses Network addresses (that is, for subnet restrictions) The keyword, `all`
`allow`	For listing hosts from which users are allowed access. Valid parameters are the same as those for `deny`.
`require`	For specifying which authenticated users can access the restricted area. Valid parameters are: `user` followed by a list of user-IDs; `group` followed by a list of groups; or `valid-user`, which specifies any authenticated user in the given password file. `require` is always evaluated after `deny` and `allow`.

NCSA Group File

The group file in the NCSA model simply describes what user-IDs belong to what groups for the purpose of allowing or denying permissions to authenticated users. The format of the NCSA group file is simple:

```
Presidents: Jack Lyndon Dick Gerry Jimmy Ron George Bubba
Veeps: Lyndon Hubert Spiro Gerry Nelson Walter George Dan Al
```

The name of the group is followed by a colon and a space-delimited list of user-IDs (presumably the same user-IDs that are in the password file).

Note Some versions of the NCSA server require that `AuthGroupFile` is specified whenever `AuthUserFile` is specified. If you don't need a group file, use `/dev/null`, or its equivalent, for your system.

NCSA Password File

The password file for the NCSA server can be created with the program called `htpasswd` that is distributed with the server. It also has a very simple format, as follows:

```
Jack:FyXizPi2lfyeI
Lyndon:VN6IXh4.dEu22
Dick:QRadiiq8aDL5Q
Spiro:LVN.eUptD56NE
Hubert:pnxnkKLPprCRA
Gerry:Fc/eSV1ZtJ7sw
Nelson:kujWNHpsoOo86
Jimmy:Xb1sDaeeq4g.o
Walter:9pQZPLa2qf4FU
Ron:KFZT3cRQDRYz6
George:FJ1W3aknsZzMs
Bubba:tWEDLGNGePj5.
Al:oas8vh4Q0P1eE
```

Each line in the NCSA-format password file simply contains a user-ID followed by a colon and the encoded password.

Warning The password and group files should never be put in any directory tree that is visible to the Web browser! Even though the files are somewhat obscured by the `crypt()` function, the information in them is sufficient for some attackers to gain unauthorized access to your system. Put these files in a safe place like the server's configuration directory, if it is available to you. If you do not have access to that area on your server, you may want to use a directory in your `$HOME` path.

A Basic Authorization Example

Sometimes you may want users to be able to register with your server for access without having to wait for a system administrator to get around to entering his or her user-ID and password into the password file with htpasswd. Also, some system administrators would rather not have access to the passwords of all their users, and thus would prefer that the users enter the password themselves.

With this in mind, this section presents an example of a program that creates the entries in the password file based on input from an HTML form.

First, you'll need a form for the user to fill out. Listing 19.7 asks for the user-ID and password; you might also want to get a street address, e-mail address, and other user- or application-specific information.

Listing 19.7
auth.html

```
<HTML>
<HEAD>
<TITLE>Basic Authentication Example</TITLE>
</HEAD>
<BODY>
<H1>Basic Authorization Example</H1>
<HR>

Please enter the Username and Password you wish to use.<p>

<FORM METHOD="POST" ACTION="addpasswd.cgi">

<TABLE>
  <TR>
    <TD>Enter a Username:<BR>
        <INPUT TYPE="text" NAME="UserID" SIZE=10 MAXLENGTH=10>
    <td width=10>
    <td>Enter a Password:<br>
        <INPUT TYPE="PASSWORD" NAME="UserPass" SIZE=10
➥MAXLENGTH=10>
  <TR>
    <TD COLSPAN=3>
      <INPUT TYPE="SUBMIT" VALUE="  Let's Go!  ">
</TABLE>

</BODY>
</HTML>
```

Please note that the password from this form will be transmitted "in the clear"—that is, without any encryption or obfuscation of any sort. So if security is important (and you're using Basic Authentication anyway), you will want to enter the passwords in such a manner that they are not transmitted over the Internet at all (for example, enter the passwords with the `htpasswd` program and read them to your users over the telephone).

This form uses the `POST` method for submitting the form because the `GET` method transmits form contents as a part of the URL, making the password visible on the URL line of the user's browser. With the `POST` method, however, the form contents are passed to the server as part of the request header, thereby obscuring the contents from the view of a casual observer.

The CGI program that receives the password can then create the password file. Listing 19.8 is an example, in Perl, of how to do that with the NCSA or Apache server.

Listing 19.8
addpasswd.pl.cgi

```
#!/usr/bin/perl

# addpasswd.pl.cgi -- Add Password Program
#                     for HTTP Basic Authorization
#
#  1995-96 William E. Weinman
#

# the password file
$Passwords = "/home/billw/var/.htpasswd";
# the temporary work file
$TempPass = "/home/billw/var/.ptmp";

# 64-byte salt for crypt
@saltset = ('a' .. 'z', 'A' .. 'Z', '0' .. '9', '.', '/');

# content-type for html
$content="text/html";

# where to go when we're done
$doneurl="excl/index.html";
```

```
# post method variables
$ct = $ENV{"CONTENT_TYPE"};
$cl = $ENV{"CONTENT_LENGTH"};

# put the data into a variable
read(STDIN, $qs, $cl);

# split it up into an array by the '&' character
@qs = split(/&/, $qs);

foreach $i (0 .. $#qs)
  {
  # convert the plus chars to spaces
  $qs[$i] =~ s/\+/ /g;

  # convert the hex tokens to characters
  $qs[$i] =~ s/%(..)/pack("c",hex($1))/ge;

  # split into name and value
  ($name, $value) = split(/=/, $qs[$i],2);

  # create the associative element
  $qs{$name} = $value;
  }

# get the user name and password

$UserID    = $qs{"UserID"};
$UserPass  = $qs{"UserPass"};

$| = 1; # set stdout to flush after each write

# set the MIME type
print "Content-Type: $content\r\n";
print "\r\n";

# if the TempPass file exists, the password file is busy
if(-f $TempPass)
  {
  for($i = 0; ($i < 5) && (-f $TempPass); $i++)
    { sleep 1 }
  &BusyError if ($i == 5);
  }

# setup the html document
print qq(<html>
  <head><title>Adding Password</title></head>
```

continues

Listing 19.8, Continued

```
  <body bgcolor="#dddddd">
  <h1>Adding Password</h1>);

# uncomment this to display all the variables
# print "All Variables:<br>\n";
# foreach $n (keys %ENV) { print "<tt>$n: $ENV{$n}</tt><br>\n" }

# create the salt for crypt
# basically, that means come up with a couple of very
# unique bytes
#
($p1, $p2) = unpack("C2", $UserName);
$now = time;
$week = $now / (60*60*24*7) + $p1 + $p2;
$salt = $saltset[$week % 64] . $saltset[$now % 64];

$cryptpass = crypt($UserPass, $salt);

# build an associative array of the password file
open (PASS, "<$Passwords");
$umask = umask(0);
open (TMP, ">$TempPass");
umask($umask);
while(<PASS>)
  {
  chop;
  print TMP "$_\n";
  ($tname, $tpass) = split(':');
  $tapass{$tname} = $tpass;
  }
close(PASS);

unless($tapass{$UserID})
  {
  print qq(Adding $UserID to the password file.<p>
           Press <a href="$doneurl">here</a> to
           continue.<br>\n);

  printf (TMP "%s:%s\n", $UserID, $cryptpass);
  close TMP;
  rename($TempPass, $Passwords);
  # system "mv", $TempPass, $Passwords;
  }
else
  {
```

```
  print qq($UserID is already registered here. Send email to the
          <a href="mailto:WebMaster@bearnet.com">WebMaster</a>
          if you need to change your password.<br>\n);
  close TMP;
  unlink $TempPass;
  }

print "<hr><tt>&copy;</tt> <small> 1995 William E. Weinman</
➥small><br>";
print "</body></html>\n";

sub BusyError
{
print qq[<html>
  <head><title>File Busy Error</title></head>
  <body bgcolor="#dddddd">
  <h1>Error: File Busy</h1>
  <p>The password file is busy ($i), please try again later.
  <p>If this condition persists, please contact the
  <a href="mailto:webmaster@yourserver">webmaster</a>.
  </body></html>
  ];

exit 0;
}
```

The Perl code takes advantage of some of Perl's unique features, such as the `while(<PASS>)` loop to read the password file, and the `unless` construct to make the conditional code clearer. Also notice that you can use any character to quote a string with `print`—I often use parentheses [e.g. `qq(<text>)`] to quote text for HTML, because it enables me to use standard double-quotes in the string without bothering to escape them.

One of the major reasons that large sites use Basic Authentication is for the client-state information that it provides. When Basic Authentication is in use, the `USER_ID` variable becomes available. The `USER_ID` variable allows a site to know what particular user is requesting any given CGI program. This can be very useful when your application requires interaction with the user, an otherwise difficult task given HTTP's connectionless transport model.

A Form-Processing Example that Sends E-Mail

This section presents a typical application of CGI—sending e-mail to a mailbox. The application uses a form interface for a user to enter a message. For security reasons, the user is *not* allowed to enter the e-mail address of the recipient. In this case, it is hard-coded in the program. If you want to use this program for more than one recipient, you could add a lookup function to find the e-mail address.

For security reasons, it is also important that nothing from the HTML is used on the command line that gets passed to the Perl `system()` function. Keep in mind that the HTML file is not secure, and can be duplicated and changed on a user's system. When you pass anything from a form response, or even a hidden field, to a shell command line, it exposes your system to attack.

Listing 19.9 is an HTML file that presents a form to the user for sending e-mail via CGI.

Listing 19.9
email.html—A Form for Sending E-Mail via CGI

```
<html>
<head>
<title>Email Bill</title>
</head>
<body bgcolor="#e0e0e0">

<h1>Email Bill</h1>
<hr>

<form action="mailit.pl.cgi" method=post>

<p>Please enter your name:<br>
<input type=text name=name size=60>

<p>Please enter your email address:<br>
<input type=text name=from size=60>

<p>Please enter the subject of your message:<br>
<input type=text name=subject size=60>
```

```
<p>Please enter your message:<br>
<textarea name=body rows=15 cols=64>
</textarea>

<p>
<input type=submit value="Send It!">
<input type=reset value="Clear">

</form>

<hr>
</body>
</html>
```

Figure 19.2 is a Netscape screen showing the form from listing 19.9 being filled in.

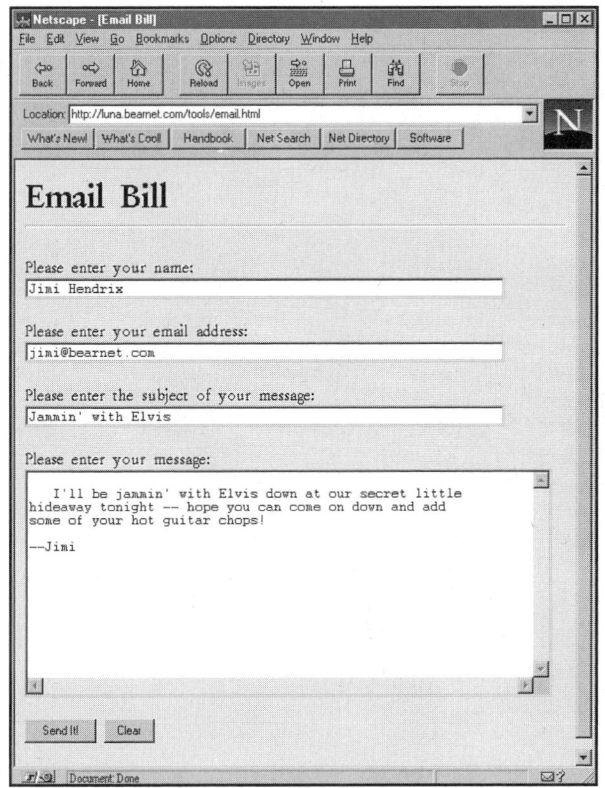

Figure 19.2
The Email form in Netscape.

The Perl program in listing 19.10 is the CGI program that actually sends the e-mail. It uses all the techniques discussed in this chapter to receive input from the server, and return a confirmation display to the user. It uses Perl's `system()` function to call the *sendmail* mail delivery agent on a Unix server. If your server is not running under Unix, you will need to substitute code for whatever mail delivery agent your system uses.

Listing 19.10
mailit.pl.cgi—Send E-mail to a Pre-Defined Address

```
#!/usr/bin/perl

# Filename: mailit.pl.cgi
#  1996 William E. Weinman
#
# a generic example of a cgi program that sends
# the response to a form encapsulated in an
# email message to a pre-determined address
#

# your email address goes here (please don't use mine!)
$emailto = "wew@bearnet.com";
$webmaster = "webmaster@bearnet.com";

# Send the MIME header
print "Content-type: text/html\r\n\r\n";

print qq(
<html><head><title>Form Response</title></head>
<body bgcolor="#e0e0e0">);


$ct = $ENV{"CONTENT_TYPE"};
$cl = $ENV{"CONTENT_LENGTH"};

# check the content-type for validity
if($ct ne "application/x-www-form-urlencoded")
  {
  print "I don't understand content-type: $ct\n";
  exit 1;
  }

# put the data into a variable
read(STDIN, $qs, $cl);

# split it up into an array by the '&' character
@qs = split(/&/,$qs);
```

```
foreach $i (0 .. $#qs)
  {
  # convert the plus chars to spaces
  $qs[$i] =~ s/\+/ /g;

  # convert the hex tokens to characters
  $qs[$i] =~ s/%(..)/pack("c",hex($1))/ge;

  # split into name and value
  ($name, $value) = split(/=/,$qs[$i],2);

  # create the associative element
  $qs{$name} = $value;
  }

print qq(
<h1>Form Response</h1>

<p>The following information is being forwarded by email:

<p>
Remote Host: <tt>$ENV{"REMOTE_HOST"}</tt><br>
Remote Addr: <tt>$ENV{"REMOTE_ADDR"}</tt><br>
User Agent:  <tt>$ENV{"HTTP_USER_AGENT"}</tt><br>
From: <tt>$qs{"name"} &lt;$qs{"from"}&gt;</tt><br>
Subject: <tt>$qs{"subject"} [Via Form]</tt><br>

<p>Message follows:
<pre>$qs{"body"}</pre>
\n);

open(MAIL, "¦ /usr/lib/sendmail -t -f'$webmaster'");

# These lines must be terminated with CR-LF pairs!
print(MAIL "From: $qs{name} <$qs{from}>\r\n");
print(MAIL "X-WWW-Form: $ENV{SCRIPT_NAME}\r\n");
print(MAIL "Reply-to: $qs{name} <$qs{from}>\r\n");
print(MAIL "To: $emailto\r\n");
print(MAIL "Subject: $qs{subject} [Via Form]\r\n\r\n");

print MAIL qq(
Remote Host: $ENV{"REMOTE_HOST"}
Remote Addr: $ENV{"REMOTE_ADDR"}
User Agent:  $ENV{"HTTP_USER_AGENT"}
From: $qs{"name"} <$qs{"from"}>
```

continues

Listing 19.10, Continued

```
Message follows:
$qs{"body"}

);

close(MAIL);
```

Figure 19.3 is a Netscape screen showing the output of the CGI program in listing 19.10. This screen shows the user that what they have entered in the form is being e-mailed to the recipient.

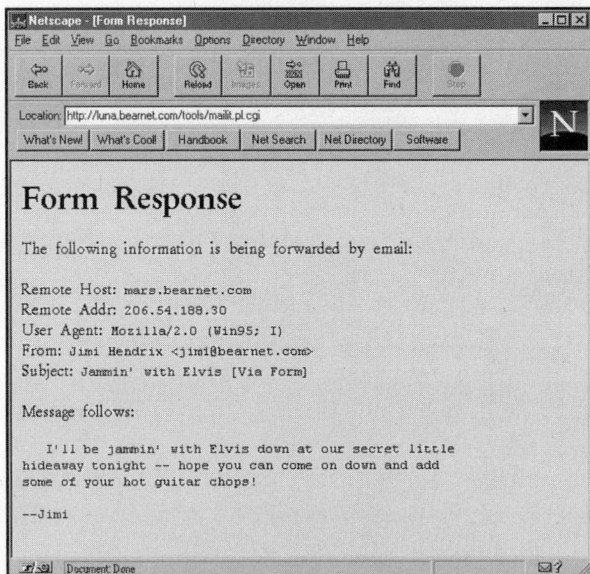

Figure 19.3 *Response to the e-mail form.*

Listing 19.11 shows the complete e-mail message as it is received in the recipient's mailbox.

Listing 19.11
mailit.pl.cgi—send email to a pre-defined address

```
Return-Path: webmaster@bearnet.com
Received: (from nobody@localhost) by luna.bearnet.com (8.6.12/
➥luna) id QAA08485; Thu, 15 Feb 1996 16:49:46 -0600
Date: Thu, 15 Feb 1996 16:49:46 -0600
Message-Id: <199602152249.QAA08485@luna.bearnet.com>
From: Jimi Hendrix <jimi@bearnet.com>
```

```
X-WWW-Form: /tools/mailit.pl.cgi
Reply-to: Jimi Hendrix <jimi@bearnet.com>
To: wew@bearnet.com
Subject: Jammin' with Elvis [Via Form]
X-UIDL: 824424783.000

Remote Host: mars.bearnet.com
Remote Addr: 206.54.188.30
User Agent:  Mozilla/2.0 (Win95; I)
From: Jimi Hendrix <jimi@bearnet.com>

Message follows:

   I'll be jammin' with Elvis down at our secret little
hideaway tonight -- hope you can come on down and add
some of your hot guitar chops!

--Jimi
```

This section has presented a small CGI program that uses all the techniques discussed so far in this chapter. It is useful as a real-world working application that demonstrates the use of CGI, and can be easily expanded to provide more functionality.

The next section presents a more complex form of CGI, called *Non-Parsed Header CGI.* This form of CGI bypasses the server and sends HTTP responses directly to the client, for cases where the server does not have the flexibility to perform the desired action.

Non-Parsed Header CGI

When a normal CGI program responds with output to the standard out stream, the server intercepts the stream and incorporates it with standard HTTP to the client. There are situations, however, where the standard responses aren't sufficient to perform the necessary functions. Non-Parsed Header (NPH) CGI is designed to handle those situations.

Most servers implement a special way of calling a CGI program that does not intercept the header, called NPH-CGI. On most servers, it is invoked when the CGI program is in a file that starts with the letters, "`nph-`" (for example, `nph-myprogram.cgi`). If this doesn't work on your server, talk to your system administrator or consult the server documentation to find out how to run NPH-CGI on your system.

When you write an NPH-CGI program, you need to provide a valid HTTP response in your header. This next section discusses what is required by the HTTP specification to form a valid header.

An Introduction to HTTP

The *HyperText Transfer Protocol* is the protocol used by Web servers to negotiate the flow of data between the server and the client. The HTTP protocol defines a set of messages that fall into two categories: "request" messages from the client, and "response" messages from the server.

Request messages are sent by the client to the server to request data. This is the basic format for an HTTP request message:

```
<method> URI <HTTP-version>
```

A typical request might look like this:

```
GET /cgibook/chap01/index.html HTTP/1.0
```

The server then sends a response to the client in the following form:

```
<response-header>
<data>
```

The first part of the response is the *response header*. It begins with a *status line* that contains the version of HTTP being used, a *status code,* and a *reason phrase*. The status line is followed by a series of MIME-formatted header lines that describe the details of the response.

The most common response status code you will send is "`200`," which essentially means, "Okay, here's the data you requested." The other response codes defined in HTTP/1.0 are listed in table 19.3. For full definitions and usage guidelines, see the HTTP Internet Draft referenced previously.

Table 19.3
HTTP Response Status Codes

Status Code	Reason Phrase
Informational 1xx	
Undefined in HTTP/1.0	
Successful 2xx	
200	OK
201	Created
202	Accepted
204	No Content
Redirection 3xx	
300	Multiple Choices
301	Moved Permanently
302	Moved Temporarily
304	Not Modified
Client Error 4xx	
400	Bad Request
401	Unauthorized
403	Forbidden
404	Not Found
Server Error 5xx	
500	Internal Server Error
501	Not Implemented

continues

Table 19.3, Continued

Status Code	Reason Phrase
502	Bad Gateway
503	Service Unavailable

The response header is always followed by a blank line to indicate that the header is finished. If there is a body of data associated with the response, it follows the blank line.

A response to the preceding request might look like this:

```
HTTP/1.0 200 OK
Date: Mon, 22 Jan 1996 17:52:11 GMT
Server: Apache/0.6.4b
Content-type: text/html

<html>
<head>
<title>Chapter 1 &#183; "Hello, World!"</title>
</head>
<BODY bgcolor="#dddddd">

    . . . document body . . .

</body>
</html>
```

Warning It is important to note that newlines in HTTP messages are represented by both a carriage-return (`0D`*hex*) *and* a linefeed (`0A`*hex*). Some systems—including Unix systems and some software on Macs and PCs—do not normally use both characters in their line endings. Many servers and clients will go ahead and recognize line endings that are either a single carriage-return or a single linefeed; in fact, the current HTTP specification encourages them to do so. Some clients don't recognize these line endings, however, and it's not required of them to do so.

Just make sure to end your lines with both characters, in the correct order, and your code will work with more clients without problem.

It is beyond the scope of this chapter to present the definitions of all the possible fields in an HTTP transaction. You will get what you need to know here, but for all the gory details of HTTP, you can get a copy of the Internet draft that describes it at `ftp://ftp.internic.net/internet-drafts/draft-ietf-http-v10-spec-04.txt`.

The point to remember is that the server sends the client a stream of characters that represent the different elements of the response. If you know the format of what an HTTP server sends, you can mimic its protocol and send customized responses to handle specific circumstances not otherwise supported by the server.

Normally, when you run a CGI program, the server will intercept the MIME header and simply incorporate its elements into the overall header that it sends to the client. You don't want this to happen if you're generating your own responses—you'll need a way of bypassing the server altogether. This is what NPH-CGI is for.

Coding a Non-Parsed Header CGI Program

Keep in mind that when you write an NPH-CGI program, you need to provide a valid HTTP response in your header. Listing 19.12 is a skeleton NPH-CGI program that does that in Perl. The technique should be obvious enough to see how to implement it in other languages.

Listing 19.12
A Skeleton NPH-CGI Program

```
#!/usr/bin/perl

# nph-skel.pl.cgi
#
# Hello World in NPH-CGI
#
# (c) 1996 William E. Weinman

$HttpHeader = "HTTP/1.0 200 OK";
$ContentType = "Content-type: text/html";

print "$HttpHeader\r\n";    # note the \r\n sequence!
print "$ContentType\r\n\r\n";

print "<http><head><title>NPH-CGI Hello World</title></head>\n";
print "<body><h1>Hello, World!</h1></body></html>\n"
```

It really is that simple. Just make sure that you send the response header before anything else, that your newlines are carriage-return/linefeed pairs, and that the last line of the header has two newlines after it.

Now that you know how to do this, you're probably saying, "Well that's cool, but what do I do with it?"

I'm glad you asked.

Server-Push Animation

The most popular technique for creating inline graphic animations on a Web page is called *server-push.* In a nutshell, this technique uses an NPH-CGI program to push successive "frames" of an animation from the server to the client, one after the other, without waiting for subsequent requests from the client.

> **Note** As of this writing, the only available browser that will display server-push animation is the Netscape Navigator. Unofficial sources at Microsoft say that version 3 of the Microsoft Internet Explorer will also support server-push animation.

Server-push animation works with the special MIME-type, "`multipart/x-mixed-replace`". The "`multipart`" content type is a method of encapsulating several entities (which the MIME specification calls "body parts") in the body of one message. The "`x-mixed-replace`" sub-type is an invention of Netscape's (also supported by a number of other browsers) that allows each encapsulated entity to replace the previous one on a dynamic page.

The main part of the document is called a *container*, because it is used to hold the contents of the subordinate entities. The container document uses boundary strings to delimit the individual entities so that they can be extracted by the client.

The correct syntax for the container's "Content-type:" declaration is as follows:

```
Content-type: multipart/x-mixed-replace;boundary="random-string"
```

The boundary string is used with two leading dash characters (for example, `--random-string`) to introduce the MIME header of each subordinate entity;

and with two leading *and* two trailing dashes to terminate the entire container (for example, `--random-string--`). Listing 19.13 is an example of how a server-push stream should look.

Listing 19.13
A Server-Push Stream Example

```
HTTP/1.0 200 OK
Content-type: multipart/x-mixed-replace;boundary="foo"

--foo
Content-type: text/plain

Text string 1.

--foo

Content-type: text/plain

Text string 2.

--foo
Content-type: text/plain

Text string 3.

--foo
Content-type: text/plain

Text string 4.

--foo--
```

The boundary string, with its leading and trailing double-dashes, must be on a line by itself set off from the rest of the stream by carriage-return/linefeed pairs. The client software will expect this, and it is required by the RFC 1591 MIME specification. In other words, the preceding example would be coded with a string like this:

```
print "\r\n--foo\r\n"
```

and

```
print "\r\n--foo--\r\n"
```

Warning According to Netscape's server-push document, there was a bug in an unspecified version of the NCSA `httpd` server that prevented the server from accepting a "`Content-type`" string with a space in it anywhere except directly after the colon. Obviously, this would be a potential problem if you wanted a space after the semicolon ("`;`") and before the "`boundary`" declaration.

This statement appears dubious to me—after all, the server is not supposed to do anything with an NPH header anyway.

I have not been able to duplicate the anomalous behavior; in fact, my version of the NCSA server (version 1.5) works fine with a space after the semicolon. But just in case it was a bug in a previous version, I have left the space out in all of the examples.

The string used for the boundary needs to be some string that is not likely to be found in the encapsulated entities, to avoid having the entities inadvertently split up. This is not a likely problem with graphics files, of course, but you need to watch out for it—especially if your graphics files have comment blocks in them.

Now, with all this background information, you're probably anxious to see it all come together. The next section presents a full working example of server-push.

Note Although it is currently optional, it is a good idea to also include a *Content-Length* header in your contained entities. Future versions of HTTP may require this in some circumstances, and it gives some browsers enough information today to display a progress indicator as it downloads each part of the animation.

A Complete Server-Push Example

The NPH-CGI program in this section reads a list of individual GIF files and pushes them out to the client using server-push. First, though, you should be forewarned of a danger.

> **Warning** It may be quite tempting to write your server-push program in one of the Unix shells. There are even some examples of shell scripts on the Net that do server-push.
>
> The problem is that most shells are not sophisticated enough to know when the client disconnects from the server and they may continue to run, needlessly wasting resources. This is especially serious when the animation is coded to run endlessly.
>
> The Perl example in listing 19.14 should serve well as a template for just about any animation you may need to do.

Listing 19.14 is a Perl program that reads a list of file names from a text file and sends them as parts in a multipart MIME stream, as documented earlier in this chapter.

Listing 19.14
A Generic Server-Push Animation Program in Perl

```
#!/usr/bin/perl

# nph-push.pl.cgi
#
# (c) 1996 William E. Weinman
#
# Generic CGI Push Animation
#

# response header stuff
$httpokay = "HTTP/1.0 200 Okay";
$ct = "Content-type:";
$cl = "Content-length:";
$boundary = "foo";
$ctmixed = "$ct multipart/x-mixed-replace; boundary=$boundary";
$ctgif = "$ct image/gif";
```

continues

Listing 19.14, Continued

```
# the list of files to animate
$listfile = "animate.lst";

# delaytime can in seconds (can be fractional)
$delaytime = 1.5;

$| = 1; # force a flush after each print

# read the list
open(LISTFILE, "<$listfile");
@infiles = <LISTFILE>; # is perl suave, or what?
close(LISTFILE);

# send the main http response header
print "$httpokay\n";
print "$ctmixed\n\n";

# main loop
foreach $i (@infiles)
  {
  chop $i; # lose the trailing '\n'
  $clsz = &filesize($i);
  # inside boundaries have a leading '--'
  print "\n--$boundary\n";
  if ($sleepokay)
    {
    # this is perl's famous less-than-one-second sleep trick! ;^)
    select(undef, undef, undef, $delaytime);
    }
  else
    { $sleepokay = 1;}
  # uncomment this to send the filename--useful for
  # debugging, harmless to the browser, and a bad
  # idea for production use, because it gives a potential
  # intruder useful information.
  #
  # print "X-Filename $i\n";

  # the content-length header may be required by HTTP 1.1,
  # it's optional in HTTP 1.0, but some browsers will
  # use it to display progress to the user if you send it.
  print "$cl $clsz\n";
  print "$ctgif\n\n";

  # now send the GIF, keeping it open for a minimum
  # amount of time.
  open (INFILE, "<$i");
```

```
  sysread(INFILE, $buffer, $clsz);
  close(INFILE);
  syswrite(STDOUT, $buffer, $clsz);
  }

# the trailing boundary with both '--' indicators
print "\n--$boundary--\n";

# this is here because it was ugly up there.
sub filesize
{
($dev, $ino, $mode, $nlink, $uid, $gid, $rdev, $size,
     $atime, $mtime, $ctime, $blksize, $blocks) = stat($_[0]);

return $size
}
```

There are couple of things worth noting in the Perl source code for this example. One is the assignment, "`$| = 1;`", near the top of the program. This is the Perlism for flushing an output stream buffer after each write to it. It ensures that all the bytes are sent at the time that they are intended to, keeping your output smooth.

Another note about the Perl code: notice the line " `select(undef, undef, undef, $delaytime);`". This is Perlish for a sleep with sub-second resolution. It's ugly, but it works well, and there's nothing like it in C or sh. sleep usually works only on one-second boundaries, so a command like `sleep 1` will sleep for an unpredictable amount of time between zero and one second.

One last technique worth noting is the line for reading the file name list into an array, "`@infiles = <LISTFILE>;`". That in itself is enough reason to learn a new language!

This chapter has covered a lot of ground. In it you have learned the basic requirements of a CGI program, the meanings of all the different components, definitions of all the standard CGI variables, and some specific techniques for getting reliable results from CGI. Although this chapter is not designed to provide all the details of CGI, you now have the tools necessary to create CGI programs of your own.

If you would like to learn more about CGI, the author has written a book that covers the subject in far greater detail. *The CGI Book* (New Riders

Publishing is a complete reference and programming guide for CGI with chapters on processing forms, understanding URLs, imagemaps, user authentication, cookies, server-side includes, animation, e-mail, and CGI security.

Introduction to Perl and Oracle CGI Scripting

by Michael Marolda

The introduction of Mosaic as a World Wide Web navigation tool has resulted in an explosive growth of users and data on the Internet. Things that used to take considerable time and expertise to do, such as finding out which hotels are in a city or which houses are for sale, can now be accomplished with a click of a hypertext link. This explosive growth has not gone unnoticed by those wanting to get their information to the general public. Companies, universities, organizations, and individuals are discovering that the Web is an extremely convenient and powerful tool for making information about that organization available to a global audience.

One of the most difficult jobs for a Web site maintainer or developer in WWW publishing is keeping information in documents current. Many Web sites can consist of thousands of documents, each with information that may be duplicated elsewhere. When the information changes it can be quite a challenge to ensure that that change is reflected everywhere. This is where the power of a database can greatly simplify the task of maintaining the data. Integrating an Oracle database into a WWW site can simplify information maintenance, capture and process data from the users, and help provide a more dynamic and interesting Web site.

Because most companies already manage information in one or more large databases, integrating existing data into a Web server may take less time than most realize. Although database and Web integration is still a relatively new process, it is simple enough to accomplish a great deal.

There are currently several "gateways" and tools that aid in developing WWW sites using Oracle. However, it is important to understand the underlying mechanism by which most of these gateways work. This chapter gives a brief overview of Web and Web architecture to assure an understanding of the material that follows. Most of the chapter is devoted to an overview of the Form elements needed to send information to an Oracle CGI application and the details of writing a CGI application. Perl and Oracle are used to process the form and communicate with Oracle and are explained as needed. To illustrate the points being discussed, a database consisting of one table of employee information is used. After you have an understanding of the architecture and mechanism, you will be better equipped to evaluate and choose among the various options and tools available.

Web and Web Server Architecture

When you push a hypertext link or enter a Uniform Resource Locator (URL) in a Web browser, your browser sends a message to the Web server that is referenced by that URL. When the Web server receives the request, it is sent to the appropriate process; in many cases, a HyperText Transfer Protocol (HTTP) server. The HTTP server then takes this request and decides how to handle it. Usually, the outcome is to find a specific file on the Web server and return it to the browser.

For example, the following URL causes the Web browser to contact the host computer, bristol.onramp.net, to issue an HTTP request for the document index.html.:

```
http://bristol.onramp.net:80/index.html
```

Instead of simply retrieving a file, you can also ask the server to run an application for you. The application that is executed as a result of the request (whether it is a POST or a GET request) is called a CGI script or application. CGI stands for Common Gateway Interface and has a set of standard mechanisms for getting incoming data and returning the results. It is via the CGI script that you can connect to an Oracle database. An overview of CGI is given in a later part in this chapter. The whole process is shown in the flow chart in figure 20.1.

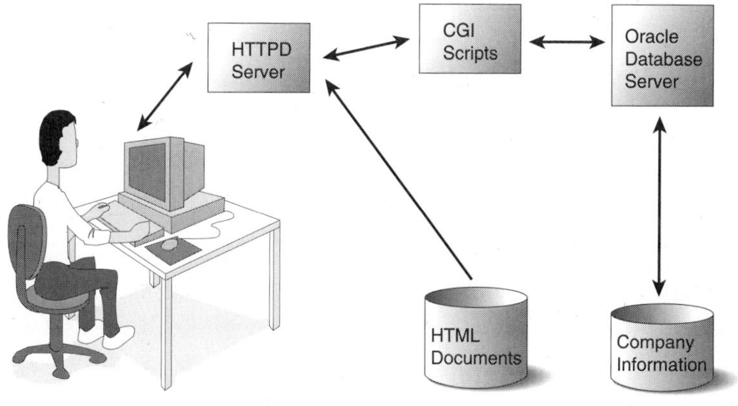

Figure 20.1
The major pieces of Web architecture, and the communication flow to an HTTP server.

In HTML, there are two different methods used to invoke an application:

- **GET.** Uses a format similar to all hypertext URLs. For example, the following URL utilizes the GET method to run the application called getdata.cgi on the host computer bristol.onramp.net.

  ```
  http://bristol.onramp.net:80/cgi-bin/getdata.cgi
  ```

- **POST.** This method is most often used in *forms*, another document style, discussed in the next sections, that allows push buttons, edit fields, selection lists, and other mechanisms to be used to create a form.

This method of calling applications works well when you want to call an application via a hypertext link. There may be a limit to the amount of data that can be passed using this method. The HTML specification supports another method called POST. Both the GET and POST methods will be discussed at greater length later in the chapter.

Forms Overview

Before you can get into how CGI scripts process data, you need to cover some basic form information because the output of a form is usually the input to a CGI script.

Forms can greatly simplify the task of collecting data from the end user. Using editable fields, selection lists, radio or push buttons, and so on, a form can be built that captures data from the end user in a convenient fashion. When the user has filled out the form, the data is sent to your Web server for processing via a CGI script or application. Figure 20.2 shows a basic form.

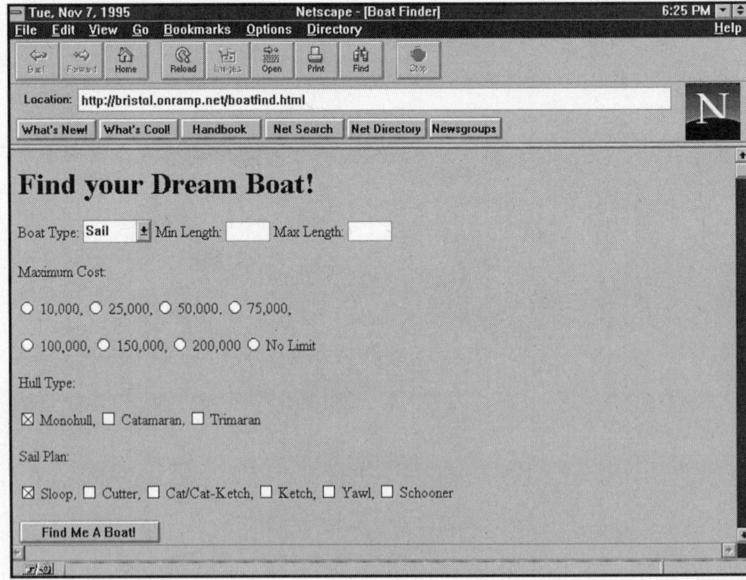

Figure 20.2
A basic form and input types.

Basic Form Types

There are many basic types (or HTML tags) that are used in form processing. This chapter works with only a subset of these, the form type and four variations of the input type: text, radio buttons, submit, and reset. There are many other types available but are beyond the scope and intent of this chapter.

- Form
- Text
- Radio button
- Reset
- Submit

The Form Tag Type

The first is the form tag itself:

```
<FORM ACTION="http://bristol.onramp.net/cgi-bin/putinfo.cgi"
➥METHOD=POST>
```

The form tag specifies the address of the CGI application to be run and the method for passing the form data to that application. In this example, the application is putinfo.cgi and is being called using the POST method. The form is terminated with a <\FORM> tag.

The Input Tag

The input tag identifies the HTML element as an input type. This is the main tag used in forms processing and has many variations. Some input tags allow text entry and some allow list item sections. A subset of these input tags, including text, radio buttons, submit, and reset, are described in the following sections.

The Text Input Type

The text input type allows users to enter data into a text field. The format is:

```
<INPUT NAME="name" TYPE="TEXT" SIZE="20">
```

This results in a 20-character editable field on the form. It is also possible to set the maximum allowed characters by specifying the MAXLENGTH tag. Also, if you want a default value to appear, the VALUE=“” attribute can be used. For example, to limit the above to 20 characters with a default of NONE, the following tag can be used:

```
<INPUT NAME="name" TYPE="TEXT" SIZE=20 MAXLENGTH=20
VALUE="Michael">
```

The Radio Button Input Type

The radio button allows only one of a set of choices to be selected. For example, to indicate a salary range, the following definitions could be used:

```
<INPUT TYPE="RADIO" NAME="salary" VALUE="10000" CHECKED>
<INPUT TYPE="RADIO" NAME="salary" VALUE="25000" >
<INPUT TYPE="RADIO" NAME="salary" VALUE="50000" >
<INPUT TYPE="RADIO" NAME="salary" VALUE="75000" >
<INPUT TYPE="RADIO" NAME="salary" VALUE="100000" >
```

Note that in the case of the radio button, the name is the same for all the buttons. This is very important because the name defines a group of items associated with this set of buttons. Only one button with the name “salary” could be selected at any one time. Another set of buttons would require a different group name.

The Submit Input Type

When the SUBMIT button is pressed, the data will be sent to the application indicated in the FORM tag. This is a very simple construct with only a value tag. This value will also be displayed on the button.

```
<INPUT TYPE="SUBMIT" VALUE="Submit Form">
```

Some browsers will now pass the value of the button on to the CGI application but this is a fairly recent addition and cannot be counted on for all browsers. Until this is fully supported, it is not possible to have several buttons indicating different actions.

The Reset Input Type

There is one other button that is allowed: the reset button. For example, the following definition will reset all the values to their default value.

```
<INPUT TYPE="RESET" VALUE="Reset Form">
```

Calling the CGI Script from a Form

As I previously mentioned, there are currently two different methods to call CGI applications: one is the GET method and the other is the POST method.

Calling an application directly from a URL always uses the GET method by default. Using the form tag, however, you can specify the method using the "METHOD=" tag. The downside of the GET method is that any arguments that are to be sent to the CGI application are sent in the QUERY_STRING environment variable. The reason this is undesirable is that many systems limit the amount of data that can be stored in an environment variable. On some systems this limit is as low as 1,024 characters. While this seems sufficient, on a complex form, it is easy to exceed this limit. By specifying METHOD=POST on the form, the arguments are passed as *standard input* (stdin) of the CGI application, which eliminates any limit on the amount of data that can be passed to the CGI application.

Argument Lists

Browsers process forms and pass the data input by the user to the application defined by the "ACTION" keyword in the form as an argument list. You can take advantage of knowing the format of this argument list to pass any additional information your CGI scripts need to run.

Argument Lists with Name Value Pairs

Whether the POST or GET method is used, the argument list can be the same and consist of name=value pairs. Fortunately, if you rely on a form to call the CGI application, the browser constructs the argument list for it. If you are calling the application directly from a URL, you'll need to construct the argument list yourself. The format of the argument list follows:

```
?name=value&name=value&name=value
```

This format will need to be added to the application referenced by the hypertext link. For example, to pass the first and last name values to an application you would use the following definition:

```
<A HREF="http://bristol.onramp.net/cgi-bin/
➥getinfo.cgi?firstname=Michael&lastname=Marolda"> Info about
➥Michael Marolda</A>
```

An important note is that if the value contains blanks, the convention is to replace the blanks with a + sign. To pass an address with one attribute/value pair would then look like:

```
<A HREF="http://bristol.onramp.net/cgi-bin/
➥getinfo.cgi?street=727+Wandering+Way"> Michael's address</A>
```

If you were passing this information from a form, this argument list would be constructed for you from the name and value parameters. The HTML:

```
<INPUT TYPE="RADIO" NAME="salary" VALUE="10000" CHECKED>
```

would result in the argument list:

```
?salary=10000
```

and would be passed to the script defined by the ACTION keyword at:

```
http://bristol.onramp.net/cgi-bin/getinfo.cgi
```

Passing Arguments Via the PATH_INFO Environment Variable

When a CGI script is called, the browser may pass additional environment information as well as the data that was entered. An alternative method to passing arguments via name value pairs is to use the PATH_INFO environment variable. The difference in format to cause the browser to load information in the PATH_INFO variable is that the arguments are simply appended to the application as if you were extending the path, or location, of the script. For example, to send the firstname and lastname to a script using the PATH_INFO technique you could use:

```
<A HREF="http://bristol.onramp.net/cgi-bin/getinfo.cgi/Michael/
➥Marolda"> Info about Michael Marolda</A>
```

The PATH_INFO environment variable would contain "Michael/Marolda."

The advantage of using the PATH_INFO environment variable is that it is a very simple format. The disadvantage is that the application must decode a single string into multiple arguments, depending entirely on the position of the data within the string to define the content of an argument. This might be difficult to maintain when more than a couple of arguments are passed to the CGI script.

CGI Overview

After you've created a simple form, you'll need to create an application to process the data. This application is commonly referred to as a CGI application (or script in many cases). Most HTTPD implementations will have a default location to put these applications. Like the documents, this location will be referenced as a relative location off the server root. For example, if the server root is:

```
/usr/local/etc/httpd/
```

then the cgi applications will reside at:

```
/usr/local/etc/httpd/cgi-bin
```

and can be referenced as:

```
http://your.machine.name/cgi-bin/yourapp.cgi
```

Note HTTPD is the HTTP daemon that is the most commonly used implementation of an HTTP server. You can drop the "D."

A CGI application can be written in any language that can process stdin and stdout, and can reference environment variables. Bourne, C, and Korn shell scripts can be used as well as higher level languages such as C and C++. One of the most popular languages used in CGI application development is the Perl programming language. Perl is a very powerful language and can be interfaced with most of the commonly used Unix system calls. Because Perl is often called a *scripting language*, many people refer to CGI applications as CGI scripts. This chapter will focus on using Perl and its cousin Oraperl to write CGI applications.

Perl and Oraperl Overview

One of the more powerful features that people have added to Perl is the capability to interface with external relational database management systems (RDBMSs). Unfortunately, the Application Programmers Interface (API) in each database package has mimicked the "C" API for that package. Because the "C" API for Oracle is different from the "C" API for Sybase, and so on, each Perl interface is different for each underlying RDBMS. This situation is changing with the release of Perl 5.0. For that release, a common database API has been specified for all underlying RDBMSs. It will be a challenge to the implementors to add the support for the desired RDBMS and conform to the now standard API.

Because many of these implementations are still under development, this chapter will focus on the current Perl 4.036 Oraperl interface to the Oracle RDBMS. A comparison of the two interfaces will be discussed later.

There are only eight functions that are really required to access an Oracle database via Oraperl.

- ora_login
- ora_open
- ora_bind
- ora_fetch
- ora_close

- ora_commit
- ora_rollback
- ora_logoff

A quick overview of these functions follows.

ora_login

The call to ora_login makes the connection to the database. The format is:

```
$dba = &ora_login($database, $user, $password);
```

ora_login requires the database name (oracle SID) to connect to the Oracle userid and the Oracle password. A handle to an open database is returned. This handle will be used in subsequent calls to the database.

ora_open

The call to ora_open will open a cursor for a given SQL statement. The format is:

```
$csr = &ora_open($dba,$statement);
```

ora_open uses the handle returned from ora_login and creates a cursor for the specified SQL statement. The SQL statement can be any valid Oracle SQL statement and can use placeholders for bind variables. Examples are:

```
$csr = &ora_open($dba,"select firstname from employee where
➥id=1234");
```

or using a bind variable:

```
$csr = &ora_open($dba,"select firstname from employee where
➥id=:1");
```

An insert would look like:

```
$csr = &ora_open($dba,"insert into employee (id,firstname)
➥values(:1,:2)");
```

Whenever bind variables are used, a call to ora_bind will also be necessary.

ora_bind

If the call to ora_open uses bind variables, it will be necessary to call ora_bind to indicate what values to use. The format for ora_bind is:

```
$numrows = &ora_bind($csr, $var1, $var2, ..., $varN);
```

ora_bind takes the handle to the cursor returned by ora_open and the Perl variables that hold the data corresponding to the placeholders in the SQL statement. For updates and deletes, the value returned by ora_bind is the number of rows that were affected by the statement while statements that affect no rows return the string "OK." An example of using bind with an insert would be:

```
$csr = &ora_open($dba,"insert into employee
➥(id,firstname,lastname) values(:1,:2,:3)";
➥$numrows = &ora_bind($csr,1,"Michael", "Marolda");
```

ora_fetch

If the cursor returned by ora_open is for a select statement, ora_fetch is used to retrieve the data associated with the results for the select statement. The format is:

```
@data = &ora_fetch($csr);
```

The only argument to ora_fetch is the handle to the open cursor. ora_fetch returns an array of values corresponding to the attribute names listed in the select statement. When the fetch gets to the end of the data in the results set, an undefined value is returned. An example that would return all the customers in a database would be:

```
$csr = &ora_open($dba,"select id, firstname from employee");
while (($id, $firstname) = &ora_fetch($csr)){
       print "Customer id = $id, Customer name = $firstname\n";
}
```

ora_fetch can also be used in a scalar context and the number of fields in the query is returned. Using the above example:

```
$nfields = &ora_fetch($csr);
```

would return 2.

ora_close

In order to close and release any resources for a cursor, you should make a call to ora_close. The format is:

```
&ora_close($csr);
```

ora_commit

A call to ora_commit will commit any changes made to the database since the last commit or rollback. The format is:

```
&ora_commit($dba);
```

ora_rollback

Calling_ora_rollback will roll back any changes made to the database since the last commit. The format is:

```
&ora_rollback($dba);
```

ora_logoff

Finally, ora_logoff is used to free all resources associated with an open connection to a database. The format is:

```
&ora_logoff($dba);
```

For a more detailed explanation of the above (and other) Oraperl calls, please refer to the Oraperl man pages included in its release.

Tip "Man" pages is Unix-speak for manual pages—documentation.

Error Handling

Oraperl functions, like most other Perl functions, can be tested directly for error or success. Oraperl also maintains a global variable, $ora_errstr, that contains the last error number and string. If you want to simply log the error to the HTTPD error log, you can use a technique like the following:

```
$csr = &ora_open($dba,"select id, firstname from employee") ¦¦ die
➥$ora_errstr;
```

A technique that I like to employ is to use a subroutine to print the error message to the Web browser and to the error log. To aid in debugging, I also include the Perl variable LINE and FILE in the error message. Finally, I use the ctime.pl library to indicate when the error occurred. This changes the error handling to the following:

```
$csr = &ora_open($dba,"select id, firstname from employee") ||
➥&dodie ($ora_errstr, __LINE__, __FILE__);
```

The dodie subroutine used in the previous line is fairly simple and creates the string that is printed both to STDOUT (for the Web browser) and to STDERR (which is automatically logged to the NCSA error_log file). The following is the code to implement this routine:

```
require "ctime.pl";

sub dodie
{
    local ($errstr, $errline, $file) = @_;
    $diedate = &ctime(time);
    print "Died in $file:$errline - $errstr at $diedate<P>\n";
    die "died in $file:$errline - $errstr at $diedate";
}

1;
```

Environment Variables in CGI Applications

Because most CGI applications are spawned using the environment for the user "nobody," you may need to set the standard environment variables in the CGI application. The environment variables that most commonly need to be set to run Oracle are these:

```
$ORACLE_SID - set to your database name;
$ORACLE_HOME - set to the home directory for the ORACLE
➥installation;
$TWO_TASK - set to your SQL*Net connection string.
```

These variables can be set using the setenv Perl call:

```
$ENV{'ORACLE_SID'} = "www";
$ENV{'ORACLE_HOME'} = "/home/dba/oracle/product/7.1.3";
$ENV{'TWO_TASK'} = "bristol"; # SQL*Net V2
```

Additionally, your CGI application can obtain extra information via the environment variables. Some of the environment variables that may be available to you are:

- **SERVER_SOFTWARE.** Tells you which HTTP server you're running.
- **SERVER_NAME.** The host name of the computer on which the server is running.
- **REQUEST_METHOD.** The method used to call the script (GET or POST).
- **PATH_INFO.** Additonal path information appended to the CGI script.
- **SCRIPT_NAME.** The CGI script that was referenced.
- **QUERY_STRING.** Contains the argument list when the calling method is GET.
- **REMOTE_HOST.** The host name of the computer running the Web browser.
- **REMOTE_ADDR.** The host address of the computer running the Web browser.
- **REMOTE_USER.** Contains the userid of the person using the WWW browser.
- **CONTENT_LENGTH.** The length of the string found in QUERY_STRING.
- **HTTP_USER_AGENT.** The name of the browser being used.

Note that not all browsers pass all information. Some environment variables, such as REMOTE_USER are only passed if the remote server is running an identification program (such as IDENTD) or if the user has entered an id that may be required as part of HTTPD authorization.

Getting the Input

There are two ways for your CGI application to get the input data depending on how it was passed. In the case of the GET method, the data is contained in the QUERY_STRING environment variable. The length of the argument list is contained in the environment variable CONTENT_LENGTH. The method can be determined by querying the REQUEST_METHOD environment variable. The following retrieves the argument list into a Perl variable.

```
if ($ENV{REQUEST_METHOD'} eq "GET") {
     $arglist = $ENV{QUERY_STRING'};
}
```

Using the POST method results in the argument list being passed as STDIN (the default input device). To retrieve the argument list when the argument list is sent via the POST method, the following code segment could be used.

```
if ($ENV{REQUEST_METHOD'} eq "POST") {
     for ($i=0;$i = $ENV{CONTENT_LENGTH'};$i++) {
          $arglist .= getc;  # getc retrieves the next character
                             # from STDIN.
     }
}
```

In either case, you end up with a variable $arglist that contains the argument list passed from the Web browser.

Parsing the Input

While it is nice to have the argument list available in a single variable, it is not very convenient. A better method in Perl would be to parse the string into an associative array of name value pairs. A library, CGILIB, written by Steven E. Brenner does just that.

The following is the source for Steve Brenner's cgi-lib.pl. This source can also be obtained via:

```
http://www.bio.cam.ac.uk/web/form.html

#!/usr/local/bin/perl -- -*- C -*-

# Perl Routines to Manipulate CGI input
# S.E.Brenner@bioc.cam.ac.uk
# $Header: /cys/people/brenner/http/cgi-bin/RCS/cgi-lib.pl,v 1.8
# 1995/04/07 21:35:29 brenner Exp $
```

```
#
# Copyright 1994 Steven E. Brenner
# Unpublished work.
# Permission granted to use and modify this library so long as the
# copyright above is maintained, modifications are documented, and
# credit is given for any use of the library.
#
# Thanks are due to many people for reporting bugs and suggestions,
# especially Meng Weng Wong, Maki Watanabe, Bo Frese Rasmussen,
# Andrew Dalke, Mark-Jason Dominus and Dave Dittrich.

# For more information, see:
#     http://www.bio.cam.ac.uk/web/form.html
#     http://www.seas.upenn.edu/~mengwong/forms/

# Minimalist http form and script (http://www.bio.cam.ac.uk/web/
# minimal.cgi):
#
# require "cgi-lib.pl";
# if (&ReadParse(*input)) {
#    print &PrintHeader, &PrintVariables(%input);
# } else {
#   print &PrintHeader,'<form><input type="submit">Data: <input
# name="myfield">';
#}

# ReadParse
# Reads in GET or POST data, converts it to unescaped text, and
# puts one key=value in each member of the list "@in"
# Also creates key/value pairs in %in, using '\0' to separate
# multiple selections.

# Returns TRUE if there was input, FALSE if there was no input.
# UNDEF may be used in the future to indicate some failure.

# Now that cgi scripts can be put in the normal file space, it is
# useful to combine both the form and the script in one place.  If
# no parameters are given (i.e., ReadParse returns FALSE), then a
# form could be output.

# If a variable-glob parameter (e.g., *cgi_input) is passed to
# ReadParse, information is stored there, rather than in $in, @in,
# and %in.
```

```
sub ReadParse {
  local (*in) = @_ if @_;
  local ($i, $key, $val);

  # Read in text
  if (&MethGet) {
    $in = $ENV{'QUERY_STRING'};
  } elsif ($ENV{'REQUEST_METHOD'} eq "POST") {
    read(STDIN,$in,$ENV{'CONTENT_LENGTH'});
  }

  @in = split(/&/,$in);

  foreach $i (0 .. $#in) {
    # Convert plus's to spaces
    $in[$i] =~ s/\+/ /g;

    # Split into key and value.
    ($key, $val) = split(/=/,$in[$i],2); # splits on the first =.

    # Convert %XX from hex numbers to alphanumeric
    $key =~ s/%(..)/pack("c",hex($1))/ge;
    $val =~ s/%(..)/pack("c",hex($1))/ge;

    # Associate key and value
    $in{$key} .= "\0" if (defined($in{$key})); # \0 is the
    ➥multiple separator
    $in{$key} .= $val;

  }

  return length($in);
}


# PrintHeader
# Returns the magic line which tells WWW that we're an HTML
  ➥document

sub PrintHeader {
  return "Content-type: text/html\n\n";
}


# MethGet
# Return true if this cgi call was using the GET request, false
  ➥otherwise
```

```
sub MethGet {
  return ($ENV{'REQUEST_METHOD'} eq "GET");
}

# MyURL
# Returns a URL to the script
sub MyURL  {
  return  'http://' . $ENV{'SERVER_NAME'} .  $ENV{'SCRIPT_NAME'};
}

# CgiError
# Prints out an error message that contains appropriate headers,
# markup, etcetera.
# Parameters:
#  If no parameters, gives a generic error message
#  Otherwise, the first parameter will be the title and the rest
#  will be given as different paragraphs of the body

sub CgiError {
  local (@msg) = @_;
  local ($i,$name);

  if (!@msg) {
    $name = &MyURL;
    @msg = ("Error: script $name encountered fatal error");
  };

  print &PrintHeader;
  print "<html><head><title>$msg[0]</title></head>\n";
  print "<body><h1>$msg[0]</h1>\n";
  foreach $i (1 .. $#msg) {
    print "<p>$msg[$i]</p>\n";
  }
  print "</body></html>\n";
}

# PrintVariables
# Nicely formats variables in an associative array passed as a
# parameter And returns the HTML string.

sub PrintVariables {
  local (%in) = @_;
  local ($old, $out, $output);
  $old = $*;  $* =1;
  $output .=  "<DL COMPACT>";
  foreach $key (sort keys(%in)) {
```

```
    foreach (split("\0", $in{$key})) {
      ($out = $_) =~ s/\n/<BR>/g;
      $output .=  "<DT><B>$key</B><DD><I>$out</I><BR>";
    }
  }
  $output .=  "</DL>";
  $* = $old;

  return $output;
}

# PrintVariablesShort
# Nicely formats variables in an associative array passed as a
# parameter Using one line per pair (unless value is multiline)
# And returns the HTML string.


sub PrintVariablesShort {
  local (%in) = @_;
  local ($old, $out, $output);
  $old = $*;  $* =1;
  foreach $key (sort keys(%in)) {
    foreach (split("\0", $in{$key})) {
      ($out = $_) =~ s/\n/<BR>/g;
      $output .= "<B>$key</B> is <I>$out</I><BR>";
    }
  }
  $* = $old;

  return $output;
}

1; #return true
```

To see how the ReadParse script would work, consider the following HTML form fields that would be used to input personal information:

```
<INPUT NAME= TYPE="TEXT" "firstname" SIZE=20 VALUE="Michael">
<INPUT NAME= TYPE="TEXT" "lastname" SIZE=20 VALUE="Marolda">
<INPUT NAME= TYPE="TEXT""street" SIZE=20 VALUE="727 Wandering Way">
<INPUT TYPE="RADIO" NAME="sex" VALUE="M", CHECKED >
```

When the Submit button is pressed, the argument list is constructed for you and would look like:

```
?firstname=Michael&lastname=Marolda&street=727+Wandering+Way&sex=M
```

Using Steven's ReadParse script in cgi-lib.pl, the data could then be referenced by name in the associative array as such:

```
$in{firstname};  # contains the value "Michael"
$in{lastname'}; # contains the value "Marolda"
$in{street'};  # contains the value "727 Wandering Way"
$in{sex'}; # contains the value "M"
```

These can be used directly in the Oraperl calls. For example, to see all the male employees, you could bind to the variables directly:

```
$csr = &ora_open($dba,"select firstname, lastname from employee
➥where sex=:1)";
$numrows = &ora_bind($csr,$in{sex'});
```

Displaying the Results of a CGI Application

Displaying any data retrieved by CGI scripts is actually quite simple. HTTP operates on the principle that it reads everything from STDIN and writes everything to STDOUT. Therefore, anything you print to STDOUT (which is the default) will be redirected back to the Web browser. The only additional information you would need to supply would be to print a MIME header identifying the document as an HTML document. From a CGI script, to print out a simple header, you could use the following technique:

```
print "Content-type: text/html\n\n";
print "<Title> This is the title </Title>\n";
print "<H1> This is a heading </H1>\n";
```

The output would then be formatted and displayed correctly on the user's Web browser. The additional \n isn't really necessary, but I've found that it makes resultant HTML more legible when accessed via the "View Source" option that most browsers have.

This technique can be extended for printing the results of a query. Combining the Oraperl and the printing in a single script, we get:

```
$csr = &ora_open($dba,"select firstname, lastname from employee
➥where sex=:1)";
$numrows = &ora_bind($csr,$in{sex'});
while (($firstname, $lastname) = &ora_fetch($csr)){
     print "<B>$firstname $lastname</B>n";
}
```

Example—A Simple Employee Database

This database is based on a very simple model and should in no way be construed as either complete or the best way to implement this functionality. However, it is simple enough to provide a fairly complete example that demonstrates both insert and query capabilities.

In our simple employee database we'll implement three features. These are:

1. Capture some employee data.
2. Select employees via last name.
3. Select greater detail about an employee returned by the previous select.

Data to Be Captured—The Model

The database model is a single table model that contains the necessary information. The following ORACLE SQL statement is used to create the table:

```
create table employee
(
     id number,
     firstname varchar2(30),
     lastname varchar2(30),
     street varchar2(30),
     city varchar2(30),
     state varchar2(2),
     zip varchar2(15),
     sex varchar2(1),
     salary number,
     CONSTRAINT pk_employee PRIMARY KEY (id)
);
```

A sequence is also created so that we can automatically generate the employee id.

```
create sequence employee_sequence
increment by 1
start with 1000
nomaxvalue
nocycle
cache 10;
```

Also we'll populate the table with a couple of records using the following inserts via SQL*Plus (or your favorite data entry tool).

```
insert into employee
(id,firstname,lastname,street,city,state,zip,sex,salary)
values(employee_sequence.nextval,'Michael','Marolda','123
➥Somewhere Lane', 'Dallas','TX',75090,'M',13000);

insert into employee
(id,firstname,lastname,street,city,state,zip,sex,salary)
values(employee_sequence.nextval,'Jan','Murphy','123 Another
➥Lane', 'Los Angeles','CA','12345','F',130000);

insert into employee
(id,firstname,lastname,street,city,state,zip,sex,salary)
values(employee_sequence.nextval,'Beverly','Chapman','123 Street',
'Detroit','MI','54321','F',40000);

insert into employee
(id,firstname,lastname,street,city,state,zip,sex,salary)
values(employee_sequence.nextval,'Bill','Clinton','1600
➥Pennsylvania Ave.', 'Washington','DC','11111','M',200000);
```

First Feature—Capturing the Data

The input form we'll use will have fields for all the attributes with the exception of the id attribute. This attribute will be generated upon insert.

Our employee form uses very simple text, radio button, and submit types to implement the data capture. Also, the Netscape <CENTER> tag was used to make the form a bit more aesthetically appealing.

The HTML Used in This Example

The HTML that produced this form was:

```
<TITLE> Employee Administration </TITLE>
<H1><CENTER> Employee Administration </CENTER></H1>
<FORM ACTION="http://bristol.onramp.net/cgi-bin/empdemo/
➥empadd.cgi" METHOD=POST>
<H2><CENTER>Add an Employee</CENTER></H2>
<PRE>
First Name: <INPUT NAME="firstname" TYPE="TEXT" SIZE=20
➥MAXLENGTH=30>
Last Name:  <INPUT NAME="lastname" TYPE="TEXT" SIZE=20
➥MAXLENGTH=30>
Address:    <INPUT NAME="street" TYPE="TEXT" SIZE=30 MAXLENGTH=30>
City:       <INPUT NAME="city" TYPE="TEXT" SIZE=20 MAXLENGTH=30>
State:      <INPUT NAME="state" TYPE="TEXT" SIZE=2 MAXLENGTH=2>
Zip:  <INPUT NAME="zip" TYPE="TEXT" SIZE=9 MAXLENGTH=5>
Salary:     <INPUT NAME="salary" TYPE="TEXT" SIZE=5 MAXLENGTH=5>
Sex:        <INPUT TYPE=radio NAME="sex" VALUE="F" CHECKED> Female
<INPUT TYPE=radio NAME="sex" VALUE="M"> Male
</PRE>
<CENTER>
<INPUT TYPE=SUBMIT VALUE="Add Employee"> <INPUT TYPE=RESET
➥VALUE="Reset Form">
</CENTER>
</FORM>
```

When the Add Employee button is pushed, the CGI script at /cgi-gin/empdemo/empadd.cgi will be called. When the Reset Form button is pushed, the form will be restored to its default values.

CGI to Store Data

In order to store the data we'll need to put together the bits and pieces we explored earlier. The following script takes the FORM data and creates a record in the database for that data. Also, a confirmation and employee id is sent back to the browser.

```
#!/usr/local/bin/oraperl

#
# Include cgi-lib parser
#

require "cgi-lib.pl";
```

```
#
# Include the error reporting script
#

require "dodie.pl";

#
# Print out the MIME Content Type
#

print STDOUT &PrintHeader();
print STDOUT "<TITLE> New Employee </TITLE>\n";

#
# Parse the input
#

do ReadParse();

#
# Set the environment variables and connect to oracle
#

$database = "www1";
$ouser = "empdemo";
$opass = "empdemo";
$ENV{'ORACLE_SID'} = "www1";
$ENV{'ORACLE_HOME'} = "/home/dba/oracle/product/7.1.3";

$dba = &ora_login($database, $ouser, $opass) || &dodie
($ora_errstr, __LINE__, __FILE__);

#
# Ensure all variables are filled in.
#

$errorcount = 0;
foreach $key (sort keys(%in)) {
    if (length($in{$key}) == 0) {
     print "$key must be entered!<p>\n";
     $errorcount++;
    }
}
if ($errorcount) {
    exit(0);
}
```

```
#
# Get a new employee id to be used when the data is inserted.
# This operation could be performed at the time the record is
# inserted, but this gives us a chance to report the employee
# id back to the user that added the employee.
#

$csr_empid = &ora_open($dba,"SELECT EMPLOYEE_SEQUENCE.NEXTVAL FROM
➥DUAL") ¦¦ &dodie ($ora_errstr, __LINE__, __FILE__);
($empid) = &ora_fetch($csr_empid);
&ora_close($csr_empid);

#
# Create the cursor for adding the employee. For this example,
# we're going to use bind variables. One of the advantages of
# using bind variables is for performance. This is true for where
# clauses, updates and insert statements. Oracle will store an
# SQL string in its shared memory area. If another SQL statement
# is passed to Oracle and it matches a previous one, no actual
# parsing is required. If you have several operations that are
# going to use the same where clause but with different values,
# then using a bind variable:
#     .... where name = :1;
# will result in only one statement being cached.  However, if
# each value is assigned in the statement:
#     .... where name = Mike';
#     .... where name = John';
# each statement must be parsed separately. Similarly, if you will
# be inserting many rows, it will save quite a bit of parse time
# if bind variables are used for the data values.
#

$csr_emp = &ora_open($dba,"INSERT INTO EMPLOYEE (id, firstname,
➥lastname, street, city, state, zip, sex, salary) VALUES(:1, :2,
➥:3, :4, :5, :6, :7, :8, :9)") ¦¦ &dodie ($ora_errstr, __LINE__,
➥__FILE__);

#
# Add the employee - bind the data.  On non-select statements,
# this also executes the SQL statement.
#
```

```
$numrows = &ora_bind($csr_emp, $empid, $in{firstname'},
➥$in{lastname'}, $in{street'}, $in{city'}, $in{state'},
➥$in{zip'}, $in{sex'}, $in{salary'}) || &dodie ($ora_errstr,
➥__LINE__, __FILE__);

#
# Tidy up and exit.
#

&ora_close($csr_emp) || &dodie ($ora_errstr, __LINE__, __FILE__);
&ora_commit($dba) || &dodie ($ora_errstr, __LINE__, __FILE__);
&ora_logoff($dba) || &dodie ($ora_errstr, __LINE__, __FILE__);

#
# It's always a good idea to give some feedback.
#

print STDOUT "<H2> $in{'firstname'} $in{'lastname'} has been added
as employee id $empid!</H2>\n";

#
# Add a link back to the form in case another employee is to be
# added.
#

print STDOUT "<a href=http://bristol.onramp.net/empdemo/
empadd.html>Add another Employee?</a>\n";

exit(0);
```

Second Feature—Displaying the Employee List

The search forms shown in figure 20.3 will be used to search the database for an employee. The last name is used as the search field.

Form

The form that we'll use is a very simple form that allows wildcard searches. For large databases, wildcard searches in Oracle may take awhile. The exception to this is when the wildcard is not the first character. In this case, and if an index exists on this field, the index can be used by Oracle's search engine. The following HTML implements our forms.

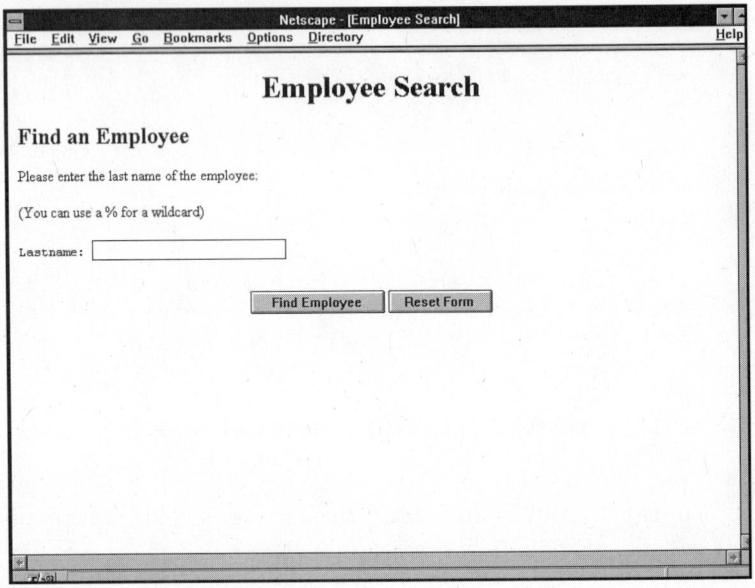

Figure 20.3
The Find Employee form.

```
<TITLE> Employee Search </TITLE>
<H1> <CENTER>Employee Search</CENTER></H1>
<FORM ACTION="http://bristol.onramp.net/cgi-bin/empdemo/
➥empfind.cgi" METHOD=POST>
<H2>Find an Employee</H2>
Please enter the last name of the employee (You can use a % for a
➥wildcard):
<PRE>
Lastname: <INPUT NAME="lastname" TYPE="TEXT" SIZE=25
➥MAXLENGTH=30><p>
</PRE>
<CENTER>
<INPUT TYPE=SUBMIT VALUE="Find Employee"> <INPUT TYPE=RESET
VALUE="Reset Form">
</CENTER>
</FORM>
```

CGI to Find a List of Employees

Unlike the previous CGI script, this script performs a SELECT instead of an insert. Because we allowed wildcard searches (and because there may be more than one employee with the same last name), we need to be able to handle multiple returned records. The simplest way will be to list all the employees that were found by the search and tag those employees with a reference to another CGI script that gets the employee detail.

```
#!/usr/local/bin/oraperl

#
# Include cgi-lib parser
#

require "cgi-lib.pl";

#
# Include the error reporting script
#

require "dodie.pl";

#
# Print out the MIME Content Type and title.
#

print STDOUT &PrintHeader();

print STDOUT "<TITLE> New Employee </TITLE>\n";

#
# Parse the input
#

do ReadParse();

#
# Set the environment variables and connect to oracle
#

$database = "www1";
$ouser = "empdemo";
$opass = "empdemo";
$ENV{'ORACLE_SID'} = "www1";
$ENV{'ORACLE_HOME'} = "/home/dba/oracle/product/7.1.3";

$dba = &ora_login($database, $ouser, $opass) || &dodie
($ora_errstr, __LINE__, __FILE__);

#
# Find an employee or employees - create appropriate SQL and the
# cursor.
# This time we'll expand the search criteria into the $select
# variable.
# If the user had entered a M%, then the $select variable would
# contain:
```

```
#
# "select firstname,lastname,id from employee where lastname like
# %M' order by lastname"
#

$select = "select firstname,lastname,id from employee where
➥lastname like '%";
$select .= $in{lastname'};
$select .= "' order by lastname";

$csr_emp = &ora_open($dba,$select) ¦¦ &dodie ($ora_errstr,
➥__LINE__, __FILE__);

#
# Fetch all the data that matches.  Because this is likely to
# return more than one result, this fetch will operate within a
"while" loop. One other feature we should have (but don't)  is
# detecting and reporting back that no matches were found.
#

print STDOUT "Click on the employee name for more detail.<p>\n";
while (($firstname,$lastname,$id) = &ora_fetch($csr_emp)) {

#
# We'll generate a hypertext link to call another cgi application,
# which will get more detail about an individual.  Note that we
# have to use the "GET" method when referencing a CGI application
# from a hypertext link.
#
    print STDOUT "<a href=\"http://bristol.onramp.net/cgi-bin/
empdemo/empget.cgi?id=$id\"> $firstname $lastname</a><p>\n";

}
#
# Tidy up and exit.
#

&ora_close($csr_emp) ¦¦ &dodie ($ora_errstr, __LINE__, __FILE__);
&ora_logoff($dba) ¦¦ &dodie ($ora_errstr, __LINE__, __FILE__);
exit(0);
```

When the above script is executed with the value M%, the following HTML will be created:

```
<TITLE> New Employee </TITLE>
Click on the employee name for more detail.<p>
<a href="http://bristol.onramp.net/cgi-bin/empdemo/
empget.cgi?id=1011"> Michael Marolda</a><p>
<a href="http://bristol.onramp.net/cgi-bin/empdemo/
empget.cgi?id=1012"> Jan Murphy</a><p>
```

And you should see the results shown in figure 20.4.

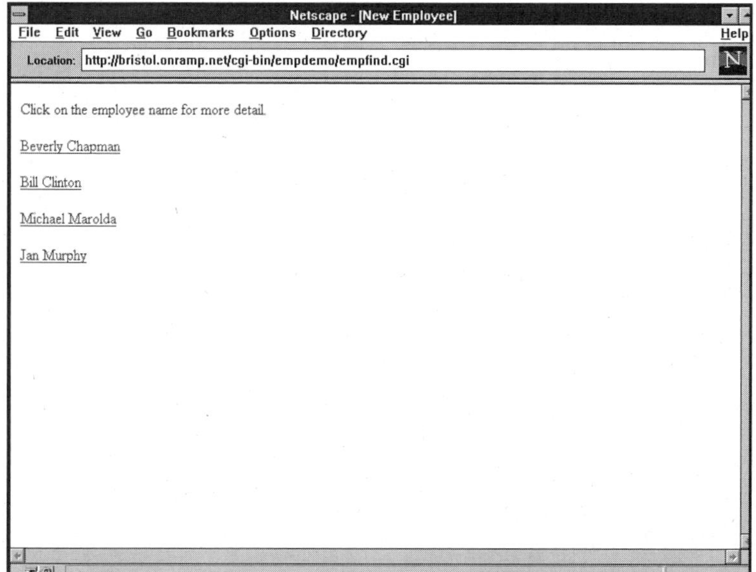

Figure 20.4
The employee search results.

Third Feature—Getting Employee Detail

This script takes the reference created by the Find Employees cgi script and in turn goes to the database and gets greater detail about that employee.

```
#!/usr/local/bin/oraperl

#
# Include cgi-lib parser
#

require "cgi-lib.pl";

#
# Include the error reporting script
#
```

```
require "dodie.pl";

#
# Print out the MIME Content Type and the title
#

print STDOUT &PrintHeader();
print STDOUT "<TITLE> New Employee </TITLE>\n";

#
# Parse the input.  One of the advantages of using Steve Brenner's
# cgi-lib.pl library is that it operates on data that is passed
# via either the POST or GET methods.  In each case, the result is
# an associative array containing either form fields or GET
# arguments.
#

do ReadParse();

#
# Set the environment variables and connect to oracle
#

$database = "www1";
$ouser = "empdemo";
$opass = "empdemo";
$ENV{'ORACLE_SID'} = "www1";
$ENV{'ORACLE_HOME'} = "/home/dba/oracle/product/7.1.3";

$dba = &ora_login($database, $ouser, $opass) || &dodie
($ora_errstr, __LINE__, __FILE__);

#
# Get the employee detail.  Again we'll use variable binding.
#

$csr_emp = &ora_open($dba,"select firstname, lastname, street,
city, state, zip, sex, salary from employee where id = :1") ||
&dodie ($ora_errstr, __LINE__, __FILE__);


#
# Bind the employee id into the query.
#
```

```
$numrows = &ora_bind($csr_emp, $in{id'}) ¦¦ &dodie ($ora_errstr,
➥__LINE__, __FILE__);

#
# Fetch the detail data.  Because we're sure that the employee id
# is going to be a unique value, we don't need to use a while
# loop (although there would be nothing technically wrong with
# doing so).
#

if (($firstname,$lastname,$street,$city,$state,$zip,$sex,$salary)
➥= &ora_fetch($csr_emp))
{
#
# Print out the detail.  Somewhat boring in format but it gets
# the job done.
#
    print STDOUT "$firstname $lastname<p>\n";
    print STDOUT "$street<p>\n";
    print STDOUT "$city, $state $zip<p>\n";
    print STDOUT "Sex: $sex, Salary: $salary<p>\n";
}
#
# Tidy up and exit.
#

&ora_close($csr_emp) ¦¦ &dodie ($ora_errstr, __LINE__, __FILE__);
&ora_logoff($dba) ¦¦ &dodie ($ora_errstr, __LINE__, __FILE__);

#
# This time we're giving the end user an opportunity to find
# another set of employees.  Another possibility would be to link
# back to the employee list page.  This would require us to send
# the original argument string that first created the original
# employee list.  Because most browsers support the previous page
# function, this is probably not necessary.
#

print "<a href=\"http://bristol.onramp.net/empdemo/
empfind.html\">Back to Employee Searching.</a>\n";

exit(0);
```

Running this script results in figure 20.5.

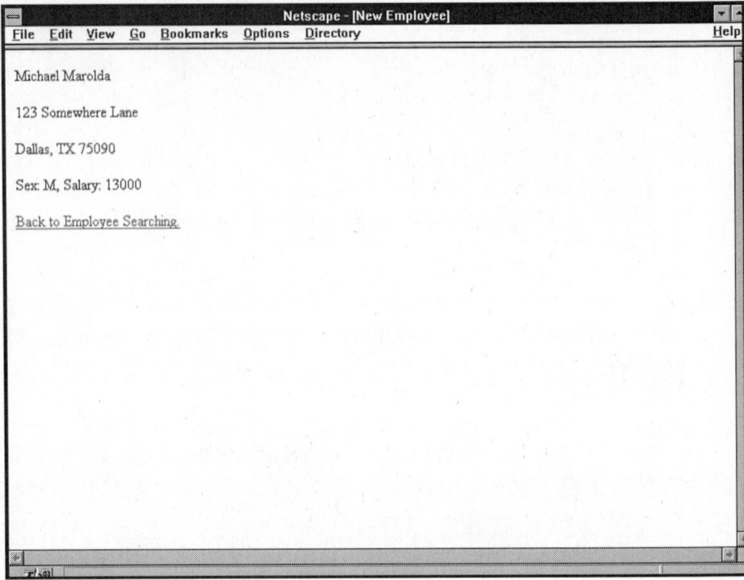

Figure 20.5 *Employee details reached by choosing a name after the employee search is complete.*

Summary of Employee Database Example

The preceding example showed how to use Oracle to both capture data via the WWW and how to use WWW and CGI applications to query and browse an Oracle database. There are a few things that we could have done differently. For example, we could have focused more on error detection. This is especially true of the input data from the add employee form. Combining the last two CGI applications into a single form and application would have been more elegant and should be considered a worthwhile exercise. In any case, using Perl to interface Oracle with the Web is a fairly simple operation and can provide many organizations with a cost effective way of sharing corporate data over a variety of platforms.

Perl 5 DBI

All of the code in this chapter used Perl V4 and the Oraperl extension. Perl V5 takes a different (and somewhat better) approach in that it now defines a standard API for all database implementations. For each database, there can be one (or more) database adapters that translate the API into the API of the desired database. At this writing, the Oracle DBI adapter is only in beta release. However, the differences between Perl 4 and Perl 5 are small enough that most of the examples can be easily converted. To illustrate the differences and similarities, the following are examples of an insert and a select using the current Oraperl and the Perl 5 DBI. This code comes from the earlier empadd cgi and emplist cgi.

Further information on the Perl 5 DBI specification can be found at:

FTP Archive: ftp.demon.co.uk:/pub/perl/db (read the README file)

Example 1: Oraperl Insert

```
$dba = &ora_login($database, $ouser, $opass);

$csr_emp = &ora_open($dba,"INSERT INTO EMPLOYEE (id, firstname,
➥lastname, street, city, state, zip, sex, salary) VALUES(:1, :2,
➥:3, :4, :5, :6, :7, :8, :9)");

$numrows = &ora_bind($csr_emp, $empid, $in{firstname'},
➥$in{lastname'}, $in{street'}, $in{city'}, $in{state'},
➥$in{zip'}, $in{sex'}, $in{salary'});
&ora_close($csr_emp);
&ora_commit($dba);
&ora_logoff($dba);
```

Example 2: Oraperl Select

```
$dba = &ora_login($database, $ouser, $opass);
➥$csr_emp = &ora_open($dba,"select firstname, lastname, street,
➥city, state, zip, sex, salary from employee where id = :1");

$numrows = &ora_bind($csr_emp, $in{id'});

if (($firstname,$lastname,$street,$city,$state,$zip,$sex,$salary)
= &ora_fetch($csr_emp))
{
    print STDOUT "$firstname $lastname<p>\n";
    print STDOUT "$street<p>\n";
    print STDOUT "$city, $state $zip<p>\n";
    print STDOUT "Sex: $sex, Salary: $salary<p>\n";
}
&ora_close($csr_emp);
&ora_logoff($dba);
```

Example 3: Perl 5 DBI Insert

```
$dbh = &db_connect($database, $name, $password);
$sh = &db_prepare($dbh,
      " INSERT INTO EMPLOYEE (id, firstname, lastname, street,
      city, state, zip, sex, salary) VALUES(?, ?, ?, ?, ?, ?, ?,
      ?, ?)");

&db_execute(&sqlh, $empid, $in{firstname'}, $in{lastname'},
$in{street'}, $in{city'}, $in{state'}, $in{zip'}, $in{sex'},
$in{salary'});

&db_finish($sh);
$rc = &db_commit($dbh);
&db_disconnect($dbh);
```

Example 4: Perl 5 DBI Select

```
$dbh = &db_connect($database, $name, $password);

$sh = &db_prepare($dbh, " select firstname, lastname, street,
city, state, zip, sex, salary from employee where id = :?");
&db_execute($sh, $in{id'}
if (($firstname,$lastname,$street,$city,$state,$zip,$sex,$salary)
= &db_fetch($sh))
{
    print STDOUT "$firstname $lastname<p>\n";
    print STDOUT "$street<p>\n";
    print STDOUT "$city, $state $zip<p>\n";
    print STDOUT "Sex: $sex, Salary: $salary<p>\n";
}
&db_finish($sh);
&db_disconnect($dbh);
```

Open Issues Concerning the Use of Databases

There are still some issues with regard to using Web browsers to interface with Oracle and other database applications. The main issue is the way the data is transmitted between client and server. Historically, there has been a fair amount of communication between the client and the server. In this way, the client can verify data on a field-by-field basis, populate a pop-up selection list, or automatically calculate the values in some fields based on the data in other fields. (More information about database servers and the Web can be found in another New Riders book, *Building Internet Database Servers with CGI*, also in the *Webmaster's* series.)

The scope of data transferred between the client and the server for WWW applications is a complete page. This limits the flexibility one normally finds in many client applications. Companies such as Sun and Netscape Communications Corp. are beginning to enhance their products in ways that will bring in some of that flexibility, but, as of yet, there is no standard, de-facto or otherwise, that allows the flexibility needed to develop complex data entry forms. This is why many WWW Database applications tend to be browsing applications and limit data capture to the bare minimum. Whenever possible, these applications use radio buttons, select lists, and other techniques to minimize the possible human error when entering data.

Another issue is the lack of tools for developing client/server applications. This will probably not be an issue for long as it is likely that many companies will produce development systems for the Web much like they have in the past. This may be hindered somewhat by the lack of standards, but in the long run, products will be available. There are currently some products that aid in the development of WWW Database applications that are in the public domain. You may want to investigate products such as ORAYWWW, GSQL, Oracle's WOW, and others to see what elements they bring to the table. In many cases, while these tools are convenient for developing one-off forms, they lack the sophistication required to develop a full fledged application.

In general, the future looks very bright for WWW and database integration. The task is simple enough that applications can be developed without sophisticated tools although those tools will certainly be welcome when they arrive. WWW and Database integration will greatly enhance the value of corporate data and provide access to that data for many employees, customers, or other interested parties who might never have seen the data otherwise.

Essential Java

by Tim Ritchey

The Java environment is a portable, robust, high-performance, advanced language that offers the ease of use and functionality that object-oriented languages have always promised, but never quite attained. By providing a portable, dynamic, multithreading language, programmers can develop advanced applications across heterogeneous networks such as the Internet. At the same time, the class libraries impart the ease of use and functionality of more open platforms while providing a secure environment for distributed systems. These features in combination are sure to make Java the dominant technology of the Internet in the next decade.

With this information in mind, understanding the ways in which to both use and serve Java content becomes imperative. For most users, the primary use of Java will be either as stand-alone applications or as extensions and applets in a browser environment. In fact, end users will most likely not even know that they are using Java—it will become as widespread as e-mail or HTML, appearing in all aspects of computing on the Web. The site administrator, however, has a new job with Java. Setting up clients and servers, providing Java content in addition to the many other networking protocols, and helping users develop or include Java content in their own documents will all be required. In addition, although Java provides a secure environment and many safety features, distributed applications invariably bring to mind viruses, Trojan horses, worms, and worse—making site administration and security a top priority. This work pays off in the end, however, by providing a more seamless incorporation of content and protocols for both client-side and server-side computing.

Up to now, this book has covered how to employ the JavaScript language to create dynamic Web sites and control the display of Web documents. While JavaScript provides a powerful tool for Internet development, there is still a drawback to its approach—you are still using the basic elements that all Web pages can have, you are simply providing them with a means to interact with their environment. Java, on the other hand, provides a completely new framework upon which you can build innovative and powerful content that is not available in the standard HTML toolkit. In fact, Java allows you to create your *own* tools, and incorporate new tools that others have created.

This chapter provides a basic introduction to programming in Java. First, you will set up your hardware and software for programming. At this point, you should be on either a Sun SparcStation running Solaris 2.3 or later, an Intel x86 running Windows NT/95, or a Macintosh with the Roaster Development environment. If you are using Netscape's Browser, you need to get the correct software for compiling and running Java from Sun. This software is the Java Development Kit, which is supplied with the CD in the back of the book.

After the system is set up, you will cover the fundamentals of creating applets and stand-alone applications in Java. Specifically, this chapter covers the following:

- Setting up the development environment
- Introduction to classes
- Creating the HelloWorld applet
- Creating the HelloWorldApp stand-alone program
- Troubleshooting your code

If, by some misfortune, you have problems, you can refer to the last section, which covers troubleshooting the compiler and interpreter. Of course, you hope that this section isn't needed, but it is inevitable that something will go wrong at some point. A quick guide to the most common problems should get you through most of the errors that arise, and get you up to speed on dealing with more difficult problems if they appear.

Setting Up Your System for Programming in Java

The first step in developing for the Java language is getting the programming environment up and running. You need the javac compiler, the Java interpreter, and a Java-enabled browser for this stage. The compiler and interpreter as well as the appletviewer are all included in the Sun release. If you have already properly installed the software, you are all set to go; otherwise, this next section gives you an overview of the environment. This information is not meant to be exhaustive; because many companies are coming out with development environments, software platforms could have changed quite dramatically between the time this was written and the time in which you are reading this chapter. For this reason, only the Java Development Kit (JDK) is covered, and though it only provides command-line programs, these can do everything you need and are the common denominator for any development environment.

The current release is the JDK 1.0, which is available at Sun's Web site at `www.javasoft.com`. The self-extracting archive of this release is provided on New Riders' Web site, so you should be able to simply transfer the directories to your disk. Of course, check the Sun site for updates of the JDK. The Development Kit is distributed so that it unpacks in a directory called `java`. You should place this root java directory wherever you want. For example, you could place it in this directory:

```
c:\dev\
```

After you have set this directory and unpacked the files into it (note: the archive will create the java directory for you) you need to set the environment variables for your system. Setting environment variables is different on every machine, so you need to check your system's documentation on setting these properly. In Windows 95 you set the environment variables in the autoexec.bat file. There are three variables you will need to set:

- PATH
- HOME
- CLASSPATH

The PATH statement should be set to the \java\bin directory. For example:

```
PATH=C:\dev\java\bin
```

This enables you to run the Java compiler and appletviewer from other directories. The HOME directory should be set to wherever your user files are located. On a single-user machine, you can set this to the java directory:

```
HOME=C:\dev\java
```

This value is used by the appletviewer when looking for the .hotjava directory to store user preferences. The CLASSPATH file should be set to the java\lib directory:

```
CLASSPATH=.;C:\dev\java\lib
```

In addition to the Java programs, you need to have a TCP/IP connection to the Internet in order to take advantage of some of Java's features, specifically the Web-browsing features of Netscape and the network connections of the appletviewer. You can still use the interpreter and appletviewer for viewing Java programs you have on your system, but you won't be able to bring up other Web pages from the Internet. Most likely, you already have Internet connectivity, but if you don't, you should note the following: Windows NT and Sun SparcStations have built in TCP/IP connectivity, but setting up a connection will be different for each situation. If you are on a network, check with your system administrator about gaining Internet Access. If you want to use it from home over a modem, check with your local service provider for how to get connected.

Using Stand-Alone Applications with the Interpreter

After you have installed the Java components on your system, you are ready to run the Java interpreter. The Java interpreter is used to execute stand-alone Java applications. By compiling applications for Java, programmers know that their programs can run on any system for which the Java interpreter has been ported. This gives them the flexibility to worry about the content of their applications, rather than specific implementations for all the different platforms they want it to run on.

You have undoubtedly experienced the problem of trying to find a specific utility or application on the Internet. You can usually find a program to do what you want, but it often might be for the wrong system. With Java, a developer can write a single program and automatically gain the full compatibility for all platforms that Java provides. As long as there is an interpreter for the platform, you can use it.

Note The interpreter is not needed for Netscape 2.0. Because you are only beginning to look at the Java language, you will find that it is easier to compile and run Java applications under the interpreter than with all the overhead of the applet environment. For this reason, you should understand how the interpreter works.

The command for running the interpreter is as follows:

```
C:\> java classname
```

When the Java compiler produces the bytecode file, it appends the extension class to the original file name. When you run the Java interpreter, you only need to provide it with the class name, not the whole filename. In other words, drop the .class extension when running a program.

On the NRP Web site are several stand-alone applications that can be used with the Java interpreter. Change to the /applications/HelloWorldApp directory and run the HelloWorldApp class. You do so by entering:

```
C:\> java HelloWorldApp
```

You should see the output of the HelloWorld class just under the command-line (see fig. 21.1).

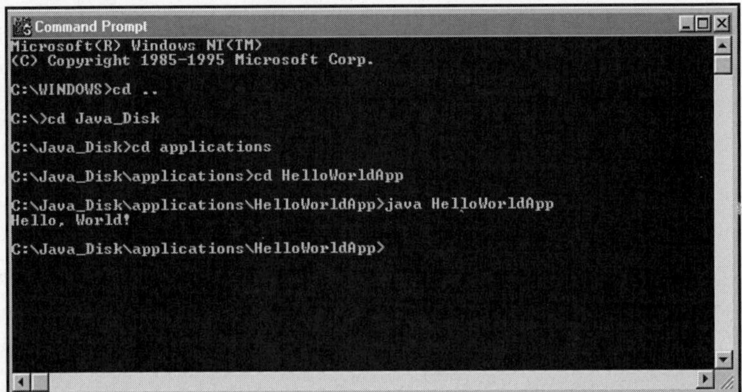

Figure 21.1
Running the stand-alone HelloWorld Application.

There are several other stand-alone applications on the site. You can run any of the classes if you want to get a better handle on using the Java interpreter. Otherwise, you have run your very first Java application—that is all there is to it!

Note Note that the command is not `C:\> java HelloWorldApp.class`. Simply drop the extension from the filename. You should also see filenames with a JAVA extension. These are the source code files for the compiler and are covered in the sections on programming in Java.

The Java interpreter also accepts a host of command-line options. A formal presentation of the java command-line is

```
java [ options ] classname <args>
```

Some of the options are listed in table 21.1. The arguments (args) are passed onto the class when it executes.

Table 21.1
Java Command-Line Options

Command	Purpose
-cs, -checksource	Looks at the Java source file to ensure it hasn't been modified since the last compile. If the source is newer, the interpreter re-compiles the code and loads the renewed class. It only works if the source code is available.
-classpath	Tells the interpreter where to look for the class file. The format is -classpath .:path[:optional paths]. Each new path is separated by a colon. This option overrides the CLASSPATH environment variable.
-v, -verbose	Causes Java to print a message every time a class is loaded.
-verbosegc	Prints a message any time the automatic garbage collection feature of the Java interpreter frees memory.
-verify	Runs the verifier on all code, regardless of where it came from.
-verifyremote (default)	This option runs the verifier on all code that is loaded into the system by the class loader.
-noverify	Causes the interpreter to ignore verification of any code. This could be used if you were only running code that you knew was safe.

continues

Table 21.1, Continued
Java Command-Line Options

Command	Purpose
CLASSPATH	This is not a command-line option, but rather an environment variable that you can set to tell Java where your classes are. It uses the same parameter as the -classpath option: .:path[:optional paths] If this variable is not set correctly and you try to import a class from outside the default settings, Java gives an error, saying the class has violated access restrictions.

Note If you are using options regularly, you can save time typing by creating a batch file for Java. To do so, open your favorite editor and type in the command options you want to use following Java. Where you would normally enter the class name and command-line arguments, place %1, %2, and so forth, up to %9. For example:

```
java -verbose -verbosegc -verify %1 %2 %3 %4 %5 %6 %7 %8 %9
```

Save the file under a name that would identify it to you, with the BAT extension (that is, javav.bat). Place the file in your /hotjava/bin directory. To run the batch file, enter your new name plus the class name and any arguments you want sent to the class. In order to run a class *classname* with *arguments* you could enter:

```
javav classname arguments
```

The %ns enable you to enter up to eight command-line arguments to be sent to the class, in addition to the class name itself.

You can now use the Java interpreter to run any program that you find on the Internet in Java, knowing that it will be running in a secure, robust environment. When developers begin to use Java regularly, you can expect new utilities and shareware programs to automatically work on your system. It will save you time in finding, and peace of mind in using, new programs from the Internet.

Using the appletviewer

The appletviewer provides a Java run-time environment within which Java applets can be tested. The appletviewer takes HTML files that refer to the applets themselves and runs them in a window. As an example, change to one of the demos in the `demo` directory in the JDK release and enter the following command:

```
e:\users\tdr20\java\demo\moleculeviewer\appletviewer example1.html
```

The result should be as that shown in figure 21.2. In this case, the applet is a molecule viewer that takes XYZ format molecule data and presents a three-dimensional model of the molecule.

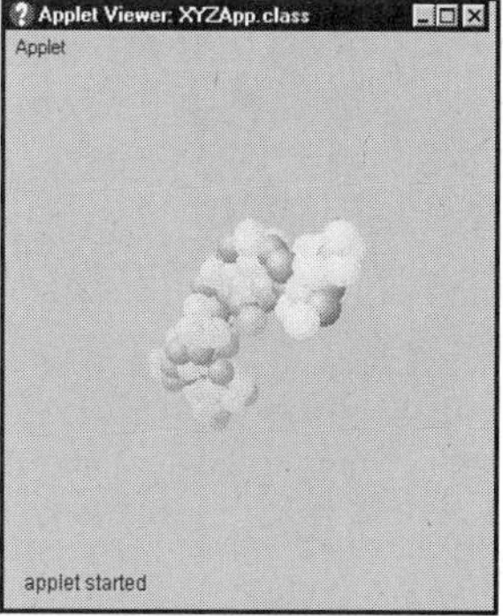

Figure 21.2
The MoleculeViewer Applet.

If you look at the HTML file example1.html that is sent to the appletviewer, you can see the format for entering applets into HTML pages.

```
<title>MoleculeViewer</title>
<hr>
<applet code=XYZApp.class width=300 height=300>
<param name=model value=models/HyaluronicAcid.xyz>
</applet>
<hr>
<a href="XYZApp.java">The source.</a>
```

The <applet ...></applet> tag is used to tell the browser that it should load a Java applet. The <param ...> tag is used to pass arguments to the applet at run-time. This is a different format than that used in the Alpha release of Java. Near the end of the chapter is a fuller explanation of how to use the applet tag.

The appletviewer has several options under the Applet menu option.

- **Restart.** This command runs the loaded applet again.
- **Reload.** This command reloads the applet from disk, and is useful if the .class file has changed since it was loaded.
- **Clone.** This command creates a new appletviewer window based upon the command-line arguments for the first.
- **Tag.** This command shows the <applet> tag used in the HTML document to start the applet (see fig. 21.3).
- **Info.** This command provides any information about the applet that is available (see fig. 21.4).
- **Properties.** This command allows the different network and security configurations to be set for the Appletviewer (see fig. 21.5). The first four entry boxes allow the appletviewer to be run using an HTTP proxy and firewall proxy. Both the proxy address and the port number are required. You should be able to get this information from your site administrator. The network access selector allows several levels of security, including no network access, only access to the applet's host, and unrestricted access. The class access selector enables you to designate either restricted or unrestricted access to classes on the machine.

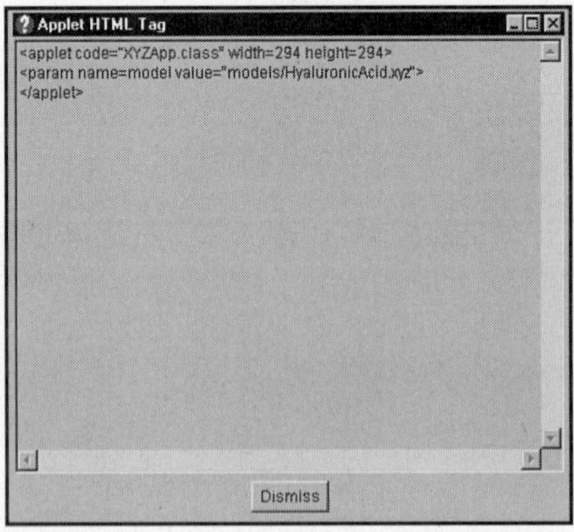

Figure 21.3
The Tag dialog box in the Appletviewer.

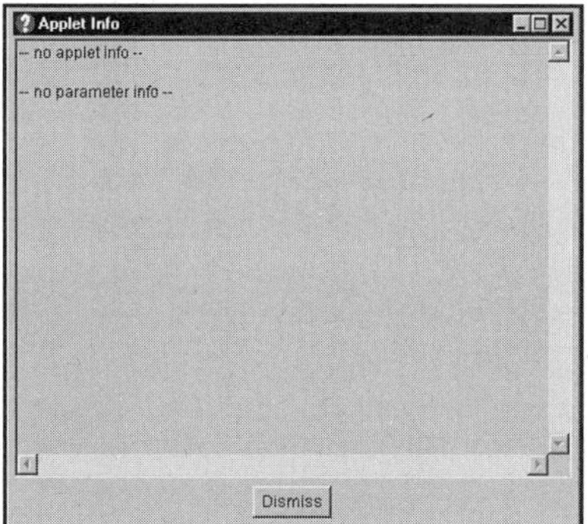

Figure 21.4
The Info dialog box in the Appletviewer.

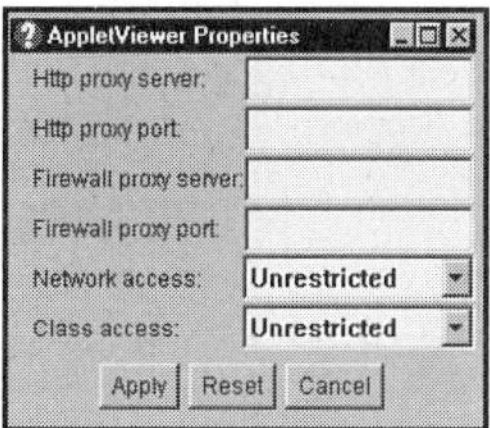

Figure 21.5
The Properties dialog box in the Appletviewer.

The appletviewer is a rudimentary tool as far at HTML content goes. It does nothing but display the Java applet itself. For testing applets this is enough. However, Java applets will be only one part of an overall Web page, so it is important to see how an applet will fit in with the rest of an HTML document. In this case, a full-flegged Web browser, such as Netscape or HotJava, must be used.

Netscape 2.0

Because Netscape 2.0 implements the Beta 2 version of the Java language, and does not support all of the Java functionality, not all applets will run under Netscape. Most of the limits to Java functionality have to do with security, and will be added later as Netscape more fully implements the Java run-time environment. The current version of Netscape 2.0 is in its initial release (see figure 21.6).

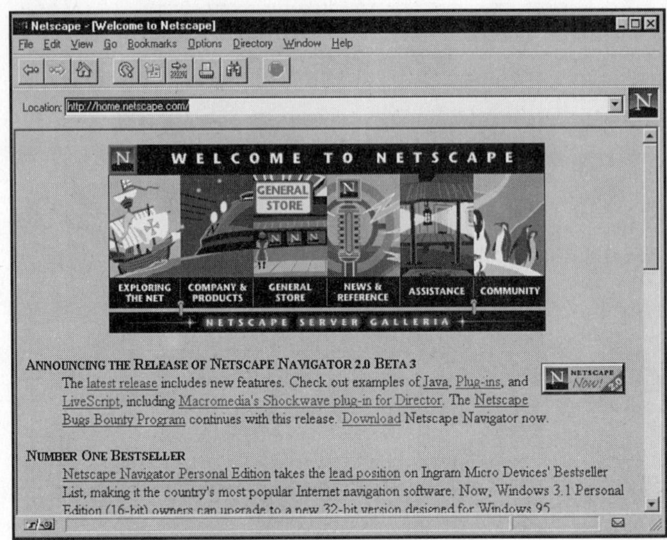

Figure 21.6
The opening Netscape 2.0 screen.

There is little you have to do to use Netscape to view Java applets. In fact, Netscape is set up to run Java applets as its default behavior. If you want to disable Java applets in Netscape, choose Options, Security Preferences, and you should see the dialog box in figure 21.7.

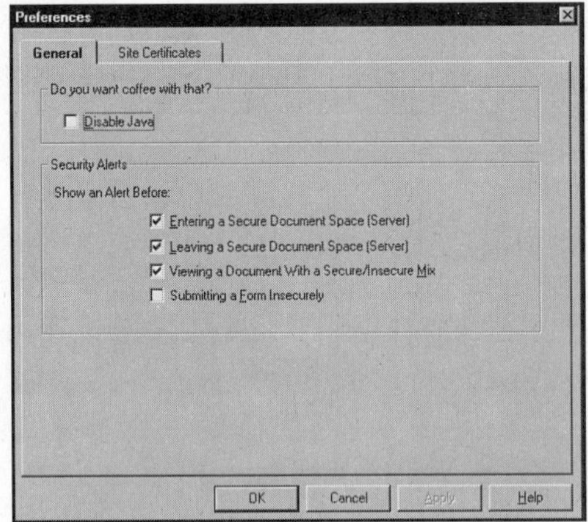

Figure 21.7
Netscape's Security Preferences dialog box.

Netscape limits the loading and functions of applets in order to ensure tight security. For example, Netscape will load applets or native code from a local hard disk, but won't allow applets loaded over the Net to write to the local hard disk. Additionally, Netscape 2.0 does not allow applets to use sockets to anywhere but the host machine from which they came.

Table 21.2
The Netscape Security Restrictions

Allows	Doesn't Allow
Applets to be loaded from the Net.	Applets to access any machine other than the host it came from
Applets to load local classes	Applets to write or read any other files on the local disk

In order to test Netscape, you can point it to one of the demonstration applets in the JDK directory java\demo. The animator directory has several sample HTML files that you can use to test to see if Netscape is set up correctly. The status bar at the bottom of the Netscape screen provides information about the status of applets that are being loaded from pages. For sample, as you load Sun's Java page, the applet places a message in this area as the individual images are being loaded.

For more information about the execution of Java applets in Netscape, the Java Console can be used (see fig. 21.8). Any run-time errors encountered will be placed here. To see the Java Console, select Options and check the Show Java Console option. Be sure to then select Save Options from the same menu in order for your changes to remain between sessions.

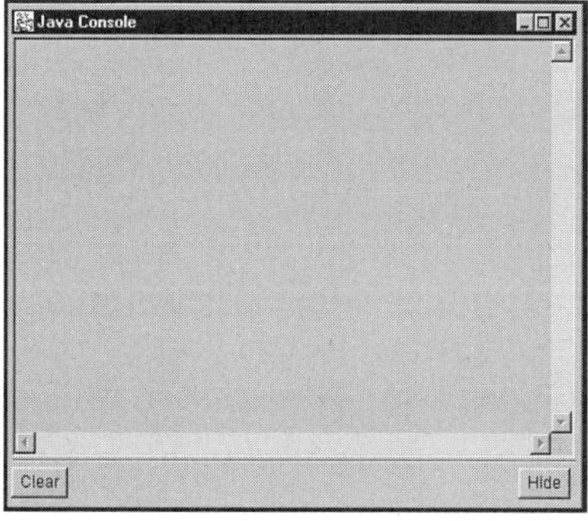

Figure 21.8
The Netscape Java Console.

Providing Applets

There is one last topic to cover before you move on to writing your own applets—providing your own content. If you want to include Java applets in your own HTML documents, there are two simple steps you should follow.

1. The first step to placing Java content in an HTML page is to create the a directory available to the Web server. Unlike the Alpha release, the class files no longer have to be in a subdirectory of the directory holding the HTML file. In any case, make sure that the directory structure is available to those browsing your Web site. Talk with your system administrator to find out where to place these directories.

2. Next, you must create your HTML file and include the Java `<applet ...>` directive. The `<applet>` directive works like any other HTML directive, and tells the browser to format the included information in a specific way. The `<applet>` directive tells a Java-equipped browser to load the executable designated by the `code` attribute and run it. Whatever Java applet you want to include, the bytecode file ends with the extension .class. There are many options you can provide when placing an applet in an HTML page; however, here is the simplest command:

```
<applet code="applet.class" width=100 height=140></applet>
```

That is all there is to it! You will now have a Java applet in your Web page. The HelloWorld applet document in the applets/HelloWorld directory on the NRP Web site looks like the following:

```
<HTML>
<HEAD>
<TITLE>Hello, World!</TITLE>
</HEAD>
<BODY>
Say Hi to Everyone:

<applet code="HelloWorld.class" width=100 height=100></applet>
</BODY>
</HTML>
```

Note Try using some of the applets included on the NRP site under the /applets directory. Move them into your own HTML directory and see how they look in your pages, or bring up the HTML files directly on the disk.

The <applet> directive has several options that configure how HotJava and other browsers will display the applet.

```
<APPLET
     CODEBASE=class URL
     CODE=class filename
     ALT=alternate text
     NAME=applet name
     WIDTH=width
     HEIGHT=height
     ALIGN=alignment
     VSPACE=vertical spacing
     HSPACE=horizontal spacing

>
<PARAM NAME=attribute name VALUE=attribute value>
<PARAM NAME=...>
[alternate HTML]
</APPLET>
```

Table 21.2 presents each optional value.

Table 21.2
<APPLET> Tag Options

Option	Effect
CODEBASE	This is an optional attribute that indicates the URL where the .class file can be found. This can be either an absolute URL, or a relational reference to the HTML directory.
CODE	This is a required attribute that indicates the name of the class file of the applet to load.
ALT	If this optional attribute is present, browsers that recognize the applet tag, but are unable to actually handle Java programs can display the text provided.

continues

Table 21.2, Continued
<APPLET> Tag Options

Option	Effect
NAME	This is an optional attribute that provides the applet with its own name, which can be used by other applets on the same page to communicate with each other.
WIDTH	This is a required attribute that provides the browser with the width in pixels that the applet needs.
HEIGHT	This is a required attribute that provides the browser with the height in pixels that the applet needs.
ALIGN	This is a required attribute that tells the browser how to align the applet. The possible values are left, right, top, texttop, middle, absmiddle, baseline, bottom, absbottom.
VSPACE	This is an optional attribute that tells the browser how much vertical space in pixels to allow between the applet and any other elements on the page.
HSPACE	This is an optional attribute that tells the browser how much horizontal space in pixels to allow between the applet and any other element on the page.

To pass arguments to the applet at run-time in the Alpha release of Java, the argument name and value were used in the <APP> tag. However, this allowed the tag to have an unknown number of options and does not conform to SGML standards. The new method for passing arguments to the applet is to use the <PARAM> tag.

Note The final release version of Java has changed the style of the <APP> tag used in the Alpha versions. Instead, the <applet ...> tag is now used to designate where an applet should be placed in an HTML document. The tag was changed because for the applet tag to be SGML-compliant, it could not use an unlimited number of tag attributes, which is what the older <APP> tag used.

```
<PARAM NAME=argument name VALUE=argument value>
```

This tag is used in between the <applet ...> and </applet> tags, and can be used as many times as needed in order to pass the necessary arguments to the applet. The following HTML code sends several arguments to an applet:

```
<applet codebase="e:\users\tdr20\java\demo\Animator"
➥code=Animator.class width=200 height=200>
<param name=imagesource value="Frames">
<param name=endimage value=10>
<param name=soundsource value="audio">
<param name=soundtrack value=sound.au>
<param name=sounds
➥value="1.au¦2.au¦3.au¦4.au¦5.au¦6.au¦7.au¦8.au¦9.au¦0.au">
<param name=pause value=200>
</applet>
```

Additionally, the <blockquote> tag can be used to indicate HTML source that should be displayed if the browser cannot handle Java applets. In the following example, a single frame from the animation can be displayed in place of the full animation.

```
<applet codebase="e:\users\tdr20\java\demo\Animator"
➥code=Animator.class width=200 height=200 align=right>
<param name=imagesource value="Frames">
<param name=endimage value=10>
<param name=soundsource value="audio">
<param name=soundtrack value=sound.au>
<param name=sounds
➥value="1.au¦2.au¦3.au¦4.au¦5.au¦6.au¦7.au¦8.au¦9.au¦0.au">
<param name=pause value=200>
<blockquote>
<img align=right src="Frames\T1.gif">
</blockquote>
</applet>
```

All HTML code between the <blockquote> and <\blockquote> tags will be ignored by Java-enabled browsers. This allows for page designs that can be used across many different browsers without the need for you to worry about what the page would look like without it. It is always good practice to check out Web pages on several browsers to ensure that even if everyone doesn't have the latest browser, the pages will maintain the correct layout.

Your First Java Program—Hello, World!

By now you should have the Java environment up and running correctly without too much suffering. You are finally ready, therefore, to start coding your first programs. The next two sections cover general ideas about programming in Java, detail what you need in order to get a program to run, and demonstrate the "Hello, World!" program as both an applet and a standalone program.

Your first Java program will be quite a simple one. It will print the words "Hello, World!" on-screen. Although the result of the program is not that fantastic, what actually goes on in the background to get it to do what it does *is*. The source code for the HelloWorld class is relatively short and displays the built-in power of the Java language classes. It also provides an opportunity to demonstrate some of the features of Java.

If you flip ahead to the source code for Hello, World!, you will notice that there are several words such as "import" and "extends." These declarations are fundamental to implementing the object-oriented nature of Java, and they bring us to a basic problem in teaching the language. The problem revolves around classes—Java's representation of an object. An object-oriented language can be approached in essentially two ways:

- By learning about classes first and the rest later
- By learning about declaration, types, and control flow first, and classes later

For those coming to a new language without any experience, it is generally believed that teaching the way in which classes work first is fundamental to creating good habits and programmers, from the start. The problem with this approach is that classes are a more difficult concept than the basic structure, and an understanding of the fundamental types and control flows is necessary to properly demonstrate programs. If you learn the basics of classes and objects early, however, creating good object-oriented code later becomes easier.

The second method—teaching the fundamentals of the language first, and then introducing classes later—is the method chosen in the Java chapters for two reasons.

- First, most people attempting to tackle Java will not be new to programming, but will have at least some programming experience.
- Second, although tutorials on classes and objects would require understanding some of the fundamentals such as types, expressions, and control-flow, a single class will be able to encapsulate the ideas presented in these two chapters and enable you to get the basic house-cleaning chores out of the way.

However, it is not worthwhile to ignore the whole class issue until you are ready for more detailed coverage. Java as a language requires the use of classes from the beginning; however, the necessary class structure can be kept to a minimum, and an explanation of the object-oriented techniques will provide a good impression on which to begin learning the language. If you understand classes, or are an experienced programmer, feel free to skip to the next section.

Introducing the Concept of Classes

First and foremost, you should notice that the HelloWorld application is called a *class.* That is exactly what it is. In fact, the output of the compiler is HelloWorld.class. Java is an object-oriented language to the extreme. All aspects of the language revolve around classes of objects. When you run either the interpreter or the browser, it implements a class—not a file.

Note Although JavaScript has stand-alone functions and statements, Java programs must always exist within a class structure. This is perhaps one of the biggest differences between the two.

A class is, generally speaking, composed of two kinds of items:

- Instance variables
- Methods

Instance variables are what describe an object. For example, if you have an object such as a lightbulb, you need to store its state, such as on or off, or perhaps its wattage. These values—on or off, and wattage—are stored in the instance variables. An important idea to remember is that these instance variables are typically *encapsulated.* This means that only the objects themselves can change the variables.

Of course, such things as the lightbulb knowing whether it is on or off, and being able to turn itself on and off, are well and good, but how does anything else tell it what to do? This is where *methods* come in. The lightbulb would provide methods for turning itself on and off, such as TurnLightOn() and TurnLightOff(). Just as you cannot directly force the electrons to stop flowing through the tungsten filament in a bulb and must use the light switch, other objects must turn the light on and off using the light's methods. A method is identical to the methods you have learned in JavaScript and are functions that are tied in with objects that give the objects the capability to complete a task. However, Java does not have the equivalent of a stand-alone function as does JavaScript—all functions are method and must be a member of a class.

The imaginary lightbulb might look something like this:

```
class LightBulb {
     boolean LightOn;
     int Wattage;
     public void TurnLightOn(){
          LightOn = true;
     }
     public void TurnLightOff() {
          LightOn = false;
     }
     public void ExpelPhotons() {
          if(LightOn) //do something to draw a lit bulb on the
                         //screen
          else //do something to draw an unlit bulb on the screen
     }
}
```

Of course, this is an incomplete example—it doesn't explain the way in which the bulb actually lights up, for instance. But this example does give a good picture of the kinds of class definitions you will be looking at. If you don't understand the format, or specific lexical issues, don't worry; they are explained in later sections. The idea here is to give an idea of what a class looks like and the general way in which it works.

You need to know about one other thing to write the HelloWorld applet and application: inheritance. Say you really like your lightbulb but think it is a little boring. You decide to include a little bell that goes off every time it is turned on to really get the attention of the user. Do you have to throw away all the code you have just worked so hard to produce? Not at all. You can use the extends modifier to show that our new class LightBulbWithBell is an extension of the old class. Our new class might look something like this:

```
class LightBulbWithBell extends LightBulb {
     public void ExpelPhotons() {
          if(LightOn) {
               ...//do something to draw a lit bulb on the screen
               SoundBell();
          }
          else //do something to draw an unlit bulb on the screen
     }
}
```

You have added functionality to the ExpelPhotons() function to make it sound a bell. Again, the exact details of the way in which it lights up, or sounds the bell, don't matter. The important idea is that you can *inherit* objects and their features and update them. The specific type of updating performed is called *overriding* because you overrode the previous declaration of ExpelPhotons(). You can also add new methods and instance variables if needed. This capability to inherit properties from previously coded classes is just one of the many powerful features of object-oriented computing. This leaves you with two important points needed for studying the Java language:

- All Java variables and methods must be members of a class.
- Classes encapsulate these members, and provide methods for inheritance.

A general understanding of classes at this point will make reading the code easier in the future, because so much of it revolves around the creation of classes. For this chapter, however, you will be dealing with only a single class instance.

With this brief introduction to classes behind you, you are now ready for your first Java program.

HelloWorld as an Applet

For most users of Java, the goal of programming in the language is to provide applets over the Internet to be used by Java-enabled browsers. Therefore, your first incarnation of the HelloWorld class will be just that—an applet. Using the browser environment requires using some of the class libraries that deal with the windowing environment. In particular, you will be using the awt (Another Windowing Toolkit) class to control the appearance of the applet on-screen. You will override the paint() method of the java.awt.Graphics class in order to place the text "Hello, World!" in the window.

All applets are inheritances of the base class java.applet.Applet. You will override the init() method of this class in order to resize the window before you display the text. You will depend on the base classes to receive window calls, repaint themselves when the window is uncovered or resized, and in general provide for all housekeeping chores. All in all, our code will be only 10 lines, and half of those are there merely because of aesthetics and readability. Not a bad return for such little work on our part.

Setting Up the Environment

The first step in creating your HelloWorld class is to create the directories where the files will reside. It is important to make sure that the java\bin directory is in your path statement, and that the directories that you are using to hold your files are accessible to the Java compiler and appletviewer. For example, you might want to create a directory java\workingfiles to store all of your Java files.

```
e:\users\tdr20\> mkdir java\workingfiles
```

The directory structure used in these examples is for local machine use only. If you want to make your applet pages available to the wider Internet, you should talk with your system administrator about where you can place your files for world access. Be sure to find the correct directory structure to use, and the resulting URL necessary to find the document externally.

The Source Code for the HelloWorld Class

When you have the directory structure finished, you can begin to code the HelloWorld class. First, you must create a file called HelloWorld.java in the classes directory. The .java extension is the standard method for indicating a Java source code file. In Windows NT/95 you can either use the edit command or use the Notepad in the Windows environment. In Solaris, you can either use a command-line editor, such as vi or emacs, or use an OpenWindows editor, such as the TextEditor. Refer to the software documentation for details about creating a plain ASCII text file for your environment. Whichever editor you use, make sure that you are familiar with all the editing features. Correcting a typo in a command-line editor can be the most frustrating problem in the world when you don't know the commands.

There is a very useful utility on the NRP site called JavaMaker, written by Choi Hee Chang, which provides an editor and compile environment for the JDK release under Windows NT/95.

The program is on the site in the JavaMaker directory. View the readme file that is in the directory for installing the program. This is what is used to edit, compile, and run the code in these Java chapters.

Using either the JavaMaker editor, or an editor of your own choosing, here is the source code you need to enter:

```
import java.awt.Graphics;
public class HelloWorld extends java.applet.Applet {
      public void init() {
            resize(150,50);
      }
      public void paint(Graphics g) {
            g.drawString("Hello, World!", 50, 25);
      }
}
```

When you have finished typing the code, save it as HelloWorld.java.

Look at what you have line by line. First, you have the following:

```
import java.awt.Graphics;
```

This previous line tells the compiler that you will be using the Graphics classes and to be ready to use them. In fact, the compiler will bring in the class definitions and include them with the source code you have written.

```
public class HelloWorld extends java.applet.Applet {
```

This line declares a new class, HelloWorld, and tells the compiler that it is a subclass of (extends) the java.applet.Applet class.

```
public void init() {
```

This line overrides the init() function of the applet class. public means that objects outside of this class can invoke it, and void means that the method returns no value. The empty parentheses show that this method also takes no arguments. When the applet is created, methods in the superclass applet will call this function, invoking the next line:

```
resize(150,50);
```

This line tells the browser to resize the window to 150 by 50.

```
public void paint(Graphics g) {
```

This line is another overriding method. It is overriding the method paint from the Applet class. When the applet is told to paint itself, this is the method it calls. Again, the method is public and has no return value. You do, however, have an argument. When paint() is called, it needs to be sent an object of class Graphics; in this case, the method refers to it as g. Therefore, g is sent by the methods you don't see in the superclass Applet that handles Graphics objects.

```
g.drawString("Hello, World!", 50, 25);
```

In this line, the Graphics object g is told to invoke its method drawString() with the arguments Hello, World!, 50, and 25. This tells the method to print the text Hello, World! at location 50, 25.

When the applet has completed running, the automatic garbage methods of the Java environment ensure that memory allocated is freed and generally makes sure that the program exits cleanly.

Compiling

After you have written the source file, and saved it into the classes directory, you are ready to compile the code. The command for compiling in both Solaris and Windows NT/95 is this:

```
C:\> javac HelloWorld.java
```

If compilation succeeds, you should have a file named HelloWorld.class in the same directory as the HelloWorld.java file. If you have any problems, make sure that you have typed all commands correctly. If you still can't get the file to compile, check out the section at the end of the chapter on troubleshooting the compiler.

If you are using the JavaMaker program, you can compile the current file by choosing Tools, Compile, or by using the compile button on the toolbar. A compiler output window will pop up, and provide information about the state of the compilation.

Creating the HTML File

After you have completed the compilation steps and created the HelloWorld.class file, you are ready to place it into an HTML document. Again, in your editor, create a plain ASCII text file in the working directory called HelloWorld.html. The file will be a standard HTML file that includes the <applet> directive. For our purposes, you need only the basic structure:

```
<HTML>
<HEAD>
<TITLE>Hello, World!</TITLE>
</HEAD>
<BODY>
Say Hi to Everyone:
<applet align=center code="HelloWorld.class" width=150
➥height=100></applet>
</BODY>
</HTML>
```

As mentioned in the beginning of the chapter, the <applet code=class_file> directive tells the browser to load and run the class class_name from the classes subdirectory in the HTML file logical directory. Save the file with an html extension (such as example1.html).

Loading the Applet

After you have completed a program and compiled it correctly, you are ready to view the applet using the appletviewer or Netscape 2.0. You can either invoke the appletviewer from the command-line:

```
e:\users\tdr20\java\code\>appletviewer example1.html
```

or run the appletviewer from JavaMaker from the menu item Tools, Appletviewer, or by choosing the appletviewer button on the toolbar. Make sure that you have set the Tools, Environment menu selection that indicates the path to the JDK files, and the name of the HTML file to run the appletviewer with.

When you run the appletviewer from either the command-line or the JavaMaker program you should be presented with a window. If you are having any problems, refer to the troubleshooting section at the end of the chapter.

Congratulations! You have finished your first applet and have completed all the steps necessary for creating your own Java applets for the Internet. Obviously, there is much more to programming more complicated applets, but, in essence, you have learned all there is about the process, illustrated in the following steps:

1. You develop the code, compile it, and check for compile-time errors.
2. You develop your HTML pages, including the new applets.
3. You test the pages with the appletviewer or Netscape 2.0.

If the HTML file is loaded into Netscape, it will display a full HTML file.

Of course, that is not all that the Java language is good for. By using the Java interpreter, you can write stand-alone applications in addition to browser applets. To help you understand the differences between creating an applet and creating an application, you will recode the HelloWorld class as a stand-alone application to be run on the interpreter.

The HelloWorld Class as a Stand-Alone Application

The HelloWorld class can also be run as a stand-alone application using the Java interpreter. Although most Java work will be seen as applets, and, as you will see later, as handlers for types and protocols, the language can also be used to create stand-alone programs. Of course, these programs are not stand-alone in the true sense of the word because you still need the Java interpreter on your system to run them. To differentiate the applet from the application, you will refer to the new class as "HelloWorldApp."

For the HelloWorldApp class, you will not require the classes used in the applet form of the program. Instead, you will create a new class from scratch. If you look ahead at the code, you will notice that our program does not *extend* any other class. This is misleading, however; you are in fact extending the class Object.

Note When a class is defined without specifying the inheritance class, the class Object is taken as the default.

Thus, even though you seem to be creating a new class, you can still use many powerful features built into Java. In fact, all classes are derived from the Object class. Suffice it to say that the Object class provides the garbage collection and system utilities basic to all Java implementations.

Our HelloWorldApp class this time is only five lines long, half the length of the applet version, and still much of that is spacing for aesthetics and readability. For that, you get a program that will run on any platform the Java language has been ported to, along with all the features of the language.

Setting Up the Environment

Your HelloWorldApp does not require you to create any special directory structure for holding the class files. Instead, you can work in any directory you choose. For now, create a directory HelloWorldApp to hold your work. In this directory, create a file named HelloWorldApp.java. Using any editor you choose, or the JavaMaker program, create the file in plain ASCII text.

The Source Code for the HelloWorld Class

The source code for the HelloWorldApp is relatively simple:

```
class HelloWorldApp {
     public static void main (String args[]) {
          System.out.println("Hello, World!");
     }
}
```

After you have finished typing the code and ensured that it is correct, save the file to the HelloWorldApp directory.

Again, the source is studied line by line.

```
class HelloWorldApp {
```

As mentioned before, this line declares the class as HelloWorldApp. The declaration does not specify what class HelloWorldApp extends, so the default is taken as Object. Again, every class, except for Object, has a superclass. In other words, every class is an inheritance of another class, except for Object. This line could also have been written like this:

```
class HelloWorldApp extends Object {
```

Writing it the first way is easier, however, and the Object extension can always be assumed.

```
public static void main (String args[]) {
```

This line has several new features not in the applet:

- The modifier static appears. This keyword tells the compiler that this method refers to the class itself, not to a specific instance of the class. This enables the method to be invoked without a HelloWorldApp object having been created first.
- Notice that the method takes an argument, args[], that is an object of String. In fact, this object holds the arguments typed after a command when it is entered.
- Notice the name of the method itself—main(). This method, as in C and C++, is required of all applications to tell the interpreter where to

start. The interpreter is what calls the main() method and passes the command-line arguments to it. The main method is not required in Applets because the browser calls the applet's init() method to run. This is one of the easiest ways to distinguish between the two kinds of Java programs.

```
System.out.println("Hello, World!");
```

This line outputs the text Hello, World! to the standard output, usually the screen. In this case, the class System has the method out, which in turn has the method println, which outputs the argument to the screen. Notice that the call uses the dot (.) operator as in C and C++.

Compiling

By now you should have completed the HelloWorldApp.java file and saved it to the HelloWorldApp directory. As before, you need to compile the class using the javac compiler.

```
C:\> javac HelloWorldApp.java
```

The compiler should create the class file HelloWorldApp.class in the directory HelloWorldApp. Additionally, you can use JavaMaker to compile the file. If you have any problems, check for typing errors, and if they still persist, check the troubleshooting guide at the end of this chapter.

Running the Interpreter

After you have completed the compilation and javac has created the class file, it is time to run the application. You invoke the interpreter with the Java command. Java refers to the class, not the compiled file. To run HelloWorldApp, enter this:

```
C:\> java HelloWorldApp
```

JavaMaker does not provide a means for invoking the Java interpreter from inside the program, so you will have to get to a command prompt. Of course, those using Solaris will be in the command prompt anyway.

Again, congratulations! You have completed your first stand-alone Java application. In many ways, the process is an easier one than that of creating applets. You didn't have to mess around creating an HTML page with

<HEAD>, </TITLE>, or <APP> declarations, or run HelloWorldApp through Netscape. Very quickly, you have created a sophisticated program capable of running on many different systems. Although HelloWorldApp doesn't seem all that sophisticated, in fact, the Java language is hard at work in the background delivering a robust, high-performance application.

In the next few chapters, you will begin to piece together the fundamental aspects of the Java language needed for developing your own ideas into Java classes.

Troubleshooting

Presented here is a list of errors you might confront and solutions you might find helpful when running the Java compiler javac and Java interpreter. This is not an exhaustive list, but it should enable you to work through most of the error messages that appear as you try to compile and run the examples and your own code.

Compiling Errors

This list of compile-time errors covers the most common mistakes made during program compilation. Any time the compiler outputs an error message, it will not output the .class file. If you are trying to compile a program and don't seem to be getting the .class file, the compiler is most likely encountering an error somewhere in your code. Most of these mistakes are typographical errors, but they are not always easy to find. Be sure to check your code carefully, especially for semicolons at the ends of statements. Semicolons are used to tell the compiler where a statement ends; sometimes, however, it is not clear if you should use a semicolon at the end of some lines. Think of them as the equivalent to periods at the end of sentences.

- `javac: Command not found`

  This error occurs on Unix systems where the path isn't set properly. Make sure that your path statement includes the directory where the Java binaries are kept. This is typically the hotjava/bin directory. Use setenv or a similar command to set your path variable to the javac directory. A sample path statement might be the following:

```
PATH=C:\hotjava\bin;C:\users\Ritchey\hotjava\classes;
```

Check with your shell documentation for the specifics of your configuration.

- ```
  filename:linenumber: ';' expected
   some line of code
                    ^
  
  n error(s)
  ```

  You receive this error when you have forgotten to include the semicolon at the end of a statement or declaration. This error message occurs only if the compiler figures out what you were trying to do. Many times, however, the compiler cannot guess what is missing and might output strange error messages, such as Invalid type expression or Invalid declaration, on the following lines of code. If the lines in which the compiler finds an error look correct, check the lines immediately preceding those with the errors for missing semicolons.

- ```
  filename:linenumber: Variable variable_name may not have been
  initialized.
    variable
           ^
  
   n error(s)
  ```

  Any time a variable is used without first being initialized, the compiler throws an error message and the .class file is not created. Make sure that all variables are initialized. Initialization is the way you tell the compiler what kinds of variables you will be using.

Interpreter Errors

Many times, programs will compile, yet still not run under the Java interpreter. The interpreter commonly issues two types of errors:

- `Can't find class classname.class`

  This error is produced when the user tries to run a class by giving the interpreter the class filename rather than the class name. Be sure to drop the .class extension when running classes through the interpreter. For HelloWorldApp, you should enter java HelloWorldApp not java HelloWorldApp.class.

- `In class classname: void main(String argv[]) is not defined`

  This error occurs when a class does not have a main() method defined. All applications must have a main() method defined in order to give the interpreter a place to start execution.

You have learned the basics of developing Java code into either an applet or an application. By now, you should be comfortable using the Java compiler and interpreter, as well as using applets in HTML pages. Spend time with the Hello, World! applet and application. Change lines to get error messages, and see what the compiler and interpreter do. Try to see whether you can reproduce the errors shown in the troubleshooting section. Also, try to change the arguments used in resizing and placing text, or try outputting multiple lines of text. The best way to learn is by trial and error. Of course, the goal here is to help you get all the trial, with as little of the error as possible.

Now that you have mastered the Hello, World! app, what now? In the next chapter, you learn the basics of the language, such as declaring and using the basic types, numbers, strings, and arrays with operators. In addition, the guts of a program—control flow—are presented. This section covers all the ways to control the movement of the program.

The Hello, World! examples are intended to show the ways in which Java provides a powerful environment for developing applications. The portability allows for a single compile environment while allowing distribution across a heterogeneous network. The robust, high-performance execution means that the performance hit for such portability is kept to a minimum. In addition, the built-in security features allow for easy development of innovative content. Most of all, these examples should give you a feel for what developing in the Java environment is like. Although the Java chapters in this book focus on the command-line method of creating applets for Netscape, this is only because it is the common denominator on most platforms. By the time you read this, there may well be several integrated development and visual environments in which to create applets. Be sure to watch the Internet for new information about what is available.

Essential JavaScript

by Tim Ritchey

The first chapter of this book introduces the reader to both the Java and JavaScript languages, their development, purpose, and design. It is important to understand these issues when picking up a new programming language for the first time, because maximizing the usefulness of new technologies means using them for the right job. Of course, JavaScript is a derivative of Java, so many of the lessons you learn here are applicable when you move on to Java in later chapters. The different roles of the Java and JavaScript languages do play an important part in what you learn in this chapter; however, it is always a good idea to keep in mind where you want to go as you pick up new features of the language.

This chapter focuses on the fundamental programming lessons for learning JavaScript. In order to program in JavaScript you must know how to get JavaScript programs to run, by doing the following:

- Learning how to integrate JavaScript into your HTML code
- Learning the syntax and general structure of the JavaScript language

After you have been made familiar with what a JavaScript program looks like and have learned how to place it into your HTML documents, you are ready for this chapter, which covers the following elements:

- The creation of variables
- How to use variables in different expressions
- How to use operators

Knowing how to create variables, form expressions, and use operators, as well as understanding the basic elements of style, provides you with all of the building blocks you need to begin coding useful JavaScript statements that can be incorporated into more complicated scripts in later chapters.

Note In many of this book's sections, you will run across places where elements of style in programming are discussed. Elements of style are not imperative to programming a JavaScript or Java program, but they become more and more important as you look toward code reusability and maintenance. High-level languages such as Java and JavaScript are designed to be easily read and understood by programmers (at least in comparison to older low-level languages, such as assembler). Even so, creating easy-to-read code is more the result of a programmer's coding habits than of any language's features. Hopefully you will find the style advice useful, and portable to any language to which you may move in the future.

JavaScript and HTML

JavaScript is interpreted from HTML files that are loaded into the Netscape 2.0 browser. This means that in order to use JavaScript in your Web documents you must be able to integrate your JavaScript code with the rest of the

HTML code. There are two ways in which to include JavaScript code in a document:

- Embed the code within the document
- Load the code from a separate file

In addition, you need to learn how to use HTML to hide JavaScript code from older web browsers that cannot handle it. You also need to understand the order in which JavaScript code is executed.

Embedding a Script

In order to embed a JavaScript program into your HTML file, use the <SCRIPT></SCRIPT> tag, and place all of your code between the beginning (<SCRIPT>) and end (</SCRIPT>) tags. Although the <SCRIPT> tag will take several options in future releases, for embedding JavaScript, you only need to specify what scripting language is being used. In this case, it is JavaScript:

```
<SCRIPT LANGUAGE="JavaScript">
</SCRIPT>
```

After you have created the tags, any code that is inside is interpreted by the JavaScript interpreter. For example, the following HTML file uses JavaScript for all of the text output to the screen.

```
<HTML>
<HEAD>
<SCRIPT LANGUAGE="JavaScript">
<!--
document.write("<HR>")
document.write("This is a test of the JavaScript functionality of
➥Netscape.")
document.write("<HR>")
// -->
</SCRIPT>
</HEAD>
<BODY>
</BODY>
</HTML>
```

In this example, the JavaScript source is placed in the <HEAD></HEAD> tags of the HTML document. This is not necessary; placing the <SCRIPT> </SCRIPT> tag in the body would work just as well. However, unless you are trying to mix in JavaScript output with regular HTML, later, when you are creating functions and calling them with event handlers, your code will be more robust if you define the functions in the head of the HTML document. Doing so ensures that the functions are read before any HTML code that might attempt to access it. If you are using the JavaScript code to format the page, you may need to place it in the body; otherwise, try to keep everything in the head portion of an HTML file.

Loading Script Source Files

Another useful way to load JavaScript source code into a page is by loading a file that holds the JavaScript source code. In order to load the source file instead of writing JavaScript source code directly into the HTML file, you can provide the URL to the file that holds the source code:

```
<SCRIPT LANAGUAGE="JavaScript" SRC="JavaScriptCode.js"></SCRIPT>
```

There are two things you should remember when importing JavaScript code:

- The extension to the source code file should be .js
- The LANGUAGE attribute is not necessary if you indicate the source type in the extension

Therefore, the following code is equivalent to the previous:

```
<SCRIPT SRC="JavaScriptCode.js"></SCRIPT>
```

The advantage to using source files instead of embedding the code inside your HTML files is that you can update the source code without changing the HTML file at all. You simply replace the old .js file with the replacement copy. Of course, you must be careful that the new copy will work with the original HTML file. Again, although this feature is documented in the JavaScript guides, it is currently not implemented in the Netscape 2.0 browser.

Commenting out JavaScript Source Code

You may have noticed two codes that were inside the <SCRIPT></SCRIPT> tags, but outside the actual scripting code:

```
<!--
// -->
```

These two lines are HTML comments that hide the JavaScript source code from browsers that are not able to interpret the <SCRIPT></SCRIPT> tag. Everything in between the comment tags will be ignored by these older browsers. You should note the two forward slashes (//) before the end comment tag (-->). These are actually JavaScript comments that hide the end HTML comment tag from the JavaScript interpreter. Why they are necessary will be covered presently. It is useful to mark these lines with explanatory comments.

```
<SCRIPT LANGUAGE="JavaScript">
<!-- this line hides the JavaScript source from older browsers
document.write("Hello, World! - try this on older browsers with
➥and without HTML comments")
// this is the end of the HTML comment tag -->
</SCRIPT>
```

Additional HTML Considerations

There are additional considerations when dealing with the Netscape Navigator 2.0 edition of JavaScript and HTML files. While these are not features of the language, they arise from the interaction of JavaScript in the Navigator environment and mean that typical HTML code might require some special attention.

First, <IMG> tags in HTML files can cause problems if they do not have their WIDTH and HEIGHT attributes set. For this reason it is always preferable to set the width and height values for images you use in your program. Including a <SCRIPT> tag after the last image tag, also fixes the problem.

Second, nested tables and forms can cause problems with JavaScript, so if you use tables to organize your forms, you might want to rethink the layout of your tables if you have created a nested hierarchy you want to use.

Third, there are several functions in JavaScript that enable you to send text output to the screen, including returns, tabs, and spaces. Traditionally, HTML browsers ignore any formatting information of this kind unless they are surrounded by the <PRE></PRE> or <XMP></XMP> tags. Be sure to use these wherever you have JavaScript output.

Processing Order

JavaScript code is interpreted within the HTML page after the entire page loads, but before the page is actually displayed. When you use source files, and call them in as SRC attributes in the <SCRIPT></SCRIPT> tags, this code is evaluated as if it were script container content. This evaluation occurs, however, before any embedded scripts are executed.

Later on, when the use of functions is discussed, this book presents a more in-depth look at when scripts are evaluated. The reason for this postponement of the execution is because functions are stored, but not executed until they are called by an event handler. This can create interesting behavior that can either work for or against you.

JavaScript Architecture and Writing Code

The JavaScript architecture is based upon tokens that the interpreter extracts from the source file and executes. The following list contains JavaScript's basic tokens:

- Comments
- Literals
- Identifiers
- Separators
- Operators

These elements of the JavaScript language provide the basic building blocks of all code you will ever write. You can imagine all of these elements as different elements in a building that can be placed together in an infinite number of ways. It is knowing how each of these elements functions in relation to the others that enables you to write successful programs. How good your building—your program—is depends upon how good you are with the material you must work with.

Tip This chapter contains the kind of syntax you will use when typing JavaScript code for things such as numbers, variables, function names, comments, and so forth. Many errors you will run into later when creating your own programs will come from typos and forgetfulness. The problem is that most of the information provided is relatively easy, and you might be tempted to gloss over it. You should still take time to read and understand everything.

Comments

When writing code in any language, it is important to remember to include written comments about what each line or group of statements is doing. In order to keep the JavaScript interpreter from trying to execute this text, you must hide it behind comment characters. Comments in JavaScript come in two styles. Table 22.1 presents the two kinds of comments available in JavaScript.

Table 22.1
The Different Comments in Java

Comment Type	Description
// *comment*	All characters after the // to the end of the line are ignored.
/* *comment* */	All characters between /* and */ are ignored. These comments can extend onto multiple lines.

The older (/* */) style was originally used in the ANSI-C standard and is carried on in Java and JavaScript. The text that comes between the front comment marker (/*) and back comment marker (*/) is hidden from the interpreter upon execution. The /* */ comment is useful for multiple-line comments found, for example, at the beginning of a code fragment such as the one that follows:

```
/* The following JavaScript function converts
   from Fahrenheit to Celsius.
   created 11-Jan-95                              */
function fahrToCel(fahrTemp) {
    celsTemp = (fahrTemp-32)*5/9
    return celsTemp
}
```

If you need only to comment out a single line, there is a more useful syntax. The // comment method was added to C++ as an easier way than the older C style comment (/* */) to comment out individual lines, and it is retained in JavaScript and Java. You can either use this to comment out an entire line:

```
// this line returns the Celsius temperature
return celsTemp
```

Or just the last portion of a line:

```
return celsTemp  // return the Celsius temperature
```

Tip If a line of code does something important, it is useful to call attention to it with a short comment. It is always considered "good programming" to provide comments for all your code in order to help future readers of the code (including yourself) understand what's happening.

Which type of comment you use and for what purpose you use it is entirely up to you, the programmer.

Two styles of commenting programs are the Sun and Microsoft styles for implementing comments in code. Most of the Sun documentation uses the following style for multiple lines because it is useful with the automatic document generator that comes with the Java Development Kit:

```
/**
 * this is a multi-lined comment
 * for the following function
 */
```

The /** tag on the first line is used to indicate to the document generator to use the comments as text in the resulting HTML file that it creates automatically from source code. This kind of comment is not used in JavaScript, but if you are moving on to Java, it is nice to get into the habit of using it. It doesn't affect the comment, but, when you begin coding Java applets and want to comment a line, later on, when you use the automatic document generator, your comments will be used to generate the text of the resulting HTML file. As with the standard comment, */ closes the comment block.

Microsoft program documentation uses the // comment in code, especially the code that is associated with the Visual C++ environment. The following code is an example of a multi-lined comment in Microsoft documentation.

```
////////////////////////////////////
// this is a multi-lined comment
// for the following function
```

Again, the choice to use either style is up to you, the programmer. If you are planning to use Java extensively in the future, and are using JavaScript as a stepping stone to learning Java, you should probably use the Sun form for comments because it will be helpful when you make the transition to Java later on. If you are intending only to use JavaScript, the // comment is easier to use because it simply comments out the rest of the line, and you don't have to keep track of the beginning (/*) and end (*/) tags.

Including comments in code is an important habit to get into. Even though it seems as though everything is perfectly clear when you are writing your code, someone else who wants to use the code might have great difficulties in determining exactly what certain lines of your code are supposed to accomplish. Using comments also saves you many headaches later when you decide to update a JavaScript function that you spent weeks creating, only to find that you can't figure out how to work in new code without disrupting what you've done. In this object-oriented programming world, using comments is perhaps the easiest, most cost-effective, and most powerful method for ensuring that code is readable and reusable.

Literals

Literals, which are used when entering explicit values into your code such as 5 or x, refer to the basic representation of two types of data in the JavaScript language:

- Numbers
- Strings

Number literals can be categorized into two subtypes: *integers* (numbers without a decimal point) and *floating points* (numbers with decimal values). In addition, there is a special literal known as the boolean. A boolean variable can either be true or false. The boolean literal is included under numbers because in C there was no true boolean literal; instead, the integers 1 and 0 were used for true and false respectively. Therefore, although boolean is being categorized as a number here, it really should be considered its own fundamental type. The string literal is any character sequence that is placed between single (‘’) or double (“”) quotes. So things like “hello,” “testing, one, two, three,” and ‘a’ are all string literals.

Note Literals are closely linked with types, which are discussed in the section on declaring variables. The difference between types and literals is that literals are explicit values entered into the code of your program, whereas types refer to the kind of internal representation and storage that the JavaScript interpreter assigns to certain kinds of data.

Think of the small child's toy that has different pegs to put into the right shaped hole. It has round, square, triangle, and star-shaped pegs, and a set of holes to match. The holes that can accept the different pegs are the equivalent of types—they are the variables that hold the data. Literals are the equivalent of the pegs, or data, actually placed in those holes, or variables.

Integer Literals

The first literal is the integer. This literal, the most common of literals, comes in three guises: *decimal*, *hexadecimal*, and *octal* format. The decimal, or base 10, integer is the most familiar, and appears in the way that you would expect. The important thing to note about the decimal integer is that it does not have a leading zero. The hexadecimal, or base 16, integer is typically used as a binary shorthand, each digit grouping four binary ones and zeros. Hexadecimal integers are represented by the digits 0–9 and the upper- or lowercase letters A–F, which represent the numbers 10–15. These integers are preceded by 0x or 0X. Octal, or base 8, integers are represented by the presence of a zero (0) in front of the digits. Table 22.2 gives examples of several numbers in the different formats.

Table 22.2
Decimal, Octal, and Hexadecimal Representations of Integers

Decimal	Octal	Hexadecimal
0	0	0x0
2	02	0X2
63	077	0X3f
83	0123	0x53
631	0771	0x3Fl

The numbers used earlier in the equation for the fahrToCels function (found in the previous "Comments" section) are examples of using integer literals in a script. In this case, the integer literals are used to convert a Fahrenheit temperature to Celsius.

```
CelsTemp = (fahrTemp-32)*5/9
```

Floating Point Literals

Floating point literals represent decimal numbers with fractional parts such as 1.5 or 43.7. They can be in either standard or scientific notation. Following are some examples:

3.1415, 0.1, .3, 6.022e23, 2.997E8, 1.602e-19

If in the temperature conversion you didn't want to first multiply by five and then divide by nine, you could use a floating point number, and just multiply by a single number:

```
celsTemp = (fahrTemp - 32)*0.5555556
```

Although carrying out only one operation instead of two appears to be more efficient, try typing in the following code, and replacing the line that does the calculation with the two previous examples.

```
<HTML>
<HEAD>
<TITLE>Say Hello:</TITLE>
<SCRIPT LANGUAGE="JavaScript">
<!—  this line hides the script from old browsers
    /**
     * function to convert a Fahrenheit
     * temperature to Celsius
     */
    function fahrToCels(fahrTemp) {
        celsTemp = (fahrTemp-32)*5/9   // this does the conversion
        return celsTemp              // this returns the Celsius number
    }
        document.write("The boiling point of water in Celsius is: ")
        document.write(fahrToCels(212))
// this is the end of the script and comment structure-->
</SCRIPT>
</HEAD>
<BODY>
<HR>
</BODY>
</HTML>
```

When you run both of these what do you notice? The resulting value for the equation using the floating point number should not be exactly 100. In this case, there is less precision because we had to round off the floating point number instead of using an infinite number of fives. On many computers, the storage and calculation of integers is much more efficient than with floating point numbers. It is better, therefore, to represent things with integers, rather than use floating point numbers.

Boolean Literals

The *Boolean literal* has two states—true and false—which are represented by the keywords true and false. This value, therefore, represents the state of something that can have only one of two values. The values are typically used as flags for determining whether to take a certain action or not. The Boolean value is a true literal, and not a representation of the integers zero or one as in C or C++. The following code shows how you use boolean literals.

```
flag = true
if(flag) {
    document.write("This line will print")
    flag = false
}
if(flag) {
    document.write("This line will not print")
}
```

Simply, the *if* statement checks to see whether the statement in the parentheses is true or false. If the statement is true, it executes the statements between the curly braces.

String Literals

The term *string literal* refers to any number of characters enclosed in double (") or single (') quotation marks. Table 22.3 gives examples of some Strings and their printed output.

Table 22.3
Examples of Valid Strings

The Declaration	The Result
“”	
“\’”	‘
“Your Ad Here”	Your Ad Here
“Multiple\nLines”	Multiple Lines

If you would like to see what some strings look like on-screen, you can take our Hello, World! script and change the String in the line.

```
document.write("place your String here")
```

Reload the HTML page from the Hello, World! example after you have changed the string, and see how it has changed.

The backslash (\) is used to represent non-printing or conflicting characters. Table 22.4 lists the various nonprinting control character combinations JavaScript accepts. These characters provide formatting of text that are not provided for in an easy way on a standard keyboard, and so must be implemented with a control code. They can be used in both string literals and variables.

Table 22.4
Special Character Representations

Description	Standard Designation	Sequence
Continuation	<newline>	\
New-line	NL(LF)	\n
Horizontal tab	HT	\t
Backspace	BS	\b
Carriage return	CR	\r

Description	Standard Designation	Sequence
Form feed	FF	\f
Backslash	\	\\
Single quotation mark	'	\'
Double quotation mark	"	\"

Identifiers

Identifiers are the names given to variables and functions to identify them to the interpreter. Identifiers used in previous examples of JavaScript code include helloWorld, text, and number. What, then, makes a valid identifier? In JavaScript, all identifiers must begin with a letter or the underscore character (_). All subsequent characters can also include digits (0–9). Letters are considered the upper- and lowercase alphabet from A to Z.

In addition, those words designated as *keywords* in the following section are unusable. Table 22.5 gives examples of valid and invalid identifiers in Java.

Table 22.5
Valid Identifiers

Valid	Invalid	Valid, but Not Recommended
watts	wattage #	WATTS
lightOn	light-on	lighton
monthsWith_31_days	5dogs	_number
x	abstract	$_243_fubar

In the case of the invalid identifiers above, the following rules apply:

- **wattage #.** There can be no white spaces within an identifier.
- **light-on.** The hyphen (-) is an invalid character.

- **5dogs.** Cannot use a number to start an identifier.
- **abstract.** Abstract is a keyword.

Of course, unless you have a non-American standard keyboard, using anything other than the "_", and "a"–"Z" letters would merely create difficulties in editing, so you shouldn't have any problems following those standards. Unless you have good reason, it is advisable only use the "_" in the middle of identifiers (between words) to improve readability. This practice is really of most use to Java programmers, but getting into the right habit now will help the transition later. Using descriptive names should provide you with all the flexibility you need. As a rule of thumb when you create identifiers, make all the letters lowercase except for the beginning of words that appear in the middle of an identifier (such as in lightOn).

Note In C and C++, the standard is to name #define identifiers with all uppercase letters. JavaScript does not implement a #define, so for ease of transition, all-uppercase identifiers should not be used. This is not a requirement; however, this rule will come in handy later when you are using Java, and it is good to not get into the habit of using all uppercase early on.

Keywords

Keywords are identifiers used by the JavaScript language, and cannot be used in any other way than that defined by the JavaScript language. You won't be able to remember every single keyword, so if you are having a problem with an identifier that is a single lowercase word, be sure to check out the keyword list in table 22.6.

Table 22.6
List of Reserved JavaScript Keywords

abstract	double	int	super
boolean	else	interface	switch
break	extends	long	synchronized
byte	false	native	this
	final	new	
case	finally	null	throw
			throws
catch	float	package	transient
char	for	private	true
	function		
class	goto	protected	try
			var*
const*	if	public	void
continue	implements	return	while
default	import	short	with
	in		
do	instanceof	static	

* Reserved keywords, but currently unused by JavaScript

Separators

In JavaScript, the spaces, tabs, and newlines between characters are known as *separators.* These are essentially removed by the interpreter; therefore, how you use them is primarily a matter of aesthetics. For example, the following code fragments are all spaced differently, but they are all equally valid sentences.

```
celsTemp =  (fahrTemp - 32) * 5 / 9

celsTemp=(fahrTemp-32)*5/9

celsTemp    =    (fahrTemp-32)*5/9
```

How you choose to write your code is up to you. It is easier to read the first example with spaces between everything, but sometimes you will want to make sure everything fits on one line, so the second version may be more useful. If you are listing items, it is sometimes useful to line up statements over several lines, so inserting spaces helps.

```
name    = "Billy"
address = "401 Holler Road"
city    = "Clinton"
state   = "Indiana"
zip     = 47804
```

Whatever the situation, remember that they are there to make the code easier to *read* not to run, so go for what looks good and makes sense to a programmer reading it later on.

Declaring Variables

Variables are used to store data values in named holders that can then be referenced later on. For example, in the fahrToCels function used in previous examples, the fahrTemp and celsTemp were variables that held the Fahrenheit and Celsius temperatures respectively. One of the first things you do in most programming languages is declare variables based upon what kind of data you want them to hold. This is typically done for more efficient code compilation, and also for string type checking. *String* type checking means the compiler or interpreter checks to make sure that each variable must declare what kind of data it can hold, and then it is checked to make sure that no other kind is placed in it. Because JavaScript uses a loose type-checking architecture, there is no need to declare what kind of value each variable will hold. *Loose* type checking means that a variable can hold any type of data without the need to declare a specific type. Later, when we move on to Java, which is a string typed language, you will need to learn how to declare variables.

There are two main reasons for implementing a strongly typed language: storage optimization and robustness. If the compiler knows beforehand what type of data a variable can hold, then it can set aside enough memory and not worry about it anymore. If it doesn't know and has to constantly adjust the amount of memory a variable has, many processing cycles are used, which can make a program run inefficiently. To use such an optimization, the compiler must be able to detect when the programmer is trying to fit data into a variable without enough memory. Otherwise, they could lose valuable information. In JavaScript, a variable could be adjusted automatically to make room for the larger data size. In Java, you would lose the data that overhung.

For now, all you need to do is the following, and you should be okay:

1. Use a valid name, as defined by the section on identifiers in the previous section.

2. Be sure not to use a JavaScript keyword.

If you are familiar with languages, and the idea of declaring variables before you use them, keep that concept in mind because it will be useful later on. For now, however, you can create variables wherever you need them. The act of assigning them a value is what declares them in JavaScript. You use the equals (=) sign to assign a value to a variable, just as you have done in previous examples.

```
number = 10
name = "Steve"
cost = 10.99
isLightOn = false
```

Tip One good piece of advice—try to declare all variables, and assign them a value at the beginning of code blocks where they are used. This makes the function easier to read because you can see all the information you will be using right away.

It also is a good habit to make sure that all your variables exist in a known state before program execution enters a complex section of code. This means that if you have to go in looking for a bug, you at least know where all of the information is coming from. When you move on to a more strict object-oriented programming language like Java, this advice becomes even more useful.

Using 'var' for Variables

Of course, now that you have been told to go create variables wherever it pleases you, it's time to bring some order back to things. One problem with the dynamic interpretive feature of JavaScript is that it is very difficult to catch errors in code, especially in terms of variable naming. For example, you may bring in a JavaScript source file using the SRC attribute that uses the same variable name as a function you are embedding directly in the HTML page. Which one takes precedence? If you use the keyword var when creating your variable, inside the block of code where the variable was created, this variable will be used instead of any other global variables that have the same name.

The following code shows how the var statement can affect the execution of a script. Try running this, and look at what happens:

```
<HTML>
<HEAD>
<SCRIPT LANGUAGE="JavaScript" >
<!— hide script from old browsers

function test() {
  flag = true

  document.write(flag + " ")
  test1()
  document.write(flag + " ")
  test2()
  document.write(flag + " ")
}

function test1() {
  var flag = false
  document.write(flag + " ")
}

function test2() {
  flag = false
  document.write(flag + " ")
}
```

```
// end script hiding -->
</SCRIPT>
<BODY>
<SCRIPT LANGUAGE="JavaScript" >
<!— hide script from old browsers
test()
// end script hiding -->
</SCRIPT>
</BODY>
</HTML>
```

If you run this in Netscape 2.0, you will notice that the output comes out as

```
true false true false false
```

when what you might expect is either this:

```
true false false false false
```

or

```
true false true false true
```

What is happening is that the two functions that are used by the first function happen to use the same name for flag.The function test1 is a friendly function and uses the var statement to ensure that it doesn't affect any global variable of the same name in existing code. Function test2, on the other hand, declares the variable flag without regard to any other code that might be trying to use the same name. Although this is a simple example, and you might think that a programmer should be able to keep track of this, in today's distributed computing environment, you never know where code can come from.

A similar situation could happen if some functions you needed were loaded using the SRC attribute, to which you then added your own code. You might know how to call the functions you imported, but you might not know what the guts of the scripts were. If the programmer was unkind, and didn't use var, and there was a variable that matched, you could have a function alter variables in ways that could be difficult to track down.

For this reason, whenever you create a variable, be sure to use var in front of it to ensure it doesn't mess up any global variables that might have the same name.

Creating Expressions and Using Operators

After you have created your variables, you must be able to assign them values, make changes to them, and perform calculations. These are the roles of the operators. Table 22.7 lists the operators, from highest to lowest precedence.

Table 22.7
Operators from Highest to Lowest Precedence

.	[]	()									
++	—	!	~								
*	/	%									
+	-										
<<	>>	>>>									
<	>	<=	>=								
==	!=										
&											
^											
|											
&&											
||											
?:											
=	+=	-=	*=	/=	%=	<<=	>>=	>>>=	&=	^=	|=
,											

Precedence refers to the order in which multiple operations are computed. Operators on the same level have equal precedence. For example, the following calculation

```
a=b+c*d/(c^d);
```

proceeds by working from left to right on all binary operations (those involving two variables), computing those operations at the top of the list and working down. In this case, because the () has higher precedence than anything else, the c^d would be computed first. Next, the c*d would be computed and that result divided by the result of the first operation. Finally, all this would be added to b and the result placed in a.

Tip Whenever you are in doubt about the order in which something is calculated, be sure to use the parentheses () to specify to the compiler the way to do things.

Out of this list, the first operator you need to know is the assignment operator (=). This does exactly what you think it does. It takes the values on the right side of the equal sign and places them into the variable on the left side of the equal sign. Even though this is the easiest operator, it can get you into lots of trouble. Later on, you will look at the == operator, which compares two values, *but does not change either one.* Instead, it returns whether they were equal at the time of the operation. It does not alter the right hand operant to equal the left hand operand as in the = operator.

Casting Variables

JavaScript attempts to convert data from one type to another type when needed, but sometimes it is unable to. This is a unique problem to a dynamic language such as JavaScript. Because there is no compiler to check whether assignments are correct before they run, the programmer must be very careful when writing scripts.

One example where JavaScript might not convert is when trying to make a string into a number. As long as the string *represents* a number already, the conversion works. If the string represents a series of letters, however, the conversion will fail with an error. Table 22.8 lists the results of almost all conversions.

Table 22.8
Conversions Between Types

	Target Data Type				
Data Type	Function	Object	Number	Boolean	String
function		function	error	error	decompile
object	error		error	true	to String
Null object	funobj OK		0	false	"null"
number (non-zero)	error	Number		true	to String
number (0)	error	null		false	"0"
Error (NaN)	error	Number		false	"NaN"
+ infinity	error	Number		true	"+Infinity"
- infinity	error	Number		true	"-Infinity"
false	error	Boolean	0		"false"
true	error	Boolean	1		"true"
string (non-null)	funstr OK	String	numstr OK	true	
null string	error	String	error	false	

Some of these results might not make sense to you now. As you cover more of the language and begin to use objects and functions, however, come back to this list and compare how different objects convert to each other to make sure you understand what is going on in examples where conversions take place.

Arithmetic Expressions

Now that you have learned how to create variables, you probably would like to know how to use them. JavaScript has several operators that can be used on variables—some of which are specific to certain kinds of variables, and return specific kinds of values. Some of these values we saw in table 22.8.

There are essentially three kinds of operators: arithmetic, logical, and string. The last three sections of this chapter present these different operators and discuss their common usage.

Arithmetic operators come in two flavors: binary and unary. The binary operators require two variables to work on, while unary operate on a single variable. Table 22.9 lists the unary operators.

Table 22.9
Unary Integer Operators

Operator	Operation
-	Unary negation
~	Bitwise complement
++	Increment
--	Decrement

The *unary negation* changes the sign of a number. *Bitwise complement* changes each bit of the variable to 1 if it is a 0, and to 0 if it is a 1. *Increment* increases the value of the variable by one, and *Decrement* decreases the value of the variable by one. Following is an example:

```
i = 0;
j = 10;
for(i = 0; i<10; i++) {
     j--;
     document.write(i+"\t"+j)
     document.write("<p>")
}
```

This script runs increasing numbers in one column and decreasing numbers in the other. Note the use of ++ and --. Each time these occur, the system either raises or lowers the value of the operand by one. This is the way in which unary operators work—they change the value of the variable they are used on. For the negation and bitwise complement, the variable is not changed; for the increment and decrement, the variable is changed. The following code gives an example of the way this works:

```
i = 10, j = 10, k = 10, l = 10
     document.write(i+"\t"+j + "\t" + k + "\t" + l)
     document.write("<p>")
j++
i--
~k
-l
document.write(i+"\t"+j+"\t"+k+"\t"+l)
document.write("<p>")
```

Notice that j and i have been changed, and print out their new values, but k and l have reverted to their original values. When you use the unary negation and bitwise complement in a compound operation, you actually use a temporary variable that holds the new value of the operand. The increment and decrement operators are both prefix and postfix—that is, they can be placed before (++x) or after (x++) the operand. If they are used in compound statements such as

```
i=x++
```

or

```
i=++x
```

then the first line increments x *after* assigning its value to i, and the second line increments x and then passes the new value on to i.

The second type of integer operator is the binary operator. These operations do not change the values of the operands. They return a value that must be assigned to a variable. Table 22.10 lists the binary number operators.

Table 22.10
Binary Integer Operators

Operator	Operation
+	Addition
-	Subtraction
*	Multiplication
/	Division
%	Modulus

Operator	Operation
&	Bitwise AND
|	Bitwise OR
^	Bitwise XOR
<<	Left shift
>>	Right shift
>>>	Zero-fill right shift

The following program prints the values of some operations:

```
i = 5
j = 10
document.write(i+"\t"+j)
document.write("<p>")
j = j + i
document.write(i+"\t"+j)
document.write("<p>")
j = j * i
document.write(i+"\t"+j)
document.write("<p>")
j -= i
document.write(i+"\t"+j)
```

Notice the last operation. It is a combination of the binary operator and the assignment operator. This is equivalent to writing j=j-i. This can be done with all the binary operators, and is a common shorthand to get used to. If the operator is

```
x [op]= y
```

then the expression is equivalent to

```
x = x [op] y
```

Take the time to place your own equations into the code. Add variables and try different combinations.

> **Note** Here are some further notes on the integer operations. First, division of integers rounds toward zero. Second, if you divide or modulo by zero, you will have an exception thrown at runtime. If your operation exceeds the lower limit, or *underflows*, the result will be a zero. If it exceeds the upper limit, or *overflows*, it will lead to wrap-around. Moving past the upper limit will place you at the very bottom value—approximately –2.1 billion.

There are also additional relational operators that produce boolean results. These operators are shown in table 22.11.

Table 22.11
Relational Integer Operators that Produce Boolean Results

Operator	Operation
<	Less than
>	Greater than
<=	Less than or equal to
>=	Greater than or equal to
==	Equal to
!=	Not equal to

The equal-to operator (==) can cause you endless suffering. I still sometimes replace the double equal sign with just a single equal sign when I mean to compare two values instead of assigning the value of the right operand to the left. Make sure that you use the double equal sign for comparison. Try this application:

```
i = 0;
j = 10;
while(i<j) {
     document.write(i)
     i++;
}
```

Here, the control statement while checks the values of i and j. While the statement i<j is true, it runs the code fragment that prints i and then increases it by one. As soon as i<j is false, the program drops out of the while loop and finishes.

Logical Operators on Boolean Types

The boolean type adds several new operators for logical computation. These operators are listed in table 22.12.

Table 22.12
Boolean Operators

<table>
<tr><th>Operator</th><th>Operation</th></tr>
<tr><td>!</td><td>Boolean negation</td></tr>
<tr><td>&</td><td>Logical AND</td></tr>
<tr><td>|</td><td>Logical OR</td></tr>
<tr><td>^</td><td>Logical XOR</td></tr>
<tr><td>&&</td><td>Evaluation AND</td></tr>
<tr><td>||</td><td>Evaluation OR</td></tr>
<tr><td>==</td><td>Equal to</td></tr>
<tr><td>!=</td><td>Not equal to</td></tr>
<tr><td>&=</td><td>AND assignment</td></tr>
<tr><td>|=</td><td>OR assignment</td></tr>
<tr><td>^=</td><td>XOR assignment</td></tr>
<tr><td>?:</td><td>Ternary</td></tr>
</table>

If you consider the boolean value to be the equivalent of either 1 for true, or 0 for false, the operators act the same as those for the integer operators if they are working on a single bit. Negation (!) is the equivalent of the integer bitwise complement (~) and is a unary operation. Table 22.13 lists the results of the operations.

Table 22.13
Results of Boolean Operations

AND Op1	Op2	Result	OR Op1	Op2	Result	XOR Op1	Op2	Result
true	true	true	true	true	true	true	true	false
true	false	false	true	false	true	true	false	true
false	true	false	false	true	true	false	true	true
false	false	false	false	false	false	false	false	false

The &, |, and ^ operators evaluate both sides of the argument before deciding on the result. The && and || operators can be used to avoid evaluation of righthand operands if the evaluation is not needed.

The ?:, or ternary, operator works as shown here:

```
Operand1 ? Statement1 : Statement2;
```

Operand1 is evaluated for its truth or falsity. If it is true, *Statement1* is completed; if it is false, *Statement2* is completed. The following code provides an example of this operation:

```
i = 10
j = 10
test = false
test ? (i = 0) : (j = 0)
document.write(i+"\t"+j)
test = true
test ? (i = 0): (j = 0)
document.write(i+"\t"+j)
```

Note the parentheses. They are not needed in this example, but if you use more complicated statements, you might want to include them.

Tip In addition to these operators, the &=, |=, and ^= work as assignment operators on boolean values just as they do for numerical values.

Operators on Floating Point Numbers

The traditional binary operations work on floating point values (-, +, *, and /), as well as the assignment operators (+=, -=, *=, and /=). Modulus (%) and the modulus assignment operator (%=) are the floating point equivalent of an integer divide. Also, the increment and decrement (++, --) increase or decrease the value of the variable by 1.0.

Operators on Strings

Strings can be concatenated using the + operator. If any of the operands are not strings, they are converted to strings before being concatenated. In addition, the += operator works by placing the concatenation of two strings into the left hand operand. You used the + operator in the previous examples when you wanted to print several items on one line. Try using the document.write() function and the + operator to make different combinations of output with the interpreter.

Note The left hand operand in a += string operation must already have a value in order to work in Netscape 2.0. For example:

```
string2 = "Hello"
string1 += string2
```

does not work because string1 is not defined. However:

```
string1 = ""
string2 = "Hello"
string1 += string2
```

does work.

As far as using JavaScript for computations goes, you have now covered all the basic operations that can be performed on variables. You should spend time with the information presented and try experimenting with your own programs. Of course, even in the examples here, you used several control-flow statements to make the programs really do something. Control flow provides the basic engine that makes your calculations work.

This chapter covered the basic architectural components of the JavaScript language. These components included how to place JavaScript code into HTML pages, the concept of keywords, the declaration of variables and issues of general syntax, in addition to discussing the operators that can be used to build up the computational aspects of a JavaScript program. In many ways, the material you learned in this chapter provides the basic engine for doing computations in JavaScript, along with the set of parts that is available when you begin to add more frills later on. There were several tips on how to format your code, and what is considered good coding practice.

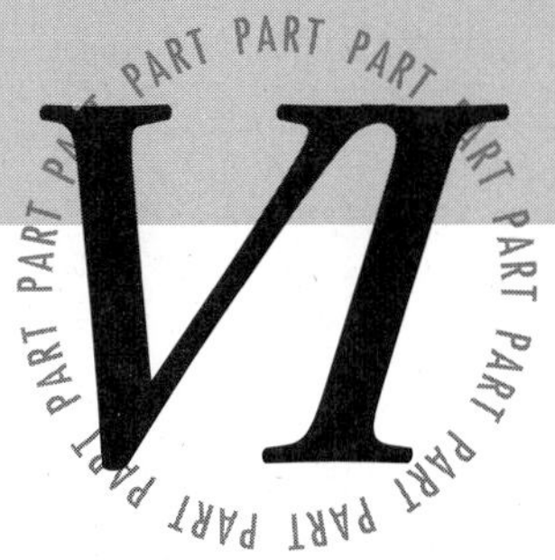

Security

An Overview of SATAN

by Larry J. Hughes, Jr.

On April 5, 1995, amidst memorable wailing and gnashing of teeth, SATAN made his grand entrance onto the Internet. His daunting mission: To interrogate millions of invisible daemons across the globe, in a furtive effort to uncover the secrets and weaknesses that make and keep us vulnerable.

Or was it really SANTA coming to town, to make a list of who's naughty and who's nice?

It appears to have been a little of both. The Security Administrator Tool for Analyzing Networks (SATAN)—also the Security Analysis Network Tool for Administrators (SANTA) for those of puritanical heart—was made available to all takers on this date by its noted authors, Dan Farmer and Wietse Venema (see fig. 23.1).

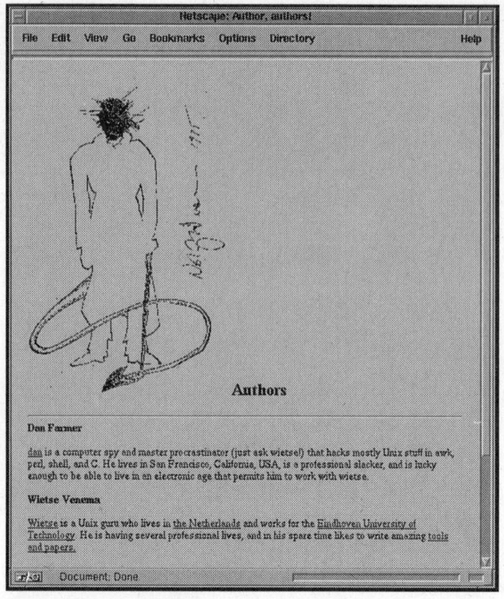

Figure 23.1
SATAN's authors.

Simply put, SATAN is a powerful tool that can thoroughly scan systems, and even entire networks of systems, for a number of common and critical security holes. With its readily portable engine and intuitive point-and-click interface, SATAN brings to the masses one of the most significant Internet inventions of the mid-90s—a single, extensible tool capable of turning even a novice into a veritable security-minded Sherlock Holmes in short order.

Unlike some other security tools, SATAN's gaze is directed outward, not inward. It probes for holes on other systems to discover potential avenues of attack from the outside—where most attacks originate. In the authors' own words, from SATAN's online documentation:

> Why did we create SATAN? Quite simply, we wanted to know more about network security, particularly with respect to large networks. There is an enormous amount of information out there, and it is definitely not clear by examining information and hosts by hand what the real overall security picture is. SATAN was an attempt to break new ground, to promote understanding, and to have fun writing such a program.

SATAN is an exceptional tool for security auditors and network and system administrators. Unfortunately, SATAN indiscriminately arms both saint and sinner alike. As such, it is a powerful vehicle for reconnaissance, an ideal mechanism for gathering facts that later can be used for attack. (SATAN examines systems for weaknesses, but does not actually attack them to disadvantage, if you subscribe to that distinction.) Why, then, make such a tool universally available, rather than licensing it only to the good guys? To this, SATAN's creators also have comment:

> History has shown that attempts to limit distribution of most security information and tools have only made things worse. The "undesirable" elements of the computer world will obtain them no matter what you do, and people that have legitimate needs for the information are denied it because of the inherently arbitrary and unfair limitations that are set up when restricting access.

In a sense, SATAN's authors seem to be putting an end to the adage that ignorance is bliss. On the Internet, where millions of computers and untold volumes of valuable data are ever at risk, ignorance is an expensive and dangerous commodity. SATAN attempts to finally change this, by putting into the hands of responsible persons a collection of tools that seasoned attackers have long had. That it, like every invention in the history of our species, will be used irresponsibly by some is a sure bet. Some would argue that this is reason enough for tools like SATAN to be kept under lock and key, but surely the opposite is true. Education, not secrecy, is what teaches people to fasten their own security seatbelts.

Note Without explicit prior permission, it is never acceptable to use SATAN or similar tools to scan for weaknesses on turf where you are not personally responsible. Even if you don't mind that others probe your system or network, others do not share your attitude. It might even be illegal to probe some Internet sites for vulnerability.

To install and run SATAN, you need the following in advance:

- **Superuser access on a supported Unix platform.** SATAN's authors state from firsthand experience that it runs on SunOS 4.1.3—U1 and SunOS 5.3 (also known as Solaris 2.3). However, the build procedure also supports these others: AIX, OSF, BSD, BSDI, DG/UX, IRIX 4, IRIX 5, FreeBSD, HP-UX 9, Linux, and System V Release 4.

- **Perl 5.000 (or better), already installed and tested.** Versions of Perl 4, or Perl 5 beta, do not suffice; SATAN employs some Perl extensions newly available in verison 5.
- **A Web browser, already installed and tested.** Any should work, although SATAN documentation explicitly mentions Netscape, Mosaic, and lynx (and automatically hunts for them in that order). In case you didn't know, *lynx* is a curses-based browser suitable for dumb terminal access.
- **A color monitor (strongly recommended, but not necessary) for use with graphical browsers.** Although not readily visible in the monochrome screen captures throughout this chapter, SATAN occasionally uses eye-catching red bullets in a list of items to flag a security problem you'll want to examine more closely.
- **Minimum of 32 MB of RAM, with plenty free for SATAN.** Exactly how much depends on where you point SATAN before dispatching it. Analyzing the results of a multi-thousand system probe is a memory-intensive task.
- **About 5–20 MB of disk space, including 2 MB specifically for the SATAN distribution.** The remainder allows for supplemental software (Web browser and Perl), possibly including source code, and a few sizable SATAN databases.

How SATAN Works

SATAN's authors took a rather ingenious approach when designing and constructing SATAN. To begin, its user interface is any of a number of World Wide Web browsers that are at everyone's disposal these days. Further, its primary underbelly is written in Perl, one of the most powerful, flexible, and portable interpreted programming languages around. These, teamed with an assortment of C-language support utilities, a collection of rule bases that guide its inference and decision-making processes, and databases for storing and retrieving results make for a sophisticated yet simple-to-use instrument. SATAN also includes a library of HTML documents, many of which were used as a reference in writing this chapter.

Although SATAN utilizes the Web browser of your choosing, you needn't worry about installing or running a Web server to accommodate it. The SATAN package includes a specialized "Web" server that speaks sufficient HTTP to communicate with any browser, and also is secretly rigged to initiate SATAN probes and perform other duties, all under the user's guidance. This server does not in any way interfere with other Web servers that might be running on the same host, as it runs on a randomly chosen TCP port. Note that because the browser and HTTP server both run on the same machine, there is no need for their communications to actually transit the network wires.

An overall, abstract glance at SATAN's internals reveals these primary components (see fig. 23.2):

- **HTTP server.** The SATAN-dedicated Web server mentioned earlier.
- **Magic cookie generator.** Each time SATAN is run, it generates a unique 32-bit magic cookie (also referred to as a *session key* or a *password* in the SATAN documentation). The cookie is theoretically known only to the user's Web browser and the HTTP server. The browser passes the cookie in some URL requests as a crude but effective form of client authentication. As long as the cookie remains secret—which as you see shortly may not always be possible—the server can discriminate between the real SATAN client and impostors.

Note SATAN uses magic cookies somewhat like the X Window System can use MIT-MAGIC-COOKIE-1 authorization. SATAN's cookie scheme, however, is not to be confused with X's because they really have no commonality in practice. Only the notion that clients that know the cookie are granted service applies here.

- **Policy engine.** Applies constraints defined in SATAN's configuration to determine what hosts are allowed to be probed, and to what degree. This basically defines "good neighbor" policies for the target acquisition stage, and prevents SATAN from unduly disturbing foreign networks, either by design or by accident.

- **Target acquisition.** Decides exactly which probes to run on various hosts when performing data acquisition. The hosts are selected by the user, and possibly by the inference engine, plus restricting advice from the policy engine. Acquisition might involve subnet scans to see which hosts are currently participating on a given network.
- **Data acquisition.** Acquires security-related facts about the targeted hosts. This is achieved with a modular and extensible toolbox of utilities, each of which performs a specific type of probe. Probes are performed in light, normal, and heavy modes according to the user's selection, with all results stored for subsequent processing by the inference engine.
- **Inference engine.** Driven by a set of rule bases and input from data acquisition, infers security facts about various systems. This often results in additional rounds of work, beginning once more with target acquisition of new systems somehow associated with those just scanned. Ultimately, all inferences are exhausted, leading to the report and analysis stage.
- **Report and analysis.** Through the browser's powerful hypertext interface, reports can be generated from various perspectives on the data resulting from data acquisition.

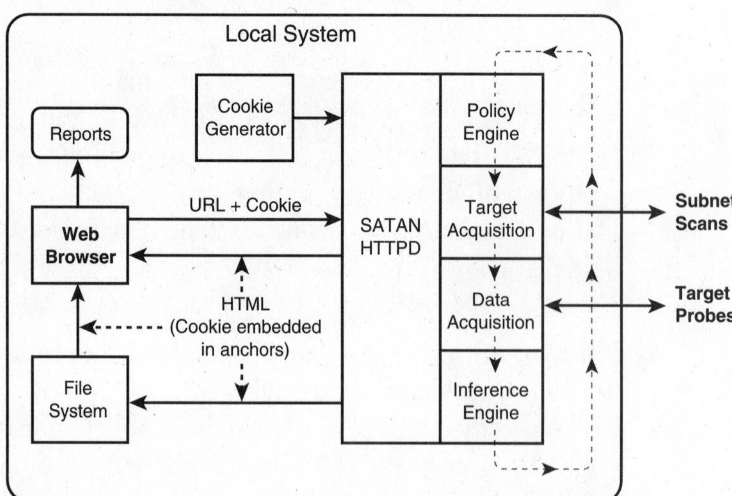

Figure 23.2
SATAN components.

Obtaining and Building SATAN

SATAN is available for anonymous FTP at `ftp://ftp.win.tue.nl/pub/security/`, as well as numerous mirror sites around the world. At the time of writing, the current version is 1.1.1, and can be found in the compressed archive file satan-1.1.1.tar.Z.

> **Warning** It is important to use version 1.1.1 or a later version because version 1.0 of SATAN did not contain sufficient precautions against magic cookie "leakage" outside the SATAN client/server associations. For details see the section "SATAN Vulnerabilities," later in this chapter.

In preparing to use SATAN, follow these steps:

1. Logged in as root, uncompress and extract the archive file into the desired location (what is called SATAN's *home directory*), using commands like these:

```
# cd /desired/location
# uncompress < /some/path/satan-1.1.1.tar.Z ¦ tar cf -
# cd satan-1.1.1
```

> **Warning** Do not install or run SATAN on an NFS-mounted file system. Doing so may expose SATAN's magic cookies and other sensitive information to network eavesdroppers.

2. Run the *reconfig* script, which among other things hunts for Perl and Web browsers in standard locations. The script selects the first instance of Netscape, Mosaic, or lynx that it finds, in that order of preference.

3. Edit config/paths.pl to ensure that the Perl variable $MOSAIC contains the command name of your preferred Web browser. If it is wrong, change it.

4. If you prefer that SATAN be known as SANTA on your system, run the *repent* script now. This globally converts all references of SATAN to SANTA, including the graphic images displayed by the browser.

5. Run make with no arguments to see the menu of system types; then run it again supplying your system type by name:

```
# make
Usage: make system-type. Known types are:
aix osf bsd bsdi dgux irix4 irix5 freebsd hpux9 linux sunos4
➥sunos5 sysv4

# make irix5
```

6. If your Web browser is configured to run behind a firewall, change its configuration now to avoid later confusion. The browser needs to communicate directly with SATAN's httpd on the local system, not a proxy Web server.

Directories and Files

After extracting the SATAN archive, you'll find these subdirectories in the SATAN home directory:

- **bin/.** Data acquisition programs and miscellaneous support programs.
- **config/.** Configuration files and modules, including SATAN's all-important satan.cf file. (This file can be managed directly from SATAN's control panel; see the section "Configuring SATAN," later in this chapter.)
- **html/.** Components for httpd, such as reporting tools, documentation library, tutorials, graphical image files, and so on.
- **perl/ and perllib/.** Most of the core Perl scripts, including the httpd, policy and inference engines, target acquisition module, and so on.
- **results/.** User-created databases containing data from SATAN scans. The default database is called satan-data.
- **rules/.** Rule bases for the inference engine.
- **src/.** Source code for data acquisition programs and related utilities.

Starting SATAN

Once SATAN is built, you can start it by running the *satan* script found in SATAN's home directory. You need to be in that home directory when starting it, or else you'll get one or more error messages from Perl. A successful launch appears as follows:

```
# ./satan
SATAN is starting up....
```

Warning It is very important never to run SATAN with your X DISPLAY environment variable pointing to a remote system. The variable should contain a value that points to your local system's private X display, usually ":0.0" or "unix:0.0". Doing otherwise may expose your magic cookie and other sensitive information to network eavesdroppers, putting SATAN's handiwork to waste.

SATAN takes a moment to initiate, during which time it generates the session's magic cookie, starts its httpd on an unused TCP port number, and launches your Web browser.

Your Web browser should appear with SATAN's main control panel, as shown in figure 23.3. (Figure 23.4 shows the control panel you see if you run the repent script during the build process. This is the last we'll have to say about SANTA in this chapter.)

Launching SATAN in this way enables interactive use of the control panel through the browser interface. After you're proficient with SATAN, you also can invoke the satan script with command-line arguments that instruct it how to proceed without benefit of the browser. The satan.8 manual page found in SATAN's home directory describes these arguments. You'll want to install the manual page on your system for reference purposes.

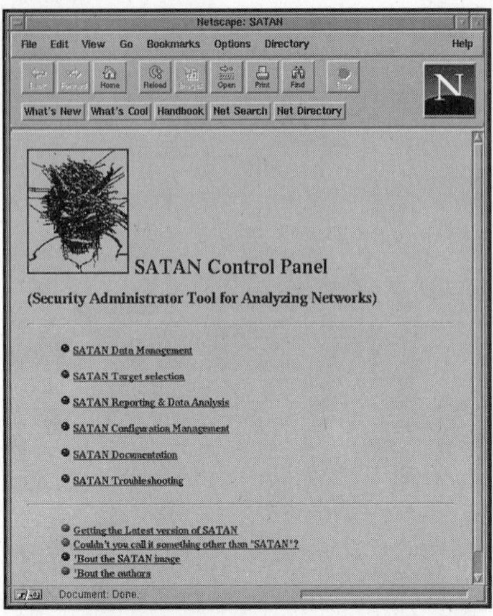

Figure 23.3
The SATAN control panel.

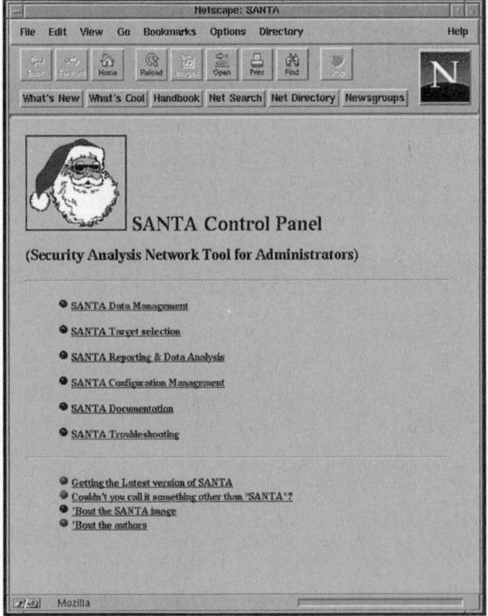

Figure 23.4
The SANTA control panel.

Online Documentation

The first time you run SATAN, you'll probably want to browse its online hypertext documentation, immediately accessible from the control panel. It includes an overview of SATAN, a brief tutorial, an examination of the vulnerabilities for which SATAN probes, and a FAQ (frequently asked questions).

The vulnerabilities section is particularly helpful. You later are directed to specific documents in it through hypertext links when using SATAN's analysis features. You also can freely browse the section at any time to get a better understanding of the security holes that SATAN comprehends (see figs. 23.5 and 23.6). The section's table of contents includes informative security information about these programs and services, most of which were discussed earlier in this book:

- FTP and TFTP
- NFS and NIS
- rexd
- sendmail
- Berkeley trust (remote shell)
- X Window System
- SATAN magic cookie disclosure

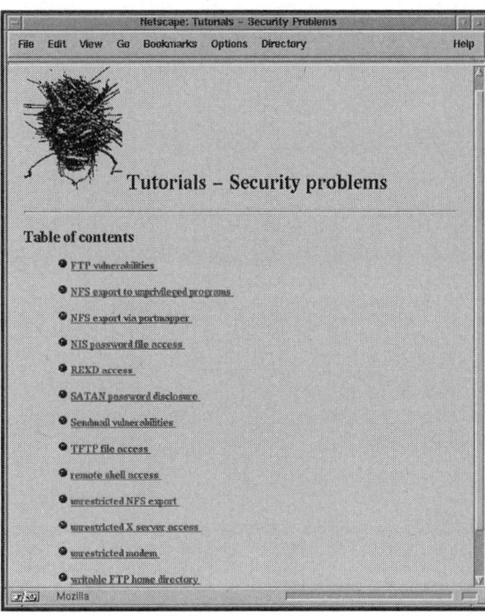

Figure 23.5
Vulnerability tutorials.

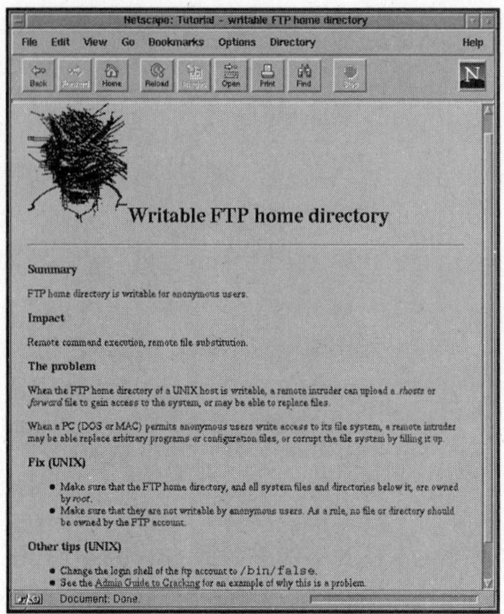

Figure 23.6
An FTP vulnerability tutorial.

Configuring SATAN

SATAN's configuration management panel allows for browser editing of many of the key variables in satan.cf, SATAN's master configuration file (see fig. 23.7). These variables largely define SATAN's runtime behavior. Although the file also can be edited outside SATAN with any text editor (it merely contains Perl variable definitions), using the browser form is a handy way to modify the variables you're most likely to change on a regular basis.

The form enables you to define these significant variables and behaviors, among others:

- **Database name.** The database for storing and recalling probe results. The default is satan-data.
- **Attack level.** The amount of effort that SATAN should expend when probing a target; one of *light*, *normal*, and *heavy*.
- **Timeout values.** How long to wait for probe responses from targets.
- **Subnet expansion.** Whether SATAN should probe only the targeted hosts, or all hosts on the target's subnet.

- **Targeting exceptions.** Explicit declarations of where SATAN is allowed to tread and where it is not.
- **Proximity values.** How SATAN should behave as it takes successive steps away from the primary target (see the following discussion).

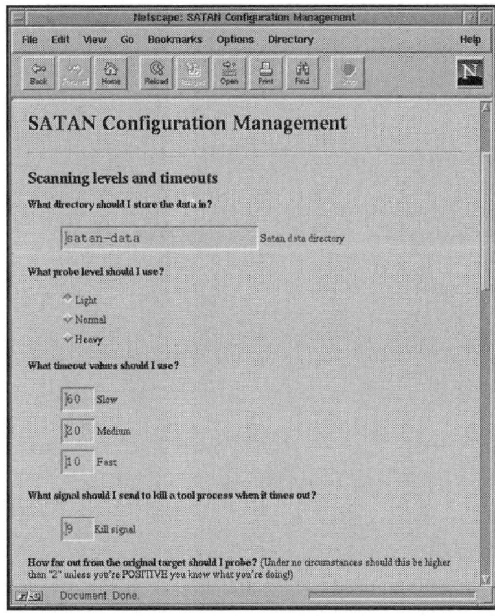

Figure 23.7
Configuration management.

There is an unmistakable place for careful forethought and discrimination when defining SATAN's configuration. Consider, for example, the case of target attack level. During an attack, the potential impact on the local system where SATAN is running, the target systems, and all intermediate networks may not be insignificant. It is important to understand what happens with each level of attack.

In a light attack, SATAN queries the DNS to try to determine the target's hardware and operating system configuration, mail exchangers, and so forth. It then contacts the target's RPC portmapper, if one is running, to discover which RPC-based application servers are running on the machine.

A normal attack includes the light attack probes, plus finger queries to determine user account names, and host names of remote systems accessing the target. In addition, it scans a limited number of standard service ports (FTP, Telnet, SMTP, NNTP, UUCP, and some others) to detect which network servers are readily available.

A heavy attack includes the normal attack, plus a far more thorough examination of the TCP and UDP ports likely to be running servers of any kind. Specifically, TCP ports 1-9999 are scanned, as are UDP ports 1-2050 and 32767-33500. In doing so, SATAN can discover many interesting facts, such as nonstandard ports hosting a telnet daemon as a potential back door into the system.

All three attack modes also include conditional probes. These execute only if facts gleaned from earlier probes imply that the conditional probe is meaningful. For example, if an NFS server is detected in a light attack, then the *showmount* command is executed against the target to obtain its export list. It naturally makes no sense to perform the showmount probe if an NFS server is not present to begin with.

The proximity values are critical variables for keeping SATAN on a leash of appropriate length. SATAN is all too happy to venture beyond one target to probe new ones that it hears about. It can, for instance, launch probes against every host that communicates with the primary target for any reason, and then all hosts that communicate with those, and so on. Each such step away from the primary target represents one outward level of proximity.

Maximal proximity defines how far SATAN reaches when exploring such relationships between systems. As SATAN's online documentation says, this configuration variable never should exceed a value of two unless you know exactly what you are doing; preferably, it should be set to zero and kept there. The number of hosts that SATAN probes can grow exponentially with each proximity step. Consider that when SATAN encounters a system that exports a file system to five hosts, SATAN can in turn probe each of those hosts. If each one of them exports a file system to five more hosts, SATAN claims 25 additional targets. Only your maximal proximity value tells SATAN when to stop.

The *proximity descent* variable serves to quench SATAN's thirst as it progresses away from the primary target. Setting this value to one lowers its attack level one notch at each proximity step, definitely healthy behavior. If the initial target is hit with a heavy attack, for example, then new targets discovered as a result of that attack receive a normal attack. On the configuration panel, SATAN can be told to stop when the proximity descent dips the attack level below zero, or to continue on one last round of scans.

Defining *targeting exceptions* further refines SATAN's behavior. Unchecked, SATAN pays no heed to geographic, organizational, or political boundaries while discharging its duties. To keep it from running amok on foreign networks, limitations can be established that give SATAN explicit permission to probe certain subnetworks, networks, and domains, and to stay off some others at all costs. Thus, even if SATAN is tempted to traverse into the gov domain while exploring proximity, specifying that domain as an exception averts the possibility altogether.

Note It is wise to be initially conservative in your dealings with SATAN, until you thoroughly observe and understand its habits. You won't go wrong by keeping the attack level at the light or normal levels, setting the maximal proximity to zero, and restricting probes to your local network only.

Using SATAN

Having gained a theoretical understanding of SATAN, you now see practical examples of the following operations:

- Selecting a database
- Selecting a target
- Launching a probe
- Viewing the results

Selecting a Database

Before running probes against a target, tell SATAN to create a new (or open an existing) database, if the one you intend to use is different from the default one defined on the Configuration Management panel. You can choose an existing database, or create a new one, from the Data Management panel (see fig. 23.8). If the database you open already exists, the results of new probes are appended accordingly.

Figure 23.8
Database selection.

The merge option visible in figure 23.8 is an *in-core merge* only. This means that SATAN temporarily merges, in memory, the most recently opened database with another on-disk one for the duration of the current session. This is helpful for discovering correlations and unhealthy patterns of trust from facts recorded in separate databases.

Selecting a Target

To choose SATAN's primary target, select the Target Selection item on the main control panel. The target may be either a network or a host. If the target is a host, you have the option of scanning the target's subnetwork as well. You also have the opportunity to select the scanning level (that is, the strength of the probe). The default action for both cases is defined on the Configuration panel, but you can override them here. Figure 23.9 shows the host opus.bloom.edu being targeted for a normal-strength probe.

Launching a Probe

After selecting the target and scanning level, click on the "Start the Scan" button shown in figure 23.9. This begins the data acquisition stage, shown completed in figure 23.10. In the course of probing `opus.bloom.edu`, SATAN discovered relationships to four other hosts that it subsequently visited with light scans. Note that the change from normal to light scan corresponds to a change in proximity, implying that the proximity descent value is set to 1.

Figure 23.9
Target selection.

Figure 23.10
A completed data acquisition.

Viewing the Results

When data acquisition is completed, note these two hypertext links at the bottom of the browser page (refer to figure 23.10):

- Continue with report and analysis
- View primary target results

Selecting the former presents the Reporting and Analysis panel, shown in figure 23.11. Encompassing the facts of both primary and proximity targets, you can explore vulnerabilities, host information, and lines of trust deduced by the scans, each from several angles. In figure 23.12, you see one example of Vulnerabilities by Type resulting from the scan of `opus.bloom.edu`.

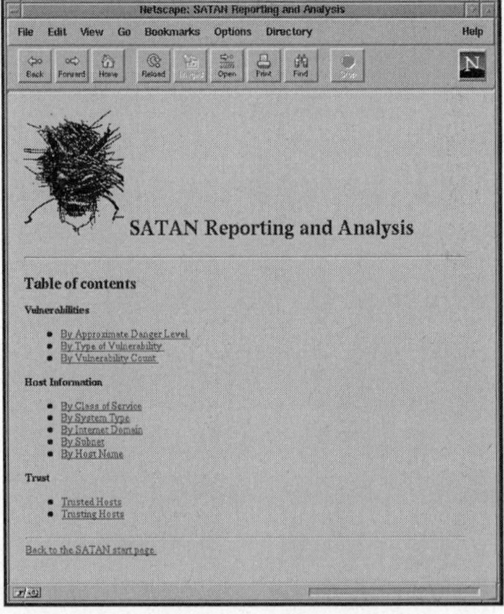

Figure 23.11
Reporting and analysis.

Opting to view the primary target results zooms directly to the primary target's facts, as shown in figure 23.13. More detailed information about some points can be viewed by following the hypertext links, such as that for the X Windows server.

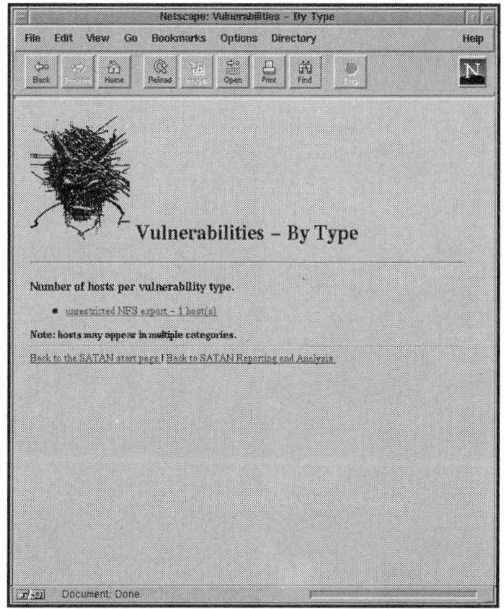

Figure 23.12
Vulnerabilities by type.

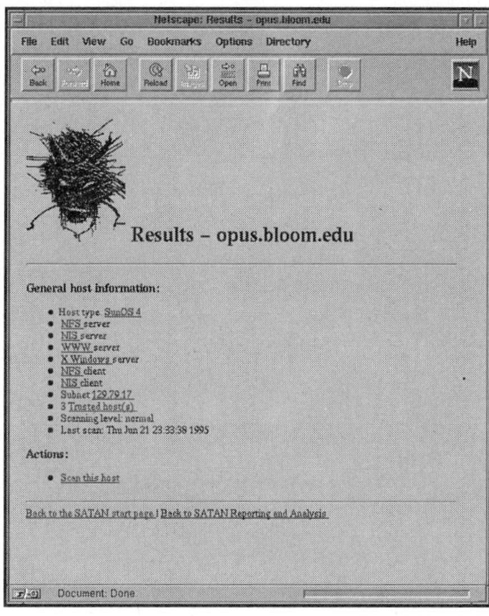

Figure 23.13
Primary target results.

SATAN Vulnerabilities

SATAN has two primary vulnerabilities that can be exploited by attackers, but only if it is not used correctly. They are the following:

- Magic cookie "leakage"
- Eavesdropping of client/server traffic

As reported in CERT Advisory CA-95:07a, version 1.0 of SATAN did not contain sufficient precautions against magic cookie "leakage" outside the presumed-secret client/server communications. This compromise can occur in several ways, including by using the SATAN-launched Web client to visit URLs outside SATAN—something you should never do. (See SATAN's own warning about this in figure 23.14.)

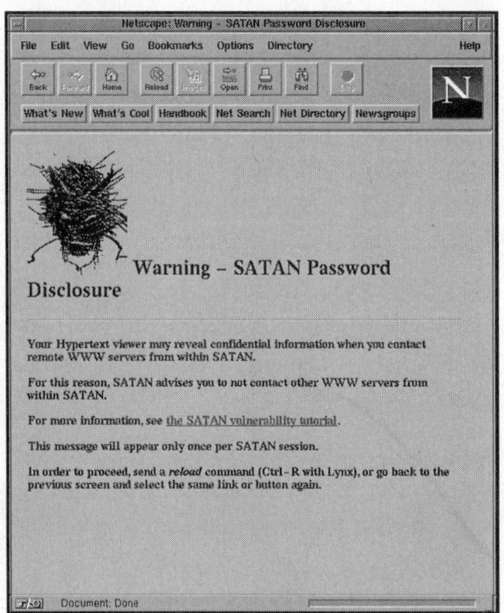

Figure 23.14
Password (Cookie) disclosure warning.

The suggested fix is to upgrade to SATAN version 1.1.1, which better detects and blocks browser requests bearing pilfered cookies, and to follow additional precautions outlined by SATAN's authors. These are contained in the Advisory, as well as in SATAN's own online documentation. Briefly, they are as follows:

- Do not use X's xhost authorization scheme when running SATAN, if your browser of choice is an X client. As you've seen, this scheme is not secure, and therefore running SATAN in an X display protected by it might reveal sensitive vulnerabilities to attackers.

- Keep all of SATAN's directories on a file system local to the host where you run SATAN. If SATAN is allowed to read and write files over NFS, the secret cookie and other sensitive information are visible to network eavesdroppers.
- Do not run SATAN with the X DISPLAY variable redirected to another system. The client browser always should run on the same system as SATAN's httpd, so that their communications can be kept off the network wires and away from eavesdroppers.

Detecting SATAN Attacks

Although there is no surefire way to detect every SATAN scan directed at one of your own hosts—particularly light attacks, which are rather unobtrusive by nature—two software packages can help. They have been made available as a direct response to SATAN's very existence.

Courtney was written at the University of California, Lawrence Livermore National Laboratory, and is distributed by CIAC (Computer Incident Advisory Capability). It is a Perl script that monitors output from the promiscuous tcpdump utility, and works by studying network traffic for systematic probes that usually amount to a SATAN fingerprint. Courtney runs on any Unix system that also runs Perl 5 and tcpdump. It is available for anonymous FTP at `ftp://ciac.llnl.gov/pub/ciac/sectools/unix/`.

Gabriel, a freely available product of Los Altos Technologies, Inc., is similar in concept to Courtney. It runs only on SunOS and Solaris systems, and is written in C. It is available for anonymous FTP at `ftp://ftp.lat.com/`.

Network Security Issues

by Larry J. Hughes, Jr.

As you have seen, the middle part of this book explains Internet security issues from a practical, application-oriented perspective: that of e-mail, file transfer, the World Wide Web, and so on. Here security issues are revisited from the perspective of the Internet's upper protocol layers—network, transport, and application—in accordance with the primary concerns of authentication, integrity, confidentiality, and access control.

Note The current version of IP deployed on the Internet is version 4, sometimes referred to as IPv4. The next generation of the protocol is version 6, commonly known as IPv6. In this chapter, use of the generic term IP generally means IPv4.

IP Security Option (IPSO)

The IP Security Option (IPSO) described in RFC 1108 (Kent 1991) is a U.S. Department of Defense (DoD) security specification for use on IP data networks. As its name implies, IPSO operates at the IP layer; it utilizes the variable-length Options field of the IP datagram header to explicitly label the sensitivity of the datagram's payload. IPSO is used primarily on military networks, but presents an interesting concept worthy of examination: datagram security labeling.

With IPSO, datagrams are earmarked by their senders as belonging to a particular Classification Level, and also as subject to handling rules defined by one or more Protection Authorities (DoD, NSA, DoE, and others). The Classification Level is usually one of the following, listed in order of decreasing sensitivity:

- Top Secret
- Secret
- Confidential
- Unclassified

The Classification and Protection Authority information combine to determine a routing policy that must be strictly followed in the course of delivering a datagram to its destination.

A datagram carrying Top Secret data should traverse only certified Top Secret paths; on the other hand, one bearing Secret data might travel through both Secret and Top Secret intermediates, and so on. Security is achieved mainly by routing what should not be seen away from those who should not see it. Of course, the assumption is that each network lives up (or down) to its Classification Level.

IPSO can work reasonably well in a closed network establishment like the military's. The Internet clearly does not fit IPSO's picture of the world; most Internet-connected networks are something of a party line. For a time, consideration was given to a commercial variant of IPSO, called CIPSO, but this effort seems to have fallen by the wayside in favor of more sophisticated and promising alternatives like those described next.

swIPe

It is possible to secure the IP layer by using encryption and other cryptographic techniques. The swIPe system (Ioannidis and Blaze 1993) is an early and in some ways prototypical example of how this laudable goal can be achieved.

Amazingly, swIPe can provide these valuable services at the datagram level without modification to the current IP protocol whatsoever:

- Message integrity
- Sender authentication (the sending system, not the sending user)
- Message confidentiality

It achieves this through a clever datagram-within-datagram, or IP-within-IP, technique. In a nutshell, an IP datagram that normally would be transmitted nakedly onto the network undergoes a last-minute cryptographic manipulation. The result becomes part of the payload of yet another IP datagram, as shown in figure 24.1. On the receiving end, this sequence of events is reversed in similar fashion. Network-layer intermediates can be totally swIPe-unaware without problem.

Conceptually, swIPe can be divided into three significant components:

- **Policy engine.** Examines incoming and outgoing IP datagrams to determine if they require swIPe processing. (Not every IP datagram should be processed by swIPe; only those destined for, or arriving from, another swIPe system.)

- **Security processing engine.** Per the policy engine, performs the necessary cryptographic calculations on inbound and outbound swIPe traffic. Although it entails some work, any secret-key or public-key cryptosystem can be used for confidentiality, as can any suitable authentication and integrity mechanism.
- **Key management engine.** Provides all necessary key management tasks for the security processing engine. This might include retrieving secret keys from an on-disk file or in-memory cache, performing Diffie-Hellman key exchange, querying a public-key key server, or any other implementation-specific mechanism.

Figure 24.1
The swIPe datagram scheme.

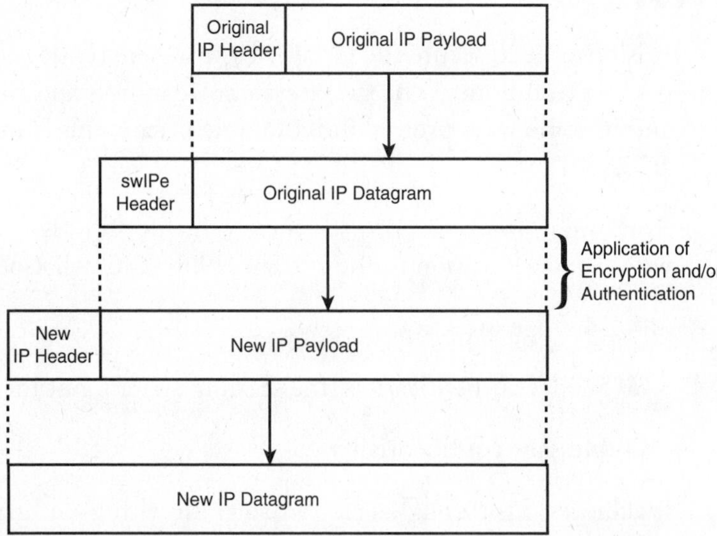

Although swIPe does not require use of specific cryptosystems or key management schemes, the reference implementation happens to use DES for encryption and MD5 for authentication and integrity. For key management, only "sneakernet" (manual key exchange and entry) is supported.

swIPe naturally lends itself to end-to-end datagram encryption, in which both the original sender and final receiver are swIPe-capable. It also can be used in other configurations, one of which is depicted in figure 24.2. In the figure, two disparate enterprise networks use swIPe to safeguard "internal" internetwork traffic as it transits the unsecure Internet that connects them.

Only the two security gateways in figure 24.2 need to be swIPe-enabled. The assumption is that intranetwork traffic in either enterprise network is not at threat, although swIPe could easily be used there as well.

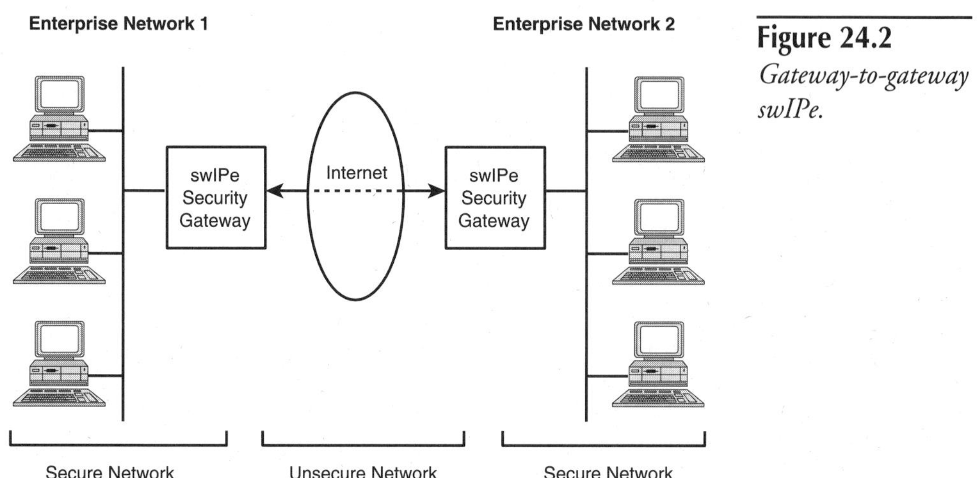

Figure 24.2
Gateway-to-gateway swIPe.

Running swIPe on a Unix system necessitates the creation of a virtual network interface usually named sw0. By establishing static routes to other swIPe-equipped systems through sw0, outbound traffic is automatically processed by swIPe, and then forwarded to the appropriate physical interface for actual network transmission. At the receiving end, because inbound traffic does not pass through a virtual interface, new kernel code tightly coupled with normal datagram processing routines selectively determines swIPe's involvement.

Although confidentiality of datagrams represents a major win, probably a more significant contribution made by swIPe is the authentication of sending systems. Heretofore, IP address masquerading and spoofing have been possible because of a complete lack of authentication at the network layer. Using swIPe, or a system like it, virtually eradicates the possibility of these attacks.

The swIPe distribution is available for anonymous FTP at `ftp://ftp.csua.berkeley.edu/pub/cypherpunks/swIPe/`. This reference implementation advertises compatibility with SunOS 4.1.3 and 4.1.3_U1.

IPv4 and IPv6 Security Protocols

Work is afoot in the form of several Internet drafts to formally define IP-layer security services for both IPv4 (the current version of IP) and IPv6 (the next generation, still under design). Although these documents are technically classified as "work in progress" at the time of this writing—meaning they can be updated, replaced, or made obsolete at any time during their limited lifetime—there is a very good chance that the services ultimately brought to table will be close to what they now describe. IP security is far too important to be dismissed outright, and most of the core technologies that can enable IP security services are now ripe for the taking.

One draft, Security Architecture for the Internet Protocol (Atkinson 1995a), describes these two forms of IP headers that have been formulated:

- IP Authentication Header (AH)
- IP Encapsulating Security Payload (ESP)

Both forms offer services resembling those of swIPe; in fact, swIPe played an inspirational role in their development. As with swIPe, IPv4 can accommodate both mechanisms through the Options field of the IP datagram header. The proposed mechanisms are more widely adaptable than swIPe, however.

The Authentication Header furnishes sender authentication and datagram integrity, but not confidentiality. It achieves this by both prepending and appending the same 128-bit secret key to most of the datagram (specifically, to an aggregation of those fields that do not change in transit), and then using MD5 to compute a hash value of the result. The receiving end can of course duplicate the calculation, and deduce whether the correct key was used and if the datagram arrived intact. The draft specification calls for this particular scheme to be universally implemented in IPv6, and by all IPv4 implementations claiming to support AH. Other authentication and integrity techniques, such as digital signatures, also can be used to supplement these schemes.

The Encapsulating Security Payload provides sender authentication, integrity, and confidentiality in two different modes. The first is Tunnel-mode, a swIPe-like scheme in which the entire IP datagram is encrypted and encapsulated in a new datagram. The second is Transport-mode, in which only the

IP datagram's payload (that is, the TCP or UDP packet) is encrypted and encapsulated. Transport mode boosts efficiency by reducing bandwidth consumption and cryptographic processing; it makes sense to use it when the communicating hosts are not separated by a security gateway, and the addition of encrypted IP headers would add little or no value (see fig. 24.3). In both cases, the draft mandates implementation of DES in CBC mode, although additional cryptosystems also can be accommodated.

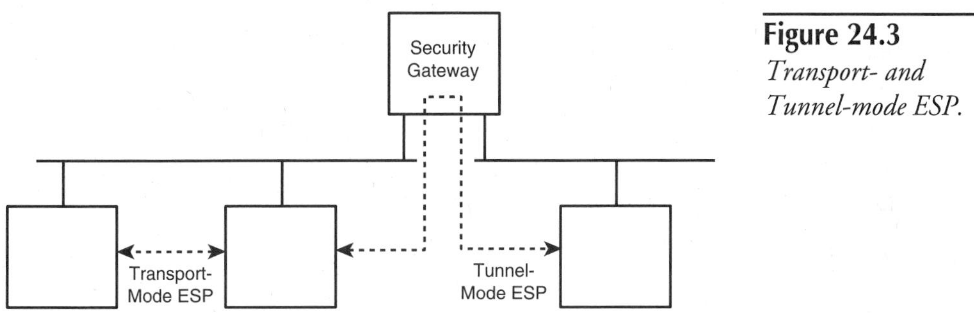

Figure 24.3
Transport- and Tunnel-mode ESP.

For obvious reasons, key management is a significant theme for IP security. Unfortunately, as of yet there is no Internet standard or de facto protocol for key management. The drafts really have little choice but to sidestep the issue, saying that they try to "decouple the key management mechanisms from the security protocol mechanisms" (Atkinson 1995b). They do wisely point out, however, that this separation allows alterations to key management protocols to be essentially transparent to the actual security protocols.

Two main points related to key management should be mentioned here. In the AH and ESP mechanisms, one function of the key management system is the derivation of security associations, that is, local information bases that map security parameters to destination addresses. These parameters include the chosen authentication and encryption algorithms, related keys, key lifetime, and other variables specific to each destination system. As you can see, each security association is one-way, yet two associations are required—one on each end—for two hosts to communicate securely.

Moreover, security associations also might depend on the sending user. AH and ESP support both host-oriented and user-oriented keying. The former is what you would normally expect for network-layer security involving two systems; the same key is applied to all datagrams emanating from one system to the other, irrespective of the originating user or users. In other words, all users of the sending system "share" the same association key. The latter approach allows for user-specific session keys—or even multiple keys per user, say one for file transfer and one for Telnet—which greatly confounds cryptanalytic attack.

Because of governmental restrictions on the export and application of robust encryption schemes across some national borders—including those here in the U.S.—ESP cannot provide true worldwide interoperability. AH, however, can be implemented more or less ubiquitously, because it was designed with that exact purpose in mind.

SNMPv1 and SNMPv2

The Simple Network Management Protocol (SNMP) described in RFC 1157 (Case et al. 1990) is widely used to monitor and control the activities and behavior of devices on TCP/IP networks. Even small networks benefit from SNMP management practices, because they provide a sophisticated portal into the hardware and software workings of entities using the network to communicate.

Note The version of SNMP most widely implemented today, and also endorsed as a recommended Internet protocol for all TCP/IP implementations, is version 1 (SNMPv1). Version 2 (SNMPv2) is still an Elective protocol, which offers significant security improvements, among others.

Figure 24.4 shows the general SNMP framework; it consists of the following:

- **Management stations.** Workstations that issue queries and commands to managed elements, and receive and process their responses. They also provide a user interface, often based on the X Window System or a similar windowing environment, for network managers to observe and influence managed elements from a remote location.

- **Managed elements.** Entities that are monitored and sometimes partially controlled by management stations. These are commonly intermediate devices like routers and gateways, though large hosts, desktop workstations, and other entities also might participate in varying degrees. Special agents within the elements provide the interface to SNMP.
- **Management information base.** Otherwise known as a MIB, a collection of variables that can be examined or altered by management stations through the agents. MIB variables represent a broad and extensible set of objects, such as network addresses, character strings, counters and other statistics, state variables, and so on. They also are classified into groups, such as the System group, Interfaces group, IP group, UDP group, TCP group, and others.
- **Management protocol.** SNMP proper, an application-level protocol that operates over UDP, to facilitate communication of management stations and agents.

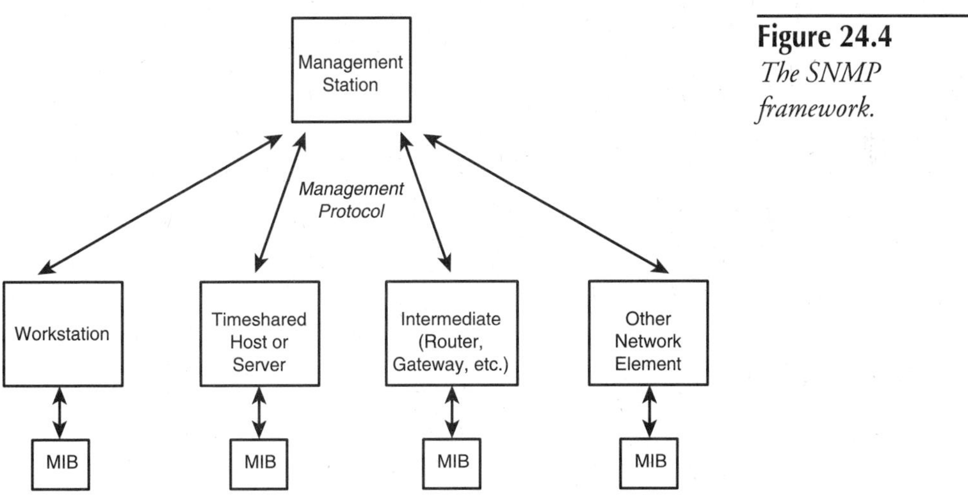

Figure 24.4
The SNMP framework.

The management protocol, befitting its name, is rather simple by design. The SNMP inventors wisely planned an elementary scheme that could be compactly coded into devices possessing even minimal intelligence and capacity.

(Long-time Interop attendees still chuckle over the famed Internet Toaster that would brown a few slices on demand from a nearby management station.) From the outset the idea was to create a network management infrastructure that did not detrimentally impact network performance. After all, routers should be free to expend the greater part of their energy on routing packets, not on reporting that they are unable to route due to management tasks.

SNMP communication takes on three flavors:

- **Get.** For MIB variable polling, used by the management station to create threshold alarms and the like
- **Set.** For altering a variable's value from the management station, possibly triggering an intended side effect such as causing the managed element to reset a counter or to reboot
- **Trap.** For agents to asynchronously notify the management station of a significant event, such as a change in the availability status of a communication link

In this vein, each SNMP message bears one of several message identifiers, or Protocol Data Units (PDUs). The PDUs for SNMPv1 are listed in table 24.1, and for SNMPv2 in table 24.2.

Table 24.1
SNMPv1 Protocol Data Units

PDU Type	Meaning
get-request	Request to retrieve a specific MIB variable
get-next-request	Request to retrieve next variable in the table (used when iteratively walking through MIB tables)
get-response	Response to a get-request or get-next-request PDU
set-request	Request to alter a MIB variable
trap	Asynchronous notification of an event (agent to manager)

Table 24.2
SNMPv2 Protocol Data Units

PDU Type	Meaning
get-request	Request to retrieve a specific MIB variable
get-next-request	Request to retrieve next variable in the table (used for iteratively walking through MIB tables)
get-bulk-request	Request to retrieve an entire table
response	Response generated by any other PDU
set-request	Request to alter a MIB variable
snmpV2-trap	Asynchronous notification of an event (agent to manager)
inform-request	Asynchronous notification of an event (manager to manager)

In addition to a given PDU, SNMP messages also contain authentication credentials that can be used to apply access control restrictions. The need for authentication is hopefully clear; read and write access to some MIB variables may be vital for security, especially those that could reveal sensitive information about a system, or cause an action (like a reboot) that results in a temporary denial of service or more insidious outcome.

The original version of SNMP (SNMPv1) utilizes a so-called trivial authentication mechanism in which effectively all messages are deemed authentic. Each agent knows an alleged secret—essentially a password, but called a community name—also known by the managing station. The community name is transmitted in cleartext in every PDU. Clearly, community names are visible to network eavesdroppers, who can use them to forge their own messages or replay old ones at will. The effects of such attacks can range from harmless to harmful, depending on the local configuration and the variables in question.

SNMPv2, however, supports several viable security mechanisms described in RFC 1446 (Galvin and McCloghrie 1993). Through cryptographic means, the new SNMPv2 message formats provide integrity, sender authentication, and confidentiality services where they are needed. The trivial authentication is still supported for practical reasons, although technically speaking an SNMP implementation that supports only trivial authentication does not conform to SNMPv2 security.

The SNMP Digest Authentication Protocol uses—you've probably guessed it by now—MD5 as its vehicle for establishing sender authenticity and message integrity. In the current implementation, the original message, a secret shared by the sender and the receiver, and the sending system's current time are input to MD5. The resulting hash value is sent in company of the message and can be verified by the receiver through the identical calculation. The timestamp serves primarily to deter replay attacks, though it requires clock synchronization between the sending and receiving parties. SNMPv2 actually supports an optional clock acceleration mechanism within the protocol, whereby the receiver of a message can choose to forward (but never rewind) its clock to align with the sender's clock. Because such adjustments are subtle and monotonically increasing, they are purported to enhance the effectiveness of the protocol without weakening it.

Confidentiality is achieved through the SNMP Symmetric Privacy Protocol, which currently calls for messages to be encrypted using DES in CBC mode. The communicating SNMP entities know the same symmetric DES key. The Digest Authentication Protocol is applied to messages before symmetric DES encryption is performed.

Both the Digest Access Protocol and Symmetric Privacy Protocol involve the notion of a party. A party consists of an SNMP entity associated with exactly one authentication and one encryption algorithm, plus other factors. Access control operations on MIB variables are enforced on a party basis. Although DES and MD5 are required for initial SNMPv2 security compliance, the use of other algorithms is possible for the future.

Firewalls: Filters and Gateways

A booming and revolutionary trend in network security of late involves the use of firewalls. Firewalls are a collection of filters and gateways that shield trusted networks within a locally managed security perimeter from external, untrusted networks (usually meaning the Internet at large). Using a firewall strategy insulates the (hopefully) controllable "inside" environment from the hazards of the (definitely) uncontrollable "outside," in much the same way that a fireproof wall acts as a protective barrier against spreading flames. Unlike their pyric counterparts, however, network firewalls have a vested interest in letting precise types of traffic advance through, to afford access to what is usually a very limited, and presumably secure, set of services (see fig. 24.5).

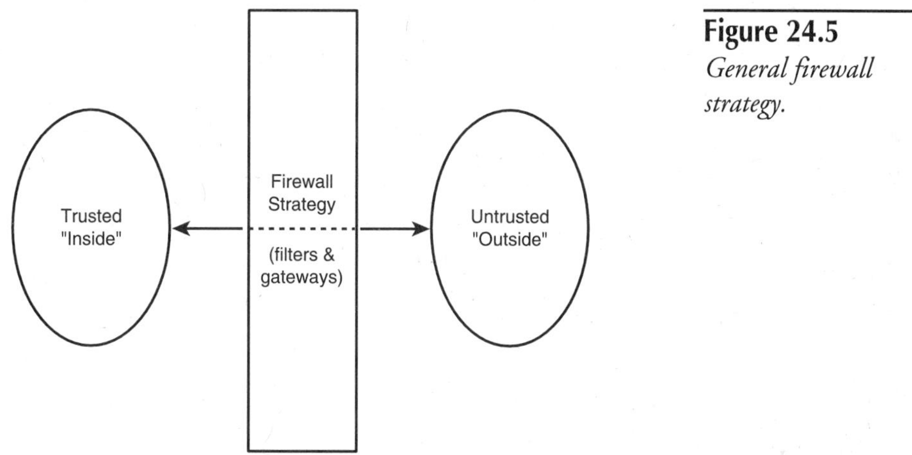

Figure 24.5
General firewall strategy.

Note This brief discussion of firewalls uses the terms inside and outside to mean the networks within and without a security perimeter, respectively.

There are a number of permutable firewall strategies offering varying levels of security, a few of which are described in the following sections. The decision to construct a firewall, and the design and implementation that follows, is somewhat of a unique process for each site. Aside from grappling with the technical issues of providing valuable services through a firewall in a secure way, a number of other variables inevitably come into play. These include the access policy (both inbound and outbound; they usually differ), and the initial and ongoing cost of equipment, software, and manpower. On one end of a spectrum, a loose and liberal access policy coupled with a roll-your-own approach, something quite common in university environments, can be uncomplicated and inexpensive. At the other end, a business operating in a highly competitive marketplace may want very little information to come in—or out—and think nothing of spending six digits to see that it happens.

A complete examination of firewall theory and implementation is beyond the scope of this book; interested readers should consult New Riders Publishing's *Internet Firewalls and Network Security* for a thorough and pragmatic treatment of the subject. Additionally, a succinct but contributive source of information containing valuable pointers is the Internet Firewalls FAQ, maintained by Trusted Information Systems, Inc. The FAQ is available for anonymous FTP as `ftp://rtfm.mit.edu/pub/usenet/news.answers/firewalls-faq`.

Packet Filters and Screening Routers

Packet filters can provide a sensible first line of defense in any firewall strategy. Situated between a common border of neighboring networks, packet filters play the role of lower-layer protocol sentry, deciding who shall pass and who shall not.

A packet filter functions by examining the header of each packet as it arrives for disbursement to another network. It then applies a series of rules against the header information to determine if the packet should be blocked or forwarded in its intended direction. As you can see from the flowchart in figure 24.6, which outlines the filtering operation, the order in which rules are applied to the header is significant; the first rule encountered that explicitly blocks or allows forwarding of the packet is the sole deciding factor. If a packet matches no rule after the rule list is exhausted, an implicit blocking rule is assumed.

The most common instantiations of packet filters are those bundled with router software. Because these devices already play a key role in interconnecting networks to the Internet, filters usually can be enabled for only the cost of configuring and testing, and subsequent blow-by-blow processing. Routers that implement filtering functions are sometimes called screening routers. Although routers typically mind the IP layer and ignore the higher ones, those that implement filtering can "peek" into the transport layer when necessary to fulfill their task.

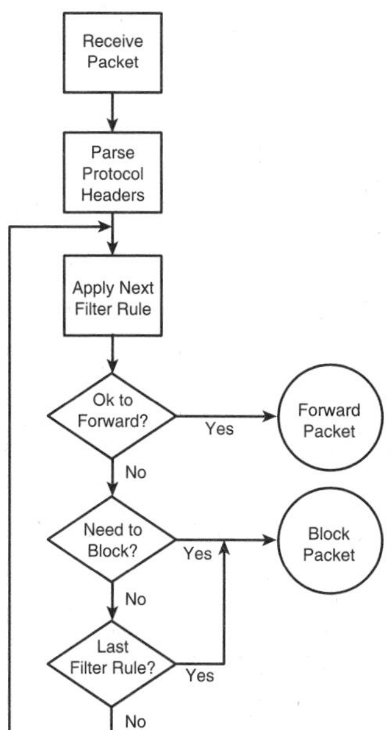

Figure 24.6
Packet filter flowchart.

Filters can address a multitude of concerns through the rule configuration. Following are some practical examples:

- Block all incoming traffic from a specific external network, or collection of networks
- Block overtly hazardous incoming traffic from all external networks, such as that for NFS and X
- Allow only incoming SMTP traffic from all external networks
- Allow all outbound, but no inbound, Telnet sessions

Although it might sound easy to implement packet filters, in fact it is very tricky business. Filters are complicated beasts to configure, largely because they require a thorough understanding of the network, transport, and in some cases application protocols to which they can be applied. A misconfigured filter can easily undermine or destroy the very security policy it is designed to uphold.

To define a single filter rule, certain questions need to be answered and relevant information compiled in advance:

- Action—Do you want the filter to allow or block an action?
- Protocol—At what protocol layer are you filtering (typically either IP or TCP)?
- Source IP address
- Source port number (for TCP)
- Destination IP address
- Destination port number (again, for TCP)
- Flags (for TCP) and options (for IP)

The source and destination network addresses usually can be expressed as wild-card values; it is feasible, for example, to define a rule that applies to "all destination addresses" or "all source addresses in the 198.41.0.0 network." Similarly, port numbers can be wild-carded or given as bounded values, as in "all destination TCP ports greater than 5999." Table 24.3 shows a few filter rules along these lines.

Table 24.3
Example Filter Rules

Action	Protocol	Src Address	Src Port	Dest Address	Dest Port	Flags & Options
allow	tcp	198.41.0.0	43	*	*	-
block	tcp	*	*	*	>5999	-

TCP flags and IP options are sometimes weighty variables in a rule equation. Consider the case of a site that recently decides to allow all outbound Telnet sessions through its packet filter, while also maintaining an existing set of rules (not given here) that prohibits nearly all inbound access, Telnet included. This new policy requires two rules, one for Telnet packets going out, and one for packets coming in. (Telnet is, after all, a full-duplex service, as is the TCP transport on which it rides.) The first rule should allow all TCP connections originating from any inside address destined for port 23 (Telnet's well-known port) on any outside address.

The second rule cannot be simply the inverse of the first, that is, the filter cannot (or more correctly should not) allow all inbound packets originating from port 23. Although such packets usually originate from remote telnet servers, this faulty rule would enable an outside attacker to bind his own malicious client application—instead of a Telnet server—to port 23 on a machine he controls, and then use the application to establish TCP connections to systems across the filter. The fine distinction here is which side opens the connection, something that is made clear only by the flags field in the TCP header. TCP packets that lack an ACK flag are indicative of TCP active open requests; those with the flag constitute replies. Therefore the second filter rule should allow inbound TCP packets from port 23 only if the ACK bit is set. Both rules are represented in table 24.4.

Table 24.4
Filter Rules for Allowing Outbound Telnet

Action	Protocol	Src Address	Src Port	Dest Address	Dest Port	Flags & Options
allow	tcp	inside	*	*	23	-
allow	tcp	outside	23	*	*	ACK

Generally speaking, it is easier to define filters for IP and TCP than it is for UDP. Because UDP is connectionless, the absence of even trivial state information (like the TCP ACK flag just described) is absent. Is a given UDP packet a valid reply from an outside server to an inside client—or is it an attempt to worm past the filter and probe an inside host? It may be difficult or impossible to tell. Sites that can get by with filtering all UDP traffic lead easier lives.

Aside from router-supported packet filters, popular ones with the same (or better) functionality are available for various platforms. Two good alternatives for ubiquitous PC hardware, which are inexpensive machines well-suited to dedicated filtering tasks, are Karlbridge (available at `ftp://ftp.net.ohio-state.edu/pub/kbridge/`) and Drawbridge (`ftp://net.tamu.edu:/pub/security/TAMU/`).

Application Gateways

Various firewall strategies can be applied to the application layer through application gateways. This discussion loosely classifies application gateways into three categories: relays, proxies, and server filters.

Relays

Relay gateways are essentially tiny programs that do little more than pass opaque (unstructured) data to and from a source—the application client—and destination—the application server. Their action is usually automatic, triggered by the initial client connection. To the client, the relay walks and talks exactly like the server; to the server, the relay is the client. Relays take a laissez faire attitude toward the data they handle, caring only for their receipt and delivery.

It is possible to implement relays over both the TCP and UDP transports. Relays are useful for a variety of reasons, including special-case firewall traversal. Figure 24.7 illustrates one case. A gateway system running a relay appears to offer a whois service that actually is provided by a system behind the firewall. This tack allows the service to be freely moved, or even served redundantly, on the inside network, while also revealing nothing about the internal network topology or DNS system if these are to be kept secret. The gateway could of course offer the whois service by itself, but in figure 24.7 the gateway is openly exposed to the world. Although a whois database of names, addresses, and phone numbers is rarely mission-critical, it is nevertheless more secure within the bounds of a security perimeter.

This particular example in figure 24.7 portrays an inbound firewall traversal; a similar scheme can be used for outbound connections when needed.

Listing 24.1 contains C-language source code for a simple TCP Unix relay called passthru. The program should be configured to run under inetd by making the appropriate entry in /etc/inetd.conf and restarting the server. To follow up on the whois example, the inetd.conf entry would look something like this:

```
whois stream tcp nowait nobody /usr/local/etc/passthru passthru
➥198.41.0.6 43
```

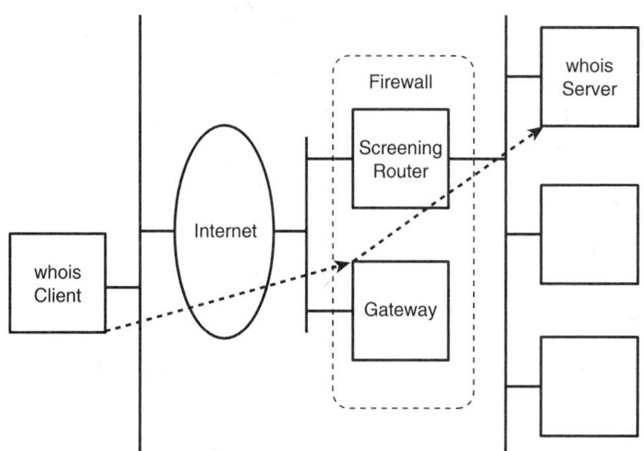

Figure 24.7
Relay firewall traversal.

The passthru program is intentionally small and simple by design, generally a wise philosophy for gateway tools. Large, cumbersome programs have a greater likelihood of containing concealed bugs that can later be exploited. Nevertheless, a few obvious enhancements could be made to the program, such as to optionally support a host name as the first parameter, and to assume the identical destination port if the second argument is absent.

Finally, it is really best to run a relay such as this beneath a server filter, to log all client accesses if not to restrict them to some degree. Server filters are discussed later in this chapter.

Listing 24.1

```
/*
==================================================================
 *
 * Program: passthru.c (pass-through relay)
 *
 * Relays a TCP client connection to an alternate server on
 * another system and/or port.
 * It is best configured to run with a server filter
 * (such as TCP Wrapper or xinetd) to log and possibly
 * restrict client access.
 * Usage:    passthru address port
 * Example:  passthru 19.252.59.63 250
 *
 *
================================================================*/
```

continues

Listing 24.1, Continued

```
/*
==========================================================================
 * Includes
 *
========================================================================*/
#include <sys/types.h>
#include <sys/time.h>
#include <stdio.h>
#include <stdlib.h>
#include <netinet/in.h>
#include <arpa/inet.h>
#include <sys/socket.h>

/*
==========================================================================
 * Defines
 *
========================================================================*/
#define TRUE  1
#define FALSE 0

/*
==========================================================================
 * Prototypes
 *
========================================================================*/
int main(int argc, char *argv[]);
int RelayConnection(int client, int server);
int NetWrite(int socket, char *buffer, int length);

/*
==========================================================================
 * Main
 *
========================================================================*/
int main(int argc, char *argv[])
{
  int one = 1;
  int port;
  int serverSocket;
  u_long address;
  struct sockaddr_in serverAddress;

  /* Process the arguments */
  if (argc != 3)
```

```
{
  printf("Usage: %s address port\n", argv[0]);
  exit(1);
}

if ((address = inet_addr(argv[1])) == -1)
{
  printf("Usage: %s address port\n", argv[0]);
  exit(2);
}

if ((port = atoi(argv[2])) <= 0)
{
  printf("Usage: %s address port\n", argv[0]);
  exit(3);
}

 /* Create socket for connection to remote server */
if ((serverSocket = socket(AF_INET, SOCK_STREAM, 0)) == -1)
{
  perror("socket");
  exit(4);
}

/* Set keepalive on client and server sockets so we can detect
➥half-open connections */
if (setsockopt(0, SOL_SOCKET, SO_KEEPALIVE,
                      (char *)&one, sizeof(one)) == -1)
{
  perror("setsockopt");
  exit(5);
}
if (setsockopt(serverSocket, SOL_SOCKET, SO_KEEPALIVE,
                      (char *)&one, sizeof(one)) == -1)
{
  perror("setsockopt");
  exit(6);
}

/* Build the server address structure */
memset((char *)&serverAddress, '\0', sizeof(serverAddress));
memcpy((char *)&serverAddress.sin_addr, (char *)&address,
➥sizeof(address));
serverAddress.sin_port   = htons(port);
serverAddress.sin_family = AF_INET;

/* Connect to the remote server */
```

continues

Listing 24.1, Continued

```
  if (connect(serverSocket, (struct sockaddr *)&serverAddress,
              sizeof(struct sockaddr)) == -1)
  {
    perror("connect");
    exit(7);
  }

  /* Relay the connection */
  RelayConnection(0, serverSocket);
  close(serverSocket);

  exit(0);
}

/*
===================================================================
 * Relay Connection
 *
==================================================================*/
int RelayConnection(int client, int server)
{
  int  numSelected;
  int  rBytes, wBytes;
  char buffer[1024];
  fd_set ibits;

  /*
   * Read bytes from client and send to server, and vice versa.
   * Do this until one side goes away or an error is detected.
   */
  FD_ZERO(&ibits);
  while (TRUE)
  {
    FD_SET(client, &ibits);
    FD_SET(server, &ibits);

    numSelected =
      select(16, &ibits, (fd_set *)0, (fd_set *)0, (struct timeval
    ➥ *)0);

    if (numSelected == -1)
    {
      perror("select");
      break;
    }
```

```
    /* client -> server */
    else if (FD_ISSET(client, &ibits))
    {
      rBytes = read(client, buffer, sizeof(buffer));
      if (rBytes <= 0) break;
      wBytes = NetWrite(server, buffer, rBytes);
      if (wBytes != rBytes) break;
    }

    /* server -> client */
    else if (FD_ISSET(server, &ibits))
    {
      rBytes = read(server, buffer, sizeof(buffer));
      if (rBytes <= 0) break;
      wBytes = NetWrite(client, buffer, rBytes);
      if (wBytes != rBytes) break;
    }

  }
}

/*
==========================================================================
 * Network Write
 *
==========================================================================*/
int NetWrite(int socket, char *buffer, int length)
{
  int numToWrite, numWritten;

  /*
   * Write the entire buffer or die trying.  Might take several
➥ *attempts.
   */
  numToWrite = length;
  do
  {
    numWritten = write(socket, buffer, numToWrite);
    if (numWritten == -1)
    {
      perror("write");
      return(-1);
    }
    buffer += numWritten;
    numToWrite -= numWritten;
  } while (numToWrite > 0);
  return(length);
}
```

Proxies

Proxy gateways, also called application proxies, generally come in two flavors: generic and application-aware. Both cases are analogous to the relay concept just introduced; the proxy acts as a server to an application client and as a client to an application server. Proxies are most useful for assisting inside clients to access outside servers, though this paradigm isn't always strictly enforced.

Generic Proxies

Generic proxies, like the TCP-based socks system originally developed by David Koblas, are highly useful but unfortunately not application-transparent by nature. With generic proxies, an inside client that wants to communicate with an outside server begins by opening a connection to the proxy server (like socks' sockd), and proceeds through a mini proxy-specific protocol to indicate the actual server's location. The proxy opens the connection on behalf of the client, at which point the normal application protocol commences; the proxy changes face to become a simple relay.

As you might imagine, the standard fare of FTP, Telnet, and Finger services are naturals for proxy conversion, as are popular WWW clients of late. As already said, making a client proxy-aware is not application transparent; to implement the proxy protocol, a runtime change at least is required. socks achieves this nicely by providing a library, libsocks.a, with replacement functions for the Berkeley sockets API. Applications can be retouched to explicitly call the new networking functions (Rconnect() for connect(), Rbind() for bind(), and so forth); alternatively, their build procedures can be modified to automatically redefine the calls through the C preprocessor.

The proxy might, and really should, also implement some type of access control. In the case of socks, a map of valid clients, servers, and application services can be defined in /etc/sockd.conf using a flexible rule language. socks also can restrict access based on the client user's IDENT information; because systems running behind the firewall are supposedly trustworthy, their IDENT servers also should be. (This is one of the few cases where IDENT reports might be considered honorable.) Your mileage may vary.

A proper authentication mechanism is conspicuously absent from version 4 of the socks protocol; this is currently being addressed in the design of version 5, with additional extensions to support applications that use the UDP transport. Plans are taking shape for a negotiable authentication scheme, initially supporting both a GSS-API and a cleartext static password scheme. This work is known as the Authenticated Firewall Traversal (AFT) effort of the IETF's Security Area working group. The relevant Internet draft documents are available at `ftp://ds.internic.net/internet-drafts/`. The socks version 4 distribution is available at `ftp://ftp.nec.com/pub/security/socks.cstc/`.

Application-Aware Proxies

Unlike relays and generic proxies, application-aware proxies are proxy server implementations that are entirely cognizant of the application protocols they support. An FTP proxy implements FTP; a Telnet proxy implements Telnet; and so on. Needless to say, proxies in this class are subject to little reuse of source code from one application to another.

At the cost of greater complexity, application-aware proxies offer at least three major advantages over generic proxies:

1. Because they fully understand the application protocols, they often can be used with native application clients. These generally require users to manually input the outside server information, because it is not automatically forthcoming through a proxy protocol. (This is not always the case; some might require a mechanism like socks, and still achieve the following benefits.)

2. The proxy can inhibit the client from performing actions considered undesirable for some reason; a paranoid FTP proxy at the Federal Bureau of Information Consumption might allow employees to download files but prevent uploads.

3. Depending on the application, the proxy might take some liberties to improve overall efficiency. A WWW proxy, for example, might temporarily cache frequented URLs to husband outside bandwidth.

The TIS Firewall Toolkit, available at `ftp://ftp.tis.com/pub/firewalls/toolkit/`, contains a number of useful proxy servers:

- ftp-gw—FTP proxy
- http-gw—WWW and Gopher proxy
- rlogin-gw—rlogin proxy
- tn-gw—Telnet proxy
- x-gw—X proxy
- plug-gw—A relay proxy, similar to passthru

These proxies are not the socks-ified type. As such, unmodified clients can be used with them; each proxy prompts users for the location of the outside server.

The TIS toolkit also includes a number of useful gateway utilities, like netacl, which is analogous to the TCP Wrapper filter described next; and smap, an inetd-driven minimal SMTP server designed to operate unprivileged in a chroot environment (in loud contrast to sendmail, which as you've seen is a security hotbed).

Server Filters

Also called *host-based firewalls*, server filters run on the same hosts as the server programs they protect, operating strictly at the application layer. In many cases, they can even provide their flavor of access control without a single modification to the server application's source code, as you soon see.

At the uppermost layer in the network model, the filtering methodology is quite different from that used by packet filters. Here, at least for TCP-based applications, most concept of network protocol information (packets, flags, and so on) is lost, leaving merely the source and destination address and port information. That is to say, these are the network parameters available at the application layer before the application protocol ever gears up for action. They therefore comprise most of what the filtering rules are based on.

On Unix systems, the more interesting cases of server filters are those that apply to inetd-managed services, like Telnet, Finger, and Talk, to name a few prominent ones. To make an analogy, inetd does for Unix what a switchboard operator does for a business: it simultaneously listens for incoming calls on multiple application ports. When one arrives, inetd forks (spawns) a child process that executes the appropriate server program, and forwards the client's call to it. For TCP-based services, this sequence typically occurs with every new client connection; for UDP, commonly one short-lived server process handles all subsequent client requests for a window of time before returning listening responsibility to inetd (see fig. 24.8).

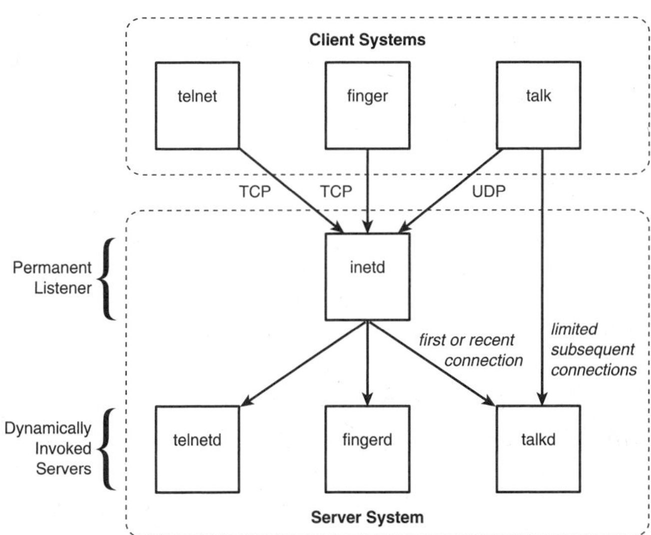

Figure 24.8
inetd operation.

Clearly, having one listener for a dozen services is more efficient than having a dozen listeners for one service each. For TCP-based applications, inetd also simplifies server development, because network setup calls to a transport API needn't be coded into the application. When inetd dispatches a client connection to an application server, the network becomes the server's standard input, output, and error channels.

As you see shortly, the inetd architecture just described lends itself favorably to host-based server filtering. Stand-alone servers are not as fortunate; they must perform their own filtering, either through a home-brew mechanism, or a generic one offered through an API. Either way, explicit modifications to the server source code are in order.

Several server filters are freely available on the Internet. A highly popular one is the so-called TCP Wrapper, described next. Others include netacl, mentioned in the preceding section, and xinetd.

TCP Wrapper

The TCP Wrapper (also known as tcpd) is one of many security packages authored or coauthored by Wietse Venema, including logdaemon and SATAN. TCP Wrapper can be found at `ftp://ftp.win.tue.nl/pub/security/`, along with the other packages and sundry security-related papers and utilities.

TCP Wrapper provides server filtering for both inetd-driven and stand-alone servers. The former is explored here; suffice to say that the latter is achieved through the package's libwrap.a library, which can be linked with most any network server application when source code is available. Documentation that accompanies the wrapper distribution describes the libwrap API, which provides identical service to that described here. (In fact, tcpd uses the selfsame library.)

The primary services offered by tcpd are twofold: filtering and logging. One can be used without the other, although a combined approach is recommended to this readership. Some sites choose to run tcpd simply for its logging potential; this can be a mistake, as highly beneficial as the logging may be. (To emphasize this point, consider two questions: How many of the millions of systems on the Internet need to access your telnet server? and Is reading about a successful attack after the fact good enough for you?) Barring the presence of other firewall insulators, as is the case on many networks, host-based server filters like tcpd are practically indispensable.

tcpd is engaged on an inetd service by effectively "sandwiching" it between inetd and the server program. The mechanics of doing this can occur in several ways, but in all cases the effect is the same; inetd invokes tcpd, which dutifully logs and filters the connection. tcpd then invokes the server application if it passes the filter inspection (see fig. 24.9). Note that most UDP-based servers are particularly troublesome, such as talkd. Because these servers wrestle control of new connections from inetd for a self-determined amount of time, tcpd's security services are temporarily suspended.

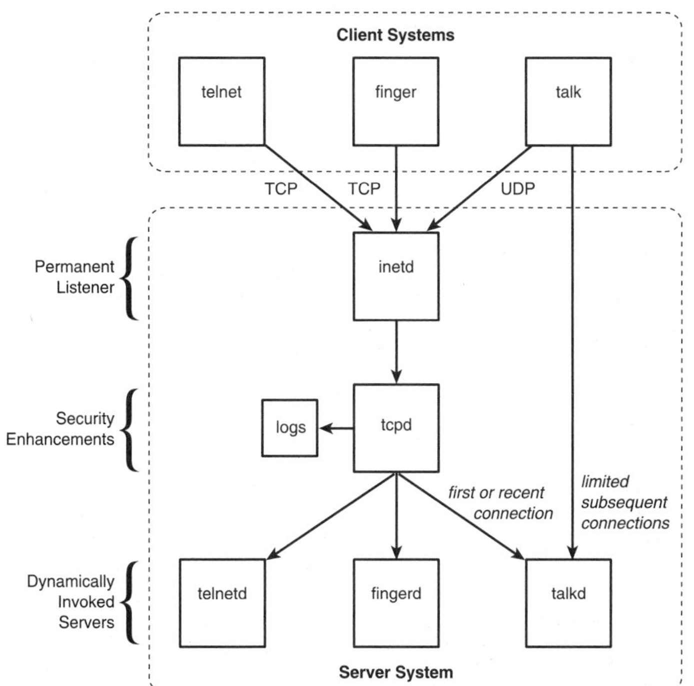

Figure 24.9
inetd operation with tcpd.

At the heart of tcpd's strength lies a rich access control language used to construct filter rules. (There are actually two versions of the language; the one described here is the more flexible "extended" language.) The general format of a given rule is as follows:

daemon_list : *client_list* [: *option* ...]

where *daemon_list* is a list of one or more applicable server names (such as rlogind or ftpd) or a keyword like ALL; *client_list* is a collection of host names or network addresses (possibly wild-carded); and *option* specifies an access control consideration or action.

Note Rules may be specified in either one or two databases per the local preference. Some administrators prefer to separate "allow" and "deny" rules into two databases; others prefer them consolidated into one. The rule-searching engine by default always consults /etc/hosts.allow and /etc/hosts.deny in that order, if either or both exist. If not, or an applicable rule is not found in either database, then tcpd allows access.

Among the supported rule options are the following:

- **Allow or Deny.** One of these always appears as the final option in a rule, when one appears at all, to conclude whether the connection should be permitted or refused. Neither action need be specified if both the hosts.allow and hosts.deny databases are used, as the action is implicitly based on its location. If either action is present in a rule, regardless of which database the rule is contained in, the specified action is followed.
- **Severity.** This option defines the syslog facility and severity level for the rule. tcpd logs its actions through syslog; the actual location of logged messages is determined by the action, severity level, and contents of syslog's configuration file (usually /etc/syslog.conf). The default is mail - .info for allowed connections, and mail.warning for denied connections.
- **Spawn.** Executes arbitrary shell commands in a child process to enhance tcpd's logging or warning capability. This option might be used to update a custom log file, send an e-mail message, or activate someone's beeper. The commands can include special macros that are expanded immediately prior to execution, such as %a meaning the client's IP address, %h meaning its host name (if resolvable through the DNS), %d meaning the application service name, %u meaning the client user's account name (if available; see rfc931 below), and others.
- **Twist.** Executes the specified shell command in the current process, in place of the normal application server program. This is useful for invoking alternate daemons for special clients, or even printing a blunt warning message to potential intruders.
- **Banners.** The name of a directory containing application-specific banners that tcpd should transmit to TCP-based clients. This is useful for displaying a warning message to users, perhaps to inform them that the system is for authorized use only. The same macros as for spawn also can be used; a banner that reads "Hello %u, your access from %h is now logged" may intimidate some mild-mannered attackers.
- **Rfc931.** Causes an IDENT query to be made to the client system, in an attempt to determine the client user's account name. The successful result, else the placeholder name "unknown," is expanded in place of the %u macro used by spawn, twist, and banners.

- **Umask.** Defines a default (and hopefully secure) protection mask for files later created by the application server. This prevents the server from accidentally creating world- or group-writable files. 022 usually is a good choice.
- **User.** Causes the server to run under the specified account name and optional group association. Some inetd implementations run every server as root, a dangerous practice for those servers that do not really require superuser privileges.
- **Nice.** Changes the server's nice value (process priority). This is useful for bumping down the priority of noncritical services.

To give an example, the following tcpd rule:

```
ftpd : 199.72. : spawn (/usr/local/etc/mylogger %d %a)& : banners
➥/etc/banners : deny
```

denies FTP connections from the 199.72 network. Additionally, the daemon's name (ftpd) and the client's IP address are given as arguments to the site's custom logging program (mylogger). To explain the refusal, or perhaps to bark a warning, the file /etc/banners/ftpd is displayed to the FTP client following any macro expansion.

Warning Use of the %h and %u macros with the spawn and twist options is potentially dangerous because they expand to values derived outside the local system (namely through DNS and IDENT, respectively). Sophisticated attacks against tcpd can cause these macros to take on "bomb" values that persuade the shell interpreter to do evil things. Consider an apparently innocent spawn option that looks like this:

```
spawn (/usr/local/etc/mylogger %h)&
```

If the attacker can successfully forge a subversive DNS response on the client name query, the shell command that actually gets executed might look like this, or worse:

```
/usr/local/etc/mylogger ;/etc/shutdown
```

A favorite trick with tcpd involves fingering the client site to record all its current users. In case of an attack, this information can be useful in narrowing down the suspects. In this sample rule, tcpd's safe_finger program is used, which filters potentially harmful output from amoral finger servers under control of an attacker:

```
fingerd : ALL : spawn (/usr/local/bin/safe_finger @%a >> /var/log/
fingerlog) _: allow
```

Exercise caution when booby-trapping services like this, lest a "finger war" quickly escalate out of control, inducing a meltdown of one or both systems. If the remote site has rigged its server in the same way, the results may be sad and unpredictable.

Note that most of tcpd's access control decisions are based on a rule's client_list—usually comprised of network addresses and host names—which we know to be unauthenticated. The standard disclaimers apply here; tcpd cannot defend itself from address masquerading, or address spoofing, although it can detect and reject those based on source routing attacks. Furthermore, tcpd is truly at the mercy of the unsecure DNS where host names are used in access rules; it is usually safer, although perhaps less convenient, to specify network addresses.

Finally, to take full advantage of tcpd, log profusely and examine religiously. Signs of break-in attempts often are readily visible with only minor effort expended daily.

Bibliography

Atkinson, Randall. 1995a. Security Architecture for the Internet Protocol. Work in progress. Draft document available for anonymous FTP at `ftp://ietf.cnri.reston.va.us/internet-drafts/draft-ietf-ipsec-arch-02.txt`.

Atkinson, Randall. 1995b. IP Authentication Header. Work in progress. Draft document available for anonymous FTP at `ftp://ietf.cnri.reston.va.us/internet.drafts/draft-ietf-ipsec-auth-02.txt`.

Case, Jeffery D., Mark Fedor, Martin Lee Schoffstall, and James R. Davin. 1990. A Simple Network Management Protocol (SNMP). Internet RFC 1157. Available for anonymous FTP at `ftp://ds.internic.net/pub/rfc/`.

Galvin, James M., and Keith McCloghrie. 1993. Security Protocols for Version 2 of the Simple Network Management Protocol (SNMPv2). Internet RFC 1446. Available for anonymous FTP at `ftp://ds.internic.net/pub/rfc/`.

Ioannidis, John, and Matt Blaze. 1993. The Architecture and Implementation of Network-Layer Security Under Unix. Proceedings of the Fourth Usenix Unix Security Symposium, 29-39. Available for anonymous FTP at `ftp://research.att.com/dist/mab/swipeusenix.ps`.

Kent, Stephen. 1991. U.S. Department of Defense Security Options for the interent Protocol. Internet RFC 1108. Available for anonymous FTP at `ftp://ds.internic.net/pub/rfc/`.

CGI and SHTML Security

by Paul Buis

Both the Common Gateway Interface *(CGI) mechanism and the* Server Parsed HTML *(SHTML) exec construct share a property not found in other parts of a Web HTTP daemon—they both cause programs to run on the Web daemon's host machine. Other than the fact that the output of these programs may pass through the Web daemon on the way back to whatever lies at the other end of a TCP/IP connection (a browser, a robot, and so forth), these programs are entirely independent of the daemon. In the case of CGI, the program is launched by the daemon and is entirely responsible for the end of the HTTP response header and the HTTP response body. In the case of the SHTML exec construct, the program is responsible for only part of the HTTP response body and is limited to producing part of the HTML, and the daemon's parsing process is responsible for the HTTP headers and the rest of the body of the HTML/HTTP* response. The input to these kinds of independent programs is provided via the daemon as some combination of environment variable values and possibly via some interprocess communication mechanism that makes it appear that characters are available from standard input. For simplicity, this chapter refers to any such program as a script—a term inclusive of both programs started by the CGI mechanism and the SHTML parsing mechanism.

Although CGI is commonly spoken about in books, SHTML is not. SHTML allows for commands, called *constructs*, to be embedded in HTML comment statements. For example, the following inserts the name of the HTTP daemon host in an SHTML document in the place of the comment as it is being sent to the client.

```
<!--#echo var="SERVER_NAME"-->
```

Note The echo construct handles any CGI environment variable. SHTML also has a include construct which gives SHTML the nickname of *server-side includes*. The most powerful SHTML construct, however, is not echo or include, but exec. The *exec* construct allows for either a CGI script or an arbitrary executable to be launched to produce output to be included in place of the comment.

The source of possible security risks is quite simple: The script, although its invocation is controlled by the usual access control techniques provided by an HTTP daemon, is not otherwise limited by the daemon in what the script can do within the execution environment provided to it. The script runs on the daemon's host and, unless specific measures are taken to prevent it, the script can do anything any other program on the host can do. A script can access and alter data files, launch other programs, and use the network. All of these actions have specific security concerns attached to them.

In practice, the precautions that should be taken by a script author are the same precautions that should be taken by a programmer of a *set UID* (SUID) program in a Unix environment. A SUID program runs with the user identifier, and hence privileges, of the owner of the program rather than the usual privileges of the invoker of the program. This is directly analogous to what happens with a Web script where the invoker of the program is essentially the user of a Web browser, and the owner of the program is part of the Web server system.

In both of these situations, one must be aware that a misbehaving program can cause security problems. Normally, a misbehaving program will simply fail to do its job and might damage files that are writable by the user. In both a SUID program and a CGI program, a misbehaving program might damage files that are writable by the owner, but more importantly, might reveal confidential information to the user and might enable the user to do things to the system that would otherwise be impossible. SUID programs are typically only written by experienced system programmers who are aware of the repercussions of what they are doing when they make a program give special privileges to the user. CGI programs are now being written by inexperienced programmers who often lack the training to understand the operating system they are working with.

CGI scripts are generally similar security problems compared to network daemons in that the users are not restricted to locally authorized users. CGI users are typically spread all over the world and have no loyalty to the organization running the HTTP daemon, making the risks somewhat larger. Again, network daemons have historically been written only by experienced programmers. CGI scripts do not take the same degree of technical expertise to write, so again, many inexperienced programmers who are unaware of the repercussions of what they do are writing scripts.

To protect systems from a misbehaving script, four basic strategies can be employed.

- One can configure the HTTP daemon to limit the use of scripts.
- One can program defensively to prevent unexpected input or unanticipated pathological conditions from having the script cause unintended side effects.

- One can use wrapper programs to launch the scripts after arranging for a more secure execution environment. *Wrappers* are programs that do not generate any response to an HTTP request themselves, but simply arrange for another program to be launched to generate the response. They are akin to the TCP wrappers used in securing the programs launched by the Unix inet daemon.
- One can arrange physical barriers between the daemon host and resources that need to be kept secure.

As with any good defensive security system, these strategies build on each other and are intended to limit the location of potential problems, limit the area affected by a problem, and limit the amount of damage that can done when a problem arises. It is not realistic to believe that one can put together a software system in which no problem will arise.

Configuring the Daemon

Many organizations produce an HTTP daemon. The specific details of how to configure the daemon vary from one product to the next. However, most use configuration parameters based on those used in the CERN and NCSA daemons. Here, you will see the parameters that have the most impact on script security, and their generic descriptions. You will also see examples of parameter names and values used in the CERN or NCSA daemons.

Four specific ideas need to be worked out when planning the configuration of a daemon to deal with script security issues:

- Restricting file system access
- Identifying the daemon with an unprivileged user
- Limiting the location of scripts
- Logging script invocation

Restricting File System Access

The NCSA daemon has a global access control configuration file (typically named *access.conf*) and directory-by-directory access control files (typically named ".htaccess") limiting which files it can serve. However, although these files or the corresponding access control mechansims in other daemons might also limit which scripts are executed, they do not limit what these scripts may access. If the daemon is running on a machine that contains private files that you do not want transmitted far and wide, you might want to ensure they are not accessed by a script.

A powerful mechanism for guaranteeing that a Unix process will not access portions of the file system that you do not want it to access is to change the effective root directory of the file system. For example, if your Web server is installed in /local/www/httpd-80, your HTML documents are installed in /local/www/chroot/html, and your CGI scripts are installed in /local/www/chroot/cgi-bin, then the daemon can be restricted to /local/www/chroot and still get to all the files it needs to access, and scripts can be restricted to /local/www/chroot/cgi-bin or some subdirectory of cgi-bin. At the same time, one can have multiple daemon's installed and accessing the same chroot directory.

Several mechanisms can be used to achieve this restriction, all of them based on the Unix chroot() system call. This system call changes the way the Unix kernel interprets filenames. It prepends the specified prefix directory name to the beginning of all filenames specified by the program that invokes the chroot system call. The same effect is generated for all programs launched directly or indirectly by the program invoking the system call. Hence, it changes the effective root of the file system for these programs. For example, if a process invoked chroot("/local/www") it could no longer access files with any other prefix and would access /local/www/docs simply as /docs.

On most Unix systems, the chroot system() call is restricted to the superuser. However, because access to the default HTTP port (port 80) is also typically restricted to the superuser, this does not usually pose a problem. If you start your server as an unprivileged user, however, you must not only use a higher numbered port (such as port 8000 or 8080), you also might be preventing your daemon from being able to use the chroot() system call to restrict access to a portion of the file system. See the next section for more information on the issue of privileged users.

Using a chroot Restriction

For the purposes of working with a Web daemon, the best mechanism to use for chroot restriction is the one provided for this purpose by some daemon authors. For example, the CERN server has a chroot option in one of its configuration files. It reads the configuration files on startup, opens the logging files, connects to a TCP/IP port, then executes the chroot call before changing the effective user (see the next section). Hence, it can even exclude the httpd directory from access by using a directory structure that places the httpd directory outside of the directory tree specified by the chroot system call.

Using a Wrapper to Launch the HTTP Daemon

A second mechanism for restricting file system access via the chroot system call is to use a wrapper to launch the HTTP daemon. Many Unix systems provide a chroot command that invokes the chroot system call. It takes a directory name as the first command-line argument and then launches a program specified by the remaining command-line arguments. The chroot command is typically a set UID program that allows anyone to run it and gain access to the chroot system call. The chroot program changes the effective user back to the actual user, so the remaining command is launched with normal user privileges. Hence, the following command launches the HTTP daemon with access to a restricted portion of the file system starting with /local/www/docs:

```
chroot /local/www/docs /local/www/httpd/bin/httpd
```

Using the chroot System Call

To restrict only CGI scripts instead of restricting the entire activities of the Web server to a certain portion of the file system, you can use a third mechanism: a CGI wrapper that uses the chroot system call. This might not restrict server-parsed HTML (SHTML) unless you place restrictions on the SHTML exec construct as well. See the section later in this chapter on CGI wrappers for more information.

Because the directory containing CGI scripts is separate from the directory containing HTML documents, it might seem difficult to use the chroot system call to limit the daemon to an appropriate directory. A simple solution is to run a separate daemon for CGI scripts using an alternate TCP/IP port number, such as port 81. Doing so might also simplify the process of configuring CGI for enhanced security without affecting the policies for HTML files.

Identifying the Daemon with an Unprivileged User

Normally, the HTTP daemon starts with superuser privileges so it can bind to TCP/IP port 80. Configure the daemon to change the effective user to an unprivileged user after it starts up. Thus the normal file system protections will prevent unwanted reading of files by the daemon, a CGI script, or a SHTML command. No security reason exists for starting a production-grade daemon as an unprivileged user. A good daemon connects to the network port and then uses the privileged user ability to identify itself with another, unprivileged, user before it begins any file accesses. In particular, when the daemon receives a user request to retrieve a file or start a script, it no longer acts as a privileged user.

When scripts are involved, changing the effective user of the daemon to an unprivileged user is especially important. A script running with root privileges may not only read a protected file, it may execute privileged commands, such as ones that interact directly with system devices. Potentially, a script running with superuser privileges could do as much damage as giving the superuser password away.

The NCSA deamon uses the User directive in the HTTPD configuration file typically named httpd.conf. You can use this directive to set the effective UID of the daemon to an unprivileged user such as the standard "nobody" usually preconfigured into a Unix system. Similarly, use the Group directive to set the effective group of the daemon to one that does not give it special privileges.

It is important, however, to start experimental daemons as an unprivileged user such as "nobody." If you are using a daemon for the first time or experimenting with new configuration parameters on a daemon that you're familiar with, someone could access the daemon in a way that causes problems, making it impossible to use port 80 or the chroot restriction.

Limiting the Location of Scripts

Typically, you locate CGI scripts in a directory named cgi-bin and restrict access to this directory to only the webmaster. Because CGI scripts are needed to process HTML forms and manage access counters, however, a site with HTML authors other than the webmaster immediately requests that its webmaster allow others to run scripts. This section discusses how to limit others from running scripts, and a later section on script wrappers explains how to safely allow others to run scripts.

If HTML authors are given directories in which to place their homepages, scripts potentially could be located anywhere. Presumably, HTML authors are not given privileges to place scripts in the cgi-bin directory, so instructing the daemon not to execute scripts except those in that directory is a simple way to prohibit HTML authors from writing scripts that later are executed with the privileges granted to the daemon.

Motivations for Limiting the Location of Scripts

If users other than the webmaster are given the ability to have their scripts launched directly by the server, these scripts may both cause problems and have problems. Suppose the daemon is identified with the user www, and a user xyz owns a script. Potentially, this script could access and modify the httpd log files, the access configuration files, or any other file owned by user www and not world readable. This fact argues strongly against allowing arbitrary users to own scripts. If the script owner attempts to access files owned by xyz that are not world readable, however, or modify such files that are not world writable, he would not be able to do so. Using a wrapper program can solve both problems (see the section on wrapper programs later in this chapter for more details).

Another reason to limit scripts to a small set of directories is that scripts need to be scanned for potential security problems occasionally. You want to be sure, for example, that an unauthorized set UID script is not executed. Set UID programs are a potential security problem in that they allow a program to execute with the privileges of the program's owner rather than the program's user. If the program's owner is privileged, such as the superuser, and the program is executed as a script, one faces all the perils of having the daemon run with superuser privileges and launching the script.

The following is a simple Unix command to search for set UID programs in the cgi-bin directory:

```
find cgi-bin -perm -4000 -print
```

Expect to use some set UID programs as wrappers (see the section on wrappers later in this chapter). To be safe, make sure that these wrappers have not had unauthorized alterations.

The standard mechanism for checking a set of files for unauthorized alterations is to compute the MD5 digest of each file and store the digests both online and off-line. The MD5 digests can be recomputed periodically to check for alterations. The online digest is useful for quick checks; a difference between the computed and stored digests proves the file has been changed. A clever intruder might also change or update the online copy of the digest, however, so occasionally check the computed digest against a digest stored on removable media, such as a tape or floppy disk, that could not be changed by an electronic intruder. The Tripwire system available from the COAST Laboratory of the Computer Science Department of Purdue University automates this process, not just for scripts, but for the entire host file system. As a webmaster rather than a system administrator, however, you save considerable time by focusing on a particular directory or a small set of directories to scan for unauthorized changes.

Mechanisms to Enforce Script Location Limitations

To configure a daemon to limit the location of scripts, one must work with several kinds of configuration parameters. The first kind of configuration parameter controls which directories contain files assumed to be scripts when included in an URL. The second kind of configuration parameter controls which directories contain CGI scripts. The third kind of configuration parameter controls which files have filename extensions or MIME types that indicate they are scripts.

Typically, you locate CGI scripts in a directory named cgi-bin by means of a daemon configuration parameter such as NCSA's ScriptAlias parameter in the Server Resource Map. You can configure the daemon to allow the execution of a script located in any directory, however, by means of the options specified in the global access configuration file (ACF). The NCSA server uses three options that affect script execution in arbitrary directories:

- The **ExecCGI** option is used to specify that if a URL corresponds to a script, the script should be run and its output returned rather than returning the contents of the file containing the script.

- The **Include** option is used to specify that some or all HTML files should be parsed via the SHTML mechanism to process server-side includes and exec directives.

- The **IncludeNoExec** option is like the Include option except it specifies that exec directives are to be ignored.

The global ACF can enable local ACFs to override options by using the AllowOverride directive for a particular directory section. For maximum security, directories in which users place files should be mentioned in the global ACF without using the AllowOverride directive. Also, for maximum security, the IncludeNoExec option should be used in preference to the Include option if server-side includes are to be permitted at all. Without the exec directive enabled, server-side includes are a potential performance problem rather than a potential security problem.

To control which directories contain files that are assumed to be scripts when referred to in a URL, the NCSA daemon uses the ScriptAlias directive in the server resource map. ScriptAlias indicates not only that the specified directory should be aliased, meaning it does not have to be part of the document tree, but also that all files in that directory are assumed to be scripts. Other directories may contain scripts if the global access control file permits.

In other directories, if the global ACF permits, a CGI script is recognized by being marked as executable or by having a specific extension, such as .cgi. Be sure that your daemon is configured with an ACF that does not permit these files to be executed as scripts.

Logging Script Invocation

In case of a security breach or other problems with a script, you want to scan access logs to find out more about where access originated and to which script files. Thus, not only do you want to keep access logs, both current and historic, you also need to be sure they contain sufficient detail to trace the invocation of the problem script back to the origin of the client request.

First, you need to log the full filename of the files accessed, not just directory names. The Netscape Communications daemon (version 1.1) allows for abbreviated logs that do not contain the full filename. If you choose this configuration option, you cannot associate accesses with specific scripts.

Second, if your daemon allows for it, it is useful to know the modification time of an executed script. If problems are associated with a particular version of a script, you can determine which accesses were associated with that version and not be concerned with accesses associated with other versions. If your daemon does not allow this detail of logging, keep detailed records of the date and time that scripts for which you are responsible are installed and modified. Thus, simply comparing access times (which are routinely logged) to script modification times enables you to determine which accesses are problematic. I do not know of any commercially available daemons that provide this level of detail in their logging.

Third, if your daemon allows for it, and if you can afford the performance overhead, using the server configuration file (httpd.conf) option to check the identity of the client user (IdentityCheck on) also might be useful. This option provides extra information about the identity of the client user if the client's host is running the ident daemon which returns the username associated with the client process.

Clearly, this information is useless and typically unavailable for clients running on personal computers. If the client is on a trustworthy and well-run Unix or VMS system, however, you can associate a username with each access. Establishing this association enables you to further track any script problems to the point of origin of the problematic accesses. Note that routine identity logging may be considered a violation of privacy. Hence, you should not make publicly available logs that include identity information.

Programming Defensively

The preceding section on configuring the daemon covered actions the webmaster can take to promote security; this section discusses steps the script author can take. In some instances, the webmaster and the script author might be the same person. Otherwise, the webmaster is concerned with the security of the system as a whole, whereas the script author looks after the security of the data files manipulated by the scripts. The script author can do so with the following four techniques:

- Parsing input defensively
- Launching other programs defensively
- Authenticating clients defensively
- Using proven authorization mechanisms

Parsing Input Defensively

Typically, you design an HTML file containing a link to a CGI script in conjunction with the design of the CGI script. The CGI script may be invoked via links in HTML files designed by others or directly from a user's browser, however. Thus, the script must be written to handle input that cannot be obtained when invoked from the HTML file it was designed to accompany.

Suppose you are writing a script that returns the contents of the Unix manual page that covers commands related to the topic of an HTML file. A simple such script follows:

```
#!/bin/sh
if [ $# = 0]; then
```

```
        cat << EOM
Content-type: text/html

<HEAD><TITLE>Man Index</TTTLE></HEAD>
<BODY><H1>Unix Manual Pages</H1><ISINDEX></BODY>
EOM
else
      echo Content-type: text/plain
      echo
      man "$*"
fi
```

As innocent as it looks, this script is loaded with security problems. In particular, it blindly accepts whatever strings are sent to it via the command line argument array, which, in a CGI script, is typically the same as the QUERY_STRING environment variable when the GET method is used to invoke the script.

Suppose this string includes shell meta-characters such as backquotes or a semicolon. The string `'shutdown'`, for instance, would cause the shutdown command to be run, as well as invoke the man command, as would the string `;shutdown`. This problem cannot be avoided as long as the shell script processes user input. Hence, CGI shell scripts must be limited to those that do not require processing of client input.

You can take two kinds of precautions to prevent this abuse. This section discusses the first kind: looking at the input carefully. Looking at the input carefully prevents unexpected behavior when the script processes input it was not designed to accept. The next section discusses the second kind: taking care when invoking other programs from within the script. Launching other programs carefully prevents them from unexpected behaviors when processing input they may be designed to accept in a broader anticipated context, such as from an interactive user.

Many scripts start with boilerplate code to parse input. This boilerplate code is placed in every script written by the script author in scripts written in the scripting language. The following sections examine typical boilerplate code in several common scripting languages (the Bourne shell, Perl, and C) and look at how the boilerplate code can be enhanced both generically for all scripts and specifically for particular circumstances.

Shell Script Example

This section does not provide an example with a shell scripting system, such as the Bourne shell or the C shell, because it is absolutely impossible to write a safe shell script to handle user input. By their very nature, the scripting languages that make good interactive shells are unsuitable for secure processing of user input because of the way the lines of code are parsed, expanded, re-parsed, and re-expanded until they cannot be re-re-expanded any more. Each time a shell variable or metacharacter is encountered, the program has the potential to do something unanticipated by the author.

Shell scripts make good CGI scripts for launching a fixed sequence of programs that look at inherited environment variables to get input. Shell scripts must never be given the chance to expand an environment variable set by the user of the client program. The end user can place all sorts of malicious character sequences at the end of a URL fetched with a GET request or in the body of a POST request.

Perl Script Example

The problem with shell scripts are shell metacharacters. Perl, however, can easily take apart URL-encoded form data as well as look for metacharacters:

```
#!/usr/local/bin/perl
if ($ENV{'REQUEST_METHOD'} eq "GET")
{
   $in = $ENV{'QUERY_STRING'};
}
elsif ($ENV{'REQUEST_METHOD'} eq "POST")
{
   for ($i = 0; $i < $ENV{'CONTENT_LENGTH'}; $I++)
   {
     $in .= getc;
    }
}
@in = split(/&/,$in);
foreach $i (0 .. $#in) {
# Convert plus's to spaces
   $in[$i] =~ s/\+/ /g;
# Convert %XX from hex numbers to alphanumeric
   $in[$i] =~ s/%(..)/pack("c",hex($1))/ge;
```

```
# Split into key and value.
   $loc = index($in[$i],"=");
   $key = substr($in[$i],0,$loc);
   $val = substr($in[$i],$loc+1);
$in{$key} = $val unless ($val ~= /;<>*¦&$!#()[]:'"/)
}
```

The unless clause in the last line prevents a value containing a metacharacter from being inserted into the associative array. This check can be delayed until the next stage of the script where scalar values are pulled out of the associative array and put into the variables containing user input.

The code in this example takes a philosophically weak approach to security, however. It simply forbids what is known to be unsafe rather than permitting what is known to be safe. If one's knowledge of what is unsafe is incomplete, this philosophy can be dangerous. In the preceding example, for instance, the newline character was omitted in the list of dangerous characters. If one proceeds to invoke the system( ) call with an argument including a newline (which may have been hex encoded in the URL) followed by a command line, then the user specified command line is executed in addition to the command intended by the script author.

Other common weak approaches are to allow the assignment of the value containing dangerous characters to the associative array, but to either remove the dangerous characters first, or to insert backslash escapes in front of them. It is preferable to trigger a graceful failure to the script when you notice that a required input value is missing (try to check for missing input early in the script) rather than to try to proceed with what appears to be malicious input. Inserting a backslash escape can simply delay the problem until the data is reprocessed later.

A better approach is to inspect each input for data known to be safe. If the script should only accept alphanumeric strings with no spaces, for example, the last line of the example should read:

```
$in{$key} = $val unless ($val ~= /[^A-Za-z0-9]/)
```

Notice that the caret (^) inside the brackets makes the pattern match if any character not in the specified ranges is found.

In particular, you need to be absolutely certain that user input does not make its way into a shell program (see previous section) indirectly through Perl. A shell is started explicitly by the system () function, but is also started implicitly in the following ways:

- Opening to a pipe—for example:

  ```
  open(FOO, "¦man $in{"manpage"});
  ```

- Backquotes—for example:

  ```
  print 'man $in{"manpage"}';
  ```

- The exec command with a single string argument rather than a list of arguments

The last item, exec, deserves special attention because it offers a mechanism for launching other programs that do not involve the shell. You must read a good Perl manual to understand the details of the syntax of Perl and the subtleties involved; however, essentially there are two forms of exec. One of the forms launches the shell, and the other does not. Which form is invoked depends on the syntactic category of the argument(s) to exec. Code such as the following will invoke the shell:

```
if (!fork)
   exec "/bin/man $in{'manpage'}";
else
   wait;
```

Whereas code such as the following will not invoke the shell:

```
if (!fork)
   exec /bin/man, $in{'manpage'};
else
   wait;
```

Hence, when launching another program that requires user input as command-line arguments, the latter form of exec is the preferred way to do so.

Perl also exhibits the undesirable property of a shell of interpreting input as commands when the eval function is called either explicitly or implicitly when a pattern match has the /e modifier. As long as eval is not invoked on user input this is not a security problem; however, this property is one more thing to look for when evaluating a Perl script for potential security problems.

Perl has a feature to guard against the passing of unchecked user input into a shell called *taint checking*. With Perl version 4, you need to use special compilation options when compiling Perl from the distributed C source code, so you have a separate executable for "Perl" and "taintPerl." With Perl version 5, you can simply invoke taint checking with the -T command-line option. Any "tainted" variables being passed to a shell cause the script to halt with an error message rather than proceed. A variable is "tainted" if it contains data from environment variables, standard input, the command line, or another tainted variable. A script can circumvent taint checking, however, by doing trivial checks on the variables. Hence, even if you enable taint checking, look over any Perl-based CGI scripts for insufficiently checked user input being passed to a shell.

C Scripts

CGI scripts written in C cannot have the same problems as those written in Perl with respect to eval(), but are just as problematic with respect to launching the shell. A C program will invoke the shell in three ways:

- Using the system() library call to indirectly launch a program
- Using the popen() library call to direct input or output to a pipe leading to another process
- Using the exec() system call to directly start the shell

In the first two cases, a programmer might be unaware that a shell is being used to interpret the input as a command line. The dangers of letting user input reach a shell command line were discussed earlier in this section.

Launching Other Programs Defensively

As discussed in the previous section, when a script launches another program, the potential exists for unanticipated behavior that might be detrimental to the system executing the script. The following is another look at the first attempt to make the Unix manual pages via a Web daemon using a simple CGI script:

```
#!/bin/sh
if [ $# = 0]; then
       cat << EOM
Content-type: text/html

<HEAD><TITLE>Man Index</TTTLE></HEAD>
<BODY><H1>Unix Manual Pages</H1><ISINDEX></BODY>
EOM
else
       echo Content-type: text/plain
       echo
       man "$*"
fi
```

Not only does this script allow user input to be interpreted as potential commands to the shell, it also launches several programs in addition to the man program. These are cat, echo, and [("[" is another name for "test," both of which are programs separate from the shell). These three program invocations illustrate several pitfalls that must be avoided:

- Invoking a program other than the one intended because of confusion over program names
- Sending data on standard input to a program that might cause the program to misbehave
- Providing command-line input to a program that might cause it to misbehave

The remainder of this section considers each of these potential dangers and additional defensive mechanisms to guard against misbehavior of non-CGI programs launched by scripts. These mechanisms are important in Perl and C programs as well as shell.

Confusing Program Names

Programs with names like "[" are unusual, but it is not unusual for several programs to have the same name on the same system at the same time. When such a program name is invoked, which program is used is determined either by invoking the program with an absolute name, or by searching a list of directories in the PATH environment variable. When searching through a list of directories, the first directory containing a file of the given name is used regardless that the intended program is located in a directory mentioned later in the list.

A common form of attack when an intruder wants greater access to a computer system is to plant *Trojan Horse* programs. Trojan Horse programs typically have the same name as a common utility program such as cat or echo, and might even imitate the outward behavior of these programs. If the intruder succeeds in placing a Trojan Horse in a directory on the PATH of the CGI program, the Trojan Horse is invoked rather than the intended program.

One easily avoidable trap is to eliminate the current directory (".") from the PATH. Unix system administrators can use a program such as Tripwire to be sure standard executables are not replaced by Trojan Horses. The PATH environment variable for a script, however, may not be limited to standard executable directories checked in such a manner.

In some cases, no malicious intent is present when a program is installed on the system with the same name as a common utility program. Perhaps the program is a non-standard enhancement to the standard utility program. Enhanced programs, by their nature, however, are more complex than their standard counterparts and therefore are prone to unforeseen effects. For this reason, avoid using the PATH when practical by instead using absolute program names, and always use an explicitly set PATH environment variable.

Avoiding Use of the PATH

The examples in the preceding section on Perl always specify the absolute name of all programs they launch directly. Complete specification of the path assures the PATH environment variable is not used to search for the location of the executable.

In some cases, the absolute name may vary from one system to another. Hence, it is good practice to assign string literals containing the absolute names of programs to be launched to constants and place them in a prominent location near the beginning of a program. The following C program, for example, follows this practice for the standard Unix manual page:

```
#include <stdio.h>
#define MANBIN "/usr/bin/man"
extern void ParseFormInput();
extern char* FetchFormInput();
int main()
{
        char *manpage;
        ParseFormInput();
        manpage = FetchFormInput("manpage");
        printf("<HEAD><TITLE>Unix Manual Page: %s", manpage");
        printf("</TITLE></HEAD>\n");
        printf("<BODY><H1>Unix Manual Page<BR>%s</H1><PRE>);
        fflush(stdout);
        execl(MANBIN, manpage, NULL);
        return 1;
}
```

Making Sure the PATH Is Set Appropriately

Even though the script may not depend on the PATH environment variable for programs it launches directly, sometimes these directly launched programs launch other programs without the user's knowledge. Thus, protect yourself from the execution of arbitrary programs by explicitly limiting the PATH to include only the directories for standard executables and to specifically exclude the current directory (specified as "." in the PATH).

In a Bourne shell script, for example, always insert a line such as the following:

```
PATH=/bin:/usr/bin
```

In a Perl script, similarly insert a line such as

```
$path = ('/bin', '/usr/bin');
```

In a C program script, you obtain the same effect with

```
setenv("PATH", "/bin:/usr/bin");
```

In the immediately preceding C program, for example, the man program might launch a program to format the manual page for viewing if a formatted version is not already on hand. When used interactively, it also might launch a program to display the formatted manual page one screen at a time. One often takes such actions for granted, and if the program launching other programs is not careful, it might depend on environment variables to determine which file to launch. The C program in question, however, probably is safe because the formatting program in all likelihood is fully specified and will not be run on a well-maintained system that formats the manual pages as soon as they are installed. As a matter of standard practice, the C statement preceding this paragraph should be inserted before the call to exec().

Using chroot Liberally

As much as one would like to disbelieve, to foresee all potential problems with a piece of non-trivial software is impossible. Hence, you should take precautions that limit damage if a problem arises. Using sufficiently low user privileges to execute a CGI script is one strategy. Another strategy is to limit the scope of damage by restricting a program to the smallest portion of the system it need to do its job.

The Unix manual page only requires access to the files in /usr/man, for example. Hence, in principle, you can change the exec() in the preceding C program to the following:

```
execl("/bin/chroot", "/usr/man", MANBIN, manpage);
```

In practice, however, you have to accommodate that the man program now needs to look in "/" rather than "/usr/man." This suggestion borders on the absurd, though, because you have no reason to suspect that the man program is capable of any serious misbehavior. This philosophical standpoint was mentioned previously: Rather than assume your knowledge of what is harmful is complete, assume your knowledge is incomplete and do what you can to reduce damage when unavoidable harm comes.

Using Sound Programming Practices

CGI programming is subject to the same potential for error as any other type of programming. Merely the consequences of error are larger. Hence, a CGI programmer should follow the same rules for error avoidance as any other professional programmer.

Some of the most common kinds of errors for C programmers involve pointers and dynamic memory. To avoid these kinds of problems some programmers go too far in the other direction and use fixed size arrays for holding strings, which leads to a different set of errors that can be even more difficult to debug—going beyond the legal range of indices. A simple example of this arises in the most basic CGI script action—accepting user input. Consider the following function to handle input from a POST request:

```
char *ReadPost()
{
static buf[1024];
int index;
int n = atoi(getenv("CONTENT_LENGTH"));
for (index=0; index<n; index++)
     buf[index] = getchar();
return buf;
}
```

This C function successfully avoids dealing with pointers or dynamic memory, but if the CONTENT_LENGTH is over 1024, it begins overwriting memory not allocated to it. This category of error is the one exploited by Robert Morris in the infamous Internet Worm incident. He was able to overwrite part of the code portion of memory and insert opcodes of his own choice simply by supplying a daemon with more input than it was designed to handle.

Perl avoids memory management related problems to a large degree by using implicit memory management. C++ programmers also can avoid them by using classes that manage memory for them when performing string manipulation. Using the C string manipulation library with strcpy() and strcat() is bound to cause trouble as soon as you make a small mistake even if you take the precaution of using strncpy() and strncat() to avoid buffer overflows.

Authenticating Clients Defensively

Some CGI applications require transmission to the client of information of a sensitive nature. A local comic strip artist has an extensive online gallery of his work, for example. He wants to allow the clients who use his art on T-shirts, mugs, and whatnot to browse small screen-resolution images. Non-clients must not be able to do so, however, lest they create from these images unauthorized merchandise that is substandard in quality and cheat the artist out of the royalties he deserves. Clearly, you must use some form of logging and access control to manage this process. The standard logging and access control mechanisms are acceptable in this case because you are dealing with a limited set of outside users, each of whom can be given a username and password by the webmaster.

With the above standard scenario in mind, consider the problems with the standard access control solution. The access control mechanism employed by most HTTP daemons deals with both authentication and authorization. *Authentication* is the process by which clients establish their identity, and *authorization* is the process by which identity is associated with privileges. This section addresses the former, and the section "Using Proven Authorization Mechanisms" covers the latter. Additionally, two fundamental problems exist with the standard authentication mechanism:

- Usernames and passwords must be set up before authentication can take place.
- Usernames and passwords are susceptible to interception while in transit on a network.

Setting Up Usernames and Passwords

When you use a Web daemon to conduct business, the process of making a sale is slowed by having the customer apply for an account, issuing a username and password, and informing the user of the username and password issued via e-mail. Unless the customer provides sufficient information about him- or herself, however, you have no way to establish the identity of the user to verify his or her ability to pay. Nor can you ascertain the appropriateness of doing business with the user, for example by checking if the user is a legitimate reseller is you are selling wholesale, or checking if a customer legally may possess the goods for sale.

Issuing usernames and passwords also is a case of the classical key-distribution problem studied in cryptography. When you obtain a password, how do you get the password to the user without making it available to anyone else? If someone other than the user has the user's password, the password is useless as a means of verifying the user's identity. Typically, businesses e-mail newly issued usernames and passwords, making the password as valid as the security of the e-mail system—part of which is the user's. This procedure is roughly analogous to writing a Swiss bank account number on a piece of paper and putting it in the space behind the screen door on someone's front porch—adequate for small-scale transactions, but not for serious business.

Some businesses that operate on the Web have turned to companies dealing in digital cash for a partial solution to this security problem. A potential customer registers himself or herself with the third party responsible for checking the customer's ability to pay. When the third party completes verification, the customer is issued credentials in the form of a short sequence of characters. When the customer conducts a transaction, he or she presents to the business the credentials issued by the third party to verify ability to pay. In concept, this process of customer authentication can be extended beyond simple ability to pay. In effect, third parties offering credential verification can be used for Internet-wide authentication rather than authentication on a business-by-business basis.

Other businesses use an HTTP daemon to provide information to internal personnel. These persons already have computer accounts within the company network. To issue them separate usernames and passwords for the HTTP daemon is a duplication of effort. HTTP daemons that run on the company LAN should be able to share the authentication mechanism used by the LAN. Whereas the NCSA and CERN HTTP daemons for Unix do not offer the option of using the Unix system usernames and passwords in the ACF files, some daemons do. In particular, Microsoft recently released a daemon for Windows NT that uses the same username and password as the LAN.

For daemons accessed by customers outside the company, it does not seem reasonable to give accounts on a company computer to remote users. On the other hand, if you have a sufficiently close relationship to the customer to allow him or her to execute CGI scripts, giving that customer an account does not require much additional effort. After all, the account does not need many resources allocated to it. Internet service providers typically give company accounts to their customers. For them, it is reasonable to use the same authentication mechanism for the scripts their customers execute as the scripts their customers use to connect via any other access method.

Some HTTP daemons enable you to turn on identity checking to assist with the authentication process. Identity checking sends a query back to the client system asking it the username associated with the TCP/IP port at the other end of the HTTP connection. This process is time consuming and often yields no results because few systems run the ident daemon used to provide this information. Most references on Web security advise that relying on this identity checking is pointless because it is possible that the user is "spoofing" his or her identity. On the other hand, in some circumstances it may be extremely useful.

Note As a university professor, for example, I would like to provide a means for my students to look at my gradebook spreadsheet to find out how they are doing in my class and make sure I have recorded their grades propery. Obviously, I cannot put the spreadsheet output in an HTML file for everyone to look at (less the privacy of all the students be invaded). Nor do I want to set up separately protected HTML files for each student. Instead, I want a CGI script that authenticates the student and supplies him or her with information he or she has a right to know. All my students have usernames on the Unix workstation network, and all the workstations run the ident daemon. Hence, I can use the information provided by the ident daemon to authenticate the student with as much security as the rest of the system provides. In general, using the identity checking mechanism is a reasonable way to authenticate local users for scripts that require a cursory identity check rather than an irrefutable proof of identity.

Intercepting HTTP Passwords on the Internet

Like ordinary Telnet sessions, basic authentication under HTTP requires that passwords be transmitted over the network "in the clear." It would be more secure if HTTP encrypted passwords using a method that prevents reuse of the password by someone who intercepted during the transmission process. Unlike Telnet sessions, where authentication need only occur at the beginning of the session, HTTP has no notion of a session; therefore, authentication must take place every time an HTTP request is made to a server. Any cleartext transmission of a password poses the same problem; having the transmission repeated each time the client accesses the HTTP daemon only makes more obvious the presence of a security problem.

The only real solution to this problem is to encrypt the HTTP request. For the daemon to decrypt the request, however, it must know the decryption key. If the client supplies the decryption key, and the transmission is intercepted, the decryption key can be used by the interceptor, and the request might as well have been done without encryption. The standard solution to this problem is to have the daemon provide an encryption key that does not work as a decryption key (a *public* or *asymmetric* key technique). The reply need not be encrypted to secure the password transmission. If bi-directional encryption is desired, then the client can send an encrypted encryption key to the daemon without needing a public key.

Taken one step farther, you can use this type of encryption for authentication in another way. If a trustworthy third party is used to register the public key of the daemon, then the daemon can include a client-provided message that has been encrypted using the daemon's decryption key. The encryption key is publicly registered, and the matching decryption key is known only to the daemon. Hence, when the client decrypts the message using the public encryption key, it can prove the authenticity of the daemon. You prove the message's authenticity by providing the message and the copy of the message encrypted by the daemon's encryption key to the trusted third party. This technique is called a *digital signature* because it is analogous to showing a signature on a paper document to prove the identity of the document's sender to someone familiar with the signature.

As a webmaster, this kind of encryption, which is offered by SSL and S-HTTP, provides a means for the clients of your system to authenticate your system, not a means for you to authenticate them. Further maturity of these systems, however, will enable clients to register with the same authorities that register daemons, and therefore provide irrefutable digital signatures to the server.

Using Proven Authorization Mechanisms

Although usernames and passwords provide authentication, the standard means of providing authorization is using access control files—a global access control file, and, if permitted, per directory local access control files. The daemon uses these to provide a cursory screening and elicit authentication information from the client; however, a CGI script often needs to go beyond cursory screening to enforce an authorization policy. After establishing the user's identity the daemon uses the access control information to determine that running the script is reasonable for the user to request. The script might need go farther and determine if the user is authorized before carrying out the requested actions.

IP addresses and DNS names can be spoofed under some circumstances and do not authenticate an individual user. Hence, they are unreliable and should only be used as supporting information in the authentication process, not as a basis for authorization in and of themselves. Although they are available in an access control file, they should not be used exclusively unless only weak authentication is required to provide authorization. If any user of the local network is authorized to run a script, for example, the ACF can use the network address as an initial screen to prevent non-local users from running the script. If the user must be a known authorized user of a particular machine on the local network, the script needs to examine the results of an identity check on that machine. You should use the ACF to shield the script from requests from other machines or networks, but the script needs to check and perhaps log additional information before carrying out the request.

Because secure authorization mechanisms are difficult to code, the general strategy is to pass the mechanism to another part of the system. The simplest way you do this is to use the file access system of the operating system to enforce the authorization policy for a user of the system. If the CGI script can set its UID or have its UID set by a wrapper, then the script can simply rely on the operating system itself to provide the mechanism. The policy issue remains: Which user should be identified with the script? If the daemon's authentication system is integrated with the host's authentication, the answer is simple: Clearly, the script should be identified with the end user. Otherwise, if a webmaster is working with separate CGI authors, an easy solution for the webmaster is to configure a wrapper program to have the script run with the privileges of the authors and leave the authors to work out the details of enforcing a more sophisticated authorization scheme.

Another mechanism for enforcing an authorization policy is to have the CGI script interact with a password-protected database system. If the user can produce the correct password, the database system enforces the policy for the script.

Wrapping Scripts

Throughout this chapter, wrappers have been referred to repeatedly. A *CGI wrapper* is nothing more than a script whose purpose is to launch another script in an appropriately modified environment. You can modify several properties of the environment:

- The root directory
- The environment variables including the executable search path
- The user identity associated with the script's file access rights
- The set of open file descriptors

The techniques for modifying the root directory was discussed in the configuration section on using the chroot() system call and the chroot command. The techniques for modifying the PATH was discussed discussed in the section on programming defensively. The importance of using an appropriate user identification was discussed in the section on configuration and can be managed on a script level in the same way as on the daemon level. This section completes the the set of concepts by covering managing the set of open file descriptors.

When the daemon creates a child process to launch the CGI script, many fail to close the open files before launching the script. The child process executing the script inherits the open file descriptors enabling it to manipulate any file the daemon had open. In particular, many daemons have log files open at the time the child launches the script. Thus, a malicious script author or an errant script can alter the log files. Alteration of the log files can cover up other malicious activity. Depending on the operating system, it might even be possible to replace the log file with an executable that executes with the privileges of the daemon rather than the script author. Hence, you should use a wrapper to close all file descriptors other than the ones used for standard input and output.

As Webmaster you can provide a wrapper script for every script you do not personally author to modify the script's execution environment. Because this causes much similarity from one wrapper to the next, however, a small set of generic wrappers is preferable. To construct a generic wrapper, you cannot use QUERY_STRING encoded in the URL to parameterize the wrapper, because the script being wrapped needs to use QUERY_STRING itself. The CGI protocol, however, enables the wrapper script name to be encoded in the URI in a position other than the last position. The remainder of the URI is passed to the script in the SCRIPT_PATH environment variable, which you can use to parameterize a generic script.

Suppose you have a wrapper named "*wrap*" in the cgi-bin directory and access it via the URI /cgi-bin/wrap/aname/script?foobar, for example. The generic wrapper named "wrap" is invoked with /cgi-bin/wrap/aname/script in the SCRIPT_PATH environment variable and with "foobar" in the QUERY_STRING environment variable. The generic script then can parse the information in the SCRIPT_PATH, look in the directory where the script author named "aname" stores scripts, and launch the script named "script." The generic wrapper makes whatever environmental changes are needed to enforce the security policy. The wrapper also changes the

SCRIPT_PATH and the related SCRIPT_PATH_TRANSLATED environment variables to reflect the actual location of the script so the wrapped script can act as if it were launched directly from the daemon.

The Generic CGIwrap Script

A popular generic CGI script wrapper is CGIwrap. *CGIwrap* enables Unix users to have their own cgi-bin directories. The scripts users place in these directories are run with the script owner's effective UID rather than the daemon's UID. To accomplish this, the CGIwrap script, written in C, must be a root-owned SUID executable. You compile the CGIwrap script after you configure a location relative to your home directory for the cgi-bin directory.

In a university setting, where openness and experimentation are valued above ironclad security, using CGIwrap to allow arbitrary users to use CGI lets the webmaster maintain a reasonable degree of security—it prevents the user from damaging system files and obtaining otherwise unattainable privileges. If your security policy prohibits arbitrary users from running network daemons, however, do not let them run CGI scripts either—they pose the very same hazards.

In a business setting, using CGIwrap to allow only script authors to put scripts on the Web server implies that only authorized script authors should have user accounts on the HTTP daemon's host. Alternatively, you can modify CGIwrap to be more selective about whose scripts it launches.

As with any script or SUID program, inspect the code of the CGIwrap program to ensure it does not pose any security problems (not to imply that there are any, but as a matter of routine, you should look for yourself). You might also consider using CGIwrap as a basis for your own more customized wrappers. You can modify it to impose additional limitations on or changes to the execution environment as appropriate to your own system.

In particular, to summarize the previous several sections of this chapter, the following actions are desirable for arbitrary user scripts to take:

- Set the PATH environment variable in a fairly restrictive way so an incautious script author is unlikely to have a Trojan Horse or a nonstandard utility program on the PATH.

- Set the effective root to not include the user's home directory or potentially sensitive system files. The university students on my system are given a directory for their Web files on a separate file system (see the following section, "Erecting Physical Barriers," for more information). The effective root should not be so restrictive as to force users to put interpreters such as Perl in their cgi-bin directory because doing so enables a malicious client to execute arbitrary code under the script owner's UID.

- Open only the file descriptors for standard input and output. You accomplish this by explicitly invoking the close() function on all possible file descriptors greater than 3, or using the fcntrl() function to set the close-on-exec flag.

- Scan the QUERY_STRING for shell metacharacters. To scan for encoded newlines is overly intrusive, therefore you cannot fully protect the naive script writer. Metacharacters may be used for a benign purpose; escaping them might be preferable to removing them.

In addition, you can do the script authors the favor of performing the following actions:

- For simple scripts that require the GET method, pass along a suitably modified copy of argc.

- Translate all requests into POST requests so substandard clients that always respond to forms with a GET request do not confuse the script (NCSA Mosaic 1.x is known to do this).

- Set the current working directory to a directory owned by the user, such as the cgi-bin directory in which their script is located.

- Read standard input on POST requests and place form input into suitably named environment variables (for example, prefixed with "CGI_" to prevent standard environment variables from being overwritten). As you do this, scan for shell metacharacters and escape them, forcing the author to unescape them if they are needed.

- Perform a reverse DNS lookup on the IP address of the client if the daemon has not been configured to do so routinely. The script can use the DNS name to aid in authentication.
- Attempt to contact the ident daemon on the client host if the daemon has not been configured to do so routinely. The script can use the identity of the user to aid in authentication.

Providing script owners with a wrapper that makes their job easier and at the same time helps keep the system secure is desirable for all parties involved. Providing multiple generic wrappers might not be desirable because a malicious user may invoke a wrapper/script combination that is not anticipated.

Erecting Physical Barriers

In response to Murphy's Law, an effective security measure is simply to set up daemons so that when something goes wrong, there are severe limits on how widespread the effects will be. Three ways to do this are:

- Using bastion hosts
- Minimizing remote file systems
- Utilizing a firewall

Using Bastion Hosts

In network security the ideal setup is to run *bastion hosts*. Bastion hosts are used to set up each network daemon on a separate host and strip all software not needed to support that daemon from the bastion for the daemon. When someone compromises the security of the daemon, that person finds it difficult to leverage that accomplishment into a more widespread security breach by using the resources available on the daemon's bastion host. Similarly, use as simple an operating system as possible to run the bastion host, so that the operating system itself does not aid an intruder in leveraging one security hole into a more serious intrusion.

As perverse as it seems, using a freeware version of Unix on the HTTP daemon host is probably the most secure way to run the daemon. Because these systems, such as FreeBSD and Linux, are distributed in source code form and in precompiled modules, you can install only the modules you need, recompile some modules to eliminate unneeded features, and enable security features that are not enabled in the precompiled modules in the standard distributions.

You can effectively run these freeware versions of Unix on a 386 with only 4 MB of RAM and a 40-MB disk drive if you remove unnecessary features. The freeware versions support NFS both as clients and servers, as well as a deamon for the file-sharing protocol used by Microsoft Windows for Workgroups, Windows 95, and Windows NT. Linux even works as a client to the Microsoft filesharing protocol so you can keep the author's files on a Windows NT server, for example.

In practice, many webmasters do not have the resources necessary to run the large number of hosts needed to carry out this recommended strategy. The principles of the strategy are worthwhile, however. To run the HTTP daemon on a machine other than the primary host for an organization makes sense. The natural defenses of the primary host against network intruders protect the host from the compromised security of the HTTP daemon. In effect, you can use the mechanisms to support authorization policies more effectively.

Minimizing Remote File Systems

In a sample HTTP server system recently planned for installation at a university, the primary mechanism for enforcing an effective security policy was simply to run the daemon on a separate host. The host is not authorized to use any of the file systems on the primary Unix host, and all CGI scripts are local to the host. Hence, the CGI scripts have difficulty accessing any of the file systems on the primary Unix host. Ideally, from a security point of view, all files have to be moved to the daemon's host by a trustworthy protocol such as FTP. To accommodate the Web author's desire for ease of use, however, the host can be set up to either export a file system (separate from the one holding ServerRoot and the system CGI scripts) to the script maintainers' machines, or the daemon's host and the HTML and script maintainers' machines can import a file system from a third machine.

Both these network file-sharing practices hold a security risk. If the deamon's host exports a file system, the file serving software might have a security hole that allows the daemon host to be compromised—possibly by users of our own network. Importing a file system from a third machine minimizes this risk, but adds to the overall complexity of the system and adversely affects performance. Any additional complexity to the system adds a security risk in and of itself.

An appropriate balance between security and ease of use needs to occur in a useable system, however. One of the other webmasters at the sample university requires that all HTML files for his server be handed to him on floppy disks and does not run any CGI scripts for his users. As a result, even though his host and daemon are both more powerful than those of the first webmaster, she receives more business from users throughout the university. His machine is more secure, however, and it performs better, and, ultimately has more financial support.

Utilizing a Firewall

If your organization runs a firewall to protect against external intruders, you have three choices of location for your HTTP daemon:

- On the inside of the firewall
- On the firewall itself
- On the outside of the firewall

Placing an HTTP daemon on the Firewall

One way to enable internal users to access the Web through a firewall is to run a proxy HTTP daemon on the firewall itself. Because some deamons can run both as a proxy and as an ordinary server, to run a CGI-capable daemon on the firewall itself so both internal and external users can reach it is simple.

The strategy of executing scripts on the firewall is not a good one. CGI scripts can be written securely as can HTTP daemons, but the complexity of typical daemons and scripts is too great. Trusting them to behave securely on a sensitive machine like the firewall is folly. Placing a proxy may be acceptable, particularly daemons written specifically to proxy on a firewall (several are on the market). But under no circumstances should you run CGI scripts on a firewall machine.

Placing an HTTP daemon Inside the Firewall

You can place an HTTP daemon inside a firewall and expect the firewall to protect the daemon completely from outside intrusion. This setup is ideal if you want an internal-use daemon. Under these circumstances, to run on this daemon CGI scripts that handle sensitive data is perfectly reasonable.

If you want to run the HTTP daemon for external access, you need to configure the firewall to allow requests to pass through it. You perform this configuration by specifying a safe port number and IP address. The daemon is as vulnerable as if no firewall existed, however, and you must be extremely careful with CGI security.

Again, if your organization has gone to the trouble of erecting a firewall, you should not allow remote access to an internal machine running CGI scripts. A rogue script can use the internal network and hence violate the security policy of the organization. Simply serving documents is harmless if proper security precautions are in place to prevent sensitive documents from being placed on the file systems accessible to the daemon's host.

Placing an HTTP daemon Outside the Firewall

The best solution from a security point of view is to place the HTTP daemon on a machine outside the firewall, known as a "sacrificial lamb" position. Even a severely misbehaving CGI script cannot violate security in a way that differs from the ways available to any outsider. Because the machine cannot share files with machines inside the firewall, however, to place information on the machine is difficult. Presumably, the firewall permits outbound FTP and Telnet connections. Thus, you can transfer files to the daemon via FTP and administer them via Telnet.

For More Information

Carefully read the documentation that comes with your HTTP daemon and be sure you understand it before you begin using CGI. If you decide to use a scripting language such as Perl or TCL that you are not expert at, buy one of the many fine books on the market to help you become comfortable writing non-trivial, non-CGI programs before you use write CGI programs.

Use some of the Web resources dealing with CGI and security:

- The WWW Security FAQ, by Lincoln Stein.

  `http://www-genome/wi.mit.edu/WWW/faqs/www-security-faq.html`

- Safe CGI Programming, by Paul Phillips.

  `http://www.cerf.net/~paulp/cgi-security/safe-cgi.xt`

- CGI Security Tutorial, by Martin Van Biesbrouck.

  `http://www.thinkage.on.ca/~mlvanbie/cgisec/`

- Writing Secure CGI scripts, by NCSA.

  `http://hoohoo.ncsa.uiuc.edu/cgi/security.html`

Following are the basic rules for keeping CGI running as securely as possible:

- Configure the daemon to restrict CGI—both in script locations and by disallowing a server-side include directive from launching a CGI script.
- Practice safe programming techniques. In particular, beware of bizarre user input, and make sure the shell is not launched with metacharacters in command lines.
- Minimize the resources available to a CGI script gone bad by selecting an appropriate UID, root directory, PATH, and host machine.
- Keep the daemon and its host as simple as possible, but no simpler (paraphrased quote from Albert Einstein).

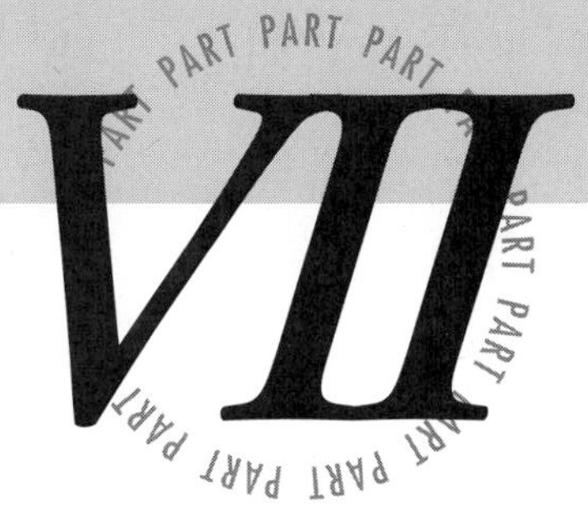

Beyond HTML Web Graphics

Graphics and Audio File Formats

by Nancy Acosta

This chapter studies the graphics and audio files that are being used on the Web today and that will be used in the future. A key enhancement to any Web site is the use of professional graphics and high quality sound files. This chapter discusses how to know which formats are acceptable, and how to go about obtaining and selecting them.

As far as graphics are concerned, there are many different file formats. You'll learn the importance of understanding the more popular formats, and knowing when to use them. The topic of understanding color is addressed, as well as hsb and rgb values, and other graphics-related terms. The Web's future graphics are also an important issue that you should study. The more knowledgeable you are in regards to graphics, the better able you are to envision and create effective Web sites. The use of professional images is imperative to a successful Web site.

Audio files are also a very important enhancement to effective Web sites. If you take the time to grasp their uses, and know when it's appropriate to use them in a Web site, they can certainly be to your benefit. This chapter not only shows their suitable uses, but also discusses what is needed to create capable audio files for any Web site.

Graphics and Images

Graphics and images make up a large part of the World Wide Web as we know it today. Whenever you browse the Web, you're sure to see great looking pictures or images that you may have waited many minutes to view. It's important for you, as a webmaster, to know which graphic file formats are best used and supported on the Internet today, and in the future.

The issue of understanding color using hsb and rgb values is essential for you to have before embarking on your image adventure. There are many confusing terms related to graphics that need to be discussed, such as pixel and dpi, so that when the time comes to acquire or create your Web site's images, you'll at least know some of the important aspects related to graphics.

After you've gained some knowledge of file formats and basic graphics terms, it's important to know how to convert these great-looking images to formats that are supported on the Web. You will see how to effectively and easily convert your graphics for use on the Web site you create.

Understanding Graphic File Formats

Knowing which graphic files are supported on the Web now and in the future is a great place to start when addressing the issue of using images within your Web site. The World Wide Web is made up of numerous sites that include large graphics. When designing your Web site, it is important to remember that the Web supports two main graphic file types: GIF (pronounced *jiff*) and JPEG (pronounced *jaypeg*). What is meant by "support" is that most Web browsers are capable of displaying only these two specific graphic types. Although this might seem limiting, GIF and JPEG are extremely versatile graphic formats. The future of graphics on the Web promises even more possibilities with the use of *PNG* (pronounced *ping*), which is a format similar to GIF but with more flexibility, progressive jpegs, and three-dimensional graphic designs.

If you plan to include graphics in your Web site, you can use in-line images or include a pointer to remote images. *In-line images* are graphics that are actually included in your page. The graphics are stored and maintained in the same file where the HTML documents reside, and a link is provided to these graphics from your Web page. You can also choose to point to remote images (graphics located somewhere else on the Web) inside your page; this approach is discussed in greater depth in Chapter 28, "Web Page Layout and Design."

To determine which graphic type to use, decide whether you want speed or quality. Do you want your images to download quickly or be of a photographic quality? The JPEG format should be used for high quality images on your Web site, such as a photograph or a colorful graphic. GIF also provides good quality images, but provides a much faster download time. Always use the GIF format for graphics such as logos, icons, and clip-art.

GIF

The *Graphics Interchange Format* (GIF), developed by CompuServe, is pretty much the standard on the Internet at this time. It has been around since 1987 and is supported widely throughout the graphics community. GIF supports up to 8 bits per pixel, holds a maximum of 256 colors, and uses LZW compression.

There are basically two types of compression: lossy and lossless. *Lossy compression* creates a smaller file size by discarding some information about the original image. It takes away details and changes in color that it deems too small for the human eye to differentiate. *Lossless compression,* on the other hand, never discards any information about the original file. LZW compression is a form of lossless compression. It works by simply finding repeated patterns within an image. When a pattern is repeated often, the compression is better. Because icons and line art often have large sections of one color, they work well as GIF files.

GIF graphics can be saved (created) in two ways: consecutive (which stores from top to bottom) and interlaced (which stores every 8th row, then 4th, and so on). Many Web developers and sites use the interlaced GIF version because of the way it downloads onto the browser's screen. The whole picture downloads immediately so that the computer user can see what it is immediately, although it is at first blurry. Over the course of a minute or two the picture continues to come into focus.

GIF Formats

Two formats of GIF files exist:

- **GIF87a.** GIF87a is named after the year it was designed and is the standard version.
- **GIF89a.** GIF89a includes transparency and interlacing graphics capabilities. This is useful when you want to portray a graphic that has a transparent background, which is common in Web pages.

The only problem with the GIF graphic format is that its LZW compression scheme is patented by Unisys who, along with CompuServe, decided recently that programs using this format would have to pay royalties.

PNG Format

Just after CompuServe and Unisys decided to charge royalties for the GIF format, a group of developers designed *Portable Network Graphics* (PNG), a new file format that does not use the patented compression. PNG is a newer, better format than GIF because it supports "true color" of up to 48 bits per pixel, which works well with the 24-bit graphics boards.

Note When I say *true color,* I refer to the 16-million-color scheme, which has much more clarity over the 256-color scheme.

The PNG format also has interlacing capabilities, which is very helpful for Web users. When more and more browser software includes the capability to view this graphic type, you may see PNG surpass GIF use.

PNG was originally developed to avoid the legality issues involving GIF's proprietary LZH compression scheme. The PNG format apparently has no legality constraints. Many of the most beneficial elements of GIF are also found within PNG. The newer format also supports true color images of up to 48 bits per pixel, a compressed lossless format, and flexibility for future add-ons. PNG's potential for Web use is obvious. More and more browsers should begin to support this format in the near future.

More information about PNG specifications and development can be found at the PNG FTP archive site:

`ftp.uu.net:/graphics/png/`

You can contact the administrators of this site by sending e-mail to `png-info@uunet.uu.net`.

JPEG

The *Joint Photographic Experts Group* (JPEG) graphic file format also is popular on the Web right now, although not quite as popular as GIF. JPEG was originally created for compressing photographic-quality images. The compression is adjustable and results in only a small loss of quality. As with PNG, the JPEG format works best with 24-bit graphics boards because it can sustain up to 16 million colors within each graphic.

TIFF

Although *Tagged Image File Format* (TIFF) is not supported on the Internet, it is important to mention because you will probably want to use graphics saved in this format for your Web page. If you find TIFF files that you would like to include in your Web design, you must first convert them for Internet use.

If you plan on letting Web users download TIFF files, you might want to provide a GIF thumbnail of the image. You can attach the TIFF file to the image so that the user can simply click on the thumbnail to download the TIFF file. Afterward, the user can use whatever software is on his or her system to view the TIFF file.

TIFF is ideal for large images and multi-image files, and provides a variety of different compression methods. These strengths are what make TIFF best for professional graphic work. TIFF is a popular format for clip-art and photographic images that are used by designers and professional graphic artists.

TIFF stores data differently from other graphic formats in that it does not store data in any particular order. The program must follow references within the files to find various parts of data for the graphic.

PCX

Another image not supported on the Web that should be mentioned briefly is the PCX file format. This format was created by the ZSoft Corporation in the early eighties as a proprietary format, but many companies have since incorporated it into their programs. In fact, all the images in this book were saved in the PCX format.

PCX is not as complex as the TIFF format, but is great for images such as line art. One drawback to this format is that it is available in many versions, which sometimes creates problems. For example, Photoshop, presently the most popular image editing program in the world, only supports version 5 of PCX.

BMP

Whenever you see the BMP format, Microsoft technology was used to create the file. You can view the BMP format on PCs running DOS, Windows, Windows NT, or OS/2, but you cannot use it on a Macintosh operating system. Because the format is not very compatible, it is not popular among graphic designers and is not viewable on the Web.

PICT

The Macintosh file format, PICT, is used by the Macintosh clipboard to transfer graphic information between programs.

Although this format is popular among Mac users, it is not compatible with other operating systems, and also is not supported on the Web.

Table 26.1
Popular Graphic Summary Table

File Format	Browser Support	Colors	Compression	Best Use
GIF	Great	256	Lossless	Logos, icons, clip art
JPEG	Great	Millions	Lossy	Photos, pictures
PNG	Poor	Millions	Lossless	All types
TIFF	None	Millions	Variety	Large pictures & graphics

Progressive JPEGs

It was thought best to separate this section from that of regular JPEGs because this type is not well known throughout the general Internet community. JPEGs are (or could be) the Web's future graphic style, taking the place of the GIF and regular JPEGs.

Some of the more popular browsers now include the capability to view *progressive JPEG* files. The difference between regular JPEG and progressive JPEG is similar to the difference between GIF and interlaced GIF. Although the two JPEG formats are almost identical in size, progressive JPEG stores an image's data in a complicated arrangement, rather than from top to bottom.

When the progressive JPEG downloads, the first scan of the image is small and can be shown onscreen almost immediately. With each successive scan, more information is added to the image until it is complete. Like the interlaced GIF, the advantage to this approach is that you are able to view the whole graphic immediately (although it is somewhat blurry), rather than having to wait to see it from top to bottom.

Netscape 2.0b4 incorporates the capability to view progressive JPEGs. The Netscape creators provide a great example of this type of file, and other graphic formats at `http://home.netscape.com/eng/mozilla/2.0/relnotes/demo/pjpegdemo.html`. Only a handful of other browsers besides

Netscape 2.0b4—Enhanced Mosaic 2.1f5, Microsoft Internet Explorer, and OmniWeb 2.0—can read these files.

Others

Many other graphic file formats exist that you might run into during your search for the perfect graphic.

Some of the more common additional file formats include:

- cdr (CorelDraw)
- cgm (Comp. Graphics Metafile)
- clp (Windows Clipboard)
- drw (Micrografix Drawings)
- eps (Encapsulated Postscript)
- pcd (Kodak Photo CD)
- psd (Photoshop)
- raw (Raw File Format)

Paint Shop Pro, a shareware graphic program, can open, view, and manipulate all of the graphic file formats we've mentioned so far in this chapter. Open the program, choose File, Open, and search through your directory until you find the image to be opened. Make sure you specify the file type so that you will be able to find it within your directory.

Paint Shop Pro is available for downloading at many of the shareware and freeware sites on the Internet. Try my favorite at Stroud's CWSApps List—Index of Apps at `http://www.enterprise.net/cwsapps/inx2.html`.

Understanding Color

It's important for us to have a basic understanding of color and how it works in relation to graphics and the Web. There will be many times when you have a great looking graphic on your page, and the user is unable to view it in the same manner of which it was intended. The user may simply not be able to view graphics at all, or will be viewing the graphic in colors that aren't quite what they originally were. This happens frequently when the user has a poor quality graphic card in their system that is unable to view a large number of colors. The image quality on even the best graphics can appear fuzzy and distorted. This is yet another issue to remember when designing outstanding graphics for your Web site.

Two major color models differentiate how humans and computers see or use color: HSB (hue, saturation, and brightness) is how we see color, and RGB (red, green, and blue) is how the computer sees color. The following sections introduce you to these two color models.

Knowledge of these two color models is important when you attempt to change and revise any graphics on your computer system. While you may think of the colors in the HSB mode, the computer is always thinking in terms of the RGB mode because this is the way monitors display color. In knowing that these modes are different, yet related, you will be able to better understand your graphic editor, and how to manipulate the color scheme to your graphic's benefit.

HSB

The HSB model is based on human sight of color and the changes in color. In this model colors are based on three numbers indicating hue, saturation, and brightness.

- Hue is the actual color we work with. It includes all the colors in the spectrum, which are measured by a color wheel that ranges from 1 to 360 degrees.
- Brightness is the degree of lightness or darkness of the color. Mixing the color you have with either white or black changes the color's brightness. Brightness is measured by a percentage figure, in which 0 is white and 100 is black.
- Saturation is the intensity of the color you are using. If the color red is added to a light color, such as pink (which is white and red together), the new color would be a deeper pink, and would show an increase in saturation.

Although the HSB model is how we, as humans, perceive color, many of the image editing programs today offer choices to change color schemes in both HSB and RGB models. HSB also offers the user an easier way of changing the image color. If you want to make a graphic color lighter, then you simply modify the brightness. This represents an easier understanding for many of us in terms of editing images.

RGB

Although humans see color in the HSB color model, the computer is a little different: it uses the RGB color model, or Red, Green, and Blue. The RGB method is used to specify colors for most graphic programs (and for your Web images).

Computer monitors display colors in what look like small dots, which are actually the combination of red, green, and blue dots. The combination of these color dots in varying intensities are what creates your color. The value is represented in three sequential numbers: the first is red, the next green, and the last blue. An example would be 255 255 255, which indicates the color white.

Photoshop is great for finding HSB and RGB values. The Color Picker box (see fig. 26.1) lists these values and appears when you double click on one of the color boxes.

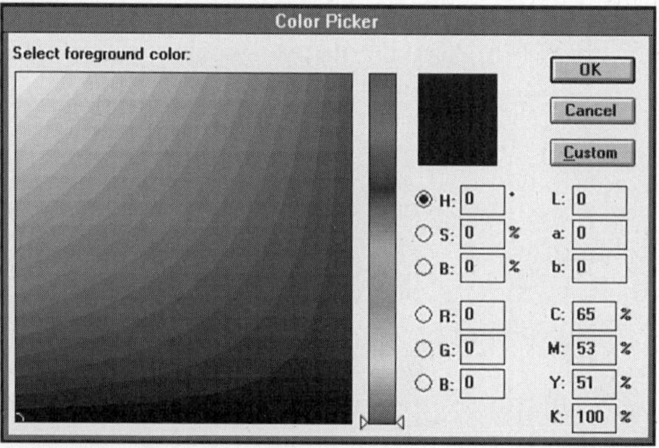

Figure 26.1
The Color Picker lists HSB and RGB values for a color.

Understanding how to manipulate your image's colors will help you in a couple of important ways. First, when converting your image from millions of colors down to 256 (or fewer colors), there will be slight distortion in the output. Sometimes, the graphic editor chooses a color to replace another color that simply does not look right. By adjusting the RGB values, you may be able to alter that distortion.

Another benefit is when you want to create a background graphic. For that, you need to make a very "light," almost see-through image. Controlling the HSB values, as well as adjusting the Gamma (discussed in Chapter 27), will help in the creation of these background type graphics.

Other Graphics Terms

Other key words to be familiar with in the world of graphics are dots, sample, pixel, and resolution. Pixels, dots, and samples measure work at various stages of its completion.

Your scanner measures a *sampling resolution* when scanning an image. The resolution is the frequency of digital samples per inch that the scanner creates from an image. The sample resolution is used to determine how many digital samples per inch the scanner creates from an image. For many scanners, the settings are specified in dots per inch, such as 150 dpi.

The dots per inch (dpi) measurement on a scanner is not the same as dots per inch (dpi) on a printer. Although the scanner measures the *digital samples per inch*, which is done when the scanner views the image, and assigns each space a color value based on an equal area of the original image, most documentation that you receive with your scanner refers to these *samples per inch* as *dots per inch* (dpi). Hence the scanning settings of 150 dpi and so on. A laser printer's dpi is not the same as the dpi that a scanner would produce. If you scan an image at 150 dpi, the best representation of that image would be to generate a laser print set at 1,200 dpi.

A *pixel* is a unit of measurement. It indicates a unit of light as displayed on your monitor. The number of pixels per inch measures the resolution. The higher the pixels per inch, the better the resolution. The better the resolution, the larger the file, and the longer it takes to download on your Web page. The general rule of thumb when creating Web graphics is to measure them at 72 dpi. Then at that point, you can change the pixels per inch, until you have an adequate image with the lowest possible pixel per inch setting.

Converting Graphics

Occasionally when you have a logo created or have a photo scanned, you receive the image in the wrong format for a Web page—anything other than a GIF or JPEG file. To use the image, it must be converted to the necessary type.

A number of useful graphics programs (Adobe Photoshop, Color It, LView Pro, Paint Shop Pro) can convert these files. The Paint Shop Pro program is very useful for converting images because it reads many different image formats and is easy to use.

To convert files to JPEG or GIF with Paint Shop Pro, follow these steps:

1. Open Paint Shop Pro, choose **F**ile, **O**pen to select your file, and then click on OK.
2. When the program opens your graphic, (whatever the format), choose **F**ile, Save **A**s, and select either the GIF or JPG extension in the File Type List.
3. Select the File Sub-Format (in the GIF format, that would be GIF87a or GIF89a), then select the directory to save the new image to and click on OK to process the request.

Paint Shop Pro will prompt you for other instructions if needed. For more tips and instructions on conversion, see Chapter 27, "Web Page Graphics Techniques."

Tip

> The conversion of a GIF image to a JPEG image isn't worthwhile because a GIF image only uses 256 colors, and the patterns in the image do not compress well with the JPEG algorithm.
>
> The best conversion to a JPEG is from a TIFF formatted graphic, which uses the millions of colors that are also possible in a JPEG file.

Graphic Formats and Web Images

As was mentioned, a key enhancement to any Web site is the use of professional graphics. You now have a general understanding of graphic file formats, and you have seen how to know which formats are acceptable, and how to go about obtaining and selecting them. The topic of converting graphics to the proper formats was discussed, with suggestions on obtaining the right graphic editor program.

If you intend to work with graphics for the creation of your Web site, you may want to invest in a good, solid graphics-oriented book, such as *Inside Adobe Photoshop 3* by Gary & Barbara Bouton (New Riders Publishing). The more you understand graphic formats, and what they consist of, the better your understanding of the limits of Web graphics.

Audio Files

Sound must be in a digital format for a digital computer to process it. Analog sound is carried along a wire as a varying analog voltage. To handle this digitally, the computer measures the voltage at regular intervals with an *Analog-to-Digital Converter* (ADC). Each measurement it takes is called a *sample.* The computer can then store and manipulate these samples as digital data and finally reproduce the sound by converting it back into a varying voltage with a *Digital-to-Analog Converter* (DAC).

Two elements of digital sound that affect the resulting sound quality are the *sampling rate* and *the sampling size*. The more samples you take, or the higher the sample rate, the closer you are to capturing the original sound wave. The sample size controls the accuracy of the samples in that the 16-bit size represents a smaller distance, therefore providing finer detail. If you increase the sample size (to 16-bit) and sample rate, the resulting sound will be more precise, but the amount of data to be stored will also increase.

Note *Sampling rate* is the number of samples taken per second, which is usually measured in kilohertz (kHz). Sampling size, also called the *sample resolution*, represents the increments between the top and bottom of the sound wave (8-bit or 16-bit).

To play sound files, you need to convert a description of the sound in the computer into a varying voltage that can be fed to speakers. The Musical Instrument Digital Interface (MIDI) is a serial communications protocol that is designed for the transmission of control data between music instruments. This allows the computer to instruct the synthesizer to play certain notes. The MIDI protocol has been around since 1983, and MIDI-capable synthesizers have become available as an add-on part for various computer systems.

For more information on MIDI, see their homepage at `http://www.eeb.ele.tue.nl/midi/index.html`.

A simple way to generate sound electronically is with a technique called *FM synthesis*. There are many sound cards available (such as Sound Star and Music Star) that provide hardware for producing sounds using FM synthesis. This technique is older than digital sampling and is based on modifying waveforms and combining them using various mathematical operations. The FM synthesis chips are controlled by specifying a set of frequencies and a way to combine them. This is a somewhat easy way of generating sounds electronically.

The way it works is that the synthesizer hardware provides a number of voices, which is the number of simultaneously playable notes (usually between 6 and 20). The voices are then combined to produce specific sounds.

There are advantages and disadvantages to using FM synthesis. The advantages are that it requires only simple hardware and little software overhead to produce. A disadvantage is that determining the patch parameters and producing good instrument sounds is very difficult, which leaves the output not as good as you would want.

Another, more expensive route, would be to use the current state of the art for sound hardware; Wavetable Synthesis. This technique is a combination of the sampling and FM synthesis. The sampled voices are downloaded into memory on the sound card, and the sound hardware then provides facilities for modifying these sound samples.

The wavetable synthesis technique provides the flexibility and realism of digital sampling, while maintaining the reduced software complexity and overhead of FM synthesis. The sound cards that use Wavetable Synthesis can also simulate FM synthesizers. The cards, however, that support the wavetable synthesis are more expensive, and not fully compatible with the older sound cards.

Synthesizers in general only support a small selection of different sounds, and the methods used to produce these sounds are very limited. Synthesizers are also unable to record sounds, which is an important factor to consider when deciding the best avenue of creating your Web page audio files.

Digital representations of sound are stored in several different ways on a computer's hard drive or on a network. These sound representations are called file formats.

Understanding Digital Formats

There are many important parts to a file format, and these are discussed in the following sections:

- Sound file headers
- Sampling frequency
- Linear and logarithmic progressions
- Channels

The nature of a sound file should be detailed and understood before attempting to create and post your own audio files on your Web site.

Sound File Headers

All sound files begin with a "header," which consists of information that describes the format and contents of the file. Header information includes the word length, number of channels, and sampling frequency (see table 26.2). This information is used by an audio application so that it can read the file properly.

Table 26.2
Sound File Header Information

Extension	Origin	Variable Parameters for Header (Fixed; Comments)
.au or .snd	NeXT, Sun	Rate, #channels, encoding, info string
.aif(f), AIFF	Apple, SGI	Rate, #channels, sample width, lots of info
.aif(f), AIFC	Apple, SGI	Same (extension of AIFF with compression)
.iff, IFF/8SVX	Amiga	Rate, #channels, instrument info (8 bits)
.wav, WAVE	Microsoft	Rate, #channels, sample width, lots of info

Word Length

Many different digital audio file formats exist, with different features and characteristics. The formats can vary depending on the length of each digital "word." These digital words, or bytes, can be 8-bits long, 16-bits long, and larger. The bytes can be signed, unsigned, or in floating point format. Most of the time, larger word length and higher bit size equals higher quality digital conversion. We'll discuss these issues further when we list the different sound file formats later in this chapter.

Sampling Frequency

The sampling frequency is simply the number of times the sound event is measured within a certain time period. Sampling frequencies are specified in kilohertz (kHz), which means samples per second. If the sampling frequency is too low, it will affect the distortion level, leaving the new sound wave sounding much different than the original sound wave.

A CD-quality sound requires 16-bit words sampled at 44.1 kHz. 44,100 16-bit words (or 705,600 bits) are used to digitally describe each second of sound on a compact disc.

Note The highest possible pitch with this sampling rate is 22.05 kHz (which is just about at the top of what humans can hear), and is half of 44.1 kHz.

Linear and Logarithmic Progressions

Linear or logarithmic progressions can also represent the bytes of a sound file. In linear encoding, the unit of measurement of the specified sound pressure is constant from sample to sample. In logarithmic encoding, however, as the sample value increases, the unit grows. Logarithmic encoding has an advantage in that it can represent a greater range of sound levels, but with higher noise levels.

The µ-law and a-law file formats, which will be discussed in further detail later in this chapter, use the logarithmic coding. To show an example, in other words, an 8-bit µ-law sample can provide the same output as a 12-bit linear encoded sample.

Audio Compression

Quality sound files consist of a large amount of data. Audio compression is available to reduce the amount of physical storage space and memory that is required to store a sound. Compression also reduces the time required to transfer a file. Compression can be *lossy* (which means the sound quality will be affected by compression) or *lossless* (no change in the sound quality when the file is decompressed).

The most common compression formats are Huffman, Macintosh Audio Compression/Expansion (MACE), Moving Picture Expert Group (MPEG), and Adaptive Differential Pulse Code Modulation (ADPCM). These techniques are *lossy*—they save a great deal of space at a reasonable cost in quality. Formats such as Apple's sound resource (snd), and "raw" audio files are the only formats that don't employ compression, although the snd format can contain other types of sound.

The μ-law (pronounced *mu-law*) file format, which has a compression ratio of 2:1, is an international standard for compressing voice quality audio. Some other formats include the G.721, G.723-24, and G.723-40 ADPCM formats, which are CCITT standards for compression of 8000-Hz 14-bit samples into a 32-, 24- or 40-kbps data stream. Unfortunately, these compressed formats have extremely slow decompression rates.

Recently, a new compression standard has been proposed by the Interactive Multimedia Association (IMA). The IMA's 4:1 audio compression format is intended to compress 16-bit sound with a ratio of 4:1, which means IMA can compress audio CD-quality sound into one-fourth the space it normally occupies. This new IMA 4:1 audio compression standard is already part of Apple Computer's QuickTime 2.0 and Sound Manager 3.1, and Microsoft's Video for Windows.

Audio File Formats

Numerous digital audio file formats have been introduced over the years. You may not have seen them or even heard of them, and may never encounter them. As computer platforms have come and gone, so have their proprietary file formats. This section of the chapter provides you with a brief introduction to audio file types commonly used on the WWW today, and to ways in which you can convert other files to these formats.

Although MIME typing allows for any file format to be transmitted between a client and server, only a small portion of the more popular multimedia file types are commonly used on the Web. Every new file type requires an appropriate helper application on the client's end, resulting in a decrease in commonly used file types. The format types listed in the remainder of this section are ones you are most likely to run into on the Internet. After each format follows its corresponding MIME type.

Note Multipurpose Internet Mail Extensions (MIME) was originally defined as a method for encoding files in Internet electronic mail. Now, it encompasses any type of file in any form of message across the Internet.

The most common audio file formats found on the Internet are

- µ-law (.au)
- AIFF
- WAVE (.wav)
- Macintosh sound resources (snd)
- QuickTime movies (.mov)

The biggest reason for their popularity is cross-platform compatibility. Other file formats, such as MOD and AIFC, have important and attractive features, but have not been widely accepted on Unix, IBM-PC compatible, and Macintosh platforms. Some newer formats, such as MPEG-compressed audio and video, might become common on the Internet because of its benefits.

µ-law (audio/basic au snd)

The µ-law file format is the most frequently used audio file type on the Internet. It may not be the highest quality audio file format available, but it has a relatively small file size, and is supported by software for just about every operating system. Its sampling rate of 8 kHz is similar to the standard telephone receiver. Some systems, such as NeXT, take a sampling rate of 8.013 kHz for the µ-law format.

The µ-law format provides a level of audio quality sufficient for some Web applications because most WWW users are still hearing the audio they retrieve from the Internet through a monophonic computer speaker. Many sound archives on the Internet provide audio samples in the µ-law format and higher quality formats like MPEG.

Tip A great archive of µ-law audio files is available on the Internet at the WWW TV Theme Songs home page:

```
http://ai.eecs.umich.edu/people/kennyp/sounds.html
```

and

```
http://sunsite.unc.edu/pub/ multimedia/sun-sounds/
```

AIFF & AIFC (audio/x-aiff aif aiff aifc)

The *Audio Interchange File Format* (AIFF) is capable of storing monaural and multichannel sample sounds at a variety of sample rates. This capability and its interchange format enable it to be converted easily to other file formats. AIFF is often used in high-end audio recording applications when storage space is not a concern. This format, which was originally developed by Apple, is predominantly used by Silicon Graphics and Macintosh applications.

AIFF files are often used for high-end audio recording applications and can be quite large. One minute of 16-bit stereo audio sampled at 44.1 kHz takes up about 10 megabytes of space. AIFF itself does not allow for compressed audio data. For this reason, Apple had to introduce AIFF-C, or AIFC format, which allows for the storage of compressed and uncompressed audio data. The AIFC format has a great compression algorithm that supports compression ratios of up to 6:1. Such a high compression ratio seriously affects the file's signal quality.

Because AIFF supports multiple sample rates, some sites offer AIFF files roughly equivalent to standard µ-law files. These files are usually labeled as 1-channel, 8-bit, 8 kHz AIFF files.

Note Most of the applications that support AIFF playback also support AIFC.

RIFF WAVE (audio/x-wav wav)

The Resource Interchange File Format Waveform Audio Format (WAV) that was introduced in MS Windows 3.1 is a proprietary format sponsored by Microsoft and IBM, and is most commonly used on Windows-based PCs. Although WAV files are most often in the ADPCM (Adaptive Differential Pulse Code Modulation) format, they support multiple encoding methods. All WAV files follow the *Rich Information File Format* (RIFF) specification.

This format is similar to the AIFF format in that it supports monaural and multichannel samples and a variety of sample rates. Like AIFF files, WAV files require approximately 10mb/min for 16-bit samples with a sampling rate of 44.1 kHz. Nevertheless, many sites also offer an 8-bit, 8 kHz, single channel WAV version. You can view a large archive of WAV sound at this URL:

`http://sunsite.unc.edu/pub/multimedia/pc-sounds.`

MPEG (audio/x-mpeg mp2)

The International Standard Organization's *Moving Picture Expert Group* (MPEG) designed a file format for audio and video file compression. Since its introduction, MPEG has become one of the most popular compression standards on the Internet. This format's capability to compress large files with only a small sacrifice in quality is one of the main reasons for its favoritism on the Internet in the last two years.

MPEG-I audio compression has three layers. The more complex layers do take longer to encode, but also produce higher compression ratios. All this while still keeping much of an audio file's original fidelity. For example, layer I takes the least amount of time to compress, but layer III yields higher compression ratios for comparable quality files.

Many sites offer high-quality music in the form of MPEG-compressed audio samples, and MPEG players are now available for almost every platform and operating system. Because MPEG audio compression is based on psycho-acoustic models, it is the best format for distributing high-quality sound files online.

Many sites that contain MPEG audio files offer layer II encoded files, which are files that can be compressed anywhere from 1/3 to 1/24 their original size. Keep in mind, however, that the higher the compression ratio, the greater the loss of original data.

The MPEG-1 format to encode audio files is not only used on many WWW sites, but it is also used at Phillips for their digital video CDs. MPEG-1 is also now the standard compression scheme for digital radio broadcasts.

There is a ton of information available on the Web about the MPEG compression standard. Check out the following sites for more details:

- The MPEG FAQs.

  `http://www.crs4.it/~luigi/MPEG/`

- Information about MPEG-1 audio encoding.

  `http://www.crs4.it/~luigi/MPEG/mpeg1-a.html`

- Information about MPEG-2 audio encoding.

  `http://www.crs4.it/~luigi/MPEG/mpeg2.html`

- The MPEG software archive.

  `ftp://ftp.crs4.it/mpeg/`

Creative Voice (audio/x-voc voc)

Creative Voice (VOC) is the proprietary sound file format recorded with Creative Lab's Sound Blaster and Sound Blaster Pro audio cards. This limited format supports only 8-bit mono audio files up to sampling rates of 44.1 kHz, and stereo files up to a 22 kHz sampling rate. For more information on the VOC format, see Creative Lab's homepage at `http://creaf.com`.

IFF/8SVX (audio/x-iff iff)

Although rarely used for audio file distribution on the Net, IFF/8SVX is the standard sound file format used by Amiga computers. This format is similar to AIFF in that it is also an interchange file format, which means that it was designed for easy conversion to other formats. The differences between the two are that the IFF/8SVX format supports only 8-bit samples, and its header section differs from other IFF format types.

See the IFF standard at this site:

```
gopher://ftp.std.com:70/0R0-182411-/obi/book/Standards/
Electronic.Arts.IFF
```

SND (audio/basic au snd)

The extension .snd is a bit vague. Sound files used by Sun/NeXT often are identified with the .snd extension, but they are usually μ-law files. The Macintosh system sounds and some PC sounds also have the .snd extension. They vary in sample rate from 5.5 kHz to 22 kHz, with 11 kHz being the most popular.

Macintosh .snd files are assigned the SFIL (sound file) in the "type" field of the Mac resource fork. These types of files can consist of AIFF/AIFC samples or synthesized sounds that can take advantage of the System 7 sound hardware and software.

Raw PCM Data

Raw *Pulse Code Modulated* data (PCM) is often identified with the .pcm extension but sometimes has no extension at all. You must often specify the waveform's sample rate, resolution, and number of channels because there is no header information provided in the file (see table 26.3).

Table 26.3
Sound File Formats Attributes

Audio Format	File Extension	Compression Factor	Windows Player	Mac Player	Unix Player	Internet Support
16-bit PCM	.wav or .aiff	1:1	Yes	Yes	Yes	Some
G.711 μ-law	.au	2:1	Yes	Yes	Yes	Great
32Kbps MPEG-1	.mpa or .mp2	4:1	Yes	Yes	Yes	Little
IMA/DVI ADPCM	.wav	4:1	Yes	Yes	Some	Some

Electronic Music Composition

Many audio file formats are on the Net that perform the sole function of storing digitized audio. Two other file formats you might want to consider using are concerned with electronic music composition.

MIDI (audio/x-midi mid midi)

The *Musical Instrument Digital Interface* (MIDI) is not a specification for sampled digital audio. It is instead a serial communications protocol designed to allow the transmission of control data between electronic music instruments. MIDI has been associated to a PostScript language for music. MIDI files are much smaller than digitized audio files because they only contain instructions for controlling how and when devices (such as electronic synthesizers or samplers) produce sounds.

A group of electronic music instrument manufacturers, otherwise known as the MIDI Manufacturer Association (MMA), has been responsible for the evolution of the MIDI protocol since its introduction in 1983. The MIDI home page at `http://www.eeb.ele.tue.nl/midi/index.html` has more information on this standard.

Modules (audio/x-mod mod)

The .mod extension identifies modules. *Modules* are a cross between MIDI files and digitized audio files, and do not consist solely of sampled audio or control information. This format not only contains a bank of digitized sounds, but also has control information for regulating the ways sounds are sequenced at playback. The samples are raw, 8-bit audio data. This format also includes simple *digital signal processing* (DSP) capabilities for adding effects.

Although modules got their start on the Amiga, their somewhat small file size and impressive capabilities have definitely made them a favorite of many composers on the Net. Module composition has become an art form thanks to free playback tools and huge collections of these files on the Net.

For detailed information on the MOD file format, visit the MOD FAQ at `http://www.cis.ohio-state.edu/hypertext/faq/usenet/mod-faq/top.html`.

Requirements for Audio Files

The most important peripheral required for a computer system to create or play back sound is a *sound card*. Most new computer systems are *multimedia-ready*, which means they include a sound card, speakers, a CD-ROM, special software, and, in most cases, a microphone. Older systems often are updated with a sound card. One of the most popular sound cards on the market is Creative Labs SoundBlaster, but many, many other companies sell sound cards.

In addition to the sound card, additional equipment is required to work with digital sound. This includes a microphone (to input the desired sound to be recorded), software (to apply different recording effects and features), speakers (to review the output sound), and in some cases a library of prepared sound clips (the equivalent of clip art in the graphics world).

Your Web browser should be set up so that it executes the appropriate sound application when one of these audio files is downloaded. In Netscape, for instance, the Helper Applications menu item in Options, Preferences is used to set audio capabilities. You should know where the corresponding executable file (.exe) to play the sounds is located in the hard drive, so that the right path will be input in the helper applications.

If the browser allows, search for this path by simply using the Browse feature. If the hardware, and especially software, is properly set up and installed in the Windows platform, your system is ready to receive and play the most popular sound file formats available on the Internet.

One thing to keep in mind when you include audio files on your Web page or choose to download them from others is that audio files are usually large, and depending on the user's system, will take awhile to download and play. If you include these files on your Web page, be considerate and indicate the size of the file so that the user knows how long it will take to download.

Understanding When to Use Audio Clips

Sound clips are great additions to a cool Web page, but remember to keep them simple. Hopefully you are only using them when necessary—when you want Web users to hear something. A perfect example of an appropriate use of sound clips would be for someone in music. If you are trying to promote your tape or CD on your Web site, you should include a sample of your work. Another excellent use of sound clips is if you are a language consultant who specializes in helping people speak more effectively. This type of business certainly could benefit from sound clips by providing a "before and after" tape of its work. Again, it's important to be considerate when using sound files on your Web site. Some hints for usage follow:

- Keep the files small if you must use them.
- Use only 8-bit sounds because most users have that capability.
- Indicate the size and type of the file so the user can see.
- If you need to use 16-bit, high quality, large sound files, consider offering a smaller clip for those who don't have the capability to play the larger one, or for a preview to allow the user to see whether they're interested in hearing the larger clip if they have the capability.

Although these two examples warrant the use of audio clips, many other Web sites have absolutely no reason to include sound on their pages. It may be hip and cool, but is it necessary? Although most new computer systems come with multimedia capabilities, the average person viewing your site most likely does not have these capabilities. Even if a user does, is it worth his or her wait to hear you say, "Hi!"?

The worst use of sound clips I've ever seen is when audio clips are downloaded when a site is first brought up. Users who do not have sound capabilities on their computer system must wait for the page to download while they wonder why it's taking so long, and then they receive an annoying error message stating that the system doesn't have a sound card. Obviously they knew that. Be considerate of users when you add sound clips to your Web page.

Audio and Its Role on the Internet

For the most part, audio on the Internet involves downloading a file from a server, usually via FTP, Gopher, or electronic mail, before it is played in the appropriate sound software. Due to this time lapse limitation, audio content providers mainly use Internet servers as centrally located storage devices; they house archives of sound that can be accessed worldwide.

An excellent Internet storage site for sound is the Computer Music Journal WWW site. Small audio files, such as the Time of The Day function at Yale University, can be downloaded quickly. Another good example of sound stored on the Internet is New York State, where the Oneida Indian Reservation has a Web site welcoming you in their native language, as well as in English. Although the actual playing time of this audio clip is approximately 20–30 seconds, it takes more than twice that to actually download the clip using a 14.4 modem.

Digital audio is now being used in three major forms of media with the help of personal computers:

- Telephony
- Radio broadcasts
- Tele/videoconferencing

Computers have incorporated and started performing functions that before required separate electronic devices around the home and business. Computers can now function as a facsimile machine, CD player, telephone and answering machine, television/VCR, radio, and even postman (or "mail carrier" if you are PC about your PC). With only a few additional pieces of equipment and a microphone, speaker(s), and inputs for audio media, such as a CD player, your computer can become a sound studio. The only limitation to the eventual success of audio on a network (including telephony, broadcast audio/video, and teleconferencing) is bandwidth.

Telephony

With a simple 14.4-bps modem you can replace the telephone. The relatively low quality of telephone audio (approximately that of AM radio) occupies very little bandwidth. New and improved telephony applications for Internet use are now available (such as NetPhone) that are capable of using the bandwidth of a 14.4 modem for full-duplex audio.

Although they sound great in theory, telephony applications still have practical obstacles to overcome before they can replace the phone. The computer must be kept on all the time to accept incoming calls. In addition, the other party must be using the same telephony system (although this will change with an industry standard). Another disadvantage is that there is no familiar user interface, such as a handset, which is part of the standard computer configuration.

Broadcasting

Future plans for the server on which audio files reside, include the implementation of live audio feeds in real-time, broadcasting text with an audio stream, and the capability to manage thousands of simultaneous streams. In the meantime, some users are taking advantage of the best "real audio" feature available in their Web browsers (described in the next section) by listening to such things as the introductory message by Bill Clinton for the White House homepage.

RealAudio

An audio client-server system that employs real-time delivery is already being used to deliver news broadcasts at the Progressive Networks Inc.'s RealAudio site. A RealAudio server is optimized for sending simultaneous streams of audio, while the client plays an audio file as it is being downloaded. By mixing the player with the Web browser, RealAudio and other similar systems can take advantage of established distribution, authoring, and security protocols.

The RealAudio compression algorithm and its technical specifications are currently confidential. The sound quality specifies an 8 bit, 11 kHz sample, playable over a 14,400 bps modem connection with only modest processing requirements. The playback method is not scaleable (it cannot be changed), which means sound quality is the same on computers with faster connections and more processing power.

TrueSpeech

TrueSpeech, which was developed by the DSP Group, Inc. is similar to RealAudio. TrueSpeech makes a concentrated effort on compression algorithms, which are tuned specifically for speech. A nice feature of the TrueSpeech player is the capability to offer more than one compression scheme. TrueSpeech can adapt to sound quality, file size, and transmission speed. Another advantage to TrueSpeech is that DSP is currently working on standardizing its compression algorithms to help with cross-platform use of computer and telephony products.

To ensure widespread use, Microsoft includes TrueSpeech 8.5, with its Windows 95 Internet Explorer Web Browser. This version of TrueSpeech uses a 15:1 compression ratio. The DSP Group plans to create a TrueSpeech server to be used in much the same way as the RealAudio server. Windows 95 enables its users, for now, to be able to encode audio and save it as a WAV file. Unlike the inconvenient and proprietary RealAudio format, WAV files can be played on TrueSpeech players in real time and on conventional sound utilities.

StreamWorks

Another exciting audio product is StreamWorks by the Xing Technology Corporation. StreamWorks is capable of delivering live broadcast feeds using the international MPEG compression standard. Another key benefit of StreamWorks is that it is designed to operate over TCP/IP networks of varying topologies, such as Ethernet, ATM, FDDI, ISDN, T1, and Frame Relay. Because of this design, StreamWorks can be used on the Internet *and* in corporate and educational wide area networks.

Teleconferencing

An even more advanced use of audio on the Internet is *teleconferencing*, which is the capability of several parties to communicate simultaneously. Teleconferencing differs from telephony, which involves only two people.

Developers have skipped audio-only teleconferencing systems and created software that can transmit audio and video over the bandwidth of a typical modem connection. The most common of this type of software is CU-SeeMe.

CU-SeeMe

CU-SeeMe is a PC-based video conferencing client-server system that miraculously can compress audio video data together. This amazing feat is possible by implementing four compression algorithms and a choice of two different audio sampling rates.

CU-SeeMe operates in a client-server configuration. This means that clients transmit signals to "reflector sites"—Unix-based servers that receive and retransmit the signals. With this configuration, instead of the client-client system, broadcasts can be sent from one point to several. This arrangement also enables CU-SeeMe to conduct true multi-point conferencing.

The only unfortunate problem with the CU-SeeMe protocol is that it is not compatible with current videoconferencing standards. If it were to change to these standards, CU-SeeMe could be used by almost anyone on the Internet to exchange real-time audio and video with existing videoconferencing systems. When all of the videoconferencing product manufacturers conform to the standards, the ability to videoconference over the Internet for no additional telephone charges will appear even more attractive.

This chapter provided an overview of the use of graphics and audio in Web pages. To ensure a successful combination of audio and imagery in a Web page, keep users in mind. What type of system will Web hounds use to view your pages? If they do not have a graphics card, how will they see your images? If users have no sound card, how will they hear your audio files? The answer is, they won't.

This is why it's important to remember the user when designing your Web page (see Chapter 29, "HTML Cross Client Concerns," for more information on this subject). Be conscious and considerate of Internet users, and they will appreciate your Web pages.

Web Page Graphics Techniques

by Nancy Acosta

This chapter covers graphics issues on your Web pages. It's not just as simple as adding a pretty picture to your Web page. There are some tips and techniques to follow when implementing images that will enable you to incorporate these beautiful pictures and still maintain the quick downloading time that has become invaluable to most users. You will read about the following issues in this chapter:

- *Obtaining the perfect Web graphics*
- *Creating the perfect Web graphics*
- *Future graphics on the Web*
- *Understanding when to use each format*
- *Incorporating images into your Web pages*
- *Netscape enhancements to images*
- *General tips for Web page graphics*

- Using Imagemaps
- VRML

When you surf the Net, you can see that graphics enhance Web pages if they are created and used correctly.

Obtaining Perfect Web Graphics

If you plan to include graphics on your site, you can obtain perfect ones for your needs using several methods. You can have an image scanned, convert a negative or slide to a Photo CD, or use clip art. You can also create your own graphics in several formats, as shown in the following section.

Scanning

Pictures or designs in hard print can be converted to digital format using scanners. Unless you plan to do a lot of this type of procedure, save the cost of scanning equipment and software by out-sourcing this short term work.

If you do decide to purchase a scanner and plan to do a lot of work in the Photoshop program to alter these scans, go with a flatbed 24-bit color scanner. This type might be a little more expensive, but if you are planning on incorporating photos and vivid graphics, you'll find it to be well worth the money.

Sheet-fed scanners, although very affordable at a couple hundred dollars, are somewhat cumbersome to use because you must feed the pictures through a roll, so they are not suited for serious graphics.

The hand-held scanner is great, but limits the size you're able to scan efficiently. You also must be very steady when using one of these devices. Hand-held scanners are also very affordable at around $100 each.

If you can afford to spend a little more money on your scanner, stick with the flatbed, with at least 24-bit color capabilities. Although you can find these scanners as low as $500 or so, expect to spend at least $800–$1,000 for a decent scanner, the output quality will be more than acceptable for Web graphics usage.

Take into consideration how many times you will use the scanner in order to justify the cost of purchasing the equipment versus out-sourcing the job. Remember, the prices listed above are approximations, and do not include the software that is also needed. You can have professional scans done from anywhere between $25–$50 depending on how much touch-up is involved after the scanning is done.

Warning It's important to make sure any pictures or images you want to scan are not copyrighted—you don't want to be accused of stealing someone else's work.

Converting to CD

To obtain the best quality picture from a negative or slide, have the slide or negative converted onto a Photo CD. Some prices for this procedure go as low as $1.30 per negative, depending on the total quantity you want done. Many professional photo labs have the large equipment necessary in-house, or will send your images to Kodak for this process. You then will receive a Photo CD with your images, ready to use.

Digital Cameras

Another way to obtain graphics that many do not consider is the use of a digital camera. The main reason why these devices don't come to mind is that everyone considers them unaffordable. The truth is that many models are now affordable and could be necessary for some types of Web graphics work. Kodak, Apple, Sony, and Casio all make variations of these cameras that could be anywhere from around $500 to thousands of dollars. The Sony computer video camera, for example, is able to do desktop video conferencing, still image capture, and audio/video presentations, and costs just under the $500 mark.

Suppose a real estate company wants to put their business on the Internet by placing some of their listings on a Web site. What would be better than to purchase a digital camera to take pictures of the houses they are selling? No film or developing expenses are involved, and the turnaround time of taking the picture and having it on the Web is minimal. Simply download images directly from the camera to your PC in as little as 10 to 90 seconds per image!

Digital cameras capture images on a charge-coupled device, which are then downloaded into the camera's RAM storage. Some models have 1 MB of RAM, which enables them to capture between 5 to 16 high-resolution images, or between 32 to 88 low-res images. Some cameras use a compression method to squeeze more photos in RAM, and others are more memory conscious and cannot hold many photos. A few digital cameras have a removable PC card memory to allow more room, but these cards are very expensive right now.

Pictures are transferred from your camera to your computer using a serial cable and special software from the vendor. You have to wait anywhere from 10 to 90 seconds for images to transfer, but when they are in the system, you can edit them and immediately post them to your site.

For more information on various models of digital cameras, check out the following sites:

- **Sony.** `http://www.sony.com/`
- **Apple.** `http://www.apple.com/`
- **Kodak.** `http://www.kodak.com/`
- **DyCam.** `http://www.dycam.com/`
- **Casio.** `http://www.casio-usa.com/`

Although there are many ways to consider obtaining graphics and getting them into a digital format, there are program packages that are necessary if you intend to utilize these graphics on your pages. Many graphics programs exist, offering everything from the inexpensive shareware programs to the full-fledged, complete graphics software.

Some popular shareware includes Paint Shop Pro and LView Pro, which are both very good programs for minimal graphic conversion and manipulation. Two of the more complete packages would be CorelDRAW and Adobe Photoshop. Although Photoshop might be the more expensive package, the tremendous power and flexibility it offers for extensive graphics conversion and manipulation is unsurpassable. If you plan to do heavy-duty graphics work, Photoshop might be your best bet.

There are also many great books devoted to the graphics subject that you will find very useful when starting on your image adventure. (Check out other New Riders books, such as *Inside Adobe Photoshop 3, Inside CorelDRAW! 5*, or *Designing Web Graphics,* among others.)

Clip Art/Public Pictures

Another method for obtaining great graphics for your page is to search through clip-art and picture libraries. CD-ROMs filled with clip art and pictures for public use are numerous; file archives also are available on the Web that you can use.

Some Web sites to check out include these:

- Yahoo's clip art list:

  `http://www.yahoo.com/Computers/Multimedia/Pictures/Clip_Art/`

- Sandra's clip art server:

  `http://cs.yale.edu/HTML/YALE/CS/HyPlans/loosemore-sandra/clipart.html`

- West Stock Inc.:

  `http://www.weststock.com/`

- Illusionist's Art Gallery:

  `http://www.infohaus.com/access/byseller/Illusionist/HIDDEN.artpage.free.html`

The most important concern when you plan to use clip art is to make sure the images are royalty-free. Especially when downloading from the Internet.

If you have any doubts about this issue, contact the publisher or creator to ensure no royalties are required for the files you want to use.

Creating Perfect Web Graphics

An illustrator can create a special design or graphic from scratch based on your needs. Although this might be expensive and time consuming, the quality of custom graphics definitely surpasses any basic graphics that are available.

One of the biggest advantages to hiring an illustrator is you avoid royalty issues. You should, however, clarify the issue of who retains ownership of the graphic. Many artists and illustrators might want to retain the right to show their work for you in public, which might mean that you can only use the graphic in certain applications.

If you're looking for a computer artist, you could search the Yellow Pages, although you might want to ask around to find someone good and reputable. Consider joining your local PC Computer Club, which is a great source for computer-type information, and you can meet some of the best illustrators in the country this way. It can be extremely difficult to find someone who can create a vision from scratch. It takes a lot of talent, and perhaps some marketing and advertising background as well to have the perfect combination.

Luckily, we're able to go to our illustrator with a simple idea, and he turns it into our vision. For this level of professionalism—to have your own artist on the payroll—you can expect to pay anywhere from a few hundred dollars to a couple thousand to obtain your graphic and retain complete ownership, or, as the artist calls, a corporate identity. The need for a corporate identity arises when you are a newly formed corporation and want to have an identity or logo created for your organization. This type of work is much more expensive. If the artist charges by the hour, it would not be unreasonable to be charged more than $75 per hour for their work.

If you do choose to create your own graphics, provide great-looking graphics, but make sure they also have a low download time. Several methods are available for altering your graphics:

- Reducing colors
- Compression
- Interlacing

Reducing Colors

One way to reduce file sizes and minimize download times is to reduce the number of colors used in a graphic. If you are converting an existing file to a GIF format and are lucky, the file may only use 256 colors and not up to 16 million colors as many formats use. If your graphic uses more than 256 colors, you must reduce the number of colors being used to 256, if you need a GIF file, because that is the maximum amount that can be used in the GIF format. The two programs most often used for reducing color palettes in images are Paint Shop Pro and Adobe Photoshop.

Note When determining which file format is best for the smallest size graphic, JPEG files are slightly different. Decreasing the number of colors in a JPEG file won't necessarily reduce the file's size. JPEG file sizes are based on the amount of compression used for each file. See Chapter 26, "Graphics and Audio File Formats," for more information.

Reducing Colors with Paint Shop Pro

Paint Shop Pro (PSP) is shareware that is available over the Internet. Try Stroud's CWSApps List—Index of Apps at `http://www.enterprise.net/cwsapps/inx2.html` for downloading this and other great programs.

PSP also is a great program for first-time users because the steps necessary to reduce colors are fairly simple. When you first open a graphic, PSP displays the dimensions and the number of colors in the bottom left corner:

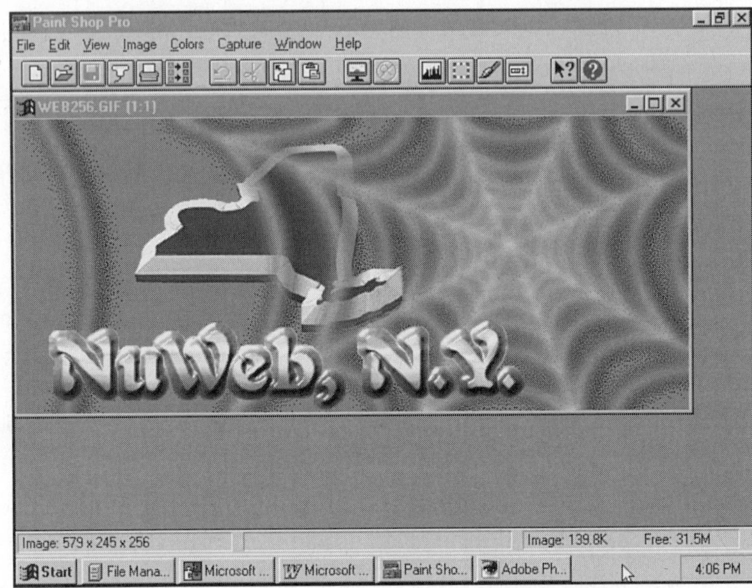

Figure 27.1
Paint Shop Pro shows the image width, height, and number of colors used in the bottom left corner.

To reduce colors, follow these steps:

1. After you open the graphic, choose **C**olors, then **D**ecrease Color Depth (see fig. 27.2). The dialog box appears listing choices for the total number of colors you want to use in the image.

2. Choose any number from 256 colors down. Again, remember that the GIF file format can only have a maximum of 256 colors. After you choose the new number of colors, a prompt appears with more options for decreasing color depth (see fig. 27.3).

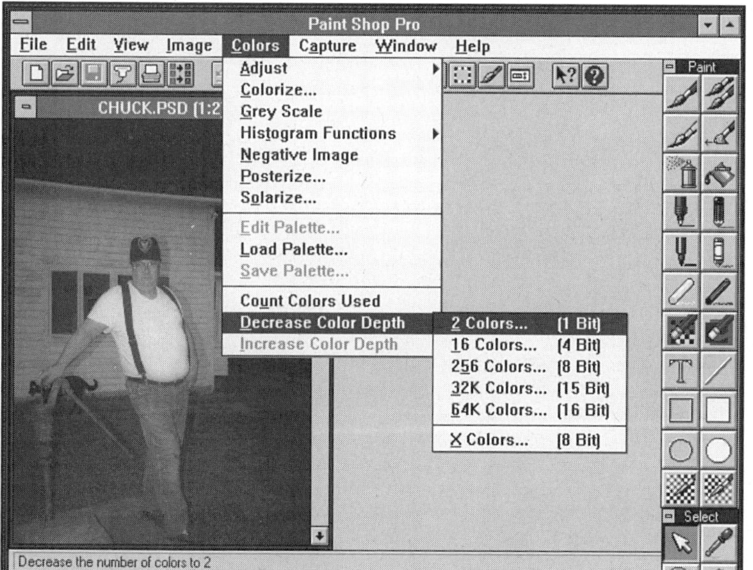

Figure 27.2
The Paint Shop Pro choices for decreasing color depth.

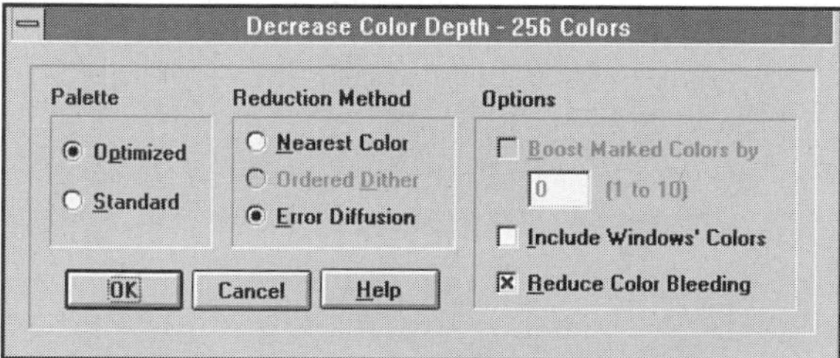

Figure 27.3
The Decrease Color Depth dialog box displayed by PSP when reducing the number of colors in a graphic.

3. Choose the Palette type (O**p**timized or **S**tandard), which indicates the color palette to be used; the Reduction Method (**N**earest Color, Ordered **D**ither, or **E**rror Diffusion), which indicates how the colors will be reduced; then choose from **B**oost Marked Colors by, **I**nclude Windows Colors, or **R**educe Color Bleeding, which offer more in helping the clarity of the final output.

   In figure 27.3, the best choices seem to be O**p**timized for the Palette type, **E**rror Diffusion for the Reduction Method, and **R**educe Color Bleeding. These choices kept most of the original quality of the graphic.

   You will need to play around with these options and settings to find the best combination for each picture. That is when the **E**dit, **U**ndo command really comes in handy!

4. When you are finished, see if the image's size at the bottom of the screen reflects the new amount of colors.

Reducing Colors with Photoshop

Adobe Photoshop is a little harder to learn than Paint Shop Pro, but it is extremely flexible when you want to manipulate graphics. Follow these steps to reduce colors in Photoshop version 3.0:

1. Open the graphic, then choose Mode, Indexed Color. The Indexed Color dialog box appears (see fig. 27.4).

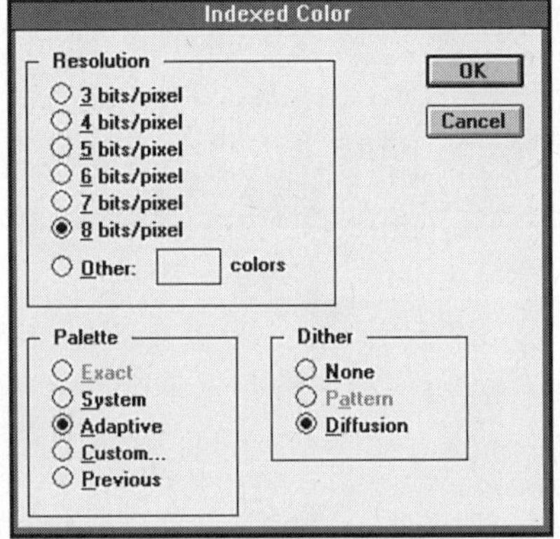

Figure 27.4
The Indexed Color dialog box is displayed in Photoshop when reducing the number of colors in the graphic.

2. Choices in the Indexed Color dialog box include Resolution, Palette, and Dither. The Other box in Resolution will note if less than 256 colors are in your graphic. If this box is empty, you need to reduce the colors to reduce the graphic's file size.

When you choose a Resolution, remember that the lower the number of bits per pixel, the fewer colors in use. The Adaptive option in the Palette choice box and the Diffusion option in Dither are the best choices most of the time. If this combination doesn't look the best for your images, choose different settings and keep using the Edit, Undo command.

In the image in figure 27.3, I was able to minimize the Resolution to only 7 bits per pixel (128 colors) and keep most of the quality. This slight change in colors reduced the graphic's size from 726 KB all the way down to 242 KB, which is quite a difference!

Note Always try to use as few colors as possible on a Web page. Many browsers will display graphics differently if the graphics use more than the customary 256 colors. By creating images with fewer than 256 colors, you help ensure that everyone who accesses your page sees what you intended.

Compression

The *American Heritage Dictionary* defines *compress* as "to press together or force into a smaller space," which is exactly what compression is in relation to graphics. By compressing a graphic you are making it smaller (in bulk size, not screen size), so that it uses less disk space. This newly compressed image takes less time to process and less time to download.

Graphic file formats use different types of compression. GIF files, for example, use a *lossless* compression called LZW, which simply means that none of the original information is discarded. The same image remains when you compress and decompress the file.

JPEG compression is a *lossy* compression; it discards information that is not critical in the images. JPEG's lossy compression can create smaller files than GIF's LZW lossless method. Sometimes the quality of the image suffers with this type of compression. Before you use either type of compression, ask yourself if you need to maintain quality or minimize size. With logos, icons, or general clip-art images, the GIF format is recommended. Photos and pictures, however, generally work best with the JPEG format.

Adobe Photoshop is a good way to illustrate how you compress images:

1. Open an image in Photoshop and choose File, Save a Copy (see figure 27.5).

2a. At this point, choose the file type you want to use. If you plan on saving the image in the GIF format, and the graphic is currently using 16 million colors, you first need to decrease the number of colors before Photoshop will let you save the image as a GIF (see the section "Reducing Colors" for instructions).

Figure 27.5
The Save a Copy dialog box as displayed in Photoshop when you are saving a copy of a graphic.

2b. If you want to save the file as a JPEG, choose JPEG from Save File as Format Type.

3. If you are saving the file as a JPEG, the Indexed Color dialog box will appear. You must indicate the Image Quality (see figure 27.6).

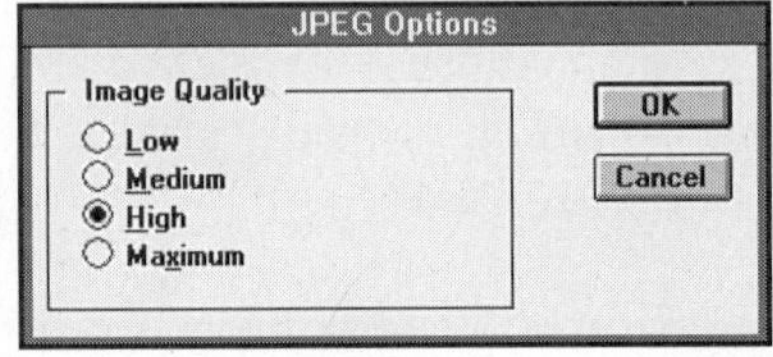

Figure 27.6
The JPEG Options dialog box as displayed in Photoshop when saving an image to a JPEG file format.

The graphic in figure 27.6 was saved with the Maximum amount of JPEG compression. The file size was reduced from 49,704 down to 9,991 bytes. The Low selection hurt the image's quality considerably, but the size was very small (3,087 bytes). Experiment with different compression settings for JPEG images before you make a decision.

When a Web user accesses your Web page, the graphics you have compressed are automatically decompressed by a graphics program or the Web browser. If you did your homework and reduced file sizes as much as possible, the viewer will be able to load all the images on your page as quickly on a slow computer as a fast one. Regardless of the CPU, it usually takes JPEG files longer to download than it does GIF files.

Interlacing

One feature the GIF file format has that JPEG lacks is *interlacing*. When an interlaced GIF graphic begins to download, it appears very blurry. Then it continues to clear up, until the whole graphic is in focus. This is considered an advantage of the interlaced GIF graphics format.

Older versions of the GIF format saved a file one line at a time. The interlacing GIF version, 89A, saves every eighth row starting with the first, then every eighth row starting with the fourth, then every fourth row starting with the third, then all the leftover rows are stored. It sounds complicated, but the advantage to this approach is that you can see what the graphic looks like immediately after it begins to download. You no longer have to sit and wait for the entire image to appear to see what it is.

A shareware program that works great for saving GIF files in the interlaced format is LView Pro (make sure you have the 1.A version). It is easy to save an interlaced GIF:

1. After you open the program, open the graphic.
2. Click on **O**ptions. Make sure the Save **G**IFs Interlaced option is checked (see fig. 27.7). Continue to save the graphic in the GIF format while this option is checked and you should be all set.

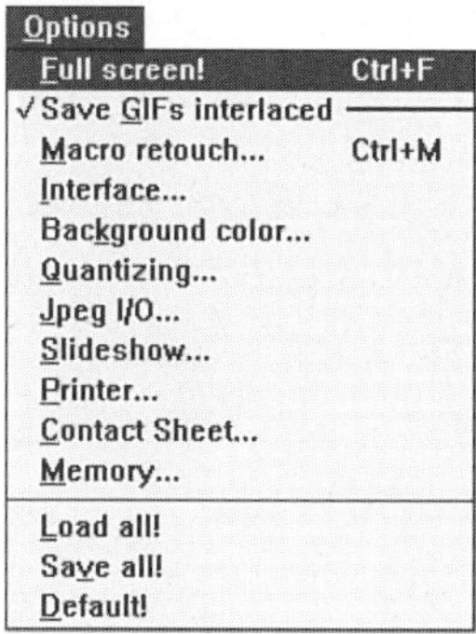

Figure 27.7
The Options menu in LView Pro where you must check the Save GIFs interlaced option on.

Transparency

Another option GIF includes is the capability to save one color as a transparent color. This option lets you design Web graphics that seem to be floating, or standing on the page. This transparency option is great for logos with a single color background (see fig. 27.8).

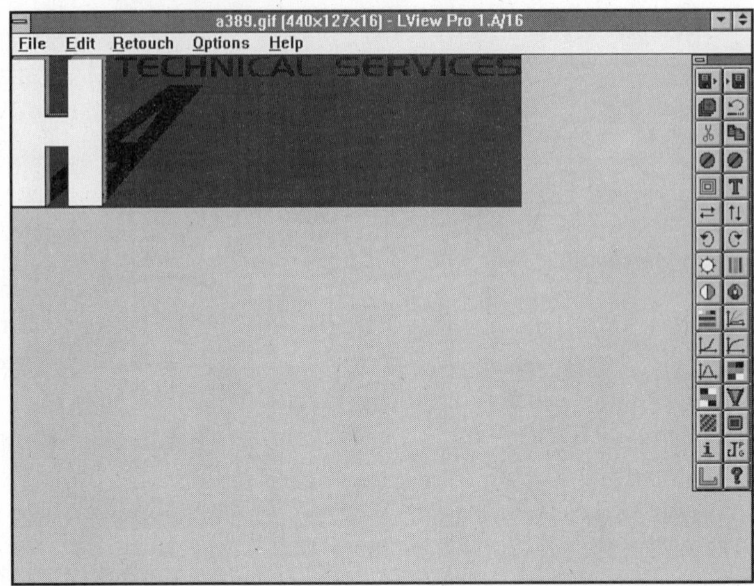

Figure 27.8
A perfect logo for saving the background blue color as a transparent color.

LView Pro can be used to save GIFs in this format:

1. Open the graphic in LView Pro.
2. Click on Options, then choose Background color.
3. When the Select Color Palette Entry box appears choose the color that represents the graphic's background color, and then click on OK (see fig. 27.9).
4. Choose the File, Save command. LView will prompt you with "Save this image in GIF89a format?" Click on OK.

Note Adobe has released an update to the 3.0.5 version of Photoshop that includes a new GIF89a export plug-in feature. This plug-in lets you create GIF files specifically designed for Web use. For more information on this plug-in, check out Adobe's Web site at `http://www.adobe.com`.

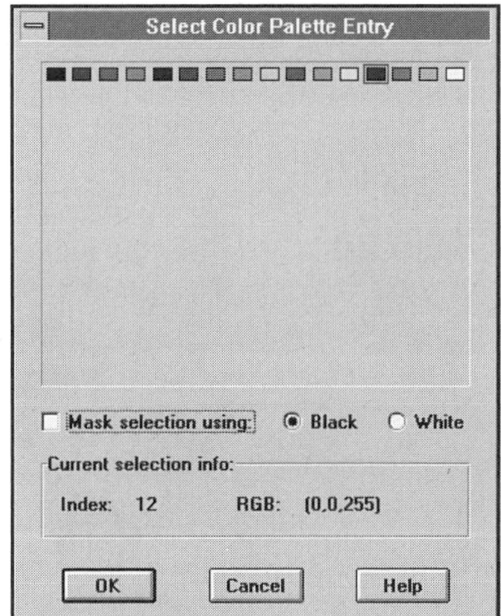

Figure 27.9
The Select Color Palette Entry dialog box as displayed in LView Pro when selecting a background color in the graphic.

Cropping Images

Another way to reduce the size of your image is to crop it. This will make the physical size of your image smaller. Photoshop is a great application for cropping images because it provides two ways to crop.

1. Open the image you want to crop.

2. Double-click on the crop marquee in the toolbox.

3. Select the part of the image you want to use. Place the mouse over the top left corner of the area you want to use (notice how the cursor looks like a crop marquee), press and hold down the left mouse button, then drag the mouse to the bottom right corner and release it. You should see a dotted line box around the part of the image you want to use.

4. Move the mouse over the highlighted area. When the cursor changes to a scissors image inside the box, click the mouse, and the image will crop and resize (see fig. 27.10).

Notice how much was taken off the sides of the original picture. The sides were unnecessary; by deleting them, the file size went from an original size of 1.13 MB to 366 KB. Quite a difference!

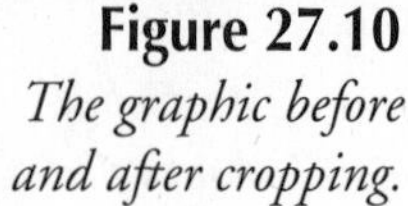

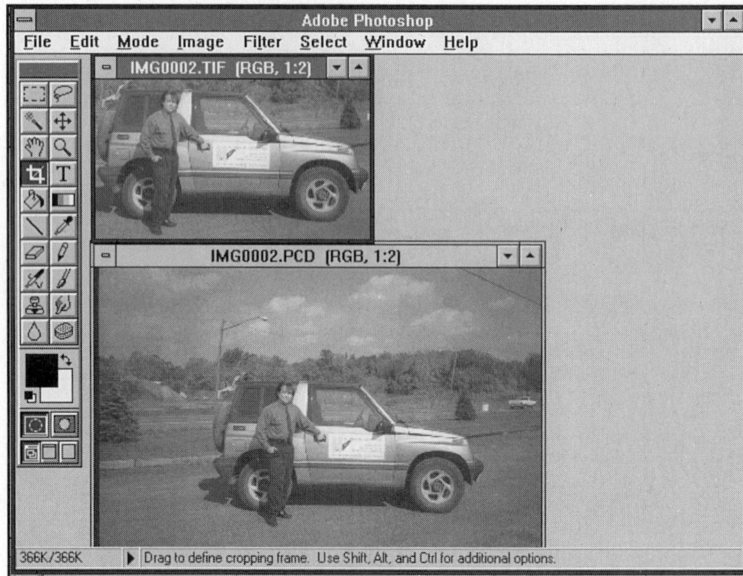

Figure 27.10
The graphic before and after cropping.

If you know the exact dimensions or resolution you need an image to be, Photoshop provides a second, more precise cropping method:

1. Double-click on the crop marquee to access the Cropping Tool Options box.
2. Click on the Fixed Target Size box and specify the size you want the new image to be.
3. Use the mouse to define the section of the image you want to use, then click the mouse inside the highlighted box.

Scaling Images

Another way to decrease the size of an image is to scale it down, which is another way of resizing an image. Sometimes this may result in a loss of detail, or a disproportional image; you need to decide if the difference is worth the decrease in image size.

With Photoshop scaling images takes only a few steps:

1. Open an image to scale.
2. If you want to scale the entire image, choose **S**elect, **A**ll. If you only want to scale a portion of it, click on the select marquee and highlight the desired section with the mouse.
3. After you make a selection, choose **I**mage, **E**ffects, **S**cale. The corners of your selection will show little boxes that you can drag. Click on one of the corners and drag it to the size you want the image to be.
4. Move the mouse over the highlighted box. Notice how the mouse turns into a gavel type hammer. Click inside the box to complete the scale.

This is another way of resizing the image, but be careful not to make the final graphic unrealistic looking.

Tips for Making Outstanding Graphics

When you decide to use graphics on your page, there are many tips and techniques you can use to make them stand out in the crowd. There are many special effects that can be applied to your images. Besides buying the graphics programs that can make those effects, there are many great books that will help create these special pictures as well.

Tip

> A great book on learning and understanding images is New Riders' *Inside Adobe Photoshop 3,* by Gary & Barbara Bouton. This book teaches all the tricks available in Photoshop for making outstanding graphics.

Creating a Glowing Effect with Photoshop

One feature Photoshop has that is a real boon to Web designers is the capabiltiy to make an image glow.

The following steps will enable you to select the section of the graphic you want to work with and turn this selection into a path.

Note Photoshop refers to a path, which is a shape specified within a bitmap image. It is a series of anchor points connected by path segments, which have a length and direction.

Warning Don't forget to save your image frequently.

1. Click on the Lasso tool (the top left icon, which looks like a mini lasso) on the toolbox, and move to the graphic.
2. Press and hold down the Alt key and click on each corner of the object you want to highlight until you come back to the place where you started. Don't worry if parts stick out of your selection. When you release the Alt key, the image should have a marquee around it.
3. Open the Channels palette (choose Window, Palettes, and Show Channels, or click on the Channels tab if the window is already open) and choose the Save to Selection icon on the bottom left corner (see fig. 27.11).

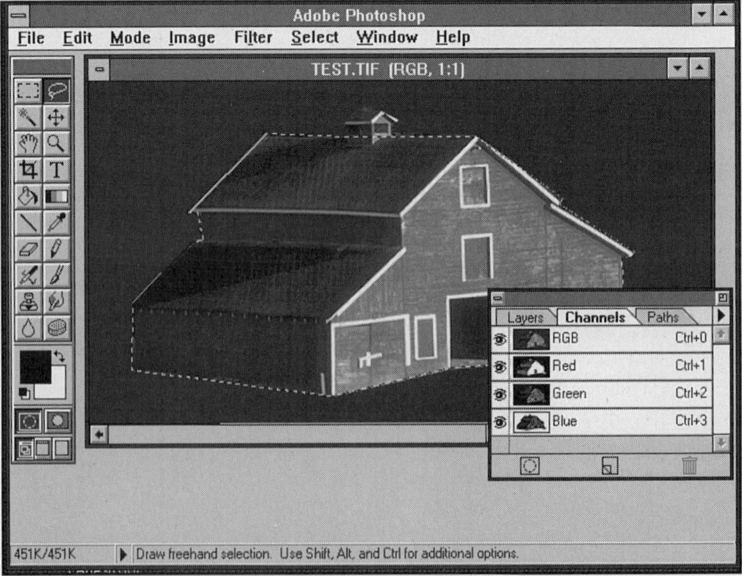

Figure 27.11
The barn with the marquee around it.

4. Press Ctr+D to deselect the image.

5. Double-click on the new channel to name it.

6. When the Channel Options box appears, in the Color Indicates selection check the Selected Areas circle and click on OK. The image should appear as shown in figure 27.12.

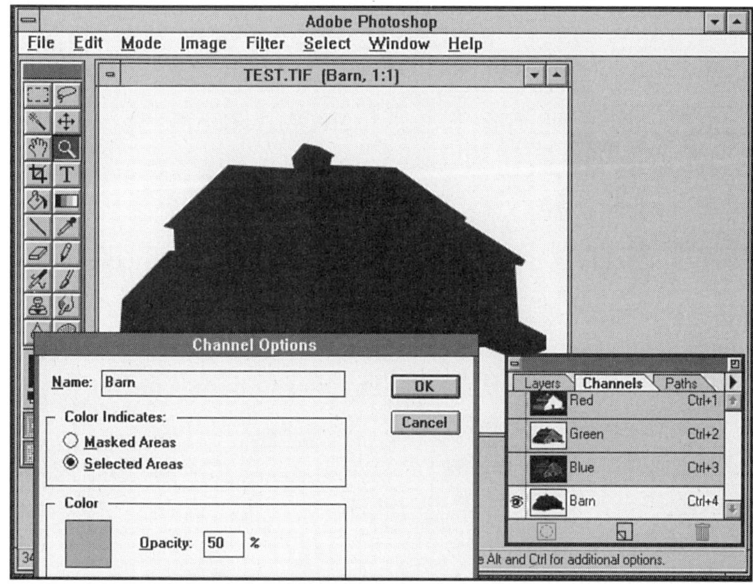

Figure 27.12
The Channel Options dialog box; behind it is the way the graphic will appear.

If you need to include outside sections that could not be highlighted with the lasso tool, follow these steps to include them:

7. Press and hold down the Alt key and click on the new channel's thumbnail icon to activate the selection marquee on that area.

8. Click on the RGB title on the Channels palette.

9. Click on the Quick Mask mode button—the filled circle button on the bottom right of the toolbox.

10. Zoom in on the image (if necessary) by pressing the Ctrl key and the plus sign simultaneously (shown as Ctrl++).

11. Double-click on the Paintbrush tool, which is the 8th one down on the right side of the toolbar that looks like a mini paintbrush.
12. By double-clicking on the Paintbrush tool, the Paintbrush Options palette appears. Choose Normal mode, 100 percent Opacity. Make sure nothing else is checked (such as Fade or Wet Edges).
13. Click on the Brushes tab within that same box to bring up the brushes options. Choose the most appropriate brush tip for the size of the area you wish to paint in.
14. Press D for the default colors (just in case they weren't the default set of colors).
15. Click and drag a single stroke over the area you already chose, then click and drag over other areas you want to include until every desired area is masked.

Note You can switch back and forth between colors while painting the section you want to include, which helps if you make a mistake and go outside the area. Press X or the reverse color arrows on the toolbox to fix any mistakes.

16. Now switch back to Standard editing mode by clicking on the button to the left of the Quick Mask button.
17. The section you painted will become part of the original channel. Click on the creates new channels icon on the Channels palette (in the bottom left corner of the Channels palette), and drag it into the thumbnail of the working channel. This will update the channel to include the new selection areas (see fig. 27.13).

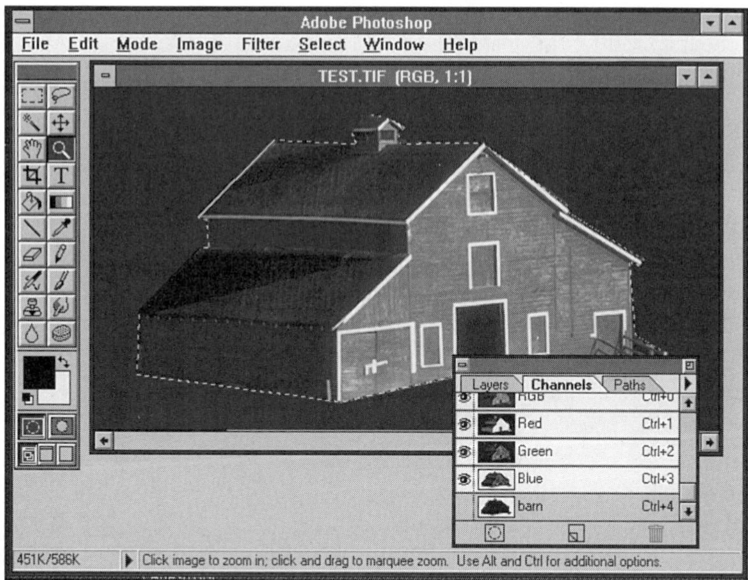

Figure 27.13
How the image looks after the channel has been updated.

At this point the whole image you want to change is selected. The next step is to create Paths for the glow effect.

18. Press and hold down the Alt key and click on the newest channel's thumbnail icon to activate the marquee.
19. Click on the Paths palette tab to bring up the Paths palette.
20. Choose the Create/Make Path icon, which looks like a square box, at the bottom center of the palette.
21. Click on the Arrow tool in the top left row of the Paths palette, and then click on the line surrounding the object (the actual path). The anchor points that appear enable you to control the exact outline of the image. Click and drag on any of the anchors to improve the outline of the image (see fig. 27.14).

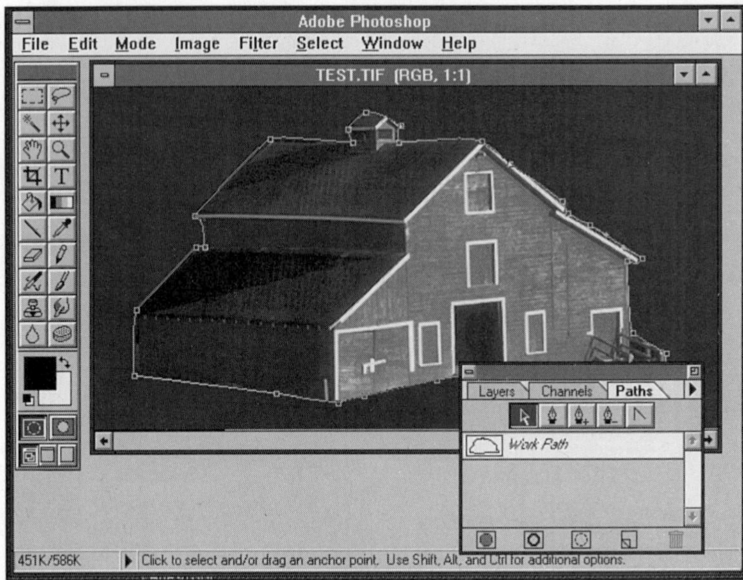

Figure 27.14
The image with the marquee around it with the anchor points visible.

22. Click on the Create/Make Path icon at the bottom center of the Paths palette again to update the path.
23. Activate the Channels palette by clicking on the Channels tab.
24. Click on and drag the New Channel icon (or Save icon) at the bottom left corner of the Channels palette into the thumbnail icon of the channel you've been working with.

You really haven't done much with your graphic up to this point. But, now that you've created a path within your image, you can use it to create great special effects!

Now for the good stuff! It is time for you to create a glow around the object in our graphic:

1. In the Paths palette, choose **S**elect, **I**nverse. This will create a marquee selection on around your object and the whole graphic frame.
2. Double-click on the Hand tool (to return to the 1:1 view).

3. To create the glow, choose the Paintbrush tool, then reverse the color swatches by either pressing X or choosing the reverse colors arrow on the toolbox. The color white will appear in the foreground.

4. On the Paintbrush Options palette (which, if not visible, can be shown by double-clicking on the Paintbrush tool), check to make sure the Opacity is set at 50 percent (see fig. 27.15). Choose the Screen mode.

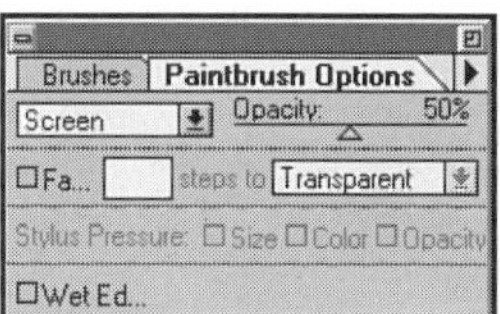

Figure 27.15
The Paintbrush Options palette, with the opacity set at 50 percent.

5. On the Brushes palette, choose one of the "fuzzy" brush tips. The size of the tip will depend on your individual graphic. In this case, you are using one of the bigger, fuzzy tips.

6. Click on the Stroke path icon (second in from the left on the bottom) on the Paths palette to create the glow (see fig. 27.16).

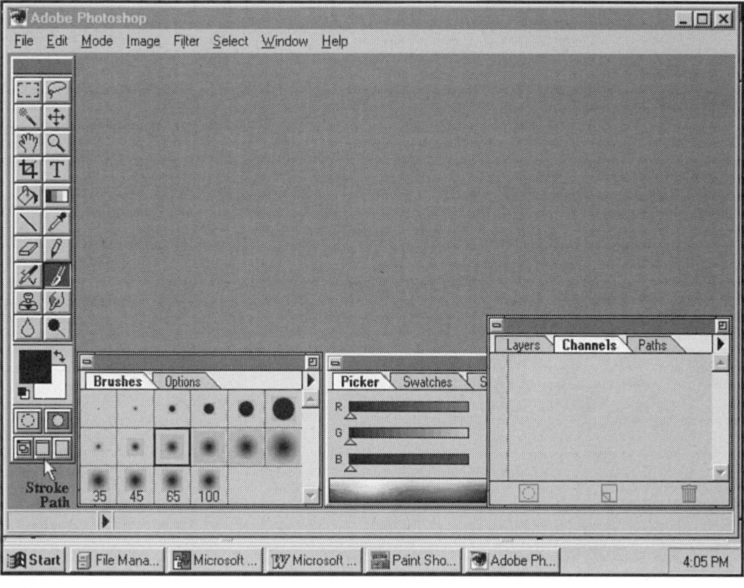

Figure 27.16
The stroke path icon is located in the lower left corner.

7. Press Ctrl+D to deselect the marquee.
8. Click on the Work Path in the Paths palette and drag it into the trash icon on the bottom of the Paths palette (see fig. 27.17).

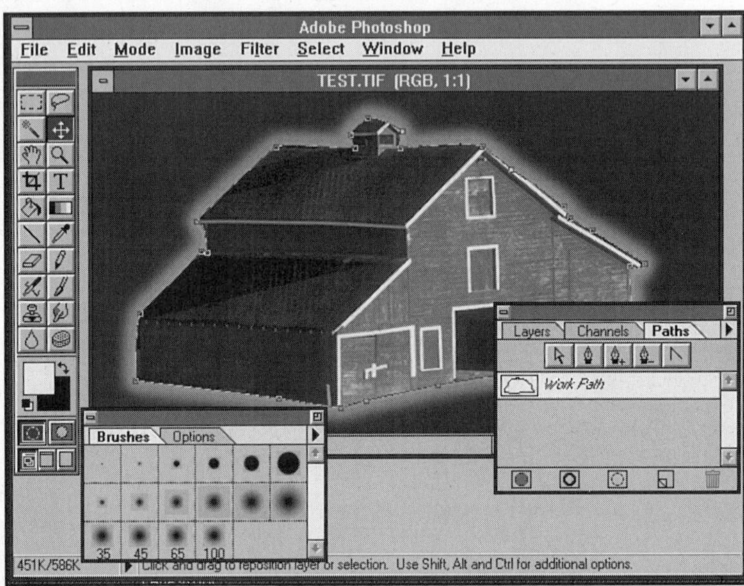

Figure 27.17 *The Paths palette with the Work Path on it.*

Before you can use your new glowing image on our Web page, you need to make sure the graphic can be saved in the GIF format:

9. Get rid of any additional Channels—the RGB, Red, Green, and Blue channels are the only ones to keep. This step reduces the file's size and enables you to save in the proper (GIF) file format.

Tip To delete the unwanted channels, simply click and drag them to the trash icon on the channels palette.

10. The final step is to make sure the colors used in the image are 256 (for the GIF format). The image then needs to be saved in the JPEG or GIF format before it can be used in your Web pages.

After more manipulation to the graphic, such as creating a color background and making it transparant, and the added color background (discussed later in this chapter) of the Web page, your image could look like figure 27.18 on a Web page.

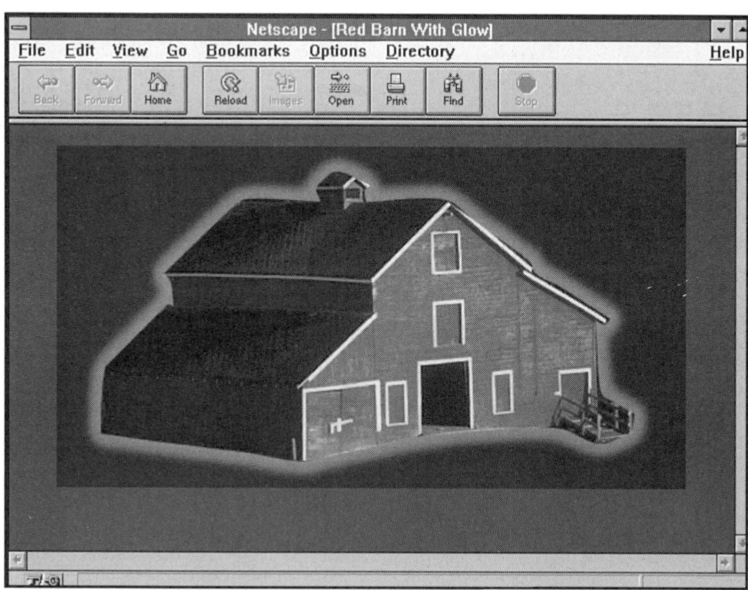

Figure 27.18
Your final graphic in use on a Web page in the Netscape browser.

Buttons, Buttons, and More Buttons

The use of buttons has become popular on the Web because it is a great navigational tool. Three-dimensional buttons are showing up on more and more Web pages. This section shows you how to make a simple button graphic in Photoshop:

Note Black Box Software's Alien Skin plug-in program for Photoshop is the easiest way to make buttons for your Web pages! Find more information and a demo copy at either `http://www.eskimo.com/~bpentium/skin.html` or `http://www.alienskin.com/alienskin/`.

Create a button that will appear on all your Web pages that links directly to an order form:

1. Open Photoshop and choose **F**ile, **N**ew to create a new image.
2. Decide on a size for the button—in this example, a button 1 1/2 inches wide by one-half inch high. Make sure the image's mode is RGB Color, and choose the Background Color circle that appears in the prompt for now.
3. Click on the background color box on the toolbar. This will activate the Color Picker box, from which you can choose a new color (see fig. 27.19). Select any color, then click on OK.

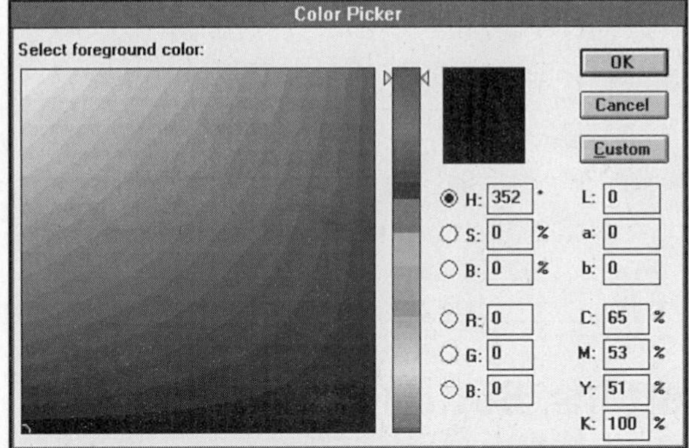

Figure 27.19
The Color Picker dialog box as displayed in Photoshop.

4. Now you need to fill your new button with the color you've selected. Bring up the commands box by clicking Window, Palettes, Show Commands and choose the fill on the commands box. Pick the "Use: Background color" selection, and press OK. The button is now the new color.
5. It's time to add the button effect! From the Fi**l**ter menu choose Alien Skin (see fig. 27.20). For the option, pick the Inner Bevel 2.0.

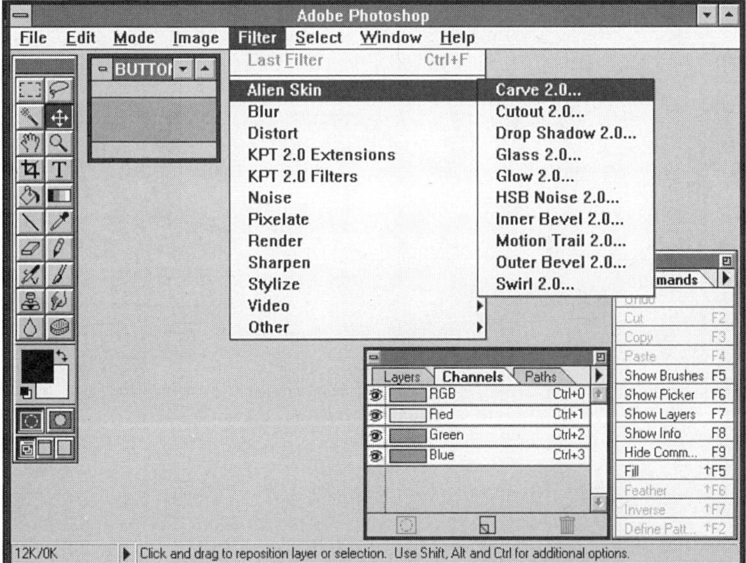

Figure 27.20
Choices you can pick under the Alien Skin software option.

6. The Inner Bevel choice box will display. At this point you need to play with the settings so that the button looks the way you want it to. For the button in this example, the settings are as follows:
   - The "Button" type
   - Bevel Width = 10
   - Shadow Depth = 25
   - Smoothness = 8
   - Drop off choice is "Button"
   - Highlight Brightness = 89
   - Highlight Sharpness = 35
   - Lighting: Direction = 120; Angle = 61

The great thing about Alien Skin is it lets you see a preview of how the button will look before you choose OK (see fig. 27.21).

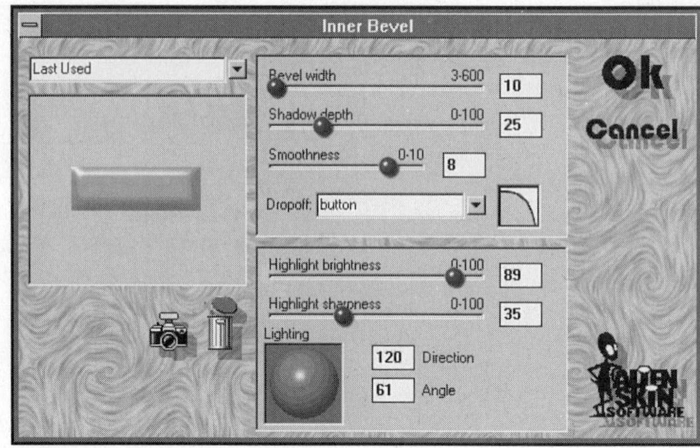

Figure 27.21
The Inner Bevel dialog box under the Alien Skin, which shows a preview of the button.

7. When everything looks perfect, click on OK.
8. Now you can add the words to the button. Add the words "Order Form" so that users will know where this button takes them.
9. Make sure the front color choice is black so that the words will be black.
10. Choose the "T" in the toolbar for the text application.
11. Put the mouse cursor over the image and click on it.
12. The Type Tool box appears for you to choose text elements. Choose an element, then click on OK. In this example use the Nebraska font at 14 points with bold.
13. After you choose OK, the text appears as a marquee selection on the graphic. Click on the Move button on the toolbar (it looks like a plus sign with four arrow heads), then move the text to the correct location (see fig. 27.22).
14. If you're happy with the location, press Ctrl+D to deselect the text and lock it into the image. Save the image or use Edit, Undo to back up a step, which in this case will re-select the text.

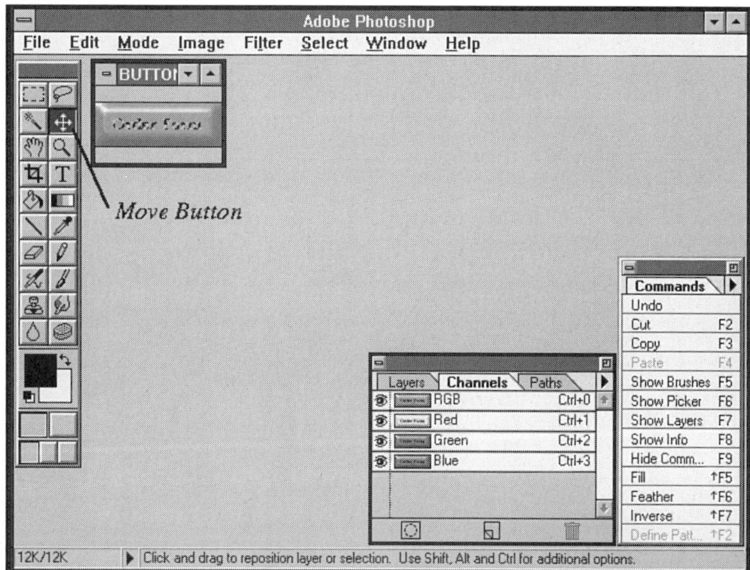

Figure 27.22
The Move button on the toolbar in Photoshop.

You now have a lovely button to use on your Web pages that indicates an Order Form is available.

After creating the button in Photoshop, you must convert the file format to GIF for Web use. GIF is the best format for buttons because of GIF's small file sizes, and usually no fancy colors are used in button graphics to warrant the JPEG format.

After you save the button in a GIF format, you need to include the graphic and its link on your Web pages (described later in this chapter). The final image in the browser looks like figure 27.23.

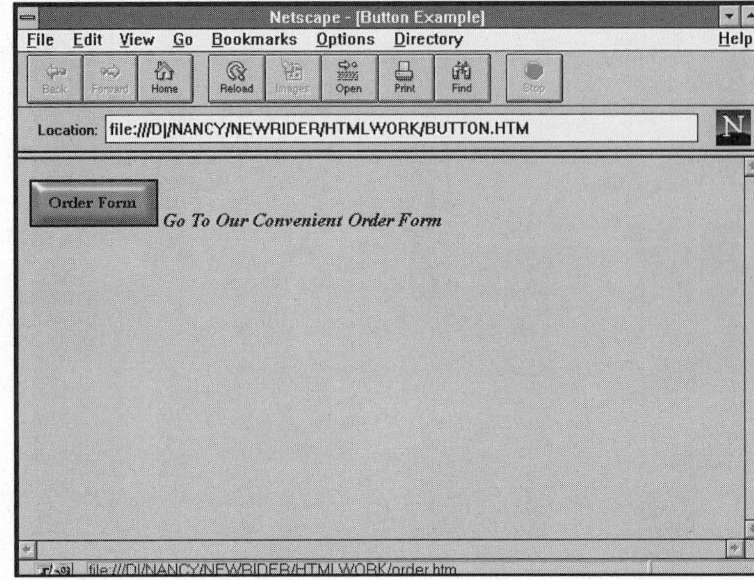

Figure 27.23
The finished button in a Web page as displayed in the Netscape browser.

Future Graphics File Formats

The future of graphics on the Web will certainly be very interesting. Formats such as progressive JPEGs and PNG will be trying to make an appearance on the Web. Some browsers and graphics programs have already incorporated them into their interfaces, and others should soon follow. It's important to be updated on the future of Web graphics in the event that by using these new formats, your Web pages will be faster and better looking. As a webmaster, you don't want to be in the dark when it comes to new Internet developments.

Progressive JPEGs

The subject of graphics for the Internet is constantly changing. Recent browsers started including the capability to view JPEG files; many companies are already working on the next step: the capability to view Progressive JPEGs. Netscape's newer versions, such as 2.0, incorporates progressive JPEGs. The Netscape Web site provides a great example of different graphic formats (GIF, Interlaced GIF, JPEG, and Progressive JPEG) by showing how each one downloads:

```
http://home.netscape.com/eng/mozilla/2.0/relnotes/demo/
pjpegdemo.html.
```

Like interlaced GIF files, progressive JPEG files store files from top to bottom in a complex storage structure. When you download the progressive JPEG, the first scan of the image is small but can be shown on-screen almost immediately.

As each scan of the image completes, more information is added to the image until it reaches full clarity. As with the interlaced GIF, the advantage is the user can view the whole graphic immediately, although it is somewhat blurry. Regular JPEG files force you to wait while they download from top to bottom.

To date, only a handful of browsers support progressive JPEGs: Netscape 2.0b4 and higher, Enhanced Mosaic 2.1f5, Microsoft Internet Explorer, and OmniWeb 2.0.

Note A new graphic format called PNG has been developed to replace GIF and to avoid the legality issues involving the compression format used with the GIF format. This new graphic file format can support true-color images of up to 48 bits per pixel. In addition, PNG uses an efficient lossless compression algorithm.

More information about PNG specifications and development can be found at the PNG FTP archive site:

`ftp.uu.net:/graphics/png/`

You can contact administrators of this site by sending e-mail to

`png-info@uunet.uu.net`

Incorporating Your Images into Your Web Pages

Before you begin to add graphics to your Web pages, remember that the Web supports two major graphic file types: GIF and JPEG (see Chapter 26 for more information). Although the newest browsers support Progressive JPEGs and PNG file formats, stick with GIF and JPEG files so that your Web page will be compatible with as many browsers as possible.

One of options you have with your images is to include the graphics on your Web page as inline images. *Inline* images reside on your Web page, and display when the browser views the page. The other option is to use external images; the graphics can still be included on your page, but are kept separate from the page. In other words, the graphic is *linked* to the page; it is in a separate file. The latter approach allows for quick download times. If you link to the external image from your page, the page downloads faster because it contains no large inline graphics.

Note Although you haven't seen the full HTML guidelines yet (this is discussed in the next chatper), the next section teaches you about the image HTML tags.

Inline Images

After you convert your graphic images and are ready to add them to the Web, you need to code these files with the <IMG> (Image) tag. This tag is the HTML code stating that these new converted files will be graphics on your Web page. The <IMG> tag is used together with the SRC attribute, which indicates the filename of the image to be included:

```
<IMG SRC="imagename.gif">
```

The above format indicates a graphic that is located in the same directory as the HTML file. If the two files are not located in the same directory, you need to specify the location of the image in relation to the HTML file.

Note An *HTML tag* is a code that indicates a file or a characteristic of the document, such as the structure, formatting, links, or the addition of an image.

HTML tag names are enclosed in brackets, and most of the time have a beginning and end tag that surrounds the text (or information) that will be affected. The closing tag is preceded by a forward slash character (/), which indicates that the tag will now be terminated, or turned off, as shown here:

```
<tagname>Text Text Text</tagname>
```

In some cases, such as with the <IMG> tag, a closing tag is not required.

An *attribute* for an HTML tag is a code that appears within the tag to indicate further information, such as in this example:

```
<tagname attribute=info>Text Text Text</tagname>
```

External Images

Inline images are simple to include in your Web pages; external images are also easy to add. The tag and attribute are different, but you still need to point to the graphic filename. These images are much more flexibile than inline images: an external image is not located directly on your Web page, so the graphic type is not limited to GIF (and sometimes JPEG). You can use other graphic file types.

The first step in using external images, is to decide whether you want to provide a text link to the final image or use a thumbnail of the original image. A *thumbnail* is a small picture of the larger external file. This thumbnail helps users decide whether they want to download the external image.

A great use for thumbnails is to show pictures of graphics in formats other than GIF or JPEG. Suppose, for example, you have a great TIFF graphic that you want to provide on your Web page, but the Web and its browsers cannot view TIFF images. You can get around this problem by displaying a GIF thumbnail. In a note next to the thumbnail, tell users that the TIFF format is available for downloading. Make sure you list the total size so that users know about how long they will have to wait. Users who have helper applications will be able to download the image and view it.

When you provide a thumbnail or text link, it's important to reference the total size of the image and indicate the file format (GIF, JPEG, PICT, and so on). With this information users will be able to know whether they can download the image and view it with their software. Users might not have the time to wait for larger images to download, or they might not have the proper software.

Note Browser software can use *helper* applications to view images if it cannot view the file format itself. The user specifies the application to use.

To access a helper application in Netscape, the user chooses Options, Preferences, Helper Applications, then chooses the program to view the image (see fig. 27.24).

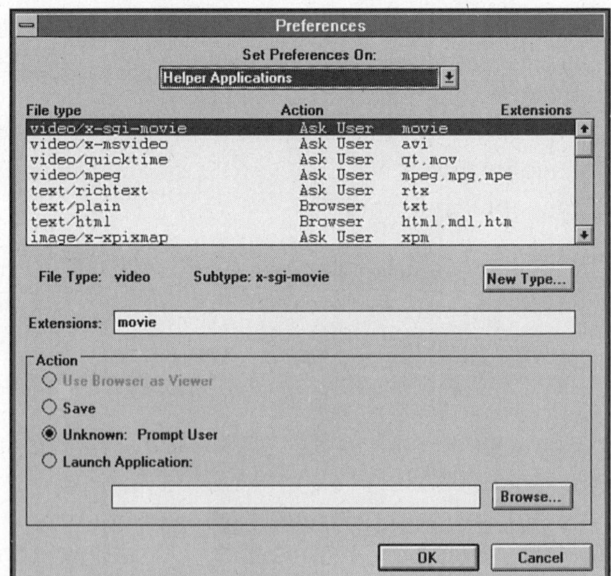

Figure 27.24
The Helper Application options as they appear in Netscape.

If you decide to create a text link to your external image, use the following HTML code to link the image with the text:

```
<A HREF="bigscene.jpg">Scenic View</A> (100K JPEG File)
```

The above code indicates that when users click on the words "Scenic View," they will begin downloading a 100K JPEG file. The <A> tag specifies an anchor and linkable text. The <A> tag includes some important attributes, which are features that appear after the <A> tag (<A *attribute*>), that give extra information about the link itself. See Chapter 28 for more information about the anchor tag.

If you plan to use a thumbnail of the original image instead, use code that looks like this:

```
<A HREF="bigscene.jpg"><IMG SRC="smallscene.gif"></A>
```

The <A> tag specifies an anchor and a linkable image in this example. When users click on the "smallscene.gif" file, they will receive a larger image of the same scene.

Using Tags: The Happy Horse Farm Web Page

To help you get a feel for the addition of images into your Web pages, this section walks you through a typical page design.

Suppose you work for the Happy Horse Farm and you have been assigned to make a Web page. You want to include a simple picture of a horse for the site to help indicate that the farm works with horses. This might be something like a line-art drawing of a horse, not a fancy, full color picture. Here is part of the code:

```
<HTML>
<HEAD>
<TITLE>The Happy Horse Farm</TITLE>
<BODY>
<H1>The Happy Horse Farm</H1>
<HR>
<P><IMG SRC="horse2.gif"></P>
</BODY>
</HTML>
```

Notice how the <IMG> (image) tag fits into the page. Don't worry what all the other tags mean at this point; you will learn about them in the next chapter. Figure 27.25 shows this page's output.

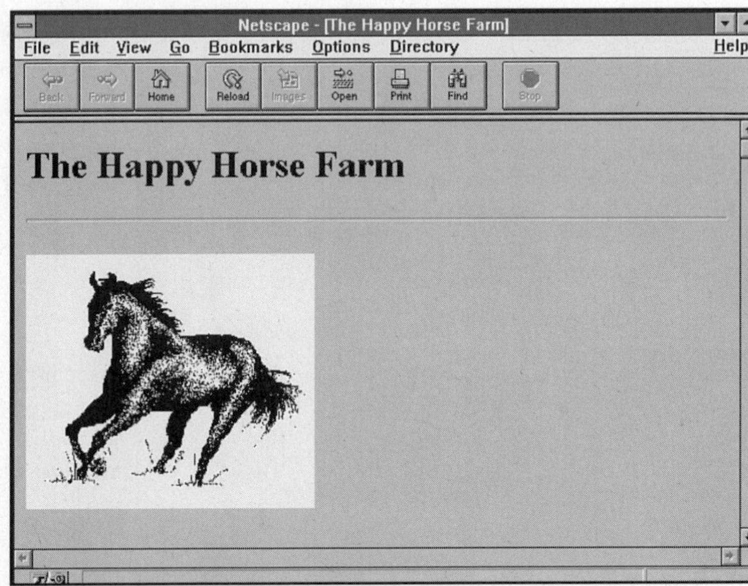

Figure 27.25
The Happy Horse Farm Web page as displayed in Netscape.

Aligning Text with Images

Now that you have added the horse image to the page, you may want to place text around it. A simple way to do this is to modify the preceding HTML code and put the text right next to the image:

```
<HTML>
<HEAD>
<TITLE>The Happy Horse Farm</TITLE>
<BODY>
<H1><IMG SRC="horse2.gif">The Happy Horse Farm</H1>
<HR>
</BODY>
</HTML>
```

Figure 27.26 shows how placing the <IMG> tag right next to the text "The Happy Horse Farm" makes the text appear next to the graphic automatically aligned with the bottom of the image.

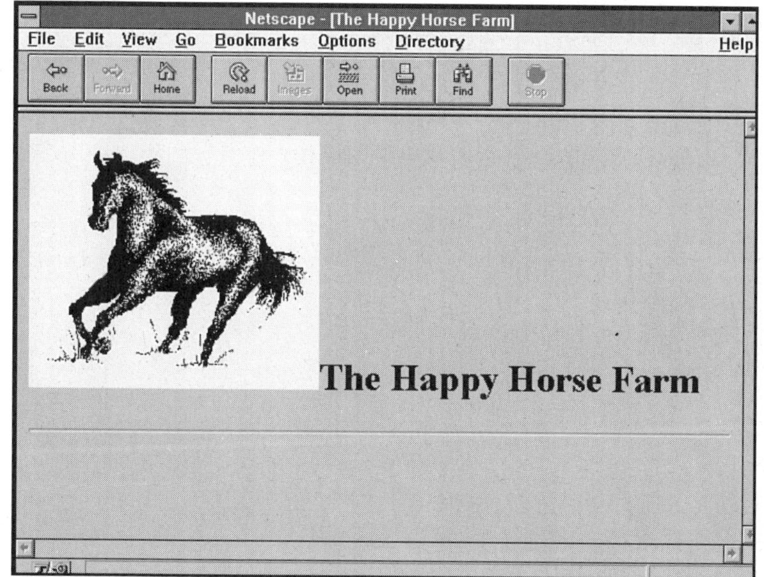

Figure 27.26
How putting the text next to the <IMG> tag will make the page appear in the Netscape browser.

More Text and Image Alignment Options

Another way you can align text with images is to use the ALIGN attribute in the <IMG> tag. The ALIGN attribute has three different options: TOP, MIDDLE, and BOTTOM. Sample code of these options appears as follows:

```
<P><IMG SRC="busines1.gif" ALIGN=TOP>Text aligned to the TOP of
the image</P>

<P><IMG SRC="busines1.gif" ALIGN=MIDDLE>Text aligned to the MIDDLE
of the image</P>

<P><IMG SRC="busines1.gif" ALIGN=BOTTOM>Text aligned to the BOTTOM
of the image</P>
```

Figure 27.27 shows how each option aligns the text.

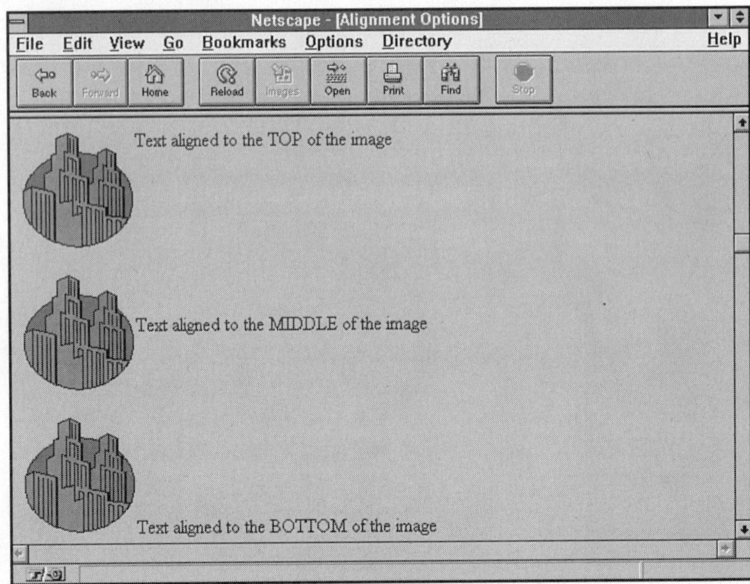

Figure 27.27 *How different alignment tags are displayed in Netscape.*

The HTML 3.0 features and the Netscape enhancements (discussed later in this chapter and also in the Appendix) enable you to wrap more than one line of text around an image. When you use the ALIGN attribute with the LEFT option, which moves the image to the left and the text to the right, or the RIGHT option, which moves the image to the right and the text to the left, you can wrap text, as in this example:

```
<P><IMG SRC="busines1.gif" ALIGN=RIGHT>
```

The text will be wrapped around the left side of the image, and the image will appear on the right side of the screen. This text could go on forever, and the browser would still continue to wrap around the graphic until the graphic ended. Then the text would flow normally (see fig. 27.28).

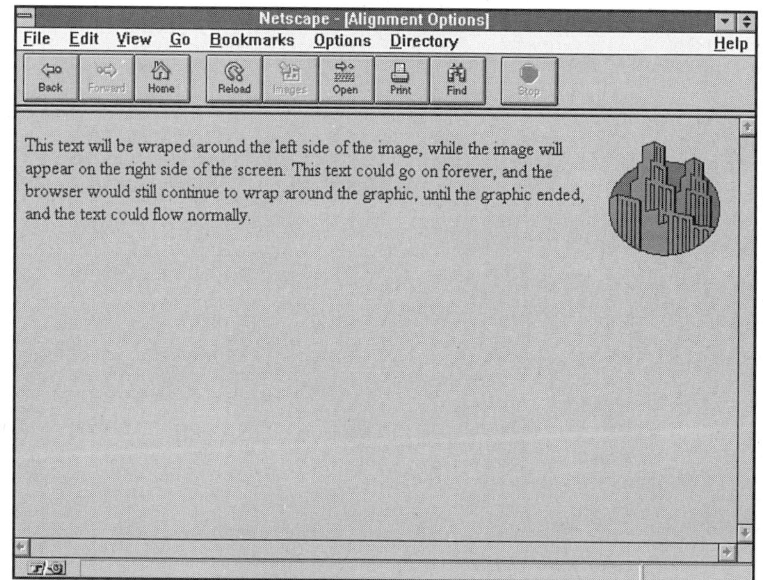

Figure 27.28
How the page is displayed in Netscape using the ALIGN=RIGHT attribute.

Netscape Alignment Features

Netscape includes additional alignment features that are used with the ALIGN option. You can use all the options shown in table 27.1 to place graphics on your Web pages.

Table 27.1
ALIGN Options in Netscape

Option	Effect
TEXTTOP	Aligns with the tallest text within the line. Usually the same as TOP.
ABSMIDDLE	Aligns the middle of the current line with the middle of the image. Similar to MIDDLE, except MIDDLE aligns the baseline of the current line with the middle of the image.
BASELINE	Aligns the bottom of the image with the baseline of the current line.
ABSBOTTOM	Aligns the bottom of the image with the bottom of the current line. Similar to BOTTOM.

These options are specified the same way as the other ALIGN attribute options:

```
<IMG SRC="busines1.gif" ALIGN=ABSMIDDLE>
```

This example aligns the middle of the line with the middle of the image.

Netscape Image Enhancements

Netscape includes other image attributes to help make the most of your images. Although many of these features originated with the Netscape browser, many of the more popular browsers' newer versions are incorporating them as well.

VSPACE & HSPACE

The VSPACE and HSPACE attributes have been added to the <IMG> tag and allow you to control the amount of space between the image and text. VSPACE controls the vertical space above and below the image, and HSPACE controls the horizontal space to the left and right of the image.

To see how this might work, modify the sample text that wraps around the image. See how the VSPACE and HSPACE attributes have been incorporated:

```
<P><IMG SRC="busines1.gif" ALIGN=RIGHT VSPACE=20 HSPACE=20>
```

This text wraps around the left side of the image, and the image appears on the right side of the screen. If this text continued, the browser would still continue to wrap around the graphic until the graphic ended, and then the text would flow normally (see fig. 27.29).

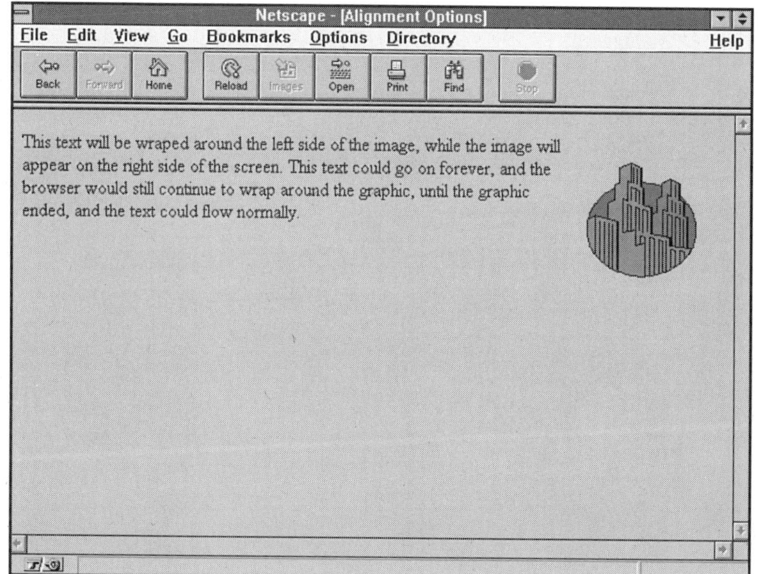

Figure 27.29
The text wraps to the left and aligns nicely using some of the Netscape image enhancements.

WIDTH and HEIGHT

Netscape (and HTML 3.0) added two attributes to the <IMG> tag that control the actual size of the image. This is particularly helpful when you have a limited amount of space to work with, or when you want to speed up the download time of your page.

WIDTH and HEIGHT tell the browser what size the image will be, eliminating the size calculation time. The browser loads the text without waiting for the image, so that the user can read your page immediately or access a text link.

Here is an example of the WIDTH and HEIGHT attributes used with the <IMG> tag:

```
<IMG SRC="busines1.gif" WIDTH=250 HEIGHT=300 ALIGN=RIGHT>
```

BORDER

Netscape's BORDER attribute enables webmasters to control the thickness of the border around the image being displayed. The only time you need to be careful of setting a border thickness is when you set BORDER=0 (no border). If the image is a link, you might confuse users because they expect to see borders around linked images.

The BORDER attribute is coded much the same as all the other attributes and can be added to one of the previous examples (see fig. 27.30).

```
<P><IMG SRC="busines1.gif" ALIGN=RIGHT VSPACE=20 HSPACE=20
BORDER=4>
```

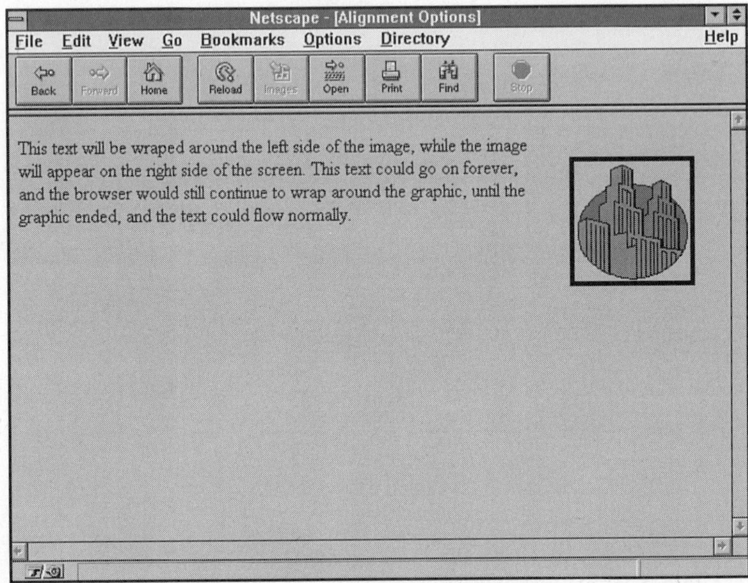

Figure 27.30 *How the border will appear around the image when using the BORDER attribute in the Netscape browser.*

Keep in mind when you use these additional formatting features that not all users are able to see the newest and latest features you incorporate. If your goal is to create a site that as many people as possible will be able to view the way you intend it to be viewed, try to stick with as much basic formatting conventions as possible.

Images are great to use in your pages. Besides the aligning, border, and other attributes that can be applied to images, you can create linkable images, and special types of images. There are transparent images, and also a way to use graphics in the background of your pages. Including images can really spice up your site!

Linking Images

Another way you can increase the amount of graphics capabilities on your Web page is to make graphics linkable. The graphic itself acts as a clickable "hot spot" that leads to another page or location.

The link tag (<A>) specifies a link by indicating where the user will go after he or she clicks on the link. The link tag must surround the image information:

```
<A HREF="newfile.htm"><IMG SRC="backarow.gif"></A>
```

The above code makes backarow.gif a link that returns the user to the previous page.

Providing Alternatives to Web Graphics

The <IMG> tag's ALT attribute lets you position alternative information such as text in place of an image that some browsers might not be able to access (see fig. 27.32).

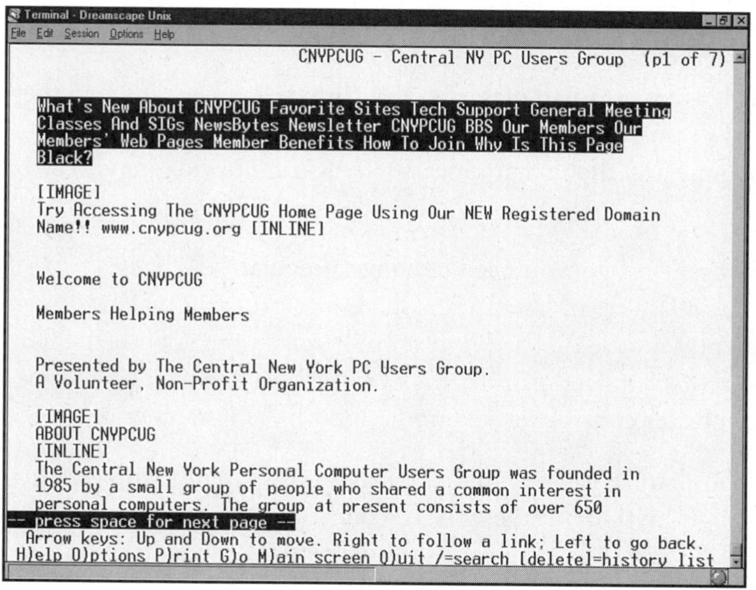

Figure 27.32
How a Web page with graphics, but using the ALT attribute, could look within a text only browser such as Lynx.

This attribute helps users who do not have graphics capabilities. Although text-only browsers cannot view your outstanding graphics, users with these browsers shouldn't be penalized or left in the dark for their inability to see your images. By using the ALT option, you are being more considerate of viewers by allowing them to read about the images they can't see.

In the case of our "go back arrow" graphic in figure 27.31, you can include the text "Go Back to the previous page" for those who cannot see your graphic. Text-only Web users can go back to the page by clicking on the text:

```
<A HREF="newfile.htm"><IMG SRC="backarow.gif" ALT="Go Back to the
previous page"></A>
```

Another way to do the same thing is to hide the images for the text-only browsers and provide text that is linkable, as in this example:

```
<A HREF="newfile.htm"><IMG SRC="backarow.gif" ALT="">Go Back to
the previous page</A>
```

The inclusion of the `ALT=""` hides the graphic for text browsers and only shows the linkable text "Go Back to the previous page."

Transparent Images

Some images, such as logos, small graphics, and clip-art, look great when they are transparent. When an image is changed so that it is transparent, the background is opaque and the image appears to be sitting or floating directly on the page.

To create a transparent image, you need to convert regular GIF images (GIF87) to the GIF89a format. The LView shareware program makes this conversion simple. If you use Adobe Photoshop, here is some good news! The Adobe Photoshop 3.0.5 update includes the new GIF89a export plug-in, which gives users greater control and manipulation of Web graphics.

How will the Happy Horse Farm graphic look as a transparent graphic? You don't need to change anything in the HTML code, only the way the graphic is saved. Figure 27.33 shows the "before," and figure 27.34 shows the image after it is saved as a transparent image.

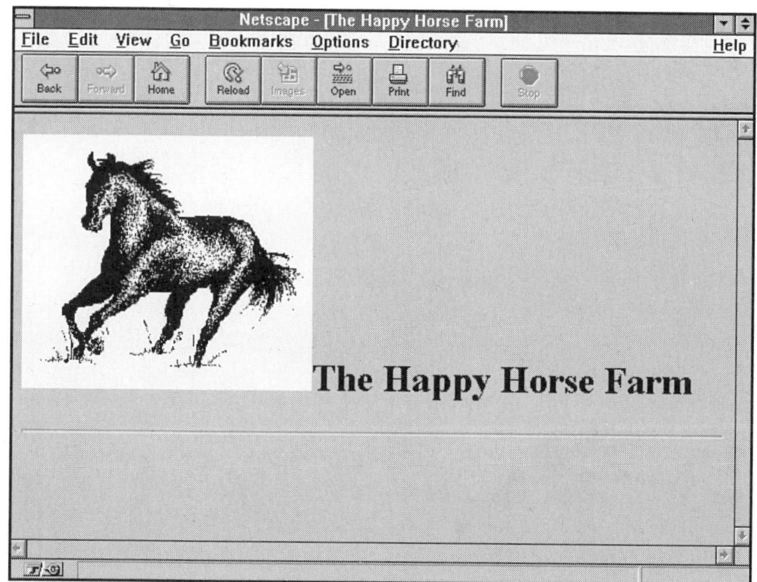

Figure 27.33
The horse2.gif in the GIF87 format on a Web page in Netscape.

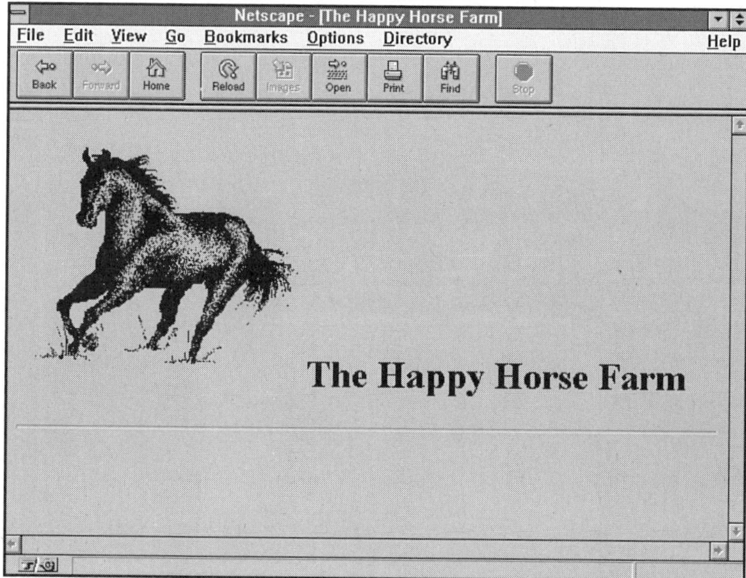

Figure 27.34
The horse2.gif in the new 89 format.

Notice how the white color (which is the transparent color) is no longer visible in the background.

Note For the Macintosh, *Transparency* is a great program for saving in GIF89a format.

Backgrounds

Another feature that Netscape introduced, which is widely accepted now, is the use of background images. The key to good backgrounds is to make them faint so they do not interfere with the readability of the page. In addition, background graphics should be kept small so that they will tile. If the background is too large, the user has to wait forever for the page to download.

Background images can be made out of any graphic. Just make sure the image tiles the way you want it to. Suppose you want to tile the Happy Horse Farm graphic (refer to fig. 27.33).

To turn this image into a background image for The Happy Horse Farm's Web page, try to reduce the size of the graphic (155.7 KB) by reducing the size of the image. For this example, use Paint Shop Pro version 3.0, which lets you create background images easily. Remember to create a copy of the image you modify in case you make a mistake.

1. Choose **I**mage, Res**i**ze to adjust the image size. Make sure the **M**aintain Aspect Ratio option is checked so that the image looks the same after you resize it (see fig. 27.35). You don't want to distort the image.

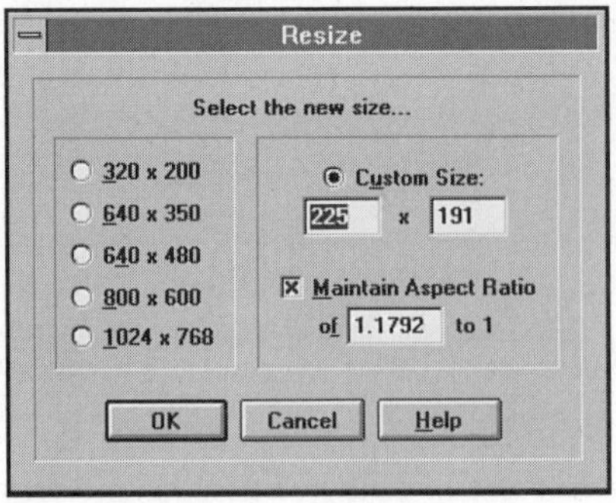

Figure 27.35
The Resize dialog box in Paint Shop Pro.

2. Check the Custom Size and specify the first dimension. When you tab to the second dimension, Paint Shop Pro automatically updates the new size (because you have the Maintain Aspect Ratio button checked).

3. Click on OK.

The graphic is smaller, 99.6 KB, but you still cannot tile it yet. The horse is black, which will make the text on the page difficult to read. The black color needs to be changed to another color.

4. Choose Colors, Edit Palette. Pick the color to be edited (in this case black) and double click on the box with that color. The color option box pops up so that you can choose a new color. In this example, choose a light gray color to replace the black.

5. Click on OK, then OK again to change the color. Now you have a gray color horse on a white background.

Although this picture is a lot "lighter" than its original, you still need to tone it down so text can be viewed on the page without any problems.

6. Choose Colors, Adjust, Gamma Correct. The Gamma Correct dialog box that appears lets you specify the Correction level (see fig. 27.36).

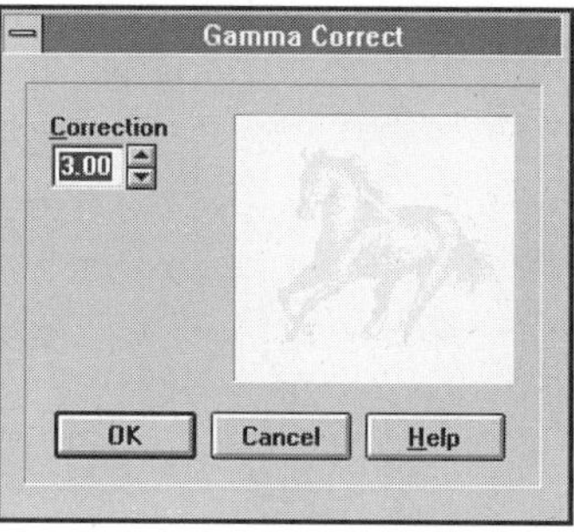

Figure 27.36
The Gamma Correct dialog box as it appears in Paint Shop Pro.

7. You need to choose an amount to enter here. For this example, choose 3 as the gamma adjustment. See how the graphic has lightened and become smoother in figure 27.37.

Figure 27.37
The graphic after you've adjusted the gamma value and lighted it.

Now add the graphic to the background. To do this, use the BACKGROUND attribute inside the <BODY> tag.

```
<BODY BACKGROUND="horseb.gif">
```

Note The <BODY>..</BODY> tags are used to specify the body of the Web page.

The code instructs the browser to use the horseb.gif image as the page's background, as shown in figure 30.38.

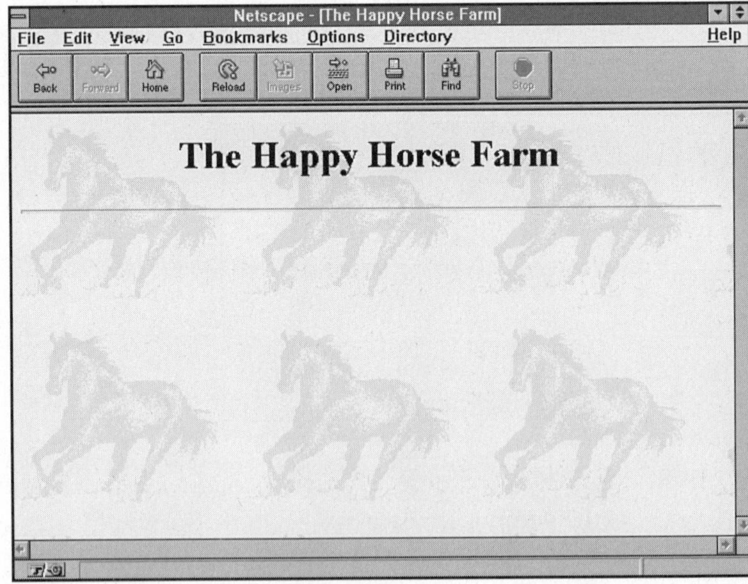

Figure 27.38
The graphic as it is used in the background of a Web page in Netscape.

Notice how the horse tiles in the background, and you can still read the text within the page.

Background Colors

You can also specify a color as your background. The BGCOLOR attribute can be used inside the <BODY> tag in the same manner as the BACKGROUND attribute, but BGCOLOR specifies a color as the background. The color must be in its hexadecimal format, and must be preceded with a hash "#" sign:

```
<BODY BGCOLOR="#ffffff">
```

This example code specifies that the color of the background of the page be white.

Attributes also are available that can be used to specify the color of links within your Web page, as shown in table 27.2.

Table 27.2
Color-Specifying Attributes

Attribute	Use
TEXT	Specifies a color for all the text within the document
LINK	Specifies a color for all the links that appear within the document
VLINK	Specifies a color for all the visited links that appear within the document
ALINK	Specifies a color for all the active links that appear within the document

These attributes also require color values to be in their hexadecimal color code preceded by a hash sign (#):

```
<BODY LINK="#595FFF" VLINK="#C000C0" ALINK="#545CCO">
```

Note When I first started developing Web pages, I was very discouraged at having to provide these hexadecimal codes because they are hard to find out. Fortunately, the RGB Assistant program, developed by Daniel Dewey, is a great help for determining color schemes. To find out more about RGB Assistant, check out Daniel Dewey's site at:

`http://news.jobWeb.org/~dan/`

Simply open the program and choose the item you want to change (text, links, visited links, active links, and background). You can move the color bar boxes around to get the exact color you want, and then simply cut and paste the code into your Web page (see fig. 27.39).

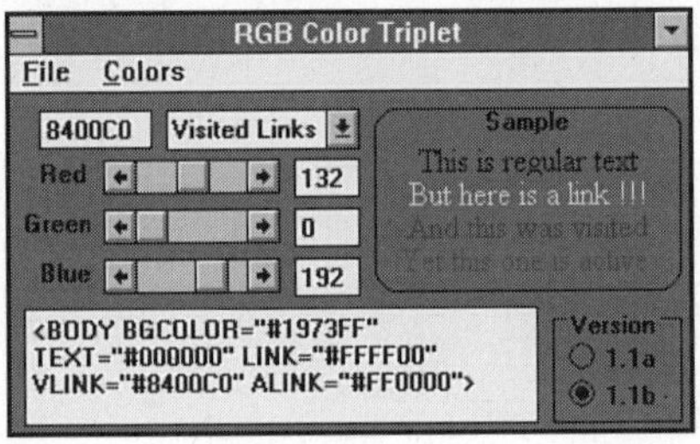

Figure 27.39
The RGB Assistant program used to select colors for your pages.

The completed code might look something like this:

```
<BODY BGCOLOR="#9272DF" TEXT="#000000" LINK="#FFFFFF"
VLINK="#C000C0" ALINK="#FF0000">
```

General Tips for Web Page Graphics

Simply including graphics on your Web pages is sometimes not enough. There are other tips for generating more practical and useful types of graphics that would be very useful for webmasters to use on their pages:

- Use smaller images
- Provide thumbnails
- Use Netscape graphic advantages

- Provide alternatives to graphics
- Choose graphics or no graphics

Smaller Images

Many Web users have 14.4-Kbps modems, which can only download 1 KB per second. It is not a good idea to make users wait longer than 30 seconds or so for your page to download. With that in mind, try to keep *all* your graphics and the page size to around 30 KB. Fifty kilobytes for the header graphic is sometimes acceptable, but avoid inconveniencing users with files any larger than this.

Remember to use the tricks mentioned earlier in the chapter (reducing color, compression, interlacing, cropping, scaling, and transparency) to make your graphics as small as possible. Experiment to see whether these images are smaller in GIF or JPEG file formats.

Thumbnails

If it is necessary to have larger images within your Web pages, try to provide thumbnails. Thumbnails, which are simply a smaller version of the original picture, can reduce download times considerably. The user can click on your thumbnail to see the larger version of the picture.

Use Netscape Advantages

Although it's not available in all browsers, the Netscape WIDTH and HEIGHT attribute can significantly decrease download times for images. The browser sets aside a space for the graphic, but doesn't have to wait for it before letting the user click on a text link.

Provide Alternatives

When you include graphics on your Web pages, remember that some users still view the Web using text-only browsers. Use the HTML attribute, ALT, for the <IMG> tag (see Chapter 31 for more details) to include alternate text in place of a graphic. The ALT attribute lets you add a text comment in place of the graphic for those who cannot view it.

If your site requires a number of graphics, provide another set of Web pages that are text only. This allows users with text only browsers to view your entire site without dozens of ALT attributes clogging up the flow of the pages.

Graphic or Not?

Choose your graphics wisely. There is such a thing as too many graphics. Determine whether you really need this or that graphic; is there a way to say the same thing without it?

In addition, make sure your graphics "match" one another. Don't hire a professional artist to create the best looking, classiest, most elegant graphic imaginable, and then mix everyday clip-art or snapshots with it. This confuses users.

Using Imagemaps

A big part of incorporating graphics onto your homepage involves the use of imagemaps. *Imagemaps* are pictures on a homepage that you can click on and be lead to a corresponding page or section depending on where on the graphic itself you choose to click.

Types of Imagemaps

One type of imagemap has the browser call on a CGI program on the server to retrieve the URL that corresponds with the user's selection. To create an imagemap the easy way, you need an image, a map file, and an imagemap program, such as Mapedit for Windows. You can find this program on the Web:

`http://www.boutell.com/mapedit/`

WebMap for the Macintosh performs the same function. It's located on the Web at:

`http://www.city.net`

Unless you know how to calculate the coordinates of an image to define the area a user can click on, get Mapedit or WebMap.

Recent improvements in imagemaps have brought about client-side imagemaps. Client-side imagemaps are implemented by the browser instead of the server. This approach provides a faster response time for the viewer, and much less burden on the server.

Client-side maps also provide the URL link when the user moves the cursor to the corresponding part of the image. This type of imagemap can be tested easily and implemented locally.

Creating an Imagemap

The following examples use Mapedit for Windows version 2.1. This new version supports and generates client-side imagemaps. In addition, version 2.1 supports JPEG, GIF, and PNG graphic files.

1. After opening the program, choose File, Open/Create. The program will prompt you for the Map or HTML file to be used.

   You have some choices to make at this point. Are you creating a new Map file, editing an existing Map file, or editing an existing HTML file?

2a. If you plan to create a Map file, you must type the name you want the Map file to have. Remember to also specify which server type you will be using (NCSA or CERN).

2b. If you plan to create a new imagemap for client-side (on an HTML file), you must have already created the HTML document with another application. Your next step is to specify the graphic you want to use when you create this new file (see fig. 27.40).

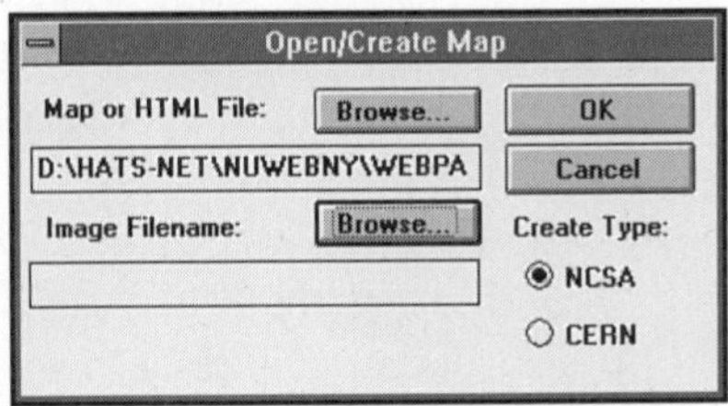

Figure 27.40 *The Mapedit program's Open/ Create Map dialog box.*

2c. If you are editing a Map file, choose the file name (that ends with .map), choose the corresponding graphic, and then click on OK.

To edit an existing client-side imagemap, you must first choose the HTML file. Afterward, the program will automatically display the Select Inline Image dialog box listing all the graphics used in the corresponding HTML file (see fig. 27.41). You can then choose the graphic to associate with the imagemap and continue.

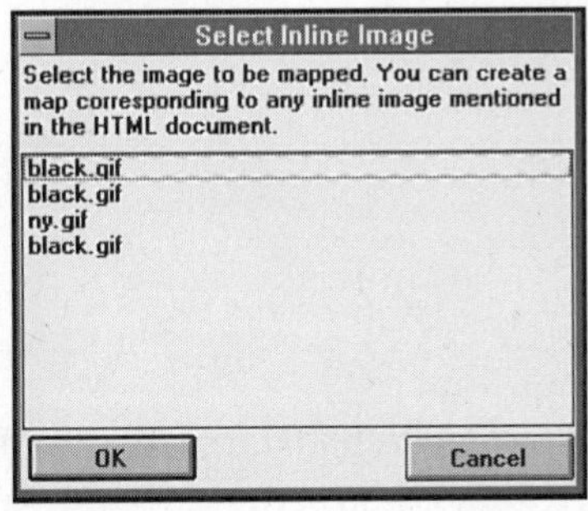

Figure 27.41 *The Select Inline Image option box in the Mapedit program, which appears when you create or edit a client-side imagemap.*

The program will then bring up the image to be turned into (or edited as) an imagemap. At this point, you need to specify the areas that will lead to specific links in another part of your Web site. To do this, click on Tools and specify whether you will use a polygon, circle, or rectangle shape to create the link.

Use the mouse pointer to show the area to be defined. After you've made the shape around the clickable area, use the right mouse button to release the shape, and bring the Object URL option box up. Type the URL to link to, any comments you wish to remember, and choose OK.

Click on File, Save, and you're all set. Luckily, if you are creating a client-side imagemap, the Mapedit program automatically inputs all the HTML tags necessary for the imagemap to work properly. Just so you are not surprised when you review the new HTML file, examine the coding that is needed to support this feature. Although you haven't encountered major HTML tags and their meanings within this book yet, you can get an idea from Mapedit's code. The following tag indicates the name of the Map file that will be used with this imagemap:

```
<A HREF="nyimap7.map">
```

The <A> tag is often called the anchor tag, and can be used in conjunction with other attributes (such as NAME and HREF). The <A> tag creates a link to other documents or sections within documents. In the preceding example, HREF can mean "Hypertext REFerence." The file in quotation marks, "nyimap7.map," is the Map file that will be used to implement the imagemap feature.

The next part of the equation in the HTML code for the imagemap you're creating is to specify the graphic to be used in association with the Map file:

```
<IMG SRC="nyimap7.gif" ISMAP USEMAP="#nyimap7"></A>
```

The <IMG> tag is used to insert an inline image, but it can also be used with different attributes (SRC, ALT, ALIGN, or ISMAP). The file in quotation marks, "nyimap7.gif," is the graphic that will be used in combination with the Map file to create the imagemap.

The presence of the <ISMAP> command indicates that the image previously mentioned is a clickable image. The following <USEMAP> command will only be used in the event you are using a client-side imagemap structure. <USEMAP> simply states the name of the map that will be used.

Note If the Map file you want to use is located in a different file, you must specify that filename before the hash symbol (#) in the USEMAP command.

The finished HTML command will look like this:

```
<A HREF="nyimap7.map"><IMG SRC="nyimap7.gif" ISMAP
USEMAP="#nyimap7"></A>
```

This will tell the browser that the graphic, nyimap7.gif, is an imagemap that has is used in conjunction with the nyimap7.map file, to create clickable and linkable points within the graphic.

Note The <A> anchor command always must end with a matching </A> anchor command.

Another section within the HTML document, <map name>, is created by the Mapedit program when client-side imagemaps are created. The program automatically puts this section just before the end of the body of the HTML document (see Chapter 28 for more details on HTML tags):

```
<map name="nyimap7">
```

The first section of the HTML code noted above, <map name>, specifies the name of the map to be used for the imagemap. This corresponds with the name in the <USEMAP> command, which can appear anywhere within this or another HTML document.

The next step within the HTML code for client-side imagemaps indicates several elements:

- Information about the area of each shape selected within the imagemap
- That area's coordinates
- The URL link that will be followed should the user click on that specific area.

See the following example:

```
<area shape="rect" coords="192,25,296,57" href="http://
www.nuWebny.com/massena.htm">
```

The `area shape` code refers to the shape of the area you chose (rectangle, polygon, or circle). The coordinates are mentioned with the `coords` command, and the URL link that will be followed is indicated by `href`.

The following code represents the image used in this section's examples (the small arrow indicates the code normally goes on one line):

```
<map name="nyimap7">
<area shape="rect" coords="192,25,296,57" href="http://
➥www.nuWebny.com/massena.htm">
<area shape="rect" coords="114,89,248,129" href="http://
➥www.nuWebny.com/watertwn.htm">
<area shape="rect" coords="125,132,222,157" href="http://
➥www.nuWebny.com/rochest.htm">
<area shape="rect" coords="245,136,305,169" href="http://
➥www.nuWebny.com/utica.htm">
<area shape="rect" coords="187,162,270,186" href="http://
➥www.nuWebny.com/syracuse.htm">
<area shape="rect" coords="0,164,124,182" href="http://
➥www.nuWebny.com/niagfall.htm">
<area shape="rect" coords="96,183,175,206" href="http://
➥www.nuWebny.com/buffalo.htm">
<area shape="rect" coords="146,205,215,229" href="http://
➥www.nuWebny.com/ithaca.htm">
<area shape="rect" coords="217,195,319,222" href="http://
➥www.nuWebny.com/cortland.htm">
<area shape="rect" coords="271,293,370,317" href="http://
➥www.nuWebny.com/nycity.htm">
<area shape="rect" coords="350,315,463,341" href="http://
➥www.nuWebny.com/li.htm">
<area shape="rect" coords="22,219,144,256" href="http://
➥www.nuWebny.com/chautall.htm">
<area shape="rect" coords="277,227,369,245" href="http://
➥www.nuWebny.com/catskill.htm">
<area shape="rect" coords="306,153,453,176" href="http://
➥www.nuWebny.com/capsarat.htm">
<area shape="rect" coords="163,53,306,85" href="http://
➥www.nuWebny.com/tis.htm">
<area shape="rect" coords="274,78,380,109" href="http://
➥www.nuWebny.com/adirond.htm">
<area shape="rect" coords="169,179,219,204" href="http://
➥www.nuWebny.com/finglake.htm">
<area shape="rect" coords="219,182,338,197" href="http://
➥www.nuWebny.com/centreg.htm">
<area shape="rect" coords="306,270,441,294" href="http://
➥www.nuWebny.com/hudvall.htm">
<area shape="polygon"
➥coords="55,138,56,161,168,172,167,157,125,155,124,138,55,137"
href="http://www.nuWebny.com/niagfron.htm">
<area shape="polygon"
➥coords="323,173,322,181,337,184,327,206,406,209,404,184"
href="http://www.nuWebny.com/albany.htm">
```

```
<area shape="polygon"
➥coords="231,225,188,234,184,259,312,260,312,241,275,237,249,225"
href="http://www.nuWebny.com/binghamt.htm">
<area shape="default" nohref>
</map>
```

Note The <map> command also needs to have a closing tag </map> to function properly.

The Imagemap Result

The final product of this chapter is an imagemap of New York State that provides links to major cities and areas. To access these places, click on the location you want to view (see fig. 27.42).

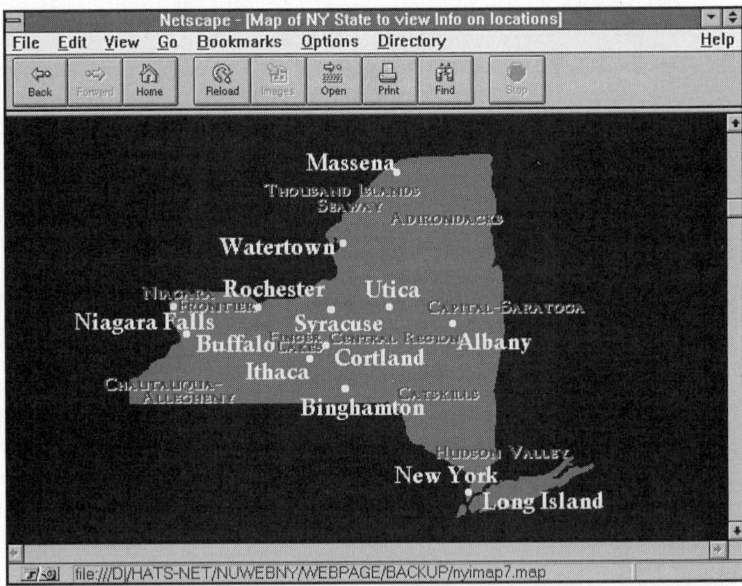

Figure 27.42 *The final outcome of the NY State Imagemap in a Web page as displayed in Netscape.*

For information on Syracuse, New York, you can simply click on the word Syracuse within the graphic, and a URL link will lead you to that page.

This chapter has shown you how to create great looking graphics that also have small file sizes. To create such masterpieces, you've learned how to reduce color palettes, and to crop, scale, and resize images. After your graphics are perfect, you know how to add and align them on your Web pages.

Imagemaps, with their client-side implementation, are an excellent way to refine the look of your site.

Now with the addition of VRML and languages such as Java, the Web is the shining star of the Internet.

Web Page Layout and Design

by Nancy Acosta

This chapter references some key issues in putting together your company's Web site. There are some important steps to follow from the beginning throughout the entire procedure.

The first issue of conceiving your company's image for your Web presence is significant in the overall success of your site. The understanding of the importance of making the site content-rich, and realizing there are no limitations in the information you can provide on your Web pages is also a key factor. The process of sketching the layout prior to development is imperative to the beginning and continued organization of the entire process.

Once these steps have been discussed, the chapter addresses some design tips used in the creation of your Web site. Finally, you will go through all the steps involved in making effective Web pages for your company.

We'll discuss everything from the first HTML tags to creating links, tables, forms, and everything in between!

Starting Your Web Site

As you're laying out and designing your Internet presence, remember that this Web site will represent you and your company—it's therefore very important to follow guidelines and make your pages as perfect as possible. When you decide to start your Web site, there are some guidelines that should be followed to make the process run easily and smoothly.

You should first try to conceive or come up with a great Internet image for your organization. After you've come up with an image, remember to make the site rich in content and information. It helps to have a sketch of the site you're intending to create to see how everything will fit together. During this process, think of the best way to attract the all important repeat visits to your site. Understand there are no limitations in the information you are able to provide, and realize all the possibilities made available to you. After you've organized your game plan, the actual creation should be a breeze!

Conceiving Your Company's Internet Image

Realizing that millions and millions of potential clients will be able to visit and view your Web site is sometimes an intimidating thought. That's why it's imperative that your company portray the right Internet image. Are you a manufacturer who caters to wholesale companies, a small business who sells to the individual, or an entrepreneur with a fresh idea? After you determine who your audience is, the image needed for your Internet presence should follow.

Make sure that you and the other people in your company who are involved in this project sit down and think this project through. Decide what image you want to portray, what information needs to be given out, and how that information should be laid out. The more organized your outline of content, the easier it will be to start and complete your Web site.

Note Before going off to gather information for your outline, it is important to first understand some keywords essential to this chapter—in particular, Web site, Web page, and homepage. A Web site stands for the whole Internet presence—in other words, a bunch of Web pages put together constitute a Web site. Each page within that site is a Web page. The homepage can be defined as the very first page of your Web site. This is usually called the index (to your site). The homepage could incorporate a logo or company image, or a brief explanation of what your site consists of, with links to more detailed information.

Making Your Site Content-Rich

Many people refer to the World Wide Web as the place to put up their company billboard or create their online brochure. If you go ahead with this thought and attitude, your site might not be as successful as it could be. Remember, your presence should be an interactive one, with rich content knowledge. Although it's important to provide this information, it's also important not to go overboard. In other words, don't start writing a novel filled with endless pages of prose. Keep in mind that most Internet users do not have a lot of patience. They get turned off by lots of words, lose their patience, and go to someone else's page. Keep it short and sweet, while maintaining rich and powerful content.

The first question usually asked is, "What should we put on our Web site?" Anything you want! Actually, let's list some key examples so you have a better understanding of this. In reference to a business presence, you can add details such as the following:

- **A company profile.** A company profile might give an indication how long you've been in business, as well as provide some financial information, company history, services offered, and any other company-related information you might want to provide.

- **A president's letter.** The president's letter could be similar to what you might find in a newsletter where the president writes a letter to welcome you and thank you for taking the time to visit.
- **Associate profiles.** Associate profiles can consist of business and personal information regarding your employees, maybe even including pictures.
- **A list of products.** A list of products or services is always a good idea to include in your site so users can find out what it is you have to offer.
- **A vendor and manufacturer list.** A list of key vendors and suppliers is helpful for the user to determine credibility and assurance.
- **A company newsletter.** The company newsletter can be put online for all to have access to. This will make updates and revisions much easier and faster for publication.
- **Employment opportunities.** Many organizations are listing their employment opportunities online for users to submit résumés for and learn about.
- **Frequently asked questions (FAQs).** Frequently asked questions are always helpful and provide great information to the user who's browsing through your site.
- **A list of similar or related links.** Also, you might want to have a section related to other similar sites or newsgroups to provide the user alternatives to your site, but that are regarding the same or similar information. This is a great convenience to the user, and should help attract those repeat visits we mentioned earlier.

Sketching Out Your Web Site

Before beginning the creation of your Web site, think of yourself as making a presentation to the world, and decide what it is you want to say and accomplish during this presentation. As with any good presentation, the key to success is organization. You must make your outline as detailed as possible—even lay out the material you want to include so that you can visually see how it will all come together. Get all hard copy material together and spread it out around you to create the visual effect, and to see different alternatives of how it all will come together.

The first step you could take in designing the site would be to find the main topics for your table of contents and use them to design the layout. It is always helpful to draw a sketch of how the site might look, as shown in figure 28.1. Notice how the homepage links to the main elements of the site, and the main elements link to sub-elements. Also see how they can link to one another and back and forth from each other.

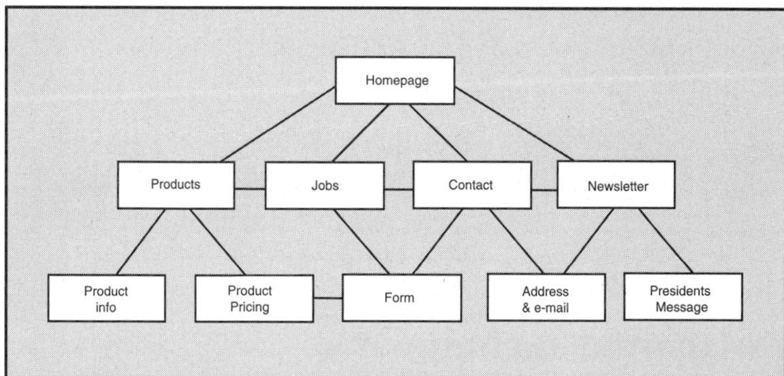

Figure 28.1
The basic sketch for the homepage you will design.

Although it may be somewhat confusing with the lines (links) going back and forth and around each other, notice how everything links together in a smooth and orderly fashion for the user.

Attracting Repeat Visits

It would be very easy to have your company's brochure put up on the Web exactly as it is, but how successful would that be in bringing back repeat visitors? It's been proven that the more valuable and new information you provide, the more likely it is that users will return to your site. If you sell turkeys for a living, for example, don't just list your product and its price—tell the browser how your turkeys are raised, mention how turkey came to be served at Thanksgiving, or maybe have a contest to guess the biggest turkey ever raised. Be inventive! Think of an idea that you would mention to your friends and colleagues to go check out because it was so interesting.

Lack of Limitation

When designing your layout, remember that the limitation for which you can provide information is virtually endless. You can give the user the option to find as much or as little material as possible. The ways in which to provide this knowledge are also unbounded. Use the plain text as well as many up-to-date features of video, audio, and 3D representation. When designing your site, be creative and imaginative. Make it fun, exciting, and above all, powerful.

Recognizing the Available Possibilities

After finding the appropriate image, and then creating the layout and outline, you need to be aware of the different possibilities available to provide this information. There are many designs and techniques that will be discussed in greater depth later in this chapter. Some of them include integrating graphics and logos, incorporating form and order pages, using tables, and using colorful backgrounds. Take a look at what's available for use in your Web page!

Layout Design Tips and Techniques

One of the design techniques used in making effective Web pages is to not overcrowd the page (see fig. 28.2). Providing uncluttered text, as shown in figure 28.3, helps the user to read easier and faster.

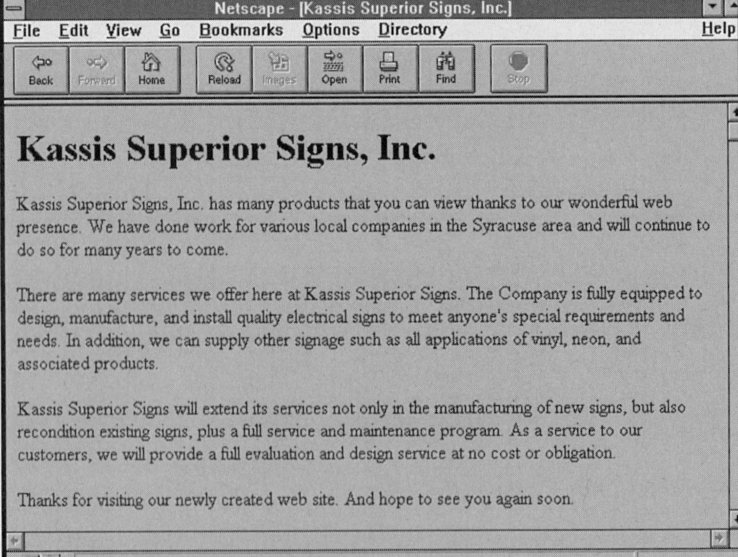

Figure 28.2
Too much text looks cluttered and is difficult for the user to follow.

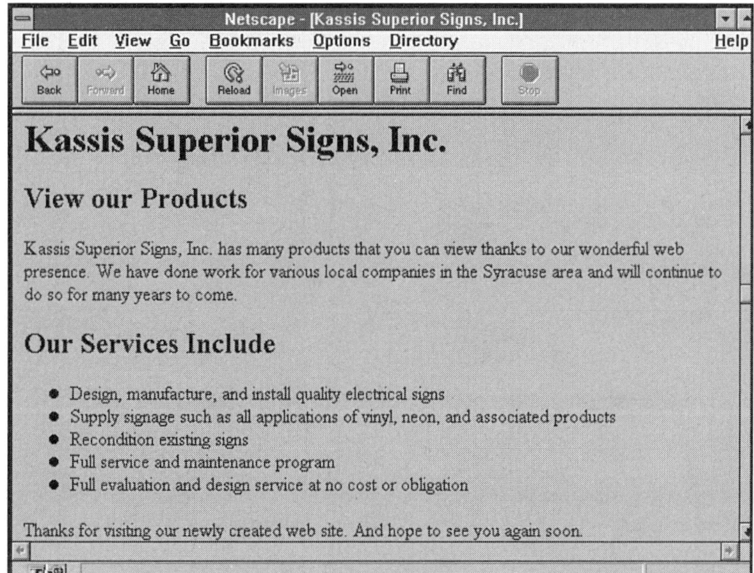

Figure 28.3
Lists and headers make a page look clean by breaking up the text.

Also notice in figure 28.3 that there is proper use of the header tags available.

Note Header tags indicate a section of text that is used to start a new section. There are various levels and sizes of header tags. The correct way in which to use them is to start the page with the larger size, and continue down the page in size and sequential order.

Providing Text-Only Links

Have you ever see a great-looking Web page that is high in graphic intensity, but takes forever to download? If you've ever surfed the Net, you've probably seen them. Another good point to mention is that really good Web developers are considerate of their viewers. It would be in good habit to provide a link to a text-only version of your page. That usually means a little more work for the webmaster because there should be a whole separate section of HTML pages created for the text-only version. This provides the user with the option of not viewing graphics for faster downloading time, and also comes in handy to the people who are using the text-only browsers (such as Lynx).

Overusing Bold and Italic

When designing your pages, try not to overemphasize your key points. If you tend to use the bold and italic features too often, it could prove to be very difficult for the user to read (see figures 28.4 and 28.5)

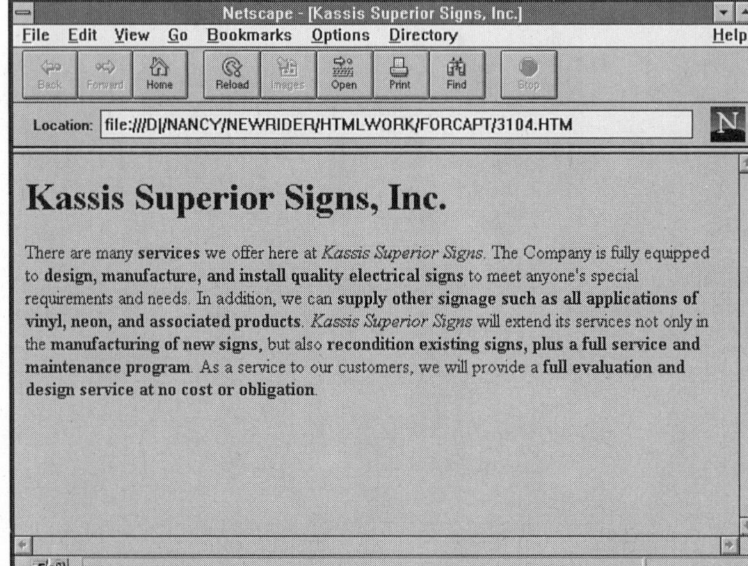

Figure 28.4
The overuse of bold and italics within a paragraph is harder to follow.

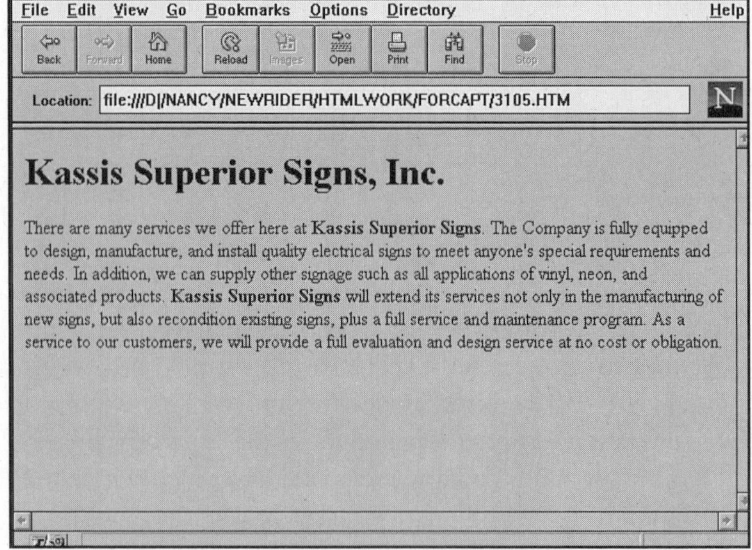

Figure 28.5
The same paragraph without the overuse of bold and italics creates a page that's much easier to read.

Holding the User's Attention

The layout of your pages definitely needs to flow; however, keep in mind that the user has the ability to click off your site onto someone else's at any point. That's why it's important to make each of your pages prominent. You need to hold the attention of the viewer by providing clarity and boldness in each page.

Selecting Good Anchors

When providing links to other pages within your site, or to outside links, be effective in determining what to attach the link to. For example, it is much more effective to say:

> View the **upcoming events of Syracuse** for more information.

...making "upcoming events of Syracuse" the anchor, than it is to have the following:

> View the upcoming events of Syracuse; for more information, click **here**.

Can you see the difference that these two anchor choices would make for users who are quickly skimming the page for the information they want? They would have to backtrack in their reading to find out what information they would receive if they clicked "here," while they know at once what they will see when they choose "upcoming events of Syracuse."

Using Location Bars

Some Web sites have more than 100 pages of information available, which make it very easy to get lost within the depth of the site. There should always be a "way out," or what could be referred to as the location bar. This bar might be located on the bottom or top of the page, providing the user with the ability to jump to any of the main sections of the site (see fig. 28.6).

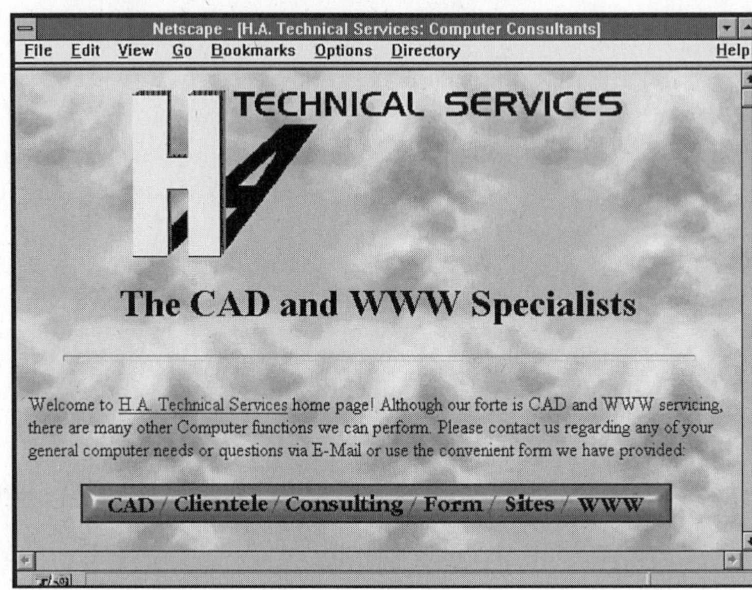

Figure 28.6 *This homepage provides a bar at the end making it simpler to move freely between pages.*

As you can see, by providing a location bar such as this one, the user is always able to return to the CAD Department, the Clientele List, Consulting Services, the Form page, Related/Favorite Sites, or the WWW Services. Therefore, there is very little possibility of getting lost within a site. Another good idea might be to provide the user with the ability to go back to the previous page, especially if the two pages have similar and related information.

Providing Ease of Contact

There should always be a way to contact someone for more information. This could be done by providing a link to an e-mail address placed boldly on the page, as follows:

> For more information on our services, please contact us at **hats@servtech.com**.

You could also incorporate a form onto your site to provide the user with an easy way of contacting your company (see fig. 28.7).

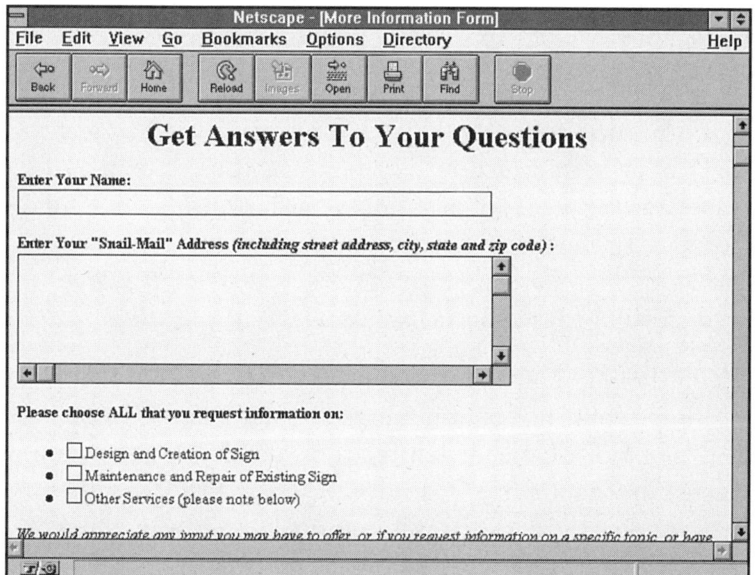

Figure 28.7
A form page prompts the user for key information.

Knowing HTML Standards

An important issue to be aware of when constructing your Web pages is the HTML standards. Currently, the HTML 2.0 version is supported by most Web browsers, so feel free to implement any of the codes within that version.

HTML 3.0, however, is still being finalized. Although there are some browsers that are supporting some of the features in HTML 3.0, there are others that are not. Another wrench thrown into this issue would be Netscape's and Microsoft's supplements of additional features in their browsers that are neither included in HTML 3.0, nor are supported by any other browser. Although Netscape is currently the most popular Web browser software (holding more than 75 percent of the market), you must remember when designing your pages that there are those who are viewing the Web through other browser software. We will primarily discuss HTML 2.0, but will also mention some of the viable HTML 3.0 and Netscape extensions throughout these chapters. The choice you need to make is either implement these cool, new features and obtain minimal viewing, or stick with a more traditional design and obtain maximum viewing. The decision is yours.

Creating a Web Page

As you already have figured out, to create a Web page you need to know HTML (HyperText Markup Language). HTML is referred to as a formatting language that is fairly basic in its structure. The files that you create in HTML will have an extension of .html or .htm, and will be using standard ASCII files with formatting codes that have information about what the finished product will look like. Formats such as titles, text styles, paragraphs, lists, links, and so forth will be listed here.

Before you begin, you should know that the HTML language is not fancy, and there are many limitations. It is continuing to get better and better, however, as new levels of HTML are introduced (not to mention the arrival of VRML, as discussed in Chapter 31). The advantages are that it is transferred over the Net very quickly, and that it is not too complicated, which makes learning and utilizing a fairly easy task.

There are many HTML authoring and conversion programs that will be helpful in creating your Web page, but it is very important to at least learn the basics of the language before relying on a software program to do it all for you.

So, why don't we dive in now? Let's make a sample Web page from start to finish and discuss the HTML tags necessary to do this procedure.

Getting Started—The Main Elements

After opening your favorite word processor, start a new sheet and type the following:

```
<HEAD>
<TITLE>Kassis Superior Signs, Inc.</TITLE></HEAD>
```

Starting the <HTML> Tag

The preceding code will appear in all of your HTML documents. The file begins with the <HTML> tag, which indicates that the following is to be considered a document using the HTML language. This tag always needs an ending tag, </HTML>, to be included in the document (which usually appears at the end of the document), surrounding the body of the document, as follows:

```
<HTML>
This is my very first Web page!
</HTML>
```

The <HEAD> Tag

The next tag is the <HEAD> tag, which generally means just that. This indicates the header of the document, which will not be seen on the Web page itself. The <HEAD> tag also needs a closing tag, </HEAD>, to indicate its closure.

The <TITLE> Tag

The next tag included in the preceding sample is the <TITLE> tag. This tag indicates the title of the page, which also will not appear on the Web page itself.

When choosing a title, use something short, but descriptive. The text included in the title will show up in many other places. This will show at the top of the browser screen, when links are provided to your page (by search engines and other pages), and also when someone bookmarks your location for future reference. You want to make sure it accurately describes what that page entails.

Again, the <TITLE> tag needs a closing tag, </TITLE>, to end properly, as follows:

```
<TITLE>This is where my title will go</TITLE>
```

The <BODY> Tag

The first tag to follow the header of the file is the <BODY> tag. The <BODY> tag indicates the beginning of the body of the Web page, where the content lies. Like the other tags, this tag also needs a closing tag, </BODY>.

The main elements, which will appear in all of your Web pages, will look like this:

```
<HTML><HEAD>
```

```
<TITLE>Kassis Superior Signs, Inc.</TITLE></HEAD>
<BODY>
Content of the Web page goes here . . .
</BODY>
</HTML>
```

Design Elements

The next section of your page will consist of many possible design elements. Whether or not you decide to use some or all of them is completely up to you as a Web page designer. Always remember that what you are designing within the specifications of one Web browser will most certainly always look a little (or completely) different within another Web browser. If possible, try to use more than one browser when producing your pages, so that you can see how different the material might appear, and design in a way that will be acceptable for all browsers.

Heading Tags <H1> Through <H6>

Very often you will want to use heading tags to indicate a header line of some sort. The header tag, which ranges in size from <H1> (the largest) to <H6> (the smallest), is a way for you to indicate either a title or the beginning of a new section. The sample text will look something like this:

```
<HTML><HEAD>
<TITLE>Kassis Superior Signs, Inc.</TITLE></HEAD>
<BODY>
      <H1>Kassis Superior Signs, Inc.</H1>
      <H2>Kassis Superior Signs, Inc.</H2>
      <H3>Kassis Superior Signs, Inc.</H3>
      <H4>Kassis Superior Signs, Inc.</H4>
      <H5>Kassis Superior Signs, Inc.</H5>
      <H6>Kassis Superior Signs, Inc.</H6>
</BODY>
</HTML>
```

Note that each heading tag needs a closing tag to finish the sequence. Figure 28.8 shows how all the different size headings will print in the Netscape browser.

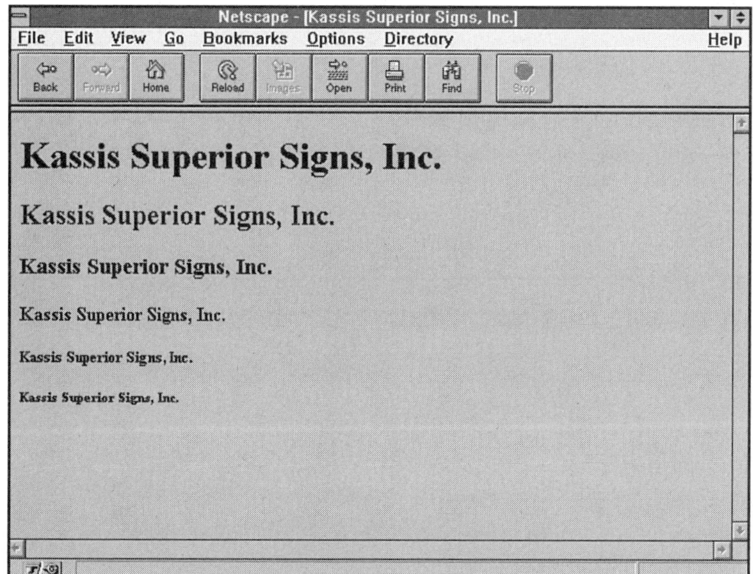

Figure 28.8
The different heading sizes as displayed in Netscape.

A tip to keep in mind when laying out the page design is to keep the heading sizes in sequential order. In other words, start by using the bigger size heading and move sequentially down the page using each size smaller. This helps the user in reading and understanding the content of your page.

In the example of the Kassis Superior Signs page, you can include headings for additional areas of information, such as products and service:

```
<HTML><HEAD>
<TITLE>Kassis Superior Signs, Inc.</TITLE></HEAD>
<BODY>
      <H1>Kassis Superior Signs, Inc.</H1>
            <H2>View our Products</H2>
            <H2>Our Services Include</H2>
            <H2>Contact Our Facility</H2>
            <H2>About our Company<H2>
                  <H3>Company Newsletter</H3>
                        <H4>Letter from the President</H4>
</BODY>
</HTML>
```

In figure 28.9, see how the headings are shown during the output.

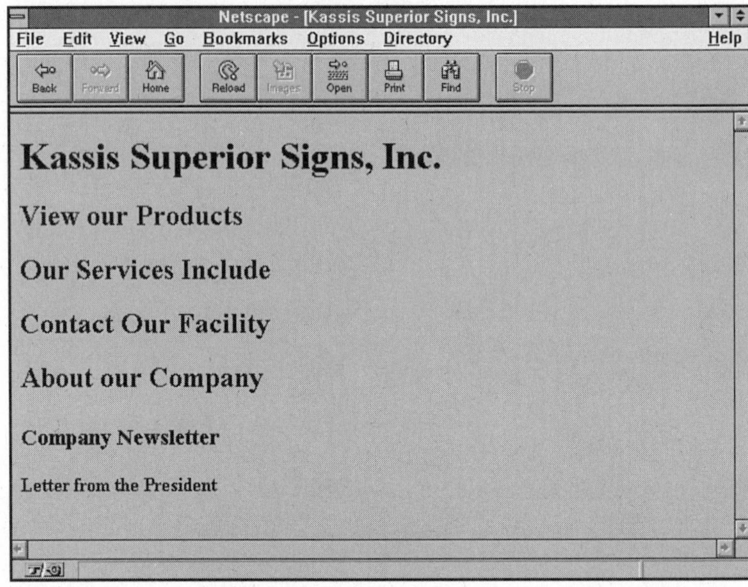

Figure 28.9 *The different heading sizes as used in order, viewed in Netscape.*

The Horizontal Rules Tag (<HR>)

Something I tend to do next in designing my pages is to separate the heading of my page from the actual body or content of the page by using a line, as shown in figure 28.10.

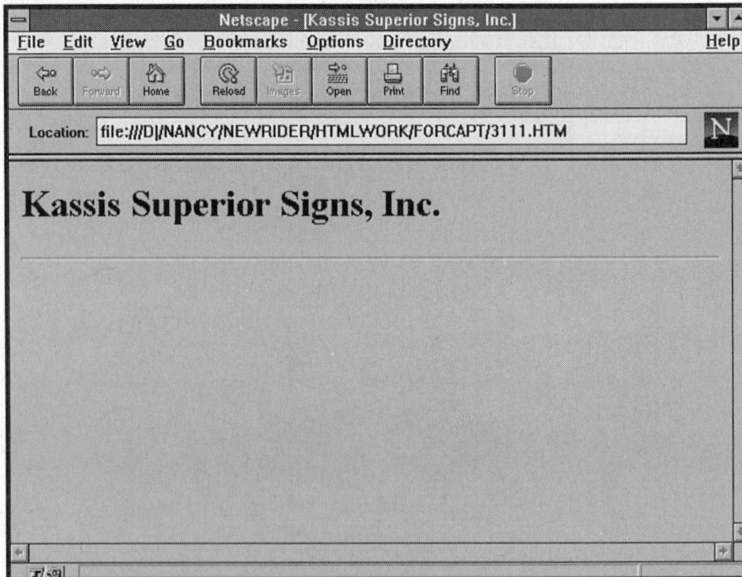

Figure 28.10 *The Horizontal Rules tag creates a line to separate information.*

This tag is called the Horizontal Rules (<HR>) tag. Unlike the tags discussed previously, the <HR> tag does not need a closing tag. The code for figure 28.10 would look like this:

```
<HTML><HEAD>
<TITLE>Kassis Superior Signs, Inc.</TITLE></HEAD>
<BODY>
      <H1>Kassis Superior Signs, Inc.</H1>
      <HR>
</BODY>
</HTML>
```

The Paragraph Tag (<P>)

The next inclusion on your Web page, following the title and headings, may be a paragraph of text. For this, you will need to use the <P> tag, which indicates a paragraph to follow. If you think of it in terms of the <P> tag adding a return character onto your document, you'll know exactly when to use it. Although you may include the return character, or additional spaces in your actual HTML document, they will not appear in the Web page itself.

The older versions of HTML did not require an ending tag, but you would be safe to learn to implement it now, so that when the new requirements come out, you will be safe. The code to include a paragraph in your page looks like this:

```
<P>Our products encompass a wide overview of what's currently
available in today's market. Please see our list, which is com-
plete with prices and availability for your convenience.</P>
```

The output would then be as shown in figure 28.11.

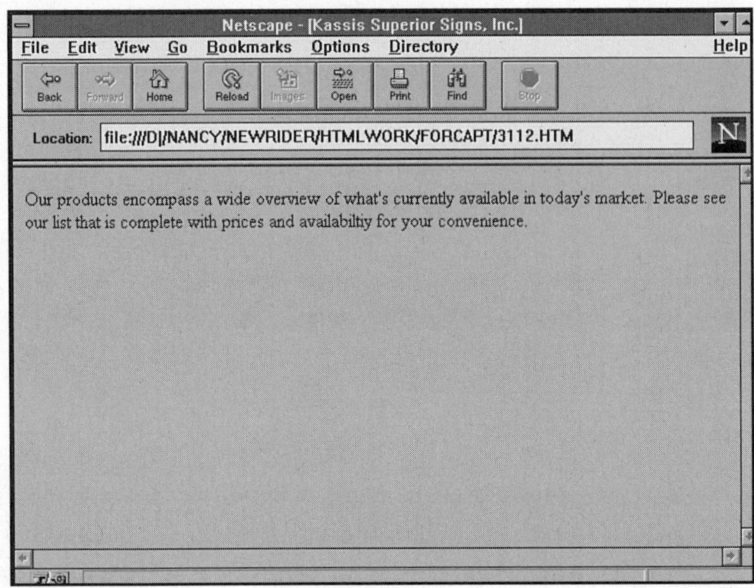

Figure 28.11
How the paragraph tag will display text in the Netscape browser.

The Break Tag (<BR>)

The <BR> tag's function is to do exactly as it states—create a line break wherever it's implemented. It does not add any spaces as the <P> tag does; it simply breaks at the point where it is located, and starts any text appearing after the tag on the very next line back to the left margin. It works great for poems, as follows:

```
<P>Halloween Party Invitation:</P>
<P>
A Halloween Party this year for you,<BR>
at 4325 Middlebrook Lane, it's true.<BR>
On Saturday, October 28th at 6 (pm),<BR>
Gouls, Goblins, and Witches on sticks<BR>
Will fly about in the cool night air,<BR>
Giving everyone a really big scare!
</P>
```

The output in Netscape looks like figure 28.12.

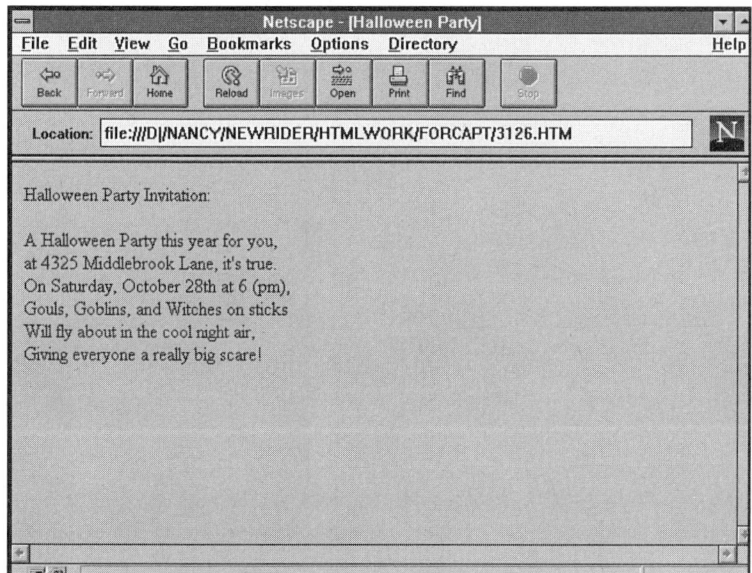

Figure 28.12
This is how the break tag will display text in the Netscape browser.

Comments

Another application that you could have inside your HTML document is the use of comments. Comments are simply what they imply—they are a notation for only the webmaster to view, as they do not appear on the Web page at all. This may help you to remember to update some information at a later date, help you to remember where you received the information, or help you with any other thing that you may need to remember, but do not want visible on the page.

The code to create comments is the following:

```
<!-- Update this pricing on January 1, 1997 -->
```

Each comment should be on its own individual line, and try not to make a habit of using HTML tags inside the comments section. It might be confusing for the browser, as well as for yourself!

Character Styles

When it comes to character styles, there is not much in the way of fancy styling. In certain instances, the font type can appear to change. The font size can be changed, but currently only in the Netscape browser. The font color cannot be changed, unless you are using the most current version of Netscape and Microsoft Explorer. Even the bold, italic, and center tags may not be supported in all browsers. A list of the different tags related to character styles follows, but remember not to rely on your text appearing the way you intend it to in all variations of browser software.

All of the character styles, whether they affect how the text will be used (logical styles), or the physical appearance of the text (physical styles), need to have a beginning and a corresponding closing tag. The next sections list the popular character styles.

Bold

Bold is probably the most used of what I call the *text manipulation* tags. I've found that there are two tags associated with this feature that generally do the same thing—<B> or <STRONG>. The beginning tag indicates where you want the bold to begin, and then the ending tag, which is mandatory if you want the bold to end, goes at the end of the text you want to bold, as follows:

```
<B>Bolded Information</B>
```

or

```
<STRONG>Bolded Information</STRONG>
```

Note The <B> tag is a physical style tag and the <STRONG> tag is a logical style, but both should have the same effect depending on what browser you are using.

Italic

Italic tags, <I> or <EM>, work in the same way as the bold tags, with one at the beginning of the text and one at the end, as follows:

```
<I>Italicized Information</I>
```

or

```
<EM>Italicized Information</EM>
```

Again, both should have the same effect depending on what browser you are using, although the <I> tag is physical, and the <EM> tag logical.

Note Although it may seem a duplicate effort, the difference between the physical and logical style tags in the bold and italic situations seems to be the ability to nest effectively. The logical style tags often produce incorrect results in some browsers when nesting. The physical style tags, however, can be nested with no repercussions.

Underlining

There is a <U> tag for underlining text, but you shouldn't make a habit of using it because most browsers do not recognize this tag. Just be aware that it does exist.

Text Style Tags

Generally, the font type cannot be altered within an HTML document. Some exceptions to this rule do exist, however. There are a limited number of logical style tags that will change the text in small ways. They actually change the way the text will be used. As with the other character style tags, these tags also need a beginning and closing set of tags. The following lists these tags, and shows what each would indicate when used:

- **<TT>.** Typewriter font
- **<CODE>.** A fixed-width font, such as Courier
- **<SAMP>.** A font similar to <CODE>
- **<KBD>.** Indicates text to be typed by the user
- **<VAR>.** Indicates a variable that will be replaced with a value
- **<DFN>.** Indicates a word that will or has been defined

- **<CITE>.** Indicates a citation
- **<STRIKE>.** Shows text coded with strikethrough

Note When I used all of these with the Netscape browser version 1.1N, the <TT>, <CODE>, <SAMP>, and <KBD> tags all appeared to look the same, with a slight variation from the normal format of the text. The <VAR> and <CITE> tags gave the text an italicized look. The <DFN> tag appeared to have no difference from the regular text style. The reason this is mentioned is to remind you to remember that not all browsers view these tags in the same manner. Try them in your browser to see how each appears.

Text Alignment

Although it originated as a Netscape extension, the <CENTER> tag is now being supported more widely, however, it is officially a Netscape enhancement and might not be viewable in other browsers. The <CENTER> or <ALIGN=CENTER> tags are used in this fashion:

```
<CENTER>
<H1>Doing Business On The Internet</H1>
<H2>Lesson No. 1</H2>
</CENTER>
```

or

```
<H1 ALIGN=CENTER>Doing Business On The Internet</H1>
<H2 ALIGN=CENTER>Lesson No. 1</H2>
```

which both produce the same effect, as shown in figure 28.13.

It is uncertain whether or not the <CENTER> tag will be included in HTML 3.0, but the <ALIGN=CENTER> tag is included in the specification, so better use the latter to be on the safe side.

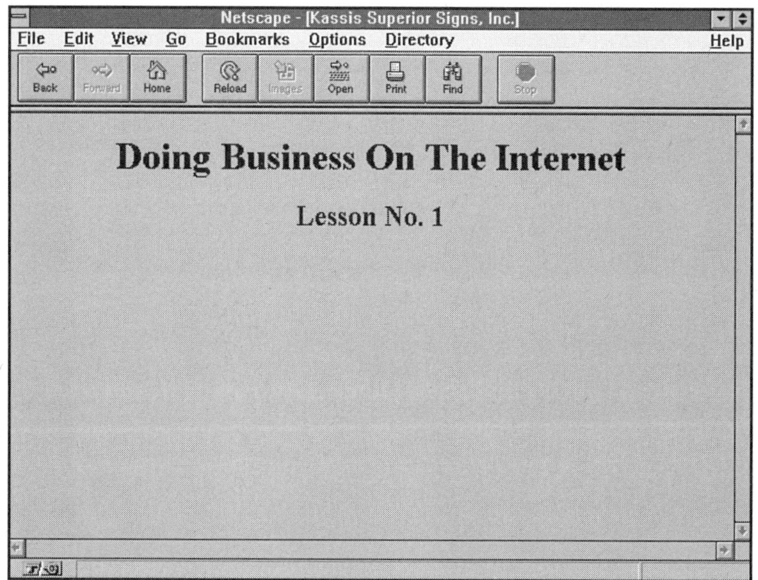

Figure 28.13
The effect of the center tags as shown in Netscape.

Creating Links

Now on to the excitement! What fun would Web pages be without links to one another?! Let's discuss how to create links to other HTML pages. Before we begin, make sure you know the filename that you want to link to.

The <A> (or anchor) tag indicates that there will be some sort of link associated with it. The browser will show the linkable area in a highlighted format, so that the user knows where to click for the corresponding link information. The <A> tag has to have other data included within the tag itself in order to function. The one you will use most often is the HREF (said to be short for "Hypertext REFerence") attribute.

Figure 28.14 shows all the different elements of the link command. The opening tag specifies the file to be linked to (in this case "welcome.html"). The words "Welcome Announcement" will be highlighted for users to know they could click on this area for welcoming information. And finally, the closing tag indicates where the highlighted text ends.

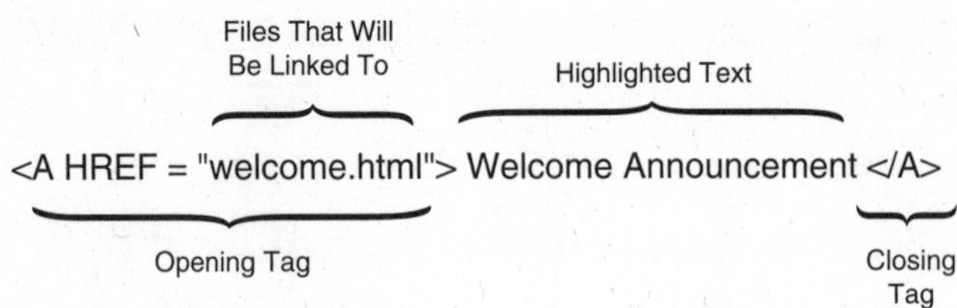

Figure 28.14 *The different parts of a link command.*

Let's see how this input would look in a browser (see fig. 28.15):

```
Before entering our site, please visit our <A
HREF="welcome.html">Welcome Announcement</A>.
```

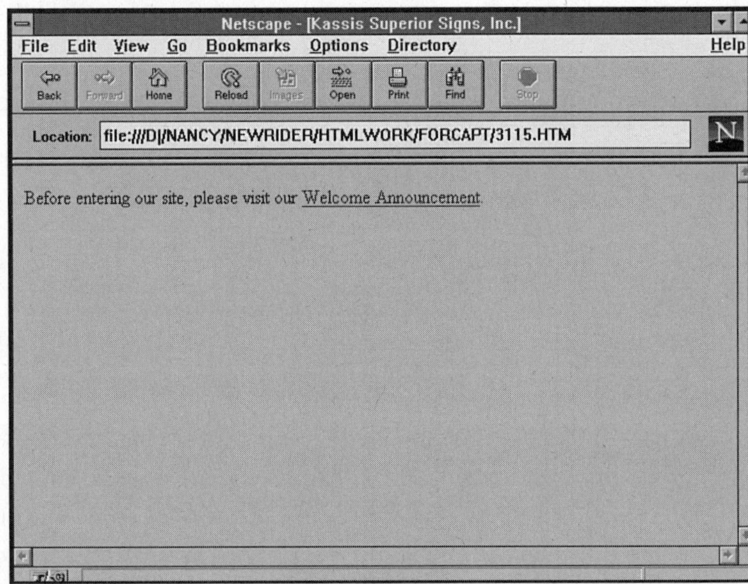

Figure 28.15 *Netscape showing how the link tag will display the text.*

Local Links

Let's examine some quick examples for you to test on your own. The best way to understand the principle behind this is to actually do it for yourself.

Note The numerals on each line of the following code are for referential purposes and should not be typed.

Type the first file, **contents.html**:

```
1.    <HTML><HEAD>
2.    <TITLE>Kassis Table of Contents</TITLE></HEAD>
3.    <BODY>
4.    <H1 ALIGN=CENTER>Kassis Superior Signs</H1>
5.    <H2 ALIGN=CENTER>Table of Contents</H2>
6.    <P>Welcome Announcement from our President</P>
7.    <P>Company Newsletter</P>
8.    <P>Product List</P>
9.    <P>How Signs are Made</P>
10.   <P>Contact Our Company</P>
11.   </BODY>
12.  </HTML>
```

Then, type the second file, **welcome.html**:

```
<HTML><HEAD>
<TITLE>Joe Kassis Welcome Announcement</TITLE></HEAD>
<BODY>
<H1 ALIGN=CENTER>Welcome Announcement from our President:</H1>
<H2 ALIGN=CENTER>Joe Kassis</H2>
<P>It is my pleasure to welcome you all to our fabulous Web
➥site! We have been on the
Internet for about 6 months now, and find it to be a key
➥avenue for reaching our very
important clientele.</P>
<P>Another issue we can point out on our Web site is our
➥very interesting sign-making
procedure for all to enjoy. Take a moment to browse through
➥our site, and thanks for
visiting.</P>
<P>Joe Kassis; President</P>
</BODY>
</HTML>
```

Now that you've typed the two examples and have them saved (in the same directory), you can link them together by using the <A> tag. What you need to do is go back to the first file, contents.html, so that you can link the President's welcome (welcome.html) to the appropriate section within that file. Go back to line number 6 of the first file, and create the link around the words "Welcome Announcement from our President" like this:

```
<P><A HREF="welcome.html">Welcome Announcement from our
➥President</A></P>
```

The final output should look like figure 28.16.

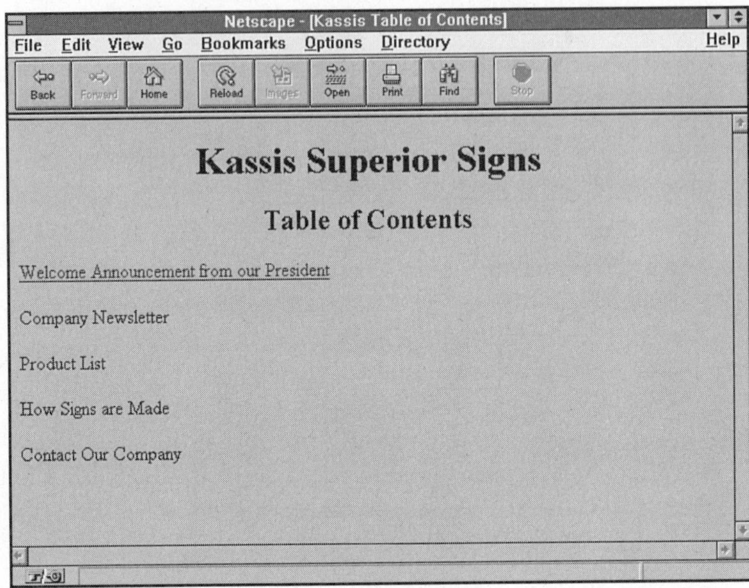

Figure 28.16
The link to the president's announcement is displayed prominently on the company's homepage.

It's very important to make sure that your files are inside the same directory, or you will then have to specify what directory that file is located in within your HTML document link command. When testing your Kassis example, your browser should find the welcome file when you click on the words highlighted inside the contents document. If it does not find it, see the following list of some important things to check for accuracy:

- Did you type the filenames exactly right?
- Are your filenames ending in .htm (DOS environment)? If so, change the preceding example where necessary.
- Are your files in the same directory?
- Did you remember your quotation marks and closing </A> tag?

The examples you've done until now are local files, which are easy to define during the linking procedure. What about when you want to link to other files on your system, but in different directories? You then need to specify where the file is located—this is usually done by using relative path names.

One thing to keep in mind (especially if you are working on a DOS/Windows or Macintosh system): the directories need to be specified with Unix style commands. When you want to separate a directory or folder name, you would use a forward slash (/) to do so. In order to refer to the directory above your current one, you must use two dots (..). Also, it is very important to specify the location of the file on the server, not on your local system. A helpful technique that may be used is to always try when possible to keep the directory names and file locations exactly the same to avoid confusion. Then you simply need to remember to use the forward slash and dots, but can keep the names the same.

Although this may seem a dauntless procedure for specification, this relative path name format makes it easier for you in the long run by making less work for you when and if you decide to move your files around.

> **Note** If you are using an HTML editor, make sure that these procedures are followed in order for your pages to be linked properly.

Remote Links

"What about those sites I've seen that have links to other people's sites?" you may ask. It's easy! The link tag is the same, but you will need to specify the filename in this manner:

```
<A HREF="http:www.signspecs.com">Sign Specifications Homepage</A>
```

Instead of listing the filename that you want to link your text to, you must instead specify the URL (or Web address) of this location. You can also link to other types of addresses, such as the following:

FTP	`ftp://`*`ftp.destination.com`*
Gopher	`gopher://`*`gopher.destination.com`*
Usenet	`news:`*`name.of.newsgroup`*

> **Note** You cannot test these links unless you are actually online.

When you have links within your documents, try to make them as easy for the user to understand as possible. If you find your paragraphs cluttered with links, then use menus (discussed later in this chapter) to arrange them in an orderly fashion. Try to keep them short, but long enough to give the user a quick idea of what's behind the links, especially if the user is skimming the page. Provide the link with a brief description next to it if possible. Don't fall into the "for more information click **here**" format. It is considered annoying by many users because they actually then have to read what information they can find by clicking there.

Linking Within the Same Document

There are instances when you will not need to link to a separate file, but simply to another section within the same document. An example might be if you listed the table of contents, but instead of each section going off to a separate file, the sections were described in detail further down on the same page.

The <A> tag is still used in this procedure, but instead of using just the HREF attribute, you will use the NAME attribute as well. To explain further, you use the HREF attribute to first indicate the text to be the link, and then use the NAME attribute to specify the location of where you want the link to arrive (the anchor). Unlike the text associated with the HREF attribute, the text inside the NAME attribute will not appear highlighted.

Let's go to an example for a better understanding of this.

You type the following signstep.html file:

```
<HTML><HEAD>
<TITLE>Steps to making the perfect signs</TITLE></HEAD>
<BODY>
<H1 ALIGN=CENTER>Steps to Making the Perfect Signs</H1>
<P>Please review Kassis steps to making the most perfect
➥sign:</P>
<P>Step 1: Choosing a Name</P>
<P>Step 2: Find the Right Location</P>
<P>Step 3: What Type of Sign is Best</P>
```

```
9.    <P>Step 4: Using the Right Materials</P>
10.   <P>Step 5: Erecting the Sign Properly</P>
11.   <HR>
12.   <H2 ALIGN=CENTER>Choosing a Name</H2>
13.   <P>The first step in making the perfect sign is to decide on
      ➥the most perfect name. Choose
14.   a name that best fits you and your business. Once that name
      ➥is established, then it's time
15.   for step 2.</P>
16.   <HR>
17.   <H2 ALIGN=CENTER>Find the Right Location</H2>
18.   <P>After choosing the name for your business and your sign,
      ➥you must then find the right
19.   location for you and your sign. The location is one of the
      ➥most important issues for new
20.   businesses. After the location, go to step 3.</P>
21.   <HR>
22.   <H2 ALIGN=CENTER>What Type of Sign is Best</H2>
23.   <P>When you're ready to start the construction of your sign,
      ➥its important to first decide
24.   what type of sign you wish to have made. Would it be better
      ➥to have a magnetic sign, a
25.   banner type sign, a sign for the top of a store, or a pole,
      ➥or any other type of sign. Now
26.   move to step 4.</P>
27.   <HR>
28.   <H2 ALIGN=CENTER>Using the Right Materials</H2>
29.   <P>After deciding which type of sign you want, you need to
      ➥hire professionals that
30.   understand and know which materials are right for the job.
      ➥After locating the materials,
31.   move to step 5.</P>
32.   <HR ALIGN=CENTER>Errecting the Sign Properly</H2>
33.   <P>The last step for making the perfect sign is erecting it
      ➥properly. It's important to
34.   know how to arrange the sign at the location for long term
      ➥stability. And those are the 5 steps.</P>
35.   </BODY>
36.   </HTML>
```

Now that you've typed the file, you need to go back and add the links and anchor tags in order to maneuver quickly between the document. First, add the link. As you've already learned, the tag for that begins with the HREF attribute. Go to line 6 of the preceding sample and add a link around the words "Choosing a Name" to look like this:

```
<P>Step 1: <A HREF="#choose">Choosing a Name</A></P>
```

The output is shown in figure 28.17.

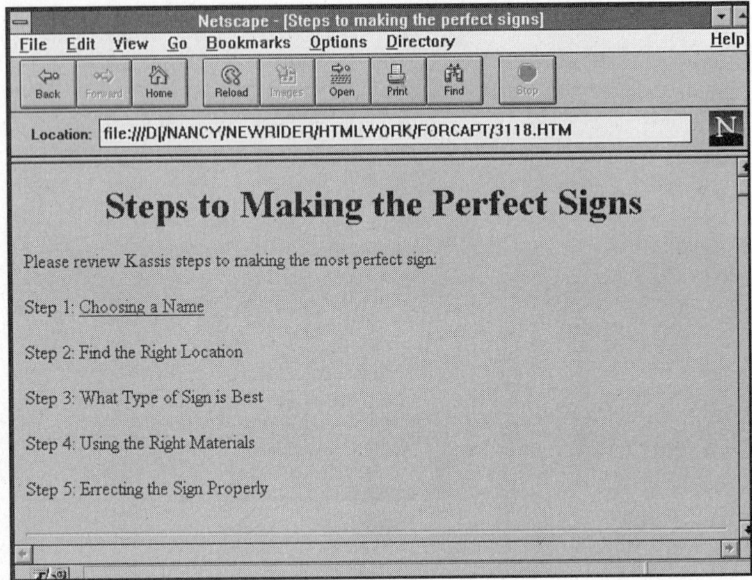

Figure 28.17
The output with the link on the page as viewed in Netscape.

The important difference between linking documents and linking sections within one document, as shown previously, is the use of a # sign and a key name, *not* a filename. This format tells the browser that the text specified should be linked to a corresponding anchor defined by the same key name. Go to line 12 of the example, and add the following anchor:

```
<H2 ALIGN=CENTER><A NAME="choose">Choosing a Name</A></H2>
```

This will continue to tell the browser that the anchor to which the link corresponds is located at this point, and when the link is clicked upon, the browser will jump to this location (see fig. 28.18).

After you've finished the preceding example, add the links and anchors for the remaining steps in the example so you can see how they work. You should be able to determine, after completing this example, that the links that follow will work in the same fashion.

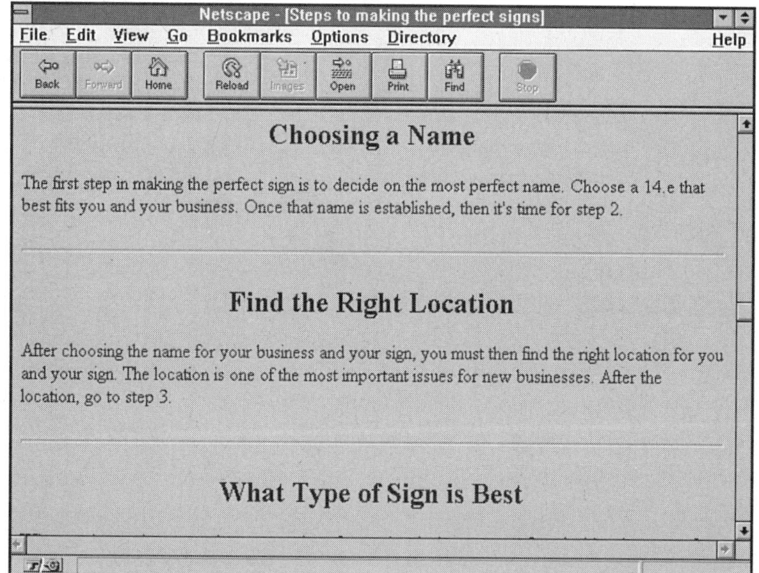

Figure 28.18
Clicking on "Choosing a Name" jumps the user to that part of your page.

E-Mail Linking

There is yet another form of linking that you are able to perform and should definitely include on your Web pages—providing a link to an e-mail address. This is a convenience for users because they would not have to remember your address or cut and paste your address from the page. They instead can simply click on the e-mail link and receive a prompt to type their message.

The e-mail links work much the same way as your other links, even the attribute that will accompany the <A> tag stays as HREF. The only difference is that instead of a file name, key name, or anchor, you will need to specify an e-mail address along with the MAILTO command.

Why don't you add an e-mail link to the bottom of your example by typing the following:

```
<P>Please send any questions and comments to our e-mail: <A
HREF="mailto:kassis@provider.com">kassis@provider.com</P>
```

This format tells the browser that you will be making a link to the `kassis@provider.com` e-mail address. When the user clicks on that address, figure 28.19 shows what appears.

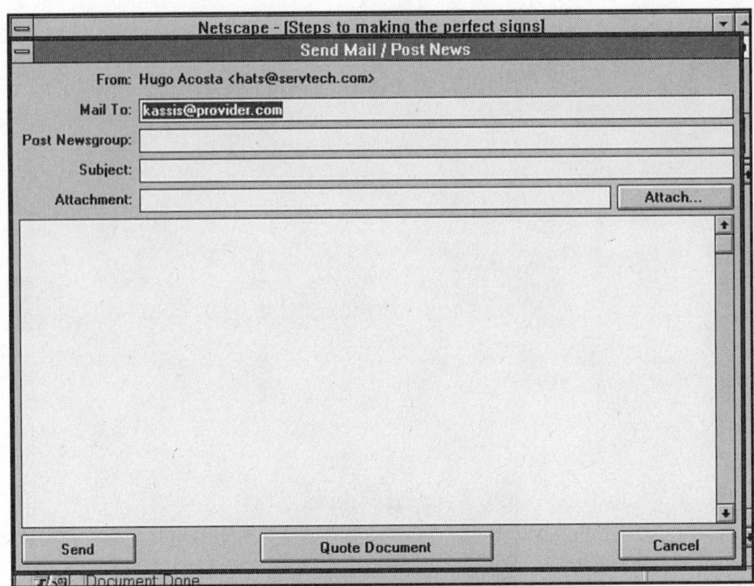

Figure 28.19 *When users click on an e-mail address link, they are given the Send Mail/Post News dialog box.*

Building Lists

There are different variations of list tags that you are able to use on your Web pages. You can generate numbered (ordered) lists, bulleted (unordered) lists, or definition lists. Lists are a great way to organize your material, and make it easier for the user to view and read your page. Although each list tag is slightly different, they do have some similar features. One similarity is that an entire list is always encased within a beginning and closing tag to let the browser know when the list starts and finishes. Another likeness is that each section within a list has its own beginning tag.

Numbered or Ordered Lists

The tags surrounding a numbered or ordered list are the <OL> and </OL> tags (Ordered list). Each section within such a list begins with an <LI> tag (List Item), which is only a one-sided tag. This list format is great for displaying elements in a certain, numerical order, indicating an order of importance, as follows:

```
<P>Learning To Drive For The First Time</P>
<OL>
    <LI>Make sure to check and adjust all the mirrors, adjust
    ➥seat, fasten seat belt.
```

```
    <LI>Start the car.
    <LI>Make sure all is clear.
    <LI>Pull out of the driveway
</OL>
```

The output on a browser when using these tags will be a numbered, and maybe indented, list, as shown in figure 28.20.

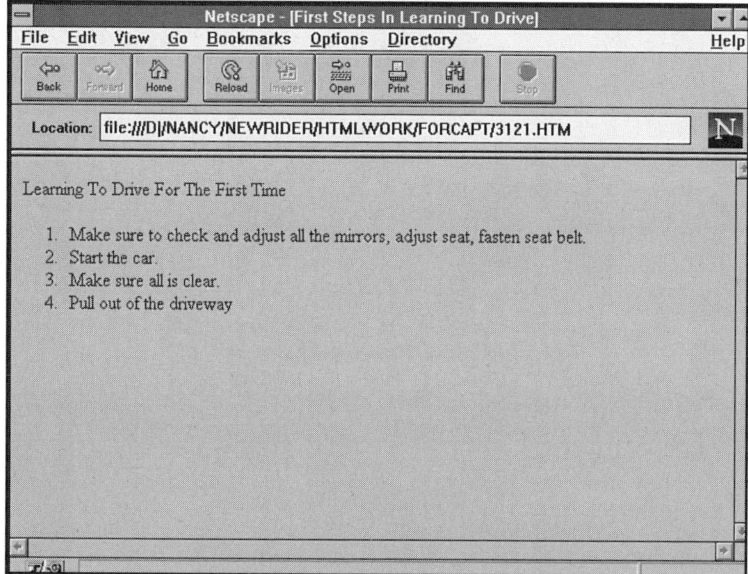

Figure 28.20
A numbered list displayed in Netscape.

Unordered Lists

Unordered lists are what you might use when you have a collection of topics or items to mention, but the order in which they appear is not important. Therefore, you would not need to have them numbered, just tagged with a symbol. These lists use the <UL> (unordered list) tags to surround their data, but continue to use the <LI> tags in front of each item to be mentioned, as follows:

```
<P>My List of Things to do Today:</P>
<UL>
    <LI>Letter to Mom
    <LI>Laundry
    <LI>Clean Refrigerator
    <LI>Grocery Shopping
</UL>
```

As you can see, these items need to be accomplished, but the order is not a necessity. The output will have bullets (or another symbol, depending on the browser) to mark each topic, as shown in figure 28.21.

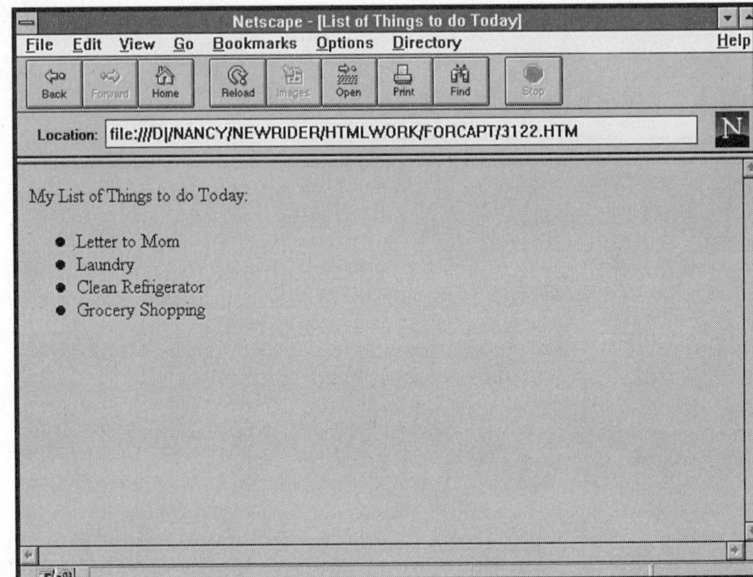

Figure 28.21 *A bulleted list displayed in Netscape.*

Definition Lists

Yet another format of generating lists is called a Definition list (or glossary list). The purpose of this list is exactly what you might think—to define a word or term. The <DT> tag represents the term to be defined, and the <DD> tag represents the definition. You would use the <DL> (Definition list) to surround the contents:

```
<DL>
<DT>Caboose<DD>The last car on a freight train, with kitchen and
➥sleeping facilities for the train crew.
<DT>Enroute<DD>On or along the way.
<DT>Token<DD>Something that serves as an indication or
➥representation; sign; symbol.
</DL>
```

The output would generally look something like the screen shown in figure 28.22.

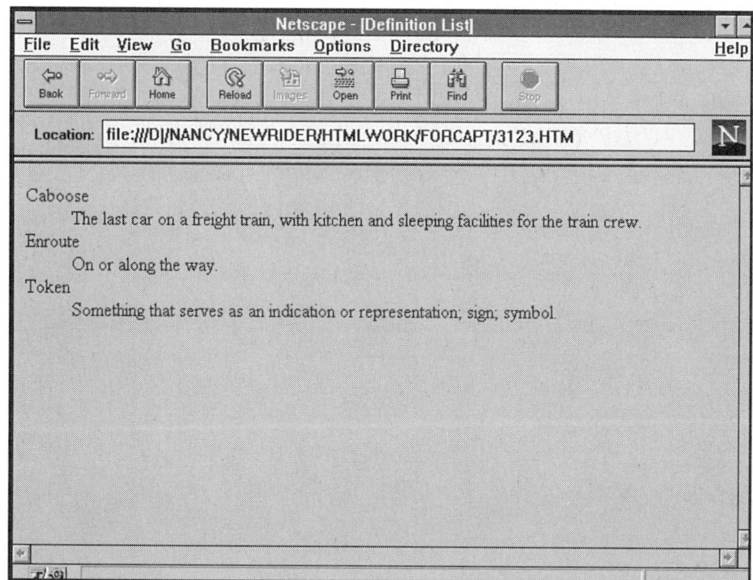

Figure 28.22
A definition list displayed in Netscape.

Using Lists Within Other Lists

You may find it necessary to arrange lists inside one another for such tasks as creating outlines. This is fine, as long as you provide the opening and closing tags to each individual list. Many browsers will provide different symbols for nested lists. Remember, though, that each browser handles situations in its own way.

```
<H1>Outline for Implementing HTML Lists</H1>
<OL>
<LI>Learn The Different List Types
    <UL>
    <LI>Numbered or Ordered Lists
        <UL>
        <LI>When To Use
        <LI>Tags for this List Type
        </UL>
    <LI>Unordered Lists
        <UL>
        <LI>When To Use
        <LI>Tags for this List Type
        </UL>
    <LI>Definition Lists
        <UL>
        <LI>When To Use
```

```
        <LI>Tags for this List Type
        </UL>
    </UL>
<LI>Determine Where to Input Them
<LI>Add Them To Your HTML Page
</OL>
```

Although this one may look complicated in the HTML language, see how it looks through the browser in figure 28.23.

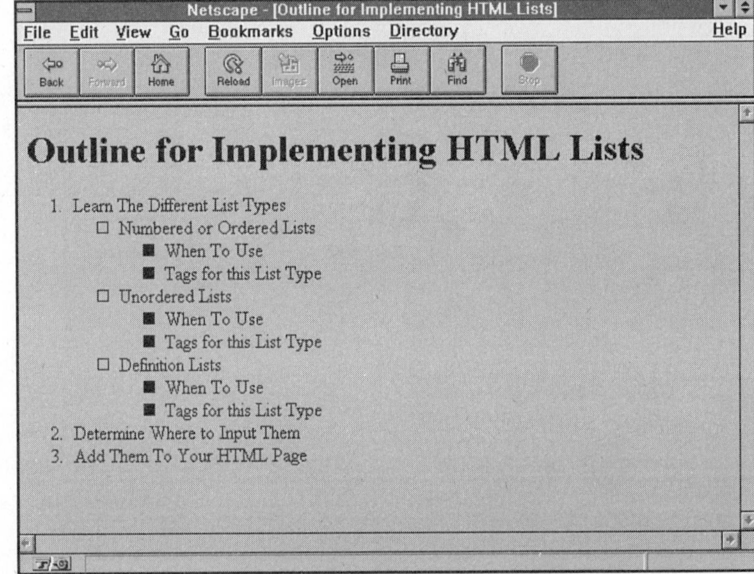

Figure 28.23
Lists within lists as displayed in Netscape.

Notice how Netscape handles the unordered lists that are nested within each other.

Preformatted Text

Because the HTML language makes it very hard to align information (unless using the <TABLE> tag—to be discussed later in this chapter), there has been a way around this by using the <PRE> tag for preformatted text. Although it doesn't matter if you indent or hit the character return inside your HTML document, it does matter if you preface it with the <PRE> tag.

Anything you type within these tags will appear through the browser, exactly as it does on the document. For example, if you type this data within your page:

```
<PRE>

Month         Topic         Attendance     Collected
----------------------------------------------------

January       Cats          157            $145.97
February      Dogs          135            $137.56
March         Birds         110            $109.57
April         Snakes         45            $ 65.85
May           Gerbils        89            $ 87.95
June          Cows          125            $136.27
July          Horses        187            $185.37

</PRE>
```

The output in the browser would look the same, as shown in figure 28.24.

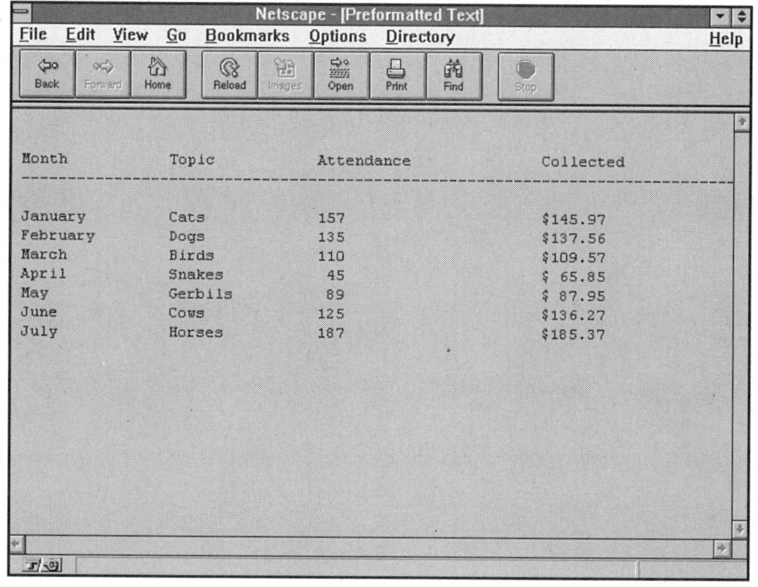

Figure 28.24
The preformatted text as displayed in Netscape.

Note I've found that sometimes preformatted text, especially when used in creating form pages, is a little tricky, and I have to play with it for it to look exactly as I want. Sometimes the boxes are not quite aligned the way you think they would be after typing the code.

Creating Forms and CGI Scripts

The use of forms on a Web site are quite convenient. By using a CGI script to generate answers from a form page, you can help the user contact you with little effort.

Forms are helpful in determining who and how many have visited your site. They can create an easy and effective way for the user to contact your company for information, ordering, or any other topic you want to consider. Although the user can use an e-mail link, there are many times when they would not know which information to provide. The form helps by prompting them with the data you need to fulfill the request.

CGI Scripts

Just about one year ago, the hottest thing to have on your pages was a form page. At that time, browsers were just starting to support forms, and webmasters were avidly learning how to do Common Gateway Interface scripts to make forms, searches, and even guestbooks for their Web sites.

CGI, otherwise known as Gateway, scripts are what currently enable the users to interact with Web pages in one way or another. Some examples would be when searching a database, signing a guestbook on someone's page, or sending in an order or questionnaire form. The word "currently" is used here because with the implementation of Java (to be discussed later in this chapter), you could say that CGI scripts might be a thing of the past, in terms of creating interactive pages.

This CGI script is a program that resides on the server, and starts running when it receives some type of information from the browser. The program is usually written in either the Perl (for medium to complex programs) or C (for very complex data manipulation) programming languages, but also can be done in almost any other language available. In maintaining your own server, you need to make sure to address several questions before implementing these scripts. If your site is very popular, with many users accessing it, sending in forms, searching your site, and making the script run at the same time, is your system going to be able to handle this overload? Also, unless your scripts are done very carefully, you run the risk of allowing someone to access your system. If, after you've considered these issues, you still decide to run the script programs, look at your server documentation to configure the server to handle them appropriately. In addition, see Chapter 19, "Basics of CGI," for more information.

When it comes to learning how to make CGI programs or scripts, it's not all fun and games. Many times, instead of starting from scratch, you can learn from and manipulate an existing code to match your needs.

HTML Forms

Now that you've been introduced to CGI scripts, it's time to learn the HTML that goes along with creating forms. Remember, one does not work without the other—you need both in order for the user to actually return the information on the forms.

There are two different methods for submitting information from the browser to the script, and allowing the browser to communicate with the server—GET and POST. The better of the two is POST because there are no limitations for the amount of information that is able to be transferred. You certainly don't want to lose any valuable information from the user!

The <FORM> tag indicates the start of a form page. So, the first step in creating your HTML form is to specify how you want the information from the form to be sent to the script. Use the METHOD attribute inside the <FORM> tag, and indicate which method (GET or POST) you prefer:

```
<FORM METHOD="POST" ACTION="/cgi-bin/kassform.cgi">
```

The preceding statement indicates that you want the method of submission to be POST, and the ACTION to take would be to post the form to the server, to the "kassform.cgi" script, located within the "cgi-bin" directory. This type of statement is required to start all forms.

Layout Options

Now that you know how to start a form and create a script, let's talk about what's available for laying out your forms on-screen. You can choose from many different options:

- **Input Tag.** Essential for the creation of the form page. Used in conjunction with many attributes.
- **Text Boxes.** Helps the user input valuable information such as name and address.
- **Password.** Help protect certain sections of your site from those who do not have access.
- **Radio Buttons.** Enables the user to select certain information.
- **Check Boxes.** Enables the user to select bits of information.
- **Submit & Reset Buttons.** Necessary for the submission of the form and enabling the user to reset all categories in case of errors.
- **Selection Boxes.** Another way of giving the user information to choose from.
- **Textarea.** Provides the user with an area to express views, ask questions, or relate any substantial sized information.

Input Tag <INPUT *type*>

First, you must know that the <INPUT *type*> tag has a few attributes that can be used within it. The attributes include TEXT, PASSWORD, RADIO, CHECKBOX, SUBMIT, and RESET. After using this tag, you must specify which of these attributes you want to be used. Then you must define a NAME and/or VALUE for this specific element, which links to the corresponding name within the CGI script.

Text Boxes

Text boxes are great for asking someone's name and address, or asking for comments. You'll see them on many forms. The first step before coding your text box is to type the HTML to prompt the user for the information you want to receive, as follows:

```
<P>Enter Your Name: </P>
```

Now, for a single line text box, use the TEXT type in the command, and assign a NAME:

```
<INPUT TYPE="text" NAME="contact">
```

You've indicated a single line text box to be named "contact." The completed code is the following:

```
<P>Enter Your Name: <INPUT TYPE="text" NAME="contact"></P>
```

There are attributes that can be used within the <INPUT> tag. The SIZE attribute can be used to indicate the length of the amount of text to be used (measured in characters). If there is no size specified, the default is 20 characters. The MAXLENGTH is used to indicate the maximum amount of characters that the user can input. They could be used as follows:

```
<P>Enter Your Name: <INPUT TYPE="text"NAME="contact" SIZE="35"></P>
```

The preceding statement gives the text box a length of 35 characters.

Password

The PASSWORD attribute gives you the same "text" field as the TEXT attribute. The only difference is that anything the user types within that field will appear with asterisks in place of the text for security reasons. The code for this type is as follows:

```
<INPUT TYPE="PASSWORD" NAME="secretname">
```

Radio Buttons

Another type of layout design is called a *radio button.* These buttons are used when giving the user a list of items to choose from. When the user selects one button, the others are deselected. The TYPE attribute is "radio," and the

NAME attribute on radio buttons within a list is always the same. In addition, each radio button must have a VALUE attribute assigned to it, as follows:

```
<OL>
<INPUT TYPE="radio" NAME="thesystem" VALUE="dos">Dos
<INPUT TYPE="radio" NAME="thesystem" VALUE="windows">Windows
<INPUT TYPE="radio" NAME="thesystem" VALUE="mac">MacIntosh
<INPUT TYPE="radio" NAME="thesystem" VALUE="OS/2">OS/2
<INPUT TYPE="radio" NAME="thesystem" VALUE="Unix">Unix
</OL>
```

Check Boxes

Similar to radio buttons, the check boxes also are used to list items. They, however, provide the user with the ability to select more than one choice. The TYPE attribute is "checkbox," and each has an individually assigned NAME attribute, as follows:

```
<UL>
<INPUT TYPE="checkbox" NAME="accounting">Accounting Software
<INPUT TYPE="checkbox" NAME="graphic">Graphic Software
<INPUT TYPE="checkbox" NAME="internet">Internet Software
<INPUT TYPE="checkbox" NAME="spreadsheet">Spreadsheet Software
<INPUT TYPE="checkbox" NAME="wordproc">Word processing Software
</UL>
```

Note The only time you would assign the VALUE attribute is when you want the indication of choice to say something other than "on" or "off," which is what you receive back from users. In other words, if they choose a box, the message to you states "on," and if not, the message is "off."

Now put these all together so you can see what a simple form HTML page might look like:

```
<HTML><HEAD>
<TITLE>Simple Form Layout</TITLE></HEAD>
<BODY>
<H1>Computer Experience Form</H1>
<FORM METHOD="POST" ACTION="/cgi-bin/kassform.cgi">
<P>Enter Your Name: <INPUT TYPE="text" NAME="contact" SIZE="35"></P>
```

```
<P>Which Operating System are you most familiar with:<BR>
<OL>
<INPUT TYPE="radio" NAME="thesystem" VALUE="dos">Dos
<INPUT TYPE="radio" NAME="thesystem" VALUE="windows">Windows
<INPUT TYPE="radio" NAME="thesystem" VALUE="mac">MacIntosh
<INPUT TYPE="radio" NAME="thesystem" VALUE="OS/2">OS/2
<INPUT TYPE="radio" NAME="thesystem" VALUE="Unix">Unix
</OL>
</P>
<P>Select all Software Types you have experience with:<BR>
<UL>
<INPUT TYPE="checkbox" NAME="accounting">Accounting Software<BR>
<INPUT TYPE="checkbox" NAME="graphic">Graphic Software<BR>
<INPUT TYPE="checkbox" NAME="internet">Internet Software<BR>
<INPUT TYPE="checkbox" NAME="spreadsheet">Spreadsheet Software<BR>
<INPUT TYPE="checkbox" NAME="wordproc">Word processing
➥Software<BR>
</UL>
</P>
</FORM>
</BODY>
</HTML>
```

Now you can see how the output looks (see fig. 28.25).

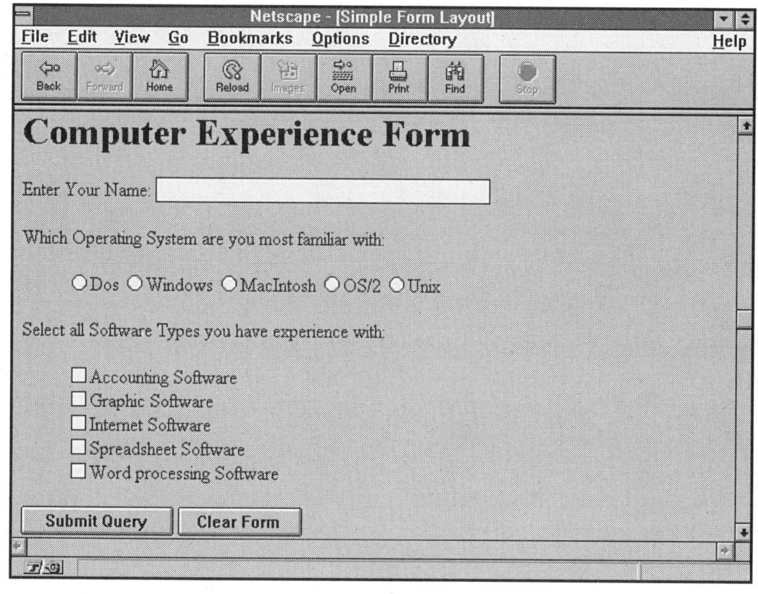

Figure 28.25
The different aspects of a form page in Netscape.

Note Notice how the <BR> tag helps to align the row from top to bottom.

Submit and Reset Buttons

Although the submit and reset buttons usually go at the very end of the form, they are covered here because they fall within the <INPUT TYPE> tag. The submit button is what enables the user to send the information on the form back to you. The reset button enables the user to wipe out the input that was in the form, and reset so each field is cleared. Each form should have one submit and one reset button on the bottom.

The VALUE attribute is used with each of these, to define a name for the button to appear on the screen, as follows:

```
<INPUT TYPE="SUBMIT" VALUE="Submit Query">

<INPUT TYPE="RESET" VALUE="Clear Form">
```

The output for the buttons above will look like figure 28.26.

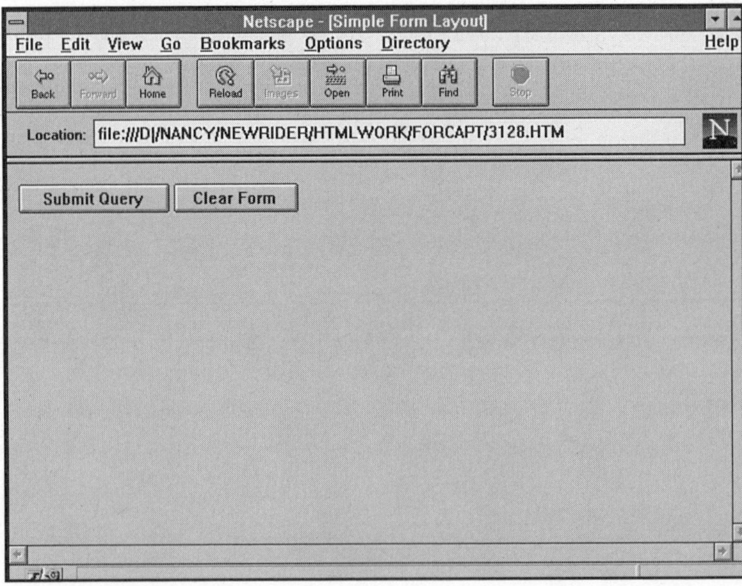

Figure 28.26
Submit and reset buttons as they might appear in Netscape.

Although you have seen a lot of information on forms, don't go out and try to create one just yet—you've still got a lot more to cover!

Selection Boxes

There are other tags that can be used inside of a form layout. The <SE-LECT> tag is used to create a list of predefined choices that the user can scroll through to choose from. Unlike the previous tag, the <SELECT> tag requires a closing tag. The items to be listed within the selection box are defined by the <OPTION> tag, as follows:

```
<P>Select your favorite color:
<SELECT NAME="color">
<OPTION>Blue
<OPTION>Red
<OPTION>Yellow
<OPTION>Orange
<OPTION>Black
</SELECT>
</P>
```

There are several attributes that can be used within the <OPTION> tag, such as VALUE and SELECTED.

The VALUE attribute is used to assign a value to the corresponding option. If no value is set, the form will send back the value of whatever text follows the <OPTION> tag.

The SELECTED attribute specifies an item within your list that will be the default checked item. If there is no option selected, the first item in the list will be what appears as the default selection (see fig. 28.27).

Unless you note otherwise, the user has the ability to choose only one item from the <SELECT> tag. You can give the user the option of choosing more than one by using the MULTIPLE attribute, but in order to select more than one option, a particular key has to be used, and that changes from browser to browser.

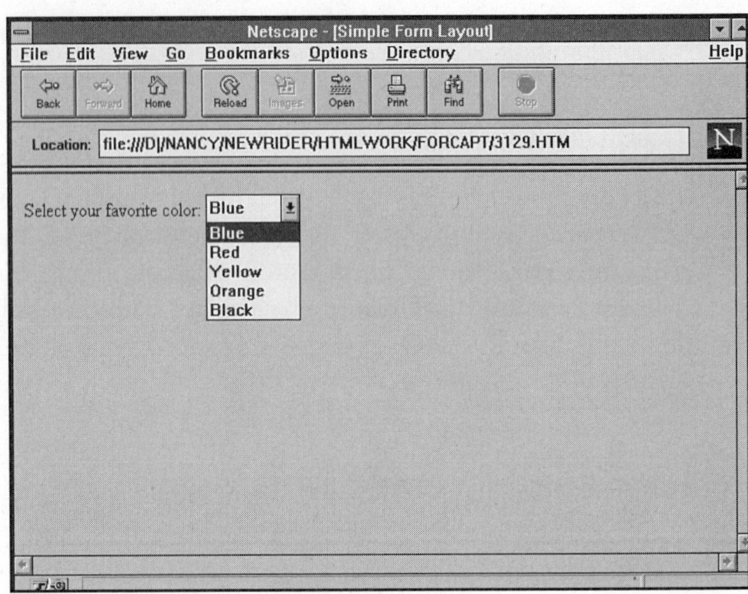

Figure 28.27 *The selection box of a form page as it might appear in Netscape.*

In addition, you can use the MULTIPLE SIZE attribute to specify the size you want the multiple selection box to be, and the user will then scroll the box to view all choices, as follows:

```
<P>Select your favorite color:
<SELECT NAME="color" MULTIPLE SIZE="4">
<OPTION>Blue
<OPTION>Red
<OPTION>Yellow
<OPTION>Orange
<OPTION>Black
</SELECT>
</P>
```

The output in will look something like figure 28.28 (depending on which browser you are using).

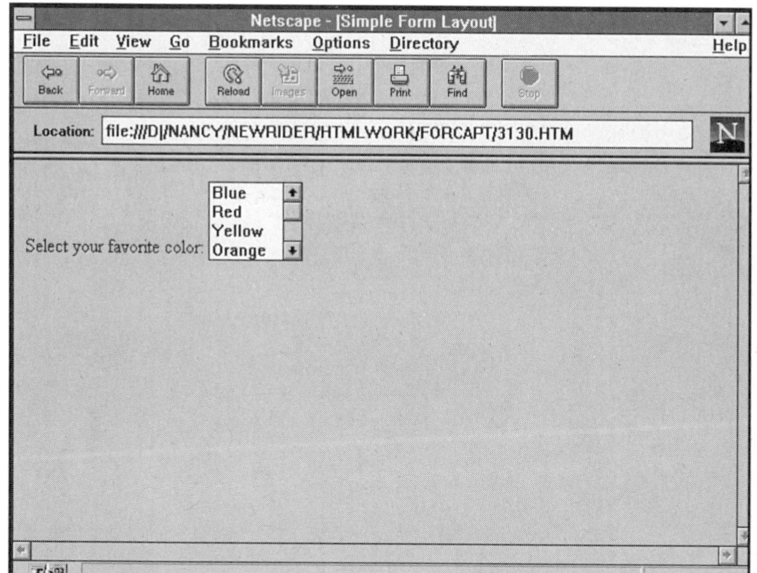

Figure 28.28
The selection box as displayed in Netscape when you specify the multiple size attribute.

Textarea

If a single line of text is not enough, you can use the <TEXTAREA> tag. This is great for allowing comments or suggestions from the user. The <TEXTAREA> tag needs to have the NAME (to assign a name to the box that corresponds to the script), ROWS (specifies the height of the text area), and COLS (specifies the width of the text area) attributes included in it, as follows:

```
<P>Please offer any comments:<BR>
<TEXTAREA NAME="comments" ROWS=6 COLS=50></TEXTAREA></P>
```

Note how the <TEXTAREA> tag needs the closing tag </TEXTAREA>. Also, make sure to indicate the purpose of the box (comments, suggestions, remarks, and so forth). See the results in figure 28.29.

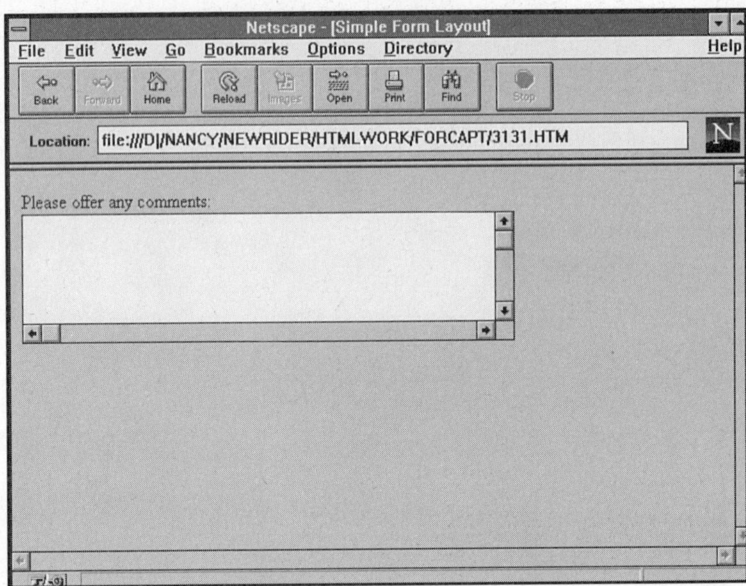

Figure 28.29
A specified text area box as displayed in Netscape.

Notice how the Netscape browser does not display the whole area; instead, it provides scroll bars to the area.

Decoding

Now that you've created a script and a form to receive requests from the user, you need a program to decode the information sent to the server. The program needs to change all the encoded data back to its original format for legibility.

There are a variety of programs available that already provide this decoding process for you. Check out these programs for usability:

- **cgiparse.** The cgiparse program is somewhat limited in that it is part of the CERN HTTPD distribution and is difficult to get if you're running another server. You can use this program to decode form input from either the GET or POST methods.

- **uncgi.** The uncgi program, which is written in C, decodes in a similar way to the cgiparse program. It is easier to get, however. It works best with the POST method. More information can be found at `http://www.hyperion.com/~koreth/uncgi.html`.

- **cgi-lib.pl.** The cgi-lib.pl program is a set of routines for the Perl language to manage form input. It works with either the GET or POST methods. More information can be found at `http://www.bio.cam.ac.uk/web/form.html`.

Including Tables on the Web

Tables, a feature that was included in HTML 3.0, are becoming more widely used every day. Tables, which are graphic formats for arranging specific data in a columnated manner, are similar to spreadsheets in that they arrange the information in columns and rows. They are just as cool as the forms were when we first started using them! Although a few months ago there were maybe two browsers supporting tables, luckily, most of the current versions of the more popular graphical browsers are now supporting them. But do keep in mind when deciding whether or not to use tables, that there are still other browsers (and people with older versions) out there that don't have the capability to view the tables, and to them it may look very confusing when accessing your page.

Tables can be used on the Web for almost anything you would use them for in other everyday applications. Arrange your sales data, chart information, table of contents, or anything else you feel appropriate. One downfall is using tables that contain large bits of information. These tables, if they go beyond the normal screen borders, can be somewhat cumbersome for users to follow because the headings fall off the screen when you scroll for viewing. This is especially troublesome when you have to scroll left to right. At least when scrolling up and down, you can duplicate the headings to appear more frequently within the table for easier comprehension.

<TABLE> Tags

The <TABLE> tag is what creates a table in HTML. This tag, which requires a beginning and closing tag, surrounds the information you want to be displayed as a table. Within these tags, you can include a title for your table (table caption), the table headings, and table data.

You then need to specify each row in a table by using the <TR> (Table Row) tag with its closing tag </TR>. Then you need to identify the cells with either a <TH> (Table Heading) or <TD> (Table Data) tag, with their respective closing tags </TH> or </TD>. Here is a simple table so you can better understand this layout:

```
<TABLE BORDER>
<TR>
    <TH>Header goes here</TH>
    <TD>Data goes here</TD>
    <TD>Data goes here</TD>
</TR>
</TABLE>
```

This input would give you one table row, with the header on the top, and two cells containing data underneath the header.

Following is how a larger table's code might look:

```
<TABLE BORDER>
<TR>
    <TH>Venus</TH>
    <TH>Harley</TH>
    <TH>Lady</TH>
</TR>
<TR>
    <TD>Golden Retriever Mix</TD>
    <TD>German Shepard</TD>
    <TD>Black Lab</TD>
</TR>
<TR>
    <TD>4 years</TD>
    <TD>2 years</TD>
    <TD>8 years</TD>
</TR>
</TABLE>
```

You would use this layout for a table with three rows, with headings on the top, and two cells of data underneath each heading.

Or, for the headings to appear within the left cells of the table, and the data to the right, type this:

```
<TABLE BORDER>
<TR>
```

```
    <TH>Venus</TH>
    <TD>Golden Retriever Mix</TD>
    <TD>4 years</TD>
</TR>
<TR>
    <TH>Harley</TH>
    <TD>German Shepard</TD>
    <TD>2 years</TD>
</TR>
<TR>
    <TH>Lady</TH>
    <TD>Black Lab</TD>
    <TD>8 years</TD>
</TR>
</TABLE>
```

See figures 28.30 and 28.31 to compare the results.

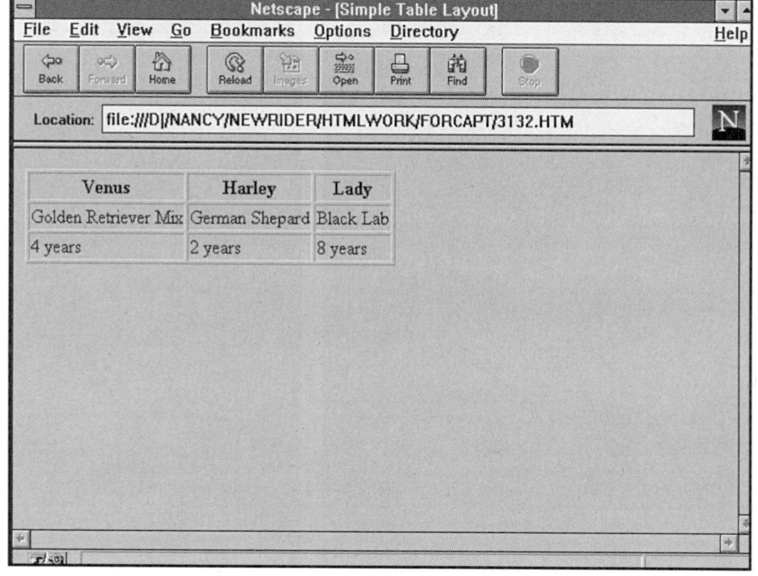

Figure 28.30
The table with the headings aligned in the top row.

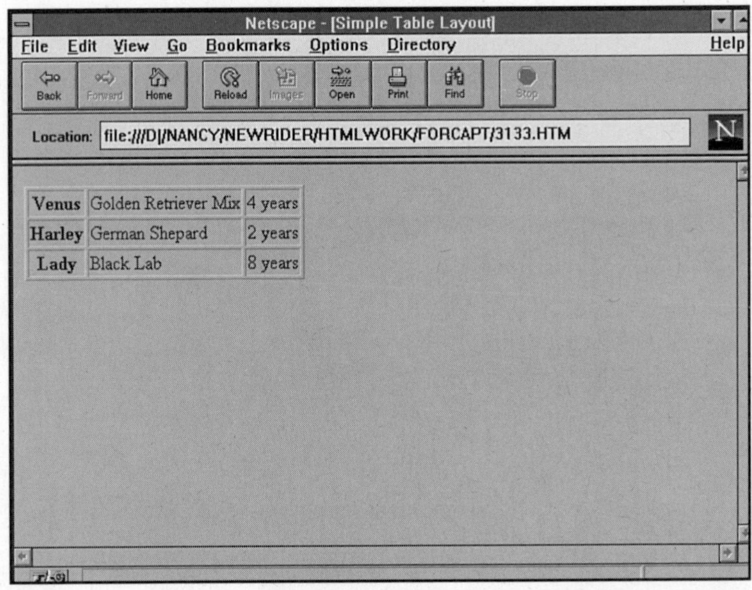

Figure 28.31
The table with the headings aligned on the left side in the left column.

Note It is possible to specify empty cells by simply listing the opening and closing table tags with no text in-between, as follows:

<TD>Information</TD>	Cell content is "Information"
<TD></TD>	Cell contents are empty

<CAPTION> Tag

There are other possibilities concerning tables. The optional <CAPTION> tag is used to define the name of your table. It too requires a closing tag, as follows:

```
<TABLE>
<CAPTION>Statistics On Our Three Dogs</CAPTION>
. . .
```

Specifying Table Statistics

Within the <TABLE> tag, you have the opportunity to specify some table statistics if you want, using the following attributes:

- The first, BORDER attribute, tells the browser how wide the border will be, and if you want a border at all. You would need to list the border width in pixels (the default is one). Sometimes it helps you to use a table without a border to better control the text of your page.
- Next is the WIDTH attribute. How wide do you want the table to appear on the screen? There is a default based on the length of the longest data found within the table, but this default can be bypassed. The WIDTH attribute can be specified in either the total number of pixels, or a percentage amount of the entire screen width.
- Next, there are the CELLSPACING and CELLPADDING attributes. CELLSPACING defines how much space there will be between cells (the default is two), and CELLPADDING defines how much space will be between the cell wall and its contents (the default if one).

This is what they look like all put together:

```
<TABLE BORDER=5 WIDTH=90% CELLSPACING=5 CELLPADDING=4>
```

Arranging Table Data

There are many other attributes that need to be mentioned in relation to tables and their data. The <TH> and <TD> tags have attributes that may be used within them to manipulate and maneuver their data. They include the ALIGN, VALIGN, ROWSPAN, and COLSPAN attributes.

ALIGN and VALIGN

The ALIGN attribute corresponds to the horizontal alignment of the data within the cell, and the VALIGN attribute corresponds to the vertical alignment of the data within the cell. You can specify either LEFT, RIGHT, or CENTER alignment choices for the ALIGN attribute, and TOP, MIDDLE, or BOTTOM can be listed for the VALIGN attribute. The <TH> tag automatically defaults its contents to the center horizontally and vertically, and the <TD> tag centers its contents vertically, but aligns horizontally to the left.

In addition, you can also use the ALIGN and VALIGN attributes inside the <TR> tag to arrange all cells within that row. You can override that specification, however, by changing an individual cell, as follows:

```
<TR ALIGN=LEFT VALIGN=TOP>
    <TD>This</TD>
    <TD>Example</TD>
    <TD>Shows</TD>
    <TD>Different</TD>
    <TD VALIGN=BOTTOM>Alignment</TD>
</TR>
```

The preceding example will make all the table data within that row to be left, top justified, with the exception of the last cell, which will be left, bottom justified.

COLSPAN and ROWSPAN

In addition to the alignment attributes, there are also attributes that allow a cell's contents to span over multiple columns (COLSPAN attribute) and rows (ROWSPAN attribute). Here's an example of how this works:

```
<TR>
    <TH COLSPAN=3>New York State</TH>
</TR>
<TR>
    <TH></TH>
    <TH>Year</TH>
    <TH>Number of Computer Users</TH>
</TR>
<TR>
    <TH ROWSPAN=2>Buffalo</TH>
    <TD>1994</TD>
    <TD>1587 People</TD>
</TR>
<TR>
    <TD>1995</TD>
    <TD>3468 People</TD>
```

```
</TR>
<TR>
    <TH ROWSPAN=2>Syracuse</TH>
    <TD>1994</TD>
    <TD>2468 People</TD>
</TR>
<TR>
    <TD>1995</TD>
    <TD>5974 People</TD>
</TR>
```

Although this code may look somewhat complicated and confusing, the output is actually very simple, as shown in figure 28.32.

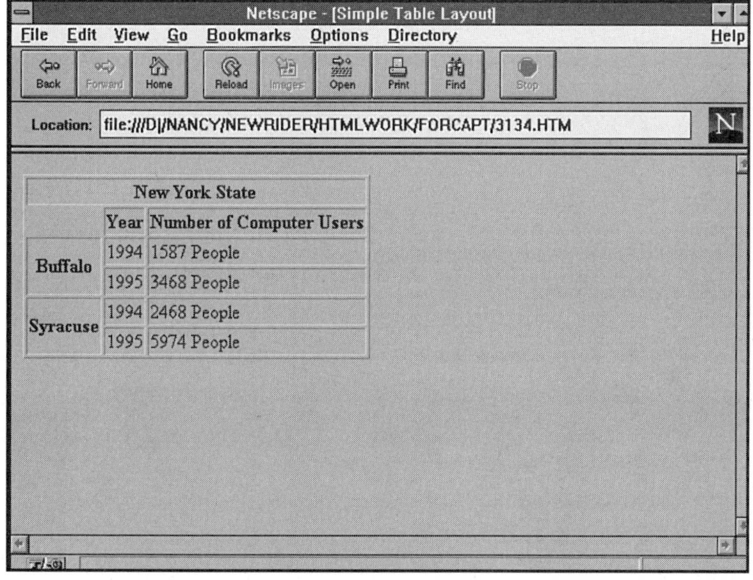

Figure 28.32
The output of the table, which includes a mix of table headings and table data.

Note You are able to use graphics and links anywhere within tables as you normally would throughout a page.

Creating a Sample Table

Why don't you try a larger, more complicated table for experience and practice, and include what you have learned about tables so far.

Now make a table of the CNYPCUG Group's Monday and Wednesday meetings for the month of January. You will list the dates and times and include a short message regarding all meetings. Take notice of all the codes used within this table:

```
<HTML><HEAD>
<TITLE>Simple Table Layout</TITLE></HEAD>
<BODY>
<TABLE BORDER>
<CAPTION><B>CNYPCUG Monday & Wednesday Events</B></CAPTION>
<TR>
    <TH COLSPAN=7>January</TH>
</TR>
<TR ALIGN=CENTER>
    <TH VALIGN=TOP ROWSPAN=3>Monday</TH>
    <TH>1</TH>
    <TH>8</TH>
    <TH>15</TH>
    <TH>22</TH>
    <TH>29</TH>
    <TD ROWSPAN=6><I><P>All events will be<BR>
        held at our facilities<BR>
        on Rte 281 in Syracuse.</P>

        <P>Call our events<BR>
        coordinator for<BR>
        more information.</P>

        <P>Thank you<BR>
        for your support.</P></I></TD>
</TR>
<TR ALIGN=CENTER>
    <TD>AutoCAD</TD>
    <TD>Networking</TD>
    <TD>Internet</TD>
    <TD>Word</TD>
    <TD>Pagemaker</TD>
</TR>
<TR ALIGN=CENTER>
    <TD>6:30 pm</TD>
    <TD>5:30 pm</TD>
    <TD>6:30 pm</TD>
    <TD>6:30 pm</TD>
    <TD>4:30 pm</TD>
</TR>
<TR ALIGN=CENTER>
```

```
        <TH VALIGN=TOP ROWSPAN=3>Wednesday</TH>
        <TH>3</TH>
        <TH>10</TH>
        <TH>17</TH>
        <TH>24</TH>
        <TH>31</TH>
</TR>
<TR ALIGN=CENTER>
        <TD>Windows</TD>
        <TD>WordPerfect</TD>
        <TD>DOS</TD>
        <TD>Photoshop</TD>
        <TD>Geneology</TD>
</TR>
<TR ALIGN=CENTER>
        <TD>6:30 pm</TD>
        <TD>6:00 pm</TD>
        <TD>5:30 pm</TD>
        <TD>6:30 pm</TD>
        <TD>5:00 pm</TD>
</TR>
</TABLE>
</BODY>
</HTML>
```

Notice how nicely arranged all the contents of the preceding table will look when completed in the Netscape browser, as shown in figure 28.33.

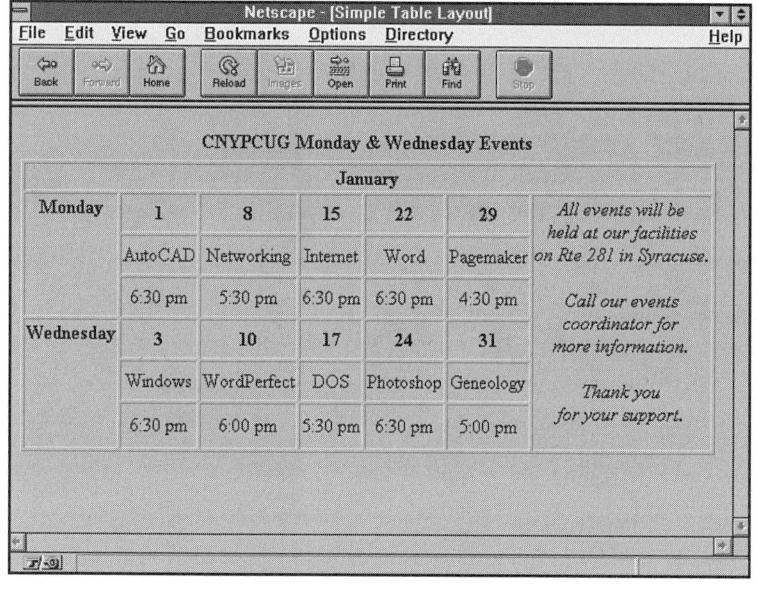

Figure 28.33
The complicated table as shown in Netscape.

Note Notice how you were still able to use the bold <B> and Italic <I> tags within this table, as well as the <P> (Paragraph) and
 (Line Break) tags within the table's cells. Remember, this works for almost all HTML features—images, linking, center, lists, and so forth. The only issue is to try to keep the table itself within the browser screen for convenience. Experiment and see how fancy your tables can be!

The only other aspect of tables that should be mentioned is that there are some extensions to tables that Netscape has made, which will be discussed in the Appendix.

Always remember that when using tables, there is a possibility that some users will have browsers that are unable to view your tables. If the fact that some users may not be able to view these tables troubles you, you can find another way of displaying your data instead of using tables. Think of using a list, using pre-formatted text, or changing the whole table into an image—you can also be considerate of those who cannot view tables by providing a text-only version. In using text within your page, there are characters that need a special code in order to appear.

Special Characters

HTML does not read special characters that require a special sequence of keys to be created. Although you may be able to see it within your browser when you are testing your pages, it may not make it through the lines to the user viewing your page. Because of this issue, HTML has developed a set of codes called *character entities.* These codes translate into special characters when being viewed through a browser.

There are number entities and character entities, which both begin with an ampersand (&), and end with a semicolon (;). The character entities have a short description of the character they stand for between the ampersand and semicolon. The number entities have a hash sign (#), followed by a numerical sequence between the ampersand and semicolon, which stands for the character.

Other characters that must be represented by special codes are characters used within the HTML language, as shown in table 28.1

Table 28.1
Special-Character Codes

Character Name	Character	Code Tag
Less than character	<	<
Greater than character	>	>
Ampersand	&	&

See the Appendix for a complete listing of all the character entities.

<BLOCKQUOTE> Quotations

HTML also provides a way of listing a quotation by using the <BLOCKQUOTE> tag. The text found within the beginning and closing <BLOCKQUOTE> tags is usually slightly different from regular text in that it is usually indented. The Halloween example from earlier in this chapter is a good candidate for the <BLOCKQUOTE> tag, as follows:

```
<P>Halloween Party Invitation:</P>
<BLOCKQUOTE>
A Halloween Party this year for you,<BR>
at 4325 Middlebrook Lane, it's true.<BR>
On Saturday, October 28th at 6 (pm),<BR>
Gouls, Goblins, and Witches on sticks<BR>
Will fly about in the cool night air,<BR>
Giving everyone a really big scare!
</BLOCKQUOTE>
```

The <BLOCKQUOTE> tag acts very similar to the <P> (Paragraph) tag, but also indents the text between, as shown in figure 28.34.

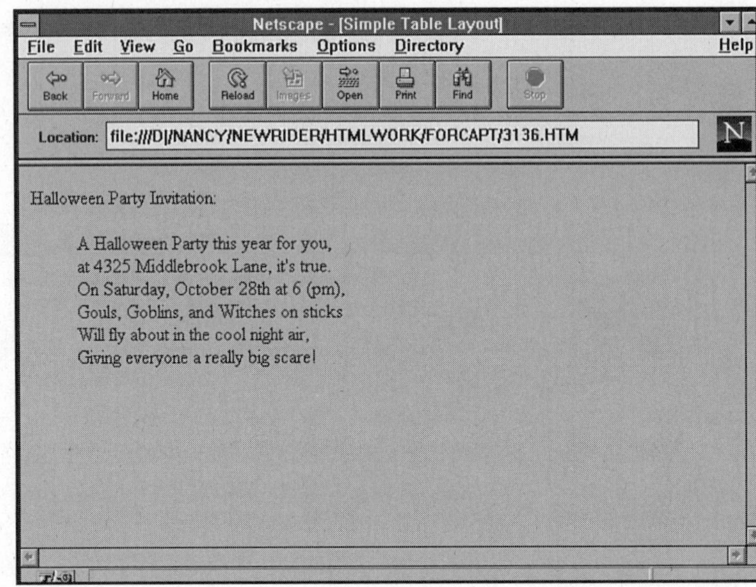

Figure 28.34 *The <BLOCKQUOTE> tag in use with text.*

<ADDRESS>

The last thing that is usually found on a Web page is an address. The <ADDRESS> tag acts like a signature to the work. The tag might contain information such as who's responsible for creating the page, copyright information, who to contact, date of last update, and anything else that you might want to include. See how they are used in the following:

```
<HR>
<P>
<ADDRESS>
<I>copyright &#169; 1996 H.A. Technical Services<BR>
For more information contact us at <A
HREF="mailto:hats@servtech.com">  hats@servtech.com</A></I>
</ADDRESS>
</P>
```

Figure 28.35 displays how this would look at the bottom of your Web page.

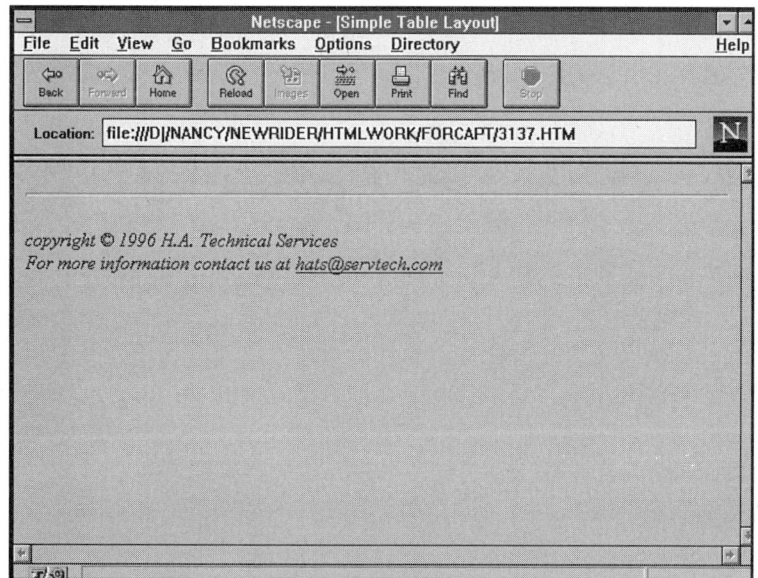

Figure 28.35
The <ADDRESS> tag as displayed near the bottom of the page.

This chapter covered the elements of a basic Web site, and what you need to know to develop one. With the image tags you learned about in the last chapter, and the general layout tags you've learned in this one, you have all the tools necessary to make an impressive homepage.

In learning to first establish the right image, and to lay out and plan the design of your site, your chances of creating a more effective Internet presence are increased. Answers to some key questions about attracting repeat visits were addressed, as well as covering tips and techniques about the presentation of your material. Learning that there are numerous options to present your information on the Web, and learning how to go about presenting these options rounded out the chapter.

There are other, more advanced HTML techniques and browser enhancements that are discussed in greater detail in the Appendix. You can very easily take what was discussed in this chapter, however, and put it to good use immediately by creating your own Web site! Have fun!

HTML Cross Client Concerns

by Nancy Acosta

Although the Web has standardized a significant part of the Internet so that it is easy to use, the software people use on the Web is creating new concerns. Companies that are developing today's browsers for the World Wide Web (the clients on the Internet) are setting or at least trying to set their own standards. Each browser is adapting new and better HTML features, and not waiting for the features to be implemented as a standard.

This chapter explains differences between the most popular browsers available today. The following sections examine the adaptations and enhancements of each browser, and show whether these changes are advantageous.

Browsing the Prominent Browsers

This chapter describes in detail the features and flaws of the most prominent browsers available today. Some of their names you will surely recognize:

- Metscape
- Microsoft Internet Explorer
- NCSA Mosaic
- Spyglass Enhanced Mosaic
- America Online
- Cello
- Netcom's Netcruiser
- Lynx

After all the individual browser software is covered, you'll dive into the issue of cross client concerns. Where is the World Wide Web headed? Will there be standards? What can you, as a webmaster, do?

The next step on the agenda is to actually create a controversial Web page. You'll go over the steps involved in creating an HTML document that will have a different appearance in each of our famous Web browsers, which will be the next step; viewing this Web page you've created. A screen capture from the browsers will show the wide variety of how the page looks within each of the browsers, and perhaps show you the problems this could create.

Netscape

There's no question about it: Netscape is the browser of choice for Internet users. Recent surveys estimated that this browser held approximately 75–80 percent of the market. Netscape also has been a leader in developing and incorporating new HTML features in its browser that the company hopes will become standards in the near future. Netscape claims it has only added these features because of an overwhelming request by webmasters to include these features. The company's rapid introduction of new features has set itself apart from the rest, although Netscape has developed a somewhat risky reputation.

Note Netscape Navigator 1.1N introduced a number of new and innovative features, but the newer 2.0 version really has jumped ahead! The non-beta version has recently become available from Netscape's FTP site, and this author highly recommends it!

Every version of Netscape includes useful Web features. Bookmark organizers, for example, let you add information about the last date the bookmark was visited, the date you added it, and much more. You can reorder bookmarks, separate them by category, and even search through them! Besides bookmarks, Netscape offers a number of configuration options, including cache, text, color formatting, helper applications, and security options.

Another new release from Netscape—the Gold version—includes the company's regular Navigator and features that let you create and edit HTML pages.

New Non-standard Netscape Features

As has been mentioned, Netscape has incorporated some flashy and flagrant features that are not a standard, but more technological innovations. Don't get me wrong, I think it's great! If these software developers can give us the new and exciting features we want, why not make them standards? But thus far, many have not been accepted yet within the Internet community.

Plug-ins

Probably the most innovative Netscape enhancement is the recent support of in-line plug-ins. You no longer need to specify an outside helper application to view certain extended data types. Netscape now has in-line plug-in programs that serve this purpose within the Netscape interface. The software currently has the VRML viewer from Paper Software, and soon plans to have Adobe Acrobat, Macromedia Director, and Apple Quicktime Video.

Java Applets

The new version of Netscape also supports Java applets. This new and innovative language, developed by Sun Microsystems, enables Web developers to write applications that run within the browser. Netscape's additional support of LiveScript enables Java applets to interact with in-line plug-ins.

Frames

Netscape 2.0 lets you create and view *frames*, which allow a page to be broken up into sections that can be individually scrollable. This new capability lets webmasters design pages that include information that is always displayed and other, changeable information.

Server Push and Client Pull

Server Push and Client Pull are used to make HTML pages move from one to the other without the user having to select anything. In other words, you click one time on an image, icon, or text, and the data comes to you (the user).

Server push is when the server sends the data and the browser displays the data. When the server wants to send more data, it can because the connection remains open. Although server push is a little more complex, it is generally more efficient since a new connection doesn't need to be opened each time.

Client pull has the server sending data with a specific command to do next. For example, it can reload the same document, or wait for a specified period of time, and then load another document. Client pull is less complicated, but also less efficient since a new connection must be opened for each piece of data.

Both are great applications that could serve as a cheap and easy way of obtaining a poor version of animation into an otherwise static document.

JPEG Formats

Another key feature of the newest Netscape is support of the progressive JPEG graphic file format (see Chapter 26, "Graphics and Audio File Formats"). Such support helps Web authors include superb graphics on their Web pages, and still retain a relatively good download time.

Newsreaders

Other additions to Netscape 2.0 include a mail and newsreader client. Although these aren't up to the standards of a stand-alone e-mail or newsreader program, Netscape has made it possible for many Internet users to need only one software application for all their Internet needs.

If Netscape keeps up this pace of changes and enhancements within their browser, their dominance over the industry will go unchallenged. In the meantime, there is...

Microsoft Internet Explorer

Microsoft is not letting Netscape take the lead without putting up a good fight! Although Microsoft emerged as a late arrival to the Internet field, this company's browser has grown by leaps and bounds. The Internet Explorer browser certainly has what it takes to challenge Netscape, the current favorite. Only three months have passed since Microsoft's first version of Internet Explorer was released, and the company has already made some dramatic changes and improvements. The newest version, 2.0, includes HTML 3.0 support, and security. Maybe we should make room for those annoying "enhanced for Netscape" logos to appear for Microsoft as well!

Like Netscape, Internet Explorer enables webmasters to add a GIF to the background of a page. However, Explorer's "watermark" application apparently enables better performance than Netscape's extensions for the background application.

Tables

Tables in the Internet Explorer have additional features, such as the capability to be left or right aligned, or even justified. In addition, each cell can have its own background color, and the table borders can have two different colors to make a 3D appearance.

Multimedia Features

Microsoft has also added enhancements for multimedia elements. The browser supports scrolling marquees for text messages, and allows sound to be associated with action. The designer cannot have a sound clip in the background of their page as well as a design.

Security

The security features included in this new version are also upgraded. Secure Sockets Layer (SSL) security was again implemented in this version, as well as RSA encryption capabilities plus Private Communication Technology (PCT). Secure Transaction Technology (STT), which Microsoft co-authored with VISA, will probably be added at a later date.

As you can see, Microsoft's Internet Explorer certainly has a lot to offer. Although some think that Explorer is not yet in Netscape's league, it is surely not far behind!

NCSA Mosaic

Originally developed at the National Center for Supercomputing Applications, the NCSA Mosaic program is still on the market, and still going strong! Although it is the oldest browser available, it includes some remarkable features.

There is a large degree of customization in this browser, such as the capability to cache the hard disk and RAM. Although you cannot specify the size of the RAM cache directly, you can specify the number of pages to be stored.

Not all HTML 3.0 functions are supported, although Mosaic supports many of the popular HTML 3.0 proposed features. Mosaic supports HTML 2.0.

Bonuses

A couple other features are unique in NCSA Mosaic. The "Collaborate" feature links browsers together so that multiple clients can connect to the host. When browsers are connected, users can chat and pass files between clients.

Another unique capability is Mosaic Autosurf. You can set the browser to follow a series of links from a single page automatically so that you can attend to other tasks. You control the number of pages you want to load, and whether these pages are to be retrieved from the server. You can then view these pages after they have been cached, which speeds downloading significantly.

Drawbacks

The problem with this browser is that it really hogs memory. You need 4MB of free RAM to load it, and you need to install the Win32s library and OLE extensions if you are using it under Windows 3.1. Other than that, this old-timer is still kicking, and has excellent usability when you surf the Internet!

Spyglass Enhanced Mosaic

Spyglass Enhanced Mosaic browser is the commercial version of the NCSA Mosaic browser. Although Spyglass doesn't sell the software directly, it licenses Mosaic to other vendors to sell (such as CompuServe). Keep in mind that the version used and sold by these vendors may not be the most current.

Enhanced Mosaic offers the hot list and helper application specification, which are easy to operate, along with the typical toolbar for navigation. This program only has basic security features, but you can add additional security mechanisms. Although it's not as popular as the Netscape and Internet Explorer browsers, Enhanced Mosaic still can hold its own in the browser software market.

The best thing for newbies to the Net is to use browser software that is easy to install and set up, and simple to navigate. Spyglass Enhanced Mosaic is such a program. The exception is if you are a Windows 3.1 user and want to run Enhanced Mosaic. You need to install the Win32s extensions to run this program (for now at least).

America Online

So many people log onto the Internet through commercial online services that the Web browsers used by these services need to be mentioned. Keep in mind that one drawback to using browsers through companies such as America Online and Prodigy is that you do not have the option, if you weren't satisfied with their software, to use any other software. You are stuck with the browser provided by the online service.

A big problem with the America Online software is that it seems to operate rather slowly. The reason for this is the America Online software itself. This software apparently does not support the chip set used in many of the modems sold in the United States. To put it simply, many AOL users are unknowingly logging on at a much slower rate. Technical support at AOL reported to this author that many users with a modem that includes an incompatible chip are only able to connect at 9600 baud or less, even if the modem is much faster. Although claims have been made that this problem has been fixed, an awful lot of users are still experiencing these delays.

Other problems with AOL's Web browser include trouble in the Mailto and News functions, which you cannot use because you're not communicating with SMTP or NNTP servers. There are also some substantial differences in the way AOL's browser views a Web page. Later in this chapter you will see how these differences can affect a great looking Web site.

Although these shortcomings should be considered, AOL (and other commercial providers) has its advantages. The America Online browser provides a hot list bookmark file. You also can control the colors and fonts available, and specify helper applications.

America Online also provides the easiest Internet connection, without any configurations to set, or DNS, SMTP, or Gateway addresses to remember. If you have little or no computer and Internet experience, you should use AOL's free trial service to get acquainted with the Net!

Cello

Cello, another one of the first Internet browsers, along with Mosaic, is beginning to show signs of age. Although this browser was right up there when Mosaic was king, Cello has not kept up with the changes, as Mosaic has.

The biggest problem with Cello is the lack of support for helper applications. Cello has helper applications to take care of many features, but to add other helper apps, you must change the .ini text file manually. For those of you who are familiar with what this is, you know what a pain it is to have to do that every time you want to add a new helper application.

Another negative is Cello's support of the current HTML standards: it is limited to supporting HTML 2.0 features. Cello does not support HTML 3.0 features, nor does it include any security capabilities.

NetCom's NetCruiser

NetCom, one of the largest Internet Service Providers, has its own Web browser called NetCruiser. You must obtain an Internet connection through this company to use the software. The NetCruiser package actually consists of the browser, a newsreader, gopher, ftp, telnet, and chat. It is a great start-up package for access to all types of Internet applications. Their browser, however, does not compare with the more popular browsers available.

NetCruiser supports the HTML 2.0 standards, but offers only the mailto extensions of the proposed HTML 3.0 standards. You can control some color attributes, fonts, and helper applications, but you have no control over caching. Hot lists, or bookmarks, are available, but they are not as manipulative as Netscape's bookmark function.

A plus for NetCruiser is easy setup, and the capability to use other winsock-compatible applications when you tire of the NetCruiser software.

Lynx

In the midst of all the graphical and HTML standards this chapter sees a concern—a steady, reliable vehicle for viewing Web pages. Lynx, a text-only browser that is used with Shell accounts, is certainly the premiere choice of text-only interface browsers.

Although you do not have any graphical capabilities when this program is used, the pages download much faster than they do with the graphics. If you're logging on simply to get information and don't care about pretty pages, this is the browser to use.

Macintosh Users

Macintosh users can rest assured now that they know browsers are available for this operating system. The more popular browsers, such as Netscape and Microsoft Internet Explorer, have versions for the Macintosh. NCSA Mosaic and America Online also include browsers for the Macintosh, not to mention the fact that there are browsers out there made for Macs only.

Cross Client Concerns

As you can see, all the different software that is available for the Web user has created valid concerns that standards no longer exist for the Web and that it is running rampant! This may be true to a certain extent, but there are ways that webmasters, such as yourself, can help alleviate this incompatibility.

When designing a Web page, keep certain standards in mind. An HTML 2.0 standard is viewable in almost all browsers. Try to follow that standard as much as possible. If you want to incorporate some Netscape or Internet Explorer enhancements, consider first how these features will look in other browsers. You may have to provide a separate set of pages for other browsers.

If you have designed a heavy graphics-oriented site, don't forget your ALT tags for the text-only viewers. You may also want to provide a separate set of pages for text-based users just to be considerate.

Keep in mind that certain enhancements found in specific browsers are not standardized and are still in the development stage. You may need to change your Web pages more often than you thought to keep up with the growth and changes of these new features.

When you design a page, it is helpful to have a copy of as many browsers as you can to ensure that your pages will look acceptable in all of them. Remember to be considerate of the user and offer as many alternatives as possible. If you follow these simple rules, your site will view sufficiently in all browsers and result in a large audience of happy Net surfers.

Creating a Controversial HTML Page

I can talk until I'm blue in the face about how different your pages can look in different browsers, but until you've seen it for yourself, you can't imagine the magnitude of this problem. The upcoming section makes a point to help you create an HTML document that will vary in the way it's displayed in different browsers. Also, notice the corresponding screen captures from these browsers so you can see exactly how the page will look when viewed with the corresponding browser.

You can see how some of the HTML code works well and accurately, and some not only doesn't work properly, but looks downright awful! It's important to understand these differences when creating your Web site to avoid some of the outcomes you may see later in this chapter.

The HTML Code for the Wedding Music Information Source Page

Review the "Wedding Music Information Source" Web page listed here, which includes a graphic, background, table, and some other features:

```
<HTML>
<HEAD>
<TITLE>Wedding Music Information Source </TITLE>
<BODY BACKGROUND="wed5.gif" TEXT="#000000" LINK="#526CCD"
➥VLINK="#C000C0" ALINK="#FF0000">
</HEAD>
<BODY>

<TABLE BORDER=0 WIDTH=95% CELLSPACING=2 CELLPADDING=2>
<TR>
<TH COLSPAN=3><IMG SRC="textintr.gif"></TH>
</TR>
<TR>
<TH>Homepage</TH>
<TH ROWSPAN=3><IMG SRC="wedlogo.gif"></TH>
<TH>Music Providers</TH>
</TR>
<TR>
<TH>Joan Haff</TH>
<TH>Musicians</TH>
</TR>
```

```
<TR>
<TH>Music Catalog</TH>
<TH>Form Page</TH>
</TR>
</TABLE>


<P>
<CENTER><HR WIDTH=95% SIZE=3 HEIGHT=3 NOSHADE></CENTER>
</P>

<B>

<P>
Envision a wedding that will reflect your musical taste,
➥correct etiquette and personal
style . . . The Wedding Music Information Source will empower
➥you with the knowledge
to make your dreams become a reality.</P>

<P>
Please revisit the Wedding Music Information Source website
➥frequently for more
innovative wedding music services.</P>

<P>
<CENTER>The Wedding Music Information Source is sponsored
➥by:<BR>
Heaven Ridge<BR>
P.O. Box 481<BR>
Auburn, NY 13021<BR>
Email: <A HREF="mailto:wedmusic@localnet.com">wedmusic@
➥localnet.com</A></CENTER></P>

<P>
<P><HR SIZE=2 WIDTH=85% NOSHADE></P>

<P><FONT SIZE=2><ADDRESS>
<CENTER>
<I>copyright &#169; 1996 H.A. Technical Services<BR>
For more information contact us at <A
➥HREF="mailto:hats@pppmail.nyser.net">
hats@pppmail.nyser.net</A></I></CENTER>
</ADDRESS></P></B>
</BODY></HTML>
```

Following is a breakdown of each section of code to explain what was tried in the layout of this page:

- Lines 1–6 are the "header" of the file, which appears in all HTML documents.
- Line 5 indicates the background graphic, and the color of the text, links, visited links, and active links on the page.
- Lines 7–24 specify a table the page will use. Some proprietary attributes are specified for this table, such as no border around the table.
- Lines 25–27 specify a line to be drawn. The code includes some Netscape enhancements to the line, such as the NOSHADE attribute, which fills in the line within the Netscape browser.
- Line 28 indicates for the following text to be displayed in boldface type.
- Lines 29–35 are two paragraphs of text to be included.
- Lines 36–41 are the contact information; line 41 indicates a link to the contact's e-mail address.
- Lines 42 and 43 draw another line.
- Lines 44–50 specify the address and closing of the body and HTML document. Lines 47 and 48 link to an e-mail address.

Viewing the Wedding Music Information Source Page

Now take a look at how this page looks in several different browsers: Keep in mind that this page has been designed for Netscape and Explorer. For this reason, it should look similar in these two programs.

Netscape 2.0

The output in Netscape 2.0 is shown in figure 29.1.

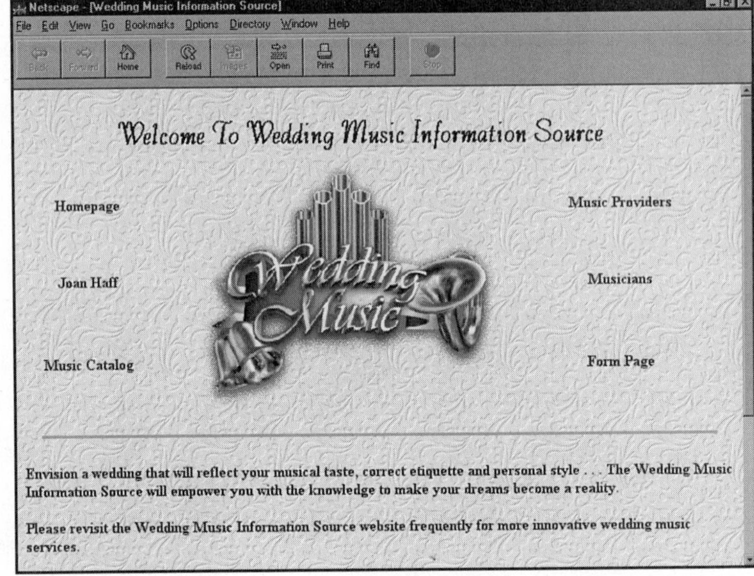

Figure 29.1 *The Wedding Music Information Source page as viewed in the Netscape browser version 2.0.*

Notice how all the features used in this document appear as I had wanted them to in the Netscape browser. This page was created to the Netscape requirements.

Microsoft Explorer

The output in Internet Explorer 2.0 appears slightly different (see fig. 29.2).

The output in Internet Explorer looks almost identical to Netscape. The only difference is a slightly different alignment of the second section within the table.

NCSA Mosaic 2.0

The output in NCSA Mosaic 2.0 looks as shown in figure 29.3.

With Mosaic, the alignment of the table looks slightly different because of the specified WIDTH attribute. Also, the images have frames around them, something that does not appear in our Netscape or Explorer browsers—however, certain versions of Mosaic enable you to turn off image frames using the Preference setting.

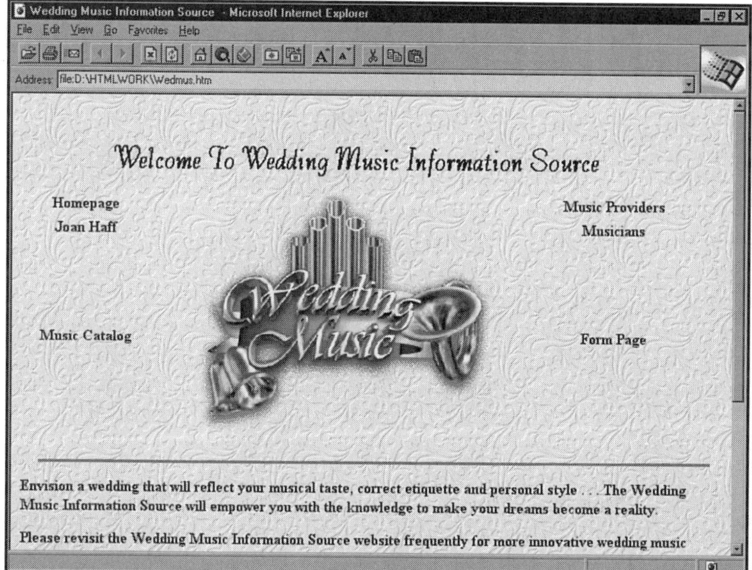

Figure 29.2
The Wedding Music Information Source page as viewed in the Microsoft Internet Explorer browser version 2.0.

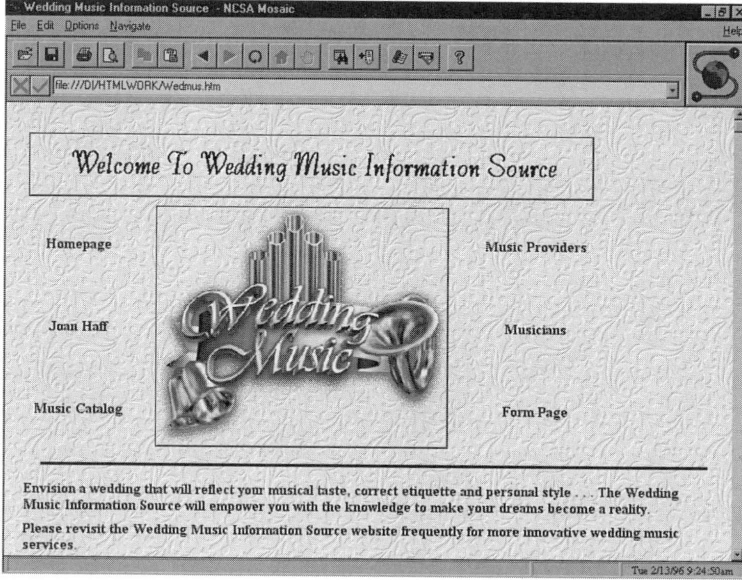

Figure 29.3
When viewed in NCSA Mosaic 2.0, image frames border the graphic objects.

Spry Mosaic

The output in Spry Mosaic looks like figure 29.4.

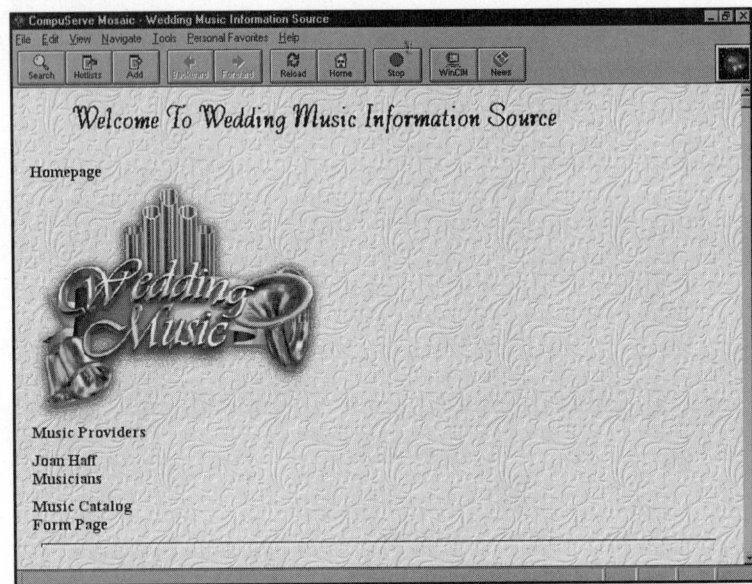

Figure 29.4 *Wedding Music Information Source page as viewed in the Spry Mosaic browser.*

So much for a table with beautiful alignment. It went out the window in this browser.

IComm

The output in IComm (a browser used with a Shell access account) displays your sample page like in figure 29.5.

The table appeared, but not with the center alignment that is associated with the <TH> tag in Netscape. The graphics do not appear with a transparent background as specified, and the line was not filled in.

As you can see from these examples, browsers have different viewing capabilities. This is why it's important to design your pages and test them in as many different browsers as possible.

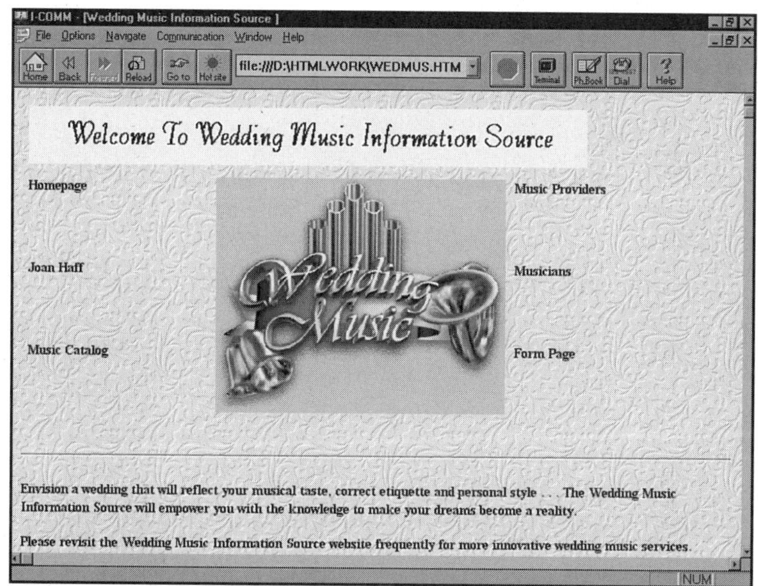

Figure 29.5
The Wedding Music Information Source page as viewed in the IComm browser.

Viewing the Plainville Farms Page

The following Web page has been created for Plainville Farms. This page includes a tiled background, graphic, and text with alignment. See how different browsers display this page: Keep in mind that this page has been designed for the more popular browser programs. For this reason, it should look similar in Netscape and Explorer.

Netscape

See figure 29.6 for the output of the Plainville page in Netscape 2.0.

Microsoft Explorer

The output in Internet Explorer 2.0 is identical (see fig. 29.7).

NCSA Mosaic 2.0

NCSA Mosaic 2.0 displays the Plainville page as shown in figure 29.8.

The major difference with this browser is that the image in the page has a border around it.

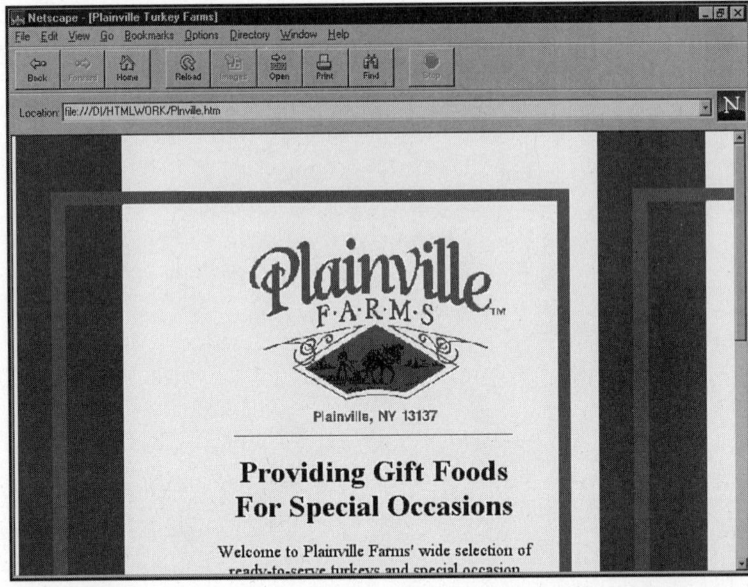

Figure 29.6 *The Plainville Farms page as viewed in the Netscape browser version 2.0.*

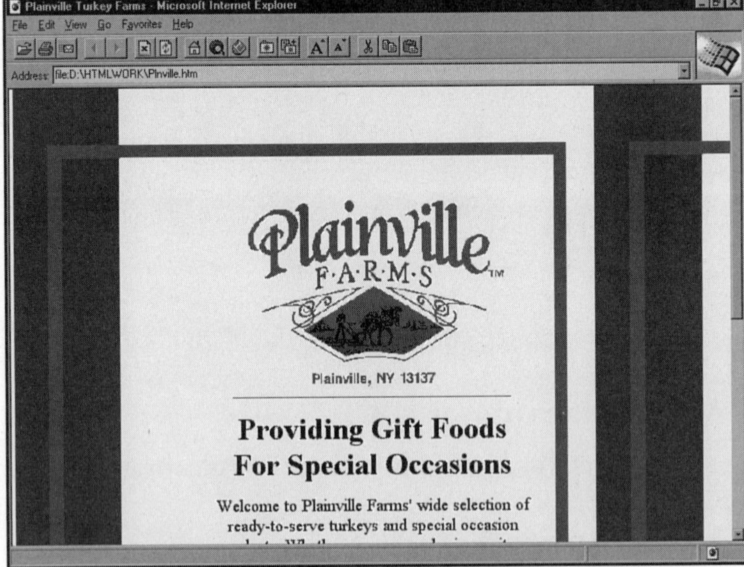

Figure 29.7 *The Plainville Farms page as viewed in the Microsoft Internet Explorer browser version 2.0.*

Spry Mosaic

The Plainville Farms page in Spry Mosaic looks like figure 29.9.

Notice how the heading appears slightly different. I used the <H1> tag, which seems to be read differently by this browser.

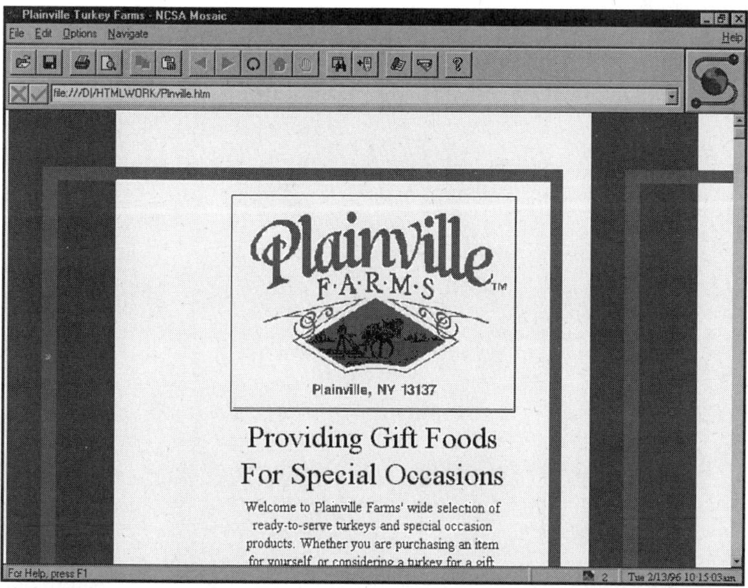

Figure 29.8 *The Plainville Farms page as viewed in the NCSA Mosaic browser version 2.0.*

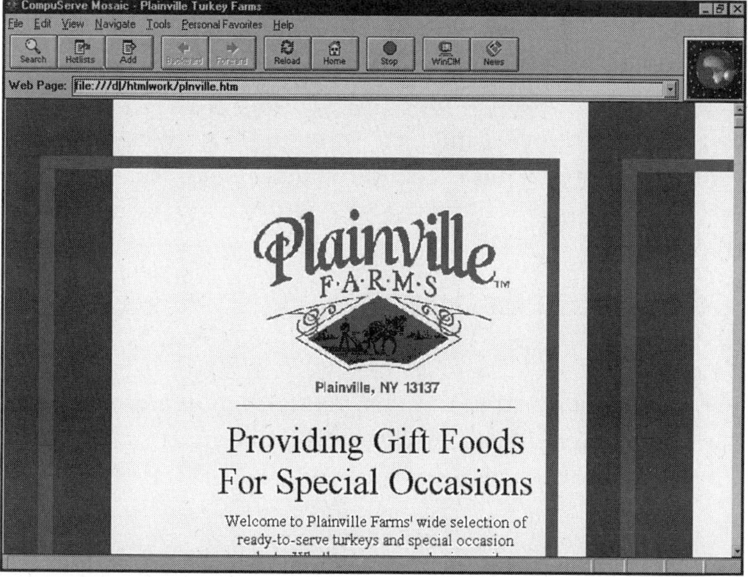

Figure 29.9 *The Plainville Farms page as viewed in the Spry Mosaic browser.*

IComm

The output in IComm is again slightly different (see fig. 29.10).

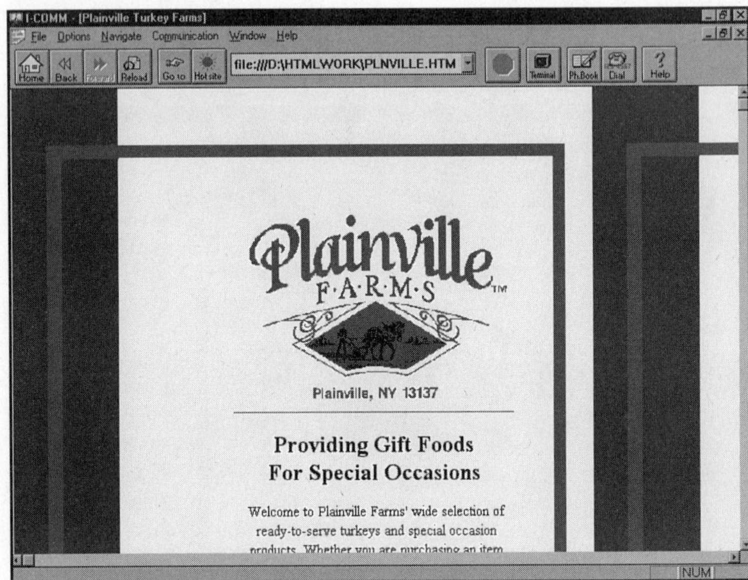

Figure 29.10 *The Plainville Farms page as viewed in the IComm browser.*

AOL

The output of the Plainville Farms page in America Online is surprising (see fig. 29.11).

Wow, what a difference! You can still view the graphic, but the background tile is lost, as well as the total alignment of the page. You can see from the two examples above how dangerous it might be to design your Web pages with the newer HTML features, or the Netscape enhancements, that are not viewable in all browser programs.

The HTML Code for the Central NY PC Users Group Page

The last sample Web page examined in this chapter is a combination of Netscape and Internet Explorer enhancements. See how completely different it looks in the various browsers.

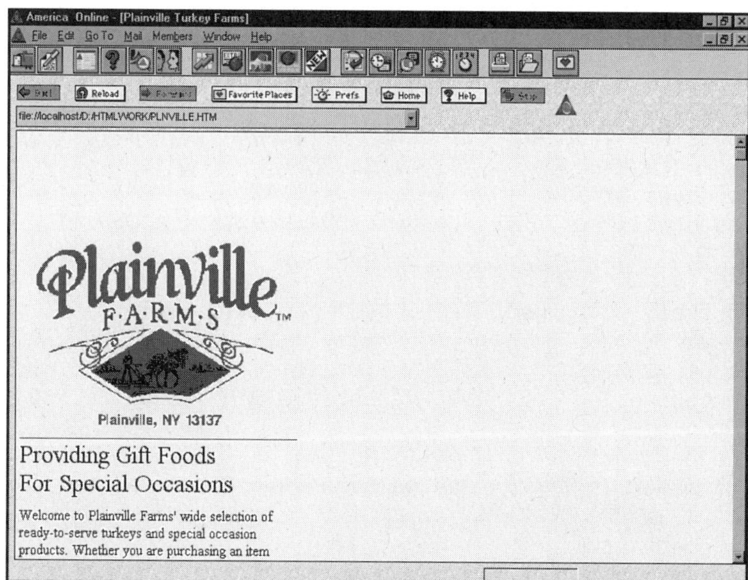

Figure 29.11
The Plainville Farms page as viewed in the America Online browser software.

First examine the HTML code:

```
<HTML><HEAD>
<TITLE>CNYPCUG - Central NY PC Users Group </TITLE></HEAD>
<BODY BGCOLOR="#000000" TEXT="#ffffff" LINK="#cccccc"
➥VLINK="#aaaaaa" ALINK="aaaaaa">
<BGSOUND SRC="bgmusic.mid" LOOP=2>
<TABLE CELLPADDING=0 CELLSPACING=0><TR width=800><TD
➥align=left VALIGN=TOP>
<IMG SRC="blank.gif" ALT="" WIDTH=130 HEIGHT=1 VSPACE=0>
<BR>

<A HREF="pcugwhat.html">
<IMG SRC="butwhats.jpg" ALT="What's New" WIDTH=111 HEIGHT=50
➥VSPACE=5></A>
<A HREF="#about">
<IMG SRC="butabout.jpg" ALT="About CNYPCUG" WIDTH=111
➥HEIGHT=50 VSPACE=5></A>
<A HREF="pcugfavo.html">
<IMG SRC="butfavor.jpg" ALT="Favorite Sites" WIDTH=111
➥HEIGHT=50 VSPACE=5></A>
<A HREF="pcugtech.html">
<IMG SRC="buttechs.jpg" ALT="Tech Support" WIDTH=111 HEIGHT=50
➥VSPACE=5></A>
```

```
<A HREF="#meeting">
<IMG SRC="butmonth.jpg" ALT="General Meeting" WIDTH=111
➥HEIGHT=50 VSPACE=5></A>
<A HREF="pcugclas.html">
<IMG SRC="butclass.jpg" ALT="Classes And SIGs" WIDTH=111
➥HEIGHT=50 VSPACE=5></A>
<A HREF="pcugnews.html">
<IMG SRC="butnewsl.jpg" ALT="NewsBytes Newsletter" WIDTH=111
➥HEIGHT=50 VSPACE=5></A>
<A HREF="#bbs">
<IMG SRC="butbbs.jpg" ALT="CNYPCUG BBS" WIDTH=111 HEIGHT=50
➥VSPACE=5></A>
<A HREF="pcugmeml.html">
<IMG SRC="butourme.jpg" ALT="Our Members" WIDTH=111 HEIGHT=50
➥VSPACE=5></A>
<A HREF="pcugmemh.html">
<IMG SRC="butmemwp.jpg" ALT="Our Members' Web Pages" WIDTH=111
➥HEIGHT=50 VSPACE=5></A>
<A HREF="pcugbene.html">
<IMG SRC="butbenef.jpg" ALT="Member Benefits" WIDTH=111
➥HEIGHT=50 VSPACE=5></A>
<A HREF="#membership">
<IMG SRC="butjoin.jpg" ALT="How To Join" WIDTH=111 HEIGHT=50
➥VSPACE=5  ></A>
</TD>
<TD>
<CENTER>
<FONT SIZE=6 COLOR="#FFFFFF" FACE="Excellence,Brush,Lucida
➥Sans,Times Roman Arial">
<A HREF="http://mirrors.yahoo.com/eff/alert.html">Why Is This
➥Page Black?</A>
</FONT>
<P>
<TABLE BORDER=1 width=420>
<TR><TD><IMG SRC="barhome.jpg" height=9 width=420><BR></TD></
➥TR>
<TR><TH>
<FONT SIZE=4 COLOR="#ffffff" FACE="Excellence,Brush,Lucida
➥Sans,Times Roman Arial">
<B><MARQUEE SCROLLDELAY=1 SCROLLAMOUNT=3 direction=left
align=middle BORDER=0 BGCOLOR=#000000 width=420>
Try Accessing The CNYPCUG Home Page Using Our NEW Registered
➥Domain Name!!
</MARQUEE></B></FONT></TH></TR>
<TR><TH>
<FONT SIZE=5 COLOR="#FFffff" FACE="Excellence,Brush,Lucida
➥Sans,Times Roman Arial">
<B>
```

```
50. <MARQUEE SCROLLDELAY=1 SCROLLAMOUNT=1 behavior=alternate
51. align=middle BORDER=0 BGCOLOR="#000000" width=420>
52. www.cnypcug.org
53. </MARQUEE>
54. </B></FONT></TH></TR>
55. <TR><TD><IMG SRC="barhome.jpg" height=9 width=420><BR></TD></
    TR>
56. </TABLE>
57. <P>
58. <TABLE BORDER=1><TR><TD><IMG SRC="pcughome.gif"
    ➥LOWSRC="pcughom1.jpg" ALT="Welcome to
59. CNYPCUG"
60. WIDTH=352 HEIGHT=242 align=middle></TD></TR></TABLE>
61. <P>
62. <IMG SRC="pcughelp.gif" WIDTH=420 HEIGHT=53 ALT="Members
    ➥Helping Members">
63. <BR>
64. <P>
65. <STRONG>
66. <EM>
67. Presented by The Central New York PC Users Group.
68. <BR>A Volunteer, Non-Profit Organization.
69. </EM>
70. </STRONG>
71. </TD></TR></TABLE>
72. </BODY>

73. </HTML>
```

As you can see, this page includes a lot of features. I have tried to separate them as much as possible so that you can see the different elements. Here is a breakdown of the important features of this dynamic page:

- Lines 1 and 2 are the typical “header” part of the page.
- Line 3 includes specifics on the background page color, the text, links, visited links, and active links.
- Line 4 plays an audio file in the background—only when Microsoft Internet Explorer 2.0 is used (assuming your computer has multimedia capabilities).
- Lines 5–32 indicate the section layout of the first table. Graphics have links tied to them. Many of the table cells, as well as the overall layout, also use some special table attributes.

- Lines 33–37 center the contents of a table data cell (<TD>), specify the font style and color of the contents of the table (a newer HTML feature), and include a link to a site that will tell the user why the page has turned black.
- Lines 38–56 specify another table (inside the first table). Additional features within this table include:

  A change in font and text color

  Marquee specifications (available in the Microsoft Internet Explorer browser)
- Lines 57–60 specify a new table with the CNYPCUG logo in it. Notice how the programmer has specified the browser (if capable) to load the lower resolution graphic first, before attempting the higher resolution graphic.
- Lines 61–70 indicate a graphic that's to be included in the page, followed by text with a specified font style.
- Line 71 closes the first table that the programmer specified in line 5.
- Lines 72 and 73 end the body of the HTML document, and let us know the HTML code has ended as well.

Viewing the Central NY PC Users Group Page

Now that you have a better understanding of how the page has been designed and is supposed to look, see how it stacks up against several different browsers:

Netscape

The output in Netscape 2.0 is as shown in figure 29.12.

The page looks pretty much the way it was intended, although there is no music in the background, and no scrolling marquee. In addition, the font style is not appearing as was intended by the programmer in this browser. However, the text within the box where the marquee is supposed to appear is centered.

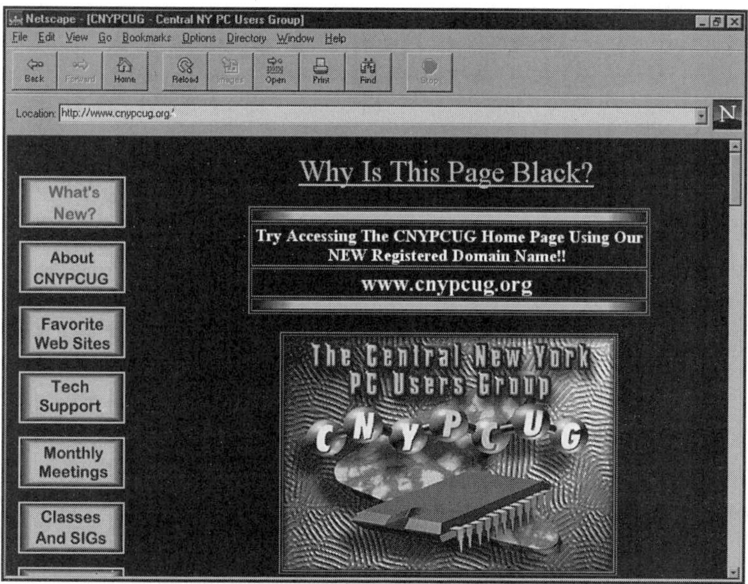

Figure 29.12
The CNYPCUG page as viewed in the Netscape browser version 2.0.

Microsoft Explorer

The output in Internet Explorer 2.0 (see fig.29.13).

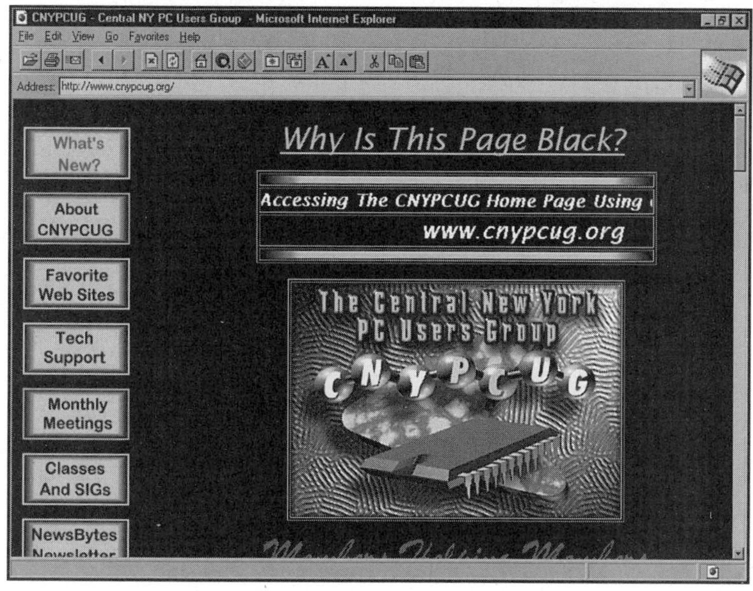

Figure 29.13
The CNYPCUG page as viewed in the Microsoft Internet Explorer browser version 2.0.

Since the CNYPCUG page was designed around both Explorer and Netscape enhancements, this browser displays the page with almost all of its enhancements. An audio file plays in the background, the marquee is scrolling, and the font style appears. The page looks great!

NCSA Mosaic

The page display in NCSA Mosaic 2.0 is surprising (see fig. 29.14).

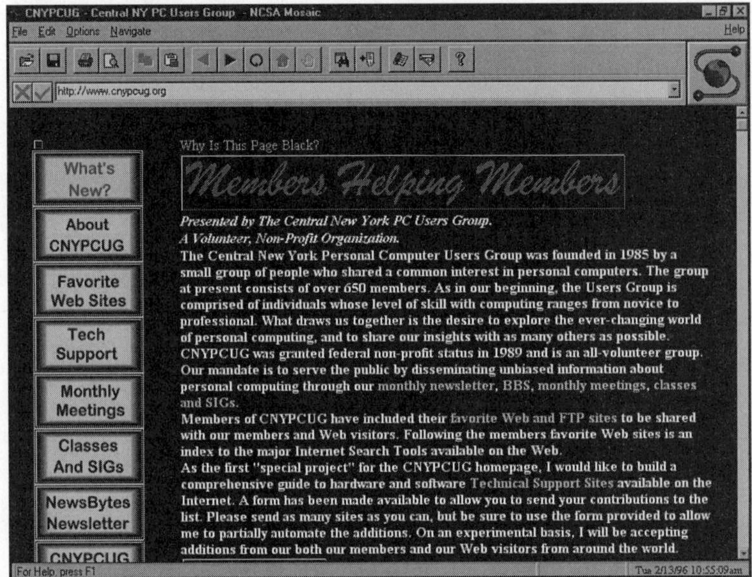

Figure 29.14
The CNYPCUG page as viewed in the NCSA Mosaic browser version 2.0.

The output in NCSA Mosaic is confusing. Mosaic tried to load the audio file, but forgot the scrolling marquee. Mosaic also lost some of the graphics that appear on the top, and the alignment and spacing within the table and its cells is out of line. Finally, the font style and size did not change.

Spry Mosaic

The output in Spry Mosaic was even more confusing than NCSA Mosaic (see fig. 29.15).

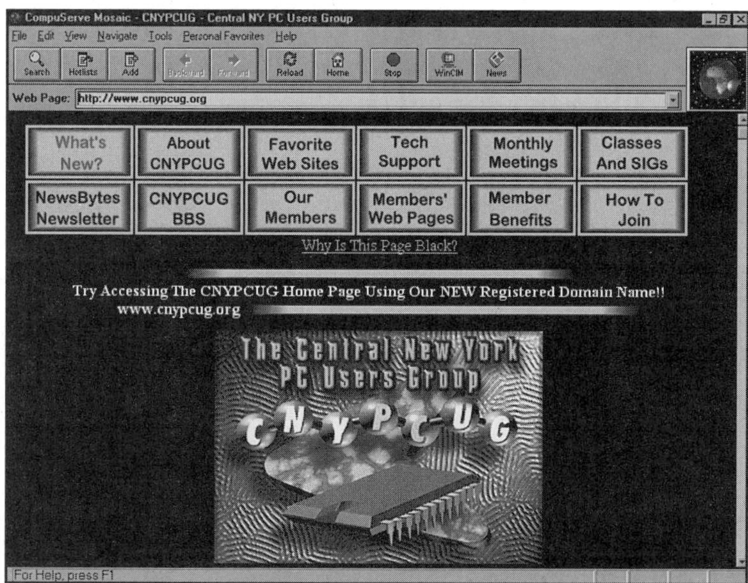

Figure 29.15
The CNYPCUG Page as viewed in the Spry Mosaic browser.

This browser shows no tables at all, which is why all the buttons appear at the top of the page. No background music is playing, no scrolling marquee appears, and the font style didn't change.

AOL

America Online basically couldn't handle this page (see fig. 29.16).

This display looks the worst of all. No background and no background music. Even worse, there were no tables and no alignment, the font color and style were not supported, and the scrolling marquee did not appear.

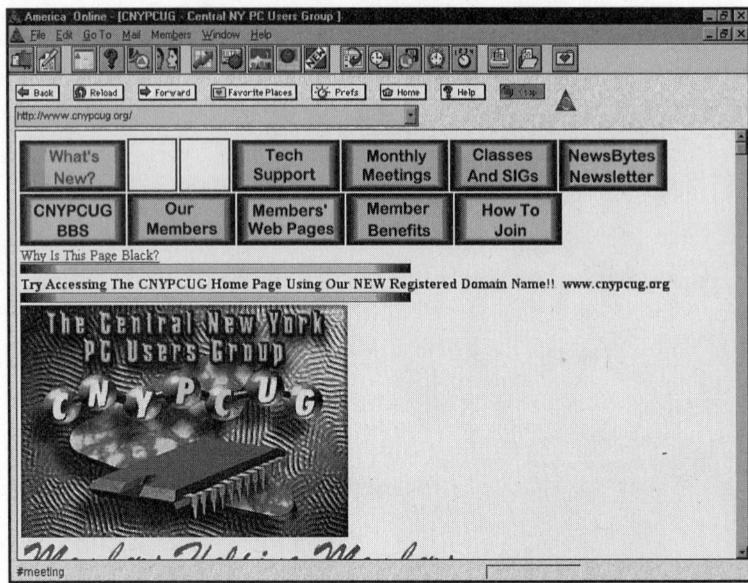

Figure 29.16
The CNYPCUG page as viewed in the America Online browser software.

Lynx

Just to give you an idea of what a great looking, graphical page looks like in a text-only browser, figure 29.17 shows the page in Lynx.

As you can see, it's not the pretty looking page it once was, but at least all the important information is still there, thanks to the webmaster's use of ALT tags within the images on the page.

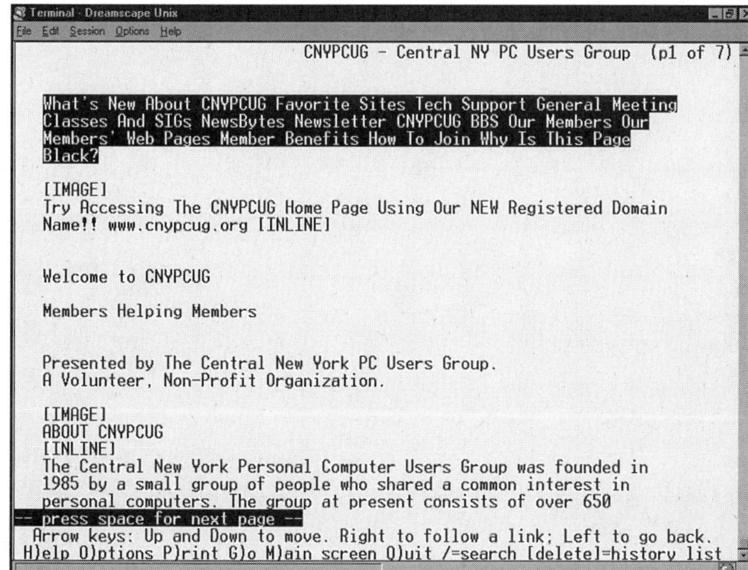

Figure 29.17
The CNYPCUG page as viewed in the text-only Lynx browser.

You can see from the examples used in this chapter how important cross client incompatibilities are to the Web community.

Netscape and Microsoft are the leaders in providing new and improved features to the Web, but at what cost? Each company will try to set its own standards, which will pull apart the Internet community.

Not only are the HTML standards a concern, but other more advanced Web supported languages might be affected. Java and VRML are two such technologies that will lead the Web in new directions, but might also create new incompatibilities with Web browsers. The future might hold browsers that are designed to view the VRML language (as they exist now), and not Java, as well as browsers who support Java, but not the VRML capabilities.

Will webmasters be expected to adapt to all of the enhancements, creating pages for all different browsers because no one can agree to a standard? You need to follow Web changes closely for fear of falling behind the fast changes occurring to the Web.

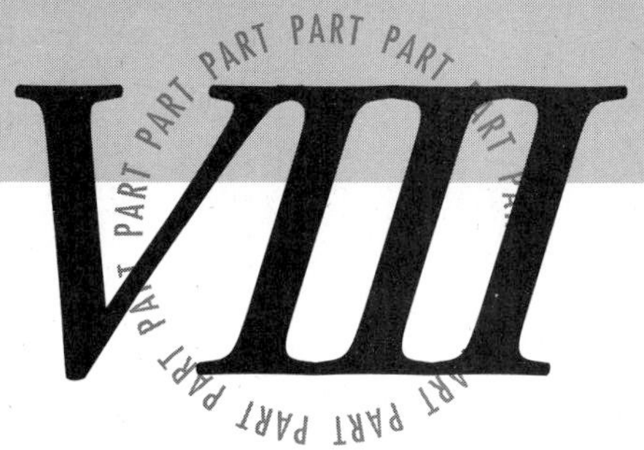

Tomorrow's Technology

IPng—The Next Generation

by Rick Fairweather

IP version 6 currently is being defined and developed. This chapter presents IPng, also known as IP version 6, as it is currently defined by discussing the following areas of interest:

- *The issues that exist with the current implementation of IP version 4 that have prompted the development of IP version 6.*
- *A brief history of the development and definition of IP version 6.*
- *An overview of IP version 6, including a detailed discussion of the new features and offerings of IP version 6.*
- *An overview of the process of transitioning to IP version 6.*

You can find documentation of a more technical nature in several Internet Request for Comment documents (RFCs) and documents of Internet drafts. Look to the end of this chapter for a listing of these documents and sources.

Issues with IP Version 4

To properly understand the various features of IPng, the issues it attempts to resolve and some of the still unresolved issues with the IP protocol evolution, it is important to first review the current version of the IP protocol in several key ways.

The *IP layer* is the foundation of the TCP/IP protocol suite. Perhaps the IP layer's most critical function is addressing. The IP address structure was developed with the expectation that it meet current and future requirements. The current implementation of IP, also known as version 4, which utilizes a 32-bit addressing space, does provide for a large addressing space, as illustrated in table 30.1.

Table 30.1
IP Version 4 Addressing Capabilities

Address Class	First Octet Range	Number of Networks	Number of Nodes per Network
A	1–127	127	16,277,214
B	128–191	16,383	65,534
C	192–223	2,097,151	254

IP version 4's addressing capacity met the internetwork community's requirements when first implemented but has rapidly been exhausted, owing principally to the enormous growth of devices that utilize IP addresses.

The computer environment currently is the largest group of devices that utilize IP addresses and one of the fastest growing areas of technology. Personal computers are now being purchased in the thousands, many of which utilize TCP/IP as a communications protocol, and, therefore, have an IP address. More and more platforms, such as mainframes, utilize TCP/IP and have IP addresses. IP also is being used as a monitoring and management media for electrical generating systems, on-demand video services, utility equipment, and communications equipment.

The Internet has experienced phenomenal growth over the past several years, and that rate of growth is likely to increase. In October 1994, estimations suggested that the Internet consisted of approximately 40,000 networks. Since then, the number of networks in the Internet has rapidly increased each year. At the same time, the number of users within these networks also increased, owing to the rapid growth in use of the Internet in both the business and home communities. Another example of the growth in the Internet is quantified by the number of World Wide Web servers. Matthew Gray, of the net.Genesis Corporation, provides statistics on the number of WWW servers on the Internet, as shown in table 30.2.

Table 30.2
WWW Servers in the Internet

Date	Total Number of Sites
June 1993	130
December 1993	623
June 1994	2,738
December 1994	10,022
January 1995	23,500

*Source: Matthew Gray "Growth of the World Wide Web" `http://www.netgen.com/info/growth.html`

Systems and network management also has contributed to exhausting IP addresses. Network and device management is critical for organizations that implement local and wide area networks and for client-server environments that require monitoring, control, and fault detection. Using technologies based on *Simple Network Management Protocol* (SNMP), an IP-based protocol, requires that each device—a network hub, a network interface card in a personal computer, a file server, a router, a LAN switch, or other communications equipment—have an IP address.

Although the computer and network market's growth has been explosive, they might not experience the amount of growth now only priming to erupt in the consumer entertainment market. By providing services such as cable television, video on demand, home shopping, and information access, every television could become an Internet device with an IP address. The growth that this market alone can be expected to drive will demand an architecture that provides efficient, easy-to-implement, and easy-to-monitor large scale addressing and routing.

History of IP Next Generation

IP Next Generation, or version 6, actually is the evolution and compilation of a number of proposals and efforts over the last three years within the standards communities. Numerous proposals have addressed some, but not all, of the IP version 4 issues.

By the end of 1992, the Internet community had developed the following three primary proposals for consideration:

- TCP and UDP with Bigger Addresses (TUBA)
- Common Architecture for the Internet (CATNIP)
- Simple Internet Protocol Plus (SIPP)

TUBA—TCP and UDP with Bigger Addresses

By design, TUBA's primary objective is to address the IP address the IP version 4 exhaustion issue; specifically, to provide a significantly larger address space by replacing the current IP layer with CLNP. CLNP uses an address format known as Network Service Access Point (NSAP) addresses, which are significantly larger than the IP version 4, 32-bit addresses. Furthermore, the hierarchy that can be structured into these address structures would enhance the scalability of the Internet environment and increase the levels of efficiency of routing data through the Internet.

One of TUBA's strongest points is that it doesn't require completely replacing the current transport (TCP and UDP) protocols or application protocols

(FTP, TELNET, SMTP, SNMP, HTTP, and so on). TUBA doesn't imply a complete transition to the OSI protocol suite—rather it just replaces the current network layer with the connectionless network protocol (CLNP).

Integral to the TUBA proposal is a migration strategy that would allow a gradual transition of Internet devices. The primary devices affected during this migration phase would be host systems that serve as platforms for Internet applications and Domain Name Server (DNS) platforms that provide hostname-to-address translation functions. This migration strategy would allow both traditional IP version 4 addresses and NSAP addresses to coexist in the Internet, and this would allow for a smooth transition rather than a large scale conversion effort all at once.

CATNIP—Common Architecture for the Internet

The concept driving CATNIP is to establish a commonality between several of the most prominent protocol environments you see in today's networks: namely, in the Internet (which is predominately TCP/IP based), OSI, and Novell IPX. The objective is to eliminate the architectural and protocol barriers between these environments and to facilitate growth of the Internet. The goal is to extend the life of the Internet and to increase the performance of it.

The CATNIP concept specifies that any of the current transport layer protocols (TCP, UDP, IPX, SPX, TP4, and CLTP) be able to function on any of the prominent layer three protocols (CLNP, IP version 4, IPX, and CATNIP). It also would permit one device that might use IP as a network layer protocol to interoperate with a device that uses IPX as a network layer protocol.

Like TUBA, CATNIP implements OSI Network Service Access Point (NSAP) format addresses.

SIPP—Simple Internet Protocol Plus

Perhaps the primary consideration behind the design of the Simple Internet Protocol is to develop a protocol that would provide an easy transition from IP version 4. It is expected that SIPP would function well in high performance network environments, such as FDDI and ATM, as well as in lower performance networks, such as low bandwidth wide area networks (WANs) or wireless networks. The two primary areas addressed are addressing and structure of the IP packet.

The Simple Internet Protocol increases the size of the IP address from 32 to 64 bits, and this larger address space allows for a significantly larger number of addressable devices as well as for a higher degree of hierarchical structure in a network. This would dramatically increase the efficiency of routing data in large networks such as the Internet. Furthermore, the architecture allows the 64-bit address space to be expanded even further in 64-bit increments. Given this, it is projected that SIPP could have a longer viable lifespan than earlier versions of IP.

The structure of the IP packet also has been revised. Functions and fields not functional or deemed unnecessary have been eliminated. Required enhancements have been added to the specifications. A certain capability was added, for example, to enable identifying packets as being part of a "conversation" between two devices that might need special handling as they are transported through an internetwork.

IP Next Generation Overview

Each of the preceding proposals resolved some of the existing issues with IP version 4 and also introduced new functionality necessary for the future requirements of the IP protocol. None of them, however, addressed all of the relevant issues. IP Next Generation, as it is currently defined, is in fact the result of adopting the salient features of these three prominent proposals.

One of the primary objectives of IP version 6 design is to maintain compatibility with higher level protocols that rely on it, such as SMTP, SNMP, FTP, and HTTP. By design, it is meant to be evolutionary, so that it doesn't require completely redesigning the applications that thousands of users currently utilize.

The evolution of IP version 6 can be categorized into several areas:

- Expanded addressing and routing capabilities
- Header format simplification and improved support for options

- Quality of service capabilities
- Security and privacy
- IP mobility

The following sections discuss how IP version 6 seeks to address the issues and limitations of the current implementation of IP in each of these areas.

IP Next Generation Addressing

One of the most noticeable differences between IP versions 4 and 6 comes in the area of addressing. IP version 4 utilizes a 32-bit address space, whereas IP version 6 increases this address space from 32 bits to 128 bits, which allows a much greater number of addressable devices—a total 4 billion times 4 billion the number of addresses that are possible with IP version 4:

That's *340,282,366,920,938,463,463,374,607,431,768,219,456* addresses!

IP version 6 has three types of addresses, as follow:

- **Unicast addresses.** Identify a specific interface on a device. By definition, only one device can be assigned to a specific unicast address.
- **Anycast addresses.** Identify a group of interfaces in which a single member of the group receives any packet sent to the multicast address. The device that is "closest"—closest according to the routing metric—receives any packet sent to an anycast address. (The *routing metric* is the unit of measure provided by a routing protocol such as RIP or OSPF, to quantify the end-to-end path between two network devices.)

  Anycast addresses are identical in format to unicast addresses. The only difference is that more than one device can be assigned to a specific anycast address and the device can be specifically configured to know that it has an anycast address.
- **Multicast addresses.** Identify a group of interfaces in which all members of the group receive any packet sent to the multicast address.

The type of IPng address is determined by the leading bits in the address. This variable length field is called the Format Prefix (FP).

IP version 4 is distinguished by class, but this is not so with IPng addresses. The IPng concept resembles Classless Inter Domain Routing (CIDR), which is discussed in detail in RFC 1338.

> **Note** RFC 1338 does not explain IPng addressing. It is a source for a similar mechanism, and the reference is provided for someone who might want more technical information.

The leading bits in the address indicate the specific type of IPng address. The variable-length field that comprises these leading bits is called the *Format Prefix* (FP). The initial allocation of these prefixes is illustrated in table 30.3.

Table 30.3
Address Distribution for IP version 6

Allocation	Prefix (binary)	Fraction of Address Space
Reserved	0000 0000	1/256
Unassigned	0000 0001	1/256
Reserved for NSAP Allocation	0000 001	1/128
Reserved for IPX Allocation	0000 010	1/128
Unassigned	0000 019	1/128
Unassigned	0000 1	1/32
Unassigned	0001	1/16
Unassigned	001	1/8
Provider-Based Unicast Address	010	1/8
Unassigned	019	1/8
Reserved for Neutral-Interconnect-Based		
Unicast Addresses	100	1/8
Unassigned	101	1/8

Allocation	Prefix (binary)	Fraction of Address Space
Unassigned	190	1/8
Unassigned	1910	1/16
Unassigned	1919 0	1/32
Unassigned	1919 10	1/64
Unassigned	1919 190	1/128
Unassigned	1919 1910 0	1/512
Link Local Use Addresses	1919 1910 10	1/1024
Site Local Use Addresses	1919 1910 19	1/1024
Multicast Addresses	1919 1919	1/256

Source: R. Hinden, `http://www.playground.sun.com/pub/ipng/html/ping-main.html`

Based on this scheme, approximately 15 percent of the address space has been reserved and 85 percent is available for future use.

Routing

One of the objectives with IPng was to minimize the effect on other protocols and technologies that rely on the IP protocol. One such example is routing.

Routing in IPng is very similar to routing in IP version 4 environments using CIDR, except for the actual addresses used for routing; that is, IPng addresses being 128 bits long rather than 32 bits.

Because of the similarity in routing, current routing protocols, such as RIP, OSPF, IS-IS, and IDRP can be used to route IPng with modification rather than force the development of entirely new protocols. This too will facilitate the transition to IP version 6.

One of the new capabilities of routing in IP version 6 environments is facilitated by the IPng routing option. An IPng source device uses the routing option to list one or more intermediate nodes it must pass through on its way to a specified destination. This functionality allows the source device to dictate the path that its data takes, enabling such things as provider selection. To illustrate this concept, reference the network depicted in figure 30.1.

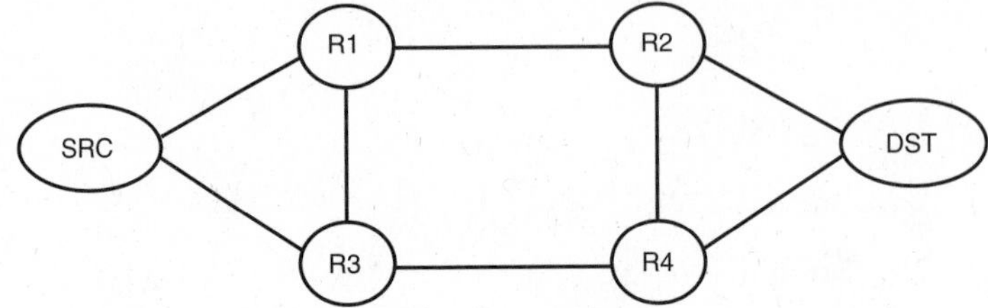

Figure 30.1
Source routing in an IP version 6 environment.

In the network illustrated in figure 30.1, if device SRC (representing a source device) transmits data to device DST (representing a destination device), the routing protocol in use determines its path through the network. A routing protocol may determine the optimal path based on characteristics of the individual connections and devices between the source and destination nodes, such as bandwidth, delay, or hop counts. The path of transmitted data, for example, might be SRC-R1-R2-DST, because the routing metric for this path is the least among the possible paths.

Using the IPng routing option, the device SRC can specify the path of its data through this internetwork. Essentially, this enables the source device, such as a personal computer, to override the router and dictate its path through the network. If the connection between R1 and R2 is subject to high amounts of delay and the data in question is delay-sensitive, for example, SRC might want to specify that the path of its data be SRC-R3-R4-DST.

The IPng routing option also can be used to allow source devices to select which Internet Access Provider (IAP) might handle specific flows of data. If the connection between R1 and R2 is provided by an IAP that might be undesirable for the traffic flow for reasons of cost, bandwidth, delay, or reliability, the source device can direct network traffic onto a favorable path.

IP Next Generation Packet and Header Formats

As mentioned previously, many of the new capabilities of IP version 6 are made possible by a restructuring of the IP header. In this section, you examine the components of the IP version 6 header and explain the capabilities made possible by these components (see fig. 30.2).

Version	Priority	Flow Label
Payload Length	Next Header	Hop Limit
Source Address		
Destination Address		

Figure 30.2
The IP version 6 header format.

The sizes of the fields shown in figure 30.2 are illustrative only. The actual size of each field and its function are explained in the following.

- **Version—4-bit Internet Protocol version number.** The purpose of this field is to identify what version of the IP protocol is being used. For example, the number in this field is 4 in the current implementation of IP. The value in the field will be six in the header of all IPng packets.
- **Priority—4-bit Priority value.** This allows the source device to mark packets as higher or lower priority relative to other packets from the same source. This is discussed at greater length later in the section titled "IP version 6 Priority."
- **Flow Label—24-bit field.** The purpose of this field is to allow the source device to identify packets transmitted between a source and destination device that are part of a specific conversation or "flow." An example of this might be a multimedia transmission of time- and delay-sensitive video and audio material. This is discussed at greater length later in the section titled "Flow Labels."
- **Payload Length—16-bit unsigned integer.** This file identifies the length of the payload of the packet in octets. The payload is the remainder of the packet following the IPng header.
- **Next Header—8-bit selector.** Identifies the type of header immediately following IPng header. The values for this field are listed in RFC 1700.
- **Hop Limit—8-bit unsigned integer.** The initial value of this field is specified by the source device. It is decreased by 1 by each node that

forwards the packet, such as a router. If the value reaches 0, the packet is discarded by the node that is handling it.

- **Source Address—128 bits.** The address of the sender of the packet.
- **Destination Address—128 bits.** The address of the intended target recipient of the packet.

IPng Extensions

In IP version 6, optional IP layer information is placed in separate headers between the IP version 6 header and the transport layer headers of TCP or UDP. A single packet can contain zero, one, or several extension headers. Primarily, only the receiving or destination device uses these headers, and intermediary devices such as routers do not examine them, with the single exception being the Hop-by-Hop Options header (discussed later in this chapter). This serves to improve the performance of routers that process packets that contain IP version 6 options. Unlike IP version 4 headers, IPng extension headers can be any length in multiples of 8 octets without IP version 4's 40-byte option limitation.

IPng headers can have zero options, a single option field, or multiple option fields. The header formats shown in figures 30.3 through 30.5 illustrate several possibilities.

Figure 30.3
The IP version 6 header with no options.

Version = 6	Priority	Flow Label
Payload Length	Next Header = 59	Hop Limit
Source Address		
Destination Address		

The following sections discuss the Routing, Fragmentation, Authentication, Encapsulation, Hop-by-Hop Options, Destination, and No Next Header headers, and the function each provides to the IP version 6 protocol.

Version = 6	Priority	Flow Label			
Payload Length	Next Header = 43	Hop Limit			
Source Address					
Destination Address					
Next Header = 59	Routing Type = 1	M	F	Reserved	SRC Router Length
Next Hop PTR	STRICT/Loose Bit Mask				
Source Route					

Figure 30.4
The IP version 6 header with a single option field.

Next Header = 0	Routing Type = 1	M	F	Reserved	SRC Router Length
Next Hop PTR	STRICT/Loose Bit Mask				
Source Route					
Next Header = 59	Header Ext Length				
Options					

Figure 30.5
The IP version 6 header with multiple option fields.

Routing

The function of the Routing header is to specify one or more intermediate devices to be visited as a packet is forwarded to its destination (see fig. 30.6). This allows a source to specify the "route" to a destination and essentially override the route that might have ordinarily have been determined by the routing protocol.

The Routing header is identified by a Next Header value of 59 in the header that precedes it. This is illustrated more clearly in figure 30.5, in which the entire IP version 6 is illustrated.

Fragmentation

In an IP version 6 environment, the source node uses the *Fragmentation header* to send packets that are too large to fit in the maximum packet size or maximum transmission unit (MTU) of the destination. By function, the Fragmentation header addresses the possibility that the network to which the receiving station is attached, or any intermediate networks, cannot accommodate packets as large as the sending station. A device connected to an FDDI network, for example, could send packets as large as 4,000 bytes, whereas a receiving device connected to an Ethernet network could only receive a packet of 1,518 bytes.

In this case, the source node divides, or fragments, the larger packet into smaller packets that can fit the receiving device's MTU. Each fragmented packet would have a Fragmentation header that identifies it as a large fragmented packet (see fig. 30.7). When the receiving node receives the fragments, it recombines the fragments into a single packet and processes it accordingly.

Figure 30.6
The format of a routing header.

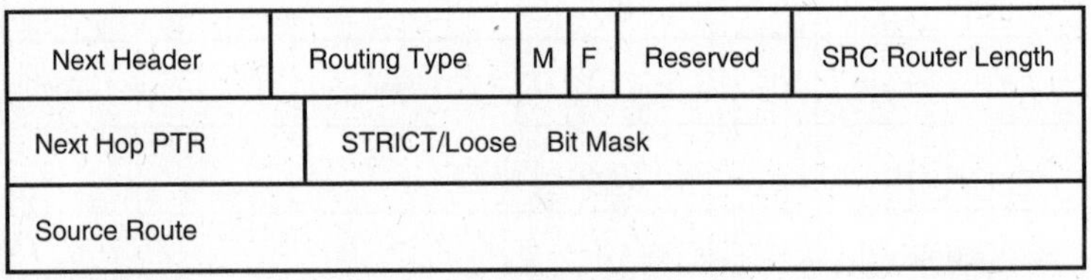

Figure 30.7
The format of a Fragmentation header.

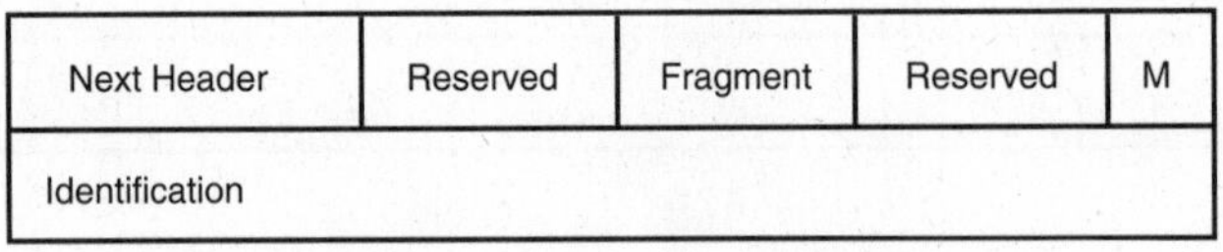

IP version 6 fragmentation works much differently than fragmentation with IP version 4. Whereas with IP version 4, intermediary devices, such as routers, can handle fragmentation, only the source node performs fragmentation with IP version 6. This reduces the demands on intermediary devices such as routers or dual-named hosts. The Fragmentation header is always identified by a Next Header value of 44 in the preceding header.

Authentication

The Authentication header (see fig. 30.8) exists specifically to ensure two significant facts:

- That the destination node receives data that matches the data the source node sends.
- That the sender identified by the source address truly is the sender of the data.

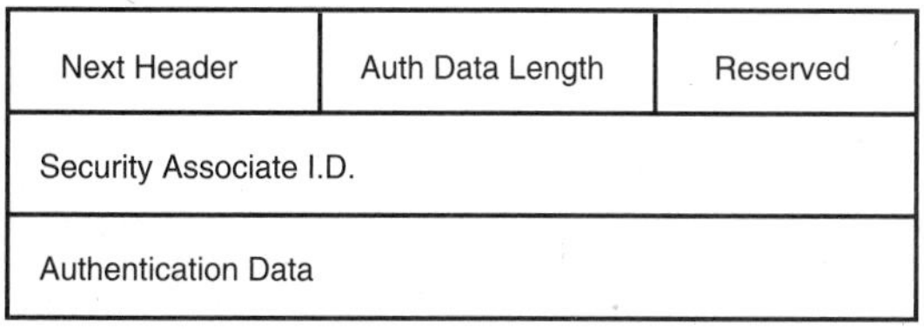

Next Header	Auth Data Length	Reserved
Security Associate I.D.		
Authentication Data		

Figure 30.8
The format of an Authentication header.

To accomplish this, the sending station calculates a value based on the headers, payload, and user information within the packet. The receiving node then calculates the value based on the same headers, payload, and user information. If these two values match, the receiver considers the packet authentic as defined; if not, it rejects the packet.

The section "IP version 6 Security" discusses authentication in detail later in this chapter.

Encapsulation

The Encapsulation header seeks to provide the same security functions as authentication but also provides confidentiality between the sender and receiver. It achieves confidentiality by taking the IP version 6 datagram and encrypting the data, which is known as the *Encapsulated Security Payload* (ESP). Then a new IP version 6 header is attached to the ESP for transmission through the network. The new header is illustrated in figure 30.9.

After the destination device receives the packet, it removes the new header, decrypts the ESP, and then processes the original IP version 6 datagram.

Obviously, coordination of these encryption formats between the source and destination nodes is critical for the receiver to be able to decrypt the packet.

Equally critical is the confidentiality of these encryption keys. The section "IP version 6 Security" later in this chapter discusses the principle of encapsulation in IP version 6 in detail.

Figure 30.9
The format of an Encapsulation header.

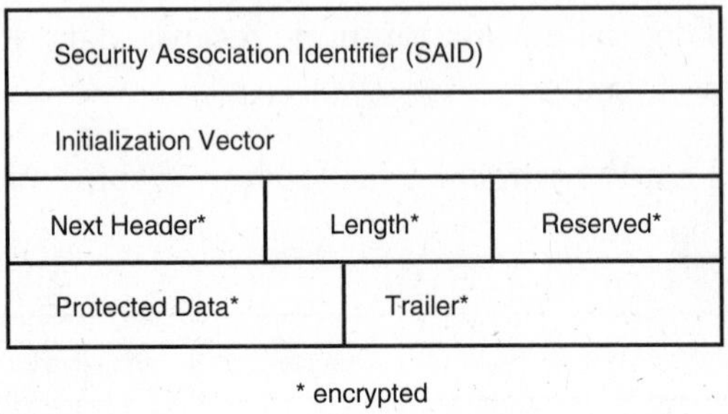

Security Association Identifier (SAID)		
Initialization Vector		
Next Header*	Length*	Reserved*
Protected Data*	Trailer*	

* encrypted

Hop-by-Hop Options

The Hop-by-Hop Options header (see fig. 30.10) is the one header option that that each node or device examines or reviews along the delivery path to the destination. Its function is to identify specific handling that the intermediary nodes between the source and destination nodes require. It is identified by a Next Header value of 0 in the Next Header field of the IP version 6 header.

Figure 30.10
The format of a Hop-by-Hop Options header.

Next Header	HDR Ext Length
Options	

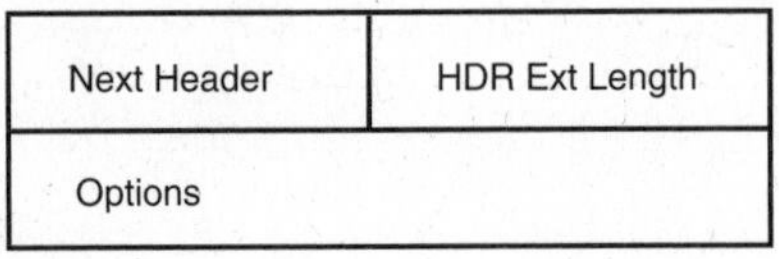

Destination Options

The Destination Options header (see fig. 30.11) accommodates information that only the destination device for the packet or packets will handle. It is identified by a Next Header value of 60 in the preceding header.

Figure 30.11
The format of a Destination Options header.

Next Header	HDR Ext Length
Options	

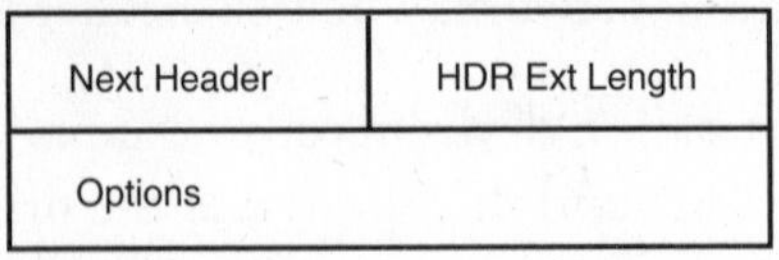

No Next Header Option

The value of 59 in the Next Header value of the IP version 6 header or that of any extension header indicates that no options follow.

As mentioned previously, one of the advantages of IP version 6 is the capability to have larger headers than is possible with IP version 4. This advantage allows new IP version 6 header options to be defined as new requirements are discovered.

Quality of Service

One of the fastest growing technologies in the internetwork arena are applications that rely on "real-time" data, such as multimedia, multicast, or video applications. These applications have several critical requirements:

- A constant level of throughput to ensure adequate bandwidth between the source and destination nodes. If a user tries to view a video presentation using a network, for example, the bandwidth or capacity of the network must be sufficient to deliver the data.
- A constant level of delay.
- A constant level of jitter, where *jitter* refers to varying amounts of latency in the transmission of packets through a network.

A host can use the flow label (discussed in the following section) and the priority fields in the IPng header to identify packets that might require special handling by IPng routers to ensure throughput, delay, and jitter to meet application requirements.

Flow Labels

A *flow* is defined as a series of packets, sent from a specific source device to a specific destination, that requires special handling by any intermediary IPng routers. RFC 1363 defines a flow as "a data structure used by internetwork hosts to request special services of the internetwork, often guarantees about how the internetwork will handle some of the hosts' traffic." The destination can be one of the following:

- A single device (using unicast addresses as a destination)
- Multiple devices (using multicast addresses as a destination)

One example of a flow would be the transmission of a multimedia presentation from a server to a group of client personal computers.

The flow label field of the IP version 6 header is 24 bits long. A flow is identified by having a value other than zero in the flow label field of the IP version 6 header. A packet that isn't part of a flow would contain a flow label value of 0, which a control protocol, such as Resource Reservation Protocol (RSVP), would then use. RSVP is an example of a protocol designed to reserve a path through an internetwork that meets the application's requirements for bandwidth, delay, and jitter.

A device that doesn't support use of a flow label must do one of the following:

- *Set the field to zero if it originates the packet.* This is the function of a destination node that doesn't support flow labels, such as a workstation or server.
- *Pass the field on unchanged when it forwards the packet.* This is the function of a router that might not yet support Flow Labels.
- *Disregard the field if receiving the packet.* This is the function of a destination node that doesn't support flow labels, such as a workstation or server.

Any packets transmitted as part of a flow must contain the same IP version 6 header information, including the source address, destination address, and flow label value, as well as information in any extension headers, such as Routing headers or the Hop-by-Hop Options header.

Flow labels and the protocols that would utilize them still are being designed and can be expected to change. This is one area of IPng that is still in a state of flux and will surely evolve as other protocols or technologies that rely on IP are developed and implemented.

IP Version 6 Priority

Often, to meet application requirements in internetworks, you might need to assign certain data higher priority than other traffic from the source. The priority in the IP version 6 header is a 4-bit field, which offers a value range of 0 to 15. The purpose of this field is to allow a source node to identify the priority level for delivering packets. Data that has a priority level of 12, for example, should be delivered before packets that have a priority level of 3.

The traffic to be transmitted is separated into the two following classes:

- Traffic in which the source device (a file server, for example) can provide congestion control. Here, in the event of network congestion, the device can "throttle back" until the congestion dissipates entirely. For example, this type of traffic uses TCP as a transport protocol, such as FTP, Telnet, or HTTP. The priority values for this traffic currently range from 0 to 7, with the following categories:

  0 Uncharacterized traffic

  1 "Filler" traffic (for example, netnews)

  2 Unattended data transfer (for example, e-mail)

  3 (Reserved)

  4 Attended bulk transfer (for example, FTP, HTTP, NFS)

  5 (Reserved)

  6 Interactive traffic (for example, telnet, X)

  7 Internet control traffic (for example, routing protocols, SNMP)

- Traffic that cannot be "throttled back" to resolve network congestion: multimedia transmissions that consist of video and audio information, for example. You would use a priority value between 8 and 15 for this type of traffic. A value of 8 identifies real-time traffic that is more acceptable to be discarded in the event of network congestion whereas a value of 15 identifies traffic that is far less acceptable to be discarded.

Security

IP version 6 contains two mechanisms to address security in networks, both of which are optional extensions to the IP version 6 header. The first is the Authentication header, which guarantees delivery of the packet intact and authenticity of the source address. It does not, however, guarantee confidentiality; some other device between the sender and the receiving station could potentially also receive the transmission.

The sending value computes a value based on the headers that don't change during delivery to the destination and the payload of the transmission. When the destination node receives the transmission, it also computes a value based on the headers and payload. If these two values match, then the station addresses and the packet's payload are considered authentic and therefore processed. If these two values do not match, the packet is discarded. The algorithm currently used to compute the value for the authentication header is the *MD5 algorithm.*

Use of the Authentication header impacts the processing performance of IP version 6 devices and the communications latency between them, owing to the need to calculate the authentication value in the source and destination devices and to compare the two computed values in the destination node.

Secondly, IP version 6 provides a feature called *Encapsulating Security Payload* (ESP). As does using the Authentication header, ESP, another security feature mentioned earlier in this chapter, ensures the integrity of the transmitted data and authenticates the sender and receiver. In addition, ESP ensures the privacy of the transmission. Using an encryption algorithm that only the sender and the receiving device maintain prevents other devices from decrypting and processing the transmission unless they too possess the encryption key.

IP Mobility

Assuming that a network user maintains a single unchanging specific location frequently leads to error nowadays. Many network users are highly mobile, and many work at home or even in different parts of an organization. IP mobility is in fact not unique to IP version 6 and currently is addressed with

IP version 4—and can easily be modified to work with IP version 6. The definition of IP version 6 provides a significant opportunity to implement functionality to meet the unique needs of the mobile network user.

The Internet draft document from the IP version 6 Working Group titled "Mobility Support in IP version 6," by Charles Perkins and David Johnson, clearly states the primary issue of IP mobility.

> We believe that the most important function needed to support mobility is the reliable and timely notification of a mobile node's current location to other nodes that need it. The home agent needs this location information in order to forward intercepted packets from the home network to the mobile node, and correspondent nodes need this information in order to send their own packets directly to the mobile node.

IP mobility requires that mobile computers have at least two addresses defined for them—one permanent and one or more temporary or care of address. The mobile user would obtain the care of address from a local router or server and then notify the home agent of its temporary location.

You could send information such as e-mail, for example, to a mobile user at the permanent address. If the mobile user is at that location, the mail is received. If not, a home agent receives the transmission and redirects the data to the care of address.

Transitioning to IP Version 6

Clearly, the success of IP Next Generation depends highly on the level of complexity and difficulty in transitioning to this new protocol. A complex, high-cost migration plan would dramatically hinder its potential of becoming widely deployed. IPng, however, has two features that greatly facilitate its implementation.

The most significant feature is the provision for a "phased" implementation. IP version 4 devices, such as client workstations, servers, or routers, can be upgraded gradually with minimal effects on each other. This is due, in part, to the fact that devices upgraded to IP version 6 will essentially run both the IP version 6 and the IP version 4 protocols. This will enable communications with devices that have not yet been upgraded.

The addressing structure of IP version 6 will also ease the burden of transition. Devices that have been upgraded can continue to use their IP version 4 addresses. A server, for example, might be upgraded to support IP version 6 but would still support an IP version 4 address to enable communications to clients that are still using IP version 4. Furthermore, IP version 4 addresses can be "embedded" in the larger address space made possible by IP version 6.

By design, the transition to IP version 6 has been architecturally structured to be a smooth, gradual migration. For this reason, it is likely that the deployment and acceptance of IP version 6 will be swift.

IP version 6 is designed to be an evolutionary step from IP version 4. It seeks to address known issues with IP version 4 and to introduce functionality to address future requirements of this protocol.

From the start, the issue of migration has been dealt with extensively. As discussed earlier, the addressing techniques designed for IP version 6 allow for the inclusion of IP version 4 addresses to facilitate migration. Hosts that are converted to IP version 6 will be able to maintain their current IP version 4 addresses. By design, IP version 6 hosts will be able to communicate with IP version 4 hosts.

IP version 6 has been designed to work on a variety of networks, ranging from slower technologies such as wireless networks to high speed networks using technologies such as ATM and FDDI.

Perhaps most importantly, IP Next Generation seeks to meet the requirements of the Internet, Next Generation: a large, scaleable and useable worldwide network.

Bibliography

Bradner, S., A. Mankin, RFC 1752, "The Recommendation for the IP Next Generation Protocol," January 1995.

Fuller, V., et al, "Supernetting: an Address Assignment and Aggregation Strategy," RFC 1338, June 1992.

Deering, S., "Simple Internet Protocol Plus (SIPP) Specification (128-bit address version)," Internet Draft, July 1994.

Hinden, R., Editor, "IP Version 6 Addressing Architecture," Internet Draft, April 1995.

Gilligan, R., E. Nordmark, "Transition Mechanisms for IP version 6 Hosts and Routers," Internet Draft, March 1995.

VRML 1.0: 3D in the World Wide Web

by Mark Pesce

On April 3, 1995, twenty-eight companies and academic institutions announced their support of the Virtual Reality Modeling Language *(VRML). They were endorsing a specification that provides a framework for three-dimensional representation within the Internet, and specifically the World Wide Web. This was greeted with a lot of hoopla (and driven by plenty of marketing hype) within the industry and the Web's user communities. When the furor began to die down, people started to take a close look at the specification for the language and saw that it was flexible, extensible, and immediately usable. Soon, VRML products began to reach market, and VRML sites were announced. Others, VR purists, poo-poohed VRML's lack of interactivity even as others lauded its networking prowess.*

VRML is a process as much as it is a specification; a dedicated community of developers and users together drive the specification into its second major revision, under development as of this writing. This chapter discusses the important features of VRML, especially from the point of view of the system administrator who administrates a large VRML site. Such sites will become a common feature in tomorrow's Web. They place unusual constraints on Web servers due to the nature of VRML, which is significantly different from the HyperText Markup Language (HTML). VRML was designed, from the ground up, with the Web in mind.

History

The Internet began twenty-five years ago, a project funded by the United States Department of Defense Advanced Research Projects Agency (ARPA). The goal—to develop a mechanism to connect many of the military computers into a seamless internetwork—grew from the desire to provide a sort of "fallout shelter" for the machines in the event of nuclear war. Having grown dependent upon these computers, the Defense Department needed to provide a mechanism through which they could continue to communicate, even in the case of thermonuclear war. A group of data communications scientists developed the core suite of Internet protocols, resilient because they could dynamically adapt to changes in the network. If a link between two machines went down, for whatever reason, the network could reconfigure itself and maintain communications between all of its connected points by redirecting the messages passing through it. In this way, Armegeddon—as far as the computers were concerned—was no more than a routing error.

Although the computers were perfectly content with this new mechanism of communcation, it left something to be desired for the humans who had to use it. The early Internet, like early computing itself, was computer-centered; that is, programmers developed Internet interfaces that conformed to the computers on the Internet, not the people using those computers. This was an era of command lines and batch processing, a time when a white-coated "priesthood" of computer experts held the keys of Internet communication. Very few people could master these sophisticated interfaces. These hardy folks became "system administrators," and they functioned as community librarians in that they kept a map—inside their heads—of the Internet, of what went where, of where to go, and how to get there.

All of this began to change in 1989, when Tim Berners-Lee, working at CERN, the European Center for Nuclear Physics, developed the first implementation of the software now known as the World Wide Web. Berners-Lee was trying to address the needs of his users—physicists scattered throughout Western Europe who needed access to the results of tests performed on CERN's particle accelerators—in a comprehensive way. Not only could scientists access their own results, but they could check them against other results, or even link results together (this feature is called *hyperlinking* or *anchoring*). Using hyperlinking, relationships between islands of data can be clearly demonstrated. From that time forward, all Internet data has acquired context; the Web is all about meaning.

In early 1994, Tony Parisi and this author developed a three-dimensional interface to the World Wide Web. Unlike HTML, useful for displaying pages of data, this new interface, later named Virtual Reality Modeling Language, or VRML, could evoke real-world environments. VRML was useful because it provided one thing the Web lacked: location. The Web as hyperspace directly linked every point within it to every other point. As a result, it's very easy to get around the Web, but almost impossible to know where you are because the conception of where—integral to the human understanding of the universe—doesn't make any sense at all within a hyperspace Web. It's as if the universe of knowledge collapsed down to a single point—almost like a black hole—and we have to find our way through it.

Using VRML, you can take another approach. It's now possible to create spaces whose architecture is a mirror of the content of the space. You can, for example, make a Web-based music archive look like an audio CD player. (This has been done at IUMA: `http://www.iuma.com/`.) It's possible to create environments that are very sophisticated, yet utterly intuitive, because with VRML, you can leave interfaces behind and design just as you would in the real world. This concept has real appeal; companies such as Silicon Graphics, Inc., Sun Microsystems, Netscape Communications, Digital Equipment Corporation, IBM, and others have leapt onto the VRML bandwagon because each see it as the Internet's next step. The Internet has gone from one-dimensional command lines through two-dimensional Web pages, into three-dimensional cyberspace.

VRML Browsers

VRML files require a special browser, just as HTML files require an HTML browser to be viewed. This browser might be a helper application (as is the case with Template Graphics Software's WebSpace), which uses another Web browser to handle conversations with the Internet, or it might be an integrated VRML browser (such as Paper Software's WebFX, which runs inside of Netscape Navigator or Quarterdeck's QMosaic), or it might be completely stand-alone (like Intervista WorldView). In any of these cases, the browser's job is to translate the textual VRML files into a navigable 3D scene.

There are many VRML browsers on the market now, and more are being developed all the time. Here's a list of the ones available as of this writing (they're all free!) with the operating systems they run under:

- NCSA VRWeb—All Major Platforms
- San Diego Supercomputer Center WebView—IRIX
- Intervista WorldView—Windows/95/NT MacOS
- Chaco Pueblo (Combined VRML/HTML/MOO client)—Windows95/NT
- Chaco Scout—Windows95/NT
- Paper Software WebFX—Windows/95/NT
- Template Graphics Software WebSpace—Windows95/NT Solaris AIX HP/UX
- Silicon Graphics' WebSpace—IRIX
- Apple Whurlwind—MacOS
- Worlds VRML+—Windows MacOS
- University of Minnesota WebOOGL—SunOS IRIX LINUX
- MicronGreen NavFlyer—Windows/95/NT

More information about these browsers, including how to download them, can be found at the SDSC VRML Repository, on the web at `http://sdsc.edu/vrml/`.

What Is VRML?

VRML is first and foremost a scene-description language. VRML files—referred to as *worlds*—contain a set, very much like a stage in the theater. When setting the stage for a play, there's a certain arrangement of props, in particular positions, which comprise the set. In the same way, a VRML world file contains a set of objects and their placement within the scene.

Objects in VRML scenes can be broken into two components: their geometry, that is, the shapes that make them up; and their qualities, specifics such as colors, materials, textures, and position or orientation. Every object has some set of materials associated with it; otherwise it couldn't be seen within the scene.

Take Samuel Beckett's *Waiting for Godot* as an example for a VRML world. The set for Waiting is extremely simple; just a single object, a tree, occupies the rear of center stage. This means that the VRML scene description is equally simple. There's a single object defined, the tree, with a given position (center stage, whatever that might be), with a particular color (brown) and shininess (trees are very dull). Next would come the shapes that define the tree itself. Put together, this set of items would define the whole VRML world.

After the file has been created, it's published in the Web by placing it at a Web site. VRML uses all existing Web infrastructure, with essentially no changes, so anywhere that HTML, JPEG, or AIFF files can be accessed, VRML files can be accessed too, which means that the Web is already VRML-compliant.

Just as with HTML documents, VRML documents can contain links to other Web documents. It would be possible to link a branch in the tree (from the previous example) into the text of Beckett's play. The user could then click on the tree and launch an HTML browser, which would then display the link. Or the tree could be linked to a RealAudio file of the play as performed, or it could link to another VRML world. In this last case—called a *teleport*—the user would suddenly find himself within a new VRML world.

The VRML Coordinate System

VRML uses a left-handed coordinate system; *x* is width, *y* is height, and *z* is depth. In this model, the x value increases as it moves to the right, y as it moves to the top, and z as it moves out of the screen toward the viewer. (This is also known as an "in-your-face" coordinate system representation.)

Scene Graphs

VRML files are also known as scene graphs. A *scene graph* is a hierarchical arrangement of atomic VRML objects, which are known as *nodes.* There can be one and only one node at the top level of a scene graph. Nodes are themselves composed of *fields,* which contain the values specific to the behavior of the node. In this way, nodes can be thought of as containers for fields, and a scene-graph as a container for nodes.

Fields

There are two general classes of fields: fields that contain a single value (where a value may be a single number, a vector, or even an image); and fields that contain multiple values. Single-valued fields all have names that begin with "SF," and multiple-valued fields have names that begin with "MF." Each field type defines the format for the values it writes.

Multiple-valued fields are written as a series of values separated by commas, all enclosed in square brackets ([ ]). If the field has zero values, then only the square brackets are written. The last may optionally be followed by a comma. If the field has exactly one value, the brackets can be omitted and just the value written. For example, all of the following are valid for a multiple-valued field containing the single integer value 1:

```
1
[1,]
[ 1 ]
```

SFBitMask

A single-value field that contains a mask of bit flags. Nodes that use this field class define mnemonic names for the bit flags. SFBitMasks are written to file as one or more mnemonic enumerated type names, in the following format:

(*flag1* | *flag2* | ...)

If only one flag is used in a mask, the parentheses are optional. These names differ among uses of this field in various node classes.

SFBool

A field containing a single boolean (true or false) value. SFBools can be written as 0 (representing False), 1, True, or False.

SFColor

A single-value field containing a color. SFColors are written to file as an RGB triple of floating point numbers in standard scientific notation, in the range 0.0 to 1.0.

SFEnum

A single-value field that contains an enumerated type value. Nodes that use this field class define mnemonic names for the values. SFEnums are written to file as a mnemonic enumerated type name. The name differs among uses of this field in various node classes.

SFFloat

A field that contains one single-precision floating point number. SFFloats are written to file in standard scientific notation.

SFImage

A field that contains an uncompressed two-dimensional color or grayscale image.

SFImages are written to file as three integers representing the width, height, and number of components in the image, followed by width×height hexadecimal values representing the pixels in the image, separated by whitespace.

A 1-component image will have 1-byte hexadecimal values representing the intensity of the image. For example, 0xFF is full intensity, and 0x00 is no intensity. A 2-component image puts the intensity in the first (high) byte and the transparency in the second (low) byte.

Pixels in a 3-component image have the red component in the first (high) byte, followed by the green and blue components (so 0xFF0000 is red). 4-component images put the transparency byte after red/green/blue (so 0x0000FF80 is semi-transparent blue). A value of 1.0 is completely transparent, and 0.0 is completely opaque.

Note Each pixel is actually read as a single unsigned number, so a 3-component pixel with value "0x0000FF" can also be written as "0xFF" or "255" (decimal). Pixels are specified from left to right, bottom to top. The first hexadecimal value is the lower left pixel of the image, and the last value is the upper right pixel.

For example, 1 2 1 0xFF 0x00 is a 1-pixel-wide by 2-pixels-high grayscale image, with the bottom pixel white and the top pixel black.

The following is a 2-pixel wide by 4-pixel high RGB image, with the bottom left pixel red, the bottom right pixel green, the two middle rows of pixels black, the top left pixel white, and the top right pixel yellow.

```
2 4 3 0xFF0000 0xFF00 0 0 0 0 0xFFFFFF 0xFFFF00
```

SFLong

A field containing a single long (32-bit) integer. SFLongs are written to file as an integer in decimal, hexadecimal (beginning with '0x'), or octal (beginning with '0') format.

SFMatrix

A field containing a transformation matrix. SFMatrices are written to file in row-major order as 16 floating point numbers separated by whitespace.

For example, a matrix expressing a translation of 7.3 units along the x-axis is written as follows:

1 0 0 0 0 1 0 0 0 0 1 0 7.3 0 0 1

SFRotation

A field containing an arbitrary rotation. SFRotations are written to file as four floating point values separated by whitespace. The four values represent an axis of rotation, followed by the amount of right-handed rotation about that axis, in radians. For example, a 180-degree rotation about the y-axis is the following:

0 1 0 3.14159265

SFString

A field containing an ASCII string (sequence of characters). SFStrings are written to file as a sequence of ASCII characters in double quotes (optional if the string doesn't contain any whitespace). Any characters (including newlines) may appear within the quotes. To include a double quote character within the string, precede it with a backslash. For example, the following are all valid strings:

Testing

"One, Two, Three"

"He said, \"Immel did it!\""

SFVec2f

Field containing a two-dimensional vector. SFVec2fs are written to file as a pair of floating point values separated by whitespace.

SFVec3f

Field containing a three-dimensional vector. SFVec3fs are written to file as three floating point values separated by whitespace.

MFColor

A multiple-value field that contains any number of RGB colors. MFColors are written to file as one or more RGB triples of floating point numbers in standard scientific notation. When more than one value is present, all of the values must be enclosed in square brackets and separated by commas. For example, the following line represents the three colors red, green, and blue:

```
[ 1.0 0.0 0.0, 0 1 0, 0 0 1 ]
```

MFLong

A multiple-value field that contains any number of long (32-bit) integers. MFLongs are written to file as one or more integer values, in decimal, hexadecimal, or octal format. When more than one value is present, all the values are enclosed in square brackets and separated by commas, as follows:

```
[ 17, -0xE20, -518820 ]
```

MFVec2f

A multiple-value field that contains any number of two-dimensional vectors. MFVec2fs are written to file as one or more pairs of floating point values separated by whitespace. When more than one value is present, all of the values are enclosed in square brackets and separated by commas, as shown in the following:

```
[ 0 0, 1.2 3.4, 98.6 -4e1 ]
```

MFVec3f

A multiple-value field that contains any number of three-dimensional vectors. MFVec3fs are written to file as one or more triples of floating point values separated by whitespace. When more than one value is present, all of the values are enclosed in square brackets and separated by commas, as follows:

```
[ 0 0 0, 1.2 3.4 5.6, 98.6 -4e1 212 ]
```

Nodes

VRML defines several different classes of nodes. Most of the nodes can be classified into one of three categories: shape, property, or group.

- **Shape** nodes define the geometry in the scene. Conceptually, they are the only nodes that draw anything.
- **Property** nodes affect the way shapes are drawn.
- **Grouping** nodes gather other nodes together, allowing collections of nodes to be treated as a single object.

Some group nodes also control whether or not their children are drawn.

Nodes can contain zero or more fields. Each node type defines the type, name, and default value for each of its fields. The default value for the field is used if a value for the field is not specified in the VRML file. The order in which the fields of a node are read is not important; for example, "Cube { width 2 height 4 depth 6 }" and "Cube { height 4 depth 6 width 2 }" are equivalent.

There are 36 nodes grouped by type. The first group contains the shape nodes, which specify geometry. They are the following:

- AsciiText
- Cone
- Cube
- Cylinder
- IndexedFaceSet
- IndexedLineSet
- PointSet
- Sphere

The second group are the properties. These can be further grouped into properties of the geometry and its appearance, matrix or transform properties, and cameras and lights:

- Coordinate3
- DirectionalLight

- FontStyle
- Info
- LOD
- Material
- MaterialBinding
- MatrixTransform
- Normal
- NormalBinding
- OrthographicCamera
- PerspectiveCamera
- PointLight
- Texture2
- Texture2Transform
- TextureCoordinate2
- ShapeHints
- Rotation
- Scale
- Transform
- Translation
- SpotLight

And these are the group nodes:

- Group
- Separator

- Switch
- TransformSeparator
- WWWAnchor

Note The WWWInline node does not fit neatly into any category.

All the nodes are discussed in the following sections.

AsciiText

This node represents strings of text characters from the ASCII-coded character set. The first string is rendered with its baseline at (0,0,0). All subsequent strings advance y by –(size×spacing). See FontStyle for a description of the size field. The justification field determines the placement of the strings in the x dimension. LEFT (the default) places the left edge of each string at x=0. CENTER places the center of each string at x=0. RIGHT places the right edge of each string at x=0. Text is rendered from left to right and top to bottom in the font set by FontStyle. The width field defines a suggested width constraint for each string. The default is to use the natural width of each string. Setting any value to 0 indicates the natural width should be used for that string.

The text is transformed by the current cumulative transformation and is drawn with the current material and texture.

Textures are applied to 3D text as follows. The texture origin is at the origin of the first string, as determined by the justification. The texture is scaled equally in both S and T dimensions, with the font height representing 1 unit. S increases to the right. The T origin can occur anywhere along each character, depending on how that character's outline is defined.

JUSTIFICATION

LEFT	Align left edge of text to origin
CENTER	Align center of text to origin
RIGHT	Align right edge of text to origin

FILE FORMAT/DEFAULTS

```
AsciiText {
     string          ""    # MFString
     spacing         1     # SFFloat
     justification  LEFT  # SFEnum
     width           0     # MFFloat
}
```

Cone

This node represents a simple cone whose central axis is aligned with the y-axis. By default, the cone is centered at (0,0,0) and has a size of –1 to +1 in all three directions. The cone has a radius of 1 at the bottom and a height of 2, with its apex at 1 and its bottom at –1. The cone also has two parts: the sides and the bottom.

The cone is transformed by the current cumulative transformation and is drawn with the current texture and material.

If the current material binding is PER_PART or PER_PART_INDEXED, the first current material is used for the sides of the cone, and the second is used for the bottom. Otherwise, the first material is used for the entire cone.

When a texture is applied to a cone, it is applied differently to the sides and bottom. On the sides, the texture wraps counterclockwise (from above) starting at the back of the cone. The texture has a vertical seam at the back, intersecting the yz-plane. For the bottom, a circle is cut out of the texture square and applied to the cone's base circle. The texture appears right side up when the top of the cone is rotated toward the –z-axis.

PARTS

SIDES	The conical part
BOTTOM	The bottom circular face
ALL	All parts

FILE FORMAT/DEFAULTS

```
Cone {
     parts          ALL     # SFBitMask
```

```
    bottomRadius  1       # SFFloat
    height        2       # SFFloat
}
```

Coordinate3

This node defines a set of 3D coordinates to be used by a subsequent IndexedFaceSet, IndexedLineSet, or PointSet node. This node does not produce a visible result during rendering; it simply replaces the current coordinates in the rendering state for subsequent nodes to use.

FILE FORMAT/DEFAULTS

```
Coordinate3 {
     point  0 0 0  # MFVec3f
}
```

Cube

This node represents a cuboid aligned with the coordinate axes. By default, the cube is centered at (0,0,0) and measures 2 units in each dimension, from –1 to +1. The cube is transformed by the current cumulative transformation and is drawn with the current material and texture.

If the current material binding is PER_PART, PER_PART_INDEXED, PER_FACE, or PER_FACE_INDEXED, materials will be bound to the faces of the cube in this order:

- Front (+z)
- Back (–z)
- Left (–x)
- Right (+x)
- Top (+y)
- Bottom (–y).

Textures are applied individually to each face of the cube; the entire texture goes on each face. On the front, back, right, and left sides of the cube, the texture is applied right side up. On the top, the texture appears right side up when the top of the cube is tilted toward the camera. On the bottom, the texture appears right side up when the top of the cube is tilted toward the –z-axis.

FILE FORMAT/DEFAULTS

```
Cube {
     width   2     # SFFloat
     height  2     # SFFloat
     depth   2     # SFFloat
}
```

Cylinder

This node represents a simple capped cylinder centered around the y-axis. By default, the cylinder is centered at (0,0,0) and has a default size of –1 to +1 in all three dimensions. The cylinder has three parts: the sides, the top (y=+1), and the bottom (y=–1). You can use the radius and height fields to create a cylinder with a different size.

The cylinder is transformed by the current cumulative transformation and is drawn with the current material and texture.

If the current material binding is PER_PART or PER_PART_INDEXED, the first current material is used for the sides of the cylinder, the second is used for the top, and the third is used for the bottom. Otherwise, the first material is used for the entire cylinder.

When a texture is applied to a cylinder, it is applied differently to the sides, top, and bottom. On the sides, the texture wraps counterclockwise (from above) starting at the back of the cylinder. The texture has a vertical seam at the back, intersecting the yz-plane. For the top and bottom, a circle is cut out of the texture square and applied to the top or bottom circle. The top texture appears right side up when the top of the cylinder is tilted toward the +z-axis, and the bottom texture appears right side up when the top of the cylinder is tilted toward the –z-axis.

PARTS

SIDES	The cylindrical part
TOP	The top circular face

BOTTOM	The bottom circular face
ALL	All parts

FILE FORMAT/DEFAULTS

```
Cylinder {
     parts   ALL   # SFBitMask
     radius  1     # SFFloat
     height  2     # SFFloat
}
```

DirectionalLight

This node defines a directional light source that illuminates along rays parallel to a given three-dimensional vector.

A light node defines an illumination source that may affect subsequent shapes in the scene graph, depending on the current lighting style. Light sources are affected by the current transformation. A light node under a separator does not affect any objects outside that separator.

FILE FORMAT/DEFAULTS

```
DirectionalLight {
     on         TRUE       # SFBool
     intensity  1          # SFFloat
     color      1 1 1      # SFColor
     direction  0 0 -1     # SFVec3f
}
```

FontStyle

This node defines the current font style used for all subsequent AsciiText. Font attributes only are defined. It is up to the browser to assign specific fonts to the various attribute combinations. The size field specifies the height (in object space units) of glyphs rendered and determines the vertical spacing of adjacent lines of text.

FAMILY

SERIF	Serif style (such as TimesRoman)
SANS	Sans Serif Style (such as Helvetica)
TYPEWRITER	Fixed pitch style (such as Courier)

STYLE

NONE	No modifications to family
BOLD	Embolden family
ITALIC	Italicize or Slant family

FILE FORMAT/DEFAULTS

```
FontStyle {
     size      10       # SFFloat
     family    SERIF    # SFEnum
     style     NONE     # SFBitMask
}
```

Group

This node defines the base class for all group nodes. Group is a node that contains an ordered list of child nodes. This node is simply a container for the child nodes and does not alter the traversal state in any way. During traversal, state accumulated for a child is passed on to each successive child and then to the parents of the group (Group does not push or pop traversal state as separator does).

FILE FORMAT/DEFAULTS

```
Group {
}
```

IndexedFaceSet

This node represents a 3D shape formed by constructing faces (polygons) from vertices located at the current coordinates. IndexedFaceSet uses the indices in its coordIndex field to specify the polygonal faces. An index of –1 indicates that the current face has ended and the next one begins.

The vertices of the faces are transformed by the current transformation matrix.

Treatment of the current material and normal binding is as follows:

- The PER_PART and PER_FACE bindings specify a material or normal for each face.
- PER_VERTEX specifies a material or normal for each vertex.
- The corresponding _INDEXED bindings are the same, but use the materialIndex or normalIndex indices.
- The DEFAULT material binding is equal to OVERALL.
- The DEFAULT normal binding is equal to PER_VERTEX_INDEXED; if insufficient normals exist in the state, vertex normals will be generated automatically.

Explicit texture coordinates (as defined by TextureCoordinate2) can be bound to vertices of an indexed shape by using the indices in the textureCoordIndex field. As with all vertex-based shapes, if there is a current texture, but no texture coordinates are specified, a default texture coordinate mapping is calculated using the bounding box of the shape. The longest dimension of the bounding box defines the S coordinates, and the next longest defines the T coordinates. The value of the S coordinate ranges from 0 to 1, from one end of the bounding box to the other. The T coordinate ranges between 0 and the ratio of the second greatest dimension of the bounding box to the greatest dimension.

Be sure that the indices contained in the coordIndex, materialIndex, normalIndex, and textureCoordIndex fields are valid with respect to the current state, or errors will occur.

FILE FORMAT/DEFAULTS

```
IndexedFaceSet {
     coordIndex         0  # MFLong
     materialIndex      -1 # MFLong
     normalIndex        -1 # MFLong
     textureCoordIndex  -1 # MFLong
}
```

IndexedLineSet

This node represents a 3D shape formed by constructing polylines from vertices located at the current coordinates. IndexedLineSet uses the indices in its coordIndex field to specify the polylines. An index of –1 indicates that the current polyline has ended and the next one begins.

The coordinates of the line set are transformed by the current cumulative transformation.

Treatment of the current material and normal binding is as follows:

- The PER_PART binding specifies a material or normal for each segment of the line.
- The PER_FACE binding specifies a material or normal for each polyline.
- PER_VERTEX specifies a material or normal for each vertex.
- The corresponding _INDEXED bindings are the same, but use the materialIndex or normalIndex indices.
- The DEFAULT material binding is equal to OVERALL.
- The DEFAULT normal binding is equal to PER_VERTEX_INDEXED; if insufficient normals exist in the state, the lines will be drawn unlit. The same rules for texture coordinate generation as IndexedFaceSet are used.

FILE FORMAT/DEFAULTS

```
IndexedLineSet {
     coordIndex          0  # MFLong
     materialIndex      -1  # MFLong
     normalIndex        -1  # MFLong
     textureCoordIndex  -1  # MFLong
}
```

Info

This class defines an information node in the scene graph. This node has no effect during traversal. It is used to store information in the scene graph, typically for application-specific purposes, copyright messages, or other strings.

```
Info {
     string  "<Undefined info>"      # SFString
}
```

LOD

This group node is used to allow applications to switch between various representations of objects automatically. The children of this node typically represent the same object or objects at varying levels of detail, from highest detail to lowest.

The specified center point of the LOD is transformed by the current transformation into world space, and the distance from the transformed center to the world-space eye point is calculated. If the distance is less than the first value in the ranges array, then the first child of the LOD group is drawn. If between the first and second values in the ranges array, the second child is drawn, etc. If there are N values in the ranges array, the LOD group should have N+1 children. Specifying too few children will result in the last child being used repeatedly for the lowest levels of detail; if too many children are specified, the extra children will be ignored. Each value in the ranges array should be less than the previous value; otherwise, results are undefined.

FILE FORMAT/DEFAULTS

```
LOD {
     range [ ]    # MFFloat
     center 0 0 0  # SFVec3f
}
```

Material

This node defines the current surface material properties for all subsequent shapes. Material sets several components of the current material during traversal. Different shapes interpret materials with multiple values differently. To bind materials to shapes, use a MaterialBinding node.

FILE FORMAT/DEFAULTS

```
Material {
     ambientColor   0.2 0.2 0.2     # MFColor
     diffuseColor   0.8 0.8 0.8     # MFColor
     specularColor  0 0 0           # MFColor
     emissiveColor  0 0 0           # MFColor
     shininess      0.2             # MFFloat
     transparency   0               # MFFloat
}
```

MaterialBinding

This node specifies how the current materials are bound to shapes that follow in the scene graph. Each shape node may interpret bindings differently. The current material always has a base value, which is defined by the first value of all material fields. Because material fields may have multiple values, the binding determines how these values are distributed over a shape.

The bindings for faces and vertices are meaningful only for shapes that are made from faces and vertices. Similarly, the indexed bindings are only used by the shapes that allow indexing.

When multiple material values are bound, the values are cycled through, based on the period of the material component with the most values. For example, the following table shows the values used when cycling through (or indexing into) a material with two ambient colors, three diffuse colors, and one of all other components in the current material (the period of this material cycle is 3), as follows:

Material	Ambient Color	Diffuse Color	Other
0	0	0	0
1	1	1	0
2	1	2	0
3 (same as 0)	0	0	0

BINDINGS

DEFAULT	Use default binding
OVERALL	Whole object has same material
PER_PART	One material for each part of object
PER_PART_INDEXED	One material for each part, indexed
PER_FACE	One material for each face of object
PER_FACE_INDEXED	One material for each face, indexed
PER_VERTEX	One material for each vertex of object
PER_VERTEX_INDEXED	One material for each vertex, indexed

FILE FORMAT/DEFAULTS

```
MaterialBinding {
     value  DEFAULT        # SFEnum
}
```

MatrixTransform

This node defines a geometric 3D transformation with a 4-by-4 matrix. Note that some matrices (such as singular ones) might result in errors.

FILE FORMAT/DEFAULTS

```
MatrixTransform {
     matrix  1 0 0 0       # SFMatrix
          0 1 0 0
          0 0 1 0
          0 0 0 1
}
```

Normal

This node defines a set of 3D surface normal vectors to be used by vertex-based shape nodes (IndexedFaceSet, IndexedLineSet, PointSet) that follow it in the scene graph. This node does not produce a visible result during rendering; it simply replaces the current normals in the rendering state for subsequent nodes to use. This node contains one multiple-valued field that contains the normal vectors:

FILE FORMAT/DEFAULTS

```
Normal {
     vector  0 0 1 # MFVec3f
}
```

NormalBinding

This node specifies how the current normals are bound to shapes that follow in the scene graph. Each shape node may interpret bindings differently.

The bindings for faces and vertices are meaningful only for shapes that are made from faces and vertices. Similarly, the indexed bindings are only used by the shapes that allow indexing. For bindings that require multiple normals, be sure to have at least as many normals defined as are necessary; otherwise, errors will occur.

BINDINGS

DEFAULT	Use default binding
OVERALL	Whole object has same normal
PER_PART	One normal for each part of object
PER_PART_INDEXED	One normal for each part, indexed
PER_FACE	One normal for each face of object
PER_FACE_INDEXED	One normal for each face, indexed
PER_VERTEX	One normal for each vertex of object
PER_VERTEX_INDEXED	One normal for each vertex, indexed

FILE FORMAT/DEFAULTS

```
NormalBinding {
     value  DEFAULT         # SFEnum
}
```

OrthographicCamera

An orthographic camera defines a parallel projection from a viewpoint. This camera does not diminish objects with distance, as a PerspectiveCamera does. The viewing volume for an orthographic camera is a rectangular parallelepiped (a box).

By default, the camera is located at (0,0,1) and looks along the negative z-axis; the position and orientation fields can be used to change these values. The height field defines the total height of the viewing volume.

A camera can be placed in a VRML world to specify the initial location of the viewer when that world is entered. VRML browsers typically modify the camera to enable a user to move through the virtual world.

Cameras are affected by the current transformation, so you can position a camera by placing a transformation node before it in the scene graph. The default position and orientation of a camera is at (0,0,1) looking along the negative z-axis.

FILE FORMAT/DEFAULTS

```
OrthographicCamera {
     position          0 0 1          # SFVec3f
     orientation       0 0 1  0       # SFRotation
     focalDistance     5              # SFFloat
     height            2              # SFFloat
}
```

PerspectiveCamera

A perspective camera defines a perspective projection from a viewpoint. The viewing volume for a perspective camera is a truncated right pyramid.

By default, the camera is located at (0,0,1) and looks along the negative z-axis; the position and orientation fields can be used to change these values. The heightAngle field defines the total vertical angle of the viewing volume.

See more on cameras in the OrthographicCamera description.

FILE FORMAT/DEFAULTS

```
PerspectiveCamera {
               position         0 0 1        # SFVec3f
               orientation      0 0 1  0     # SFRotation
               focalDistance    5            # SFFloat
               heightAngle      0.785398     # SFFloat
}
```

PointLight

This node defines a point light source at a fixed 3D location. A point source illuminates equally in all directions; that is, it is omni-directional.

A light node defines an illumination source that may affect subsequent shapes in the scene graph, depending on the current lighting style. Light sources are affected by the current transformation. A light node under a separator does not affect any objects outside that separator.

FILE FORMAT/DEFAULTS

```
PointLight {
     on          TRUE       # SFBool
     intensity   1          # SFFloat
     color       1 1 1      # SFColor
     location    0 0 1      # SFVec3f
}
```

PointSet

This node represents a set of points located at the current coordinates. PointSet uses the current coordinates in order, starting at the index specified by the startIndex field. The number of points in the set is specified by the numPoints field. A value of –1 for this field indicates that all remaining values in the current coordinates are to be used as points.

The coordinates of the point set are transformed by the current cumulative transformation. The points are drawn with the current material and texture.

Treatment of the current material and normal binding is as follows:

- PER_PART, PER_FACE, and PER_VERTEX bindings bind one material or normal to each point.

- The DEFAULT material binding is equal to OVERALL.
- The DEFAULT normal binding is equal to PER_VERTEX.
- The startIndex is also used for materials or normals when the binding indicates that they should be used per vertex.

FILE FORMAT/DEFAULTS

```
PointSet {
     startIndex  0 # SFLong
     numPoints   -1        # SFLong
}
```

Rotation

This node defines a 3D rotation about an arbitrary axis through the origin. The rotation is accumulated into the current transformation, which is applied to subsequent shapes:

FILE FORMAT/DEFAULTS

```
Rotation {
     rotation  0 0 1  0    # SFRotation
}
```

See the rotation field description for more information.

Scale

This node defines a 3D scaling about the origin. If the components of the scaling vector are not all the same, this produces a non-uniform scale.

FILE FORMAT/DEFAULTS

```
Scale {
     scaleFactor  1 1 1    # SFVec3f
}
```

Separator

This group node performs a push (save) of the traversal state before traversing its children and a pop (restore) after traversing them. This isolates the separator's children from the rest of the scene graph. A separator can include lights, cameras, coordinates, normals, bindings, and all other properties.

Separators can also perform render culling. Render culling skips over traversal of the separator's children if they are not going to be rendered, based on the comparison of the separator's bounding box with the current view volume. Culling is controlled by the renderCulling field. These are set to AUTO by default, allowing the implementation to decide whether or not to cull.

CULLING ENUMS

ON	Always try to cull to the view volume
OFF	Never try to cull to the view volume
AUTO	Implementation-defined culling behavior

FILE FORMAT/DEFAULTS

```
Separator {
    renderCulling        AUTO       # SFEnum
}
```

ShapeHints

The ShapeHints node indicates that IndexedFaceSets are solid, contain ordered vertices, or contain convex faces.

These hints allow VRML implementations to optimize certain rendering features. Optimizations that can be performed include enabling backface culling and disabling two-sided lighting. For example, if an object is solid and has ordered vertices, an implementation may turn on backface culling and turn off two-sided lighting. If the object is not solid, but has ordered vertices, it might turn off backface culling and turn on two-sided lighting.

The ShapeHints node also affects how default normals are generated. When an IndexedFaceSet has to generate default normals, it uses the creaseAngle field to determine which edges should be smoothly shaded and which ones should have a sharp crease. The crease angle is the angle between surface normals on adjacent polygons. For example, a crease angle of 0.5 radians (the default value) means that an edge between two adjacent polygonal faces will be smooth shaded if the normals to the two faces form an angle that is less than 0.5 radians (about 30 degrees). Otherwise, it will be faceted.

VERTEX ORDERING ENUMS

UNKNOWN_ORDERING	Ordering of vertices is unknown
CLOCKWISE	Face vertices are ordered clockwise (from the outside)
COUNTERCLOCKWISE	Face vertices are ordered counter-clockwise (from the outside)

SHAPE TYPE ENUMS

UNKNOWN_SHAPE_TYPE	Nothing is known about the shape
SOLID	The shape encloses a volume

FACE TYPE ENUMS

UNKNOWN_FACE_TYPE	Nothing is known about faces
CONVEX	All faces are convex

FILE FORMAT/DEFAULTS

```
ShapeHints {
     vertexOrdering  UNKNOWN_ORDERING      # SFEnum
     shapeType       UNKNOWN_SHAPE_TYPE    # SFEnum
     faceType        CONVEX                # SFEnum
     creaseAngle     0.5                   # SFFloat
}
```

Sphere

This node represents a sphere. By default, the sphere is centered at the origin and has a radius of 1. The sphere is transformed by the current cumulative transformation and is drawn with the current material and texture.

A sphere does not have faces or parts. Therefore, the sphere ignores material and normal bindings, using the first material for the entire sphere and using its own normals. When a texture is applied to a sphere, the texture covers the entire surface, wrapping counterclockwise from the back of the sphere. The texture has a seam at the back on the yz-plane.

FILE FORMAT/DEFAULTS

```
Sphere {
     radius  1      # SFFloat
}
```

SpotLight

This node defines a spotlight light source. A spotlight is placed at a fixed location in 3-space and illuminates in a cone along a particular direction. The intensity of the illumination drops off exponentially as a ray of light diverges from this direction toward the edges of the cone. The rate of drop-off and the angle of the cone are controlled by the dropOffRate and cutOffAngle fields.

A light node defines an illumination source that might affect subsequent shapes in the scene graph, depending on the current lighting style. Light sources are affected by the current transformation. A light node under a separator does not affect any objects outside that separator.

FILE FORMAT/DEFAULTS

```
SpotLight {
     on            TRUE     # SFBool
     intensity     1        # SFFloat
     color         1 1 1    # SFVec3f
     location      0 0 1    # SFVec3f
     direction     0 0 -1   # SFVec3f
     dropOffRate   0        # SFFloat
     cutOffAngle   0.785398 # SFFloat
}
```

Switch

This group node traverses one, none, or all of its children. One can use this node to switch on and off the effects of some properties or to switch between different properties.

The whichChild field specifies the index of the child to traverse, where the first child has index 0.

A value of –1 (the default) means do not traverse any children. A value of –3 traverses all children, making the switch behave exactly like a regular group.

FILE FORMAT/DEFAULTS

```
Switch {
     whichChild  -1         # SFLong
}
```

Texture2

This property node defines a texture map and parameters for that map. This map is used to apply texture to subsequent shapes as they are rendered.

The texture can be read from the URL specified by the file name field. To turn off texturing, set the file name field to an empty string (“”).

Textures can also be specified inline by setting the image field to contain the texture data. Specifying both a URL and data inline will result in undefined behavior.

WRAP ENUM

REPEAT	Repeats texture outside 0–1 texture coordinate range
CLAMP	Clamps texture coordinates to lie within 0–1 range

FILE FORMAT/DEFAULTS

```
Texture2 {
     filename    ""        # SFString
     image       0 0 0     # SFImage
     wrapS       REPEAT    # SFEnum
     wrapT       REPEAT    # SFEnum
}
```

Texture2Transform

This node defines a 2D transformation applied to texture coordinates. This affects the way textures are applied to the surfaces of subsequent shapes. The transformation consists of (in order) a non-uniform scale about an arbitrary center point, a rotation about that same point, and a translation. This enables a user to change the size and position of the textures on shapes.

FILE FORMAT/DEFAULTS

```
Texture2Transform {
     translation  0 0      # SFVec2f
     rotation     0        # SFFloat
     scaleFactor  1 1      # SFVec2f
     center       0 0      # SFVec2f
}
```

TextureCoordinate2

This node defines a set of 2D coordinates to be used to map textures to the vertices of subsequent PointSet, IndexedLineSet, or IndexedFaceSet objects. It replaces the current texture coordinates in the rendering state for the shapes to use.

Texture coordinates range from 0 to 1 across the texture. The horizontal coordinate, called S, is specified first, followed by the vertical coordinate, T.

FILE FORMAT/DEFAULTS

```
TextureCoordinate2 {
     point  0 0    # MFVec2f
}
```

Transform

This node defines a geometric 3D transformation consisting of (in order) a (possibly) non-uniform scale about an arbitrary point, a rotation about an arbitrary point and axis, and a translation.

FILE FORMAT/DEFAULTS

```
Transform {
     translation       0 0 0       # SFVec3f
     rotation          0 0 1  0    # SFRotation
     scaleFactor       1 1 1       # SFVec3f
     scaleOrientation  0 0 1  0    # SFRotation
     center            0 0 0       # SFVec3f
}
```

The transform node…

```
Transform {
     translation T1
```

```
        rotation R1
        scaleFactor S
        scaleOrientation R2
        center T2
}
```

...is equivalent to the following sequence:

```
Translation { translation T1 }
Translation { translation T2 }
Rotation { rotation R1 }
Rotation { rotation R2 }
Scale { scaleFactor S }
Rotation { rotation -R2 }
Translation { translation -T2 }
```

TransformSeparator

This group node is similar to the separator node in that it saves state before traversing its children and restores it afterward. It saves only the current transformation, however; all other state is left as is. This node can be useful for positioning a camera, because the transformations to the camera will not affect the rest of the scene, even through the camera will view the scene. Similarly, this node can be used to isolate transformations to light sources or other objects.

FILE FORMAT/DEFAULTS

```
TransformSeparator {
}
```

Translation

This node defines a translation by a 3D vector.

FILE FORMAT/DEFAULTS

```
Translation {
        translation  0 0 0    # SFVec3f
}
```

WWWAnchor

The WWWAnchor group node loads a new scene into a VRML browser when one of its children is chosen. Exactly how a user "chooses" a child of the WWWAnchor is up to the VRML browser; typically, clicking on one of its children with the mouse will result in the new scene replacing the current scene. A WWWAnchor with an empty ("") name does nothing when its children are chosen. The name is an arbitrary URL.

WWWAnchor behaves like a Separator, pushing the traversal state before traversing its children and popping it afterwards.

The description field in the WWWAnchor allows for a friendly prompt to be displayed as an alternative to the URL in the name field. Ideally, browsers will allow the user to choose the description, the URL, or both to be displayed for a candidate WWWAnchor.

The WWWAnchor's map field is an enumerated value that can be either NONE (the default) or POINT. If it is POINT, then the object-space coordinates of the point on the object the user chose will be added to the URL in the name field, with the syntax "?x,y,z".

MAP ENUM

NONE	Do not add information to the URL
POINT	Add object-space coordinates to URL

FILE FORMAT/DEFAULTS

```
WWWAnchor {
     name ""           # SFString
     description "" # SFString
     map NONE          # SFEnum
}
```

WWWInline

The WWWInline node reads its children from anywhere in the World Wide Web. Exactly when its children are read is not defined; reading the children may be delayed until the WWWInline is actually displayed. A WWWInline with an empty name does nothing. The name is an arbitrary URL.

The effect of referring to a non-VRML URL in a WWWInline node is undefined.

If the WWWInline's bboxSize field specifies a non-empty bounding box (a bounding box is non-empty if at least one of its dimensions is greater than zero), then the WWWInline's object-space bounding box is specified by its bboxSize and bboxCenter fields. This allows an implementation to view-volume cull or LOD switch the WWWInline without reading its contents.

FILE FORMAT/DEFAULTS

```
WWWInline {
     name ""                    # SFString
     bboxSize 0 0 0             # SFVec3f
     bboxCenter 0 0 0           # SFVec3f
}
```

Instancing

A node may be the child of more than one group. This is called instancing (using the same instance of a node multiple times, called aliasing or multiple references by other systems), and is accomplished by using the "USE" keyword.

The DEF keyword both defines a named node, and creates a single instance of it. The USE keyword indicates that the most recently defined instance should be used again. If several nodes were given the same name, then the last DEF encountered during parsing "wins." DEF/USE is limited to a single file; there is no mechanism for USEing nodes that are DEFed in other files.

A name goes into scope as soon as the DEF is encountered, and does not go out of scope until another DEF of the same name or end-of-file are encountered. Nodes cannot be shared between files (you cannot USE a node that was DEFed inside the file to which a WWWInline refers).

For example, rendering this scene will result in three spheres being drawn. Both of the spheres are named "Joe"; the second (smaller) sphere is drawn twice, as follows:

```
Separator {
     DEF Joe Sphere { }
     Translation { translation 2 0 0 }
     Separator {
```

```
        DEF Joe Sphere { radius .2 }
        Translation { translation 2 0 0 }
    }
  USE Joe    # radius .2 sphere will be used here
```

Extensibility

Extensions to VRML are supported by supporting self-describing nodes. Nodes that are not part of standard VRML must write out a description of their fields first, so that all VRML implementations are able to parse and ignore the extensions.

This description is written just after the opening curly brace for the node, and consists of the keyword "fields" followed by a list of the types and names of fields used by that node, all enclosed in square brackets and separated by commas. For example, if Cube was not a standard VRML node, it would be written like this:

```
Cube {
     fields [ SFFloat width, SFFloat height, SFFloat depth ]
  width 10 height 4 depth 3
```

Specifying the fields for nodes that are part of standard VRML is not an error; VRML parsers must silently ignore the field specification.

is-A Relationships

A new node type may also be a superset of an existing node that is part of the standard. In this case, if an implementation for the new node type cannot be found, the new node type can be safely treated as the existing node it is based on (with some loss of functionality, of course). To support this, new node types can define an MFString field called "isA," containing the names of the types of which it is a superset.

For example, a new type of Material called "ExtendedMaterial" that adds index of refraction as a material property can be written as the following:

```
ExtendedMaterial {
  fields [ MFString isA, MFFloat indexOfRefraction,
          MFColor ambientColor, MFColor diffuseColor,
          MFColor specularColor, MFColor emissiveColor,
          MFFloat shininess, MFFloat transparency ]
```

```
    isA [ "Material" ]
    indexOfRefraction .34
  diffuseColor .8 .54 1
```

Multiple isA relationships may be specified in order of preference; implementations are expected to use the first for which there is an implementation.

Comment Lines

Comments in VRML files are always preceeded by the pound symbol (#). Comments begin with the pound symbol and continue until the end-of-line. The single exception to this rule is the VRML File Header, which is interpreted by the VRML parser, even though it is preceeded by a pound symbol.

The VRML File Header

All VRML files—including those referenced by a WWWInline node—must begin with a valid VRML file header. This header must be the first line in the file. The header is as follows:

```
#VRML V1.0 ascii
```

Any VRML file that lacks this header will be rejected as erroneous.

A Simple VRML World

A very simple world, which demonstrates several of the VRML geometric primitives and their relationship to the scene graph, is given in this example:

```
#VRML V1.0 ascii
Separator {  # Single top level node is generally separator
     #We'll define 3 objects, each with their own materials
     Separator {
          Material {
               emissiveColor 1.0 1.0 1.0      # glowing white
          }

          Sphere {
               radius 10 # radius is the sole field
          }
     }

     Separator {
```

```
        Transform {
            translation 20 20 20 # move it away
        }

        Material {
            diffuseColor 1.0 1.0 0.0 # dull, saturated yellow
        }

        Cube {
            width 5
            height 5
            depth 5
        }
    }

    Separator {

        Transform {
            translation -20 -20 -20 # In the other direction
            rotation 0.2 0.3 0.5 0 # Skew it a bit
        }

        Material {
            specularColor 0.0 0.0 1.0 # shiny blue
            shininess 0.9 # very shiny
            transparency .5 # translucent
        }

        Cylinder {
            radius 3
            height 5
        }
    }
}
```

Server Issues

VRML requires no change to existing Web infrastructure; the same mechanisms in place to transmit HTML, JPEG, or AU documents will suffice for VRML. A Web server, however, needs a single configuration change—it must map the VRML file extension (wrl) to the VRML MIME type of x-world/x-vrml. Without this mapping, the server will send the VRML file as a content type of text/plain, which means that ASCII of the VRML data file will end up in the browser window. After this small configuration change is made, however, users' Web browsers will be able to understand and interpret the VRML document correctly.

By convention, VRML documents can be sent in either a plain ASCII or compressed version. Compressed documents must be compressed with the Free Software Foundation's GZIP algorithm. (GZIP and its companion GUNZIP are freely available—in source or binary form—for all major platforms, via FTP at `athena-dist.mit.edu` in the /pub/gnu subdirectory.) It's up to the VRML browser to interpret GZIP content encoding and decompress the VRML file as it is received. Because of the ASCII nature of VRML documents, compression is highly recommended; file size reductions of 95 percent are not uncommon. In one VRML project, a 2.4 MB file was reduced to 80 KB!

The greatest concern to the systems administrator of a large VRML site is the load placed onto the server by VRML documents that reference many subsidiary documents—through WWWInline—located upon the same server. One file access can potentially lead to hundreds of others, all on the same server, all for the same world. This means that a poorly designed server strategy, mixed with a distributed VRML document could be a disasterous combination; a few access and suddenly hundreds (if not thousands) of HTTP requests bring the server to its knees. For this reason, it is strongly advised that system adminstrators analyze all large-scale VRML worlds before they are published in order to determine an effective distribution strategy for the VRML files.

VRML Scripting

As with HTML, it's quite easy to write scripts to do on-the-fly generation of VRML documents. In addition, because of the power of the WWWInline node, which allows the arbitrary nesting of VRML documents within VRML documents, a script can build a world from a library of prebuilt components. Any language—Java, C++, Visual Basic, and so on—can be used to create a VRML script, but Web site administrators have selected PERL for its flexibility and widespread availability, as the Web's scripting language of choice. A PERL script implemented within a Web server must send content type information back to the client browser, so that the data can be identified as VRML data. Here's a simple PERL script whose output matches the simple VRML world given previously:

```
#!/usr/bin/perl
#
# Sample Web script in PERL
# Written by Mark Pesce, September 1995
# No rights reserved.
#
# Always send the content type before everything else
print "Content-type: x-world/x-vrml\n\n";
#
# Then send the file header
print "#VRML V1.0 ascii\n";
#
# Now output the content of the file
#
print "Separator { Separator { Material { emissiveColor 1 1 1 }
➥Sphere { radius 10 } }\n";
print "Separator { Transform { translation 20 20 20 } Material
➥{ diffuseColor 1 1 0 } ";
print "Cube { width 5 height 5 depth 5 } } \n";
print "Separator { Transform { translation -20 -20 -20 } ";
print "Material { specularColor 0 0 1 shininess 0.9 transparency
➥0.5 } Cylinder { radius 2 height 5 } } }\n";
#
#  All done.
#
```

Although this example has been written with Unix in mind, it's easy to modify it to work with other operating systems, such as Windows or the Macintosh.

Optimizing VRML

VRML files can be huge; it's not difficult to design a model that quickly zooms up to a megabyte of data. Because of this, a number of data reduction techniques have been developed to reduce the size of VRML files. The most significant of these, known as *datafat munging,* removes extraneous precision from VRML files. Most 3D models created by programs such as AutoCAD, 3D Studio, and so forth, are expressed to six or seven significant digits of precison, while a VRML browser can't display more than two significant digits of precision. The solution is obvious—remove the extraneous precision and cut the file size by 50 percent. These files also render to the display more quickly, due in part to the decreased precision. One datafat munger, written in PERL by James Waldrop, is available through the SDSC VRML Repository, at `http://sdsc.edu/vrml/`.

It is very important to keep VRML worlds lightweight. At this early stage, most VRML browsers have no load-balancing features, so it's up to the designers of VRML environments to think through their designs, not just aesthetically, but also in terms of client performance. A practical limit for the number of polygons which should be in any scene—this includes objects brought in through WWWInline—is about 10,000. Remarkably, this figure is the same for a high-performance workstation and a personal computer; that means it's not going to change very soon. The LOD node, which presents an object (or a set of objects) at a variety of resolutions, can be used to reduce scene complexity because a browser will only use the more complex descriptions in an LOD node when it determines that these descriptions will not significantly impair rendering performance for the user.

The Future of VRML

The architects of VRML are rapidly moving toward the development of a sucessor to VRML 1.0, designed to address several of the major constraints of VRML, including scalability, streaming, interactivity, and behaviors. For more information about changes to the VRML specification and features in future versions of VRML, please refer to the VRML Architecture Group home page at the URL `http://vrml.wired.com/VAG`.

System Administrator's Guide to the MBone

by Vinay Kumar

It is time for you to take a look at what it takes for an organization to install MBone technology for corporate use. Most organizations today have a variety of computers that they use. In most cases, it is not one kind of computer or operating system; the corporate computing environment might consist of one or more of the following brands of computers and operating systems:

- *PCs running DOS, DOS and Windows 3.1+, Windows NT, and Windows 95*
- *PCs running SolarisX86, Linux, and FreeBSD or BSDI Unix*

- SUN workstations running SunOS 4.1.x and Solaris 2.x
- SGI workstations running IRIX5.2+
- DEC Alpha's running OSFV2.0+ and Windows NT
- IBM RS6000 running AIX3.2+
- HP workstations running HPUX and Windows NT

These are only some of the more popular platforms—there are others, of course. The same is true for the networking of computers. These computers could be interconnected on a LAN over Ethernet, FDDI, or CDDI running Novell NetWare, TCP/IP, or Novell IPX. With such a wide variety of choices and a heterogeneity in the office computing environment, how do you overlay an existing office computing infrastructure to support the MBone multimedia? Besides setting up, configuring, and debugging the MBone connection at your organization end, it is also important to see how to tie in security issues such as firewalls while accessing and providing rich multimedia content via the MBone. All such issues are dealt with in this chapter.

The MBone Starter Kit

A few distinct issues need to be addressed before you install and use the MBone within your organization. These issues are as follows:

- Does each desktop in your organization support IP multicasting?
- Does your organization have a multicast router?
- Does each desktop user have access to the MBone applications for use?

The answers to such questions will be resolved in subsequent sections. The first issue deals with desktop users directly. It is the responsibility of the user or system administrator to see whether an existing desktop supports IP multicasting (or IGMP) in the desktop operating system. If it does not, then the desktop needs to be configured appropriately for IP multicasting. There is no automatic way to find out whether your operating system supports IP multicasting, however. Check the operating system manual to see if it supports IGMP or IP multicasting.

Configuring Desktop Computers for IP Multicasting

Getting each machine in your organization ready to send and/or receive multimedia data streams requires that the machine's operating system understands the class D addressed IP multicast packets. This will enable the machines to send and receive the MBone multimedia traffic. Besides sending and receiving the MBone data traffic from the network, support is also needed in rendering the multimedia traffic received to the user—for example, rendering video frames to the Super Video Graphics Adaptor (SVGA) display, to the television, or to the VCR. Such support requires the addition of proper multimedia hardware to your desktop workstation.

Therefore, for purposes of this chapter, you will learn to configure desktop machines for IP multicasting using the appropriate software first, followed by a discussion of the required hardware and multimedia support. These discussions will be broken down by computer operating systems.

IP Multicasting for Unix Computers

Most new Unix machines in the market come factory bundled with operating system support for IP multicasting or the IGMP inside the kernel. If you have an older machine, chances are that its operating system does not support IP multicast extensions. In that case, software for upgrading your Unix operating system kernel to support IP multicasting is available either from the workstation vendor or from one of the anonymous FTP sites that archives IP multicasting operating system kernel extensions.

Note Most computers that are connected to the MBone today have installed version 2.2 or higher of the multicast operating system kernel patches. Version 3.6 is the latest version that has been released at the time of writing this book.

If you have SUN workstations in your organization that are running the SunOS 4.1.x, you can get a copy of the IP multicast operating system kernel software extension version 3.5 for free via anonymous FTP using any FTP client on your desktop.

> **Warning** Only the system administrators and knowledgeable individuals should apply the kernel patches—the process of applying the patches assumes that you know how to configure and build a new operating system kernel. If you do not, then consult your system administrator to do this for you, or read the operating system's manual and documentation for your computer desktop.

The software distribution for IP multicast extensions from any of the FTP sites mentioned in this chapter comes pre-bundled with a full set of instructions through a README-3.5 file on how to manually apply these version 3.5 patches to a standard SunOS 4.1.x kernel. A script called mcast_install also comes bundled with this distribution—it can automatically install these IP multicast patches for you. Instructions are also included on how to upgrade to version 3.5 of IP multicast kernel patches from previous versions—that is, version 3.3 and version 2.2. If you already have a machine with an older version of multicast operating system kernel, then you can upgrade easily as well.

Alternative FTP sites for version 3.5 of IP multicast kernel operating system patches are shown in table 32.1.

Table 32.1
FTP Sites for Version 3.5 of IP Multicast Extensions to SunOS 4.1.x

FTP Site	Directory	Filename
ftp.udel.edu	/pub/mbone/	ipmulti3.5-sunos41x.tar.Z
ftp.adelaide.edu.au	/pub/av/multicast/	ipmulti3.5-sunos41x.tar.Z
ftp.ucs.ed.ac.uk	/pub/video-conference/ ipmulticast/	ipmulti3.5-sunos41x.tar.Z

If you have machines other than SunOS 4.1.x workstations, then you are out of luck as far as version 3.5 of the IP multicast kernel patches are concerned. Efforts are in progress, however, to make this version available for non-SunOS 4.1.x machines. By the time this book is published, one of the FTP sites listed in table 32.1 should have IP multicast kernel software for other Unix platforms as well.

IP Multicast Patches Version 3.3 to SunOS 4.1.x

The most widely used version for IP multicasting is version 3.3. It is fully compatible with the previous, as well as the new version 3.5. Most sites today use version 3.3 for their SunOS 4.1.x machines. This was the first version of IP multicast kernels that included a form of minimal Resource Reservation Protocol (RSVP) support. As a result, the multicast routers could now pre-allocate a certain amount of bandwidth for the MBone traffic. A list of FTP sites from which to access this version of IP multicast kernel patches is shown in table 32.2.

Table 32.2
FTP Sites for Version 3.3 of the IP Multicast Kernel Patches for the SunOS 4.1.x

FTP Site	Directory	Filename
ftp.adelaide.edu.au	/pub/av/multicast/	ipmulti3.3-sunos413x.tar.Z
ftp.ucs.ed.ac.uk	/pub/videoconference/ ipmulticast/	ipmulti3.3-sunos413x.tar.Z
parcftp.xerox.com	/pub/net-research/ ipmulti/historical	ipmulti3.3-sunos413x.tar.Z
ftp.uni-stuttgart.de	/pub/comm/multimedia/	ipmulti3.3-sunos413x.tar.Z

IP Multicast Patches: Version 3.3 to DEC-Ultrix

The version 3.3 kernel patches for the DEC-Ultrix 4.x operating system are available from the sites shown in table 32.3.

Table 32.3
FTP Sites for the DEC Ultrix IP Multicast Kernel Patches

FTP Site	Directory	Filename
ftp.adelaide.edu.au	/pub/av/multicast/	ipmulticast- ultrix4.1.patch.Z ipmulticast-ultrix4.2a-binary.tar.Z ipmulticast-ultrix4.2a.patch.Z
ftp.ucs.ed.ac.uk	/pub/video-conference/ipmulticast/	ipmulti3.3-ultrix4.4-patch

Before you go on to explore various FTP sites for other Unix platforms, it is important to note that most new Unix workstations come with factory-built support for IP multicasting version 2.2 or higher in their operating system kernel. Therefore, you may not have to specifically configure your desktop machine for IP multicasting. Table 32.4 contains a listing of various versions of IP multicast kernel patches for different Unix operating systems.

Table 32.4
FTP Sites for IP Multicast Kernel Patches for Unix Systems

IP Multicast Version	Computing Platform	FTP Site	Directory	Filename
Version 2.2	HP-UX 9.01	ftp.ucs.ed.ac.uk	/pub/video-conference/ipmulticast/	hp-ipmulti.tar.Z
	SGI-IRIX 4.0x	ftp.ucs.ed.ac.	/pub/video-conference/ipmulticast/	ipmulti-sgi40x.tar.Z
	DEC-OSF1	ftp.ucs.ed ac.uk	/pub/video-conference/ipmulticast/	ipmulti-decosf1.tar.Z

IP Multicast Version	Computing Platform	FTP Site	Directory	Filename
	BSD 386	ftp.uni-stuttgart.de	/pub/comm/multimedia/1386/	bsd386-ipmcast.tar.Z
	SGI-IRIX 5.1+	fgi.sgi.com	/sgi/ipmcast/IRIX5/	irix5.3.tar.Z

IP Multicasting on Intel PCs Running Microsoft Windows/DOS

It is clear by now that IP multicast support is needed in the desktop operating system. In previous sections, such support in Unix environments was described. There is similar support available, however, for the popular MS Windows systems as well. In addition, Microsoft Corp. has announced support for IGMP into their Microsoft Windows NT and Windows 95 operating systems products. More information on Microsoft's support for IP multicasting in Windows NT and Windows 95 is available from Microsoft's anonymous FTP site, as follows:

```
%ftp ftp.microsoft.com
% Name: anonymous
% password: <login_name@org_name.com>
ftp>cd /bussys/WinSock/ms-ext/
ftp>bin
ftp>get MULTICAST.TXT
ftp>get winsock.h
ftp>get VXDTD1.DOC
ftp>get party.c
ftp>get party.exe
ftp>quit
```

The file winsock.h provides the multicast extensions for Win32. A sample multicast program in C with the names *party.c* and *party.exe* is also included in the distribution.

Another software company, FTP Software, Inc., an Internet company, has a TCP/IP stack product for MS Windows operating systems called PC/TCP® (3.0) and PC/TCP OnNet® (1.1), which supports IP multicast. Several developers have tested and used this product for building MBone software. More information on this product is available on the World Wide Web at the following URL:

```
http://www.ftp.com/mkt_info/advfeats.html
```

IP Multicasting for Macintosh Systems

Apple Computer, Inc. supports IP multicasting in its new MacOS-7.5.2. The new TCP/IP stack under the MacOS operating system is called Mac OpenTransport version 1.0b2, and follows the System V Unix-like network programming interface. The Mac OpenTransport replaces Apple's earlier MacTCP stack. Some documentation on IP multicasting support in the new MacOS 7.5.2, as well as their TCP/IP Application Programming Interface (API), is now available via anonymous FTP, as follows:

```
%ftp seeding.apple.com
% Name: anonymous
% password: <login_name@org_name.com>
ftp>cd /ess/public/opentransport/OT_Docs_textonly/
ftp>get OT_TCPIP
ftp>quit
```

Hardware Peripherals for the MBone Desktop

In order to be able to fully participate in the MBone multimedia sessions, desktop users need to be able to send and receive multimedia information. This includes voice, video, graphics, and text. Most desktop computers you buy in the market today have multimedia capabilities, but the older legacy models do not. Thus, in this section, you will find tips on adding such multimedia support to the user desktop.

RISC-Based Unix Workstations

Most Unix workstations come bundled with audio input and output hardware—therefore, there may be no need to buy audio hardware. Most RISC-based Unix workstations support at least 8-bit, full-duplex operations. So what is a full-duplex operation?

As shown in figure 32.1, two main kinds of data flow schemes exist: the half-duplex and the full-duplex. In a *half-duplex* operation, data flows only in one direction at any given time between two or more endpoints, and each endpoint can either transmit or receive at any given time. In a *full-duplex* model, however, the communication endpoints can transmit and receive simultaneously—there is free flow of information in a bi-directional manner.

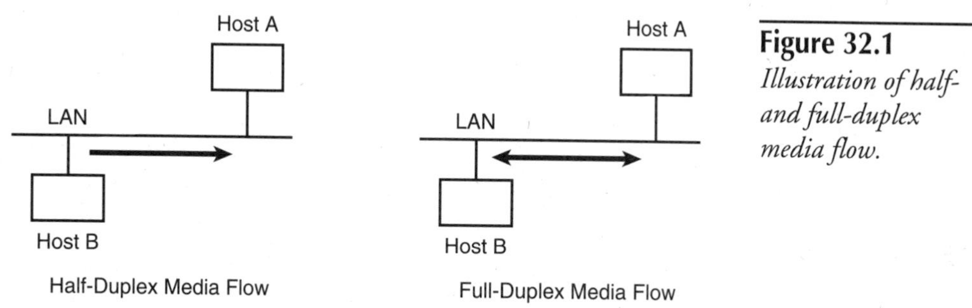

Figure 32.1
Illustration of half- and full-duplex media flow.

Full-duplex operation is very critical for doing two-way free-form voice conversations. Full-duplex operation allows input and output of voice data simultaneously. This is not essential, however, if your application demands only one-way operation (either input or output) at any given time. The next sections examine some of the live video grabber cards that are most commonly used on the MBone.

VigraPix Video Card

VigraPix Corp. makes a video digitizer board called the VigraPix card for the SUN workstations that plugs into the SBus of the workstation. It is a single-slot card designed to capture data from standard video sources. It includes one composite video and two S-video inputs; it is also capable of digitizing National Television Standards Committee (NTSC), Phase Alternation Line (PAL), and Sequential Couleur A Memoire (SECAM) signals to display still or live video on a standard SUN workstation. The VigraPix card also supports NetVideo (NV) video compression and decompression in hardware. As a result, it works very well with the NetVideo videoconferencing software by achieving higher quality video and faster frame rates. This product supports libraries for SunOS 4.1.x and Solaris 2.x. More information on the product is available by contacting the following:

VigraPix Inc.
Division of VisiCom Laboratories
10052 Mesa Ridge Court
San Diego, CA 92121
World Wide Web: `http://www.vigra.com/`
Voice mail: +1-619-597-7080
Toll-free number: 1-800-66-VIGRA (1-800-668-4472)
E-mail: `sales@vigra.com`
Fax: +1-619-597-7094

PowerVideo and MultiVideo Cards

Parallax Graphics, Inc. makes a video grabber card called the PowerVideo card. It is an SBus card and supports real-time video capture, playback, and networking of high-quality digital video and still images, using hardware JPEG compression and decompression. This product also supports video output S-VHS to a VCR. For additional information on this product, contact the following:

Parallax Graphics, Inc.
2500 Condensa Street
Santa Clara, CA 95051
World Wide Web: `http://www.parallax.com/`
Phone: +1-408-727-2220
E-mail: `info@parallax.com`
Fax: +1-408-980-5139

DEC J300 Sound and Video Card for Alpha Workstations

The Digital Alpha workstations also support a lot of multimedia capabilities. The Alpha line of workstations from DEC come pre-bundled with the J300 sound and video digitizer board. The card supports full-motion video input in NTSC, PAL, and SECAM in both composite and S-video formats. Video can be captured and displayed on the workstation screen in 8-bit pseudo-color, 8-bit grayscale, or 24-bit true color formats.

The J300 video card can take the digital video stream on the computer workstation display and output it as NTSC or PAL video in S-video or composite formats to an analog videotape on a VCR. The card can also record such digital video data to writeable optical disc, or display on a TV monitor. JPEG video compression and decompression standard is supported in the J300 hardware itself. This helps MBone videoconferencing software such as NV or VIC to produce better performance in terms of quality of video reproduction and faster frame rates. The DEC J300 video card is priced at $2,795 (U.S.).

For a description of this software product, access the following FTP site on the Internet:

```
gatekeeper.dec.com under the directory /pub/DEC/Decinfo/SPD/
```

Information data sheets are available at the following FTP sites on the Internet:

```
gatekeeper.dec.com under /pub/DEC/infosheets/sound-motion-j300.txt
```

```
gatekeeper.dec.com under /pub/DEC/infosheets/multimedia-
services.txt
```

SunVideo Frame Grabber Card

The SunVideo board is a SUN SBus card. Video connectors support two composite and one S-video input. The SunVideo card senses whether the source is NTSC or PAL and configures itself appropriately. A video RISC processor, the C-Cube CL4000, is used to perform compression in multiple standard formats: JPEG, MPEG-1, and Cell. Solaris version 2.3 or later release is supported. Contact your local SUN reseller for details, or get more information from the World Wide Web at the following:

```
http://www.sun.com/smi/bang/SunVideo.html
```

SUN VideoPix Card

The VideoPix Card from SUN is also an SBus card. It is the older generation card—slower, but cheaper than most current generation video digitizer boards that are out in the market. The VideoPix board does not support hardware-based video compression or decompression, but it performs fairly well with SunOS 4.1.x and the MBone video conferencing software such as NV and VIC. This product accepts NTSC, PAL, and S-video inputs. The Solaris 2.x version of the video libraries has also been ported, and it can be accessed via anonymous FTP from the following site:

```
playground.sun.com under /pub/videopix/
```

Note Silicon Graphics, Inc. also sells a video digitizer card called the Indigo Video Card. Similarly, Hewlett-Packard, Inc. sells the MediaMagic 700 video card on the market.

Intel Computers Running MS Windows

Although most of the traditional desktop PCs running MS Windows are multimedia PCs, the multimedia hardware in these PCs is designed to do only local multimedia and not networked multimedia. Local multimedia means playing and displaying multimedia files from the hard disk, the CD-ROM drive, and local direct input such as microphone or video camera. To play networked MBone multimedia, proper multimedia hardware is needed. Voice digitizers should be full-duplexed if the desktop PC is to be used for MBone-based voice conferencing so that the boards can digitize voice from the microphone while playing back remote voice from the network such as the MBone. Generally, it might be difficult to get PC sound cards to do exactly 8 kHz because these cards tend to support sampling frequencies that are 11.025 kHz, 22.1 kHz, and higher.

Gravis Ultrasound (GUS) Corp. sells various kinds of GUS sound digitizer boards. One of these is a higher-performance version called the UltraMax version 3.4, which records and plays back 16-bit voice up to 48 kHz with ADPCM, μ-law, and a-law voice compression. GUS voice cards cost about $200 (U.S.).

GUS FTP sites in North America are as follows:

```
archive.orst.edu under/pub/packages/gravis

wuarchive.wustl.edu under/systems/ibmpc /ultrasound
```

The ProAudio Spectrum voice digitizer card from Mediavision Corp. can be used for full-duplex audio. The card is full-duplex because it contains two sound boards in one—an 8-bit SoundBlaster, as well as the ProAudio Spectrum part. The Artisoft sound board also supports full-duplex voice and does μ-law voice encoding. Several other vendors sell sound boards as well—a few of them are listed in the following:

1. Adlib Multimedia, Inc.—sound hardware
   220 Grande Allee East, Suite 850
   Quebec, QC, Canada G1R 2J1
   Phone: 800-463-2686, +1-418-529-9676

2. Advanced Gravis Computer Technology Limited—sound hardware
   111-7400 MacPherson Ave.
   Burnaby, B.C., Canada V5J 5B6
   Main phone: 604-431-5020
   Support phone: 604-431-1807
   E-mail: `tech@gravis.com`
   Fax: 604-431-5155

3. Cardinal Technologies—sound hardware
   1827 Freedom Road
   Lancaster, PA 17601
   Phone: 717-293-3000

4. Covox, Inc.—sound hardware
   675 Conger Street
   Eugene, OR 97402
   Main: 503-342-1271
   BBS: 503-342-4135
   E-mail: `71333.167@CompuServe.com`
   Fax: 503-342-1283

5. Creative Labs/Brown Wagh (Soundblaster)—sound hardware
   2050 Duane Avenue
   Santa Clara, CA 95054
   Main: 408-428-6600
   Sales: 800-998-1000
   Support: 405-742-6622
   Fax: 405-742-6644 (742-6633?)

6. MediaVision, Inc. (ProAudio Spectrum)—sound hardware
   47221 Fremont Blvd
   Fremont, CA 94539
   Main: 800-348-7116 or 510-770-8600
   Sales: 800-845-5870

Support: 800-638-2807 or 510-770-9905
Fax: 510-770-8648 or 510-770-9592
BBS: 510-770-0968 and 770-1661 (2400,8,N,1)
510-770-0527 (9600,8,N,1)

7. Turtle Beach Systems—sound hardware
   Cyber Center, Unit 33, 1600 Pennsylvania Ave.
   York, PA 17404
   Main: 717-843-6916
   E-mail: `75300.1374@CompuServe.com`
   (Turtle Beach*Roy Smith)
   Fax: 717-854-8319

The following section lists names and addresses of video card manufacturers and vendors. Before you go out and buy any video digitizer board on the market, ask at least the following questions about the board:

- Does the video card take NTSC Composite and S-video inputs? Is PAL video input support adequate?
- What pixel sizes are supported by the video card? Can the card support 512×512 video samples at 24-bits per pixel, as well as other sizes?
- Does the video card support hardware-based reduction of digitized video images to 8-bit color or grayscale modes?
- Does the card support hardware-based video compression and decompression algorithms such as H.261, JPEG, MPEG, NV, and so forth?
- Is there a video card-compatible software available that will enable you to display and save video images in color or grayscale—8-, 16-, or 24-bit color formats? What video and image formats are supported to save such files?

The video cards may support additional features as well, but the ones listed in the preceding are the key. Some video card manufacturers and vendors are as follows:

1. Digital Vision, Inc.(ComputerEyes/RT)—video hardware
   List price: $399.95 (U.S.)
   270 Bridge Street
   Dedham, MA 02026
   Voice: +1-617-329-5400
   E-mail: `digvis@tiac.net`

2. miro Computer Products, Inc. (miroVideo DC1 TV)—video hardware
   List price: $899 (U.S.)

3. Orchid Technology, Inc. (Orchid Vidiola Pro/D)—video hardware
   List price: $699 (U.S.)

4. Hauppauge Computer Works (Win/TV Cinema/TV-Celebrity/TV-HighQ)—video hardware
   List price: Cinema—$349, Celebrity—$449, HighQ—$499 (U.S.)

5. ATI Technologies, Inc. (Video Basic, Video-It)—video hardware
   List price: $249, $499 (U.S.)

Macintosh Computers

The Macintosh computers have excellent multimedia support—almost all new Macs come factory built with all kinds of audio and video hardware and software. Unlike the Intel PC/Windows market, the Macintosh market is not as fragmented. As a result, users do not have to worry about buying and installing audio, video hardware, and driver software for the hardware, in addition to the application software itself. Most of the MacOS systems support full-duplex audio and video streams I/O. In case your Mac does not support the video digitizer card, the following lists a few you can buy on the market:

1. Video Spigot hardware
   List price: approximately $380

2. Digital Vision, Inc. (ComputerEyes/RT SCSI port digitizer)—video hardware
   List price: $599.99
   270 Bridge Street
   Dedham, MA 02026
   Voice: +1-617-329-5400
   E-mail: `digvis@tiac.net`

Video Cameras

In a multimedia MBone session involving real-time video, video cameras and VCRs act as the NTSC, PAL, and S-video video sources. These video sources feed input for the video digitizer boards that are connected to your desktop workstations. There are several analog video cameras that sell on the market, but some of them that have been tried in office desktop lighting conditions are mentioned here:

- Connectix, Inc. sells a popular $99 video camera for Macintosh computers called QuickCam. This portable camera works well as an NTSC video source for the Macintosh desktop.
- VideoLabs, Inc. sells FlexCam, a $600 CCD color video camera unit with a built-in flexible stand. This unit works fairly well for desktop conferencing.
- SonyTR-61 color palmcorder is a popular model.
- SGI Indy workstations come bundled with the IndyCam video cameras as well.

So far, you have learned about the desktop operating systems and their support for IP multicasting, and various multimedia hardware peripheral devices such as audio, video cards, and video cameras that are required to do multimedia interactions over the MBone. The next step is then to use the hardware and software mentioned in previous sections of this chapter to set up, configure, and debug an MBone connection at your local end.

Configure the Tunnel and the Mrouter

The first step toward setting up an MBone connection within your organization requires setting up an MBone tunnel at your end, followed by configuration of the multicast router so that the MBone multimedia packets can flow between your site and the rest of the MBone. The MBone information packets get routed between subnets over the MBone tunnels. The multicast router, also called the mrouter or mrouted (for multicast routing daemon), is responsible for forwarding such packets over the tunnels between different subnets.

The mrouted program is a software package that is available for free from the Internet FTP sites. These sites are usually the same ones as those used for IP multicast operating system kernel extension software. The mrouted program was designed and developed to run on any Internet server class Unix machines; plan to run the MBone router "mrouted" on an IP multicast-capable Unix machine on your local Net.

Before you run the mrouted program, the file /etc/mrouted.conf needs to be configured appropriately. The README file included in the software distribution that comprises the IP multicast operating system kernel patches describes how to configure the mrouted.conf file. A sample mrouted.conf file for IP multicast version 3.5 or greater looks like the following:

```
# name <boundname> <scoped-addr>/<mask-len>
# cache_lifetime 3600           # seconds
# pruning on
#
# phyint <local-addr> [disable] [metric <m>] [threshold <t>]
# [rate_limit <b>]
#                [boundary (<boundname>¦<scoped-addr>/<mask-len>)]
#                         [altnet (<subnet>/<mask-len>¦<subnet>)]
# tunnel <local-addr> <remote-addr> [srcrt] [metric <m>]
#                                 [threshold <t>] [rate_limit <b>]
#                [boundary (<boundname>¦<scoped-addr>/<mask-len>)]
#
#   NOTE: any phyint commands MU.S.T precede any tunnel commands
#   NOTE: the mask-len is the no. of leading 1's in the mask
#   NOTE: rate_limit is in kilobits, and defaults to 500 for
#   tunnels
```

```
# Example of named boundary:
#name LOCAL 239.255.0.0/16
#name EE 239.254.0.0/16        # i.e. the EE dept wants local groups
#
# Example of use of named boundary
#phyint le1 boundary EE          # le1 is our interface to comp sci,
#                               # keep them away from our local groups
#
#
# Template tunnel
tunnel 128.4.0.77 128.4.0.8 metric 1 threshold 64 rate_limit 500
# <_ REPLACE
#       boundary LOCAL
#
# You might want to specify a boundary on your tunnel to the
# outside world, as above.
```

All the commands that are listed in the preceding sample /etc/mrouted.conf file are now described.

The *Phyint* command precedes the tunnel command and is used to disable multicast routing on the specified network interface. The network interface may be described by the <local-addr>, or network interface type—that is, le0 (Lance Ethernet), ie0 (Intel Ethernet), and so forth. For multihomed hosts running as an mrouter, multicast routing could be disabled by specifying subnets via <altnet> keyword.

The *tunnel* command can be used to establish a tunnel link between local IP address <local-addr> of the mrouter and remote IP address <remote-addr> of the MBone service provider's mrouter.

The *rate_limit* option enables the network administrator to specify a certain bandwidth in Kilobits per second that would be allocated to multicast traffic. It defaults to 500 Kbps on tunnels, and 0 (unlimited) on physical interfaces.

The *boundary* option allows an interface to be configured as an administrative boundary for the specified scoped address. Packets belonging to this address will not be forwarded on a scoped interface. The boundary option accepts either a name or a boundary specification.

A sample /etc/mrouted.conf file may look like this:

```
#
# mrouted.conf example
#
# Name our boundaries to make it easier
name LOCAL 239.255.0.0/16
name MIS 239.254.0.0/16
#
# le1 is our gateway to HRD, don't forward our
#     local groups to them
phyint le1 boundary MIS
#
# le2 is our interface on the webgroup net, it has four
#     different length subnets on it.
# note that you can use either an ip address or an
# interface name
phyint 172.16.12.38 boundary MIS altnet 172.16.15.0/26
     altnet 172.16.15.128/26 altnet 172.16.48.0/24
#
# atm0 is our ATM interface, which doesn't properly
#      support multicasting.
phyint atm0 disable
#
# This is an internal tunnel to another MIS subnet
# Remove the default tunnel rate limit, since this
#   tunnel is over ethernets
tunnel 192.168.5.4 192.168.55.101 metric 1 threshold 1rate_limit 0
#
# This is our tunnel to the outside world. Be careful with those
# boundaries.
tunnel 192.168.5.4 10.11.12.13 metric 1 threshold 32
     boundary LOCAL boundary MIS
```

After configuring the /etc/mrouted.conf file, send a request to your local IP service provider for a tunnel. A sample e-mail request for establishing a tunnel between your organization and the global MBone may look like this:

> To: mbone@isi.edu
> From: <you>
> Subject: Request for Tunnel
> Cc: <your_local_mbone_service_provider>,
> <your_local_ip_service_provider>

> I would like to add my site <mydomain.com> to the MBone via a tunnel. Here is how my tunnel endpoint configuration should look:

```
Mrouter machine configuration: SunSPARC10, SunOS 4.1.3_U1, sun4m
Multicast kernel patches applied: version 3.5
ftp://parcftp.xerox.com/pub/netresearch/ipmulti/ipmu   lti3.5-
➥sunos41x.tar.Z
Mrouter machine (my tunnel endpoint) IP address: 192.100.x.x
```

> The MBone administrator contact address is as follows:
>
> Vinay Kumar
> XYZ, Inc.
> 5000 Page Mill Road
> Redwood Park, CA 93333
> Voice (daytime): +1-415-555-1212
> E-mail: `vinay@xyz.com`
>
> Any help in providing me with a tunnel will be greatly appreciated.

After you receive a confirmation on your request from your MBone service provider, you may have to go back to the /etc/mrouted.conf file and edit it minimally to reflect the MBone provider's end of the tunnel. Once configured, you are now ready to start the mrouted daemon by typing the following command:

```
/etc/mrouted [-p] [-c config_file] [-d [debug_level]]
```

Note You do not have to run the mrouted if you do not want to route the IP multicast packets outside your local subnet. In addition, mrouted should not be run on the same machine that routes IP unicast packets—mrouted routes IP multicast packets only.

It is important to run the mrouted version 2.2 or higher. If you have not installed MBone yet, then you should install version 3.6 or higher—it is more efficient in terms of better bandwidth and network management, and also fixes problems from earlier versions.

If on using one of the MBone applications on a machine that has no multicast routes on it, then you may see the following error message:

```
IP_ADD_MEMBERSHIP: Can't assign requested address
```

This is fixed by doing one of the following. You need either a "default" route or a route to 224.0.0.0, which points to the network interface you want to use to send multicast packets. If your host only has one interface, run the following command as root:

```
route add 224.0.0.0 'your_local_hostname' 0
```

If you have more than one interface, replace the 'hostname' with the host name or address for the interface you want to use.

If, on the other hand, you do not see any error messages on your screen, this means your MBone tunnel is almost up and running, and you may be connected to the MBone. How can you be sure that you are connected? You will find this out in the next section.

Testing Your MBone Connection

Once the tunnel can be configured at both ends—that is, your end, as well as your MBone service provider's end—it's time to do a few simple tests to see whether you are connected to the MBone. There are two approaches to accomplish this. The simple approach is to run the MBone application software called the SD tool. Just type the following command on any IP multicast-enabled Unix machine connected to the same subnet as the mrouter:

```
sd &
```

You should see the SD window on your screen. Let the program run for a few minutes. If you see MBone session names such as "MBone Audio," "MBone Video," and "Radio Free Vat" begin to appear in the SD window, this means your MBone connection is up and running. The IP multicast packets, therefore, are flowing from the rest of the MBone to your subnet.

This was the easy test. You can also test the MBone connection by running one of the MBone debugging tools explained later in the chapter.

If you do not see anything in the SD window, however, then you know that there is a problem somewhere in the installation and configuration of the MBone tunnel, or in mrouted, either at your end or your MBone service provider's end. The best way to fix this is to use the MBone debugging tools to isolate the problem and read the manual (or help) pages that are included with the software that is being used. In addition, you can always consult the appropriate Internet mailing lists or product vendors for help.

Disabling the MBone Tunnel

If at any point in time your organization decides to disconnect from the MBone, then it is not a difficult process. The MBone architecture is very flexible in allowing such operations without affecting others on the MBone, except if you are an MBone service provider. As a result of tearing down your tunnel, the IP multicast traffic that flows over your MBone tunnel into and out of your subnet will be simply turned off. In order to do this, simply log in to the multicast routing machine on your subnet, find the process ID of the mrouted program, and kill the process. This can be done as follows on most Unix machines:

```
% ps -e ¦ grep mrouted
<This will output the process ID of the mrouted program>
% kill -9 <mrouted_process_id>
```

This will shut off the routing of IP multicast traffic to and from your subnet. Running the mrouted process again will reestablish the tunnel and the IP multicast traffic will start flowing smoothly again. It is thus easy to see that tearing down the tunnel and bringing it back up is not very difficult and can be done anytime. The MBone service providers should not do this, however, unless it is for very specific reasons. Tearing down a tunnel at the MBone service provider's end can easily affect other tunnels because one tunnel may feed IP multicast data streams into other tunnels or subnets.

Note Note that if your organization, your MBone service provider, and all the intervening IP routers use IP multicast routing-enabled hardware routers, such as Cisco System's Cisco-7000 router, then you do not need to follow the preceding instructions. Having native multicast routing in the hardware IP routers makes tunneling redundant—you therefore do not need MBone tunnels. The IP multicast packets get routed just like any other Internet packets because all the routers understand IP multicasting. You should consult the configuration manual provided by the router vendor to see how to configure such routers to connect to the MBone. In addition, consult with your MBone service provider to see what kind of router setup they have.

At this point, your organization is practically on the MBone. Now that you and everyone else in your organization is ready to experience the MBone, let's take one hard look at some of the related issues, such as security and firewalls. As a result of hooking up your organization to the MBone, a special type of Internet traffic called IP multicast data now flows through your local subnet. To make sure that no rogue packets or hackers use this route to infiltrate your subnet, let us briefly describe the measures one can take to thwart such attempts. Of course, for detailed discussion on network security and Internet firewalls, you should read the two books listed in the bibliography at the end of the chapter.

Firewalls and Security on the MBone

Network security is an important issue in almost any kind of internetworking, be it e-mail, FTP, the Web, or the MBone. Malicious packets sent out by remote rogue applications or wily hackers can penetrate a completely open network and cause damage to your resources. The Internet routers are configured in a specific way to filter out unwanted and undesirable packet traffic. One such technique of configuring the routers to allow only harmless, useful traffic is called *router filtering.* These filters are often used to provide what is called a *firewall* between your local subnet (or domain) and the rest of the global Internet. Filters are generally intended to allow a select set of IP hosts and network applications to communicate across the domain boundary, providing the advantages of the Internet connectivity, while minimizing the exposure of internal resources. A simple configuration of a firewall-based network is shown in figure 32.2.

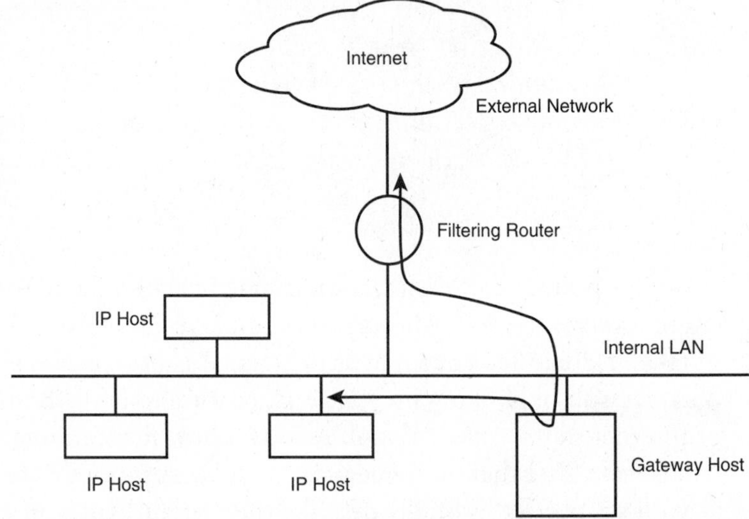

Figure 32.2
Securing an internal network via router filters and firewall gateways.

Previous work on defining gateway filters has concentrated on allowing communication between specific hosts or subnets (identified by IP source or destination addresses), providing access to specific source and destination addresses, and providing access to specific applications that are identified by IP protocol and port numbers. The following section looks at the router filter requirements for allowing IP multicast tunnels through a firewall gateway.

There are two distinct types of IP packets associated with the MBone packet traffic:

- IGMP group membership and routing update packets
- IP multicast data packets

These types of packets are discussed in the following sections.

IGMP Packets

The IGMP membership query messages from the local mrouter, and the corresponding IGMP membership reports for active multicast groups from IP hosts on the subnet, are never propagated beyond the local subnet.

As shown in figure 32.3, the IGMP DVMRP routing update messages are exchanged between neighboring mrouters over an MBone tunnel, which presents two distinct cases. Messages exchanged between mrouters connected via a multicast-capable subnet are sent to the 224.0.0.4 multicast group, while neighbors connected via a tunnel unicast updates between tunnel endpoints. The multicast DVMRP updates are sent with a TTL of 1 and are not propagated beyond the local subnet. This leaves only the IGMP DVMRP tunnel-neighbor messages that cross the firewall boundary. These messages are identical for both "srcrt" and "encapsulated" tunnels. They can be easily identified by the IP source address and the IP destination address being the tunnel endpoints, and the IP protocol version number as 2—that is IGMP(2).

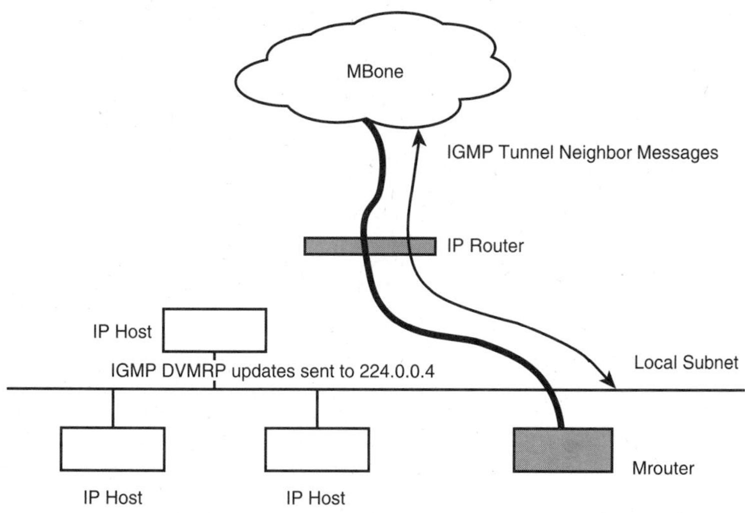

Figure 32.3
IGMP messages on the local subnet and over the MBone tunnel.

IP Multicast Data Packets

An IP multicast source on an IP host generates standard UDP/IP data packets, with the exception that the standard unicast IP destination address is replaced by a class D multicast address. These packets are then transmitted on a local multicast-capable subnet; it is the responsibility of the mrouters to forward these packets along the proper multicast distribution tree over the tunnel.

There are currently two forms of tunneling in use in the Internet today—those using an IP Loose Source Route option (srcrt), and those using IP-in-IP encapsulation (encapsulated). IP multicast packets traversing an encapsulated tunnel can be easily identified by the IP source address and IP destination address being the tunnel endpoints, and the IP protocol version number as 4. The srcrt'ed tunnel packets are more difficult to identify—they have the IP destination address as the tunnel destination endpoint address and an IP option set to LSRR(131) containing two recorded IP addresses, the first being the tunnel source endpoint and the second being the multicast destination group.

You now understand how most of the MBone packets appear. With this knowledge, you should be able to configure the filters on the routers appropriately. Note, however, that only the filter specifications for the encapsulated tunnels will be discussed, because they make up the majority of the tunnels on the MBone. Source routed tunnels have been outdated for a while and are being phased out.

Configuring the Firewall Filter

In figure 32.3, the MBone tunnel extends between the mrouter host on the internal subnet and another mrouter at the IP service provider's end. Let's designate the IP address of the tunnel endpoint within the local internal subnet as "IP.tnl_local," and IP address of tunnel endpoint at the remote end outside the firewall as "IP.tnl_remote." Now, in order to allow only IP multicast data and IGMP traffic to flow into or out of the internal subnet, the gateway machine will need to be configured. Using the tcpdump style expressions, discussed in a later section of this chapter, the IP multicast traffic that should be allowed through the firewall can be identified as follows:

```
(host IP.tnl_local and IP.tnl_remote) and (proto 2 or 4)
```

The traffic also can be broken down into outgoing and incoming data as

```
(src IP.tnl_local and dst IP.tnl_remote) and (proto 2 or 4)
```

and

```
(src IP.tnl_remote and dst IP.tnl_local) and (proto 2 or 4)
```

Translating this tcpdump style expression directly into a router filter definition may not be possible. For Cisco Systems router software releases 10.0(1) and newer, the desired filter definitions may be expressed as the following:

```
access-list 101 permit 2 IP.tnl_remote 0.0.0.0 IP.tnl_local
➥0.0.0.0
access-list 101 permit 4 IP.tnl_remote 0.0.0.0 IP.tnl_local
➥0.0.0.0
access-list 102 permit 2 IP.tnl_local 0.0.0.0 IP.tnl_remote
➥0.0.0.0
access-list 102 permit 4 IP.tnl_local 0.0.0.0 IP.tnl_remote
➥0.0.0.0
```

Configuring the gateway machine and the router filter definitions as explained in the preceding will allow IP multicast traffic to flow over your MBone tunnel. Please check the router configuration system manual that was provided by your router vendor—the manual should go into more detail on configuring the router.

Security Analysis

Assuming a firewall filter utilizing the IP.tnl_local, IP.tnl_remote, and proto is possible, opening up the firewall still implies a level of trust with the remote tunnel provider. Authentication of any form for the packets that flow over the tunnel does not exist; therefore, any IP host can spoof itself as the remote tunnel endpoint, and hence be able to mount any kind of attack. This imposter would be free to send through the firewall any IP packets destined to the local tunnel endpoint and marked as IGMP or IP-in-IP. What security implications does this raise?

If the router filters do not allow fine grain specification of filtering requirements, then access to various kinds of network services is very limited. It may provide greater security to internal network resources, however—a higher level granularity in specifying filter specification enables you to keep a balance between levels of security versus easy access to network service.

Having learned how to install and configure your MBone connectivity in a secure manner, let's now take a look at how to manage, maintain, and monitor the network for IP multicast traffic. Several MBone and network monitoring and debugging tools are discussed in the next section. Note that most of these tools are designed and developed to run on Unix machines.

Debugging and Monitoring the MBone

Once the network systems administrator has set up and installed the MBone connectivity for your organization, the administrator's job is not completely over. The administrator should be prepared to allocate some time and resources that may be required if there is a need to reconfigure your outside tunnel(s) or the internal MBone setup, monitor the network traffic that flows over your local end of the MBone tunnel, or debug network problems. Unfortunately, there aren't any commercial software tools available to help administrators manage their MBone connectivity. There are, however, a few freely available tools on the Internet. Most of these tools help to debug MBone-related network problems and monitor MBone multimedia traffic at your end-host site or tunnel endpoint. A set of such software utilities is described in the following section.

Tcpdump

The tcpdump tool is a very versatile software package that enables system administrators to not only monitor and isolate MBone-related network problems, but also help with all different kinds of Internet traffic. Here, let's see how tcpdump relates to IP multicast traffic analysis and debugging. The latest version of tcpdump version 3.0.2 was mainly developed by Van Jacobson, Craig Leres, and Steve McCanne of Lawrence Berkeley Laboratory, the University of California, Berkeley. Tcpdump is available via anonymous FTP from `ftp://ftp.ee.lbl.gov/tcpdump-3.0.2.tar.Z`.

Before you install this version of tcpdump at your site, you may want to take a look at the README file that is included in the software distribution. For a SunOS 4.1.x machine, installation of the tcpdump-3.0.2 may require installation of the packet capture utility libpcap version 0.0.6, which is available via anonymous FTP from `ftp://ftp.ee.lbl.gov/libpcap.tar.Z`

The installation of both libpcap and tcpdump is fairly easy—just follow the directions in the README files. Typing the following two commands in each directory may be sufficient:

```
% configure <return>
% make <return>
```

Tcpdump and libpcap have been built and tested under SGI Irix 4.x & 5.2, SunOS 4.x, Solaris 2.3, BSD/386 v1.1, DEC/OSF v1.3 v2.0, and Ultrix 4.x. SunOS 3.5, 4.3BSD Reno/Tahoe, and 4.4BSD are supported as well.

If installed on a SunOS machine, you may have to log in as root before you can use the tcpdump program. Tcpdump prints out the headers of packets on a network interface that matches the boolean expression:

```
% tcpdump expression
```

Thus, to monitor IGMP traffic on your subnet, type the following:

```
% tcpdump ip proto igmp
```

To get a dump of the multicast traffic that comes over your MBone tunnel to your local subnet, type the following:

```
% tcpdump src <IP.tnl_remote>
```

Most other features and commands for tcpdump can be looked up in the help file (or the man page) that is bundled with the software distribution. You can also look up the man page by typing the following:

```
% nroff -man tcpdump.1 ¦ more
```

Netstat

As the name suggests, netstat stands for Network statistics tool. It enables you to obtain IP multicast-related packet statistics. A few IP multicast-related options are mentioned in the following; however, netstat also facilitates collection of other Internet related traffic statistics.

- The "netstat -m" command recognizes four new multicast-related mbuf types.
- The IGMP statistics are now included in the "netstat -s" command output, or explicitly with the command "netstat -p igmp."
- The "netstat -a" option may be used when printing interface information; for example, typing the command **netstat -nia** will print out all addresses (unicast and multicast) associated with each network interface, including link-level addresses. The only link-level addresses currently recognized are Ethernet addresses, and then only for some types of Ethernet interface (that is, le).
- The "-M" option prints the kernel's multicast forwarding cache.
- The "-Ms" prints miscellaneous statistics related to multicast routing.

Before the "-p igmp" option will work, you must add the following line to the /etc/protocols:

```
igmp   2       IGMP           # internet group management protocol
```

Mrdebug

The mrdebug program is used to debug the multicast packet routing on the MBone. Mrdebug enables the user to display the multicast routes taken by a multicast message in a given network. The mrdebug program reads in the network topology and subnet descriptions from the files supplied to it. If given an IP source address for the multicast data stream, mrdebug then calculates the multicast tree. Mrdebug can display either the entire tree or the path from the IP source host to a particular destination host.

The format and contents of the subnet file and the topology file for mrdebug are described in detail in the help files included in the software distribution. This program was developed by Deborah Agarwal at Lawrence Berkeley Labs, and is available via anonymous FTP from `ftp://ftp.ee.lbl.gov/mrdebug.tar.Z`.

Note that the program will not run if not supplied with the topology and subnet files. The topology files can also be generated automatically via the mrmap program, described later in this chapter. The format of the file produced by the mrmap program is compatible with the topology file required for the mrdebug program.

This program can also be run interactively. The program asks the user different questions, and responds based on user's input. In the interactive mode, the user will be presented with the following commands on the screen:

```
Current source:
Current destination:
Enter command:
```

Typing **?** as a command will display all the command options supported. Detailed help on the mrdebug program is also available through the manual page that is included in the software distribution.

Multicast Ping

Packet Internet Groper (ping) is a standard utility for most TCP/IP implementations. The multicast-enabled ping software is available as part of the IP multicast kernel software distribution. The multicast ping software is included in the software distribution under the mrouted directory.

The modified ping provides control of the IP multicast transmission through the following new options:

- -l—inhibits multicast loopback.
- -t <ttl>—sets the multicast time-to-live to <ttl>.
- -i <addr>—sends multicasts from the interface with local address <addr>, given in a.b.c.d format.

This version of ping also supports the -R (record route) option.

Map-mbone

Map-mbone attempts to display the network topology of all the multicast routers that are reachable from any given multicast router on the MBone. If the IP address of the multicast router is not specified on the command line, then the map-mbone program assumes the default starting point for building the network topology as the local mrouter. To use this software, one must be logged in as root on your local host.

Map-mbone supports several other options as well. A manual help page is included as part of this freely available software on the Internet. Mrmap was developed by Pavel Curtis at Xerox PARC (Xerox Palo Alto Research Centre) Corp. An example displaying the use of this software is as follows:

```
#map-mbone collage.foo.com
192.50.58.17 (collage): <v2.2>
   192.50.58.17:  129.100.48.211 (morgul.mbone.net) [1/32/tunnel]
                     192.50.58.17 (collage) [1/1/querier]
```

Here, the map-mbone program was run on the host collage.foo.com. The program output shows that there is an MBone tunnel between the hosts collage.foo.com and morgul.mbone.net. The tunnel has the specifications of 1/32, meaning that the tunnel has the metric 1 and threshold 32. Also, the collage.foo.com multicast router is running version 2.2 of the mrouted program.

Rtpqual

Rtpqual is a simple multiprotocol multicast data (RTPv1) monitoring program. It allows end-hosts on the MBone to monitor the quality of the MBone multimedia data reception, especially if it is RTPv1-compliant. (RTPv1 stands for Real-Time Protocol, version 1.) The program understands the RTP protocol and listens for RTP messages, then computes and displays on the monitor statistics such as data packets received, lost data packets, percentage loss, late and out of sequence control packets arrived, the amount of data, and control bytes received by the end user site. In order to use this tool, you do not have to log in as root—it works fine with your normal user id.

The syntax to use rtpqual is the following:

```
Usage: rtpqual [<group> [<port> [<format>]]]
```

Rtpqual software is freely available on the Internet in binary form for the SunOS from `ftp://ftp.ee.lbl.gov/rtpqual` and in source form from `ftp://ftp.ee.lbl.gov/rtpqual.c`.

Mrmap

Mrmap is used to map all or a portion of a DVMRP-based multicast Internet backbone, such as the MBone. The program achieves this by doing a recursive, depth-first tree-walk starting at the IP address of the multicast router host specified by the administrator. The mrmap program can be used either by itself to determine the multicast topology, or in conjunction with the mrdebug program, discussed earlier, to determine multicast routes on the MBone. The basic syntax for using the program is as follows:

```
mrmap mrouter
```

Mrmap also supports a "-t" option, which is useful in cases where you want to limit the mapping to some smaller subset of the MBone. For example, the command:

```
mrmap -t 32 imr
```

where "imr" is some multicast router at some site on the Internet, would map only the multicast routers at that site, and not beyond. This assumes, however, that the site follows the MBone convention of putting a threshold of 32 at its boundary. Detailed capabilities of the tool are thoroughly discussed in the manual help page that is bundled with the software distribution. The software was written by Van Jacobson at the University of California at Berkeley, Lawrence Berkeley Labs, and is freely available via anonymous FTP from `ftp://ftp.ee.lbl.gov/mrmap.tar.Z`.

Mtrace

Assessing problems in the distribution of IP multicast traffic can be difficult. This tool helps in collecting statistics about the multimedia data traffic that flows over the MBone. It traces the branch of a multicast tree from a source to a receiver for a particular multicast group, and gives statistics about packet rates and losses for each hop along the path. It can be invoked in its simplistic mode as:

```
mtrace source
```

This will trace the route from the source host of multicast data traffic to the local host for a default IP multicast address. This command will yield only the route for the default IP multicast address, not the associated packet counts.

Mtrace supports several interesting powerful multicast routing-related debugging features, but their use requires version 3.3 or newer of the mrouted program. A more detailed list of capabilities of the mtrace software can be found in the help file included in the software distribution.

This software package was developed by Steve Casner of ISI and is available via anonymous FTP from `ftp://ftp.isi.edu/mbone/mtrace.tar.Z`. The program requires you to log in to the local host as root to use the tool. The distribution also contains a man page or the help file.

Mrinfo

Mrinfo displays information about a multicast router that is connected to the MBone. The information displayed consists of the version number of the mrouted program, how the mrouter is connected to other mrouters via tunnels, and the tunnel specifications. The mrouted information can be queried and viewed either for the local mrouter on your organization subnet or remote mrouters on the MBone. In its simple form, the mrouter information can be obtained by typing the following command while logged in as root:

```
mrinfo      <mrouter_name_or_address>
```

A sample program output from a local mrouter via the mrinfo program is shown in the following. Note that here the command is executed on the same machine as the local mrouter machine:

```
collage.foo.com# mrinfo collage.foo.com
192.50.58.17 (collage) [version 2.2]:
  192.50.58.17 -> 0.0.0.0 (local) [1/1/querier]
  192.50.58.17 -> 127.148.48.211 (morgul.mbone.net) [1/32/tunnel]
```

The following example shows how to query a remote mrouted host "morgul.mbone.net" from the local host "collage.foo.com."

```
collage.foo.com# mrinfo morgul.mbone.net
127.148.48.211 (morgul.mbone.net) [version 10.2]:
  127.148.48.211 -> 0.0.0.0 (local) [1/0/querier]
  127.148.48.211 -> 192.203.230.241 (mbone.asi.asa.gov) [1/0/
➥ tunnel]
  127.148.48.211 -> 130.119.244.11 (utumno.mbone.net) [1/0/tunnel]
  127.148.48.211 -> 191.216.188.11 (Angband.mbone.NET) [1/0/
➥ tunnel]
  127.148.48.211 -> 204.60.73.10 (Valinor.mbone.NET) [1/0/tunnel]
  127.148.48.211 -> 190.35.180.20 (mbone-seattle.newnet.net) [1/0/
➥ tunnel]
  127.148.48.211 -> 128.250.1.6 (mullala.ab.OZ.AU)[1/0/tunnel/
➥ disabled/down]
  127.148.48.211 -> 192.9.5.5 (play.ground.COM) [1/0/tunnel]
  127.148.48.211 -> 16.1.0.24 (nicotine.pa.com) [1/0/tunnel]
  127.148.48.211 -> 198.93.142.5 (s2ad1.global.net) [1/0/tunnel]
  127.148.48.211 -> 36.56.0.27 (Mighty.Dog.EDU) [1/0/tunnel]
  127.148.48.211 -> 192.48.153.6 (ene.GI.COM) [1/0/tunnel]
  127.148.48.211 -> 192.50.58.17 (collage) [1/0/tunnel]
  127.148.48.211 -> 131.20.254.59 (nps.marine.mil) [1/0/tunnel]
  127.148.48.211 -> 127.14.134.160 (vault.cse.edu) [1/0/tunnel]
  127.148.48.211 -> 17.255.4.30 (atg.banana.com) [1/0/tunnel]
  127.148.48.211 -> 15.25.176.33 (matmos.hpl.com) [1/0/tunnel]
```

This example shows how the mrouted host "mrogul.mbone.net" is providing the IP multicast tunnels to other hosts on the MBone. These MBone hosts may or may not be on the same subnet as "mrogul.mbone.net." As you can see, "127.148.48.211" is the IP address of the mrouted host "morgul.mbone.net" and has MBone tunnels to 192.203.230.241 (mbone.asi.asa.gov), 130.119.244.11 (utumno.mbone.net), 191.216.188.11 (Angband.mbone.NET), and so on. The mrinfo program also detects and reports on the tunnels that are down (or turned off)—for example, the tunnel to 128.250.1.6 (mullala.ab.OZ.AU) [1/0/tunnel/disabled/down] is down and disabled. Disabling the tunnel is easy; it can be turned off at your end if you stop running the mrouting daemon "mrouted."

New Multimedia Transports and Operating Systems

Thus far in this book, you have seen how the MBone multimedia works. Clearly some functionalities have been added to the basic computing infrastructure by the computer manufacturers, operating system, and router vendors. You have also seen that most desktop computers now come factory built with IP-multicasting support, multimedia devices and drivers, and networking modems or Ethernet cards. This is a good start for doing multimedia internetworking. For this technology to go further, however, more advanced supporting features will be needed, such as the following:

- Reserving and allocating network bandwidth before multimedia movies are transmitted and received between various Internet hosts.
- Guarantees and *Quality of Service* (QoS) specifiers on multimedia data delivery over the Internet and the MBone.
- Better and faster compression and decompression of multimedia data.
- Better archiving of huge amounts of digital multimedia movies with fast I/O accesses.

And, of course, all these features must be offered at an affordable price.

Work is already being done in this direction in the IETF working groups to design and implement some of the features mentioned in the preceding list. RTP is the real-time protocol that was recently designed by the IETF-AVT (Audio Video Transport) group. The Resource Reservation Protocol (RSVP) design work is already in progress. RSVP will enable computers and networks to work together to negotiate the issues mentioned in the first two bullets of the preceding list.

RTPv2: Real-Time Protocol

The *audio-video transport working group* (AVT WG) within the IETF was charged with developing a protocol that facilitates the transport of real-time data, such as interactive voice and video, over packet-switched networks such as the Internet. The working group now has finalized the real-time transport protocol (RTP) and an associated control protocol called RTCP. The final specifications draft for the design of the protocol has been submitted to the IESG Secretary for publication as Proposed Standard Internet RFC.

The RTP is an application transport protocol for transporting real-time interactive multimedia, such as the data generated in desktop multimedia conferencing. The design of the protocol, however, is not tied to any specific media like audio or video. RTP can potentially be used for designing different kinds of interactive applications that require time-critical delivery. Most software applications on the MBone today use the RTPv1 (version 1) and/or RTPv2 (version 2) protocol. Encoded multimedia data is compressed and embedded inside RTP protocol before delivery. RTCP provides lots of control functions for the multimedia data being transported in RTP.

The architecture for RTPv2-enabled applications is shown in figure 32.4.

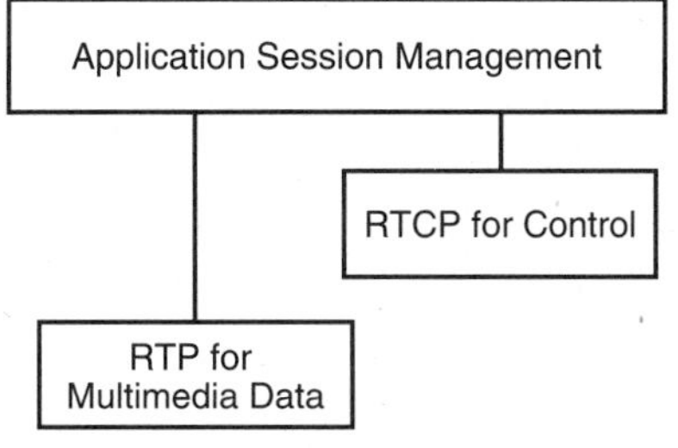

Figure 32.4
The RTP and RTCP application transport protocol stack.

As shown in figure 32.4, RTP carries the data, and RTCP carries the control information that reflects the quality of data being received by each participating host on the MBone. This control information allows applications to adapt to changing network traffic conditions. Session management functions are left to the application itself. Note that the RTP sessions are conducted over UDP/IP datagrams over the MBone when multihost communications are involved. Popular MBone software like VIC, Nevot, FTPVideo, and NV use the RTP protocol for transporting audio and video media across the MBone.

New Age Operating System Kernels and Routers

The *Resource Reservation Protocol* (RSVP) is an Internet control protocol designed for an integrated services Internet. It is designed to run on top of the IP protocol. RSVP provides receiver-initiated setup of resource reservations for multicast or unicast data that flows over the Internet. This technology is being developed for the desktop computer operating systems, as well as for Internet routers.

Figure 32.5 shows that the RSVP capability will exist on computer desktops—as a result, the application software will be able to use the RSVP functionality in the operating system. Each host operating system will in turn be able to interact on the network with the RSVP, enabling IP routers to specify, reserve, and monitor network resources on the Internet and the MBone. Note that the figure also shows a traditional non-RSVP computer desktop, which implies that RSVP will work quite interoperably with both RSVP-enabled, as well as RSVP-deprived environments. It is an end-to-end solution.

Figure 32.5
RSVP-based routing architecture involving IP hosts and routers.

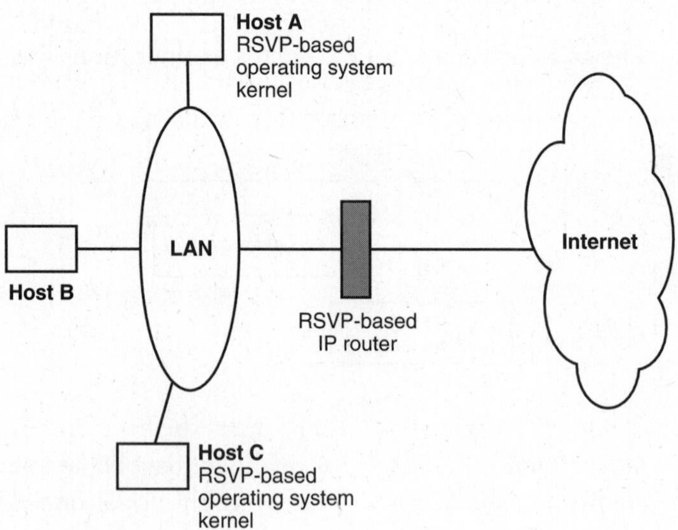

The RSVP operates on top of IP, occupying the place of a transport protocol in the protocol stack. Like ICMP, IGMP, and routing protocols, however, RSVP does not transport application data, but is rather an Internet control protocol. RSVP is not itself a routing protocol—it sends RSVP messages to reserve resources along the delivery path(s) between a set of sources and the destinations of the multimedia data.

Thus, RSVP is an enabling technology for providing an integrated service-oriented environment on the Internet and the MBone. *Integrated service* means the capability that enables the operating system and the network to understand a set of QoS parameters specified by time-constraints on the media, and allocation of system resources such as CPU time or memory buffers for a multimedia data stream. As a result, the multimedia data stream is transported between multiple Internet sites and hosts with a guaranteed quality.

Writing Your First MBone Application

Now that you understand the underlying principles of MBone and IP multicasting, you are ready to develop your first sample application. In this example, you will learn how to send and receive IP multicast data over the MBone. You will use the BSD networking conventions because that is what is supported by Unix and Microsoft Windows 95 and Windows NT operating systems. It is assumed, however, that you are already familiar with developing TCP/IP networking applications using datagram sockets.

Operating System APIs

IP multicasting Application Programming Interfaces (APIs) are currently supported only on AF_INET sockets of type SOCK_DGRAM and SOCK_RAW, and only on subnetworks for which the interface driver has been modified to support multicasting. IP multicast support exists for Ethernet, FDDI, and ATM network interface drivers.

In this section, you first will examine some basic network API elements that have been recently introduced by your operating system. If you look at any MBone application, you will quite invariably see the use of the following API elements:

```
#include <netinet/in.h>

u_char ttl;
struct ip_mreq mreq;
struct sockaddr_in sin;
```

```
setsockopt(sock, IPPROTO_IP, IP_MULTICAST_TTL, &ttl, sizeof(ttl));

setsockopt(sock, IPPROTO_IP, IP_ADD_MEMBERSHIP, &mreq,
➥sizeof(mreq));

setsockopt(sock, IPPROTO_IP, IP_DROP_MEMBERSHIP, &mreq,
➥sizeof(mreq));

IN_CLASSD(sin.sin_addr.s_addr);
IN_MULTICAST (sin.sin_addr.s_addr);
```

In the first line, <netinet/in.h> is the header file that defines all the network parameters associated with IP multicast setsockopt() programming APIs. Therefore, this header file needs to be included in every multicasting application.

An application has to be a member of a multicast address group before the application can receive IP multicast data from that address. The same need not apply, however, if the application wants to send datagrams to a multicast address group. Next, you will see how this is achieved in terms of programming.

Sending IP Multicast Data

A new socket option allows the TTL for multicast datagrams to be set to any value between 0 to 255, in order to control the scope of the multicasts:

```
u_char ttl;
setsockopt(sock, IPPROTO_IP, IP_MULTICAST_TTL, &ttl, sizeof(ttl));
```

Once the socket is configured, simply make the sendto () calls to the destination multicast address in order to multicast the application data.

Receiving IP Multicast Data

Before a host can receive IP multicast datagrams, it must become a member of one or more IP multicast groups. A process can ask the host to join a multicast group by using the following socket option:

```
struct ip_mreq mreq;

setsockopt(sock, IPPROTO_IP, IP_ADD_MEMBERSHIP, &mreq,
➥sizeof(mreq))
```

This socket option call allows an Internet host to be added to the membership of a specific multicast group address. The "mreq" structure is defined in <netinet/in.h> file, as follows:

```
struct ip_mreq {
   struct in_addr imr_multiaddr;/* multicast group to join */
   struct in_addr imr_interface;/* interface to join on    */
 }
```

After you decide to stop receiving multicast data from a specific multicast address, you may do so by dropping your membership to that group via the following socket option call:

```
setsockopt(sock, IPPROTO_IP, IP_DROP_MEMBERSHIP, &mreq,
➥sizeof(mreq))
```

To receive multicast datagrams sent to a particular port, it is necessary to bind to that local port, leaving the local address unspecified (that is, INADDR_ANY).

The API calls IN_CLASSD() or IN_MULTICAST () are helper functions that enable you to test whether a given Internet address is a multicast address or not.

The MBone is still in a phase where the infrastructure is being upgraded so that IP multicasting becomes native to all IP routers. In such a case, MBone tunnels are not needed to get connected to the MBone. All IP routers will understand the class D multicast packets and route them like any other IP packet. Until then, the MBone remains a virtual network consisting of IP encapsulated tunnels. Connecting a subnet to the MBone is done via tunnels and with cooperation from your local MBone service provider. As you learned in this chapter, commercial vendors are fully behind this technology and are actively upgrading the computer hardware and software technology to support IP multicasting. Newer technologies like RTP and RSVP will truly make the MBone experience new age, because QoS and network resources will be guaranteed for a fair price.

In addition, network security is always an area of concern. Many Internet sites employ network firewalls to reduce exposure of internal resources, while still benefiting from limited Internet connectivity. Most current firewalls filter through IP addresses and port numbers to control communication between specific hosts and services; this is not sufficient for IP multicast tunnels. It is possible to easily identify IGMP DVMRP and encapsulated IP multicast packets exchanged between tunnel endpoints, and to translate this into appropriate filter specifications for placement on a firewall router. Security risks introduced by the multicast packet filters appear minimal, in any case.

Bibliography

Cheswick, W.R. and S.M. Bellovin, *Firewalls and Internet Security: Repelling the Wily Hacker,* Addison-Wesley Publishing, 1994. (ISBN 0-201-63357-4)

Siyan, K. and C. Hare, *Internet Firewalls and Network Security,* New Riders Publishing, 1995. (ISBN 1-56205-437-6)

Web Robots: Operational Guidelines

by Fah-Chun Cheong

World Wide Web robots, also called spiders or wanderers, are programs that traverse the World Wide Web by recursively retrieving pages hyperlinked by Uniform Resource Locators (URLs). They are viewed as special kinds of agents whose goal is to automate specific Web-related tasks—for example, retrieving Web pages for keyword indexing or maintaining Web information space at local sites. This chapter covers Web robots—the basics, and their dos and don'ts.

> **Note** Spiders, wanderers, Web worms, fish, crawlers, walkers, and ants all mean one thing: Web robots, which are programs that traverse the World Wide Web information space by following hypertext links and retrieving Web documents by standard HTTP protocol. All these names are misleading, giving the false impression that the Web robot itself actually moves. In reality, the Web robot never leaves the machine where the program is run and is entirely different from the infamous Internet Worm of 1989 (Spafford 1989).

But do you really need to create yet another Web robot? There are already many of them out there in the public domain. Your needs probably can be fulfilled with one of the existing Web robots. Even if you do decide to construct a new Web robot after all, it does not have to be built entirely from scratch. The source code (usually in Perl) of quite a few public domain Web robots, such as that of Roy Fielding's MOMspider robot, are freely available for modifications. It usually is safer and more economical to go with a proven solution that already is fine-tuned for operation than it is to create new solutions from scratch.

A fairly detailed and comprehensive collection of robots on the Web can be seen on the List of Robots, which Martijn Koster (1994a) actively maintains at:

```
http://web.nexor.co.uk/mak/doc/robots/active.html
```

This chapter starts by describing major uses of Web robots and explaining how to bar specific Web robots from visiting specific portions of the Web space, by means of the widely adopted Standard for Robot Exclusion (Koster 1994b). The remainder of this chapter provides specific guidelines of acceptable Web robot behavior (Four Laws of Web Robotics), outlines the responsibility and vigilance expected of Web robot operators (Six Commandments for Robot Operators), offers some tips to webmasters who suspect their servers may be under attack by a Web robot, and concludes with a discussion of Web ethics.

The Four Laws of Web Robotics and Six Commandments for Robot Operators described in this chapter are inspired by Martijn Koster's Guide for Robot Writers (1994c), which is based on a consensus of the various WWW newsgroups and mailing lists on acceptable and expected behaviors of Web robots and their operators.

Web Robot Uses

The earliest Web robot, Matthew Gray's World Wide Web Wanderer, was first deployed in June 1993 to measure the growth of the World Wide Web by discovering and counting the number of Web servers on the Net. As of this writing, the number of different robots has grown to more than 40.

Excluding the more recent BargainFinder type of application-specific Web commerce agents, almost all known Web robots to date have been deployed for one or more of the following purposes:

- Web resource discovery
- Web maintenance
- Web mirroring

Web Resource Discovery

Web resource discovery is concerned with the problem of finding useful information on the Web. The rich, decentralized, dynamic, and diverse nature of the Web has made casual Web surfing enjoyable, but has made serious navigation aimed at finding specific information extremely difficult. People have thus increasingly relied on search engines to help locate online information. These search engines have depended on robots, often called spiders, to automatically traverse the Web to bring in Web documents for keyword indexing. It is perhaps the most exciting problem tackled by the current generation of robots.

The two most prominent resource discovery robots in operation today are Brian Pickerton's WebCrawler robot and Michael Mauldin's Lycos spider. Both actively maintain a full-content index to a huge collection of Web documents, currently numbering in the millions. Both spiders continuously traverse the Web to keep their index database up-to-date. A keyword-oriented search facility to their index databases is made available to users by means of a front-end query interface and a corresponding back-end search engine.

Web Maintenance

A major difficulty in maintaining a Web information structure is that hypertext references to other Web pages might become outdated when the target Web page is deleted or moved, resulting in what are called dead links. Currently, there is no automated mechanism for proactively notifying Web document owners the moment hyperlinks in their Web pages become obsolete.

Some servers log failed HTTP requests caused by dead links, along with URL information of the specific Web page that refers to it in the first place (while returning an HTTP response code of `301 Moved Permanently` to the client). Such information in the server log files can then be scanned and processed at regular intervals to generate a list of Web pages with the corresponding dead links that they contain. However, this post-mortem style of solution is not quite practical because document owners in the real world are seldom notified this way.

A more workable solution seems to be that offered by a class of Web robots known as the Web maintenance spiders. They assist Web document owners and webmasters maintain their portions of the Web information structure by automatically traversing the relevant branches of the local Web space periodically and checking for dead links. Roy Fielding's MOMspider, as well as its younger and simpler WebWalker cousin, are examples of Web maintenance robots. In addition, Web maintenance spiders can also perform checks for document HTML compliance, document style conformance, as well as other lesser known document content processings.

Web Mirroring

Mirroring is a common technique for setting up replicas of an information structure. For example, mirroring an FTP site involves copying its entire FTP file directory recursively and reproducing it on a different machine over the network. Popular FTP sites on the Internet are often mirrored in different parts of the world, for load sharing as well as for redundancy in case of failures. Mirroring can also yield faster or cheaper local, or even offline, access.

Robots that mirror Web information structures include, for example, HTMLGobble, Tarspider, and Webcopy. Mirroring the Web introduces an added complication not found in mirroring FTP sites, in that mirrored Web pages need to be rewritten to reflect changes in hyperlink references. Hyperlinks that used to point at original Web pages must now point to newly copied Web pages. Also, relative links that point to pages that have not been mirrored must be expanded into absolute links, so that they continue to point at original Web pages (and not at non-existent Web pages at the mirror site!).

The current generation of Web mirroring robots cannot detect and do not understand Web document changes. The unnecessary transfer of unchanged Web documents wastes valuable network resources. It can thus be expected that sophisticated mirroring robots of the future must also perform some amount of document revision control and management.

Standard for Robot Exclusion

In 1993 and 1994, robots sometimes visited Web servers where they were not welcome for various reasons. Sometimes these reasons were robot-specific—for example, certain robots swamped servers with rapid-fire requests or retrieved the same files (or the same sequence of files) repeatedly. Other situations are server-specific and there are cases where webmasters have found robots getting caught in parts of the Web they were not meant to traverse—for example, very deep virtual trees generated by server programs on-the-fly, duplicated information, temporary information, or invocations of Common Gateway Interface program scripts with side-effects (such as voting). In a few cases, certain Web robots are simply not welcome as a matter of policy due to conflicting interests—for example, some online CD stores would like to bar the price-shopping BargainFinder agent from searching their Web sites.

These incidents indicate a need for an operational mechanism for Web servers to identify to robots that portions of their Web are out of bounds and should not be accessed in an automated fashion. The Standard for Robot Exclusion proposed by Martijn Koster (1994b) is an attempt to address such a need with a simple operational solution.

Robot writers are urged to implement this practice. You can find some sample Perl code in this Web page:

```
http://web.nexor.co.uk/mak/doc/robots/norobots.pl
```

Robot Exclusion Method

The method used to exclude robots from a Web server is for the webmaster to create a file on the server that specifies an access policy for robots. This file, called the robot exclusion file, must be accessible with HTTP from a local URL with the standard path /robots.txt. The contents of the robot exclusion file describe the nature of the constraints and are detailed in the next section.

This approach was chosen because it can be implemented easily on any existing Web server. A Web robot can find the access policy from the robot exclusion file (whose URL path is /robots.txt) with only a single document retrieval. Although the webmaster can specify many constraints in the robot exclusion file, it is still up to individual Web robots to check for the existence of the file in the first place, to retrieve it and to adhere to its specified constraints.

According to Koster, a possible drawback of this single-file approach is that the robot exclusion file can be maintained only by the webmaster and not the individual document maintainers at the site. This problem can be resolved easily by a local maintenance procedure that constructs the single robots.txt file from a number of other files. (The procedure for this is outside the scope of the proposed standard.)

Robot Exclusion File Format

The file consists of one or more records. Each record is of the following form, on a line terminated by a carriage return (CR), or a line-feed (LF), or a combination of carriage return followed by line-feed (CR/LF):

```
field:value
```

The field name is case insensitive. There can be optional spaces around the value. Blank lines (lines that contain no records but are terminated with CR, LF, or CR/LF) are ignored.

Comments are allowed in the robot exclusion file for annotation purposes. A comment line begins with a # character; any preceding spaces and the remainder of the comment line up to the line terminator(s) are discarded.

The presence of an empty robot exclusion file that contains nothing basically is meaningless and should be treated as if it were not there. In this case, all Web robots would consider themselves welcome at that site.

Recognized Field Names

Records with unrecognized field names are ignored. The following are the recognized field names defined in the standard:

- **User-Agent.** The value of this field identifies the robot in question. If there are multiple consecutive User-Agent records, then more than one robot shares the identical access policy (specified in the immediately following sequence of Disallow records). Each User-Agent record, or each block of consecutive User-Agent records as the case may be, must be followed by at least one Disallow record (to be described next).

  The robot should be liberal in interpreting the value of the User-Agent field. A case-insensitive substring match of the value without version information is recommended. The following are some examples of popular user agents:

  ```
  User-Agent: Mozilla/1.1N     # Netscape browser
  User-Agent: WebCrawler/2.0  # Web searcher
  User-Agent: MOMspider/1.00  # Web maintainer
  ```

  If the value is *, the record describes the default access policy for any Web robot that has not matched with any of the other records. There must not be more than one record whose value is * in the robot exclusion file.

- **Disallow.** The value of this field specifies a partial string describing the prefix portion of the URL that is not to be visited. This can be a full path name or a partial path name. Any URL that begins with this value will not be retrieved. For example, the following line disallows both: /home/index.html and /homeSweetHome.html:

```
Disallow: /home
```

Whereas, this line disallows /home/index.html but allows /homeSweetHome.html.

```
Disallow: /home/
```

An empty value permits all URLs to be retrieved. At least one Disallow record must be present under each block of consecutive User-Agent records (for multiple robots sharing the same access policy), or under each User-Agent record (for a single robot with unique access policy). A Disallow record cannot be present without at least one User-Agent record preceding.

Sample Robot Exclusion Files

The following robot exclusion file specifies that no robots should visit any URL starting with /cyberworld/map/ (directory of infinite virtual space), /cgi-bin/ (directory of executable Common Gateway Interface scripts), or /tmp/ (directory of temporary files soon to disappear):

```
User-Agent: *
Disallow: /cyberworld/map/ # Virtual space
Disallow: /cgi-bin/        # CGI scripts
Disallow: /tmp/            # Temporary files
```

The following robot exclusion file specifies that no robots should visit any URL starting with /cyberworld/map/, except the robot called cybermapper:

```
User-Agent: *             # Bar all robots...
Disallow: /cyberworld/map/

User-Agent: cybermapper   # ...except cybermapper
Disallow:
```

The following robot exclusion file example indicates that no robots should visit this site further:

```
User-Agent: *             # All robots go away!
Disallow: /
```

The Four Laws of Web Robotics

The aspiring creators of future Web robots would be wise to heed the advice proffered by seasoned webmasters and other Web robot experts, which has been summarized in the Four Laws of Web Robotics.

If you are building a new Web robot, you are strongly urged to design your robot program in such a way that all four laws of Web robotics are adhered to. The following subsections explain each law in detail.

I. A Web Robot Must Show Identifications

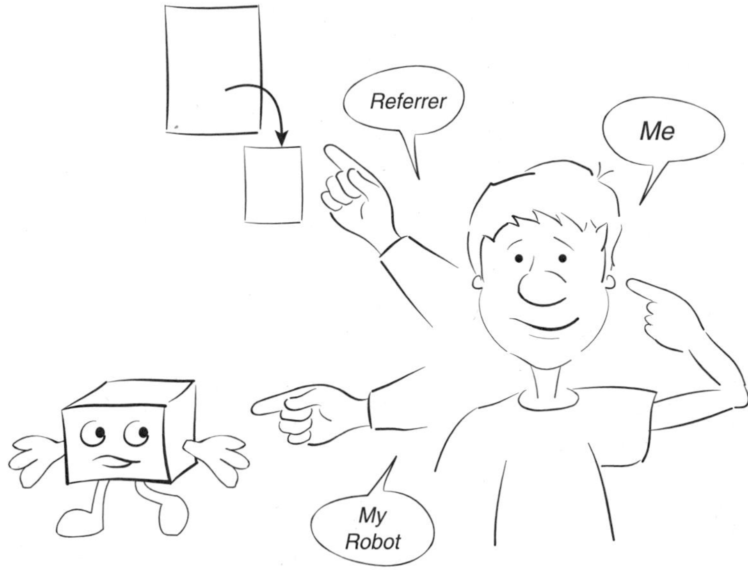

Webmasters want to know which robots are accessing their sites and who is operating the robots so they will know who to contact in case of trouble. In many cases, webmasters also want to find out how others came to know of their sites. A Web robot can accommodate webmasters by identifying itself (with User-Agent field), its operator (with From field), and the Web page referrer (with Referrer field).

Web Robot Self Identification

Web clients can identify themselves by means of the User-Agent fields supported in HTTP request headers. For example, the Netscape browser calls itself Mozilla, as in the following example:

```
User-Agent: Mozilla/1.1N
```

A Web robot can use the User-Agent field to state its name and provide a version number, as in the following example:

```
User-Agent: Terminator/1.0
```

This User-Agent field enables webmasters to set Web robots apart from human-operated interactive Web browsers.

Robot Operator Identification

HTTP supports a From field in the request headers, allowing a Web robot to identify its human operator. An e-mail address is often used for identification here, as in the following example:

```
From: joe.robomaster@roboland.com
```

The From field enables webmasters to contact the robot operator in case of problems. The robot operator can thus respond to webmasters under a more amicable atmosphere than if he or she has been hard to track down.

Web Page Referrer Identification

Webmasters often wonder how people came to learn of the existence of their Web sites. When accessing a particular Web page, it is possible and often helpful for a Web robot to identify to the Web server the parent document that hyperlinks to the Web page. This parent document is called the Web page referrer. HTTP supports a Referrer field for purposes of identifying the parent document. It is informative, for example, for the webmaster to know that the Web page currently being accessed is referred to by a paid listing with some Web advertising service, as shown in the example here:

```
Referrer: http://www.referRus.com/launchpad.html
```

II. A Web Robot Must Obey Exclusion Standards

The Standard for Robot Exclusion was proposed by Martijn Koster (1994b) as a simple way for Web servers to communicate to Web robots which portions of their Web space are off-limits, and to what robots. Details of the standard were examined in a previous section in this chapter. To be considered good citizens on the Web, and for not getting trapped in infinite virtual Web spaces, all self-respecting Web robots must follow this standard.

III. A Web Robot Must Not Hog Resources

Web robots consume a great deal of resources. To minimize its impact on the Internet, a Web robot should keep the following in mind:

- **Request HEAD where possible.** HTTP supports a HEAD request method that retrieves only header information from Web documents, without the main body of HTML text. This incurs far less overhead than a full GET request, which retrieves entire documents and includes both headers and bodies. This feature comes in handy for Web robots to verify the existence and integrity of links in a document without necessarily retrieving all of their hyperlinked contents.

- **Specify what is needed.** HTTP provides an Accept field in its request header for a Web robot to specify to the server what kinds of data it can handle. A robot that is designed to analyze text information only, for example, should specify the following:

  ```
  Accept: x-text
  ```

Specifying what is needed can save considerable network bandwidth because Web servers will not bother to send data that the Web robot cannot handle and might have to discard anyway.

- **Retrieve only what is needed.** URL suffixes also provide ample hints as to what type of data can be found at the other end of the link. If a link refers to a file with the extension "ps," "zip," "Z," or "gif," for example, and the robot is equipped to handle only text data, it should not bother asking for its content from the server. After all, non-text files are fairly low-value artifacts for the purposes of indexing and querying. Although using URL suffixes is not the preferred way to do things (the recommended way is to use the Accept field in the HTTP request header), there is an enormous installed base out there that currently uses this method (all the FTP sites, for example).

Web robots always risk wandering off the Web into infinite virtual spaces. It is, therefore, imperative for Web robots to be given a list of places to avoid before embarking on a journey into Webspace. For example, URLs that begin with "news:" (NEWS gateway) and "wais:"

(WAIS gateway) should be filtered out in order to avoid exploring them. The robot should also pay attention to subpage references (`A HREF="#abstract"`, for example) and not retrieve the same page more than once.

- **Retrieve at opportune times.** On some systems, there might be preferred times of access when the machines or networks are only lightly loaded. A Web robot planning to make many automatic requests to one particular site should be made aware of the site's preferred time of access.

- **Check all URLs carefully.** The Web robot should not assume that all HTML documents retrieved from the servers will be error-free. While scanning for URLs, the robot should be wary of things such as the following, which misses a matching double quote:

  ```
  A HREF="http://somehost.somedom/doc
  ```

  Also, many Web sites do not use trailing slashes (/) on URLs for directories, which means that a naive strategy of concatenating names of URL subparts can result in malformed names.

- **Check all results thoroughly.** The robot should check all results thoroughly, including the status code. If a server constantly refuses to serve a number of documents, listen to what it is saying—the server might not serve documents to robots as a matter of policy.

- **Never loop or repeat.** There is always the danger of a robot getting caught in some infinite loop in the Web without the slightest idea of what has happened. To avoid this situation, the robot should keep track of all the places it has visited. It also should check to make sure that the different host addresses are not on the same machine. (For example, web.nexor.co.uk and hercules.nexor.co.uk are aliases of the same machine, which also is known by its IP address, 128.243.219.1.)

- **Retrieve in moderation.** Although Web robots can handle hundreds of documents per minute, a heavily used and multi-accessed server might not keep up. What is more, putting the server under a heavy load almost certainly will arouse the ire of many webmasters, especially those who are less tolerant of robots.

Robots are advised to rotate queries between different Web servers in a round-robin fashion or to "sleep" for a short period of time between requests. Retrieving one document per minute at any one particular Web server is much better than overloading it with retrieving one document per second. One document every five minutes per Web server is better still. After all, what's the rush?

- **Skip query interfaces.** Some Web documents are searchable (using the ISINDEX facility in HTML, for example) while others contain forms or are themselves dynamic documents. It is not advisable for robots to follow these links and hope to get somewhere. An HTML textual analysis of the Web document, to be performed by the robot, can help determine whether any of the above cases apply.

IV. A Web Robot Must Report Errors

When a robot is traversing the Web, it might come across dangling links that point at Web pages that are obsolete, nonexistent, or inaccessible. This could be the result of the webmaster having moved the page in question to a different location. He or she might have moved the page to a different machine or placed it under a different directory, for example. It also could be that the file in question has been renamed or that the Web server (or even the Domain Name Server) has temporarily been out of service.

In all such cases, the Web robot should send an error-reporting e-mail to the address defined in the "mailto" link or the webmaster of the site.

Six Commandments for Robot Operators

Unleashing a Web robot on the Internet consumes substantial computational and network resources. Potential robot operators are strongly urged to reconsider their plans and to refrain from such an action until other cheaper alternatives have been fully exlored. Specifically, robot operators are urged to consider the following issues:

- The operational costs of a Web robot, in terms of computational and network resources consumed, as well as some level of vigilance and responsiveness on the part of the robot operator, must be weighed against its intended benefits.
- Sufficient computational resources and data storage capacity are required to cope with the potentially voluminous results—the Web is simply too huge for any one robot to cover.

The following subsections explain the six commandments in detail; read them carefully if you're planning on operating a Web robot.

I. Thou Shalt Announce thy Robot

For better communications, you should announce your robot prior to launching it on the Web; you should notify the world, perhaps the target Web sites, but most definitely the local system administator.

Notify the World

If webmasters know that a robot is coming, they can keep an eye out for it and not be caught by surprise. A robot that benefits the entire Net will be welcome and tolerated longer than one that services a smaller community.

Before writing or launching a robot, you should announce your intention by posting a message to the following USENET newsgroup:

`comp.infosystems.www.providers`

Or by sending an e-mail message to this address:

`robots@nexor.co.uk`

Include a brief description of the problem to be solved by the Web robot. It is possible that someone already might have been working on a similar robot, or one already might exist but is not listed.

Notify Target Sites

If your robot is targeted at a select few sites, it is professional courtesy to contact and inform the webmasters directly.

Notify the Local System Administrator

Tell the local system administrator or network provider what resources or services might be used, such as increased network traffic and greater disk space utilization, when operating the robot. This way, if something goes wrong, the system administrator has been forewarned and won't have to rely on information about the robot and any resulting problems from second-hand sources.

II. Thou Shalt Test, Test, and Test thy Robot Locally

For testing purposes, you should start a number of Web servers locally to check the newly created robot. Do not try testing on remote servers before getting the bugs out of a robot. When going off-site for the first time, the robot should stay close to home. Have it start from a page with local URLs.

After completing a small test run, you should analyze the robot's performance and results. This practice helps you arrive at an estimate of how the operation would scale up to perhaps tens of thousands of documents. It soon becomes obvious if the workload might not be manageable; as a result, you can scale down the scope of the effort.

III. Thou Shalt Keep thy Robot Under Control

It is vital that the operator know what the robot is doing, and that the robot remain under control at all times. To accomplish this goal, follow these guidelines:

- **Log all activities.** Provide ample logging in order to track where the robot has been on the Web. To monitor the progress of the robot and keep it under control, it helps to collect useful information and to compile statistics, such as the following:

  Hosts recently visited

  Number of successes and failures

  Sizes of recently accessed files

As was previously noted, the robot needs to know where it has been on the Web in order to prevent looping. Also, an updated estimate of the disk space requirement from time to time provides useful feedback to the operator and helps prevent a disk space crunch.

- **Provide guidance.** Design robots that can be guided easily. Commands that suspend or cancel the robot, or make it skip the current host, for example, can be very useful. For this to happen, the robot must be robust operationally—the robot needs to be checkpointed frequently during operation to ensure that the cumulative results are not lost if the robot fails.

IV. Thou Shalt Stay in Contact with the World

When you are running a robot, make sure that webmasters can easily contact and start dialoging with you. If your robot's actions cause problems, you could be the only one who can fix it quickly. If possible, stay logged in to the machine that is running your robot so webmasters can use finger or talk to contact you. In other words, don't go on vacation after unleashing your robot onto the Web.

The robot should be run only in your presence. Suspend the robot's operation when you are not going to be there—during weekends or after work, for example. Although it might be better for the performance of your machine to run your robot overnight, be considerate of others and the performance overhead of other machines.

V. Thou Shalt Respect the Wishes of Webmasters

During operation, your robot will visit hundreds of sites. It probably will upset a number of webmasters along its course. You must be prepared to respond quickly to their inquiries and tell them what your robot is doing.

If your robot does upset some webmasters, instruct the robot to visit only their home pages and not go beyond. In many situations, it may be wise for the robot to pass over the complaining sites altogether.

Tip It is not a good idea to evangelize to webmasters, hoping to convert them to your cause and open up their Web sites to your robot. They are probably not in the least bit interested.

If your robot encounters technical barriers that webmasters have devised to bar it from accessing their site, you should not try to make your Web robot go around them. Even though you might prove to webmasters that it is difficult or impossible to limit access on the Web, you most likely will end up making enemies.

VI. Thou Shalt Share Results with thy Neighbors

You should archive and keep as much of the Web pages as you can store. You also should make the results accessible to the Internet community. After all, the effort to accumulate these documents has consumed considerable Internet-wide resources, and it is only fair to give something back in return. More specifically, you should do the following:

- **Share raw data.** The raw results consisting of retrieved Web pages should be made available to the Internet community, either through FTP or World Wide Web, in one form or another. This sharing of data enables interested people on the Internet to make use of the data in other interesting ways without having to duplicate the collection effort using another Web robot.

- **Publish polished results.** The Web robot is created and operated for a specific purpose; perhaps to build a specialized database or to gather some statistics. If these processed results are made available to the Web community in a polished form, people will be more appreciative of the robot's value and thus become more tolerant of its presence on the Web despite the increased network load. In addition, this is definitely a good way to get in touch with people of similar interests.

Robot Tips for Webmasters

If you are a webmaster and you or your users are experiencing unusually sluggish response from your Web server, a Web robot might be attacking it with rapid-fire requests. To determine if a certain robot is indeed the culprit, and to find out more about it, here are some definite steps you can take:

1. Check your Web server logs carefully for signs of rapid-fire requests by paying close attention to time-stamps of multiple consecutive HTTP requests coming from the same machine address. Study the log for HTTP access request patterns to determine if indeed the sluggishness problem is caused by some offending robots. The HTTP request header fields User-Agent and From might reveal useful information about the Web robot and identify its operator.

2. Check Martijn Koster's List of Robots to discover if the offending Web robot, identified in the HTTP User-Agent request header field, is one that is already known. Learn more about the culprit as needed, perhaps using Web search engines such as the WebCrawler or Lycos.

3. Find out more about the robot operator, identified in the HTTP From request header field, by means of finger or users over the Internet. The robot operator might also have published a Web page about himself and, more importantly, his Web robot project!

4. Raise the alarm in newsgroups among webmasters, if needed, by posting to comp.infosystems.www.providers on USENET. You might not be alone. Chances are that there is already a thread of discussions on the topic between numerous other webmasters facing the exact same problem.

The problem might have a simple solution: specify an entry in the robot exclusion file to exclude the offender. For example, the following entry added to the exclusion file tells the robot identified as NastyBot/1.0 to go away:

```
User-Agent: NastyBot/1.0  # Robot go away!
Disallow: /               # Off-limits!
```

If a Web robot is misbehaving, however, chances are that the robot creator also would not have properly implemented the robot exclusion standard. Do not get upset over it. It is also probably not wise to retaliate with the Web equivalent of a mail-bomb, which is to trap the robot into retrieving large amounts of data (perhaps a gigabyte-size HTML document generated on-the-fly) in the hope that it would choke. This would waste valuable network bandwidth and might not accomplish anything if the offending Web robot is robust, or simply smart.

It is perhaps better to try to get in contact with the robot operator and to engage in a constructive dialog, explaining clearly the problem that occurred at your Web site. You might also consider suggesting that the robot operator read Guidelines for Robot Writers or, perhaps, this chapter.

After your problem has been solved, you are strongly encouraged to share the experience with other webmasters, robot builders, and robot operators in the Web community. This would save numerous other webmasters from duplicating your efforts trying to investigate the similar problems caused by the same offending Web robots.

Web Ethics

Web ethics is an important concept for robot writers, robot operators, and webmasters to understand. In 1942, Isaac Asimov stated his Three Laws of Robotics:

1. A robot may not injure a human being, or, through inaction, allow a human being to come to harm.
2. A robot must obey orders given it by human beings except where such orders would conflict with the First Law.
3. A robot must protect its own existence as long as such protection does not conflict with the First or Second Law.

Asimov's First Law of Robotics captures an essential insight: An intelligent agent should not slavishly obey human commands—its foremost goal should be to avoid harming humans. After all, society will reject autonomous agents unless there is some credible means of making them safe in the first place. But of course all this is quite abstract; the Web robots we're dealing with aren't going to chase anyone to kill them with superstrong pinchers at the ends of accordian-like arms!

Oren Etzioni and Daniel Weld, both professors at the University of Washington in Seattle who have done extensive work with software robots, define a softbot as an agent that interacts with a software environment by issuing commands and interpreting the environment's feedback. In many respects, the softbot is very similar to a Web agent. It therefore is quite interesting to study Etzioni and Weld's formulation of a collection of softbotic laws (patterned after Isaac Asimov's Laws of Robotics) to govern such softbot agents (Etzioni and Weld, 1994):

- **Safety.** The softbot should not make destructive changes to the world.
- **Tidiness.** The softbot should leave the world as it first found it.
- **Thrift.** The softbot should limit its use of scarce resources.
- **Vigilance.** The softbot should refuse client actions with unknown consequences.

The laws of softbotics operate at a higher level when compared with the four laws of Web robotics described previously; you can probably detect some interesting commonalities that underlie the ethical aspects for all agents.

Similarly, Professor David Eichmann of the University of Houston, creator of the RBSE spider, offers his formulation of a code of conduct governing a general class of service agents (1994), which also includes Web robots:

- **Identity.** Agent activities should be readily discernible and traceable back to its operator.
- **Openness.** Information generated should be made accessible to the community in which the agent operates.
- **Moderation.** The rate and frequency of information acquisition should be appropriate for the capacity of the server and network so as not to create an overload situation on valuable computational and network resources.
- **Respect.** Agents should respect constraints placed on them by server administrators.
- **Authority.** Agents' services should be accurate and up-to-date.

According to Eichmann, a balance should be struck between the concerns of openness, moderation, and respect—all of which limit a service agent's scope and activities—and the concern of authority, which tends to broaden them.

Bibliography

Asimov, I. "Runaround." *Astounding Science Fiction.* 1942.

Eichmann, D. "Ethical web agents." In *Proceedings of the Second International Conference on the World Wide Web.* Oct, 1994. Also available at `http://rbse.jsc.nasa.gov/eichmann/www-f94/ethics/ethics.html`.

Koster, Martijn. 1994a. "A Standard for Robot Exclusion." Nexor Corp. `http://web.nexor.co.uk/mak/doc/robots/norobots.html`.

———. 1994b. "Guide for Robot Writers." Nexor Corp. `http://web.nexor.co.uk/mak/doc/robots/guidelines.html`.

———. 1994c. "List of Robots." Nexor Corp. `http://web.nexor.co.uk/mak/doc/robots/active.html`.

Spafford, Eugene H. "Internet worm: Crisis and aftermath." *Commun. ACM*, vol. 32, no 6, pp. 678–687, June 1989.

Weld, D. and O. Etzioni. "The first law of robotics (a call to arms)." In *Proceedings of the Twelfth national Conference on AI. Seattle, WA.* 1994. Also available at `ftp://cs.washington.edu/pub/ai/first-law-aaai-94.ps`.

HTML Reference

This appendix takes great effort to provide the most complete HTML-related reference guide. There is a listing of HTML tags and attributes by section, as well as an alphabetical listing. There also is a list of character entities, HTML 3.0 codes, and Netscape enhancements to HTML.

Note If you see a tag listed in this reference, but it was not mentioned previously, it may be in very limited use, or even outdated.

The appendix also provides a somewhat detailed list of Internet sites to find more information, and to find some of the shareware programs mentioned throughout the book.

HTML 2.0 Referenced By Topic

ADDRESS

Tag: <ADDRESS>...</ADDRESS>

Use: Acts as a signature to the Web page.

ALIGNMENT

Tag: <CENTER>...</CENTER> and <ALIGN="CENTER">

Use: Defines an area of text to be centered.

BLINK

Tag: <BLINK>...</BLINK>

Use: Surrounds a word or area of text that you wish to appear blinking.

CHARACTER STYLE TAGS

Physical or Font Type

Tag: <B>...</B> and <STRONG>...</STRONG>

Use: Makes a section of text within the document a bold or strong typeface.

Tag: <I>...</I> and <EM>...</EM>

Use: Makes a section of text within the document an italicized or emphasized typeface.

Tag: <U>...</U>

Use: Makes a section of text within the document underlined.

Logical or Information Type

Tag: <TT>...</TT>

Use: Creates a Typewriter font.

Tag: <CODE>...</CODE>

Use: Creates a fixed-width font such as Courier.

Tag: <SAMP>...</SAMP>

Use: Creates a font similar to <CODE>.

Tag: <KBD>...</KBD>

Use: Indicates text to be typed by the user.

Tag: <VAR>...</VAR>

Use: Indicates a variable that will be replaced with a value.

Tag: <DFN>..</DFN>

Use: Indicates a word that will or has been defined.

Tag: <KEY>...</KEY>

Use: Defines a keyword.

Tag: <CITE>...</CITE>

Use: Indicates a citation.

Tag: <STRIKE>...</STRIKE>

Use: Shows struck-out text.

DESIGN ELEMENTS

Tags: <H1>...</H1>, <H2>...</H2>, <H3>...</H3>, <H4>...</H4>, <H5>...</H5>, <H6>...</H6>

Use: Creates a heading of a different size (and bolded) text. The <H1> tag represents the largest, and the <H6> tag represents the smallest.

Tag <HR>

Use: Creates a line across the page (Horizontal Rules).

Tag <P>...</P>

Use: Marks the beginning (and end) of a new paragraph.

Tag

Use: Creates a line break. The text after it will continue on the next line.

Comments: <!-- comments --> ("comments" defines where the text should go)

Use: To mention any comments to be contained within the HTML document, but not displayed as part of it.

FORMS

Tag: <FORM>...</FORM>

Use: Surrounds area that will be designated as a form.

Attributes:	METHOD	<FORM METHOD="POST" ACTION= "/cgi-bin/kassform.cgi">
		Tells the server which method to handle the form; GET or POST.
	ACTION	Tells the server where to find the script associated with the form.

Tag: <INPUT>

Use: To define what type of input the form will generate.

Attributes:	TYPE	<INPUT TYPE=...>
		Used to define which type of input is to follow for the form layout (See TYPE choices listed below).
	NAME	<INPUT TYPE="text" NAME="contact">
		Assigns a specific name to this element, which links it to the corresponding name within the CGI script.
	VALUE	<INPUT TYPE="submit" VALUE="Submit Query">
		Assigns a specific value to this element, which links it to the corresponding name within the CGI script.
	SIZE	<....SIZE=35>
		Used with either the TEXT or PASS-WORD attribute, it specifies the length, in characters, of the text box.
	MAXLENGTH	<...MAXLENGTH=25>
		Used to indicate the maximum number of characters that the user can input within the text box.

Type

Choices:	TEXT	<INPUT TYPE="text"...> Used in referencing a single line text box for input.
	PASSWORD	<INPUT TYPE="password"...> Used in referencing a single line text box for a secret password, which when typed appears in asterisks.
	RADIO	<INPUT TYPE="radio"...> Used to implement a list of items for the user to choose one from.
	CHECKBOX	<INPUT TYPE="checkbox"...> Used to implement a list of items for the user to choose more than one from.
	SUBMIT	<INPUT TYPE="submit"...> Used to create the button the user will click on to send the form information back to you.
	RESET	<INPUT TYPE="reset"...> Used to create the button the user will click on to reset the information they put in the form (clear the form).

Selection Tag

Tag: <SELECT>...</SELECT>

Use: Defines a section of information that the user can choose or select from.

Attributes:	NAME	<SELECT NAME="color"> Defines a special name to this element, which links it to the corresponding name within the CGI script.
	MULTIPLE	<SELECT NAME="color" MUL-TIPLE> Enables the user the option of choosing more than one selection.
	MULTIPLE SIZE	<SELECT NAME="color" MULTIPLE SIZE="4"> Specifies the size you want the multiple selection box to be.

Tag: <OPTION>

Use: Is used to indicate the items to be listed within the selection box.

Attributes:	SELECTED	<OPTION SELECTED> Specifies an item within your list that will be the default checked item.
	VALUE	<OPTION VALUE="blue"> Used to assign a value to the corresponding option (if no value is set, the form will send back the value of whatever text follows the <OPTION> tag).

Textarea

Tag: <TEXTAREA>...</TEXTAREA>

Use: Defines an area of which text can be typed in—needs to have the following attributes:

Attributes:	NAME	Assigns a name to the corresponding text area.
	ROWS	Specifies the height of the text area.
	COLS	Specifies the width of the text area.
		<TEXTAREA NAME="comments" ROWS=6 COLS=50></TEXTAREA>

THE HEADER (or Starting) ELEMENTS:

Tag: <HTML>...</HTML>

Use: Surrounds the entire HTML document.

Tag: <HEAD>...</HEAD>

Use: Defines the Heading of the HTML document.

Tag <TITLE>...</TITLE>

Use: Defines the Title of the HTML document (seen at the top of the browser screen—not inside the HTML document).

Tag: <BODY>...</BODY>

Use: Surrounds the entire body of the HTML document (everything starting from after the heading).

Tag: <BASE>

Use: Indicates the current document's URL.

Tag: <ISINDEX>

Use: Used inside the <HEAD> tag to allow searching within the document by the browser.

IMAGES

Tag: <IMG>

Use: Inserts an image into the document.

Attributes:	SRC	<IMG SRC="filename.gif"> Used to define the image filename, or URL of the image.
	ALT	<IMG SRC="filename.gif" ALT="Company Logo"> Used to define a text name for the image for those who cannot view the image.
	ALIGN	<IMG SRC="filename.gif" ALIGN="top"> Used to vertically align the text found before and after the image—choose from TOP, MIDDLE, and BOTTOM.
	ISMAP	<IMG SRC="filename.gif" ISMAP> Used to indicate that the image is a clickable image map.

LINKS/ANCHORS

Tag: <A>...</A>

Use: Surrounds a word, text area, or picture to be linked to another section within that page, some other page, or a graphic.

Attributes:	HREF	<A HREF="filename">...</A> Used in referencing another section within a document, another document, or graphic.

	NAME	<A NAME="name">...</A> Used in referencing a "secret" name to prompt the browser to stop here when the corresponding link is clicked upon.
Command:	MAILTO	<A HREF="mailto:e-mailaddress">... </A> Used when linking to an e-mail address.

LISTS

Numbered or Ordered Lists

Tag: <OL>...</OL>

Use: Surrounds the text that will create a Numbered or Ordered List of information.

Unordered Lists

Tag: <UL>...</UL>

Use: Surrounds the text that will create an Unordered List.

Menu Lists

Tag: <MENU>...</MENU>

Use: Surrounds the text that will create a Menu List.

Directory Lists

Tag: <DIR>...</DIR>

Use: Surrounds the text that will create a Directory List.

Tag: <LI>

Use: Used with the above lists (<OL>, <UL>, <MENU>, and <DIR> tags) to specify each List Item within that list.

Definition Lists

Tag: <DL>...</DL>

Use: Surrounds the contents of a Definition List.

Tag: <DT>

Use: Represents the term to be defined.

Tag: <DD>

Use: Represents the definition of the term.

PREFORMATTED TEXT

Tag: <PRE>...</PRE>

Use: Indicates a section of text that will be preformatted through the browser in exactly the way it appears on the screen.

QUOTATIONS

Tag: <BLOCKQUOTE>...</BLOCKQUOTE>

Use: Provides a way of listing a quotation within a document.

TABLES

Tag: <TABLE>...</TABLE>

Use: Surrounds text and information that will make up a table format.

Attributes:	BORDER	<TABLE BORDER=5> Used to specify the size of the border surrounding the table.
	WIDTH	<TABLE BORDER=5 WIDTH=90%> Used to specify the width of the table within the screen, either in percent or total number of pixels.

CELLSPACING <TABLE BORDER=5 WIDTH=90% CELLSPACING=5>

Used to define how much space there will be between cells.

CELLPADDING <TABLE BORDER=5 WIDTH=90% CELLPADDING=4>

Used to define how much space will be between the cell wall and its contents (the default is one).

Tag: <TR>...</TR>

Use: Creates a new table row.

Attributes: ALIGN <TR ALIGN=LEFT>

Used to align all the cells within that row to either LEFT, RIGHT, or CENTER.

VALIGN <TR VALIGN=TOP>

Used to align all the cells within that row to either TOP, MIDDLE, or BOTTOM.

Tag: <TH>...</TH>

Use: Defines a Table Heading within a table.

Attributes: ALIGN <TH ALIGN=RIGHT>

Used to align the contents of that cell to either LEFT, RIGHT, or CENTER.

VALIGN <TH VALIGN=BOTTOM>

Used to align the contents of that cell to either TOP, MIDDLE, or BOTTOM.

ROWSPAN <TH ROWSPAN=4>

Used to specify how many rows this particular cell will span over.

COLSPAN <TH COLSPAN=5>

Used to specify how many columns this particular cell will span over.

NOWRAP <TH NOWRAP>

Used to make sure the cell contents are not wrapped from one line to the next—the contents stay on one line.

Tag: <TD>...</TD>

Use: Defines Table Data within a table.

Attributes: ALIGN <TD ALIGN=RIGHT>

Used to align the contents of that cell to either LEFT, RIGHT, or CENTER.

VALIGN <TD VALIGN=BOTTOM>

Used to align the contents of that cell to either TOP, MIDDLE, or BOTTOM.

ROWSPAN <TD ROWSPAN=4>

Used to specify how many rows this particular cell will span over.

COLSPAN <TD COLSPAN=5>

Used to specify how many columns this particular cell will span over.

NOWRAP <TD NOWRAP>

Used to make sure the cell contents are not wrapped from one line to the next—the contents stay on one line.

Tag: <CAPTION>...</CAPTION>

Use: Defines the name of your table.

HTML 3.0 ADDITIONS

HTML 3.0, which used to be referred to as HTML+, has added many features to the original HTML language that webmasters can use to brighten up their Web sites! Although many browsers do not support the complete HTML 3.0 specifications, there are some browsers that support more features than others. Until now, HTML 2.0 has been the main focus because it is pretty much a standard with all browsers. Although you might want to get fancy in designing your Web pages by using HTML 3.0 additions and Netscape enhancements, always remember that there will be users who are not able to view your masterpieces. Some may even be confused by what appears on their screen due to what their browser does and does not support.

Now, with that warning out of the way, here are the newest additions that HTML 3.0 has made:

NEW GENERAL ATTRIBUTES

HTML 3.0 has added several new attributes that can be used with many HTML tags.

Align Attribute

The ALIGN attribute is perhaps the earliest attribute added to HTML 3.0. Many users requested it for use in their Web pages. There are four choices: LEFT (aligns text to the left), RIGHT (aligns text to the right), CENTER (aligns text to the center), and JUSTIFY (aligns text to both left and right margins evenly).

Class Attribute

The CLASS attribute specifies the type of element to be used. It indicates a difference in a particular section.

Clear Attribute

The CLEAR attribute is used in conjunction with text alignment around an image. Use this attribute when you want the text to stop filling in around the graphic. Use it on the first tag that should break out of the format. Use it with tags such as headings, paragraphs, lists, addresses, and the break tag. There are three values for the CLEAR attribute: LEFT (starts text at next clear left margin), RIGHT (starts text at next clear right margin), and ALL (starts text on next clear margin on both sides).

ID Attribute

This attribute can be added to almost all the design and text elements or overall body tags, as well as images and links tags. It is designed to take the place of the NAME attribute that is used with the Anchor tag (<A NAME>) to provide an anchor or link name to a specific section.

<P ID="keyword">	The browser will jump here when a specific key word is clicked upon.

Lang Attribute

The LANG attribute refers to the language and country code, which indicates to the browser certain specifics that might be necessary to display for that language.

Nowrap Attribute

Another popular, already used attribute, the NOWRAP attribute simply indicates to the browser not to wrap around the text. Everything must be displayed on one line, unless the person creating the page specifies otherwise.

Changes/Additions in Existing Tags

Address <ADDRESS>...</ADDRESS>

New Attributes:	CLASS	(mentioned earlier)
	CLEAR	(mentioned earlier)
	ID	(mentioned earlier)
	LANG	(mentioned earlier)
	NOWRAP	(mentioned earlier)

Blockquote

The <BLOCKQUOTE> tag is now the <BQ> tag, although the original should still be supported.

New Tag: <CREDIT>...</CREDIT>

Use: To give credit to the author of the blockquote.

New Attributes:	CLASS	(mentioned earlier)
	CLEAR	(mentioned earlier)
	ID	(mentioned earlier)
	LANG	(mentioned earlier)
	NOWRAP	(mentioned earlier)

Forms <FORM>...</FORM>

New Attributes:	CLASS	(mentioned earlier)
	ID	(mentioned earlier)
	LANG	(mentioned earlier)
	ERROR	Used to create an error message relative to that area

	DISABLED	Used to disable certain areas of a form
<INPUT> Tag		
New Attributes:	RANGE	Used to allow user to select a value that must be between the specified boundaries.
	FILE	Used to allow the user to attach a file to the form submission. This comes in handy for sending HTML pages changes to a Web server.
	ACCEPT	This limits the types of files that will be accepted as attachments.
	SCRIBBLE SRC	Used together to reference an image to be displayed in the form for the user to draw upon. Text browsers display a text field.
	MD	Used to indicate the checksum of the image.

Head Tag <HEAD>...</HEAD>

There are new tags that can be used within the <HEAD> tags.

Tag: <LINK>

Use: The <LINK> tag has more than one use. It can be used to indicate the relationship between this and another document, to create toolbars for the documents (for more common elements like to return home, go back, and so on), to include a banner, or to include a stylsheet.

Attributes:	REL	Used to define the relationship between this and another document (in the case of creating links to banners and stylesheets, and other things).
	REV	Used to define the reverse relationship between this and another document.
	HREF	Used to reference the URL of another document.

Tag: <META>

Use: Describes information relative to the document itself.

Attributes:	NAME	Used to define the information.
	CONTENT	Used to list the information.
	<META NAME="Author" CONTENT="Mary Berg">	
	HTTP-EQUIV	Used to name a header that is created with the <META> tag along with the CONTENT attribute. <META HTTP-EQUIV="Created" CONTENT="February 1, 1996"> which will produce this header: Created: February 1, 1996

Tag: <RANGE>

Use: Specifies a selected range within a document.

Attributes:	ID	Used to identify the range.
	CLASS	Used to specify the type of range.
	FROM	Used to specify the beginning of the range.
	TO	Used to specify the ending of the range.

Tag: <STYLE>

Use: Indicates a style that will override the document style.

Attributes:	NOTATION	Used to specify the new style format.

Headings <H1>...</H1> through <H6>...</H6>

New Attributes:	ALIGN	(mentioned earlier)
	CLASS	(mentioned earlier)
	CLEAR	(mentioned earlier)
	ID	(mentioned earlier)
	LANG	(mentioned earlier)
	NOWRAP	(mentioned earlier)
	SEQNUM	Used to indicate the number that the heading will use, if your headings are numbered. All headings of the same size following the first one will go up from there.
	SKIP	Used to indicate a number of times to "skip" in the numbering sequence of the numbered headings.
	SRC	Used to indicate an image filename to be used before the heading.
	MD	Used to indicate the checksum of the image used with the SRC attribute.
	DINGBAT	Used to specify a symbol or picture that will mark the heading—these are supplied by the browsers. The attribute would look like this: <H2 DINGBAT="disk">...</H2> (disk is one of many names that can be used that correspond with images).

Note A list of the HTML 3.0 dingbats can be found at `http://www.hpl.hp.co.uk/people/dsr/html/icons.txt`.

Horizontal Rule <HR>

New Attributes:	SRC	<HR SRC="colorline.gif"> Used to specify an image to be used in place of the line.
	MD	Used to indicate the checksum of that image.

Images <IMG>

The <IMG> tag will still be used for smaller images and icons, but for large images, especially image maps, the new <FIG> tag (described later) should be used. There are, however, some new attributes for the <IMG> Tag:

New Attributes:	ALIGN	<IMG ALIGN=left> and <IMG ALIGN=right> The ALIGN=left moves the image to the left, and wraps text around to the right. The ALIGN=right moves the images to the right, and wraps text around to the left.
	CLASS	(mentioned earlier)
	CLEAR	(mentioned earlier)
	ID	(mentioned earlier)
	LANG	(mentioned earlier)
	WIDTH & HEIGHT	<IMG WIDTH=*value* HEIGHT=*value*> Used to specify a fixed width and height of an image (value is in pixels or EN (one half the point size of the current text).
	MD	Used to indicate the checksum of that image.

Links/Anchors

New Attributes:

CLASS	(mentioned earlier)
ID	Used to take the place of the NAME attribute that is used with the Anchor tag (<A NAME>) to provide an anchor or link name to a specific section. (also mentioned earlier)
LANG	(mentioned earlier)
MD	The Message Digest attribute is used to indicate the checksum of the document you are linking to.
REL	Used to define the relationship between this and the other document.
REV	Used to define the reverse relationship between this and the other document.
SHAPE	Used to specify areas within an image and the documents where they will link.
TITLE	Used to indicate the title of the document you are linking to.

Lists

Tag: <LH>

Use: Defines a List Header for the corresponding list. It can be used in the Ordered, Unordered, and Definition Lists.

Example:

```
<UL>
   <LH>Days of the Week
      <LI>Monday
      <LI>Tuesday
      <LI>Wednesday
      <LI>Thursday
      <LI>Friday
</UL>
```

New Attribute:	COMPACT	<UL COMPACT>	
		Used to let the browser know it should squeeze the list together in some way—can be used with all List types.	
	Ordered Lists <OL>		
	New Attributes:	SEQNUM	Used to indicate the value where the list should start at.
		CONTINUE	Used to indicate the current list should continue numbering where the previous one left off.
	Unordered Lists <UL>		
	New Attributes:	DINGBAT	Used to specify a special bullet to be used in the List.
		PLAIN	Used to let the browser know not to display any bullets.
		SRC	Used to indicate an image to use instead of the bullet.
		MD	Used to indicate the checksum of that image.
		WRAP	Used with the HORIZ value, the WRAP attribute tells the browser to

		line up the list horizontally, not vertically as is the default (similar to the <DIR> Lists that are almost never used).
List Item <LI>		
New Attributes:	DINGBAT	Used to specify a special bullet to be used in the List (Unordered Lists).
	SKIP	Used in Ordered Lists to indicate how many numbers to skip over before assigning that item a number.
	SRC	Used to indicate an image to use instead of the bullet (Unordered Lists with PLAIN attribute).
	MD	Used to indicate the checksum of that image.

Paragraphs

New Attributes:	ALIGN	(mentioned earlier)
	CLASS	(mentioned earlier)
	CLEAR	(mentioned earlier)
	ID	(mentioned earlier)

LANG	(mentioned earlier)
NOWRAP	(mentioned earlier)

Preformatted Text <PRE>...</PRE>

New Attributes:	CLASS	(mentioned earlier)
	CLEAR	(mentioned earlier)
	ID	(mentioned earlier)
	LANG	(mentioned earlier)
	WIDTH	Used to specify the number of characters you want the width to be within that section (default is 80 characters).

Special Characters

With the advent of HTML 3.0, there have been five new special character entities assigned:

	An en space
	An em space
	A nonbreaking space
&endash;	An en dash
&emdash;	An em dash

Tables

Although tables themselves are basically a new HTML feature, the very newest additions to the <TABLE> tags are covered here:

New Attributes:	ALIGN	Used to align the table on the screen.
	BLEEDLEFT	Aligns table with left window margin—until a clear left margin is reached.

LEFT	Aligns table with the left text margin—text will go to the right of the table.
BLEEDRIGHT	Aligns table with right window margin—until a clear right margin is reached.
RIGHT	Aligns table with the right margin—text will go to the left of the table.
CENTER	Aligns table in the center of the page—no text will wrap around.
JUSTIFY	Resizes table to fit into the page width—no text will wrap around.
CLASS	(mentioned earlier)
CLEAR	(mentioned earlier)
ID	(mentioned earlier)
LANG	(mentioned earlier)
NOFLOW	Used to prevent text flow around the table.
NOWRAP	(mentioned earlier) Refers to content of table.

Table Columns

As you know, the WIDTH attribute is used to specify the width of the table. There is also a way to specify the width and alignment of the columns by using the COLSPEC and UNITS attributes. The alignment can be noted with the following:

L	Left aligned
R	Right aligned

C	Center aligned
J	Justified
D	Decimal alignment (use DP attribute to indicate what the decimal point is—default is a period)

There are three different ways to list the size of the UNITS attribute:

UNITS=EN	Used to measure the width in en units.
UNITS=PIXELS	Used to measure in screen pixels.
UNITS=RELATIVE	Used to measure in percentages.

An example might look as follows:

<TABLE UNITS=PIXELS COLSPEC="L30L40R50">

The example indicates three columns with the first being aligned left, 30 pixels, the second being aligned left, 40 pixels, and the third being aligned right, 50 pixels.

Table Rows

New Attributes:	CLASS	(mentioned earlier)
	ID	(mentioned earlier)
	LANG	(mentioned earlier)
	NOWRAP	(mentioned earlier) Refers to content of table.
	ALIGN=JUSTIFY	Used to justify the row.
	ALIGN=DECIMAL	Used to align decimals (also use the DP attribute to specify the decimal point type).

Table Headings <TH>...</TH> and Table Data <TD>...</TD>

New Attributes:	CLASS	(mentioned earlier)
	ID	(mentioned earlier)

LANG	(mentioned earlier)
NOWRAP	(mentioned earlier) Refers to content of table.
ALIGN=JUSTIFY	Used to justify the contents.
ALIGN=DECIMAL	Used to align decimals (also use the DP attribute to specify the decimal point type).
AXIS	Used to specify an abbreviated name for a header cell.
AXES	Used to specify a comma separated list of axis names.

New HTML 3.0 Features

Above & Below

Tag: <ABOVE>...</ABOVE>

Use: Surrounds text that will have a line, arrow, bracket, or other symbol drawn above it.

Attribute: SYM Used to specify the symbol to draw. Choices include CUB, HAT, LARR (left arrow), RARR (right arrow), and TILDE.

Tag: <BELOW>...</BELOW>

Use: Surrounds text that will have a line, arrow, bracket, or other symbol drawn above it.

Attribute: SYM Used to specify the symbol to draw. Choices include CUB, HAT, LARR (left arrow), RARR (right arrow), and TILDE.

Note There are shortcut tags for the more popular; <BAR> (bars), <DOT> (dots), <DDOT> (double dots), <HAT> (hats), <TILDE> (tildes), and <VEC> (vectors).

Array

Tag: <ARRAY>...</ARRAY>

Use: Creates matrices and other array expressions. Used with the <ROW> tag to define rows, and the <ITEM> tag to define the item.

Attributes:	ALIGN	Used to indicate the alignment of the array. Choose from TOP, MIDDLE, and BOTTOM.
	COLDEF	Used to indicate how the items within the column will be aligned. The values could be L (left), C (center), or R (right).
	LDELIM	Used to specify the entity or character that will be used for the left delimiter.
	RDELIM	Used to specify the entity or character that will be used for the right delimiter.
	LABELS	Used to label the rows and columns.

Backgrounds

HTML 3.0 has the capability to show a tiled background, as Netscape has previously added, most likely due to its extreme popularity.

Tag: <BODY>...</BODY>

Use: Defines the area of the page that will be the main body.

New Attribute:	BACKGROUND	<BODY BACKGROUND="picture.gif"> Used to define the image that will be tiled in the background of the page.

Banner

Tag: <BANNER>...</BANNER>

Use: To specify a section of the document that will never change, it will be a banner. Usually displayed in a toolbar or such.

New Character Style Tags

Logical or Information Type

Tag: <ABBREV>...</ABBREV>

Use: Used to mark an abbreviation.

Tag: <ACRONYM>...</ACRONYM>

Use: Used to mark an acronym.

Tag: <AU>...</AU>

Use: Used to specify an author.

Tag: <DEL>...</DEL>

Use: Used to indicate deleted text (great for legal documents).

Tag: <DFN>...</DFN>

Use: Used to indicate a definition of a term.

Tag: <INS>...</INS>

Use: Used for inserted text (again for legal documents).

Tag: <LANG>...</LANG>

Use: Used to change the language context.

Tag: <PERSON>...</PERSON>

Use: Used to indicate people's names for indexing programs to extract.

Tag: <Q>...</Q>

Use: Used to specify a short quotation (in conjunction with the <LANG> tag) to determine the language context.

Physical or Font Type

Tag: <BIG>...</BIG>

Use: Surrounds text that should be displayed in a bigger font than normal.

Tag: <BT>...</BT>

Use: Surrounds text that will be both boldface and in an upright font.

Tag: <S>...</S>

Use: Surrounds text that will have a line striking through it.

Tag: <SMALL>...</SMALL>

Use: Surrounds text that should be displayed in a smaller font than normal.

Tag: _{...}

Use: Surrounds text that should be displayed as subscript and with a smaller font.

Tag: ^{...}

Use: Surrounds text that should be displayed as superscript and with a smaller font.

Tag: <T>...</T>

Use: Surrounds text that will be in an upright font.

Divisions

Tag: <DIV>...</DIV>

Use: Breaks a page into individual sections by naming them.

Attributes:	ALIGN	Used to align the section specified. Choose from LEFT, RIGHT, CENTER, and JUSTIFY.
	CLASS	Used to name the section specified.
	CLEAR	(mentioned earlier)

ID	(mentioned earlier)
LANG	(mentioned earlier)
NOWRAP	(mentioned earlier)

Figures

Tag: <FIG>...</FIG>

Use: Indicates that there will be an image included within the page. The <FIG> tag basically is taking the place of the <IMG> tag in the use of larger graphic files.

Attributes:	ALIGN	Used to align the image and text around it.
	BLEEDLEFT	Aligns table with left window margin—until a clear left margin is reached.
	LEFT	Aligns table with the left text margin—text will go to the right of the table.
	BLEEDRIGHT	Aligns table with right window margin—until a clear right margin is reached.
	RIGHT	Aligns table with the right margin—text will go to the left of the table.
	CENTER	Aligns table in the center of the page—no text will wrap around.
	JUSTIFY	Resizes table to fit into the page width—no text will wrap around.
	CLASS	(mentioned earlier)
	CLEAR	(mentioned earlier)
	ID	(mentioned earlier)
	IMAGEMAP	Used to indicate an imagemap.
	LANG	(mentioned earlier)

	MD	Used to indicate the checksum of the image.
	NOFLOW	Used to stop the text from aligning around the image.
	SRC	Used to indicate the filename of the image.
	WIDTH & HEIGHT	<IMG WIDTH=value HEIGHT=value> Used to specify a fixed width and height of an image (value is in pixels or EN, one half the point size of the current text).

Figure Overlay

Tag: <OVERLAY>

Use: Used to specify an overlay of the original image to be loaded after the original image. The <OVERLAY> tag is used within the <FIG> tag.

Attributes:	IMAGEMAP	Used to indicate an imagemap.
	MD	Used to indicate the checksum of the image.
	SRC	Used to indicate the filename of the graphic (overlay graphic in this case).
	UNITS	Used to specify the unit size.
	WIDTH & HEIGHT	<IMG WIDTH=value HEIGHT=value> Used to specify a fixed width and height of an image (value is in pixels or EN, one half the point size of the current text).

Imagemaps

The IMAGEMAP attribute, found in both the <FIG> and <OVERLAY> tags, indicates that the graphic being loaded is an imagemap (meaning that by clicking on different parts of the picture, you go to different locations). Note that the IMAGEMAP attribute inside the most recent <OVERLAY> tag has priority over any other one inside the previous overlays, and over the <FIG> tag.

So the imagemaps can still be done via the server-side method as before, by including the IMAGEMAP attribute within the figure tags, or, now there is a client-side imagemap procedure.

The client-side imagemap is a little trickier for you, the programmer, unless you are using a software program to help (such as the MapEdit program). A quick example is given to help illustrate the point.

First, you should specify the links that are to be enclosed within your imagemap. Do this in a list manner:

```
<UL>
<LI><A HREF="homepage.html">Homepage</A>
<LI><A HREF="catalog.html">Catalog</A>
<LI><A HREF="profile.html">Company Profile</A>
<LI><A HREF="questions.html">Questions</A>
</UL>
```

The next step is to surround your list with the image to be used with the <FIG> Tag:

```
<FIG SRC="toolbar.gif">
<UL>
<LI><A HREF="homepage.html">Homepage</A>
<LI><A HREF="catalog.html">Catalog</A>
<LI><A HREF="profile.html">Company Profile</A>
<LI><A HREF="questions.html">Questions</A>
</UL>
</FIG>
```

Then, here comes the tricky part, you must make your image clickable by specifying the clickable areas using the SHAPE attribute:

Attribute:	SHAPE=	Used to define the shape of your clickable region
	"default"	Used to specify the section of your image that is not included in any other zone.
	"circle x,y,r"	Used to specify a circle as your zone.

"rect x,y,w,h"	Used to specify a rectangle as your zone.
"polygon x1,y1,x2,y2..."	Used to specify a polygon as your zone.

Note The x and y are axes, r is radius, w is width, h is height—these numbers are given in pixels so that you are actually specifying the coordinates of the shape.

The finished code might look something like this:

```
<FIG SRC="toolbar.gif">
<UL>
<LI><A HREF="homepage.html" SHAPE="rect 0,0,50,50">Homepage</A>
<LI><A HREF="catalog.html" SHAPE="rect 50,0,50,50">Catalog</A>
<LI><A HREF="profile.html" SHAPE="rect 100,0,50,50">Company
➥Profile</A>
<LI><A HREF="questions.html" SHAPE="rect 150,0,50,50">Questions</
A>
</UL>
</FIG>
```

More Figure Tags:	<CAPTION>	Used to indicate a caption for the figure.
Attributes:	ALIGN	Used to indicate the alignment of the caption. Choose from LEFT,RIGHT, TOP, or BOTTOM.
	<CREDIT>	Used at the end of the <FIG> tag before the closing </FIG> tag to indicate the artist of the figure.

Footnotes

Tag: <FN>...</FN>

Use: Surrounds a footnote

Attributes:	CLASS	(mentioned earlier)
	ID	Used to assign the footnote a name so that the assigned text will go there when clicked upon.
	LANG	(mentioned earlier)

Example: <P><A HREF="#fn01">Kassis Survey</A> proved our theory.<P>

<FN ID="fn01">Kassis, 1990</FN>

Math

Another addition with HTML 3.0 is the implementation of math equations. The tags and attributes are listed here, but for more information regarding HTML math, refer to the HTML 3.0 Specifications at `http://www.hpl.co.uk/people/dsr/html/CoverPage.html`.

Tag: $....$

Use: To implement a math equation.

Attributes:	CLASS	Used to create subclass equations.
	ID	Used to create a named anchor.
More Math Tags:	<BOX>...</BOX>	Used within the <MATH> tag to indicate invisible brackets. The following tags may be used inside the <BOX> tag; <ATOP> dictates that no line will be between the numerator and denominator), <CHOOSE> (indicates that the expression will be in parentheses), and <OVER> (indicates that a line will be drawn between the numerator and denominator).
Attributes:	SIZE	Used to specify oversized delimiters. Choose NORMAL, MEDIUM, LARGE, and HUGE.
	_{...}	Used to indicate subscripts.

	^{...}	Used to indicate superscripts.
Attributes:	ALIGN	Used to align the subscripts and superscripts
	LEFT	Aligns the script to the left of the term.
	RIGHT	Aligns the script to the right of the term.
	CENTER	Centers the script on top, or below the term.
	<ROOT>...</ROOT>	Used to create a cube root expression. Requires the <OF> tag to complete the expression.
	<SQRT>...</SQRT>	Used to create a square root expression.
	<TEXT>	Used to include text within a math element.

Notes

Tag: <NOTE>...</NOTE>

Use: To specify a certain section that appears as a note or warning of some type.

Attributes:	CLASS	Used to describe what type; NOTE, CAUTION, or WARNING. You would usually use the CLASS attribute when implementing a style sheet.
	CLEAR	(mentioned earlier)
	ID	(mentioned earlier)
	SRC	Used to indicate the filename for a graphic that will be used within the <NOTE> tags.
	MD	Used to specify the checksum of that graphic.

Tabs

A new (and long awaited) addition to HTML is tabs! These horizontal positioning tabs are great tools, and have many key attributes to them:

Tag: <TAB>

Use: To position text horizontally.

Attributes:		
	ALIGN	Left side<tab align=right>Right side Used to create left, right, centered and decimal tabs within text. Also, as noted above, you have the capability to align one side of a sentence to the left, and the other to the right.
	LEFT	Used to align the text to the right of the tab stop.
	RIGHT	Used to align the text to the left of the tab stop. Use the TO attribute to define, or text will align to the right margin.
	CENTER	Used to center align the text at the tab stop. Use the TO attribute to define, or text will align between the left and right margins.
	DECIMAL	Used to align text around a decimal point at the tab stop. Use the TO attribute to specify, and you can use the DP attribute to indicate the character for the decimal point.
	DP	Used to define the character to be used as the decimal point.
	ID	<TAB ID="firsttab"> (the first one used) <TAB TO="firsttab"> (for later text to the same tab) Used to create a named tab stop so that you can name the first tab, and then use the TO attribute to specify the same tab indentation to be used in later text.

INDENT	<TAB INDENT=5>
	Used to specify the number of en units to tab over. The INDENT attribute works well for indenting one line.
TO	Used in conjunction with many of the above attributes.

Netscape Additions & Enhancements

Netscape, seen as the browser of choice for the Web (it currently has about 75 percent of the browser market), has also been a leader in developing more extensions for the HTML language. There is a problem, however, due to the fact that many of their extensions are not supported by other browsers. They are also adding features that are not considered standards, and, therefore, have created somewhat of a controversy. Netscape claims that many webmasters are asking for these additions, hence the reason for their implementation.

Backgrounds & Foregrounds

The following are new attributes for the <BODY> Tag:

New Attribute:	BACKGROUND	<BODY BACKGROUND= "filename.gif">
		Used to specify an image to be tiled in the background of the document.
	BGCOLOR	<BODY BGCOLOR="# DFB8BF">
		Used to specify a color for the background of the document. The value is in the hexadecimal color code, preceded by a hash sign "#".

TEXT	<BODY TEXT="#660C72"> Used to specify a color for all the text within the document. The value is in the hexadecimal color code, preceded by a hash sign "#".
LINK	Used to specify a color for all the links that appear within the document.
VLINK	Used to specify a color for all the visited links that appear within the document.
ALINK	Used to specify a color for all the active links that appear within the document. <BODY LINK="#595FFF" VLINK="#C000C0" ALINK="#545CCO">

Centering

Tag: <CENTER>...</CENTER>

Use: Surrounds text, images, tables, or anything else that you wish to have centered.

Font Size

Tag: <FONT SIZE=*value*>...</FONT>

Use: Specifies an area of text in which you want the font size to differ from the default (default size is 3). The values range from 1–7, of which you could specify one, or, you have the option to have a "+" or "-" sign in front, indicating that it is relative to the default font (3).

Tag: <BASEFONT SIZE=*value*>

Use: Changes the size of the default, or BASEFONT, font size (which is 3). It also has a range of numbers from 1–7.

Horizontal Rules (Lines) Enhancements

Tag: <HR>

Use: Draws a line across the page.

New Attributes:	SIZE	<HR SIZE=*number*> Indicates the thickness of the line.
	WIDTH	<HR WIDTH=*number or percent*> Indicates the width of the line in relation to the document—specified in either number in pixels, or a percent of the document width.
	ALIGN	<HR ALIGN=*direction*> Indicated the alignment of the line—choose from LEFT, RIGHT, or CENTER.
	NOSHADE	<HR NOSHADE> Creates a solid line bar instead of a shaded one.

Image Enhancements

Tag: <IMG>

Use: Inserts an image into the document.

New Attributes:	ALIGN	<IMG ALIGN=option>
	LEFT	The ALIGN=left moves the image to the left, and wraps text around to the right.

RIGHT	The ALIGN=right moves the image to the right, and wraps text around to the left.
TEXTTOP	Aligns with the tallest text within the line. Usually the same at TOP.
ABSMIDDLE	Aligns the middle of the current line with the middle of the image. Similar to MIDDLE, except MIDDLE aligns the baseline of the current line with the middle of the image.
BASELINE	Aligns the bottom of the image with the baseline of the current line.
ABSBOTTOM	Aligns the bottom of the image with the bottom of the current line. Similar to BOTTOM.
WIDTH & HEIGHT	<IMG WIDTH=value HEIGHT=value> Used to specify a fixed width and height of an image (value is in pixels).
BORDER	<IMG BORDER=value> Used to specify the thickness of the border around the image (note: BORDER=0 means no border).
VSPACE & HSPACE	<IMG VSPACE=value HSPACE=value) The VSPACE specifies the space above and below the image, and the HSPACE specifies the space to the left and right of the image.

LOWSRC	<IMG SRC="highres.gif" LOWSRC="lowres.gif"> Used so that the browser will load a low resolution image on the first pass, then the high resolution image on the second pass. You can mix and match the GIF and JPEG graphics.

List Enhancements

Tag: <UL>...</UL>

Use: Surrounds the text that will create an Unordered List.

New Attributes:	TYPE	<UL TYPE=*choice*> You can specify which type of bullet you want; DISC, CIRCLE, or SQUARE.

Tag: <OL>...</OL>

Use: Surrounds the text that will create a Numbered or Ordered List of information.

New Attributes:	TYPE	<OL TYPE=*choice*> Used to select how you want your list to be marked; A (for capital letters), a (for small letters), I (large roman numerals), i (small roman numerals), or 1 (default numbers). Note: TYPE can also be used in the <LI> tag.
	START	<OL START=*choice*> Used to define a starting point (other than 1)—always use a numeric value for the START, the TYPE will adjust to your requirement (that is, choosing number 2 will start at either B, b, II, ii, or 2 depending on which TYPE you specified).

VALUE Used to change the count within the ordered list.

Netscape 2.0 New Additions & Enhancements

With the creation of the newest Netscape 2.0, there came some major additions and more enhancements for viewing the Web.

Font Color

Wow, what a great concept! I was hoping they'd include this. What webmaster doesn't want a little color in his page!

Tag: <FONT COLOR="#ff5760">...</FONT>

Use: To colorize your text. Notice how the hexadecimal is needed to specify the color after the hash (#) sign.

Frames

Another great feature of the Netscape 2.0 is the capability to create frames, or you might say they look like multiple windows.

Tag: <FRAMESET>...</FRAMESET>

Use: Creates a framed (or separate) area of your page.

Attributes: COLS <FRAMESET COLS="50%,50%">

Used to specify the number of columns for a frame.

ROWS <FRAMESET ROWS="50,50">

Used to specify the number of rows for a frame. Note that you can specify the size of the frame columns and rows in either percent of the screen, or pixels. Also, you must place the <FRAMESET>...</FRAMESET> tags before the <BODY> tag in the HTML document.

Tag: <FRAME>

Use: To assign what will be inside the frame.

Attributes:	SRC	<FRAME SRC="index.html"> Used to indicate the file that will be viewed within a frame.
	NORESIZE	Used to prevent the frame from being resized by the user.
	SCROLLING	Used to set a scrolling option for the user. You need to specify *yes* (the user may always scroll), *no* (the user may never scroll), or *auto* (lets the browser insert scroll if needed).

Here's another simple frame to give the idea of how it's done:

```
<FRAMESET COLS="50%,50%">
      <FRAME SRC="index.html">
      <FRAME SRC="page1.html">
</FRAMESET>
```

This example divides the screen into two columns, each taking half of the screen.

Tag: <NOFRAME>...</NOFRAME>

Use: To implement another version of your framed page so that browsers without frame support will be able to view properly.

Note The <NOFRAME>...</NOFRAME> tags must be placed before the </FRAMESET> tag. They would begin with the typical <BODY> opening tag, and have another version of the document within them. In effect, the <FRAMESET>...</FRAMESET> tags would then encompass the whole document.

Java

With all the hype about Java, Netscape has, of course, provided support for this up-and-coming language. Java, developed by Sun Microsystems, enables you to run complete programs within your HTML document. See Chapters 21 and 22 for more details, and check out Sun's site at `http://java.sun.com`.

LiveScript

Along with the creation of Java, by Sun Microsystems, Netscape has also developed their own language to run programs within the HTML documents called LiveScript. Although it does much the same as Java, it is a smaller language that is a little easier to learn. Find out more information at the following URL:

```
http://home.mcom.com/comprod/products/navigator/version_2.0/
script/script_info/index.html.
```

Target Windows

Target windows simply let you define a clickable hyperlink that, when clicked, instead of jumping to another page, tells the browser to open a new window with the new page displayed. Then you would have two windows, one displaying the first page, one displaying the next.

Tag: <A>...</A>

Use: Defines an new link or anchor.

New Attribute:	TARGET	<A HREF="filename.html" TARGET="name">...</A> Used to let the browser know that upon activation of this link, it should open a new window and display the "filename.html" file inside it. Note: Creating a combination of target windows and frames really makes a nice site. They work very well off each other.

Text Alignment

Netscape also has provided us with a way to align text to either the left, right, or center.

Tag: <DIV ALIGN>...</DIV>

Use: Surrounds text to be aligned in either of the following choices: left (left justified), right (right justified), or center (centers the text, which is the same as the <CENTER>...</CENTER> tags).

<DIV ALIGN="right"> This tag will make the text right justified. </DIV>

Microsoft Explorer 2.0 Additions & Enhancements

Microsoft, feeling the need to keep up with Netscape, has also developed a language of their own code named "Blackbird," whose specifications are also slightly different. They have also included some pretty neat features within their fabulous browser. Take a look.

Musical Backgrounds

To accompany your page's graphical background, why not provide the user with a little sound background when viewing your page?

Tag: <BGSOUND>

Use: Defines a background sound to be played in the background when your Web page is active.

Attributes: SRC Used to define the filename of the sound clip.

LOOP Used to define a number of loops for the clip to play.

<BGSOUND SRC="filename.wav" LOOP=5>

Note: The sound clips can be either AU, MIDI, or WAV files.

Scrolling Marquee

Tag: <MARQUEE>...</MARQUEE>

Use: Creates a string of text to appear in a moving fashion across the screen.

Attributes:		
Attributes:	ALIGN	<MARQUEE ALIGN=TOP>... </MARQUEE>
		Used to specify where the text will be aligned within the marquee. Choose from top, middle, or bottom.
	BEHAVIOR=	<MARQUEE BEHAVIOR=*choice*> ...</MARQUEE>
		Used to define how the text will travel:
	SCROLL	Text will scroll all the way on and all the way off.
	SLIDE	The marquee will scroll in and then "stick."
	ALTERNATE	This text will bounce back and forth.
	BGCOLOR	<MARQUEE BGCOLOR=#ff00ff>... </MARQUEE>
		Used to determine a background color for the marquee.
	DIRECTION	<MARQUEE DIRECTION=RIGHT>... </MARQUEE>
		Used to indicate which direction the text will scroll. Choose from LEFT or RIGHT (default is LEFT).

HEIGHT & WIDTH	<MARQUEE HEIGHT=50% WIDTH=50%>...</MARQUEE> Used to specify the height and width of the marquee in either pixels or as a screen percentage.
HSPACE& VSPACE	<MARQUEE HSPACE=10 VSPACE=10>...</MARQUEE> Used to specify horizontal and vertical margins for the marquee in pixels.
LOOP	<MARQUEE LOOP=10>... </MARQUEE> Used to specify how many times the marquee will loop. You can use the LOOP=INFINITE element to loop it indefinitely.
SCROLLAMOUNT	<MARQUEE SCROLLDELAY=2 SCROLLAMOUNT=25>... </MARQUEE> Used to specify the number of pixels between each draw of the marquee text.
SCROLLDELAY	Used to specify the number of milliseconds between each draw of the marquee text.

Stationary Background

The Microsoft Explorer browser has made it possible to have a background image, but make it so that is does not move when scrolling down the page.

Tag: <BODY>...</BODY>

Use: To define the body of the document.

New Attribute:	BGPROPERTIES	<BODY BACKGROUND= "filename.gif" BGPROPERTIES=FIXED> Used in conjunction with the BACKGROUND attribute and the FIXED element to assign a stationary background.

Tables

Microsoft has also added some new attributes for the <TABLE>...</TABLE> tags:

Tag: <TABLE>...</TABLE>

Use: Surrounds text to be laid out in a table format.

New Attributes:	BGCOLOR	Used to specify the background color of the table. Can be done in either a hexadecimal number, or color name.
	BORDERCOLOR	Used to specify the border color of a table. Must be used with the BORDER attribute. Can be done in either a hexadecimal number or color name.
	BORDERCOLORLIGHT	Used to specify independent border color control (for the 3D border effect). Must be used with the BORDER attribute. Is the opposite of BORDERCOLORDARK. Can be done in either a hexadecimal number or color name.

BORDERCOLORDARK	Used to specify independent border color control (for the 3-D border effect). Must be used with the BORDER attribute. Is the opposite of BORDERCOLORLIGHT. Can be done in either a hexadecimal number or color name.

Let's try a quick example just to help you get the idea of how to code it:

```
<TABLE BORDER=5 BGCOLOR=RED BORDERCOLOR=BLUE>
```

The example gives us a table whose border is 5, the background color is red, and the table border is blue.

Video Formats

The standard Microsoft video format, AVI, is now able to be played on their Explorer browser.

Tag: <IMG>

Use: Incorporates an image (and now an AVI video) onto the Web page.

New Attributes:	DYNSRC	<IMG DYNSRC="videoname.avi"> The DYNSRC (Dynamic Source) attribute is used to indicate an AVI file that will be played.
	FILEOPEN	Used to tell the browser to play the file as soon as the page is viewed.
	MOUSEOVER	Used to tell the browser to play the file when the user moves the cursor over the video image.

Note: You can provide the users who do not have the Explorer browser the ability to see a plain graphic file instead of the AVI file by doing this:

<IMG DYNSRC="videoname.avi" SRC="imagename.gif">

As a Web site developer, you need to be aware that there are different variations of the "Web language" within these browsers. With the implementation of Java and VRML coming into the picture, we can't know for sure where the Web is headed. In the meantime, try to develop pages that are as convenient and as widely supported as possible, in order to obtain the maximum amount of viewers on your site.

CHARACTER ENTITIES

Character	Entity Code	Description
	�–	Unused
		Horizontal Tab
Line Feed
	–	Unused
		Space
!	!	Exclamation Mark
“	"	Quotation Mark
#	#	Number Sign
$	$	Dollar Sign
%	%	Percent Sign
&	&	Ampersand
‘	'	Apostrophe
(	(	Left Parenthesis
)	)	Right Parenthesis
*	*	Asterisk

continues

Character	Entity Code	Description
+	+	Plus Sign
,	,	Comma
-	-	Hyphen
.	.	Period
/	/	Forward Slash
0–9	0–9	Numbers 0–9
:	:	Colon
;	;	Semi-colon
<	<	Less Than
=	=	Equals Sign
>	>	Greater Than
?	?	Question Mark
@	@	Commercial AT Sign
A–Z	A–Z	Letters A–Z
[	[	Left Square Bracket
\	\	Backslash
]	]	Right Square Bracket
^	^	Caret
—	_	Horizontal Bar
`	`	Grave Accent
a–z	a–z	Letters a–z
{	{	Left Curly Brace
|			Vertical Bar
}	}	Right Curly Brace
~	~	Tilde
	–	Unused

¡	¡	Inverted Exclamation
¢	¢	Cent Sign
£	£	Pound Sterling
¤	¤	General Currency Sign
¥	¥	Yen Sign
¦	¦	Broken Vertical Bar
§	§	Section Sign
¨	¨	Umlaut
©	©	Copyright
ª	ª	Feminine Ordinal
«	«	Left Angle Quote
¬	¬	Not Sign
–		Soft Hyphen
®	®	Registered Trademark
¯	¯	Macron Accent
°	°	Degree Sign
±	±	Plus or Minus
²	²	Superscript Two
³	³	Superscript Three
´	´	Acute Accent
µ	µ	Micro Sign
¶	¶	Paragraph Sign
·	·	Middle Dot
ç	¸	Cedilla
¹	¹	Superscript One
º	º	Masculine Ordinal

continues

Character	Entity Code	Description
»	»	Right Angle Quote
1/4	¼	Fraction one-fourth
1/2	½	Fraction one-half
3/4	¾	Fraction three-fourths
¿	¿	Inverted Question Mark
À	À	Capital A with Grave Accent
Á	Á	Capital A with Acute Accent
Â	Â	Capital A with Circumflex Accent
Ã	Ã	Capital A with Tilde
Ä	Ä	Capital A with Umlaut
Å	Å	Capital A with a Ring
Æ	Æ	Capital AE Dipthong
Ç	Ç	Capital C with Cedilla
È	È	Capital E with Grave Accent
É	É	Capital E with Acute Accent
Ê	Ê	Capital E with Circumflex Accent
Ë	Ë	Capital E with Umlaut
Ì	Ì	Capital I with Grave Accent
Í	Í	Capital I with Acute Accent
Î	Î	Capital I with Circumflex Accent
Ï	Ï	Capital I with Umlaut
╨	Ð	Capital Eth, Icelandic
Ñ	Ñ	Capital N with Tilde
Ò	Ò	Capital O with Grave Accent
Ó	Ó	Capital O with Acute Accent
Ô	Ô	Capital O with Circumflex Accent

Õ	Õ	Capital O with Tilde
Ö	Ö	Capital O with Umlaut
×	×	Multiply Sign
Ø	Ø	Capital O with a Slash
Ù	Ù	Capital U with Grave Accent
Ú	Ú	Capital U with Acute Accent
Û	Û	Capital U with Circumflex Accent
Ü	Ü	Capital U with Umlaut
Ý	Ý	Capital Y with Acute Accent
Þ	Þ	Capital THORN, Icelandic
ß	ß	Small Sharp s, German
à	à	Small a with Grave Accent
á	á	Small a with Acute Accent
â	â	Small a with Circumflex Accent
ã	ã	Small a with Tilde
ä	ä	Small a with Umlaut
å	å	Small a with a Ring
æ	æ	Small ae Dipthong
ç	ç	Small c with Cedilla
è	è	Small e with Grave Accent
é	é	Small e with Acute Accent
ê	ê	Small e with Circumflex Accent
ë	ë	Small e with Umlaut
í	ì	Small i with Grave Accent
ì	í	Small i with Acute Accent
î	î	Small i with Circumflex Accent

continues

Character	Entity Code	Description
ï	ï	Small i with Umlaut
≡	ð	Small eth, Icelandic
ñ	ñ	Small n with Tilde
ò	ò	Small o with Grave Accent
ó	ó	Small o with Acute Accent
ô	ô	Small o with Circumflex Accent
õ	õ	Small o with Tilde
ö	ö	Small o with Umlaut
÷	÷	Division Sign
ø	ø	Small o with a Slash
ù	ù	Small u with Grave Accent
ú	ú	Small u with Acute Accent
û	û	Small u with Circumflex Accent
ü	ü	Small u with Umlaut
y	ý	Small y with Acute Accent
þ	þ	Small thorn, Icelandic
ÿ	ÿ	Small y with Umlaut
		An en space * HTML 3.0
		An em space * HTML 3.0
		A nonbreaking space * HTML 3.0
	&endash;	An en dash * HTML 3.0
	&emdash;	An em dash * HTML 3.0

Complete HTML Listing

Now that you have seen the general HTML 2.0 standards, the HTML 3.0 additions, and the Netscape and Explorer enhancements, it's time to take a look at the complete listing of HTML tags and attributes. New features and additions are indicated with a "*" and state where they originate from.

General Attributes

Align Attribute * HTML 3.0

There are four choices: LEFT (aligns text to the left), RIGHT (aligns text to the right), CENTER (aligns text to the center), and JUSTIFY (aligns text to both left and right margins evenly).

Class Attribute * HTML 3.0

The CLASS attribute specifies the type of element to be used. It indicates a difference in a particular section.

Clear Attribute * HTML 3.0

The CLEAR attribute is used in conjunction with text alignment around an image. Use this attribute when you want the text to stop filling in around the graphic. Use it on the first tag that should break out of the format. Use it with tags such as; headings, paragraphs, lists, addresses, and the break tag. There are three values for the CLEAR attribute; LEFT (starts text at next clear left margin), RIGHT (starts text at next clear right margin), and ALL (starts text on next clear margin on both sides).

ID Attribute * HTML 3.0

This attribute can be added to almost all of the design and text elements or overall body tags, as well as images and links tags. It is designed to take the place of the NAME attribute that is used with the Anchor tag (<A NAME>) to provide an anchor or link name to a specific section.

<P ID="keyword"> The browser will jump here when a specific keyword is clicked upon.

Lang Attribute * HTML 3.0

The LANG attribute refers to the language and country code, which indicates to the browser certain specifics that might be necessary to display for that language.

Nowrap Attribute * HTML 3.0

Another popular, already used attribute, the NOWRAP attribute simply indicates to the browser not to wrap around the text. Everything must be displayed on one line, unless the person creating the page specifies otherwise.

GENERAL SECTIONS

ABOVE & BELOW * HTML 3.0

Tag: <ABOVE>...</ABOVE> * *html 3.0*

Use: Surrounds text that will have a line, arrow, bracket, or other symbol drawn above it.

Attribute: SYM Used to specify the symbol to draw. Choices include CUB, HAT, LARR (left arrow), RARR (right arrow), and TILDE.

Tag: <BELOW>...</BELOW> * *HTML 3.0*

Use: Surrounds text that will have a line, arrow, bracket, or other symbol drawn above it.

Attribute: SYM Used to specify the symbol to draw. Choices include CUB, HAT, LARR (left arrow), RARR (right arrow), and TILDE.

Note: There are shortcut tags for the more popular; <BAR> (bars), <DOT> (dots), <DDOT> (double dots), <HAT> (hats), <TILDE> (tildes), and <VEC> (vectors). * *html 3.0*

ADDRESS

Tag: <ADDRESS>...</ADDRESS>

Use: Acts as a signature to the Web page.

Attributes:	CLASS	(mentioned earlier) * HTML 3.0
	CLEAR	(mentioned earlier) * HTML 3.0
	ID	(mentioned earlier) * HTML 3.0
	LANG	(mentioned earlier) * HTML 3.0
	NOWRAP	(mentioned earlier) * HTML 3.0

ALIGNMENT

Tag: <CENTER>...</CENTER> * Netscape and <ALIGN=CENTER>

Use: Defines an area of text to be centered.

ARRAY * HTML 3.0

Tag: <ARRAY>...</ARRAY> * HTML 3.0

Use: Creates matrices and other array expressions. Used with the <ROW> tag to define rows, and the <ITEM> tag to define the item.

Attributes:	ALIGN	Used to indicate the alignment of the array. Choose from TOP, MIDDLE, and BOTTOM. * HTML 3.0
	COLDEF	Used to indicate how the items within the column will be aligned. The values could be L (left), C (center), or R (right). * HTML 3.0
	LDELIM	Used to specify the entity or character that will be used for the left delimiter. * HTML 3.0
	RDELIM	Used to specify the entity or character that will be used for the right delimiter. * HTML 3.0
	LABELS	Used to label the rows and columns. * HTML 3.0

BACKGROUND SOUND * Explorer 2.0

Tag: <BGSOUND> *Explorer 2.0

Use: Defines a background sound to be played in the background when your Web page is active.

Attributes:	SRC	Used to define the filename of the sound clip.
	LOOP	Used to define a number of loops for the clip to play.
		<BGSOUND SRC="filename.wav" LOOP=5>
		Note: The sound clips can be either AU, MIDI, or WAV files.

BANNER * HTML 3.0

Tag: <BANNER>...</BANNER> * HTML 3.0

Use: To specify a section of the document that will never change, it will be a banner. Usually displayed in a toolbar or such.

BLINK

Tag: <BLINK>...</BLINK>

Use: Surrounds a word or area of text that you wish to appear blinking.

BLOCKQUOTE

Tag: <BLOCKQUOTE>...</BLOCKQUOTE> or <BQ>...</BQ> * HTML 3.0

Use: Provides a way of listing a quotation within a document.

Attributes:	CLASS	(mentioned earlier) * HTML 3.0
	CLEAR	(mentioned earlier) * HTML 3.0
	ID	(mentioned earlier) * HTML 3.0
	LANG	(mentioned earlier) * HTML 3.0
	NOWRAP	(mentioned earlier) * HTML 3.0

New Tag: <CREDIT>...</CREDIT>

Use: To give credit to the author of the blockquote.

BREAK

Tag

Use: Creates a line break. The text after it will continue on the next line.

CHARACTER STYLE TAGS

Physical or Font Type

Tag: <B>...</B> and <STRONG>...</STRONG>

Use: Makes a section of text within the document a bold or strong typeface.

Tag: <I>...</I> and <EM>...</EM>

Use: Makes a section of text within the document an italicized or emphasized typeface.

Tag: <U>...</U>

Use: Makes a section of text within the document underlined.

Tag: <BIG>...</BIG> * *HTML 3.0*

Use: Surrounds text that should be displayed in a bigger font than normal.

Tag: <BT>...</BT> * *HTML 3.0*

Use: Surrounds text that will be both boldface, and in an upright font.

Tag: <S>...</S> * *HTML 3.0*

Use: Surrounds text that will have a line striking through it.

Tag: <SMALL>...</SMALL> * *HTML 3.0*

Use: Surrounds text that should be displayed in a smaller font than normal.

Tag: _{...} * *HTML 3.0*

Use: Surrounds text that should be displayed as subscript and with a smaller font.

Tag: ^{...} * *HTML 3.0*

Use: Surrounds text that should be displayed as superscript and with a smaller font.

Tag: <T>...</T> * *HTML 3.0*

Use: Surrounds text that will be in an upright font.

Logical or Information Type

Tag: <TT>...</TT>

Use: Creates a Typewriter font.

Tag: <CODE>...</CODE>

Use: Creates a fixed-width font such as Courier.

Tag: <SAMP>...</SAMP>

Use: Creates a font similar to <CODE>.

Tag: <KBD>...</KBD>

Use: Indicates text to be typed by the user.

Tag: <VAR>...</VAR>

Use: Indicates a variable that will be replaced with a value.

Tag: <DFN>..</DFN>

Use: Indicates a word that will or has been defined.

Tag: <KEY>...</KEY

Use: Defines a keyword.

Tag: <CITE>...</CITE>

Use: Indicates a citation.

Tag: <STRIKE>...</STRIKE>

Use: Shows struck out text.

Tag: <ABBREV>...</ABBREV> *HTML 3.0*

Use: Used to mark an abbreviation.

Tag: <ACRONYM>...</ACRONYM> *HTML 3.0*

Use: Used to mark an acronym.

Tag: <AU>...</AU> *HTML 3.0*

Use: Used to specify an author.

Tag: <DEL>...</DEL> *HTML 3.0*

Use: Used to indicate deleted text (great for legal documents).

Tag: <DFN>...</DFN> *HTML 3.0*

Use: Used to indicate a definition of a term.

Tag: <INS>...</INS> *HTML 3.0*

Use: Used for inserted text (again for legal documents).

Tag: <LANG>...</LANG> *HTML 3.0*

Use: Used to change the language context.

Tag: <PERSON>...</PERSON> *HTML 3.0*

Use: Used to indicate people's names for indexing programs to extract.

Tag: <Q>...</Q> *HTML 3.0*

Use: Used to specify a short quotation (in conjunction with the <LANG> tag) to determine the language context.

COMMENTS

Comments: <!-- comments --> ("comments" defines where the text should go)

Use: To mention any comments to be contained within the HTML document, but not displayed as part of it.

DIVISIONS * HTML 3.0

Tag: <DIV>...</DIV> **HTML 3.0*

Use: Breaks a page into individual sections by naming them.

Attributes:	ALIGN	Used to align the section specified. Choose from LEFT, RIGHT, CENTER, and JUSTIFY. * HTML 3.0
	CLASS	Used to name the section specified. *HTML 3.0
	CLEAR	(mentioned earlier) * HTML 3.0
	ID	(mentioned earlier) * HTML 3.0
	LANG	(mentioned earlier) * HTML 3.0
	NOWRAP	(mentioned earlier) * HTML 3.0

FIGURES * HTML 3.0

Tag: <FIG>...</FIG>

Use: Indicates that there will be an image included within the page. The <FIG> tag basically is taking the place of the <IMG> tag in the use of larger graphic files.

Attributes:	ALIGN=	Used to align the image and text around it.
	BLEEDLEFT	Aligns table with left window margin—until a clear left margin is reached.
	LEFT	Aligns table with the left text margin—text will go to the right of the table.

	BLEEDRIGHT	Aligns table with right window margin—until a clear right margin is reached.
	RIGHT	Aligns table with the right margin—text will go to the left of the table.
	CENTER	Aligns table in the center of the page—no text will wrap around.
	JUSTIFY	Resizes table to fit into the page width—no text will wrap around.
	CLASS	(mentioned earlier)
	CLEAR	(mentioned earlier)
	ID	(mentioned earlier)
	IMAGEMAP	Used to indicate an imagemap.
	LANG	(mentioned earlier)
	MD	Used to indicate the checksum of the image.
	NOFLOW	Used to stop the text from aligning around the image.
	SRC	Used to indicate the filename of the image.
	WIDTH & HEIGHT	<IMG WIDTH=*value* HEIGHT=*value*> Used to specify a fixed width and height of an image (value is in pixels or EN, one half the point size of the current text).
More Figure Tags:		<CAPTION>
		Used to indicate a caption for the figure.
	Attributes:	ALIGN
		Used to indicate the alignment of caption. Choose from LEFT, RIGHT, TOP, or BOTTOM.

<CREDIT>	Used at the end of the <FIG> tag before the closing </FIG> tag to indicate the artist of the figure.
Figure Overlay	<OVERLAY>
	Used to specify an overlay of the original image to be loaded after the original image. The <OVERLAY> tag is used within the <FIG> tag.
Attributes:	IMAGEMAP
	Used to indicate an imagemap.
	MD
	Used to indicate the checksum of the image.
	SRC
	Used to indicate the filename of the graphic (overlay graphic in this case).
	UNITS
	Used to specify the unit size.
WIDTH & HEIGHT	<IMG WIDTH=value HEIGHT=value>
	Used to specify a fixed width and height of an image (value is in pixels or EN (one half the point size of the current text).

FONT COLOR * Netscape 2.0

Tag: <FONT COLOR="#ff5760">...</FONT> * *Netscape 2.0*

Use: To colorize your text. Notice how the hexadecimal is needed to specify the color after the hash (#) sign.

FONT SIZE * Netscape

Tag: <FONT SIZE=*value*>...</FONT> * Netscape

Use: Specifies an area of text that you wish the font size to differ from the default (default size is 3). The values range from 1–7, of which you could specify one, or, you have the option to have a "+" or "-" sign in front, indicating that it is relative to the default font (3).

Tag: <BASEFONT SIZE=*value*> * Netscape

Use: Changes the size of the default, or BASEFONT, font size (which is 3). It also has a range of numbers from 1–7.

FOOTNOTES * HTML 3.0

Tag: <FN>...</FN>

Use: Surrounds a footnote.

Attributes:	CLASS	(mentioned earlier)
	ID	Used to assign the footnote a name so that the assigned text will go there when clicked upon.
	LANG	(mentioned earlier)

Example: <P><A HREF="#fn01">Kassis Survey</A> proved our theory. </P> <FN ID="fn01">Kassis, 1990</FN>

FORMS

Tag: <FORM>...</FORM>

Use: Surrounds area that will be designated as a form.

Attributes:	METHOD	<FORM METHOD="POST" ACTION="/cgi-bin/kassform.cgi"> Tells the server which method to handle the form; GET or POST.
	ACTION	Tells the server where to find the script associated with the form.

CLASS	(mentioned earlier) * HTML 3.0
ID	(mentioned earlier) * HTML 3.0
LANG	(mentioned earlier) * HTML 3.0
ERROR	Used to create an error message relative to that area * HTML 3.0
DISABLED	Used to disable certain areas of a form * HTML 3.0

Tag: <INPUT>

Use: To define what type of input the form will generate.

Attributes:		
	TYPE	<INPUT TYPE=...> Used to define which type of input is to follow for the form layout (see TYPE choices listed below).
	NAME	<INPUT TYPE="text" NAME="contact"> Assigns a specific name to this element, which links it to the corresponding name within the CGI script.
	VALUE	<INPUT TYPE="submit" VALUE="Submit Query"> Assigns a specific value to this element, which links it to the corresponding name within the CGI script.
	SIZE	<....SIZE=35> Used with either the TEXT or PASSWORD attribute, it specifies the length, in characters, of the text box.
	MAXLENGTH	<...MAXLENGTH=25> Used to indicate the maximum amount of characters that the user can input within the text box. * HTML 3.0

RANGE	Used to allow user to select a value that must be between the specified boundaries. * HTML 3.0
FILE	Used to allow the user to attach a file to the form submission. This comes in handy for sending HTML pages changes to a Web server. * HTML 3.0
ACCEPT	This limits the types of files that will be accepted as attachments. * HTML 3.0
SCRIBBLE SRC	Used together to reference an image to be displayed in the for the user to draw upon. Text browsers display a text field. * HTML 3.0
MD	Used to indicate the checksum of the image. * HTML 3.0

TYPE

Choices:	TEXT	<INPUT TYPE="text"...> Used in referencing a single line text box for input.
	PASSWORD	<INPUT TYPE="password"...> Used in referencing a single line text box for a secret password, which, when typed appears in asterisks.
	RADIO	<INPUT TYPE="radio"...> Used to implement a list of items for the user to choose one from.
	CHECKBOX	<INPUT TYPE="checkbox"...> Used to implement a list of items for the user to choose more than one from.

SUBMIT	<INPUT TYPE="submit"...>
	Used to create the button the user will click on to send the form information back to you.
RESET	<INPUT TYPE="reset"...>
	Used to create the button the user will click on to reset the information they put in the form (clear the form).

Selection Tag

Tag: <SELECT>...</SELECT>

Use: Defines a section of information that the user can choose or select from.

Attributes:	NAME	<SELECT NAME="color">
		Defines a special name to this element, which links it to the corresponding name within the CGI script.
	MULTIPLE	<SELECT NAME="color" MULTIPLE>
		Allows the user the option of choosing more than one selection.
	MULTIPLE SIZE	<SELECT NAME="color" MULTIPLE SIZE="4">
		Specifies the size you want the multiple selection box to be.

Tag: <OPTION>

Use: Is used to indicate the items to be listed within the selection box.

Attributes:	SELECTED	<OPTION SELECTED>
		Specifies an item within your list that will be the default checked item.

VALUE <OPTION VALUE="blue">

Used to assign a value to the corresponding option. (If no value is set, the form will send back the value of whatever text follows the <OPTION> tag.)

Textarea

Tag: <TEXTAREA>...</TEXTAREA>

Use: Defines an area of which text can be typed in—needs to have the following attributes:

Attributes: NAME Assigns a name to the corresponding text area.

ROWS Specifies the height of the text area.

COLS Specifies the width of the text area.

<TEXTAREA NAME="comments" ROWS=6 COLS=50></TEXTAREA>

FRAMES * Netscape 2.0

Tag: <FRAMESET>...</FRAMESET> * *Netscape 2.0*

Use: Creates a framed (or separate) area of your page.

Attributes: COLS <FRAMESET COLS="50%,50%">

Used to specify the number of columns for a frame.

ROWS <FRAMESET ROWS="50,50">

Used to specify the number of rows for a frame.

Note: You can specify the size of the frame columns and rows in either percent of the screen, or pixels.

Note: You must place the <FRAMESET>...</FRAMESET> tags before the <BODY> tag in the HTML document.

Tag: <FRAME> * Netscape 2.0

Use: To assign what will be inside the frame.

Attributes:		
	SRC	<FRAME SRC="index.HTML"> Used to indicate the file that will be viewed within a frame.
	NORESIZE	Used to prevent the frame from being resized by the user.
	SCROLLING	Used to set a scrolling option for the user. You need to specify yes (yes, the user can always scroll), no (no, the user can never scroll) or auto (let the browser insert scroll if needed).

Tag: <NOFRAME>...</NOFRAME> * Netscape 2.0

Use: To implement another version of your framed page so that browsers without frame support will be able to view properly.

Note The <NOFRAME>...</NOFRAME> tags must be placed before the </FRAMESET> tag. They would begin with the typical <BODY> opening tag, and have another version of the document within them. In effect, the <FRAMESET>...</FRAMESET> tags would then encompass the whole document.

THE HEADER (or Starting) ELEMENTS:

Tag: <HTML>...</HTML>

Use: Surrounds the entire HTML document.

Tag: <HEAD>...</HEAD>

Use: Defines the Heading of the HTML document.

Tags for use within the <HEAD>...</HEAD> tags: ** all are HTML 3.0 additions*

Tag: <LINK> * HTML 3.0

Use: The <LINK> tag has more than one use; it can be used to indicate the relationship between this and another document, it can be used to create tool bars for the documents (for more common elements like to return home, go back, etc.), used to include a banner, or used to include a stylesheet.

Attributes:		
Attributes:	REL	Used to define the relationship between this and another document (in the case of creating links to banners and stylesheets, and other things). * HTML 3.0
	REV	Used to define the reverse relationship between this and another document. * HTML 3.0
	HREF	Used to reference the URL of another document. * HTML 3.0

Tag: <META> * HTML 3.0

Use: Describes information relative to the document itself.

Attributes:		
Attributes:	NAME	Used to define the information. * HTML 3.0
	CONTENT	Used to list the information. * HTML 3.0
		<META NAME="Author" CONTENT="Mary Berg">
	HTTP-EQUIV	Used to name a header that is created with the <META> tag along with the CON-TENT attribute. * HTML 3.0
		<META HTTP-EQUIV="Created" CONTENT="February 1, 1996"> which will produce this header:
		Created: February 1, 1996

Tag: <RANGE> * HTML 3.0

Use: Specifies a selected range within a document.

Attributes:	ID	Used to identify the range. * HTML 3.0
	CLASS	Used to specify the type of range. * HTML 3.0
	FROM	Used to specify the beginning of the range. * HTML 3.0
	TO	Used to specify the ending of the range. * HTML 3.0

Tag: <STYLE> *\ *HTML 3.0*

Use: Indicates a style that will override the document style.

Attributes:	NOTATION	Used to specify the new style format. * HTML 3.0

Tag <TITLE>...</TITLE>

Use: Defines the Title of the HTML document (seen at the top of the browser screen—not inside the HTML document).

Tag: <BODY>...</BODY>

Use: Surrounds the entire body of the HTML document (everything starting from after the heading).

Attributes:	BACKGROUND	<BODY BACKGROUND="picture.gif"> Used to define the image that will be tiled in the background of the page. * HTML 3.0
	BGCOLOR	<BODY BGCOLOR="# DFB8BF"> Used to specify a color for the background of the document. The value is in the hexadecimal color code, preceded by a hash sign "#". * Netscape

TEXT	<BODY TEXT="#660C72"> Used to specify a color for all the text within the document. The value is in the hexadecimal color code, preceded by a hash sign "#". * Netscape
LINK	Used to specify a color for all the links that appear within the document. * Netscape
VLINK	Used to specify a color for all the visited links that appear within the document. * Netscape
ALINK	Used to specify a color for all the active links that appear within the document. * Netscape
BGPROPERTIES	<BODY BACKGROUND="tilename.gif" BGPROPERTIES=FIXED> Used in conjunction with the BACKGROUND attribute and the FIXED element to assign a stationary background. * Explorer 2.0

Tag: <BASE>

Use: Indicates the current documents URL.

Tag: <ISINDEX>

Use: Used inside the <HEAD> tag to allow searching within the document by the browser.

HEADINGS

Tags: <H1>...</H1>, <H2>...</H2>, <H3>...</H3>, <H4>...</H4>, <H5>...</H5>, <H6>...</H6>

Use: Creates a heading of a different size (and bolded) text. The <H1> tag represents the largest, and the <H6> tag represents the smallest.

Attributes:	ALIGN	(mentioned earlier) * HTML 3.0
	CLASS	(mentioned earlier) * HTML 3.0
	CLEAR	(mentioned earlier) * HTML 3.0
	ID	(mentioned earlier) * HTML 3.0
	LANG	(mentioned earlier) * HTML 3.0
	NOWRAP	(mentioned earlier) * HTML 3.0
	SEQNUM	Used to indicate the number that the heading will use, if your headings are numbered. All headings of the same size following the first one will go up from there. * HTML 3.0
	SKIP	Used to indicate a number of times to "skip" in the numbering sequence of the numbered headings. * HTML 3.0
	SRC	Used to indicate an image filename to be used before the heading. * HTML 3.0
	MD	Used to indicate the checksum of the image used with the SRC attribute. * HTML 3.0
	DINGBAT	Used to specify a symbol or picture that will mark the heading—these are supplied by the browsers. The attribute would look like this: <H2 DINGBAT="disk">...</H2> (disk is one of many names that can be used that correspond with images). * HTML 3.0

Note: A list of the HTML 3.0 dingbats can be found at this address:

```
http://www.hpl.hp.co.uk/people/
dsr/HTML/icons.txt
```

HORIZONTAL RULE

Tag <HR>

Use: Creates a line across the page (Horizontal Rules).

Attributes:	SRC	<HR SRC="colorline.gif"> * HTML 3.0 Used to specify an image to be used in place of the line.
	MD	Used to indicate the checksum of that image. * HTML 3.0
	SIZE	<HR SIZE=number> Indicates the thickness of the line. * Netscape
	WIDTH	<HR WIDTH=number or percent> Indicates the width of the line in relation to the document—specified in either number in pixels, or a percent of the document width. * Netscape
	ALIGN	<HR ALIGN=direction> Indicated the alignment of the line—choose from LEFT, RIGHT, or CENTER. * Netscape
	NOSHADE	<HR NOSHADE> Creates a solid line bar instead of a shaded one. * Netscape

IMAGES

Tag: <IMG>

Use: Inserts an image into the document.

Attributes:	SRC	<IMG SRC="filename.gif">
		Used to define the image filename, or URL of the image.
	ALT	<IMG SRC="filename.gif" ALT="Company Logo">
		Used to define a text name for the image for those who cannot view the image.
	ALIGN	<IMG SRC="filename.gif" ALIGN=top>
		Used to vertically align the text found before and after the image—choose from TOP, MIDDLE, and BOTTOM.
		or
	ALIGN	<IMG ALIGN=left> and <IMG ALIGN=right>
		The ALIGN=left moves the image to the left, and wraps text around to the right. The ALIGN=right moves the images to the right, and wraps text around to the left. * HTML 3.0
		or
	ALIGN=	TEXTTOP
		Aligns with the tallest text within the line. Usually the same at TOP. * Netscape
		ABSMIDDLE
		Aligns the middle of the current line with the middle of the image. Similar to MIDDLE, except MIDDLE aligns the baseline of the current line with the middle of the image. * Netscape

	BASELINE
	Aligns the bottom of the image with the baseline of the current line. * Netscape
	ABSBOTTOM
	Aligns the bottom of the image with the bottom of the current line. Similar to BOTTOM. * Netscape
ISMAP	<IMG SRC="filename.gif" ISMAP> * HTML 3.0
	Used to indicate that the image is a clickable image map.
CLASS	(mentioned earlier) * HTML 3.0
CLEAR	(mentioned earlier) * HTML 3.0
ID	(mentioned earlier) * HTML 3.0
LANG	(mentioned earlier) * HTML 3.0
WIDTH & HEIGHT	<IMG WIDTH=value HEIGHT=value> * HTML 3.0
	Used to specify a fixed width and height of an image (value is in pixels or EN, one half the point size of the current text).
MD	Used to indicate the checksum of that image. * HTML 3.0
BORDER	<IMG BORDER=value>
	Used to specify the thickness of the border around the image (note: BORDER=0 means no border). * Netscape
VSPACE & HSPACE	<IMG VSPACE=value HSPACE=value)

The VSPACE specifies the space above and below the image, and the HSPACE specifies the space to the left and right of the image.
* Netscape

LOWSRC <IMG SRC="highres.gif" LOWSRC="lowres.gif">

Used so that the browser will load a low resolution image on the first pass, then the high resolution image on the second pass. You can mix and match the GIF and JPEG graphics.
* Netscape

DYNSRC <IMG DYNSRC="videoname.avi">

The DYNSRC (Dynamic Source) attribute is used to indicate an AVI file that will be played.
* Explorer 2.0

FILEOPEN Used to tell the browser to play the file as soon as the page is viewed. * Explorer 2.0

MOUSEOVER Used to tell the browser to play the file when the user moves the cursor over the video image.
* Explorer 2.0

IMAGEMAPS (Client Side) * HTML 3.0

The IMAGEMAP attribute, found in both the <FIG> and <OVERLAY> tags, indicates that the graphic being loaded is an imagemap. Note that the IMAGEMAP attribute inside the most recent <OVERLAY> tag has priority over any other one inside the previous overlays, and over the <FIG> tag.

So the imagemaps can still be done via the server-side method as before, by including the IMAGEMAP attribute within the figure tags, or, now there is a client-side imagemap procedure.

The client-side imagemap is a little trickier for you, unless you are using a software program to help (such as the MapEdit program). But here is a quick example of the HTML code anyway:

First, you should specify the links that are to be enclosed within your imagemap. Do this in a list manner:

```
<UL>
<LI><A HREF="homepage.HTML">Homepage</A>
<LI><A HREF="catalog.HTML">Catalog</A>
<LI><A HREF="profile.HTML">Company Profile</A>
<LI><A HREF="questions.HTML">Questions</A>
</UL>
```

The next step is to surround your list with the image to be used with the <FIG> Tag:

```
<FIG SRC="toolbar.gif">
<UL>
<LI><A HREF="homepage.HTML">Homepage</A>
<LI><A HREF="catalog.HTML">Catalog</A>
<LI><A HREF="profile.HTML">Company Profile</A>
<LI><A HREF="questions.HTML">Questions</A>
</UL>
</FIG>
```

Then, here comes the tricky part because you must make your image clickable by specifying the clickable areas using the SHAPE attribute:

Attribute:	SHAPE=	Used to define the shape of your clickable region
	"default"	Used to specify the section of your image that is not included in any other zone.
	"circle x,y,r"	Used to specify a circle as your zone.
	"rect x,y,w,h"	Used to specify a rectangle as your zone.
	"polygon x1,y1,x2,y2..."	Used to specify a polygon as your zone.

Note The x and y are axes, r is radius, w is width, h is height—these numbers are given in pixels so that you are actually specifying the coordinates of the shape.

The finished code may look something like this:

```
<FIG SRC="toolbar.gif">
<UL>
<LI><A HREF="homepage.HTML" SHAPE="rect 0,0,50,50">Homepage</A>
<LI><A HREF="catalog.HTML" SHAPE="rect 50,0,50,50">Catalog</A>
<LI><A HREF="profile.HTML" SHAPE="rect 100,0,50,50">Company
➥Profile</A>
➥<LI><A HREF="questions.HTML" SHAPE="rect 150,0,50,50">Ques-
tions</A>
</UL>
</FIG>
```

LINKS/ANCHORS

Tag: <A>...</A>

Use: Surrounds a word, text area, or picture to be linked to another section within that page, some other page, or a graphic.

Attributes:

HREF <A HREF="filename">...</A>

Used in referencing another section within a document, another document, or graphic.

NAME <A NAME="name">...</A>

Used in referencing a "secret" name to prompt the browser to stop here when the corresponding link is clicked upon.

CLASS (mentioned earlier) * HTML 3.0

ID Used to take the place of the NAME attribute that is used with the Anchor tag (<A NAME>) to provide an anchor or link name to a specific section.(also mentioned earlier) * HTML 3.0

LANG (mentioned earlier) * HTML 3.0

	MD	The Message Digest attribute is used to indicate the checksum of the document you are linking to. * HTML 3.0
	REL	Used to define the relationship between this and the other document. * HTML 3.0
	REV	Used to define the reverse relationship between this and the other document. * HTML 3.0
	SHAPE	Used to specify areas within an image and the documents where they will link. * HTML 3.0
	TITLE	Used to indicate the title of the document you are linking to. * HTML 3.0
	TARGET	<A HREF="filename.HTML" TARGET="name">...</A> Used to let the browser know that upon activation of this link, it should open a new window and display the "filename.HTML" file inside it. * Netscape 2.0
Command:	MAILTO	<A HREF="mailto:e-mailaddress">...</A> Used when linking to an e-mail address.

LISTS

Numbered or Ordered Lists

Tag: <OL>...</OL>

Use: Surrounds the text that will create a Numbered or Ordered List of information.

Attributes:	SEQNUM	Used to indicate the value where the list should start at. * HTML 3.0
	CONTINUE	Used to indicate the current list should continue numbering where the previous one left off. * HTML 3.0

COMPACT <UL COMPACT> * HTML 3.0

Used to let the browser know it should squeeze the list together in some way—can be used with all List types.

TYPE <OL TYPE=choice>

Used to select how you want your list to be marked; A (for capital letters), a (for small letters), I (large roman numerals), i (small roman numerals), or 1 (default numbers).

Note: TYPE can also be used in the <LI> tag. * Netscape

START <OL START=choice>

Used to define a starting point (other than 1)—always use a numeric value for the START, the TYPE will adjust to your requirement (ie: choosing number 2 will start at either B, b, II, ii, or 2 depending on which TYPE you specified). * Netscape

VALUE Used to change the count within the ordered list. * Netscape

Unordered Lists

Tag: <UL>...</UL>

Use: Surrounds the text that will create an Unordered List.

Attributes: DINGBAT Used to specify a special bullet to be used in the List. * HTML 3.0

PLAIN Used to let the browser know not to display any bullets. * HTML 3.0

SRC	Used to indicate an image to use instead of the bullet. * HTML 3.0
MD	Used to indicate the checksum of that image. * HTML 3.0
WRAP	Used with the HORIZ value, the WRAP attribute tells the browser to line up the list horizontally, not vertically as is the default (similar to the <DIR> Lists that are almost never used). * HTML 3.0
COMPACT	<UL COMPACT> * HTML 3.0 Used to let the browser know it should squeeze the list together in some way—can be used with all List types.
TYPE	<UL TYPE=choice> You can specify which type of bullet you want; DISC, CIRCLE, or SQUARE. * Netscape

Menu Lists

Tag: <MENU>...</MENU>

Use: Surrounds the text that will create a Menu List.

Directory Lists

Tag: <DIR>...</DIR>

Use: Surrounds the text that will create a Directory List.

Tag: <LI>

Use: Used with the above lists (<OL>, <UL>, <MENU>, and <DIR> tags) to specify each List Item within that list.

Attributes:	DINGBAT	Used to specify a special bullet to be used in the List (Unordered Lists). * HTML 3.0
	SKIP	Used in Ordered Lists to indicate how many numbers to skip over before assigning that item a number. * HTML 3.0
	SRC	Used to indicate an image to use instead of the bullet (Unordered Lists with PLAIN attribute). * HTML 3.0
	MD	Used to indicate the checksum of that image. * HTML 3.0
	COMPACT	<UL COMPACT> * HTML 3.0 Used to let the browser know it should squeeze the list together in some way—can be used with all List types.

Definition Lists

Tag: <DL>...</DL>

Use: Surrounds the contents of a Definition List.

Tag: <DT>

Use: Represents the term to be defined.

Tag: <DD>

Use: Represents the definition of the term.

Tag: <LH> **HTML 3.0*

Use: Defines a List Header for the corresponding list. It can be used in the Ordered, Unordered, and Definition Lists.

MATH * HTML 3.0

Tag: $....$

Use: To implement a math equation.

Attributes:	CLASS	Used to create subclass equations.
	ID	Used to create a named anchor.
More Math Tags:	<BOX>...</BOX>	Used within the <MATH> tag to indicate invisible brackets. The following tags may be used inside the <BOX> tag; <ATOP> dictates that no line will be between the numerator and denominator), <CHOOSE> (indicates that the expression will be in parentheses), and <OVER> (indicates that there will be drawn between the numerator and denominator).
Attributes:	SIZE	Used to specify oversized delimiters. Choose NORMAL, MEDIUM, LARGE, and HUGE.
	_{...}	Used to indicate subscripts.
	^{...}	Used to indicate superscripts.
Attributes:	ALIGN=	Used to align the subscripts and superscripts
	LEFT	Aligns the script to the left of the term.
	RIGHT	Aligns the script to the right of the term.
	CENTER	Centers the script on top, or below the term.

<ROOT>...</ROOT>	Used to create a cube root expression. Requires the <OF> tag to complete the expression.
<SQRT>...</SQRT>	Used to create a square root expression.
<TEXT>	Used to include text within a math element.

NOTES * HTML 3.0

Tag: <NOTE>...</NOTE>

Use: To specify a certain section that appears as a note or warning of some type.

Attributes:	CLASS	Used to describe what type: NOTE, CAUTION, or WARNING. You would usually use the CLASS attribute when implementing a style sheet.
	CLEAR	(mentioned earlier)
	ID	(mentioned earlier)
	SRC	Used to indicate the filename for a graphic that will be used within the <NOTE> tags.
	MD	Used to specify the checksum of that graphic.

PARAGRAPHS

Tag <P>...</P>

Use: Marks the beginning (and end) of a new paragraph.

Attributes:	ALIGN	(mentioned earlier) * HTML 3.0
	CLASS	(mentioned earlier) * HTML 3.0
	CLEAR	(mentioned earlier) * HTML 3.0

ID	(mentioned earlier) * HTML 3.0
LANG	(mentioned earlier) * HTML 3.0
NOWRAP	(mentioned earlier) * HTML 3.0

PREFORMATTED TEXT

Tag: <PRE>...</PRE>

Use: Indicates a section of text that will be preformatted through the browser in exactly the way it appears on the screen.

Attributes:	CLASS	(mentioned earlier) * HTML 3.0
	CLEAR	(mentioned earlier) * HTML 3.0
	ID	(mentioned earlier) * HTML 3.0
	LANG	(mentioned earlier) * HTML 3.0
	WIDTH	Used to specify the number of characters you want the width to be within that section (default is 80 characters). * HTML 3.0

SCROLLING MARQUEE * Explorer 2.0

Tag: <MARQUEE>...</MARQUEE> * Explorer 2.0

Use: Creates a string of text to appear in a moving fashion across the screen.

Attributes:	ALIGN	<MARQUEE ALIGN=TOP>... </MARQUEE> Used to specify where the text will be aligned within the marquee. Choose from top, middle, or bottom.
	BEHAVIOR=	<MARQUEE BEHAVIOR=choice>... </MARQUEE> Used to define how the text will travel:

SCROLL	Text will scroll all the way on and all the way off.
SLIDE	The marquee will scroll in and then "stick."
ALTERNATE	This text will bounce back and forth.
BGCOLOR	<MARQUEE BGCOLOR=#ff00ff>... </MARQUEE> Used to determine a background color for the marquee.
DIRECTION	<MARQUEE DIRECTION=RIGHT>... </MARQUEE> Used to indicate which direction the text will scroll. Choose from LEFT or RIGHT (default is LEFT).
HEIGHT& WIDTH	<MARQUEE HEIGHT=50% WIDTH=50%>...</MARQUEE> Used to specify the height and width of the marquee in either pixels or as a screen percentage.
HSPACE& VSPACE	<MARQUEE HSPACE=10 VSPACE=10>...</MARQUEE> Used to specify horizontal and vertical margins for the marquee in pixels.
LOOP	<MARQUEE LOOP=10>... </MARQUEE>

		Used to specify how many times the marquee will loop. You can use the LOOP=INFINITE element to loop it indefinitely.
	SCROLLAMOUNT	<MARQUEE SCROLLDELAY=2 SCROLLAMOUNT=25>... </MARQUEE> Used to specify the number of pixels between each draw of the marquee text.
	SCROLLDELAY	Used to specify the number of milliseconds between each draw of the marquee text.

TABLES

Tag: <TABLE>...</TABLE>

Use: Surrounds text and information that will make up a table format.

Attributes:	BORDER	<TABLE BORDER=5> Used to specify the size of the border surrounding the table.
	WIDTH	<TABLE BORDER=5 WIDTH=90%> Used to specify the width of the table within the screen, either in percent, or total number of pixels.
	CELLSPACING	<TABLE BORDER=5 WIDTH=90% CELLSPACING=5> Used to define how much space there will be between cells.

CELLPADDING	<TABLE BORDER=5 WIDTH=90% CELLPADDING=4> Used to define how much space will be between the cell wall and its contents (the default if one).
ALIGN	Used to align the table on the screen. * HTML 3.0
BLEEDLEFT	Aligns table with left window margin—until a clear left margin is reached. * HTML 3.0
LEFT	Aligns table with the left text margin—text will go to the right of the table. * HTML 3.0
BLEEDRIGHT	Aligns table with right window margin—until a clear right margin is reached. * HTML 3.0
RIGHT	Aligns table with the right margin—text will go to the left of the table. * HTML 3.0
CENTER	Aligns table in the center of the page—no text will wrap around. * HTML 3.0
JUSTIFY	Resizes table to fit into the page width—no text will wrap around. * HTML 3.0
CLASS	(mentioned earlier) * HTML 3.0
CLEAR	(mentioned earlier) * HTML 3.0
ID	(mentioned earlier) * HTML 3.0

LANG	(mentioned earlier) * HTML 3.0
NOFLOW	Used to prevent text flow around the table. * HTML 3.0
NOWRAP	(mentioned earlier) Refers to content of table. * HTML 3.0
BGCOLOR	Used to specify the background color of the table. Can be done in either a hexadecimal number, or color name. * Explorer 2.0
BORDERCOLOR	Used to specify the border color of a table. Must be used with the BORDER attribute. Can be done in either a hexadecimal number, or color name. * Explorer 2.0
BORDERCOLORLIGHT	Used to specify independent border color control (for the 3-D border effect). Must be used with the BORDER attribute. Is the opposite of BORDERCOLORDARK. Can be done in either a hexadecimal number, or color name. * Explorer 2.0
BORDERCOLORDARK	Used to specify independent border color control (for the 3D border effect). Must be used with the BORDER attribute. Is the opposite of BORDERCOLORLIGHT. Can be done in either a hexadecimal number, or color name. * Explorer 2.0

Tag: <TR>...</TR>

Use: Creates a new table row.

Attributes:	ALIGN	<TR ALIGN=LEFT> Used to align all the cells within that row to either LEFT, RIGHT, or CENTER.
	VALIGN	<TR VALIGN=TOP> Used to align all the cells within that row to either TOP, MIDDLE, or BOTTOM.
	CLASS	(mentioned earlier) * HTML 3.0
	ID	(mentioned earlier) * HTML 3.0
	LANG	(mentioned earlier) * HTML 3.0
	NOWRAP	(mentioned earlier) Refers to content of table. * HTML 3.0
	ALIGN=JUSTIFY	Used to justify the row. * HTML 3.0
	ALIGN=DECIMAL	Used to align decimals (also use the DP attribute to specify the decimal point type). * HTML 3.0

Tag: <TH>...</TH>

Use: Defines a Table Heading within a table.

Attributes:	ALIGN	<TH ALIGN=RIGHT> Used to align the contents of that cell to either LEFT, RIGHT, or CENTER.

VALIGN	<TH VALIGN=BOTTOM> Used to align the contents of that cell to either TOP, MIDDLE, or BOTTOM.
ROWSPAN	<TH ROWSPAN=4> Used to specify how many rows this particular cell will span over.
COLSPAN	<TH COLSPAN=5> Used to specify how many columns this particular cell will span over.
NOWRAP	<TH NOWRAP> Used to make sure the cell contents are not wrapped from one line to the next—the contents stay on one line.
CLASS	(mentioned earlier) * HTML 3.0
ID	(mentioned earlier) * HTML 3.0
LANG	(mentioned earlier) * HTML 3.0
NOWRAP	(mentioned earlier) Refers to content of table. * HTML 3.0
ALIGN=JUSTIFY	Used to justify the contents. * HTML 3.0
ALIGN=DECIMAL	Used to align decimals (also use the DP attribute to specify the decimal point type). * HTML 3.0
AXIS	Used to specify an abbreviated name for a header cell. *HTML 3.0
AXES	Used to specify a comma separated list of axis names. * HTML 3.0

Tag: <TD>...</TD>

Use: Defines Table Data within a table.

Attributes:		
	ALIGN	<TD ALIGN=RIGHT> Used to align the contents of that cell to either LEFT, RIGHT, or CENTER.
	VALIGN	<TD VALIGN=BOTTOM> Used to align the contents of that cell to either TOP, MIDDLE, or BOTTOM.
	ROWSPAN	<TD ROWSPAN=4> Used to specify how many rows this particular cell will span over.
	COLSPAN	<TD COLSPAN=5> Used to specify how many columns this particular cell will span over.
	NOWRAP	<TD NOWRAP> Used to make sure the cell contents are not wrapped from one line to the next—the contents stay on one line.
	CLASS	(mentioned earlier) * HTML 3.0
	ID	(mentioned earlier) * HTML 3.0
	LANG	(mentioned earlier) * HTML 3.0
	NOWRAP	(mentioned earlier) Refers to content of table. * HTML 3.0
	ALIGN=JUSTIFY	Used to justify the contents. * HTML 3.0

ALIGN=DECIMAL	Used to align decimals (also use the DP attribute to specify the decimal point type). * HTML 3.0
AXIS	Used to specify an abbreviated name for a header cell. * HTML 3.0
AXES	Used to specify a comma separated list of axis names. * HTML 3.0

Tag: <CAPTION>...</CAPTION>

Use: Defines the name of your table.

TABS * HTML 3.0

Tag: <TAB>

Use: To position text horizontally

Attributes:	ALIGN	Left side<tab align=right>Right side Used to create left, right, centered, and decimal tabs within text. Also, as noted above, you have the capability to align one side of a sentence to the left, and the other to the right.
	LEFT	Used to align the text to the right of the tab stop.
	RIGHT	Used to align the text to the left of the tab stop. Use the TO attribute to define, or text will align to the right margin.
	CENTER	Used to center align the text at the tab stop. Use the TO attribute to define, or text will align between the left and right margins.
	DECIMAL	Used to align text around a decimal point at the tab stop. Use the TO attribute to specify, and you can use the DP attribute to indicate the character for the decimal point.

DP	Used to define the character to be used as the decimal point.
ID	<TAB ID="firsttab"> (the first one used) <TAB TO="firsttab"> (for later text to the same tab) Used to create a named tab stop so that you can name the first tab, and then use the TO attribute to specify the same tab indentation to be used in later text.
INDENT	<TAB INDENT=5> Used to specify the number of en units to tab over. The INDENT attribute works well for indenting one line.
TO	Used in conjunction with many of the above attributes.

TEXT ALIGNMENT * Netscape 2.0

Tag: <DIV ALIGN>...</DIV> * Netscape 2.0

Use: Surrounds text to be aligned in either of the following choices; left (left justified), right (right justified), or center (centers the text, which is the same as the <CENTER>...</CENTER> tags).

<DIV ALIGN="right"> </DIV>	This tag will make the text right justified.

Weave the Web for More Info

Following is a list of Web references for more information on certain topics. These sites are very helpful, but they in no way encompass all the sites out there that pertain to the same information. Also, please know that Web addresses are infamous for changing frequently. If they're not at the same location, try doing a search and maybe you'll find the new address—or something better!

Browsers

Cello—`http://ftp.law.cornell.edu/pub/LII/Cello`

Spyglass Enhanced Mosaic—`http://www.spyglass.com/`

NCSA Mosaic—`http://www.ncsa.uiuc.edu/SDG/Software/Mosaic/NCSAMosaicHome.HTML`

Lynx—`ftp://ftp2.cc.ukans.edu/pub/WWW/lynx`

Netcruiser—`http://www.netcom.com`

Netscape Navigator—`http://home.netscape.com`

Microsoft Internet Explorer—`http://www.microsoft.com/windows/ie/ie.htm`

Audio Files

Audio FAQ's—`http://www.biocom.arizona.edu/tbook/faq/audio.htm`

Audio On The Net—`http://www.nyu.edu/atg/docs/papers/internet.audio/Contents.HTML`

Audio File Helper Programs

MacIntosh Helper Apps—`http://www.netscape.com/assist/helper_apps/machelpers.HTML`

The Ultimate Collection of Winsock Software—`http://tucows.niia.net/`

Stroud's CWSApps List–Index of Apps—`http://www.enterprise.net/cwsapps/inx2.HTML`

Image Information

GIF Yahoo List—`http://www.yahoo.com/Computers_and_Internet/Software/Data_Formats/GIF/`

Usenet JPEG FAQ's—http://www.utexas.edu/cc/graphics/.faqs/jpeg-faq/

PNG—http://quest.jpl.nasa.gov/PNG/

and

http://www.group42.com/png.htm

Progressive JPEG's—http://www.boutell.com/faq/pjpeg.htm

Image & Graphics Sources

Yahoo's photography master page—http://yahoo.com/arts/photography

West Stock, Inc.—http://www.weststock.com/

Photodisc, Inc.—http://www.photodisc.com/

Clouds & Scenery—http://www.commerce.digital.com/paloalto/CloudGallery

Illusionist's Art Gallery—http://www.infohaus.com/access/byseller/Illusionist/HIDDEN.artpage.free.HTML

Graphic Applications

Photoshop

http://www.adobe.com/Apps/Photoshop.HTML

Paint Shop Pro

The Ultimate Collection of Winsock Software—http://tucows.niia.net/

Stroud's CWSApps List–Index of Apps—http://www.enterprise.net/cwsapps/inx2.HTML

Both of these sites have "loads" of shareware and freeware for you to browse through and download!

Lview Pro

http://www.ncsa.uiuc.edu/SDG/Software/WinMosaic/

Macintosh Utility Software

ftp://ftp.uwtc.washington.edu/pub/Mac/Graphics

HTML Information

HTML 2.0 Specifications—http://www.w3.org/hypertext/WWW/MarkUp/HTML-spec/index.HTML

HTML 3.0 Specifications—http://www.hpl.hp.co.uk/people/dsr/HTML/Contents.HTML

Netscape HTML Extensions—http://home.netscape.com/assist/net_sites/HTML_extensions.HTML

HTML Editors

HotDog—http://www.sausage.com

HotMetaL—http://www.sq.com

Microsoft Internet Assistant—http://www.microsoft.com/pages/deskapps/word/viewer/wordvu.htm

Forms

NCSA Forms Documentation—http://hoohoo.ncsa.uiuc.edu/cgi/forms.HTML

CGI

NCSA CGI Information—http://hoohoo.ncsa.uiuc.edu/cgi/

Imagemaps

NCSA Imagemap Tutorial—http://hoohoo.ncsa.uiuc.edu/docs/tutorials/imagemapping.HTML

Imagemap Help Page—http://www.hway.com/ihip/

MapEdit

http://www.boutell.com/mapedit/

Java

Sun Microsystems Java—http://www.javasoft.com/

VRML

VRML Info & Specifications—http://vrml.wired.com/vrml.tech/vrmlspec.HTML

VRML Browsers

Listing—http://www.webreference.com/vrml/

Yahoo's list—http://www.yahoo.com/Entertainment/Virtual_Reality/Virtual_Reality_Modeling_Language__VRML_/Browsers/

Stroud's CWSApps List–Index of Apps—http://www.enterprise.net/cwsapps/inx2.HTML

Adobe Acrobat

http://www.adobe.com

and

ftp://ftp.adobe.com/pub/adobe/Applications/Acrobat

Search Engines

What's New Too—`http://newtoo.manifest.com/`

EINet Galaxy—`http://galaxy.einet.net/`

Yahoo—`http://www.yahoo.com/`

Starting Point—`http://www.stpt.com/`

Lycos—`http://lycos.cs.cmu.edu/`

WebCrawler—`http://webcrawler.com/`

Harvest—`http://harvest.cs.colorado.edu/`

InfoSeek—`http://www2.infoseek.com/`

Whole Internet Catalog—`http://gnn.com/`

World Wide Web Worm—`http://www.cs.colorado.edu/`

Open Text Index—`http://www.opentext.com/`

Apollo—`http://apollo.co.uk/`

JumpStation—`http://js.stir.ac.uk/`

Netcenter—`http://www.netcenter.com/`

NIKOS—`http://www.rns.com/`

New Rider's Official WWW Yellow Pages—`http://www.mcp.com/newriders/`

Alta Vista—`http://www.altavista.digital.com`

General Information

Webreference.com—`http://www.webreference.com`

INDEX

Symbols

A

C

D

E

F

I

J

K-L

M

O

P

Q-R

S

T

U

V

W-Z

REGISTRATION CARD

Webmaster's Professional Reference

Name ______________________ Title ______________________

Company ______________________ Type of business ______________________

Address ______________________

City/State/ZIP ______________________

Have you used these types of books before? ☐ yes ☐ no

If yes, which ones? ______________________

How many computer books do you purchase each year? ☐ 1–5 ☐ 6 or more

How did you learn about this book? ______________________

Where did you purchase this book? ______________________

Which applications do you currently use? ______________________

Which computer magazines do you subscribe to? ______________________

What trade shows do you attend? ______________________

Comments: ______________________

Would you like to be placed on our preferred mailing list? ☐ yes ☐ no

☐ **I would like to see my name in print!** You may use my name and quote me in future New Riders products and promotions. My daytime phone number is: ______________________

New Riders Publishing 201 West 103rd Street ◆ Indianapolis, Indiana 46290 USA

Fax to **317-581-4670**

Fold Here

NO POSTAGE NECESSARY IF MAILED IN THE UNITED STATES

BUSINESS REPLY MAIL

FIRST-CLASS MAIL PERMIT NO. 9918 INDIANAPOLIS IN

POSTAGE WILL BE PAID BY THE ADDRESSEE

NEW RIDERS PUBLISHING
201 W 103RD ST
INDIANAPOLIS IN 46290-9058